CW01082093

LIVING TREASURE

Studies in Indian and Tibetan Buddhism

This series was conceived to provide a forum for publishing outstanding new contributions to scholarship on Indian and Tibetan Buddhism and also to make accessible seminal research not widely known outside a narrow specialist audience, including translations of appropriate monographs and collections of articles from other languages. The series strives to shed light on the Indic Buddhist traditions by exposing them to historical-critical inquiry, illuminating through contextualization and analysis these traditions' unique heritage and the significance of their contribution to the world's religious and philosophical achievements.

STUDIES IN INDIAN AND TIBETAN BUDDHISM

Living Treasure

Tibetan and Buddhist Studies in Honor of Janet Gyatso

Edited by Holly Gayley and Andrew Quintman

Wisdom Publications
199 Elm Street
Somerville, MA 02144 USA
wisdomexperience.org

Library of Congress Cataloging-in-Publication Data
Names: Gayley, Holly, editor. | Quintman, Andrew (Andrew H.), editor. | Gyatso, Janet, honoree.
Title: Living treasure: Tibetan and Buddhist studies in honor of Janet Gyatso / edited by Holly Gayley and Andrew Quintman.
Description: First edition. | Somerville: Wisdom Publications, 2023. | Series: Studies in Indian and Tibetan Buddhism | Includes bibliographical references.
Identifiers: LCCN 2022045158 (print) | LCCN 2022045159 (ebook) | ISBN 9781614297796 (hardcover) | ISBN 9781614298007 (ebook)
Subjects: LCSH: Buddhism. | Buddhism—Tibet Region. | Tibet Autonomous Region (China)—Study and teaching.
Classification: LCC BQ120 .L59 2023 (print) | LCC BQ120 (ebook) | DDC 294.3—dc23/eng/20220928
LC record available at https://lccn.loc.gov/2022045158
LC ebook record available at https://lccn.loc.gov/2022045159

ISBN 978-1-61429-779-6   ebook ISBN 978-1-61429-800-7

27 26 25 24 23   5 4 3 2 1

Cover and design by Gopa & Ted2, Inc.

Printed on acid-free paper that meets the guidelines for permanence and durability of the Production Guidelines for Book Longevity of the Council on Library Resources.

Printed in the United States of America.

At the International Association of Tibetan Studies Conference, Oxford University, 1979. From left to right: Namgyal Gonpo Ronge, Veronica Ronge, Ngawang Thondup Narkyid, Heather Stoddard, Samten Karmay, Jampa Losang Panglung Rinpoché, Lama Chime Rata Rinpoché, Sangye Tenzin Jongdong Rinpoché, David Snellgrove, Janet Gyatso. (Photographer unknown.)

Publisher's Acknowledgment

The publisher gratefully acknowledges the generous help of the Hershey Foundation in sponsoring the production of this book.

Table of Contents

Preface

WE ARE HONORED and delighted to present this Festschrift, or celebratory volume, in honor of Janet Gyatso, the Hershey Professor of Buddhist Studies at Harvard University. Janet's prolific scholarship and influential career have had a wide-ranging impact on the fields of Tibetan and Buddhist studies. This volume is organized around several of the key themes of her research and enduring influence with essays by her close colleagues and former students.

Janet has served as teacher, advisor, mentor, and friend to each of us. Andy first studied with Janet as an undergraduate when she taught at Amherst College in the late 1980s, and later as a graduate student when she served on his doctoral dissertation committee. Holly arrived at Harvard the same year as Janet in 2001 and was fortunate to become Janet's first graduate student from the beginning to the end of the doctoral process. Indelibly influenced, we both benefited enormously from her perspicacity and nuanced reading of Tibetan texts, as well as the ways Janet both challenges her students and encourages their insights. Since those early days, we have both had the good fortune to continue to learn from and collaborate with her in a variety of settings. These have included an extended workshop on Tibetan literature that began in 2010 as a five-year seminar at the American Academy of Religion and continued through a series of meetings on five different university campuses. We have also maintained an ongoing dialogue with Janet about the literary features of Tibetan texts and their translation into English in forums such as the Tsadra Foundations' Translation and Transmission Conferences (starting in 2014) and the Lotsawa Translation Workshops (starting in 2018).

Living Treasure signals two of the subfields that Janet has opened for inquiry and led the way for the next generation to explore. As a title, it gestures to the visionary impulse of a distinctively Tibetan mode of revelation, referred to as "treasures," or *terma* (*gter ma*). This is very much a living tradition up to the present, and the great literary output of its visionaries includes an explicit concern with narrating lives, their own and those of founding figures in the lore of Buddhism's advent in Tibet. Janet made foundational contributions to understanding the treasure tradition and pioneered the study of Tibetan auto/biography. Both areas of scholarship continue to thrive as burgeoning subfields and extend from historically significant and early figures to the continued impact of treasure revelation and life writing in Tibetan and Himalayan contexts.

Janet is also of course herself a living treasure within the fields of Tibetan and Buddhist studies, where she has been a vital and consistent presence since the early 1980s. She has served in positions of leadership in the preeminent forums for the academic study of Tibet, Buddhism, and religion more broadly. These include the International Association of Tibetan Studies (where she served as president for 2000–2006), the International Association of Buddhist Studies (where she formerly served as the general secretary for the Americas), and the American Academy of Religion (where she served as co-chair of the Buddhism Section for 2005–2010). She has taught innumerable undergraduates, trained several generations of graduate students, and remains a compelling voice in pivotal conversations and conferences, encouraging the fields of Tibetan and Buddhist studies forward in persistent and generative ways.

We would like to thank Alexander Gardner and David Kittelstrom for their incisive editorial assistance. We offer special thanks to Daniel Aitken and Wisdom Publications for supporting this project from its inception and for sponsoring a memorable reception at the Prague IATS conference in celebration of Janet's illustrious career.

Holly Gayley and Andrew Quintman

Introduction

SINCE HER EARLIEST publications in the 1980s, Janet Gyatso has contributed to the fields of Tibetan and Buddhist studies as one of the most creative and influential thinkers of her generation. Her academic writing covers a wide range of Tibetan and Buddhist thought and practice, including doctrinal and literary history, medicine and modernity, poetics and the arts—as well as theoretical issues in the study of religion writ large. Her initial doctoral research on the traditions of Thangtong Gyalpo (circa 1361–1485) and writings on treasure literature (*gter ma*) and the practice of Severance (*gcod*) were followed by groundbreaking monographs on Tibetan autobiography and, more recently, systems of Tibetan medical knowledge. She is currently a leading voice in theorizing the literary dimensions of Buddhist writing as she engages in collaborative conversations around the influence of *kāvya* in Tibet and the practices and processes of translation. Her work exemplifies the marriage of philological deftness, analytical acuity, and intellectual rigor that has established novel lines of inquiry and inspired generations of scholars. In moving beyond traditional silos of academic exposition, Janet has not only opened up new intellectual terrain for exploration in the study of Buddhism and Tibet, she has also made them available to broad communities of readers.

Indeed, Janet has pushed the next generation to communicate beyond our areas of specialization and to engage more theoretically in substantive directions that matter widely across the humanities. As always, she led the way: bringing treasure revelation into conversation with semiotics, contesting Eurocentric notions of autobiography, exploring Buddhist monastic and Tibetan medical notions of the third sex, arguing for the rise of an early modern episteme in seventeenth-century Lhasa, and, most recently, tending to animal ethics within and beyond Buddhism. Across the decades, Janet has modeled an interdisciplinary approach to Tibetan studies that engages broader theoretical concerns in relationship to Buddhist discourses and practices, but not in the extractive sense of using Tibetan raw materials to distill into universalizing academic theories. To the contrary, the movement more often went the other direction, challenging the universality of Eurocentric claims and championing the sophisticated theories and rhetorical strategies of the Tibetan visionaries and cleric-scholars like Thangtong Gyalpo, Jigmé Lingpa, and Desi Sangyé Gyatso, whom she has admired and read so closely. Crucially, within the male-dominated textual tradition, Janet has always sought out women's perspectives and the destabilizing presence of the feminine and non-normative genders.

The task we gave to the contributors to this volume echoes the call Janet has made throughout her career: to write in more theoretically sophisticated and broadly relevant ways. We thus encouraged authors to write in a creative, impactful manner that highlights a specific issue or problematic, to break new theoretical ground, or offer new research data, while remaining accessible to a broad audience—in particular scholars and students outside of Tibetan and Buddhist studies.

Biographical Sketch

Growing up in a Jewish family in Philadelphia during the early 1950s, Janet Frank was "existentially obsessed," deeply immersed in questions of human suffering and death.[1] Her father attended adult classes on world religions and once declared that, if he could choose, he would be a Buddhist since it seemed the most rational of all traditions. Her father's initial encounter with Buddhism sparked a curiosity. "I can remember holding up my skinny-girl arm," she recalls, "and asking my mother, 'Where am *I*?'" This question, posed early in her childhood, marked a beginning, and set a course for the intellectual arc of Janet's career.

She started at Boston University with an interest in astronomy. It was around this time that she heard about the *Tibetan Book of the Dead*, with its promise that "all you had to do is recognize you are dead, and you'll be liberated." In the middle of her junior year in college, Janet moved to the Buddhist center in Freewood Acres, NJ, established by the Kalmyk teacher Geshe Wangyal in the late 1950s. It was there she encountered basic Buddhist ideas, such as the four noble truths, for the first time. "It was," she reflects, "such a relief to hear a recognition of human suffering." Other prominent Tibetan teachers visited and spent time in residence, including the then Ganden Tri Rinpoche, head of the Geluk sect of Tibetan Buddhism. It was while listening to a talk by the Ganden Tripa in 1969 through an American translator that she resolved she would learn to speak to such teachers directly. These encounters made clear that her astron-

1. Quotations in this section are drawn from several informal conversations with Janet in 2021–2022.

omy major was no longer suitable. "Instead of exploring the outer universe," she determined, "I would study the inner universe."

In the 1970s, Janet went to live at Evam Choden, a Dharma center started by Kunga Thartse Rinpoche north of Berkeley. There she met some of the earliest Tibetan lamas who came to North America, including Dezhung Rinpoche, Kalu Rinpoche, and Chögyam Trungpa, who all visited and taught there. Janet returned to the academic classroom at the University of California, Berkeley determined to study math, but met Lewis Lancaster who—fatefully—convinced her to major in religious studies instead. At Berkeley, she went on to earn an MA in Sanskrit (1974) and PhD in Buddhist studies (1981), studying Abhidharma with Padmanabh Jaini and Buddhism with Lancaster.

Graduating with PhD in Buddhist studies. University of California, Berkeley, 1981. (Photographer unknown.)

She met some of her long-standing close colleagues at Berkeley, including Matthew Kapstein and Carl Bielefeldt. Of those parallel experiences, in the Dharma center and in academia, Janet avers, "I felt that education in the

Dharma center was better than what I got in graduate school. Lamas know far more than scholars."

In 1973 the entire graduate program embarked on a trip to Nepal, where she met Michael Aris, Aung San Suu Kyi, and Alexander Macdonald. Janet took a leave of absence from the MA program to remain in South Asia and, while staying near the Sakya Center in Dehradun, India, she had the good fortune to meet Sakya Trizin, leader of the Sakya sect of Tibetan Buddhism, as well as Drupthob Rinpoche, a lineage holder of Thangtong Gyalpo's tradition.

At Sakya Monastery, Rajpur, India, 1973. Front standing row left to right: Janet Gyatso, Sakya Drungyig, Gyalsé Tulku, 2nd Dzongsar Khyentse Rinpoché, 41st Sakya Trizin Ngawang Kunga, Khenpo Abé, Mme. Krull, Lama Wangchuk. (Photographer unknown.)

That encounter led to her decision to pursue doctoral research on the famed Nyingma visionary and iron-bridge builder, Thangtong Gyalpo. In Dehradun, she also met Losang Gyatso, a son of the Lukhang family. In 1974 they were married in India, whereupon she returned to Berkeley to finish her MA and PhD. (She and Gyatso separated in 1985.)

After completing her doctoral exams, Janet moved to New York City, where she developed close connections with the Tibetan exile community, including prominent Tibetan aristocrats. Between 1978 and 1981, she wrote her dissertation while working for the Institute for Advanced Studies of World Religions in Stony Brook, NY, founded by philanthropist C.T. Shen.

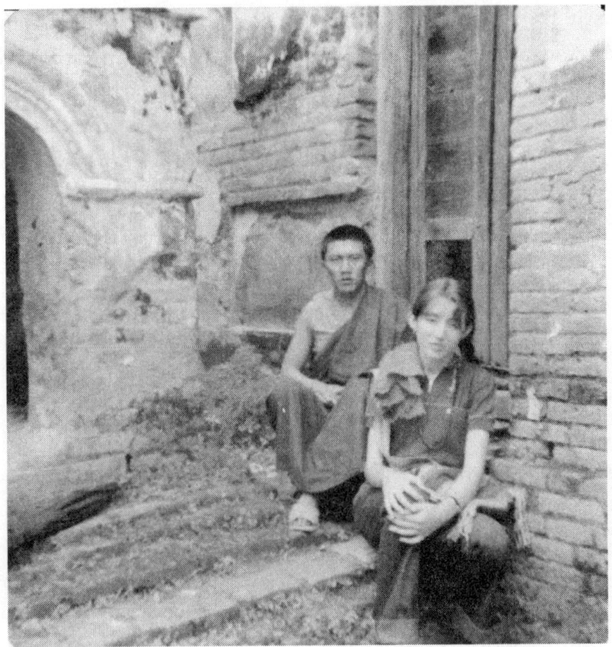

Janet at Rajpur, India, 1974. (Photographer unknown.)

Janet took her first academic job in the religious studies program at the State University of New York at Stony Brook in 1983–1988. She also had a brief stint teaching at Wesleyan University (1986–87, plus spring 1988) and then spent more than a decade at Amherst College (fall 1987, 1988–2001), with visiting positions at Harvard University and the University of Michigan, Ann Arbor. In 2001 she was appointed as the Hershey Professor of Buddhist Studies at Harvard University, where she continues to teach. She married fellow Buddhologist Charles Hallisey in 2004. In 2014 Janet became associate dean of academic affairs at Harvard Divinity School, where she has championed shifting the curriculum to a more pluralistic, diversified, and multireligious perspective. In 2017 she was elected as a fellow of the prestigious American Academy of Arts and Sciences.

Intellectual History

Early in her graduate career, Janet recalls being rebuked for emphasizing an emic Tibetan view of Buddhism. As she remembers, "all those years being married to a Tibetan and living with Tibetans had a big impact on me." Yet rather than producing a reverential tone in her work, quite the opposite occurred: she undercuts at every turn romanticized versions of Tibet to find moments that complicate and enrich understandings of the lives and writings of exalted Buddhist masters. As an intellectual impulse, Janet searched for and found voices in the Tibetan archive that mirrored her own critical perspectives, thereby breaking down a supposed divide between Western skepticism and rationality and Tibetan religiosity and devotion, the etic and the emic. Her interest in self-reflexivity and early modern impulses in Tibet literature in the seventeenth and eighteenth centuries, whether in autobiographical writings or medical treatises, exemplify this approach.

A thread running throughout Janet's work has been the human and humanizing moments in the lives of eminent Tibetan masters: whether analyzing autobiographical strategies of Jigmé Lingpa that balance the humilific dictates of first-person speech with claims to prophetic authority, seeking the historical Yeshe Tsogyal within mythologized accounts of her life, or noting the remarkable candor and critiques that Desi Sangyé Gyatso made of his teachers and peers in his medical writings. For Janet, religious masters do not hover above saṃsāra, untouched and unmoved, but are deeply enmeshed in everyday concerns and the debates of their day. They exhibit subjectivity and individuality, even within the Buddhist understanding of the self as illusory, and embody contradictory impulses of skepticism alongside deep religious commitments.

In her contribution to the fields of Tibetan and Buddhist studies, Janet's work is deeply synthetic and characterized by its ability to transect traditional modes of inquiry and suggest new analytical frames. Still, her reading practices exhibit a fine attunement to rhetorical strategies and representations in Tibetan literature, foregrounding striking claims as well as new intellectual and artistic impulses, while also reading against the grain for complexities and contradictions. Across the many fields of her scholarship, she has kept a sustained interest in diverse categories and literary features of Buddhist texts. A number of her publications highlight genres previously overlooked (or not taken seriously) in Tibetology, such as her discussion of diary-keeping practices among Tibetans in "Counting Crows Teeth" or the prophetic address (*byang bu*) in revelatory literature in "The Relic Text as Prophecy," as well as her groundbreaking work in auto/biography (*rang rnam, rnam thar*).

In her presentation of the inaugural Aris Lecture convened at Oxford (2015) titled "Beyond Representation and Identity: Opening Ways for Tibetan Studies," Janet noted that the field of Tibetan studies was at an important crossroads as it began to recognize important shifts taking place in scholarship more broadly. Foremost among them was the growing international prominence of Tibetan scholars working within the People's Republic of China. In addition, she noted that even as "we are still in the process of assessing the scope of Tibetan literature and how much of it is extant," the field was becoming increasingly interested in literary materials that lie beyond the institutionalized canons; she no doubt had in mind the medical texts that would form the basis for her subsequent monograph, among other types of literature.[2]

The synopsis of Janet's contributions to the study of Buddhist and Tibetan traditions below is organized into five major themes of her oeuvre, highlighting several of her influential publications in each area and showcasing her intellectual development over time. These are (1) women, gender, and sexuality; (2) biography and autobiography; (3) the Nyingma imaginaire; (4) literature, art, and poetry; and (5) early modernity: human and nonhuman worlds. These topics might appear at first glance to be discrete interventions, but upon close reading a clear trajectory appears, beginning with, and running through, her questions about the nature of human existence and experience—that is, the interrogation of what it means to be human. Through that central concern emerges her engagement with issues of gender and sexuality, Buddhist life writing and other genres of Tibetan literature, revelation and religious authority, artistic and poetic traditions, epistemic concerns in Tibetan medicine, and the Buddhist posthuman. The sketches that follow also introduce the twenty-nine contributions to the volume, which expand on each of these themes, directly or indirectly.

I. Women, Gender, and Sexuality

An iconic image from Janet's early publications is the "supine demoness," pinned beneath the thirteen demon-taming temples across the Tibetan plateau. It may be difficult to imagine reading feminine power into a myth of subjugation, but this is precisely what Janet does in "Down with the Demoness: Reflections on a Feminine Ground in Tibet," her earliest contribution to the study of gender in Tibetan Buddhism. In this myth of Tibet's imperial period (seventh to ninth centuries), found in later sources such as the *Maṇi Kabum*, the demoness (*srin mo*) is imagined as a chthonic force coextensive with the Tibetan plateau and its borderlands, which needs to be tamed in order for Buddhism and its civilizing effects to be established in Tibet. Only by constructing temples at her heart center (the Jokhang Temple) and three concentric squares on her shoulders and hips, elbows and knees, hands and feet, could Buddhism flourish on the plateau, or so the myth goes. Yet as Janet deftly shows, the demoness remains alive through the very narrative of her domination, and her formidable power is substantiated by the great lengths to which the masculine

2. Gyatso 2015a, 5.

religio-political structures go to keep her under control. As she concludes the essay, "the architectural erections ensure her perdurance below; she provides no less than the organic unity of the land, the totality of the context in which civilization could thrive" even as she "threatens to break loose" at any moment.[3]

José Cabezón's contribution to this volume, "The Revenge of the Demoness," takes up a parallel myth with a "demoness crucifixion motif" from the village of Kargah west of Gilgit, located in present-day Pakistan. In this case, it is a flesh-eating *yacheni* (likely a variant of the Sanskrit *yakṣinī*) nailed to and frozen in stone by a shaman, even though the associated image is clearly a standing Buddha carved in stone with his right hand at the heart in the "fear not" gesture and his left holding onto his robe. Cabezón traces the religious history of the region to argue for the myth as a local tale representing the indigenous reclamation of a Buddhist site with an attendant irony. Note the last words of his essay: "Gazing up once more at the image, with its slight smile, I wondered to myself whether it was actually the demoness who had had the last laugh, for what sweeter revenge could a demoness take on an invading Buddha than to eclipse all memory of him with a tale that's all about her?"

Women in Tibet (2005), which Janet edited with Hanna Havnevik, was in many ways a sequel to Janice Willis' *Feminine Ground: Essays on Women and Tibet* (1989), in which "Down with the Demoness" appeared. In their introduction, Gyatso and Havnevik lay out several foundational questions and lines of inquiry for the study of women and gender in Tibetan Buddhism, and their anthology helped to reignite a concern with these issues that has continued up to the present.[4] How do Tibetans define the category of "woman" in medical, religious, and linguistic terms? To what degree do Buddhist androcentric and misogynist stereotypes prevail in different types of discourses? Are their feminist or protofeminist inklings to be found in Tibetan writings? How does gender operate in tandem with class in Tibet and other markers of difference and marginality? Given the paucity of sources on the lives of Tibetan women, and the dominance of the male authorial voice in Tibetan literature, can a distinctive female voice, perspective, or literary style be identified? In addition to these questions, their introduction queries the simplistic notion that "models of female divinity in Indo-Tibetan religions have had a liberating effect on women's social status."[5] Instead of such ahistorical generalizations, Gyatso and Havnevik call for the spadework necessary to excavate historical and ethno-

3. Gyatso 1989, 51.

4. See, for example, Bessenger 2016, Diemberger 2007, Gayley 2016, Jacoby 2015, and Melnick Dyer 2022.

5. Gyatso and Havnevik 2005a, 1.

graphic specificities of women's lives, experiences, and perspectives, grounded in socio-economic conditions and/or found in literary responses to enduring stereotypes in discourse.

Several of these lines of inquiry are taken up by contributors to this volume. In "The In/Visibility of Nuns and Yoginīs in Dudjom Lingpa's Songs of Advice," Holly Gayley searches for clues about the lives of nuns and yoginīs in nomadic Golok at the margins of writings by the visionary Dudjom Lingpa (1835–1904). Examining selections from his collected songs (*mgur 'bum*) addressed to women, she finds evidence for advanced female renunciants practicing in long-term retreat, specifics about their life circumstances and challenges, the non-gendered nature of his advice on meditation practice, and idiosyncratic moments when gendered tropes and stereotypes come to the fore. In "Tibetan Nuns Writing on Equality and Education," Padma 'tsho directly addresses the question of feminist writings in contemporary Tibet. She identifies a "new education-based vision of gender equality in Buddhist terms" in essays by Tibetan nuns on women's equality (*bud med kyi 'dra mnyam*) in the journal *Gangkar Lhamo,* based at Larung Gar and founded by the female cleric-scholar Khenmo Kusum Chödrön. In addition, she provides lucid translations of several short essays so that readers can access their distinct voices and vision. In "Samtha/ the Borderlands of Tibetan Translation," Nicole Willock explores the poetry of exile Tibetan writer Nyima Tso, who convened Mayum, a group of Tibetan women writers based in India, and has served as editor of a literary magazine of the same name since 2010. Willock translates an early poem by Nyima Tso, "Life in Samtha/Borderlands" (*Sa mtha'i tsho ba*) first published in 2006, and reflects on issues of translation, hybridity, and exile through the theoretical lenses of Lawrence Venuti and Gloria Anzaldúa.

Janet's turn towards the construction of gender and sexuality in Buddhist monastic literature resulted in two groundbreaking articles on the topic, which are built upon by contributors to this volume. "Sex," the title of her chapter in *Critical Terms for the Study of Buddhism* (2005), traces the monastic preoccupation with and totalizing approach to cataloging the minutiae of sexual misconduct, from lewd innuendos and the penetration of different types of orifices to necrophilia and bestiality. In pondering the varieties of sexual transgressions and their legal consequences in the vinaya, Janet delves into the nitty gritty of what constitutes a sex act according to monastic jurisprudence as well as the possible reasons for such "obsessive analysis" in regulating celibacy well beyond pragmatic considerations of reputation and reproduction.[6] What Janet notes about the vinaya's "active sexual imagination" for the amusement and

6. Gyatso 2005b, 274.

edification of "prudent or prurient" monks,[7] Donald S. Lopez Jr. suggests in his essay here, "Sex, Part Two," can be seen as a kind of pornography. Not only are the stories of sex acts that accompany vinaya rules often fantastical, but in them repression and titillation seemingly go hand in hand, such that sex features in stories about rules quite unrelated to the topic, which Lopez likens to "hearing the punchline and then having to concoct the joke, with the requirement that the joke be about sex."

"One Plus One Makes Three: Buddhist Gender, Monasticism, and the Law of the Excluded Middle" (2003) was one of the first academic treatments on the third sex in Buddhism. Janet hones in on the category of the *paṇḍaka*, a catch-all category for people with non-conforming genders, who were excluded from monastic ordination among other forms of participation in Buddhist communal life. Yet, as she notes, the category sometimes also subsumes women who are deemed deficient in their reproductive organs and functions, leaving open the question of whether its criterion is deviance from gender binaries or normative maleness. Janet does not leave the matter there, going on to investigate how the *paṇḍaka* (Tib. *ma ning*) is valorized in Tibetan medical and tantric literature, thereby contrasting medical pragmatism and tantric inclusivity with the monastic legalistic impulse to define and regulate, excluding what is undefinable and potentially mercurial. In her inimitable and intrepid way, Janet concludes with a bold hypothesis: that the *paṇḍaka* functioned as a "scapegoat for the threat that woman was believed to pose to the monastic order," which may well have facilitated women's entry into its ranks, while simultaneously acting to "subvert the very 'order' that it created, writing slippage itself eternally into the system."[8]

Julie Regan gives Janet's investigation of the third sex contemporary relevance in her contribution, "The Possibilities of Emptiness and the Realities of (Trans) Gender," by suggesting the importance of her work to Buddhist LGBTQ+ communities today. She does this by revisiting the case of Michael Dillon, the first person to complete a modern medical gender transition, who then proceeded to become a novice monk in the Theravāda and later Tibetan traditions. In doing so, Regan reminds the reader of the ultimate fluidity and empty nature of the self and gender in classic Mahāyāna and Vajrayāna sources.

7. Gyatso 2005b, 277.

8. Gyatso 2003, 114.

II. Biography and Autobiography

"What is the nature of selfhood in Tibetan autobiography?"[9] This question sparked Janet's initial foray into Tibetan auto/biographical studies, in a paper presented at the International Association of Tibetan Studies (IATS) in Narita in 1989. She had a "near miss" with *namthar* studies early in her graduate career, during which she focused on Thangtong Gyalpo's doctrinal corpus but left the master's autobiography for another member of her graduate school cohort.[10] The IATS essay, published in 1992, noted that "autobiographical writing in Tibet is . . . unique among Asian literatures," for its "sheer quantity and relative frequency of occurrence," and differs widely in content and form from its counterparts in other Buddhist traditions.[11] The essay also raised important questions about the practice of writing one's own life story within a tradition that understands the self as "the principal villain."[12] And at its heart, her approach placed Tibetan forms of life writing in conversation with western theories of the self, self-reflection, and autowriting.

This inquiry culminated in Janet's first book *Apparitions of the Self*, published in 1998, which indelibly changed the landscape of Tibetan literary studies. It was among the first extended engagements with indigenous forms of Tibetan life writing with the aim of "draw[ing] them into the perilous domain of cross-cultural reflection" through a sustained conversation with western theories of cultural and literary criticism.[13] The book presents translations, close readings, and analyses of two secret autobiographies (*gsang ba'i rang rnam*) of the acclaimed visionary Jigmé Lingpa (1730–98). The focus was not on the form of hagiography per se, but rather the ways in which Tibetan literary self-representations express unique and individuated selves. Jigmé Lingpa's honesty and openness about his own faults and uncertainties served as an ideal platform for such reflections.

Apparitions of the Self is a work of stunning innovation. It stands among the first studies to consider Tibetan writing beyond traditional emic categories that valorize doctrinal and soteriological concerns, on the one hand, and the familiar Western approaches attending primarily to issues of history and philology on the other. It also pushed back on Eurocentric scholarly presumptions

9. Gyatso 1992a, 468.

10. She completed several short essays about Thangtong Gyalpo, including her first academic publication. See Gyatso 1980, 1986a.

11. Gyatso 1992a, 467.

12. Gyatso 1992a, 465.

13. Gyatso 1998a, xi.

Book signing for *Apparitions of the Self*, Amherst, MA, 1988. (Photographer unknown.)

about the lack of autobiographical writing beyond the West. Instead, Janet suggests that Tibetan life writing might be read, first and foremost, as literature, with works such as Jigmé Lingpa's secret autobiographies appreciated for their unique writerly qualities. These contributions have given birth to a new subfield of Tibetan auto/biographical studies—a phenomenon Janet herself identified as a "modest explosion, in Tibetan Studies, of scholarship on autobiographical writing"—demonstrated by the numerous Ph.D. dissertations and book publications over the two and a half decades since it first appeared.[14] Such work follows the trajectory of *Apparitions* with scholarship that continues to shift away from "the more traditional habits in Tibetology to read literature normatively—to establish a critical edition, or to cull and describe Buddhist doctrine, or to cull historical facts," and instead "endeavors to appreciate the idiosyncratic textures of everyday human life and values."[15]

Janet has likewise pursued an interest in the biographic literature of famous

14. Gyatso 2016, 229. Monographs that have followed in the footsteps of *Apparitions of the Self* include Bessenger 2016, Bogin 2013, Diemberger 2007, Gardner 2019, Gayley 2016, Gorvine 2018, Holmes-Tagchungdarpa 2014, Jacoby 2015, Melnick Dyer 2022, Quintman 2014, Schaeffer 2004, Yamamoto 2012.

15. Gyatso 2016, 229

women from the past, most prominently the two female masters associated with the eighth-century Indian tantric master Padmasambhava. Her introduction to an English translation of the life of Mandāravā (1998) asserts Mandāravā's status as a "female heroine in her own right," whose "connection with the famous Padmasambhava serves to enhance her image, rather than vice versa."[16] She reads Mandāravā's biography, revealed as treasure by Sangyé Lingpa (1340–1396), for its "messages about the path of female practitioners of Buddhism, its conceptions of female glory and power, its feminine and in some cases feminist sentiments, and its portrayal of the particular problems that females face in the world of Buddhism."[17] In her study on the various accounts of Yeshé Tsogyal's life story published nearly a decade later (2006), she addresses historical and philological questions about the biographical corpus of this foundational female religious figure in a search for the broader significance of her story for the Tibetan reading community. In doing so, she is admittedly reticent to read the story as evidence for a "proto-feminism," noting that the work these accounts do to create a female role model does not eradicate their evident misogyny.[18]

Matthew Kapstein's essay "How I Fell into Tulkuship: A Childhood Memoir from Northeastern Tibet," echoes Janet's work on Jigmé Lingpa. He translates a passage from the autobiography of Düjom Dorjé Rölpatsel, a late-eighteenth-century Buddhist teacher from the Rebkong region of eastern Tibet who expresses doubts about his status as a *tulku* (*sprul sku*), or recognized reincarnation of an earlier master. The author presents a critical view of the "less savory" aspects of Tibetan religion, punctuated by abandoning his position as a Geluk monk and adopting the renunciate lifestyle of a Nyingma ascetic. Elizabeth Angowski's essay "Auto/Biography for the End of the World: A Treasure Theory of Reading Revealed Life Stories" turns to the figure of Yeshé Tsogyal to offer a new theoretical framework for reading and interpreting auto/biographical literature considered to be *terma*, or treasures. Through a close examination of Yeshé Tsogyal's life story as appended to the *Testimonial Record of Padmasambhava* (*Padma bka' thang*), Angowski suggests that terma—and Buddhist scripture more broadly—implicate the reader in unique forms of world building. Samten G. Karmay highlights the biography of master painter and ritual expert Zur Chöying Rangdrol composed by none other than the Fifth Dalai Lama Lobzang Gyatso (1617–82). The essay foregrounds the Great Fifth's support of Nyingma ritual cycles even in the face of widespread Geluk

16. Gyatso 1998b, 6.

17. Gyatso 1998b, 10.

18. Gyatso 2006, 13.

sectarianism. Kurtis Schaeffer's contribution, "The Eleven Acts of Padmasambhava," turns to a work attributed to the acclaimed treasure revealer Guru Chöwang (1212–70), whose thirteenth-century survey of the terma tradition (*Gter 'byung chen mo*) was the focus of Janet's IATS presentation at Fagernes in 1992.[19] Guru Chöwang's narrative of Padmasambhava's life presents a rare example of this master's biographical corpus that uses the framing device of discrete "acts" (more commonly found in Tibetan presentations of the Buddha and Milarepa), and Schaeffer suggests this might prompt a broader comparative literary history of Tibetan narratives.

III. The Nyingma Imaginaire

Janet's forays into the secret autobiographies of Jigmé Lingpa and the historicity of Yeshé Tsogyal came as the capstone of two decades of scholarship on the treasure tradition. This is yet another subfield in Tibetan studies that she pioneered, first in her Ph.D. dissertation and later in a series of impactful articles. A number of her publications from the 1980s and '90s treat this distinctively Tibetan mode of revelation. While historians had dismissed revelatory literature as apocrypha and saw no further interest in the matter, Janet put aside the veracity of historical claims and set her sights on understanding emic theories regarding the revelation process. She inquired into the semiotics of treasure revelation, the logic of legitimation, self-representations of visionaries in claiming the mantle of tertön (*gter ston*), or "treasure revealer," and their voluminous literary production.

Many aspects of the treasure tradition, now presumed as common knowledge for scholars in the field, were first illuminated in Janet's foundational work. In "Signs, Memory, and History: A Tantric Buddhist Theory of Scriptural Transmission" (1986) she traced the transmission process from standard Nyingma paradigms to the further stages specific to treasure revelations, including the "visionary quest" itself.[20] Her primary concern was the semiotic aspects of transmission: the decoding of signs, only to encrypt and conceal them again, the prophetic clues leading up to revelation, the deciphering and translating of symbolic script (*brda yig*), and the treasure as a mnemonic device. Why the overdetermined layers of signification? Janet postulated that all this calls attention to the visionary talents of the tertön as the interpreter of signs, mediating through prophecy and memory between the authoritative past and degenerate present. As such, it is tied to issues of religious authority and legitimation.

19. Gyatso 1994.

20. Gyatso 1986c, 9.

Janet explores this last point in more detail in "The Logic of Legitimation in the Tibetan Treasure Tradition" (1993). Here she focused on the genre of history (*lo rgyus*) and its distinctive function in a revelatory context: as a mechanism to trace the tertön's literary productions back to Nyingma progenitors and, further, to propagate the lore of the imperial period itself. This genre was a crucial accompaniment to esoteric materials (tantric liturgies, yogic techniques, and advanced meditative instructions) that required legitimation in the face of sustained criticism and debates over their authenticity. Janet suggested that legitimating strategies "cannot be reduced to the matter of historical veracity, since their authenticity is also intimately tied to the authority of the Treasures' formulators, as well as their contents' soteriological virtues."[21] These strategies include prophecies and visions that alert the tertön to their calling and the location of treasures, whereby "the present individual is portrayed as fulfilling a destiny established in his [or her] own past life."[22] Moreover, various aspects of the treasure's core text (*gzhung rtsa*) signal its sanctity, including verbal formula, the inclusion of symbolic script attributed to *ḍākinīs* (tantric female deities), and the use of a special orthographical feature, the *tertsek* (*gter tsheg*). Historical accounts bolster these numinous aspects with an *origin account* of how the teaching was first transmitted and hidden during the imperial period by Padmasambhava or comparable figures and a *revelation account,* which is autobiographical on the part of the tertön, about the discovery process with all its contingencies (struggles, doubts, missed opportunities) and auspicious coincidences (success often with the aid of transempirical beings). Anticipating her study of Jigmé Lingpa's writings in *Apparitions of the Self,* Janet explores—with characteristic attention to rhetoric and shifting registers—the tensions between self-assertion and humility by tertöns: the confident tone regarding the authoritative origins of treasures and the acknowledgment of human fallibility in living up to their prophetic destiny, even while assuming the role of tertön stakes a claim to special yogic capacities and a high degree of spiritual realization.

Janet treats a host of related issues in other formative articles, too many to cover in detail here. These include questions of revelatory authorship in "Genre, Authorship, and Transmission in Visionary Buddhism: The Literary Traditions of Thang-stong Rgyal-po" (1992), tantric understandings of memory in "Letter Magic: A Pericean Perspective on the Semiotics of Rdo Grub-chen's Dhāraṇī Memory" (1992), defenses of the treasure tradition in "Guru Chos-dbang's *gTer 'byung chen mo*: An Early Survey of the Treasure Tradition and its

21. Gyatso 1993, 106.

22. Gyatso 1993, 109.

Strategies in Discussing Bon Treasure" (1994), compilations of treasures from the cycles of individual tertön up to grand anthologies such as the *Rinchen Terdzö* (*Rin chen gter mdzod*) in "Drawn from the Tibetan Treasury: The *gTer ma* Literature" (1996), and the nature of religious experience itself in "Healing Burns with Fire: The Facilitations of Experience in Tibetan Buddhism" (1999).

While the essays in this section, for the most part, do not explicitly treat topics related to treasure revelation, they illuminate issues in the broader Nyingma imaginaire in which revelation is embedded, including cosmological formulations, schemas of transmission, ritual practice and liturgies, as well as the literary legacy of tertöns. Two contributors echo Janet's research interest in the visionary Jigmé Lingpa. In "'Karma and Aspirations Converge': On Tendrel, Tsok, and Two Portraits of Jigmé Linga," Benjamin Bogin reflects on the famed "Feast Song" (*tshogs glu*) by Jigmé Lingpa used in Nyingma ritual with its emphasis on *tendrel* (*rten 'brel*), the coming together of causes and conditions in an auspicious manner. He suggests a fresh approach to understanding tendrel in ritual contexts as evoked by the haunting melodies of devotional songs like this one, as potentially transformative for the community thereby transported to a sublime state, and as conveying concise esoteric instructions encoded in its imagery. In "Jigmé Lingpa's Theology of Absence," Willa Baker explores collective memory in a recently surfaced "testament of realization" (*rtogs brjod*). She focuses on affect in memory, encapsulated in the Tibetan term *dranpa* (*dran pa*) and signifying here a "nostalgia, memory tinged with longing for an idealized past"—memory, that is, which contains not only the "shadow of absence," but also the potential for connection and realization, especially while on pilgrimage to sacred sites traversed by the great masters of yore.

The other contributions in this section deal with ritual and cosmology in the Nyingma tradition. In "Introductions in Order and Matter Out of Place: Entangled Epiphanies Between Mind and Matter," James Gentry explores how signs mediate between mind and matter in Nyingma ritual contexts, specifically the introduction to the nature of mind, which he defines as an "epiphany of nondual cognition." In "Divine Creation and Pure Lands in Renaissance Tibet," David Germano examines cosmological features in the Seminal Heart (*snying thig*) literature among the Nyingma, in particular a divine ontology deriving from gnosis, which he asserts was "born in the fertile soil of the Tibetan language and imagination." In "Evoking the Divine Human: *An Appearance of Suchness: Ornament of the Sacred*," Jacob Dalton translates and studies several versions of a versified Mahāyoga meditation manual (*sādhana*) that dates, perhaps, to the second half of the eighth century. This work draws heavily from the *Guhyagarbha Tantra*, a foundational Nyingma scripture, and thus points to materials at the heart of the Nyingma imaginaire.

IV. Literature, Art, and Poetry

Much of Janet's Tibetological scholarship has addressed literary, artistic, and poetic traditions as practices that illuminate the human qualities of life on the high plateau. These might reflect opportunities for transformation and awakening, engagements with material or visionary worlds, encounters with the wondrous or the perplexing, or even crises of identity and moments of self-doubt. Janet's interest in Tibetan art early in her career led to a fruitful collaboration with Valrae Reynolds, former curator of the Tibet collections at the Newark Museum of Art, and art historian Amy Heller (whose contribution on the sculpture portraits of the Fifth Dalai Lama appears in this volume) to produce an initial catalog of the museum's holdings.[23] Her introductory essay in that catalog, "Image as Presence: The Place of Art in Tibetan Religious Thinking," was an initial effort to articulate the social resonance of Tibetan images, not merely as symbolic representations but as living embodiments of their subject imbued with a "powerfully numinous presence."[24]

Janet's attentiveness to expressions of the human has likewise guided her career-long engagement with Tibetan and Buddhist literature. Over the past several decades she has led the field to reevaluate how Tibetan writing is assessed, interpreted, translated, and analyzed. This work has progressed along several different lines of inquiry. She has offered fresh perspectives on some of the best-known Tibetan types of literature, such as auto/biography and treasure literature, each discussed elsewhere in this introduction.[25] She has also shed light on literary forms that have remained undervalued if not altogether overlooked, as was the case with diary writing and other kinds of personal notation. Collectively, this work raises several prominent questions that have intrigued scholars of Tibet for more than a century: What constitutes the parameters of Tibetan literature? What kinds of writing are worthy of scrutiny? How might the boundaries of genre categories, and their porousness, be demarcated and understood? Yet much of Janet's work points to the more complex issue of the literary dimensions in Tibetan writing—moments of "self-conscious and even self-referential signification" that authors may use to push beyond mere reference, representation, or denotation. In her informal introductory remarks at the spring 2013 meeting of the Tibetan Literature seminar, Janet noted that

23. Gyatso 1986b.

24. Gyatso 1986b, 31.

25. Gyatso noted, however, that "The rubric gter ma, or 'Treasure,' cannot properly be characterized as representing a genre of Tibetan literature" since texts classified as such represent many different genres. See Gyatso 1996, 147.

great writing is often self-conscious of its own literary qualities, which it then uses to advantageous effect. Such works, she continued, might be approached through a variety of analytical and interpretive frames including sound, semantics, discursive forms, subjective positions, and reader reception and response.[26] These frameworks are indeed apparent in the publications surveyed here.

Several early essays in the leadup to *Apparitions* explicitly attend to the literary dimensions of Tibetan writing. Her 1992 "Genre, Authorship, and Transmission in Visionary Buddhism" (noted above) returned to the figure Thangtong Gyalpo and his literary oeuvre for a consideration of authorship and genre in the formation of treasure literature. This was, in part, an early exploration of the terma tradition more broadly, by emphasizing the literary qualities of such works. In it, she suggests identifying a corpus of texts constituting the "visionary core" of Thangtong Gyalpo's works that present "a rich array of theoretical paradigms and literary genres."[27]

Diaries and personal notation in her 1997 work "Counting Crow's Teeth: Tibetans and Their Diary-Writing Practices" serve as points of comparison to the autobiographical processes at the center of *Apparitions*. It also illustrates Janet's ethnographic research attending to contemporary literary practices (both religious and secular) as a lens for better framing historical formations. The topic, she notes, was the cause for some anxiety among her informants and elicited "a complex and sometimes conflicting set of attitudes toward diary writing," especially from her main informant Dodrupchen Rinpoché.[28] On the one hand, educated Tibetans may describe diary writing as a meaningless, even useless activity, likened to "counting the teeth on a crow (*bya rog so brtags*)." Yet the process of personal diary writing and Tibetan attitudes toward it are complex and multidimensional, from which Janet draws multiple layers of meaning. She suggests that reading personal diaries in conjunction with public autobiographies might shed light on how Tibetan authors negotiate the apparent "disparity between private preference and cultural norms."[29]

Janet's recent work has turned once again to poetry. In this case, the focus is not visionary verse forms like those in Jigmé Lingpa's secret autobiography, but rather the traditions of Tibetan *belles-lettres* known as *nyenngak* (*snyan ngag*), derived from Indian *kāvya*. In collaboration with Tibetan scholar and author Pema Bhum, "Condensed Tibetan Allusions" (2017) explores a technical aspect of Tibetan *kāvya* composition known as "condensed speech" (Tib.

26. Religion and the Literary in Tibet Seminar, Harvard University, April 13, 2013.

27. Gyatso 1992b, 100, 106.

28. Gyatso 1997, 160.

29. Gyatso 1997, 177.

bsdus brjod, Skt. *samākosti*), one of many rhetorical devices and forms of literary ornamentation (Tib. *rgyan*, Skt. *alaṃkāra*) discussed in Daṇḍin's *Mirror of Poetics* (*Kāvyādarśa*).[30] This work was deeply influential in Tibet through translations of the main text extending back to the thirteenth century, as well as a large body of commentarial literature. Her collaborative 2017 essay focuses on a specific genre of *kāvya* commentary known as the "exercise book" (*dper brjod*), which serve as practical guides to poetic composition through illustrations of the various literary devices. Like personal diaries, exercise books had previously received little scholarly attention, and this collaboration fruitfully surveys a subfield that bears further scrutiny. But this work also highlights the social and political agendas such texts supported and the programmatic functions they served, both in early modern Tibet and post-Cultural Revolution China. This ongoing collaboration has led to a more expansive study of the Kāvyādarśa in "Mirror on Fire: An Ardent Reception in Tibet and Mongolia" for a forthcoming volume *Daṇḍin in the World*.[31] This essay surveys the *Mirror*'s long, and occasionally fraught, history in Tibet and Mongolia through the premodern, early modern, and post-Mao periods, and further suggests the influence it continues to hold on the composition of poetry for contemporary Tibetan writers.

In this collection, Sonam Kachru takes *Apparitions of the Self*, described by Janet as "philosophical literature," as a starting point to consider wide-ranging relationships between literature and philosophy and, in particular, between literary aesthetics and liberative practice. "Can the ascetic," he asks, "learn anything from one who takes up an aesthetic approach to life?" Through a careful reading of Śāntideva's *Bodhicaryāvatāra*, he suggests that literary representations of bodhisattvas on the path to awakening and erotic lovers in the thrall of desire exhibit "isomorphic structures" and "similar orientations for success." Dominique Townsend continues with themes of literary affect and aesthetic resonance in "On Gutsiness: The Courageous Eloquence of *Pöpa Chenpo*," in which she reads an abecedarian poem (*ka rtsom*) by Terdak Lingpa (1646–1714) as an example of "courageous eloquence" through a careful consideration of the Tibetan term *pöpa chenpo* (*spobs pa chen po*).

Pema Bhum's "The First Tibetan Orthographical Dictionary: *Dag yig nyer mkho bsdus pa* (*Précis of Essential Orthography*)" surveys an important work by the acclaimed eleventh-century Tibetan translator Ngok Loden Sherab (1059–1109), addressing the need for uniform grammar and standardized spelling. Such texts were especially pertinent in the time before the advent of woodblock print technology in Tibet, and Bhum demonstrates that the *Précis*

30. Bhum and Gyatso 2017.

31. Bhum and Gyatso forthcoming.

exerted wide-ranging influence on Tibetan writing, especially the composition of *nyenngak*, the topic of his collaborative efforts with Janet. Nancy G. Lin likewise addresses *nyenngak* in her essay "What Language We Dare Learn and Speak: Decolonizing the Study of Tibetan Poetry." There, she is concerned not with the formal properties of Tibetan poetics but rather a reception history of *nyenngak* in European and American scholarship and the "romantic, modern, and mysticist notions" that have frequently colored such work. Attending more carefully to indigenous Tibetan notions of aesthetics and taste, she suggests, might decolonize our assumptions about Tibetan belletristic composition and bring into view new modalities of Tibetan religiosity.

Turning to examples of contemporary poetry, Lama Jabb introduces and translates three poems by the award-winning poet Chimay in "The Immortal Ring of Love, Karma, and Poetry." His analysis draws attention to the lyricism and emotional intensity of her poems, the sounds and rhythm "devised by the poet to appeal to the ear and the heart alike," and the role of love, memory, and loss at play in her poetry "like an old, open wound that refuses to heal." Andrew Quintman also takes up themes of poetry, emotion, and affect in "A Sad Song of Jonang," which translates a short verse inscribed in the margins of a Communist reeducation pamphlet. He surveys expressions of sadness in a range of poetic forms that reflect not only religious sorrow (at the suffering of others or the absence of one's guru) but also "critiques of human experience in the face of social, cultural, religious, and political forces."

Engaging with the Dynamics of Devotion panel at the first Lotsawa Translation Workshop, Boulder, CO, 2018. Photograph courtesy of the Tsadra Foundation.

In "Two Sculpture-Portraits of the Fifth Dalai Lama, His Dedications, and the People to Whom He Bestowed Them," Amy Heller examines a pair of remarkable images commissioned by two individuals in the Great Fifth's entourage. Her careful analysis suggests that such works might be understood as an extension of the autobiographical process that Janet addresses in *Apparitions*. Leonard W. J. van der Kuijp reflects Janet's engagement with Buddhist literature in his essay "Some Observations on the *Buddhāvataṃsakasūtra* in Tibet." This careful study of the *Buddhāvataṃsaka Sūtra* addresses the work's translation, reception, and transmission history in Tibet, suggesting that texts such as this made significant impacts on the religious culture of the high plateau, even as Tibetan exegetes tended to favor commentarial works.

V. Early Modernity: Human and Nonhuman Worlds

Nowhere is Janet's interest in and scholarly pursuit of the human more pronounced than her second monograph, *Being Human in a Buddhist World: An Intellectual History of Medicine in Early Modern Tibet* (2015). This is a masterful work, beautifully rendered with medical illustrations based on the original seventy-nine plates that the religio-political figure Desi Sangyé Gyatso (1653–1705) himself commissioned and oversaw. The illustrations are a jumping-off point to her analysis on medical empiricism, given their detailed attention to the practicalities and idiosyncrasies of quotidian life, their concern with botanical accuracy, their representation of the observable facets of human and animal behavior, and their displacement of religious figures and artifacts from centrality in so much Tibetan artistic and textual production. As Janet suggests, in rendering medical knowledge pedagogically visible and by championing observation and realism, the Desi positioned Tibetan medicine as a comprehensive system of knowledge on par with Buddhism and paralleling its aim to mitigate suffering. This had everything to do with state formation of the Ganden Podrang under the rule of Dalai Lamas, exercising "the power and position to know and control," projecting outwardly "medicine's responsibility for the welfare of the people," and linking medical learning to the "stability and health of the state and its ruler."[32]

In her analysis of the "medical mentality" in seventeenth-century Tibet, Janet argues for the rise of an early modern empiricism that coalesced and reinforced the state-making endeavors of the Great Fifth Dalai Lama and his regent Desi Sangyé Gyatso. With this, she undercut the long-standing habit in both popular and academic writing of referring to Tibet prior to the 1950s as

32. Gyatso 2015a, 78 and 97.

"premodern," a discourse that inadvertently reinforces Orientalist depictions of Tibet as an isolated feudal society thrust into modernity by the arrival of the People's Liberation Army, a discourse perniciously deployed by Chinese Communist propaganda. Instead, the reader encounters the cosmopolitan world of seventeenth-century Lhasa in the process of systematizing forms of knowledge as part of the state apparatus, even as it turned back toward the glory of the Tibetan empire to anchor and confer prestige on the medical tradition. Even so, Janet argues that empiricism opened a space for critique: candidness and criticalness were "the products of—and models for—professional medical ethics" as well as signs of early modernity.[33]

When Janet makes the case for early modernity in Tibet, she is focused mainly on that category in epistemic terms, or more specifically the "attitudes and values associated with modernity" such as questioning religious truths and authority based on empirical evidence.[34] In "The Authority of Empiricism and the Empiricism of Authority: Tibetan Medicine and Religion on the Eve of Modernity" (2004), for example, she discusses two types of experience within medical empiricism: "the special kind of knowledge acquired only in practice, guided by a teacher" and "the particular type of knowledge that comes from direct perception."[35] As elsewhere, Janet is attuned to specific genres that illuminate a particular theme or problematic, in this case "writing from experience" (*nyams yig*), the detailed notes from medical observation and diagnosis that came to supersede in pragmatic importance canonical formulations of medical knowledge. Unlike the Buddhist ambivalence about experience, as discussed in her article "Healing Burns with Fire: The Facilitations of Experience in Tibetan Buddhism" (1999), the medical tradition valorized the powers of observation without equivocation. Medical writers nonetheless had to carefully balance forms of authority between scriptural precedent and empirical evidence, for example with respect to the yogic channels in the subtle body of Buddhist tantra. Her focus on cultural and epistemic shifts is likewise central to her introductory essay to the anthology *Mapping the Modern in Tibet*, "Discerning Tibetan Modernities: Moments, Methods, Assumptions" (2011), in arguing that modernity did not come to Tibet all of a sudden as if "alien to its own trajectory."[36]

Emblematic of the interdisciplinary impulse behind her investigations of the human and nonhuman, and her attunement to the details in literary and

33. Gyatso 2015a, 90.

34. Gyatso 2004, 18.

35. Gyatso 2004, 19.

36. Gyatso 2011, 6.

artistic forms, Janet manages to attend to philological issues in her studies on Tibetan medicine, such as the slippage between the homophones "woman" (*bud med*) and "without sons" (*bu med*), both pronounced "bumé," in medical literature on fertility in "Spelling Mistakes, Philology, and Feminist Criticism: Women and Boys in Tibetan Medicine" (2008), while at the same time considering the artistic qualities and sensibilities of the medical paintings commissioned by Desi Sangyé Gyatso in her contribution to *Bodies in Balance: The Art of Tibetan Medicine* (2014).

Janet is currently exploring a new area of inquiry as she ventures into animal studies. Her emergent work is inspired by a Buddhist compassion for all sentient beings, especially during this period of ever-worsening brutality toward animals in the Anthropocene. She is then extending that concern into questions around new kinds of subjectivity and their relation to ethical commitment, aiming to contribute to the development of better ways of seeing, appreciating, and living with animals—and maintaining the best quality of life on our planet for all creatures. This connects to Janet's growing interest in opening new epistemologies based in bodily, aesthetic, ritual, prophetic, and other nondiscursive forms of knowledge. As with her other projects, she is contributing to contemporary intellectual and artistic conversations, using resources coming out of the Buddhist, and especially, Tibetan Buddhist world—although for the first time she will explicitly bring in her own life experience as well.

Contributors to this final section reflect on the human and nonhuman in Tibetan language, aesthetics, philosophy, and literature. In "Tendrel: Being Human in a More-than-Human World," Sarah Jacoby takes up the Tibetan term *tendrel* and its wide semantic range (from the philosophical understanding of "dependent origination" to colloquial usage as "good omens") that points to human agency intertwined with the more than human. Finding inspiration in the posthumanist and materialist turns, she explores tendrel within "Tibetan practices of geopiety" and "as a valid knowledge system that can serve as a reminder in this time of multiple crises that human flourishing is dependent on relations with others, including other animals, plants, air, water, soil, and rocks." In "The Poetry of Being Human: Toward a Tibetan Wisdom Literature," Christina Kilby finds connections between the Hebrew writing known as wisdom (*hokma*) literature and the "human dharma" (*mi chos*) discussed in Janet's *Being Human in a Buddhist World*. In particular, she suggests reading certain forms of writing (such as Mipham Dawa's instructions on human discourse and Jigmé Lingpa's letter to a young renunciate) as uniquely Tibetan expressions of wisdom literature.

In "The Buddhist Aesthetic of Replication," Jonathan Gold focuses on the ubiquitous presence of formulaic repetition in Buddhist sūtra literature. What, he asks, were the reciters and redactors of these works trying to express with "all this duplication"? Repetition, Gold suggests, lies at the center of Buddhist expression and self-representation—beginning with the Three Jewels but also including the workings of karma, experience of the self, buddha nature, emptiness, and the path to liberation—and therein, he concludes, lies the beginning of virtue. Jay Garfield extends Janet's work on Tibetan modernity into the domain of epistemology in his essay, "Knowing Knowledge: Geluk and Sellarsian Epistemology and the Emergence of Tibetan Modernity." He explores the work of the American philosopher Wilfred Sellars in conjunction with the Geluk founder Tsongkhapa in exploring the relationship between epistemology and normativity, asserting in the process that "any account of our lives that denies the reality of the norms that governs them therefore denies our very humanity."

In "My Life as a Parakeet: A Bönpo Version of the Conference of the Birds," Charles Ramble introduces and translates sections from a delightful fourteenth-century Bönpo parable in which a gathering of birds addresses the very human concerns of law, statecraft, and the maintenance of a fair and well-regulated society. Heather Stoddard addresses a puzzling detail from the life of Gendun Chöpel, often described as Tibet's "first modernist," in her essay "From the Blue Lake to the Emerald Isle via the Kingdom of Sikkim: An Offering to Janet Gyatso, a Dear Friend in Mindful Travels Around the Land of Snows." During his years of travel in India, Gendun Chöpel came into contact with a number of Theravāda monks in the Sri Lankan tradition. Most famous among them was the polyglot scholar and activist Rahul Sankrityayan, but Stoddard identifies another figure, Mahinda Thero, younger brother to the acclaimed Sikkimese scholar and translator Kazi Dawa Samdup, and recounts the circumstances through which he encountered Gendun Chöpel.

This panoramic survey of Janet's scholarly oeuvre offers a bird's-eye view of her intellectual engagements. Although the preceding pages reference some of her most important writings, they necessarily elide others that are no less consequential: these include her critique of Thomas Altizer's appeal to Buddhism in his own theological writing (famously suggesting "God is dead"), published in "Compassion at the Millenium: A Buddhist Salvo for the Ethics of the Apocalypse" (2004); her exploration of Buddhist approaches to personal transformation, making special note of transformation narratives of biography and autobiography, in "The Ins and Outs of Self-Transformation: Personal and Social Sides of Visionary Practice in Tibetan Buddhism" (2002); her analysis of the ethical import of imaginatively inhabiting the perspective of another, per the practice of "exchanging self and other" from Śāntideva's classic *Bodhi-*

caryāvatāra, in "Seeing from All Sides" (2019); and a review of recent efforts to restore the status of full ordination (*bhikṣunī*) for nuns in the Tibetan tradition drawn from her witnessing of, and behind-the-scenes participation in, a convocation held in Bodhgaya, India, in "Recently, Under the Bodhi Tree: The New Bhiksuni Trajectory in Tibetan Buddhism" (2017). The contributions to this volume likewise demonstrate reverberations of Janet's thinking across many dimensions of Tibetan and Buddhist studies today, but they also present just a partial picture. We call the reader's attention to the list of Janet's publications in the appendix to this volume.

Works Cited

Bessenger, Suzanne M. 2016. *Echoes of Enlightenment: The Life and Legacy of the Tibetan Saint Sonam Peldren*. New York: Oxford University Press.

Bhum, Pema and Janet Gyatso. 2017. "Condensed Tibetan Allusions." *Rivista Degli Studi Orientali* 90 (spring): 165–78.

———. Forthcoming. "*Mirror* on Fire: An Ardent Reception in Tibet and Mongolia." In *Daṇḍin in the World*, edited by Yigal Bronner. New York: Oxford University Press.

Bogin, Benjamin. 2013. *The Illuminated Life of the Great Yolmowa*. Chicago: Serindia Publications.

Diemberger, Hildegard. 2007. *When a Woman Becomes a Religious Dynasty: The Samding Dorje Phagmo of Tibet*. New York: Columbia University Press.

Gardner, Alexander. 2019. *The Life of Jamgon Kongtrul the Great*. Boulder, CO: Snow Lion Publications.

Gayley, Holly. 2016. *Love Letters from Golok: A Tantric Couple in Modern Tibet*. New York: Columbia University Press.

Gorvine, William M. 2018. *Envisioning a Tibetan Luminary: The Life of a Modern Bönpo Saint*. New York: Oxford University Press.

Gyatso, Janet. 1980. "The Teachings of Thang-stong rGyal-po." In *Tibetan Studies in Honour of Hugh Richardson*, edited by Michael Aris and Aung San Suu Kyi, 111–19. Warminster: Aris and Phillips.

———. 1986a. "Thang-stong rGyal-po, Father of the Tibetan Drama: The Bodhisattva as Artist." In *Zlos-gar, The Tibetan Performing Arts: Commemorative Issue on the Occasion of the 25th Anniversary of the Founding of the Tibetan Institute of Performing Arts (1959–84)*, edited by Jamyang Norbu, 91–104. Dharamsala, India: Library of Tibetan Works and Archives.

———. 1986b. "Image as Presence: The Place of the Work of Art in Tibetan Religious Thinking." In *The Newark Museum Tibetan Collection III. Sculpture and Painting*, edited by Valrae Reynolds, Amy Heller, and Janet Gyatso, 30–35. Newark, NJ: The Newark Museum of Art.

———. 1986c. "Signs, Memory and History: A Tantric Buddhist Theory of Scriptural Transmission." *Journal of the International Association of Buddhist Studies* 9.2: 7–35.

———. 1989. "Down with the Demoness: Reflections on a Feminine Ground in Tibet." In *Feminine Ground: Essays on Women and Tibet*, edited by Janice Dean Willis, 33–52. Ithaca, NY: Snow Lion Publications.

———. 1992a. "Autobiography in Tibetan Religious Literature: Reflections on Its Modes of Self-Presentation." In *Tibetan Studies: Proceedings of the 5th International Association of Tibetan Studies Seminar*, edited by Shoren Ihara and Zuiho Yamaguchi, 2: 465–78. Narita, Japan: Naritasan Institute for Buddhist Studies.

———. 1992b. "Genre, Authorship, and Transmission in Visionary Buddhism: The Literary Traditions of Thang-Stong Rgyal-Po." In *Tibetan Buddhism: Reason and Revelation*, edited by Ronald M. Davidson and Steven Goodman, 95–106. Albany: State University of New York Press.

———. 1993. "The Logic and Legitimation in the Tibetan Treasure Tradition." *History of Religions* 33.1: 97–134.

———. 1994. "Guru Chos-dbang's *gTer 'byung chen mo*: An Early Survey of the Treasure Tradition and its Strategies in Discussing Bon Treasure." In *Tibetan Studies: Proceedings of the Sixth International Association of Tibetan Studies Seminar*, edited by Per Kvaerne, 1: 275–87. Oslo: The Institute for Comparative Research in Human Culture.

———. 1996. "Drawn from the Tibetan Treasury: The *gTer ma* Literature." In *Tibetan Literature: Studies in Genre*, edited by José Ignacio Cabezón and Rodger R. Jackson, 147–69. Ithaca, NY: Snow Lion Publications.

———. 1997. "Counting Crow's Teeth: Tibetans and Their Diary-Writing Practices." In *Les Habitants Du Toit Du Monde*, edited by Samten Karmay and Philippe Sagant, 159–77. Paris: Societe d'ethnologie.

———. 1998a. *Apparitions of the Self: The Secret Autobiography of a Tibetan Visionary*. Princeton, NJ: Princeton University Press.

———. 1998b. Introduction to *The Lives and Liberation of Princess Mandarava*. Translated by Lama Chonam and Sangye Khandro, 1–17. Boston: Wisdom Publications.

———. 2002. "The Ins and Outs of Self-Transformation: Personal and Social Sides of Visionary Practice in Tibetan Buddhism." In *Self and Self-Transformation in the History of Religions*, edited by David Shulman, 183–94. Oxford: Oxford University Press.

———. 2003. "One Plus One Makes Three: Buddhist Gender, Monasticism, and the Law of the Non-Excluded Middle." *History of Religions* 43.2: 89–115.

———. 2004. "The Authority of Empiricism and the Empiricism of Authority: Tibetan Medicine and Religion in the Eve of Modernity." *Comparative Studies of South Asia, Africa, and the Middle East* 24.2: 83–96.

———. 2005a. Introduction to *Women of Tibet*, edited by Janet Gyatso and Hanna Havnevik, 1–25. New York: Columbia University Press.

———. 2005b. "Sex." In *Critical Terms for the Study of Buddhism*, edited by Donald S. Lopez Jr., 271–90.

———. 2006. "A Partial Genealogy of the Life Story of Ye shes mtsho rgyal." *Journal of the International Association of Tibetan Studies* 2: 1–27.

———. 2011. "Discerning Tibetan Modernities: Moments, Methods, and Assumptions." In *Mapping the Modern in Tibet: PIATS 2006, Tibetan Studies, Proceedings of the Eleventh Seminar of the International Association for Tibetan Studies, Königswinter 2006*, edited by Gray Tuttle, 1–37. Halle, Saale: International Association for Tibetan Studies.

———. 2015a *Being Human in a Buddhist World: An Intellectual History of Medicine in Early Modern Tibet.* New York: Columbia University Press.

———. 2015b. "Beyond Representation and Identity: Opening Ways for Tibetan Studies." Inaugural Aris Lecture, Wolfson college, Oxford, 22 October, 2015. Unpublished lecture.

———. 2016. "Turning Personal: Recent Work on Autobiography in Tibetan Studies." *The Journal of Asian Studies* 75.1, 229–35.

Holmes-Tagchungdarpa, Amy. 2014. *The Social Life of Tibetan Biography: Textuality, Community, and Authority in the Lineage of Tokden Shakya Shri.* Lanham: Lexingon Books.

Jacoby, Sarah. 2015. *Love and Liberation: Autobiographical Writings of the Tibetan Buddhist Visionary Sera Khandro.* New York: Columbia University Press.

Melnick Dyer, Alison. 2022. *The Tibetan Nun Mingyur Peldrön: A Woman of Power and Privilege.* Seattle: University of Washington Press.

Quintman, Andrew. 2014. *The Yogin and the Madman: Reading the Life of Tibet's Great Saint Milarepa.* New York: Columbia University Press.

Schaeffer, Kurtis R. 2004. *Himalayan Hermitess: The Life of a Tibetan Buddhist Nun.* Oxford: Oxford University Press.

Yamamoto, Carl. 2012. *Vision and Violence: Lama Zhang and the Politics of Charisma in Twelfth-Century Tibet.* Leiden: Brill.

I.
Women, Gender, and Sexuality

The Revenge of the Demoness

José I. Cabezón

Among Janet Gyatso's many important contributions to the field of Tibetan studies, her early article on the myth of the taming of the *sinmo* (*srin mo*) demoness is one of my personal favorites.[1] It is one of the first mature pieces of scholarship to show how the analysis of gender can illuminate Tibetan religions. Widely cited, it has influenced several generations of scholars. Thirty years after its publication, it is still discussed in the Tibetan blogosphere.[2] Gyatso's "Down with the Demoness" has certainly influenced this essay, which examines the case of a demoness who hails from Gilgit.

According to the Tibetan *sinmo* demoness myth—or at least one version of it—Kongjo, the Chinese queen of Songtsen Gampo (seventh century), discerned that the land of Tibet was actually a supine demoness who was impeding the introduction of Buddhism (see figure 1). The solution, she divined, was to build temples at specific sites throughout Tibet to pin the demoness down and render her powerless. A fourteenth-century Tibetan historian tells us that the temples acted as twelve nails (*gzer*) to render the demoness immobile.[3] Although supposedly subduing the demoness for eternity, her subjugation had to be ritually renewed on a regular basis. For example, before 1959 the Tibetan cabinet convened annual prayer assemblies, offered juniper incense, and hung prayer flags on mountains associated with the twelve sites.[4]

Rakṣa/rākṣasī (*srin po/mo*) demons of the type found in the Tibetan myth are only one of a number of different types of spirits found in the Indo-Tibetan pantheon, which also includes nāgas, piśācas, bhūtas, yakṣas, and others. *Yakṣiṇīs* (*gnod sbyin mo*) and their male counterparts, *yakṣas* (*gnod sbyin*), the

1. Gyatso 1989.

2. See, e.g., Dawa Lokyitsang 2015 and Woeser 2016.

3. Bla ma dam pa Bsod nams rgyal mtshan, 57b–58a. See also Stein 1972, 39, and Sørensen 1986, 96–101.

4. Woeser 2016 quotes "the memoirs of Ganden Paljor Shatra" to this effect but does not cite a source. It is possible that she was relying on the several hours of interviews preserved in the Library of Congress collection, "Oral history interview of Shatra Ganden Paljor."

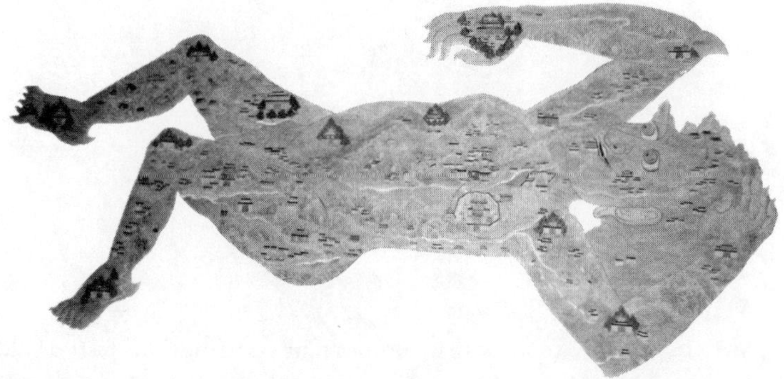

Figure 1. A painting of the supine demoness in a mural at the Khyichu Hotel, Lhasa. Photo: J. Cabezón.

kind of demon that most interests us in this essay, have a long history in Buddhism. They are usually malevolent, but the Mūlasarvāstivāda *Vinayavastu* contains various tales of the Buddha "taming" (*'dul*) these creatures.[5] For example, on the Buddha's visit to the city of Kuntī, he learns that the local yakṣiṇī and her hordes are abducting and eating newborn human children.[6] The Buddha addresses her and asks whether she will mend her ways. She agrees provided that the locals build her a temple. The Buddha encourages the city dwellers to do so, and she is thus "tamed."[7] These stories may be the Vinaya's way of incorporating local Indian spirit cults into Buddhism by having the Buddha sanction their propitiation and giving him a role in the founding of their temples. As in the Tibetan demoness myth, the building of temples is very much a part of the *Vinayavastu*'s yakṣiṇī-taming narratives, but rather than forcing a yakṣiṇī into submission, as in in the Tibetan *sinmo* myth, the Vinaya instead pacifies her by giving her a home, figuratively bringing her from the wilds of nature into the sedentary life of a home-bound spirit. In any case, the Vinaya does not advocate the kind of violent subjugation of spirits that we find in the Tibetan demoness myth.

Violence is, however, one of the ways that the tantras deal with malevolent spirits. One of the best examples is the myth of the taming of Rudra in the *Sūtra that Gathers the Intentions* (*Mdo dgongs 'dus*), purportedly translated from Burushaski (Tib. Bru sha skad), one of the languages of northern Pakistan.[8]

5. See, for example, *Vinayavastu*, vol. 2 (*kha*): 220b–222a, 224a, 225b–226b, and 236a–b.

6. *Vinayavastu*, *kha*: 225b, 226a, 236a: *bu btsas shing btsas pa dag za bar byed pa . . . 'phrog pa.*

7. *Vinayavastu*, *kha*: 225b–226b.

8. See Dalton 2016.

The violent suppression of demons is also found in other tantric works like the *Mahāmāyūrī Vidyārājñī*, a dhāraṇi text in which the Buddha teaches his audience mantras and prayers to protect them from malevolent spirits, thieves, witchcraft, diseases, and other calamities. The sūtra begins on a pacific note but later takes a more violent turn, threatening the evil spirits that their heads will burst "into seven pieces like bunches of breadfruit" if they do not obey.[9] Three copies of the *Mahāmāyūrī* dating to around the seventh or eighth century have been found among the Gilgit manuscripts. That same text also contains a long list of the names of various yakṣas who protect different cities or regions of India, including the yakṣa Mandāra, who belongs to Darada—in its broadest sense, northern Pakistan—which may help to explain the popularity of the text in this region.

Dardistan and Gilgit

Gilgit belongs to the area of the upper Indus River in what is today northern Pakistan (figure 2). It is a part of a larger area inhabited from ancient times by a people known as Dardae (Greek), Darada/Daran (Sanskrit), or Dards, the anglicized form used since the time of the British.[10] The boundaries of greater Dardistan are vague,[11] but in this essay it refers to northern Pakistan and far western Ladakh.[12]

In Chinese and Arabic documents of the eighth century, the eastern half of Dardistan is called Bolor.[13] The word Palola or Paṭola found on rock inscriptions near Gilgit refers to this same area. Chinese sources divide Bolor into two parts. "Little Bolor" refers to greater Gilgit, from Chilas up to and including Hunza in the north, and perhaps even Yasin. The language of ancient Bolor was Burushaski until the arrival of Shina-speaking people, perhaps in the tenth century.[14] Today, Gilgit is mostly Shina-speaking, while Hunza is mostly Burushaski-speaking. "Greater Bolor" is Baltistan, where Balti (Tib. Sbal ti), a form of Tibetan, is spoken. There are, however, alternative theories about the precise boundaries of ancient Bolor and its Little and Greater divisions.[15]

9. Chung 2012.

10. Leitner 1893, 2.

11. On the vexed problem of the category "Dard," see Mock and O'Neil (n.d.).

12. When treated as a linguistic area, Baltistan and the Burushaski-speaking areas of far northern Pakistan are not included in Dardistan because Balti and Burushaski are not Dardic languages, but I use the terms Dardic and Dardistan in the broader, geographic sense just mentioned.

13. Beckwith 1997, 30.

14. Nicolaus 2015, 204.

15. Zeisler (n.d.).

Figure 2: Map of northern Pakistan and surrounding areas. Modified from an original color map, "Afghanistan and Pakistan Atlas Wall Map," https://www.maps.com/products/afghanistan-and-pakistan-atlas-wall-map-910xhu.

The kingdom of Darada is mentioned in a few Sanskrit works translated into Tibetan.[16] But Tibetan sources mostly speak of the kingdom of Drusha (Bru zha or Bru sha), which corresponds to Little Bolor.[17] The *History of Domé* identifies Drusha as part of Ngari (Mnga' ris), making Drusha a part of Tibet (Bod yul), which of course it was for periods of time during the heyday of the Tibetan empire.[18]

The Karakorum Highway, which passes through Hunza Baltit, Nagar, Gilgit, and Chilas, was an important trade and pilgrimage route since ancient times, and inscriptions in Kharoṣṭhī and Brāhmī dating to before the Common Era—not to mention tens of thousands of petroglyphs—are found at various sites. Because it connected China, Tibet, Sogdiana, and the other kingdoms of the Silk Road to Gandhāra, Swat, and Kashmir, it was also strategically important and the site of many battles.[19] Tibetans sporadically controlled portions of Dardistan up to Kabul from the mid-seventh century,[20] and Tibetan

16. Darada (spelled *da ra ta*) is found, for example, among the kingdoms listed in the *Tathāgatācintyaguhyanirdeśa*, 215b.

17. Dotson 2009, 120.

18. Dkon mchog bstan pa rab rgyas 1975, 1:2a.

19. See, for example, Beckwith 1997.

20. Beckwith 1997, 30.

inscriptions are found at several sites. The Paṭola (or Palola) Ṣāhi kings, a Buddhist dynasty responsible for some of the Gilgit manuscripts as well as many religious images, ruled greater Gilgit from the sixth century, or perhaps earlier, though often as vassals of other more powerful states, including Tibet. The *Old Tibetan Annals* tells us that the Tibetan army conquered Gilgit in 737,[21] that the Tibetan princess Trimalö (Khri ma lod) was given in marriage to the king of Drusha in 740,[22] and that in the same year Drusha was lost to Chinese forces.[23] The Tang Chinese army withdrew from the region in 755 to deal with the An Lushan Rebellion, and the Tibetans likely held all of Gilgit and Baltistan from that time until the Tibetan empire collapsed in the mid-ninth century. After that, it seems that local Buddhist kings ruled Gilgit until it again came under the control of the Gugé (Gu ge) court of Western Tibet in the eleventh century.[24]

The history of Gilgit after the twelfth century is uncertain, and there are contradictory accounts.[25] One tradition, which is only preserved orally, mentions a local dynasty of Buddhist rulers called the Shahrais, whose last king, Shri Badat, was deposed, perhaps in the fourteenth century, by a Persian Zoroastrian prince, ushering in Gilgit's Trakhané (or Tarakhané) dynasty.[26] There are divergent accounts of when Islam entered the area, but by the sixteenth or seventeenth centuries, the cities of Gilgit, Nagar, and Hunza were under the control of various Muslim rulers. They held power for about two centuries, often feuding with one another, until the area came under the control of Sikh forces in the first half of the nineteenth century.[27] After the defeat of the Sikh empire at the hands of the British, Gilgit came nominally under the control of the Maharaja of Jammu and Kashmir, but from 1889 was administered by the British, who exerted increasing control over the region. After partition, it became a part of Pakistan.

21. Dotson 2009, 120; Jettmar 1993, 77–122.

22. Dotson 2009, 121.

23. Dotson 2009, 127.

24. Several Tibetan sources confirm that Ödé ('Od lde), the king of Ngari who flourished in the first half of the eleventh century, attacked Gilgit and married a Gilgit princess named Gyené (Rgyan ne); Martin 2017, 204–9.

25. See Dani 1991, 165ff.

26. Various writers consider Shri Badat to be a historical figure and date him to the thirteenth or fourteenth century. See Biddulph 1880, 20, and Jettmar 1993, 110–11. Dani (1991, 163–64), who gives the most naturalistic account of these events, considers him to be part of the Paṭola Ṣāhis and dates him to a much earlier period, circa 750. But the presuppositions required to arrive at this date seem implausible.

27. For a detailed year-by-year listing of various battles starting in 1800, see Leitner 1893, 70ff.

The Religious Landscape of Gilgit

It hardly needs saying that eastern Afghanistan and northern Pakistan—in ancient times the regions of Bactria, Gandhāra, and Swat—were important Buddhist centers from before the Common Era. Though often overshadowed by Gandhāra, Dardistan too was an important hub of Buddhism. A prince of Dardistan, the son of King Sindhugiri ("Indus Mountain") is even mentioned in the *Questions of Śrīvasu*, a Mahāyāna sūtra.[28] The *Prophecy of the Arhat Saṃghavardhana* portrays Drusha as a gathering place for monks facing persecution in other kingdoms,[29] and the *Khotanese Prophecy* identifies it as one of four kingdoms where there were many scholars learned in subjects besides Buddhism.[30] The *Avadāna Kalpalatā* of Kṣemendra (eleventh century) mentions that the Buddha "tamed two *guhyakas* [that is, yakṣas] who were Dards," suggesting that Dardistan was also known as a land of malevolent spirits.[31]

The form of Buddhism practiced in Dardistan was mostly of the exoteric variety, but the dhāraṇīs and vidyās of various deities (Hayagrīva, the Pancarakṣa, etc.) have also been found among the Gilgit manuscripts.[32] We have already mentioned the *Mahāmāyūrī*, and as we have seen, the *Sūtra that Gathers the Intentions* claims to be a translation from Burushaski. All of this suggests the presence of Vajrayāna in Gilgit from the seventh century. Despite claims that Hinduism became widespread after the decline of Buddhism, I have not found the evidence for this very convincing.

Islam entered Baltistan in the fourteenth century, carried there by Sufi preachers from Persia and Central Asia, like the famous Sayed Ali Hamdani (1314–84), who is credited with converting the Buddhists of Khaplu and Shigar, two small Balti towns. Residents of Khaplu preserve a legend of Hamdani entering into a magical contest with a "Balti lama" and converting the local people. It is possible that Islam spread from Baltistan to the Gilgit region starting in the fourteenth century, but most scholars believe that Gilgit and Hunza were not Islamized until the sixteenth century. Whatever the case, today, Twelver Shias, Nurbakshis, Ismailis, and Sunnis are all found in the region.[33]

28. *Śrīvasuparipṛcchā*, 225b–227b: *yul da ra da nas da ra da'i rgyal po sin du gi ri zhes bya ba'i bu bcom ldan 'das la blta ba dang/ phyag bya ba dang/ bsnyen bkur bya ba'i phyir wā ra ṇa sir song.* "The son of the king of Darada, called Sindhugiri, traveled from the country of Darada to Vārāṇasī in order to see, bow down to, and pay homage to the Buddha."

29. *Dgra bcom pa dge 'dun 'phel gyis lung bstan pa*, 165a.

30. *Li'i yul lung bstan pa*, 170a.

31. Das 1918, 2:44–45.

32. See Twist 2008, 278, and Kakas 2011, 427–35.

33. Lorimer 1929, 507–36; Jettmar 1961, 87; Rieck, 1995, 159–88.

The peoples of Dardistan undoubtedly had their own indigenous religious traditions before Buddhism arrived. Tibetan sources suggest that Drusha was one of the cradles of Tibet's pre-Buddhist Bön tradition. In his *Song of the Queen of Spring*, a history of Tibet, the Fifth Dalai Lama states that the "funerary Bön tradition of the Shen priests of Drusha arose [in Tibet]" at the time of the legendary Tibetan king Drigum Tsenpo (Gri gum btsan po).[34] Nor is this the only Tibetan text to mention Gilgit as a source of Bön. One Bön history states that when the god Brilliant Light ('Od zer mdangs ldan) was ready to manifest in the world, he surveyed Uḍḍiyāna, Drusha, and Tokharistan and then manifested as Drusha Namsé Chidöl (Bru sha Gnam gsas spyi rdol).[35] And as Dan Martin has shown, many Bön texts locate the Bön homeland of Ölmo Lungring ('Ol mo lung ring) in or near Dardistan.[36] Some petroglyphs found in Dardistan depict what seem to be Bön symbols.[37] Most of what we know about the beliefs and practices of early Tibetan Bönpos are from later sources, which tell us that Bön priests were called were called *shen* (*gshen*) and *aya/asha*, that they propitiated spirits, mediated between the human and spirit world, made clay effigies and thread crosses, performed animal sacrifices, played flat drums and bells, and rode on clay deer and on drums through the air.[38]

Many of these practices are also found in northern Pakistan and the Himalayas. Nowadays, the Dardic pantheon is divided into mostly malevolent male giants (*diyu*) and mostly benevolent fairies (*pari*), but a much more extensive and older pantheon in Gilgit and its surrounding villages has been document by Karl Jettmar and others.[39] It includes classes of spirits like the *devakos*, who are believed to have built the first irrigation channels and planted the first

34. Ngag dbang blo bzang rgya mtsho 1980, 13: *bru sha'i gshen gyi dur bon byung*. It is possible to read this as a general statement about the historical emergence of Dur Bön, but I here follow Per Kvaerne's reading: that the Shen arose *in Tibet* at this time to perform the funerary rituals of the slain Drigum Tsenpo. Kvaerne 1972, 33. See also Ramble 2007, 2:687.

35. See Hoffman 1969, 141. The work mentions the Tibetans' (probably Ödé's) invasion of Gilgit, how the Tibetans were defeated by a Bön priest riding a turquoise drum in space, and how four of Drusha Namsé great grandsons spread Bön in Tibet during the reign of Ödé's successor, Tsedé (spelled Btsad lde in the text).

36. Martin 1999.

37. Petroglyphs of different periods considered to be representations of shamanistic cults are found in various places in Dardistan. For a summary of those at Hodar, see Neelis 1999, 180. In Wakhan, north of Gilgit, rock carvings resemble motifs associated with Bön—specifically, a swastika with a crescent moon beneath it. On this, and for references to other research that discusses possible connections between Tibetan Bön and the pre-Buddhist religion of Dardistan, see Mock 2015, 127 and 133–34.

38. See Ramble 2007, 689–93.

39. On the pantheon of the Wakhi people of far northern Pakistan, see Mock 1998, 68–78.

corn; female *racchis*, who guide hunters; male *yamālos*, mountain demons who hunt and kill human beings with arrows; and *yachōlos*, who are household protectors.[40] Sanskrit equivalents for many of these terms—*deva*, *rākṣasī*, *yama*, *yakṣa*—suggest a relationship between the Dardic folk pantheon and that of Sanskritic traditions like Buddhism.

There are still practicing shamans throughout Dardistan, although the tradition is quickly vanishing.[41] The ones in Gilgit and Hunza, called *daiyal* or *danyal*, inhale burnt juniper to induce trance. Possessed by the fairies, they dance to beating drums and receive the fairies' messages through the drums' sound. They also travel to the spirit world.[42] *Daiyals* communicate with fairies, engage in divination, identify spells that have been cast on clients, use binding "mantras" (Shina: *gano*) to bring about desired goals, and heal the sick. Practices like those just described, which are ubiquitous throughout Dardistan and the western Himalayas, almost certainly predate the introduction of Buddhism and then coexisted alongside Buddhism (and later Islam), just as they did in Tibet.

To sum up, three distinct religious strands come together in greater Gilgit: (1) indigenous traditions that resemble the earliest forms of Bön, (2) Buddhism, especially in its Mahāyāna and early tantric forms, and (3) Islam in various sectarian forms. All of these traditions influenced one another throughout history.

The Kargah Buddha and the Yakṣinī

In 2018 I had the good fortune to travel through various part of northern Pakistan, including Gilgit.[43] Being interested in Buddhist sites, I went to see a large image of Śākyamuni carved into the side of a mountain located some six kilometers west of Gilgit between the villages of Kargah and Naupur[44] (figure 3). The standing Buddha figure, about ten feet tall, holds his right hand in the gesture of fearlessness at his heart, and clasps his lower robe with his left hand. Some art historians have dated the work to the eighth century. The Kargah Buddha is an impressive work of religious art, sculpted high on the face of a

40. Jettmar 1961, 88–89. Several decades earlier, Lorimer (1929) documented belief in various classes of spirits, some of which overlap with Jettmar's.

41. Leitner 1893, 8; and Lorimer 1929, 535–36. Lorimer (1929, 530–33) also speaks of another type of religious virtuoso called a *pashu*, "seer," who prevents witches (*rui*) from stealing and consuming the life force of their human victims.

42. See Muhammad 1905, Hussain 1998, and Nicolaus 2015.

43. I am grateful to Mr. Gul Saeed and Mr. Wazeer Shakil for their help during my visit to Gilgit.

44. The image has been discussed by Biddulph in 1880, by Stein in 1907, and by Jettmar. See Jettmar 1993, 92, for references to the earlier scholarship. It is also mentioned by Twist (2008, 188).

Figure 3. The Kargah Buddha. Photo left: J. Cabezón. Photo right: Furqan LW, CC by SA 4.0, original in color

cliff with holes around it, indicating that it was housed in a protective wooden grotto at some point.

While visiting the site, my guides and I struck up a conversation with a local man who proceeded to tell us a most interesting tale about the image. According to local legend, it is not a Buddha at all but a "*yacheni*."[45] The *yacheni* is said to be the sister of Shri Badat, the legendary king of Gilgit—purportedly its last Buddhist king—who had a predilection for eating children.[46] As others have observed, the Shri Badat legend has many elements in common with the *Mahāsutasoma Jātaka*,[47] in which Brahmadatta, king of Vārāṇasī, unwittingly becomes addicted to human flesh due to his past-life karmic seeds as a flesh-eating yakṣa. The story also has striking similarities to a story of one of the past lives of Aṅgulimāla as narrated in chapter 36 of the *Sūtra of the Wise and the Foolish*, a text with strong ties to Central Asia.[48] Finally, the Shri Badat tale is

45. The story of the *yacheni* is also found in two written sources: Muhammad 1905, 106, and Haughton 1913, 177–83. My synopsis of the story follows these written accounts, which are slightly more elaborate than, but otherwise consistent with, the one I heard at Kargah.

46. For a version of the story of Shri Badat and his expulsion from Gilgit, see Muhammad 1905, 114–19, and Leitner 1893, 9.

47. Jātaka no. 537, trans. H. T. Francis 1905.

48. *Damamukho Sūtra*, 415b–422a. There, the cannibal prince is the son of a king of Vārāṇasī, Balaṃdhara (Ba la mdar), and a lioness. His name is Spotted Feet (Kalmāṣapāda, Rkang bkra) because of a peculiar anatomical feature inherited from his mother. The story is also found in

similar to an episode in the Gilgit version of the Gesar epic.[49] In Gilgit and Hunza, the legend serves as the charter myth for the winter Taleni festival that centers on building bonfires to prevent the return of the cannibal king.

Shri Badat's sister, the *yacheni*, lived on the rock where the Buddha image is now found. Like her brother, she had a fondness for human flesh, capturing and eating men walking by her rock on their way to the high pastures. But she would only eat half the number of men, leaving the rest alone, a wise move if you hope for more human meals in years to come. A *daiyal* shaman named Soglio decided that he had to put an end to this and devised a way to kill the *yacheni*. He took some companions to the foot of the rock where the *yacheni* lived, went into trance by inhaling smoke from burning juniper, and started to sing and dance. When the *yacheni* appeared, Soglio informed her that her father had just died. Grief-stricken, she struck her chest in pain. One of the *daiyal*'s companions immediately sprang up and stabbed her raised hand with an iron spike, striking so hard that it went through her heart and pinned her to the rock. Soglio then sang another song to inform her that her brother had just died, and when she struck her thigh in grief, Soglio struck it with another nail, binding her body to the cliff and making her immobile. He then muttered a spell and turned her into stone. The story does not end there. The shaman informed the local people that in order to keep the *yacheni* permanently fixed on the mountain for eternity, he should be buried at the foot of the cliff upon his death. The townsfolk decided that it was too risky to wait for him to die, for who knew where he would be living then, so they decided to kill him right away and bury him there. Penpa Dorjee has informed me that a similar story is narrated by local people about a Maitreya statue carved on a rock near Gandhola Monastery, in Lahaul, Himachal Pradesh, India.[50]

Conclusion

The story of the Kargah *yacheni* contains both pan-Indic, Sanskritic, as well as local, shamanistic elements. *Yacheni* is almost certainly a form of Sanskrit *yakṣinī*. Given the prevalence of yakṣas in the Buddhist texts and oral lore of greater Gilgit, it is not surprising that the Kargah spirit should be identified as

Jātakamāla no. 31. Āryaśūra, *Jātakamāla*, 118a–127a. There, the cannibal's name is also Spotted Feet, but his father's name is Sudāsa. The same story is also found in the *Bhadrakalpāvadāna*, and variants of it are found in the *Mahābhārata*, the *Rāmāyaṇa*, and various Purāṇas.

49. See Mock (n.d.).

50. Penpa Dorjee, personal communication, July 21, 2019.

a *yakṣiṇī*, especially because she is also a consumer of human flesh and a blood relative of the cannibal king Shri Badat.

It is worth noting that in these yakṣa tales—and the Kargah *yacheni*'s is no exception—whatever the sex of the yakṣa, it is almost always men or children who are consumed, and not women, which points to a gendered element to these stories. Why don't yakṣas eat women? Throughout Dardistan, the high mountain pastures are considered pure because they are the abode of spirits. Menstruation is considered impure, and so women are forbidden from going there. It is men's responsibility to tend to the family's tribe of goats, and it is therefore men who overwhelmingly come into contact with spirits. Of course, the lore that associates spirits with mountains and purity (and women with impurity) is also a way to enforce women's homebound status.

Why is the Kargah image considered feminine—why is it a *yacheni* instead of a *yach*? Janet Gyatso rightly notes that nature and the earth are often portrayed as female in different religions. But as we will soon see, the Gilgit area also has tales of male *yach* being nailed to rocks. Might there be something in the appearance of the image that suggests its female gender? A mustache or beard is a ubiquitous marker of adult maleness throughout much of this region from ancient times, and Buddha images that lack facial hair may suggest femaleness to a local audience. There is one other feature of the image that may imply its femaleness to the local people, the *uṣṇīṣa*. Witches (*ruis*), who like *yachenis* eat humans, also possess, according to some Dardic traditions, a protuberance on the top of their heads, the piercing of which is said to be one of the most effective ways of killing them, and perhaps this too led local storytellers to consider the Kargah spirit (the Buddha) female.

The narrative of how the spirit came to be on the mountain is ingenious. Why is the spirit made of stone? Because the shaman recited a spell to calcify her. Why does it have one hand at its heart and the other next to its thigh? Because this is where she struck her body when she heard the calamitous news of her male relatives' demise. These details point to the fact that this is not a generic story that could be told about any mountain carving but a specific tale crafted to explain this particular image. The same is true of the Lahauli story mentioned earlier (see figure 4). As in Kargah, the Lahauli image near Gandhola Monastery is not identified as Buddhist—as a carving of the Buddha Maitreya—but as a spirit, specifically a divinity (*devatā*) or ghost (*bhoot*), and as in Gilgit, it is considered female. The Gandhola spirit is also believed to bring bad luck to the village. The carving has smaller images around it, and there is another small image below the village. For this reason, locals claim that it is a mother spirit who came down from the mountaintop to fetch water with her brood. As they were returning, one of her children lagged behind, so when they were all re-absorbed into the rocks from which they came, the mother and part of her brood merged into the upper rock, and the child who lagged behind entered the rock at the base of village.[51] The Gandhola story, like the Kargah one, explains a specific set of carvings and is not meant as a generic theory of how spirits end up on rocks.

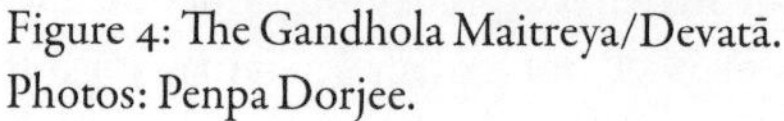

Figure 4: The Gandhola Maitreya/Devatā.
Photos: Penpa Dorjee.

Though quite different, the tales of the Tibetan *sinmo* and the Kargah *yacheni* also share some similarities. Whatever the date of the *sinmo* myth—and our earliest sources are indeed relatively late—it is projected back to the time of the Tibetan empire. Robert Miller reads the *sinmo* myth as an allegory about the expanding Yarlung empire, with a stable center at Lhasa (the *sinmo*'s heart) and a periphery (her limbs) that, marked by revolts, needed to be constantly controlled.[52] If Miller is right, then the *sinmo* myth, like the *yacheni* myth, is a story that tries to makes sense of things (the earliest Buddhist temples) for which the original justification (the need for stability in an expanding Tibetan empire) is no longer known. But while both myths may be concerned with explaining something physical whose origin has been lost to time, the concerns of the *yacheni* story are entirely local, explaining a specific remnant of Gilgit's Buddhist past by incorporating it into the local cosmology. The Tibetan *sinmo* tale valorizes a trans-local religion, Buddhism, as a way of controlling Tibetan barbarity, symbolized by the demoness. The *yacheni* myth does just the oppo-

51. My thanks to Penpa Dorjee for this information.

52. Miller 1998, 7.

site. It legitimizes the very institution—the local priestly control over indigenous deities—that the *sinmo* myth seeks to displace. History is always written by the winners, and in Gilgit, it is the indigenous religion that won.

Despite such differences, the two myths share a concern with controlling a troublesome spirit. The methods of subjugating the two demonesses are, on the surface at least, different. The *sinmo* is controlled by building Buddhist temples, whereas the *yacheni* is subjugated through a shaman's shrewdness and magical might. But the actual method of defeating the two spirits is strikingly similar: the demonesses' "crucifixion" with actual or metaphoric nails. Interestingly, another crucifixion tale is found just north of Gilgit. In Hunza cosmology, evil spirits, called *shiatus* or *bilas*, are shape-shifting malevolent beings who live on or in rocks, lying in wait to attack passersby. Shiatus are the archenemies of shamans, called *biṭan* in Burushaski, whom they constantly abuse and try to injure. M. H. Sidky reports that a legendary shaman, Shun Gakur, was renowned for trapping "a number of these demonic beings by driving iron spikes into the boulders in which they were hiding."[53] Clearly, the idea of nailing demons to the landscape is not uncommon in greater Gilgit. What are we to make of the similarities between the demon-taming myths of Gilgit-Hunza and Tibet?

John Mock has suggested that when it comes to folk tales, all that we can do is note the structural similarities between different narratives. He believes that it is both futile and inappropriate to entertain historical questions—for example, whether the tales are based on historical events or whether two geographically distant tales might have influenced one another.[54] But given the relative rarity of the demoness crucifixion motif, and the fact that it is found in two cultures (Gilgit and Tibet) that had close historical and religious ties at various points in their history, it is hard *not* to wonder whether the stories of the *sinmo* and the *yacheni* are historically related: whether tales of controlling spirits with nails were brought to Tibet by Gilgit shamans, to Gilgit by Tibetan monks, or whether both tales emerged out of a common matrix that drew on Buddhist tantric and pre-Buddhist ideas. The present state of scholarship makes it impossible to say, and Mock may be right: it may be impossible to *ever* answer such questions.

Let me conclude with one final observation. The heroes of the *sinmo* and *yacheni* tales are immortalized in physical objects. Songtsen Gampo and his heirs left behind temples, and Soglio, the image of the frozen *yacheni*. The great irony, of course, is that for Tibetans, the being on the Kargah mountainside

53. Sidky 1994, 67–96.

54. Mock (n.d.). Mock makes this claim about the Shri Badat tale, but his argument applies to the *yacheni* story as well.

is *not* a cannibal demoness, not a symbol of barbarity and chaos, but just the opposite. It is the Buddha, the embodiment of order and of the triumph of civilization over Tibetan backwardness. As Buddhism, and then Islam, entered Gilgit and began to interact with its indigenous religion, how did the practitioners of the local religion react? Did they just continue to practice their rites oblivious to the presence of the new religion? Or did they employ narrative and theological strategies to respond polemically to the foreign religion? Is the *yacheni* myth the remnant of one such strategy? After I heard the story of the *yacheni* in 2018, I found myself reflecting that while time had wiped out any memory of Buddhism in Kargah, a local spirit with Buddhist pedigree, the *yacheni*, had managed to live on in the mountains and minds of the people of Gilgit. And gazing up once more at the image, with its slight smile, I wondered to myself whether it was actually the demoness who had had the last laugh, for what sweeter revenge could a demoness take on an invading Buddha than to eclipse all memory of him with a tale that's all about her?

Works Cited

Āryaśūra. *Jātakamāla. Skyes pa'i rabs kyi rgyud.* Dergé Tengyur 4150, Skyes rabs *hu*, 1b–135a.

Beckwith, Christopher I. 1997. *The Tibetan Empire in Central Asia.* Stanford: Stanford University Press.

Biddulph, John. 1880. *Tribes of the Hindoo Koosh.* Calcutta: Office of the Superintendent of Government Printing.

Bla ma dam pa Bsod nams rgyal mtshan. *Rgyal rabs gsal ba'i me long.* Sde dge xylograph, TBRC W 00CHZ0103341.

Chung, Yeng Yew, trans. 2012. "The Mahamayuri Vidyarajni Sutra." https://mahamayurividyarajni.wordpress.com/2012/06/10/mahamayuri/.

Dalton, Jacob P. 2016. *The Gathering of Intentions: A History of a Tibetan Tantra.* New York: Columbia University Press.

Damamūko Sūtra [*Sūtra of the Wise and Foolish*]. *Mdzangs blun zhes bya ba'i mdo.* Lhasa Kangyur no. 374, Mde sde *sa*, 207b–476b.

Dani, A. H. 1991. *History of the Northern Areas of Pakistan.* Islamabad: National Institute of Historical and Cultural Research.

Das, Sarat Chandra, ed. 1918. *Bodhisattvāvadāna Kalpalatā*, 2 vols. Calcutta: Asiatic Society of Bengal.

Dawa Lokyitsang. 2015. "When Women Ruled Tibet." *Lhakar Diaries*, September 23. https://lhakardiaries.com/2015/09/23/when-tibetan-women-ruled-tibet/.

Dgra bcom pa dge 'dun 'phel gyis lung bstan pa (**Arhatsaṃghavardhanavyākaraṇa*). Dergé Tengyur no. 4201, Spring yig *nge*, 161b–168b.

Dkon mchog bstan pa rab rgyas. 1975. *Mdo smad chos 'byung* [*A History of Domé*], 3 vols. New Delhi: Sharada Rani.

Dotson, Brandon. 2009. *The Old Tibetan Annals: An Annotated Translation of Tibet's First History*. Vienna: Verlag der Österreichischen Akademie der Wissenschaften.

Gyatso, Janet. 1989. "Down with the Demoness: Reflections on a Feminine Ground in Tibet." In *Feminine Ground: Essays on Women and Tibet*, edited by Janice D. Willis, 34–51. Ithaca, NY: Snow Lion.

Haughton, Henry Lawrence. 1913. *Sport and Folklore in the Himalayas*. London: Edward Arnold.

Hoffman, Helmut H. R. 1969. "An Account of the Bon Religion in Gilgit." *Central Asiatic Journal* 13.2: 137–45.

Hussain, Altaf. 1998. "Danyalism: A Study on Spiritual Healing in Chaprote Pakistan." https://citeseerx.ist.psu.edu/viewdoc/download?doi=10.1.1.1087.8229&rep=rep1&type=pdf.

*Jayaśrījñāna. **Abhidhānaratnamāla. Mngon brjod nor bu phreng ba*. Dergé Tengyur no. 4454. Sna tshogs *po*, 164a–242a.

Jettmar, Karl. 1961. "Ethnological Research in Dardistan 1958: Preliminary Report." *Proceedings of the American Philosophical Society* 105.1: 79–97.

———. 1993. "The Paṭolas, Their Governors, and Their Successors." In *Antiquities of Northern Pakistan, Reports and Studies*, edited by Karl Jettmar, 2:77–122. Mainz: Verlag Philipp von Zabern.

Kakas, Beáta. 2011. "Hayagrīvavidyā: Spell to the Horse Necked One." *Acta Orientalia Academiae Scientiarum Hungaricae* 64.4: 427–35.

Kvaerne, Per. 1972. "Aspects of the Origin of the Buddhist Tradition in Tibet." *Numen* 19.1: 22–40.

Leitner, Gottlieb W. 1893. *Dardistan in 1866, 1886, and 1893*. Woking, England: Oriental University Institute.

Li'i yul lung bstan pa (**Kaṃsadeśavyākaraṇa*). Dergé Tengyur no. 4202, Spring yig *nge*, 168b–188a.

Lorimer, D. L. R. 1929. "The Supernatural in the Popular Belief of the Gilgit Region." *Journal of the Royal Asiatic Society* 61.3: 507–36.

Mahāsutasoma Jātaka. Jātaka no. 537. Translated by H. T. Francis (1905) and reproduced online at https://www.sacred-texts.com/bud/j5/j5030.htm.

Martin, Dan. 1999. "'Ol mo lung ring, the Original Holy Place." In *Sacred Spaces and Powerful Places in Tibetan Culture*, edited by Toni Huber, 259–301. Dharamsala: Library of Tibetan Works and Archives.

Martin, Nils. 2017. "A Solemn Praise to an 11th century West-Tibetan Councillor at Kharul, Purik." *Zentralasiatische Studien* 46: 189–232.

Miller, Robert J. 1998. "'The Supine Demoness (Srin mo) and the Consolidation of Empire." *The Tibet Journal* 23.3: 3–22.

Mock, John. 1998. "The Discursive Construction of Reality in the Wakhi Community of Northern Pakistan." PhD dissertation, University of California, Berkeley.

———. 2015. "Tibetans in Wakhan: New Information on Inscriptions and Rock Art." *Revue d'Études Tibétaines* 36: 127, 121–44.

———. n.d. "Shri Badat the Cannibal King: A Buddhist Jataka from Gilgit." http://www.mockandoneil.com/shrib.htm. Accessed December 15, 2020.

Mock, John, and Kimberley O'Neil. n.d. "Dards, Dardistan, and Dardic: An Ethnographic, Geographic, and Linguistic Conundrum." http://www.mockandoneil.com/dard.htm#Greek_and_Roman_References. Accessed December 15, 2020.

Muhammad, Ghulam. 1905. "Festivals and Folklore of Gilgit." *Memoirs of the Asiatic Society of Bengal* 1.7: 93–127.

Neelis, Jason. 1999. Review of *Die Felsbildstation Hodar*, *Bulletin of the Asia Institute*, New Series 13: 179–82.

Ngag dbang blo bzang rgya mtsho. 1980. *Bod kyi deb ther dpyid kyi rgyal mo'i klu dbyangs* [*Song of the Queen of Spring: A History of Tibet*]. Beijing: Mi rigs dpe skrun khang.

Nicolaus, Peter. 2015. "Residues of Ancient Belief among the Shin in the Gilgit-Division and Western Ladakh." *Iran and the Caucuses* 19: 201–64.

"Oral history interview of Shatra Ganden Paljor." Library of Congress: https://www.loc.gov/item/2020705818/.

Ramble, Charles. 2007. "The Aya: Fragments of an Unknown Tibetan Priesthood." In *Pramāṇakīrtiḥ: Papers Dedicated to Ernst Steinkellner on the Occasion of his 70th Birthday*, edited by Birgit Kellner et al., 2: 683–720. Vienna: Arbeitskreis für Tibetische und Buddhistische Studien Universität Wien.

Rieck, Andreas. 1995. "The Nurbakshis of Baltistan: Crisis and Revival of a Five-Centuries Old Community." *Die Welt des Islam*, New Series 35.2: 159–88.

Sidky, M. H. 1994. "Shamans and Mountain Spirits of Hunza." *Asian Folklore Studies* 53.1: 67–96.

Sørensen, Per. 1986. *A Fifteenth Century Tibetan Historical Work: Rgyal-rabs gsal-ba'i me-loṅ*. Copenhagen: Akademisk Forlag.

Śrīvasuparipṛcchā. *Dpal dbyigs gis zhus pa*. Lhasa Kangyur no. 163, Mdo sde *pa*, 221a–227b.

Stein, Rolf A. 1972. *Tibetan Civilization*. Stanford, CA: Stanford University Press.

Tathāgatācintyaguhyanirdeśa. *De bzhin gshegs pa'i gsang ba bsam gyis mi khyab pa bstan pa*. Lhasa Kangyur no. 47, Dkon brtsegs *ka*, 151a–313b.

Twist, Rebecca L. 2008. "Patronage, Devotion and Politics: A Buddhological Study of the Paṭola Śāhi Dynasty's Visual Record." PhD dissertation, Ohio State University.

Vinayavastu. *'Dul ba'i gzhi*. Lhasa Kangyur no. 1. 'Dul ba *ka–nga*.

Woeser. 2016. "The Senmo Map, or the Resurrection of the Demoness." High Peaks Pure Earth website entry for October 27, 2016: https://highpeakspureearth.com/the-senmo-map-or-the-resurrection-of-the-demoness-by-woeser/.

Zeisler, Bettina. "East of the Moon and West of the Sun? Approaches to a Land with Many Names, North of Ancient India and South of Khotan." https://www.academia.edu/6922508/2010_East_of_the_moon_and_west_of_the_sun_Approaches_to_a_land_with_many_names_north_of_ancient_India_and_south_of_Khotan. Accessed December 15, 2020.

The In/Visibility of Nuns and Yoginīs in Dudjom Lingpa's Songs of Advice

Holly Gayley

IN READING Buddhist texts, Janet Gyatso poignantly noted to her graduate students at Harvard that the idiosyncrasies in Tibetan sources—the small details beyond the usual gendered tropes—can serve as clues to the lived experiences of historical women. From her, I learned to be attuned to the deployment of gendered ideals and stereotypes, whether reinforced or contravened, across different genres and historical contexts.[1] In the wake of her groundbreaking work on Tibetan autobiography, *Apparitions of the Self* (1998), there have been a cluster of book-length studies on the auto/biographical writings of eminent female masters in Tibet,[2] and more sources have come to light in recent years.[3] Yet there is still a relative dearth of information regarding the lives of Tibetan nuns and yoginīs who were part of dedicated religious communities but did not reach the threshold of renown required to enter into the literary record as the subject of their own life story.[4]

Can we recover the presence of women in Tibetan religious circles by looking for them at the margins of writings by and about male Buddhist masters? In this essay, I am interested in how Tibetan women are rendered both visible and invisible as interlocutors to renowned male religious figures in dialogic literary works.[5] I examine a dozen songs of advice by the visionary Dudjom Lingpa

1. For more of her insights along these lines, see the introduction to *Women in Tibet* (Gyatso and Havnevik 2006).

2. For example, Schaeffer 2004, Diemberger 2007, Jacoby 2014, Bessenger 2016, Gayley 2016, and Melnick Dyer 2022.

3. This is especially the case since the *Ḍākinīs' Great Dharma Treasury* (*Mkha' 'gro'i chos mdzod chen mo*) was published in 2017 by the Ārya Tāre Book Association Editorial Office at Larung Buddhist Academy. Its first eighteen volumes include narrative accounts of Buddhist women's lives from India, Tibet, and China, first published in sixteen volumes under the title *Garland of White Lotuses: The Biographies of the Great Female Masters of India and Tibet* (2013).

4. In *Himalayan Hermitess* (2004, 4), Kurtis Schaeffer estimates that women's auto/biographical writings comprise less than one percent of an estimated two thousand Tibetan biographies.

5. This essay is a revision of a paper presented at the American Academy of Religion in November

addressed to women—nuns, yoginīs, and even a royal lady—to ask what we can discern about their religious lives through the scant information provided and certain idiosyncratic gendered moments. This recovery project is especially poignant given the lack of information in Dudjom Lingpa's autobiographical writings about the women closest to him, despite the array of female deities who appear in visions to counsel him.[6]

Dudjom Lingpa (1835–1904) became a towering figure within the Nyingma tradition in the nomadic region of Golok, revealing a sizeable corpus of esoteric teachings and spawning a family lineage that supplied the region with notable luminaries, including the Third Dodrupchen Jigmé Tenpai Nyima (1865–1926) and the visionary Drimé Özer (1881–1924). Although he grew up as an ordinary nomad tending his family's herds, Dudjom Lingpa's inner world was filled with visions of tantric deities who blessed and instructed him. As such, he had few human teachers and little by way of formal training. Nonetheless, already by his twenties, revelations in the form of "mind treasures" (*dgongs gter*) began to emerge, and he set down cycles of esoteric teachings and ritual throughout his life with the aid of a scribe. While his male companions, patrons, disciples, and scribes are mentioned by name, the women in his life are not, except obliquely in a short prophecy about his future consorts.

Adding to the challenge of identifying significant women in his religious community or learning about their lives, in a recently published family genealogy, *Wondrous Golden Ears of Grain*,[7] his three main consorts are remembered only in relation to the children they bore, while his four daughters are lost to the historical record—not even named alongside the biographies of his eight sons, despite being identified as ḍākinīs (*mkha' 'gro ma*).[8] The famous consort of Drimé Özer, namely Sera Khandro, is the only consort of any of his eight sons mentioned as such by name, and her auto/biographical writings are a key source for early twentieth-century religious life in Golok and its gendered challenges as analyzed by Sarah Jacoby.[9] Otherwise, this genealogy by the local historian Pema Ösal Thayé is concerned with family succession in patrilineal

---

2018 for a panel on *A Woman's Place in Buddhist Dialogues: Querying the Margins of Tibetan Literature for the In/Visibility of Nuns and Yoginīs*, organized by Jue Liang and Andrew Taylor.

6. His autobiographical writings have been translated by Chönyi Drolma (Anne Holland) in *A Clear Mirror: The Visionary Autobiography of a Tibetan Master* (2011).

7. Padma 'od gsal mtha' yas 2003. For a study of this genealogy, see Gayley forthcoming.

8. Exceptional Tibetan women are often regarded to be embodiments of *ḍākinīs*, a class of female tantric deities, and their title Khandro (*mkha' 'gro*) translates the Sanskrit term.

9. See Jacoby 2014. In this family genealogy, Sera Khandro is listed by an alternate name, Mkha' 'gro Bde ba'i rdo rje. Several others are mentioned as mothers to third-generation sons.

terms and focuses on short biographies for the male descendants of Dudjom Lingpa, providing data on parentage, dates of birth and death, incarnation status, teachers and disciples, major accomplishments and literary compositions. However, his female descendants are relegated to the footnotes of history, a few lines at the end of each generation; none are accorded actual biographies. This is despite the fact that, as Gyatso and Havnevik suggest in the introduction to *Women in Tibet*, yogic communities surrounding visionary Nyingma masters generally offered more opportunities for female practitioners.[10]

Dudjom Lingpa's Songs of Advice

Dudjom Lingpa's advice on meditation in the form of songs (*mgur*) can be found in volume 18 of his treasure corpus (*gter chos*) in approximately five hundred pages.[11] Within this, a dozen songs explicitly address women, which take up forty pages (less than ten percent) and are interspersed throughout the volume as a whole.[12] The gender and status of the addressee (usually a single person but sometimes a group) are evident in the names and titles of supplicants appearing in colophons. For example, one reads: "By Dudjom in response to the request of Getsunma Namdak Drolma," whereby *getsunma* (*dge btsun ma*) is one of several referents to nun found in the collection, in addition to *jomo* (*jo mo*) and *gema* (*dge ma*).[13] Another states: "Since the yoginī (*rnal 'byor ma*) Petso made insistent entreaties, the old man Dudjom Dorjé uttered these crazy things."[14] In some cases, a single-line prelude to the song announces its intended recipient(s), for example, "This is advice to devoted nuns."[15] Still others do not specify a recipient. Throughout, Dudjom Lingpa refers to himself and his advice with humility and humor as "heart advice from me, the foolish beggar" or "these crazy words and ramblings of an old man," even as he displays his virtuosity in giving nuanced advice on advanced meditation practices.[16] The

10. Gyatso and Havnevik 2006, 12.

11. Bdud 'joms gling pa 2004. There are several published versions of Dudjom Lingpa's songs. For my reading and translations, I relied primarily on the 2004 Thimphu edition of his *Collected Revelations and Writings* in *dbu can* consisting of 495 pages. There is also an *dbu med* version in 549 pages, published in Kalimpong in 1978, and a stand-alone paperback titled *Grub pa'i dbang phyug chen po bdud 'joms gling pa'i mgur bum*, published in China.

12. I would like to thank John Canti for first making me aware of the presence of these songs.

13. Bdud 'joms gling pa 2004, 18: 68.3.

14. Bdud 'joms gling pa 2004, 18: 336.3–4.

15. Bdud 'joms gling pa 2004, 18: 51.1.

16. The first phrase, *sbrang blun po bdag gi snying gtam*, occurs as a refrain in Bdud 'joms gling pa 2004, 18: 51–53, and the second, *mi rgan 'chol tshigs blun tshigs 'di*, from 18: 284.6. Usually *tshigs*

volume also includes several songs attributed to female deities as their "symbolic speech" (*brda yig*).

Below is a chart of Dudjom Lingpa's songs explicitly addressing women with page numbers drawn from volume 18 of the Thimphu edition of his treasure corpus and the penultimate volume of the 53-volume collection of writings by, about, and for Buddhist women, titled the *Ḍākinīs' Great Dharma Treasury* (*Mkha' 'gro'i chos mdzod chen mo*),[17] published at Larung Buddhist Academy, better known as Larung Gar.

Addressee in Colophon or First Line of Song	**Vol. 18**[18]	**Vol. 52**[19]
Dechen Tso (Bde chen mtsho)	43–46	264–66
Devoted Nuns (Dad ldan dge ma)	51–53	266–68
Getsunma Namdak Drölma (Dge btsun ma Rnam dag sgrol ma)	67–68	268–69
Gema Chötso (Dge ma Chos mtsho)	75–76	269–70
Jomo Lödrön (Jo mo Blos sgron)	161–62	270–71
Jomo Khandro Kyi (Jo mo Mkha' 'gro skyid)	201–4	272–74
Three Devoted Nuns (Dad ldan btsun ma gsum)	283–85	274–76
Yoginī Petso (Rnal 'byor ma Pad mtsho)	335–36	282–83
Jomo Sangyé Drönma (Jo mo Sangs rgyas sgron ma)	327–30	283–85
Gema Sangyé Drönma (Dge ma Sangs rgyas sgron ma)	331–33	285–87
Jomo Changtso (Jo mo Byang mtsho)	361–63	288–89
Sakyong Miyi Jemo Khachö Wangmo (Sa skyong mi'i rje mo Mkha' spyod dbang mo)	317–24	277–82

refers to verses and *tshig* to words, but Ringu Tulku glossed the second phrase as a kind of incoherent or rambling speech like that of a drunkard.

17. Padma 'tsho and Sarah Jacoby (2021) analyze the contents and rationale behind the creation of this unprecedented collection in "Lessons from Buddhist Foremothers."

18. See Bdud 'joms gling pa 2004.

19. See Ārya Tāre Book Association Editorial Office 2017.

While in Nepal as part of a sabbatical in 2017–18, I was fortunate to collaborate with Ringu Tulku on the translations of these dozen songs.[20] At one point, as we worked through them together, he called my project into question, saying that the meditation advice in Dudjom Lingpa's songs to nuns and yoginīs was no different from those offered to men. What was the point of focusing on his songs to women? This was early in our collaboration on this project, before we got to salient gendered moments. In hopes of redeeming the project in his eyes, I countered that this alone is significant: that we have evidence here of the existence of advanced female practitioners among Dudjom Lingpa's direct disciples and that they received comparable instructions on esoteric topics and techniques. Beyond that, although I did not think to say it at the time, the songs offer a possible window into (1) these women's life circumstances as religious practitioners, (2) male attitudes toward female practitioners in nomadic Golok, and (3) the gendered challenges that they faced, which come to the surface in several poignant passages.

In turning to these songs to recover traces of women's religious lives in nineteenth-century Golok, I felt validated after I obtained a copy of the *Ḍākinīs' Great Dharma Treasury*, thanks to my colleague Padma 'tsho. Volumes 51 and 52 (the last before the *dkar chag*, or catalog, in the final volume) contain works of advice to women, including the same dozen songs that I had labored through the five-hundred-page volume 18 in Dudjom Lingpa's corpus to find. This suggests that not only are the life stories and writings of Buddhist women important to the contemporary nuns who collected, edited, and published the *Ḍākinīs' Great Dharma Treasury* under the auspices of the Ārya Tāre Book Association, but also texts in which women serve as interlocutors for Buddhist teachings. These works, while containing comparable meditation instructions to what male disciples received, were nonetheless valued as advice tailored to female practitioners.

If we take seriously insights from the study of epistolary literature, the addressee plays a key role as intended recipient of Dudjom Lingpa's songs, whether or not those songs are specified as letters. In her seminal work *Epistolarity*, Janet Altman theorizes the "absence and presence" of the addressee, who is made present in the "I-you" context of composition while at the time remains absent by virtue of the spatial distance presumed by letter writing.[21] This absence can be heightened if only one side of the correspondence is

20. I would like to express my appreciation to Ringu Tulku for his generous time in working together on these translations. We spent several weeks meeting daily in Nepal that winter and had follow-up meetings in Boulder, Colorado, the next fall.

21. See Altman 1982, chaper 4.

preserved or, in the case of these songs of advice, there is no record of the specific requests prompting Dudjom Lingpa's advice. In fact, we know little if anything about the composition of his songs. The name of the disciple requesting advice is usually mentioned and sometimes the scribe, and a few are explicitly marked as letters, such as his reply to questions of the royal lady Sakyong Miyi Jemo Khachö Wangmo.

However, it is also possible that some of the songs were spontaneous oral compositions with the addressee present.[22] This is certainly the pretext of practice advice within the broad Tibetan genre of *shaldam*, etymologically "instructions" (*gdams*) from the "mouth" (*zhal*) of the guru, which are presented as practical instructions for a specific disciple, conveying an aura of intimacy and immediacy.[23] While *shaldam* are intended for a specific individual or group, carrying the presumption of orality in their composition and often using direct colloquial language, they are nonetheless set down in writing for the benefit of a general audience. In this case, while there are gendered moments addressing scenarios specific to women's life, Dudjom Lingpa's advice is otherwise gender-neutral with respect to the meditation instructions.[24]

Although actual women are only made present and visible as interlocutors and addressees of his advice, we can nonetheless discern certain features about their religious vocation, level of practice, and the challenges they faced. In naming the recipient for each song, Dudjom Lingpa refers to their religious vocations—as *yoginīs* or female tantric practitioners (*rnal 'byor ma*) and nuns referred to by several terms (*dge btsun ma*, *jo mo*, and *dge ma*). In the case of a royal lady (*sa skyong mi'i rje mo*), social rank takes precedence. Even so, as mentioned, his advice to them is largely comparable to his instructions to male interlocutors. Topics include exhortations to practice, reminders of the dream-like nature of appearances, refinements on how to integrate the meditation practices of calm abiding and insight, discussions of potential pitfalls and diversions in practice, and instructions on Dzogchen, the Great Perfection (*rdzogs chen*). Given the advanced nature of his advice and his encouragement to all but royalty to renounce the world and remain in solitary retreat, this sug-

22. A few of these songs are tagged as letters. Otherwise, it is not clear if they were composed in the presence of the female disciple addressed and later transcribed or whether they were dispatched as missives.

23. See my introduction co-authored with Joshua Schapiro in Gayley and Schapiro 2017.

24. Note that, for example, Dudjom Lingpa's song to Gema Chötso was used as the basis for Dzogchen teachings by Anam Thubten and Chakung Jigmé Wangdrak during an online retreat on May 13–15, 2022.

gests that there was at least a limited group of dedicated and experienced female practitioners among his direct disciples.

Gendered Moments

Let us take a closer look at moments in these songs that address the specific challenges of female practitioners, offering clues about their life circumstances and also revealing gendered perceptions and prescriptions by male teachers. Take, for example, a song titled "A Garland of Lovely Pearls: Song of Advice for Jomo Khandro Kyi," containing Dudjom Lingpa's instructions to a "devoted nun." In it, he warns about the pitfalls of bad company (*grogs ngan*), specifically a handsome bull (*glang bu ngo dkar*) in her midst. In practical terms, he cautions against her losing the opportunity for religious pursuits by falling in love and becoming pregnant. In what follows, we witness what could be a realistic dilemma for a young nun, paired with a cautionary paternalistic response that attempts to circumscribe women's mobility.

> མི་ཚེའི་སྟོད་ཆ་ཟད་ལ་ལྟོས།།
> ཚེ་མཇུག་ཆོས་ལ་དྲིལ་བར་རེམ།།
>
> Look how you've already wasted the first part of life.
> It's time to devote the rest to the Dharma.
>
> གྲོགས་ངན་འཁོར་བའི་ལྕགས་སྒྲོག་ཡིན།།
> སྡུག་རོགས་གླང་བུ་ངོ་དཀར་སྤོང་།།
>
> Beware of bad company, the iron shackle of saṃsāra.
> Give up your sweetheart,[25] the handsome bull.
>
> དྭ་ཕྲུག་འཁོར་བའི་དཔྱང་རྡོ་ཡིན།།
>
> Otherwise, a bastard child will be the stone[26]
> that drags you down and sinks you in saṃsāra's mire.

25. Ringu Tulku glossed the term *sdug rogs* as "companion in suffering," but this could also be an alternative for *snying sdug or dga' rogs*, meaning "sweetheart" as translated here.

26. The Tibetan term *dpyang rdo* refers to a stone at the end of a rope used to weigh something down. This line was shifted up for semantic clarity in the translation.

ད་ལྟ་རང་ལ་བསམ་མནོ་ཐོང་།།
འཆི་ཁ་འགྱོད་མེད་ཞིག་ལ་རེམ།།

Right now, think about yourself for a change,
so at the time of death you have no regrets.

དེང་དུས་སྔོན་ལས་བཟང་པོའི་མཐུས།།
ཆོས་ཀྱི་མཐུན་རྐྱེན་འཛོམ་ལ་ལྟོས།།

Nowadays, due to your own good deeds in the past,
look how fortunate conditions for Dharma have converged.

གནོད་སྦྱིན་གཟུགས་ལ་ཆགས་མ་བྱེད།།
མི་གྲལ་མི་སླེབ་བུད་མེད་ལུས།།

So don't get attached to the form that can harm you;[27]
a female body makes it hard to be equal among humans.

ལྷ་གྲལ་སྙོགས་དང་མོ་རབ་ཡིན།།

Instead, pursue divine rank [through the Dharma];
then you'll be the very best kind of woman.

ཕྱི་ལྟར་དགེ་མ་ཆོས་པའི་གཟུགས།།
དོན་ལ་བདུད་མོ་སྒྲོག་འཁྲོག་མས།།

Don't mimic the ways of those other nuns[28]
who outwardly appear in Dharmic form

རང་གཞན་ཐར་པའི་སྒྲོག་རྩ་བཅོད།།
དེ་འདྲའི་ལད་མོ་མ་བྱེད་རེམ།།

27. This implies that her female body is an impediment, not only because of gender inequities but because it is a source of desire for others who could tempt or force the nun away from a life devoted to practice.

28. I have shifted the order of the lines in the translation within this couplet and the next to help the semantic flow in English.

but actually are life-robbing demonesses,
who cut the root of liberation for self and other.[29]

མགོ་འཕང་མཐོ་ན་དམན་ལ་བབ།།
དམན་ས་ཟུངས་ཞིག་དགེ་བཙུན་མ།།

If you reach too high, you'll fall down low;
so be humble and take the lower seat, Getsunma.

འགྲིམ་སྒོ་ཡང་ན་ཉེས་དང་འཕྲད།།
རང་ཚོད་ཟུངས་ལ་རང་སྒོ་སྡོམ།།

If you travel around openly, you could meet with harm.
So set your boundaries: stay put and shut the door![30]

This passage from a song shows a certain realism: that sexual transgressions are more likely to ruin the spiritual careers of women in terms of both their reputation and opportunity to practice. However, his response also repeats a misogynist trope about lusty nuns, who wear the monastic robes but transgress their vows, from whom Jomo Khandro Kyi must distinguish herself. His reference to a "bastard child" (*dwa phrug*) acknowledges that men (including monks) can and do deny paternity, leaving women to bear the burdens and stigma of child rearing alone. In the name of protecting nuns on retreat, Dudjom Lingpa thereby reinscribes patriarchal limitations on nuns' mobility when he says, "If you travel around openly, you could meet with harm. / So set your boundaries: stay put and shut the door!" This is an incitement for Jomo Khandro Kyi to remain in retreat and also (potentially) a warning that women wandering around, even for religious pursuits, are asking for trouble.

At times, it is unclear if Dudjom Lingpa's advice is gendered or not—as when he advises women to be humble and take the "lower seat" (*dman sa*). Of course, humility is a Buddhist virtue, given the pernicious quality of ego-clinging (*bdag 'dzin*) as the source of suffering. Yet one cannot help but wonder if his advice would be different for a male disciple. Is his intent to keep his

29. The phrase "life-robbing demonesses" (*bdud mo srog 'phrog*) could refer to cutting short the spiritual life of monastics through breaking vows or more literally to abortion.

30. Bdud 'joms gling pa 2004, 18: 201.5–202.3. In two places in the translation of this passage, I expand a single line into a couplet to capture the fullness of its meaning and retain a structure of couplets in the English.

female disciples from being targets of criticism, while perhaps unwittingly reinforcing their inferior social status? After all, he admits the sociological reality of women's subordination when saying that "a female body makes it hard to be equal among humans"[31] and suggests that Jomo Khandro Kyi should instead achieve divine rank through mastery of tantric visualization practice, making her "the very best kind of woman" (*mo rab*).

A number of songs contain favorable assessments of the qualities of his female disciples, calling them "devoted nuns" (*dad ldan dge ma*) and warning them of more generic dangers like wasting one's life in distraction or posing as a Dharma practitioner, while not being able to put the view into practice in daily life. In complementary terms, he reinforces the tantric dictates of high regard for one's vajra "brothers and sisters" (*mched lcam*), who serve as companions on the path and should be viewed as emanations of heroes and ḍākinīs.

Other clues to the life circumstances of these female practitioners are peppered throughout. Some of the nuns he addresses appear to have come to practice late in life after having families, given his statement to Getsunma Namdak Drölma: "Look how your true purpose hasn't been achieved, / with so many years of life already passed by. / A ho! Whatever remains of this life, pursue the genuine Dharma!"[32] Likewise, to Jomo Changtso, he encourages her steadfast practice with reference to her advanced years: "With two-thirds of your life already spent, think carefully. / Now exert yourself in the Dharma without delay!"[33] With respect to a song addressed to "three devoted nuns," it seems that at least some women in his community clustered together to practice on retreat. There he advises the nuns to be "content with just enough food and clothing to survive," while also encouraging them to relax their judgments with respect to proper view, meditation, and action.[34] Still others are cast as advanced practitioners on solitary retreat, such as Yoginī Petso and Jomo Lödrön, who are given instructions on trekchö (*khregs chod*) and thögal (*thod rgal*), the most advanced meditative practices within Dzogchen.

Ḍākinī or Demoness?

There are at least two exceptional women named in the collection. One is Jomo Sangyé Drönma, to whom Dudjom Lingpa offers two songs of advice. In the

31. On the discourse of an "inferior female body," as instantiated in Golok and environs, see Jacoby 2010. Note that elsewhere in the same song Dudjom Lingpa references a precious human body (*mi lus*) possessing freedoms and advantages (*dal 'byor*) without reference to gender.

32. Bdud 'joms gling pa 2004, 18: 67.5–6.

33. Bdud 'joms gling pa 2004, 18: 361.5.

34. Bdud 'joms gling pa 2004, 18: 283.2 and 284.5–6.

first, he issues a prophecy indicating her potential status as a ḍākinī (*mkha' 'gro ma*). This term refers to a category of female tantric deity and is also commonly used to designate Tibetan women who have achieved a high degree of realization. This process of divinization, also evident in hagiographic sources, elevates certain female practitioners without challenging social biases regarding ordinary women.[35] Yet, in the process, he cautions Jomo Sangyé Drönma to cultivate renunciation and not seek fame, lest others perceive her as a "demoness" (*'dre mo*).

ཡར་སངས་རྒྱས་ཟེར་བའི་སྒྲ་བོ་ཆེ།།
ངོ་རང་ཐོག་འཕྲོད་ལས་གཞན་ན་མེད།།
མར་འཁོར་བ་ཟེར་བའི་སྡུག་བསྔལ་ཡུལ།།
མིག་འཁྲུལ་བ་ཙམ་ལས་གཞན་མ་མཆིས།།

Up there, what is exalted as "buddhahood"
is nothing other than recognizing your own nature.
Down there, what is denigrated as "saṃsāra,"
the domain of suffering, is nothing other than deluded vision.

ཆོས་དགེ་དང་སྡིག་པའི་རྒྱུ་རྣམས་ཀུན།།
ཡིད་བསམ་པ་ཙམ་ལས་གྲུབ་པ་མེད།།
བློས་བཞག་པ་ཙམ་ལས་ཡུལ་གྲུབ་མེད།།
དེ་ཡུལ་དུ་བལྟ་བ་ཐམས་ཅད་འཁྲུལ།།

All the occasions for positive and negative actions
don't exist apart from the mind and its intentions.
External things don't exist, except as imputed by mind;
to see them as real objects is utter delusion.

དེར་འཁྲུལ་པ་གཞན་གྱིས་བྱུང་མིན་ཏེ།།
གཞི་མ་རིག་པ་ཡིས་བསྐྱེད་ནས་སུ།།
དཔེ་ཆུ་ལས་གཟའ་སྐར་གཟུགས་བརྙན་བཞིན།།
ཚུལ་མེད་དང་མ་གྲུབ་ཨེ་ཐོང་སོད།།

35. See Gayley 2016, 54–61.

Not generated from somewhere else,
they arise on the basis of ignorance.
Just as the reflection of stars and planets on water,
can you see there's nothing truly existing?

དེ་མཐོང་ན་མཁའ་འགྲོ་མ་དངོས་ཡིན།།
དེ་མ་མཐོང་འཁྲུལ་པའི་སེམས་ཅན་གྱིས།།
ཆགས་སྡང་དང་ཕྲག་དོག་རྒྱུད་ཁེངས་ན།།
གདོན་མ་རིག་པས་ཟིན་བུད་མེད་ལ།།

If you see this, then you are a real *ḍākinī*.[36]
If you can't, then like confused sentient beings,
if your mind's filled with passion, aggression, and jealousy,
you're an *ordinary woman*, afflicted by the dön of ignorance.[37]

ཚེ་ཕྱི་མ་དོན་དུ་གཉེར་བ་ཡིས།།
ཚེ་འདི་སྣང་མཆིལ་མའི་ཐལ་བ་བཞིན།།
རྒྱུད་ངེས་འབྱུང་དྲག་པོས་ཁེངས་གྱུར་ཡིན།།
འདྲེ་ཟེར་ཡང་ཡེ་ཤེས་མཁའ་འགྲོ་ལགས།།

If you strive for real meaning in this life and the next,
life's circumstances are the dirt on which you spit.
If your mind is filled with intense renunciation,
even if others call you *demoness*, you're a *wisdom ḍākinī*.

མདངས་ལྷུན་གྲུབ་སྣང་བ་མངོན་བྱེད་ཅིང་།།
བདེ་སྡུག་བསྡལ་མཛེས་དང་མི་མཛེས་པའི།།
རྣམ་རྟོག་གི་ཚོ་འཕྲུལ་སྣ་ཚོགས་དང་།།
གདངས་ལུས་ཀྱི་ན་ཚ་མི་བདེ་བའི།།

Recognize appearances as spontaneous radiance.
All the joys and suffering, what has beauty or not,

36. The terms in italics are marked by dots underneath them in the Tibetan, which is a way of highlighting their importance. Often these refer to components of an individual's name when a prophecy about them is given, though that does not appear to be the case here.

37. The Tibetan term dön (*gdon*) refers to negative force or spirit.

are various expressions of conceptual thought.
So too are physical pain and sickness,

ཟུག་ཟུ་དང་མི་འདོད་ཉེར་འཚེ་བ།།
གསང་བ་ནི་སེམས་ཀྱི་དགའ་སྡུག་དང་།།
ན་ཚ་ཀུན་སོས་ཁའི་སྤྲིན་བཞིན་དུ།།
མ་ངེས་པར་འབྱུང་ཨེ་གོ་ཏོ།།

as well as aches and unwanted injuries.
The secret is: all of mind's joys and suffering,
all maladies, are like clouds in springtime,
arising unpredictably. Do you understand?[38]

In this excerpt, Jomo Sangyé Drönma is presented with a somewhat mixed assessment, alluding to her potential as a wisdom ḍākinī alongside the chance that she may just be an ordinary women, filled with delusion. Even if she does attain realization, she risks being perceived as a demoness by others—indicating an issue with the legibility of female renunciation and realization.[39] A somewhat opaque prophecy (*lung bstan*) follows, highlighting her future rebirth in the abode of Vajrapāṇi, but this outcome remains contingent on her ardent renunciation and practice. When we were translating these songs, Ringu Tulku remarked that Jomo Sangyé Drönma must have been quite a special practitioner. In the second song to her, Dudjom Lingpa goes so far as to suggest that with twelve years of solitary retreat she will attain enlightenment: "If you have the good fortune to practice continuously, / in twelve years, you'll attain the rainbow body and great transference. / You'll reach enlightenment."[40] This is promising a lot but may also be a stock phrase, since he says something similar to Jomo Lödrön: "If you practice thögal continuously for twelve years, you will awaken."[41] Yet it is still noteworthy, since as elsewhere in Tibetan literature, it represents an unequivocal affirmation of women's potential for enlightenment.

The second exceptional woman is a royal lady, referred to as the Sakyong Miyi Wangmo in the verses and Sakyong Miyi Jemo Khachö Wangmo in the

38. Bdud 'joms gling pa 2004, 18: 327.6–328.6.

39. Colloquially, the term "demoness" (*'dre mo*) is used for women who defy social conventions and exceed the gender constraints placed on them. Personal communication, Somtso Bhum.

40. Bdud 'joms gling pa 2004, 18: 332.5.

41. Bdud 'joms gling pa 2004, 18: 162.1.

colophon.[42] Rulers in various principalities in eastern Tibet went by the title of Sakyong, and her title suggests the female counterpart. This is one of the few songs to bear a title, namely "The Clear Mirror: Replies to Questions" (*Dris lan gsal ba'i me long*), and the colophon indicates that it was sent as an epistle in response to a written request. It is longer and more formal than the others under consideration here. Unlike the letter that Jigmé Lingpa (1730–98) composed to the Degé queen Tsewang Lhamo (d. 1812) a generation earlier, replete with root verses and an accompanying autocommentary,[43] this letter does not have the same poetic flourish, scriptural references, or specifically gendered language elevating her as a ḍākinī beyond the supposed faults of ordinary women.

Yet in addressing her, Dudjom Lingpa does presuppose Sakyong Miyi Wangmo's knowledge of Mahāyāna terminology and her earnest wish to practice Dzogchen. His detailed instructions on how to avoid going astray in meditation or becoming enmeshed in mental upheavals are subtle and practical, not just meant to impress. The final verses evoke the highest view in a more performative way and indicate that the letter can be regarded in exoteric terms as a blessing and vehicle for liberation through sensory contact via seeing, hearing, recalling, or touching it and thereby establishing a karmic connection with Dudjom Lingpa.[44] Thus, while the letter does not employ gendered tropes, it does suggest a certain level of interest in practicing meditation among royal women in eastern Tibet.

Conclusion

These and other moments in Dudjom Lingpa's songs provide fascinating glimpses into the religious lives of women, as well as gendered discourse and representational practices, in nineteenth-century Golok. As addressees of his songs, this cohort of nuns and yoginīs are made both present and absent in specific ways. On the one hand, they come into visibility as advanced Buddhist practitioners, who receive comparable advice to his male disciples on the subtleties of advanced meditation practice. We get some indication of the precarious margins of religious life in Golok in which at least a small group of gifted and determined nuns and yoginīs did engage in solitary retreat and form small practice communities, even as they were cautioned not to be too proud or too

42. Sa skyong mi yi dbang mo and Sa skyong mi'i rje mo Mkha' spyod dbang mo respectively. Unfortunately, I have not been able to identify this figure.

43. For an introduction and translation of this letter, see Ronis 2017.

44. This is a standard expression suggesting the liberating power of sensory contact with specifically charged sacred objects and texts.

mobile lest they become the object of scrutiny and scorn. On the other hand, these female disciples are simultaneously rendered invisible. We cannot hear their questions or concerns in their own voice, nor learn the details about who they were, how they lived, or what they achieved.

As such, the paradox of their in/visibility as Nyingma women who devoted their lives to religious practice remains, even as nuns at Larung Buddhist Academy have joined in the recovery project to seek out and make available in publication more sources by, about, and for Buddhist women in Tibet and beyond. This paradox is heightened by the enigmatic fact that, while actual women for the most part remain at the margins of Tibetan religious life, the visionary apparitions and voices of ḍākinīs feature prominently in the narrative and ritual works of male visionaries like Dudjom Lingpa.

Works Cited

Altman, Janet. 1982. *Epistolarity: Approaches to a Form*. Columbus, OH: Ohio State University Press.

Ārya Tāre Book Association Editorial Office. 2017. *Mkha' 'gro'i chos mdzod chen mo. Ḍākinīs' Great Dharma Treasury*, 53 vols. Lhasa: Bod ljongs bod yig dpe rnying dpe skrun khang.

Bdud 'joms gling pa. 2004. *Sprul pa'i gter chen bdud 'joms gling pa'i zab gter gsang ba'i chos sde. Collected Revelations and Writings of the Great Tertön Emanation Dudjom Lingpa*, 21 vols. Thimphu: Lama Kuenzang Wangdue.

Bessenger, Suzanne. 2016. *Echoes of Enlightenment: The Life and Legacy of the Tibetan Saint Sonam Peldren*. New York: Oxford University Press.

Chönyi Drolma (Anne Holland). 2011. *A Clear Mirror: The Visionary Autobiography of a Tibetan Master.* Hong Kong: Rangjung Yeshe Publications.

Diemberger, Hildegard. 2007. *When a Woman Becomes a Religious Dynasty: The Samding Dorje Phagmo of Tibet*. New York: Columbia University Press.

Gayley, Holly. 2016. *Love Letters from Golok: A Tantric Couple in Modern Tibet*. New York: Columbia University Press.

———. forthcoming. "All in the Dudjom Family: Overlapping Modes of Authority and Transmission in the Golok Treasure Scene." In *Histories of Tibet: Essays in Honor of Leonard W.J. van der Kuijp*, edited by Kurtis Schaeffer, Jue Liang, and William McGrath, 453–70. Somerville, MA: Wisdom Publications.

Gayley, Holly, and Joshua Schapiro, eds. 2017. *A Gathering of Brilliant Moons: Practice Advice by the Rimé Masters of Tibet*. Somerville, MA: Wisdom Publications.

Gyatso, Janet. 1998. *Apparitions of the Self: The Secret Autobiographies of a Tibetan Visionary*. Princeton, NJ: Princeton University Press.

Gyatso, Janet, and Hanna Havnevik, eds. 2006. *Women in Tibet: Past and Present*. New York: Columbia University Press.

Jacoby, Sarah. 2010. "'This Inferior Female Body:' Reflections on Life as a Treasure Revealer Through the Autobiographical Eyes of Se ra mkha' 'gro (Bde ba'i rdo rje, 1892–1940)." *Journal of the International Association of Buddhist Studies* 32.2: 115–50.

———. 2014. *Love and Liberation: Autobiographical Writings of the Tibetan Buddhist Visionary Sera Khandro.* New York: Columbia University Press.

Melnick Dyer, Alison. 2022. *The Tibetan Nun Mingyur Peldrön: A Woman of Power and Privilege.* Seattle: University of Washington Press.

Padma 'od gsal mtha' yas. 2003. *Ngo mtshar gser gyi snye ma.* In *Deb chung a ru ra'i dga' tshal*, 1–74. Chengdu: Si khron mi rigs dpe skrun khang.

Padma 'tsho and Sarah Jacoby. 2021. "Lessons from Buddhist Foremothers." In *Voices from Larung Gar: Shaping Tibetan Buddhism for the Twenty-First Century*, edited by Holly Gayley, 219–33. Boulder, CO: Snow Lion Publications.

Ronis, Jann. 2017. "A Letter to the Queen." In *A Gathering of Brilliant Moons: Practice Advice from the Rimé Masters of Tibet,* edited by Holly Gayley and Joshua Schapiro, 109–22. Somerville, MA: Wisdom Publications.

Schaeffer, Kurtis. 2004. *Himalayan Hermitess: The Life of a Tibetan Buddhist Nun.* New York: Oxford University Press.

Tibetan Nuns Writing on Equality and Education

Padma 'tsho (Baimacuo)

SINCE THE 1990S there have been innovations in the Buddhist monastic education system in Tibetan areas of China that have elevated the Tibetan nun or *jomo* (*jo mo*) in unprecedented ways. The most striking change in the status and role of Tibetan nuns has been the introduction of the *khenmo* (*mkhan mo*) degree at Larung Buddhist Academy (also known as Larung Gar),[1] providing nuns with a comparable education and stature as monks who reach the highest levels of monastic scholasticism.[2] Based on the khenmo degree, Tibetan nuns are gaining recognition and becoming well-known teachers and writers. As a result, a large number of publications by Larung Gar nuns have appeared in the last decade, which illustrates an improvement in their educational level, and also reflects their challenge to the traditional view of "male superiority and female inferiority" (*pho mchog mo dman*). These publications include the first extensive commentaries on all of the five major subjects of exoteric Buddhist study[3] composed by Khenmo Thupten Rikjé Lhamo (also known as Khenmo Yonten), published in 2018.[4] Another is the work of the Ārya Tāre Book Association Editorial Office in publishing the sixteen-volume *Garland of White Lotuses: The Biographies of the Great Female Masters of India and Tibet* in 2013 and the fifty-three volume *Ḍākinīs' Great Dharma Treasury*

1. On the innovative initiatives and writings by cleric-scholars at Larung Gar, see the recent anthology, *Voices from Larung Gar: Shaping Tibetan Buddhism for the Twenty-First Century* (Gayley 2021).

2. See Padma 'tsho 2021b, Liang and Taylor 2020, and Padma 'tsho 2015.

3. The five major subjects of exoteric Buddhist study (*Gzhung bka' pod lnga*) are divided into Prajñāpāramitā (*phar phyin*), Madhyamaka (*dbu ma*), Epistemology (*tshad ma*), Abhidharma (*chos mngon pa*), and Vinaya (*'dul ba*). Each of subjects follow the sūtras and corresponding commentaries to explain the main topics of the Mahāyāna path, including valid cognition and logic.

4. These can be found in *The Ḍākinīs' Great Dharma Treasury* (*Mkha' 'gro'i chos mdzod chen mo*), volumes 42–49. Chelsea Hall presented a paper about this khenmo and her writings at the panel, *Voices from Larung Gar*, at the American Academy of Religion annual meeting in November 2017.

in 2017.[5] A third example, the focus of this chapter, is the journal *Gangkar Lhamo*, the first women's journal edited by Tibetan nuns, founded in 2011 and issued annually since that time.

This essay explores writings on women's equality (*bud med kyi 'dra mnyam*) in the journal *Gangkar Lhamo,* highlighting the voices of Buddhist nuns in an emergent feminism on the Tibetan plateau.[6] What Tibetan nuns articulate in this journal is not the aspiration for full ordination, the most visible form of Buddhist feminism internationally.[7] Instead the nuns advocate uplifting the status of women, both nuns and female laity, through education and empowerment. As examples of this, I analyze a selection of essays and poems on the topic of women's equality from *Gangkar Lhamo*, providing translations for three short essays. My translations of two others are available in previous publications.[8] Here I am building on an observation made by Janet Gyatso and Hanna Havnevik in their introduction to the anthology *Women in Tibet*: "We should not be surprised to see feminist inklings among *yoginīs* and nuns in particular. There is a long history of the Buddhist monastic order (that is, despite its enduring androcentrism) and other renunciate communities serving as an alternative life-space for women, where they could escape their unhappy circumstances in society."[9] In *Gangkar Lhamo*, we can find the nuns both critiquing the "unhappy circumstances" endured by Tibetan women and also promoting a new education-based vision of gender equality in Buddhist terms.

Gangkar Lhamo *Journal*

Gangkar Lhamo, meaning "Goddess of the Snowy Range" (*Gangs dkar lha mo*), was founded by Khenmo Kusum Chödrön, a learned nun at Larung Gar, as a journal for Tibetan nuns. Initially, for the first three years, Khenmo Kusum Chödrön did all of the work by herself, but after 2014 she was joined by an editorial team of eight khenmos. The journal eventually gained the support of the Ministry of Educational Affairs at Larung Gar, and one of its leaders, Khenpo

5. On this collection, see Padma 'tsho and Jacoby 2021.

6. For a detailed discussion of terms for feminism and gender equality in Tibetan, see my coauthored article with Sarah Jacoby, "Gender Equality in and on Tibetan Buddhist Nuns' Terms" (2020).

7. A prominent example is the centrality of full ordination to the organization Sakyadhita International Association of Buddhist Women. On the various initiatives and debates over full ordination, see Mrozik 2009, Mohr and Tsedroen 2010, and Salgado 2013.

8. See Padma 'tsho and Jacoby 2020 as well as Padma 'tsho 2021a.

9. Gyatso and Havnevik 2005, 15.

Sodargye, contributed 30,000 yuan and put the journal on more sound financial footing. After 2014, the journal expanded its authorship from nuns to Tibetan laywomen and removed the "Annual Journal of Tibetan Nuns" from the cover and upper corner of the publication. Over time, the scope of the journal likewise shifted from monastic concerns to social issues, although gender equity has been a theme running through its annual publications. Since 2017, the journal has also begun to select outstanding works each year as a way to celebrate and inspire writings by Tibetan women.[10] The awards are a significant recognition and affirmation of women's contributions to Tibetan society and culture, in particular the value of their involvement in literary endeavors. The journal has also published several contributions by Jetsuma Mumtso (b. 1966), the niece and spiritual heir to Larung founder Khenpo Jigmé Phuntsok (1933–2004) and a prominent champion of the journal.[11] Her special role and status at Larung Gar embodies and bolsters the contemporary visibility of women's stature in Buddhist monasticism and tantric practice.

In the writings of nuns in the journal *Gangkar Lhamo,* gender equality surfaces as a significant issue. Here I consider a selection of essays and poems on gender equality, analyzing the themes that emerge in each. A number of nun authors highlight the importance of the inner qualities necessary for Tibetan women to achieve and realize equality and status. For example, in a brief essay titled "Our Rare Times" (*Rnyed dka' ba'i nga tsho'i dus tshod*), Kalzang Tsomo highlights four qualities that women should develop in order to advance, namely education (*shes yon*), courage (*snying stobs*), confidence (*spobs pa*), and altruism (*lhag bsam*).[12] These same qualities come up again and again in the selection of essays and poems under consideration here. Of these, the most important quality is knowledge, articulated as a human right (*'gro ba mi'i thob thang*). Education, Kalzang Tsomo argues, is key to developing confidence, not only learning about Tibetan culture but contributing to it.[13] Because knowledge is genderless—as another nun Sherab Zangmo puts it, "Even though bodies are sexed, learning is sexless"[14]—Tibetan nuns advocate for women and

10. Although the right to decide what constitutes excellence in the awards still belongs to khenpos, the awards nonetheless have encouraged Tibetan women to write and signify a turning point in the history of Tibetan nunneries, by recognizing women's contributions to and writings about Tibetan society and culture.

11. Jetsuma Mumtso's poetry can be found on the covers of the second and fifth volumes.

12. Skal bzang mtsho mo 2013, 73.

13. See Dominique Townsend's contribution in this volume on the resonances of the term *spobs pa*, which include eloquence.

14. Shes rab bzang mo 2013, 72. See also Padma 'tsho and Jacoby 2020.

nuns to have the right to study Tibetan culture and the Buddhist curriculum. If women redouble their efforts to learn and improve their capacities, as the Larung Gar nuns assert, they will truly increase their status and prove their social worth. This social worth, in turn, is an explicitly Buddhist one, based on an altruistic motive. For example, in the article "The Way Forward for You and Me" (*Nga dang khyed kyi mdun lam*)[15] Khenmo Rigzin Chödrön suggests that the point of equality should not be merely for one's own benefit, nor for the temporary equality between men and women, but for the equal opportunity to work for the advancement of Tibetans as an ethnicity or nationality (*mi rigs*) and for the benefit of the Buddhist teachings and all living beings.

A Tibetan Nun's Views on Women's Rights

In this survey of the essays from *Gangkar Lhamo,* we start with the most recent and strongest essay, "A Tibetan Nun's Views on Women's Rights" (*Bod kyi jo mo zhig gis mi'i bsam blo dang bud med kyi thob thang gleng ba*) and work our way back. This will allow the reader to trace common themes from the essays, translated into English here for the first time, back to more foundational works which I have published translations of previously.[16] This is an essay on women's rights in four pages published under the pen name Zhang Ganglung in 2017. In her essay, Zhang Ganglung takes a stark view of the challenges that women face and calls on women to step up to that challenge. As in Khenmo Rikzin Chödrön's article, the purpose of women's equality is framed as contributing to the advancement of Tibetans as a nationality.

བོད་ཀྱི་ཇོ་མོ་ཞིག་གིས་མིའི་བསམ་བློ་དང་བུད་མེད་ཀྱི་ཐོབ་ཐང་གླེང་བ།
A Tibetan Nun's Views on Women's Rights

ཞང་གངས་ལུང་།
Zhang Ganglung

I. From an honest and realistic perspective, we women need to work for equality ourselves. It will be difficult to advance if we leave it in the hands of others, even powerful officials. It's better for each of us to feel empowered and supported, and take responsibility.

15. Rig 'dzin chos sgron 2012, 13–18. My full translation of this essay can be found in *Voices from Larung Gar,* edited by Holly Gayley. See Padma 'tsho 2021a, 215–18.

16. See Padma 'tsho and Jacoby 2020 and Padma 'tsho 2021a.

From now on, strive for your rights! Then we can move in a positive direction.

II. The view of male superiority and female inferiority is a remnant from the past, like a disease that has still not been eradicated. Especially now, in the twenty-first century, when society has undergone so many changes, still in our Tibetan households and rural areas, the disease lingers on. According to tradition and customs of the past, boys are celebrated and girls denigrated. This is not only a social convention, but the attitude of even one's own kind parents. For example, in the past, whenever there was a boy and a girl in the family, and only one of them had the opportunity to go to school, then the boy would go, not the girl. The rationale was that girls could not learn or train in the domains of knowledge (*rig gnas*)—this is not right! Women were responsible for the housework, tending cattle, and other heavy tasks. They did not have equality.

Girls were also taught that they knew nothing and so walked down the road with their heads down. This was due, firstly, to obstacles caused by customs and, secondly, to the misfortune that women did not strive for equality. Today, unlike before, the state has given men and women equal rights to study, work, and engage in business, so they can choose their own path according to their abilities. But, as mentioned above, in rural areas, due to the poor understanding of family and parents, women continue to be raised to work at home as in the past. The fundamental reason for the lack of opportunities is that we women do not strive for our own rights and empowerment. It is a shortcoming to not value and diligently pursue these.

If we look down on ourselves and disrespect ourselves, this is a roadblock preventing us from taking further steps. We won't be able to make progress. As others have said, if we women believe that we are not good enough, we will not have the strength and courage to strive for equality based on such thinking. Therefore, we ourselves need to work hard for our rights and not let others treat us like objects. For example, our state cadres now have rights and status because they didn't avoid difficulties and hardships. They endeavored with great courage, so they gained equal rights.

In any case, it's important to remain hopeful about equal rights and status despite the roadblocks. We need to have faith in ourselves and great courage and commitment to take strides forward in a way that is unprecedented in preceding eras. Like others, we ourselves

> can strive for equal rights. This is the time! Thinking "we can do it," we must have unrelenting courage.
>
> III. By discussing women's rights here, I do not want to create debate or conflict between men and women. Nor, as a women, do I want to praise women and belittle men. Rather, I seek a way for Tibetans as a nationality to progress and take responsibility for our social development.
>
> The reason is that in any nationality or society, if either men or women are elevated over the other, the other falls behind. As a result, one half of the entire nationality falls behind. For the development and glory of society as a whole, men and women should make progress together. Only with both of us can we proceed. We men and women should work together for the common good and move forward in words, deeds, and ideas. To progress beyond backwardness and stupidity, we must rouse and strengthen our courage![17]

Three points stand out in this essay. The first is the way Zhang Ganglung labels sexism, or the "view of male superiority and female inferiority" (*pho mchog mo dman*), as a disease (*nad*) from the past. Never cured, it continues to infect society, culture, and family. The second point is her emphasis on the importance that women value and strive for equal rights; it is a shortcoming if they do not. This places the burden, perhaps unduly, on Tibetan women to take action despite any roadblocks (*lam 'gag*). The third point is her insistence that women's rights are not in opposition to men but are for the greater good of progress in Tibetan society. Her essay is bold, yet she takes a non-confrontational approach.

Women Raised in the Land of Snow Mountains

Next let us examine two brief essays (a single page each) and two poems published in the third issue of *Gangkar Lhamo* in 2013, all on the theme of gender equality. These contrast the "unhappy circumstances" of Tibetan women in the past and as they continue to exist in rural areas despite a new era in which it is possible to break through traditional gender roles, especially through education. Each author has a distinctive voice and emphasis. Consider the brief essay,

17. Zhang Gangs 2017, 19–21. This author uses a pen name, a sign that her essay may be controversial enough to want to protect her identity; we do not know what region she is from. The first lines of the opening are omitted in my translation.

"Women Raised in the Snow Land of Tibet" (*Kha ba gangs can ljongs nas 'tshar longs byung ba'i bud med tsho*),[18] which contrasts contemporary opportunities to study, especially for nuns, with how education was traditionally restricted as a male domain.

ཁ་བ་གངས་ཅན་ལྗོངས་ནས་འཚར་ལོངས་བྱུང་བའི་བུད་མེད་ཚོ།

Women Raised in the Land of Snow Mountains

བདེ་ཆེན་དབྱངས་སྐྱིད། སྡེ་དགེ

Dechen Yangkyi, Degé

> In the past, educated Tibetan women were rare, since there was no custom of training them in the domains of knowledge. As a result, women had no choice but to be servants of others and live under their authority. Intimidated, with little experience, they stayed out of the way, against the wall or in the corner. Now we must generate fierce courage and confidence. Due to the kindness of the Buddha and lamas, we have the opportunity to be of service to the Buddhist teachings and our nationality, and it is the responsibility of all nuns from the three Tibetan regions to do so. Today there are educational opportunities that were impossible in the past. Because of this, everyone should work hard to study. As a young *jomo* myself, I have little learning. Still, I hope that in the future I can write more about my own thoughts and sorrows. For this young nun, serving the cause of equal treatment for women, while practicing and studying Buddhism, are my sole mission and calling.[19]

In this brief essay, Dechen Yangkyi emphasizes how the lack of education limited women's choices in the past, condemning them to fear and servitude within socially prescribed duties in the household. By contrast, now that educational opportunities are more widely available for both nuns and laywomen, she encourages her readers to take advantage of it. This is something the author herself pledges to do, and her sense of commitment is palpable.

In another brief essay, "Our Rare Times" (*Rnyed dka' ba'i nga tsho'i dus tshod*), Kalzang Tsomo issues a rousing call to action for Tibetan women to seize the moment, again based on new opportunities to pursue an education. Here is my translation:

18. Bde chen dbyangs skyid 2013, 75.

19. Bde chen dbyangs skyid 2013, 75.

རྙེད་དཀའ་བའི་ང་ཚོའི་དུས་ཚོད།
Our Rare Times

སྐལ་བཟང་མཚོ་མོ། ཡུལ་ཤུལ།

Kalzang Tsomo, Yushu

> Tibetan nuns are well suited generally to serve Buddhism and specifically to lead the women of Tibet, Land of Snow Mountains. We need to orient ourselves toward our own wishes and convictions, and commit to the aspirations of others. In particular, for women who face numerous internal and external challenges, we have the chance to encounter rare opportunities. We need to seize the moment and strive for the pursuit of knowledge. This is an appropriate undertaking that need not feel burdensome. If we have courage, confidence, knowledge, and altruism, nothing can stand in our way. With knowledge, we can discern which activities to undertake and which to relinquish. With courage, we must forge ahead. Again, let's not forget that many with less experience, who have not found even a moment of time to study the domains of knowledge, are looking to us with hope.[20]

In a forthright manner, more than other authors discussed here, Kalzang Tsomo asserts the unique leadership role that nuns can play as advocates for and advisors to Tibetan women. In a Buddhist sensibility, her orientation is altruistic, committed to fulfilling the aspirations of all women. Knowledge, for Kalzang Tsomo, is the key to unlock other inner qualities, such as courage and confidence, that are traditionally coded male. The essay also embodies a certain boldness, asserting that with knowledge and the qualities that come with it "nothing can stand in our way" or more literally "there is nothing that cannot be accomplished" (*mi 'grubs pa gang yang med*).

In poems on gender equality in the 2013 issue of *Gangkar Lhamo*, nun authors address nuns and laywomen side by side with different messages, reflecting their distinct circumstances. For example, in "Conch Call from the Heart" (*Dung sems kyi 'bod brda*),[21] the nun Karma Yanglha encourages young female herders to get an education and young nuns to appreciate their education and not take it for granted. Here are just two verses by way of illustration:

20. Skal bzang mtsho mo 2013, 73.

21. Karma g.yang lha 2013, 27. My translation of the title retains the image of the conch but also the association of *dung sems* with an earnest or sincere frame of mind.

> Young sixteen-year-old girls tending cattle, rise up from your muddleheaded sleep and think for yourself! If you seek a pathway into the future, the time has come to walk in the garden of knowledge.
>
> Young nuns, aligned toward intellectual discernment, you have the opportunity to drink the elixir of the five domains of knowledge. Don't get lost in the haze of delusion! Dear sisters, please put [the teachings] into practice. Don't just recite them like a parrot!

In another poem published in the same issue, "Women" (*Skyes ma tsho*),[22] Sherab Zangmo addresses laywomen and nuns in separate sections. She too cautions young women against wasting their previous human life on tending livestock and making themselves look pretty and encourages them instead to develop their inner qualities: "Girls: It is not the case that we must only herd the livestock and till the fields . . . Girls: We also need altruism and pure intentions; shame and modesty." Meanwhile, she encourages nuns to not only study diligently but also take action: "Nuns: We must actually perform practical actions that benefit others, not just talk about doing this." In this way, she advocates for a balance of inner qualities and outer actions in cultivating gender equality.

The Way Forward for You and Me

The last, but chronologically earliest, example is "The Way Forward for You and Me" (*Nga dang khyed kyi mdun lam*) by Khenmo Rigzin Chödrön, published in 2012 in *Gangkar Lhamo*'s second issue.[23] As with Zhang Ganglung's essay above, Khenmo Rigzin Chödrön emphasizes the point that, since women are half the Tibetan population, the more empowered they are, the more benefit they can be to Tibetans as a whole:

> If laywomen don't have independence, their state of mind cannot be free from anxiety and sorrow for even a moment. The root of well-being comes from a joyful mind, and that depends on women really knowing what we want, rather than parents and relatives burdening us with a life we didn't choose. The minds and hearts of women

22. Shes rab bzang mo 2013, 72. A full translation, the result of a collaboration with Sarah Jacoby, is available in our recent co-authored article, "Gender Equality in and on Tibetan Buddhist Nun's Terms" (2020), where we discuss the publishing projects by Tibetan nuns mentioned at this outset of this chapter.

23. Rig 'dzin chos sgron 2012, 13–18. See my translation in Padma 'tsho 2021a.

> are directed toward household life rather than thinking about benefiting our nationality and studying our culture with diligence. . . . With roughly half of the Tibetan population being women, it seems to me that if most of our women are in the situation above, then half of the capacity for the development of our nationality's economy and culture declines. This is a problem for both Buddhism and secular life. So, I request everyone to be concerned about this and to consider helping as much as possible.[24]

Khenmo Rigzin Chödrön's essay is the earliest of those discussed here, and it could well be that she set the tone by drawing attention to women's lack of choice when traditionally bound to household duties and remarking on the detriment to the common cause of Tibetan progress and development. Nonetheless, the themes that echo through these selections show Tibetan nuns developing a shared discourse around gender equality through the shared medium of *Gangkar Lhamo*. As one of its leading voices, Khenmo Rigzin Chödrön has the most eloquent statement of gender equality in Buddhist terms:

> The purpose and direction of equal rights is not just for our own narrow self-interest, nor is it only for the purpose of being equal with men in terms of opportunities and circumstances. Rather, equality is most important so that we can benefit our nationality and accomplish the Dharma for sentient beings. This is equal rights in its most authentic and lasting sense.[25]

Here Khenmo Rigzin Chödrön points out that the purpose and direction of equality for nuns and laywomen are not their own advantage, but the benefit of Tibetans as a nationality and, beyond that, of all living beings. This altruistic motive behind equal rights is a distinctively Buddhist articulation by Tibetan nuns, as found in *Gangkar Lhamo.*

In "The Way Forward for You and Me," Khenmo Rigzin Chödrön insists that advocating equal rights should not become empty slogans. Instead, the key to the realization of women's rights and status is individual action. After gesturing to the international movement for women's rights and the United Nations stance of gender equality,[26] she states, "If we want to move in that direction, then we won't gain anything by advocating out of uninformed confusion

24. Rig 'dzin chos sgron 2012, 16.
25. Rig 'dzin chos sgron 2012, 16–17.
26. See https://www.un.org/en/global-issues/gender-equality (accessed on July 15, 2021).

and anger. 'We want rights. Men and women should be equal'—these are just empty words. . . . Arguing with empty words brings no benefit."[27] Her point is that if Tibetan women want to move in the direction of equality, then they need more than slogans, since those will not change the view of "male superiority and female inferiority" and the related customs. Instead, it takes hard work and planning. For the nun authors surveyed here, Tibetan women have to take action and responsibility for improving their own lot rather than relying on others to do so.

Conclusion

In the writings of Tibetan nuns, there is general agreement that the choices of Tibetan women were limited in the past, given they did not have support for equal rights in society at large or in Buddhist monasteries. Until recently, women have been confined to family roles and private spaces, and even nuns often stayed at home to take care of elderly relatives. However, nun authors contrast this with the new era and twenty-first century, a time when Tibetan women are realizing their value to society and entering more fully into public spaces. With improvements in the area of education comes a newfound confidence. According to Tibetan nuns writing in *Gangkar Lhamo*, there are several consistent themes: the need for Tibetan women to cultivate their capabilities and confidence through education, the call for women to find courage and take action instead of spouting empty slogans, and the purpose of gender equality being oriented to the greater good of Tibetans. In these ways, women can work to eliminate the view of "male superiority and female inferiority" with their own abilities and skills.

The establishment of the journal of *Gangkar Lhamo* in 2011 was a new endeavor by Tibetan nuns to lead the way in promoting publications by and for women. It remains also a potent marker of Tibetan nuns' transition from their previous lack of education, often illiterate and confined to reciting chants and caring for others, to becoming literary creators as well as learned and respected Buddhist teachers. The emergence and existence of *Gangkar Lhamo* is one important example of how the gender imbalances in Tibetan textual production are being addressed today through the efforts of Buddhist nuns. As more publications by Tibetan nuns and laywomen emerge, the traditional status and roles of women are challenged. This both reflects progress and further promotes gender equality and women's equal rights for the benefit of all Tibetans.

27. Rig 'dzin chos sgron 2012, 13–14.

Works Cited

Tibetan Sources

Ārya Tāre Book Association Editorial Office. 2017. *Mkha' 'gro'i chos mdzod chen mo. Ḍākinīs' Great Dharma Treasury*, 53 vols. Lhasa: Bod ljongs bod yig dpe rnying dpe skrun khang.

Bde chen dbyangs skyid. (བདེ་ཆེན་དབྱངས་སྐྱིད།). "Kha ba gangs can ljongs nas 'tshar longs byung ba'i bud med tsho" (ཁ་བ་གངས་ཅན་ལྗོངས་ནས་འཚར་ལོངས་བྱུང་བའི་བུད་མེད་ཚོ།). *Gangkar Lhamo* (གངས་དཀར་ལྷ་མོ།) 2013, 75.

Karma g.yang lha (ཀརྨ་གཡང་ལྷ།). "Dung sems kyi 'bod brda" (དུང་སེམས་ཀྱི་འབོད་བརྡ།). *Gangs dkar lha mo* (གངས་དཀར་ལྷ་མོ) 2013: 27.

Rig 'dzin chos sgron (རིག་འཛིན་ཆོས་སྒྲོན།). "Nga dang khyed kyi mdun lam" (ང་དང་ཁྱེད་ཀྱི་མདུན་ལམ།). *Gangs dkar lha mo* (གངས་དཀར་ལྷ་མོ།) 2012: 13–18.

Shes rab bzang mo (ཤེས་རབ་བཟང་མོ།). "Skyes ma tsho" (སྐྱེས་མ་ཚོ།). *Gangs dkar lha mo* (གངས་དཀར་ལྷ་མོ།) 2013: 72.

Skal bzang mtsho mo (སྐལ་བཟང་མཚོ་མོ།). "Rnyed dka' ba'i nga tsho'i dus tshod" (རྙེད་དཀའ་བའི་ང་ཚོའི་དུས་ཚོད།). *Gangs dkar lha mo* (གངས་དཀར་ལྷ་མོ།) 2013: 73.

Zhang Gangs 2017, 19–21. (ཞང་གངས་བླུང་།), *Bod kyi jo mo zhig gis mi'i bsam blo dang bud med kyi thob thang gleng ba* (བོད་ཀྱི་ཇོ་མོ་ཞིག་གིས་མིའི་བསམ་བློ་དང་བུད་མེད་ཀྱི་ཐོབ་ཐང་གླེང་བ།), *Gangkar Lhamo* (གངས་དཀར་ལྷ་མོ།) 2017, 19–21.

Other Works Cited

Gayley, Holly. 2021. *Voices from Larung Gar: Shaping Tibetan Buddhism for the Twenty-First Century*. Boulder, CO: Snow Lion Publications.

Gyatso, Janet, and Hannah Havnevik. 2005. *Women in Tibet*. New York: Columbia University Press.

Liang, Jue, and Andrew Taylor. 2020. "Tilling the Fields of Merit: The Institutionalization of Feminine Enlightenment in Tibet's First Khenmo Program." *Journal of Buddhist Ethics* 27: 231–62.

Mohr, Thea, and Jampa Tsedroen. 2010. *Dignity and Discipline: Reviving Full Ordination for Nuns*. Boston: Wisdom Publications.

Mrozik, Suzanne. 2009. "A Robed Revolution: The Contemporary Buddhist Nun's (*Bhikṣuṇī*) Movement." *Religion Compass* 3.3: 360–78. Doi: 10.1111/j.1749-8171.2009.00136.x.

Padma 'tsho (Baimacuo). 2015. "Dangdai Zangzu Nizhong Xinjiao Yutixi de Diaocha Yanjio" (当代藏族尼众新教育体系的调查研究) ["Investigation and Research into the Contemporary Educational System for Nuns."] *Zongjiao Xue Yanjiu* (宗教学研究) [*Religious Studies*] 3: 158–63.

———. 2021a. "The Future of Tibetan Women." In *Voices from Larung Gar: Shaping Tibetan Buddhism for the Twenty-First Century*, edited by Holly Gayley. Boulder, CO: Snow Lion Publications.

———. 2021b. "How Tibetan Nuns Become Khenmos: The History and Evolution of the Khenmo Degree for Tibetan Nuns." *Religions* 12, 1051: 1–18. Doi: 10.3390/rel12121051.

Padma 'tsho and Sarah Jacoby. 2020. "Gender Equality in and on Tibetan Buddhist Nuns' Terms." *Religions* 11, 543: 1–19. Doi:10.3390/rel11100543.

———. 2021. "Lessons from Buddhist Foremothers." In *Voices from Larung Gar: Shaping Tibetan Buddhism for the Twenty-First Century*, edited by Holly Gayley. Boulder, CO: Snow Lion Publications.

Salgado, Nirmala. 2013. *Buddhist Nuns and Gendered Practice: In Search of the Female Renunciant.* Oxford: Oxford University Press.

Samtha/the Borderlands of Tibetan Translation

Nicole Willock

Long before I met Janet, I was in awe of the way her academic writings, such as "Down with the Demoness" and *Apparitions of the Self*, on topics as varied as gender and autobiography, broke down the barriers between the field of Tibetan studies as a purely historical-philological endeavor and other categories of analysis. Aside from continuing to admire her pathbreaking research and methodologies in Tibetan studies, my respect for her engagement with Tibetan texts deepened when I had the opportunity to work with her closely in the framework of the "Religion & the Literary in Tibet" seminar at the American Academy of Religion annual meetings beginning in 2010 and continuing for the next five years.

Although I cannot recall the exact discussions, what I remember clearly is the feeling that her comments, critiques, and words of encouragement opened my mind to a new way of looking at Tibetan texts. In each session, Janet reminded us to question the category of what is meant by "the literary" and encouraged us to speak thematically and theoretically to scholars outside the field. In the session hosted at the University of Toronto in March 2012, Gedun Rabsal and I presented sections of our translation of Tseten Zhabdrung's *A General Commentary on Poetics* (*Snyan ngag spyi don*). In the ensuing discussion, Janet questioned how to create space for the Tibetanness of the text within the English translation: for example, what if we followed the syntax of Tibetan poetry more closely rather than re-ordering to match English syntax? She invited us to sense the Tibetan text and share that sensation in English. This kind of dynamic engagement with Tibetan texts opened my world.

In gratitude and recognition of Janet's stalwart support of Tibetan translation projects and her contributions to the study of Tibetan women, the goals of this essay are threefold: (1) to offer my translation of the poem, "Life in Samtha," by Nyima Tso, a contemporary Tibetan woman writer based in Dharamsala, India;[1] (2) to reflect on my own translation practices with a

1. Thanks to Tashi Dekyid, Jue Liang, and Andrew Taylor for organizing the "Tibetan Women Writing Symposium" (བོད་མོ་རྩོམ་འབྲི་བས་རྩོམ་རིག་སྒྲིང་བ།) that was the impetus for this piece.

thought experiment; and (3) to draw attention to the ethics of Tibetan translations into English-language academic discourse.

In *Feminine Ground*, one of, if not the first, critical study of the women in Tibet, Janet published "Down with the Demoness," one of her earliest analyses of gender in the Tibetan context.[2] Since then academic works on the cross-sections of gender studies and Tibetan studies have grown exponentially, seen in Janet's co-edited volume with Hannah Havnevik *Women in Tibet*, and works by Hildegard Diemberger, Charlene Mackley, Kurtis Schaeffer, Sarah Jacoby, and Holly Gayley, among others.[3] These works draw attention to writings by and about Tibetan women in the Buddhist context and the experience of Tibetan nuns.

However, far fewer studies exist on contemporary female Tibetan writers. Lauran Hartley and Lama Jabb have introduced a few key female Tibetan writers located in the People's Republic of China (PRC) into academic discourse.[4] Outside an academic context, Dechen Pemba's *High Peaks, Pure Earth* website has made an effort to bring contemporary Tibetan women writers to the fore, publishing online translations of writings in Tibetan (Jamyang Kyi) and Chinese (Woeser) and highlighting the voices of Tibetan women writers composing in English (Tashi Rabten, Tenzin Dickie, Tsering Wangmo Dhompa, and Tsering Yangzom Lama).[5] In Hortsang Jigme's assessment of "Tibetan Literature in the Diaspora," he states, "In addition to the virtual absence of Tibetan modern literature in exile until the late 1980s, another lacuna should be noted: the absence of any women writers."[6] He then lists four Tibetan women writers in exile who compose in Tibetan: Kelsang Lhamo, Chukyé Drölma, Tsering Kyi, and Zungchuk Kyi. Since his study in 2008, this group has grown with the author Nyima Tso as one of its leading figures.

2. Gyatso 1989, 33–51.

3. Havnevik and Gyatso 2005; Diemberger 2007; Makley 2005, 2007; Schaeffer 2004; Jacoby 2014, and Gayley 2016.

4. Hartley 2003, 35–36; Lama Jabb 2015, 171–72; Cf. Pema Bhum 2008, 138–40 and Hortsang Jigme 2008.

5. See, for example, "Announcing the First High Peaks Pure Earth Instagram Stories Takeover by Tibetan Women Poets," February 21, 2020: https://highpeakspureearth.com/announcing-the-first-high-peaks-pure-earth-instagram-stories-takeover-by-tibetan-women-poets/.

6. Hortsang Jigme 2008, 290–91.

Figure 1. First meeting of Mayum: Tibetan Women Writers in Exile who Write in Tibetan. Nyima Tso (left) and Tenzin Choetso (right) sit with their backs facing the camera. From the left of Nyima Tso are Tukar Tso, Gang zi, Nyig Tsema, Zungdu Kyi, and Min Nangzey. (Photo courtesy of Nyima Tso.)

Women Writing in Exile

Recognizing the need for community support in exile, several friends and colleagues convened an association called "Tibetan Women Writers in Exile who Write in Tibetan" in June 2012. (See figure 1 and plate 4.) The writer Nyima Tso is a driving force behind this group, which still continues to meet. When only fifteen years old, Nyima Tso left her native homeland of Bora village near Labrang Tashikyil Monastery in Gansu Province in 1999. After completing high school at the Tibetan Children's Village school, she went on to earn bachelor's and master's degrees from the Norbulingka Institute in Dharamsala, where she is currently employed as a production manager. She also serves as executive secretary of the Tibetan Writers Abroad PEN Centre (PEN TIBET). She is a versatile author publishing in a variety of different genres including fiction and nonfiction. Nyima Tso published a book of poems, *First Journey of this Life* (2003) with her schoolmate Jampel Drolma.[7] In addition, Nyima Tso

7. Jampel Drolma and Nyima Tso 2003.

is the author of a collection of short stories titled *A Fragment* (2009), several of which explore women's issues. She is also the editor of *Mayum*, a literary magazine which showcases female Tibetan writers in exile and has been ongoing since 2010. She also conducted research on ethnic-minority policy within China for the Tibetan-language monograph, *A Document on the Minzu Policy of Inner and Outer Tibet* (2015). When she noticed that there were too few Tibetan-language books for children, she began translating them; this has resulted in the translation of forty-four children's books into Tibetan.

I had the honor of working with Nyima Tso in the framework of the Tibetan Women Writing Symposium hosted by the University of Virginia and organized by Tashi Dekyid, Jue Liang, and Andrew Taylor (see plate 2).[8] The choice of the text for translation was not "selective" nor "densely motivated" by this translator.[9] In this case, the author herself chose the poem "Life in Samtha" (*Sa mtha'i tsho ba*) for me to translate from her body of work. This poem won the annual poetry competition at Norling College, the Academy of Tibetan Culture at Norbulingka Institute, in 2006. It was published in their literary magazine, *Norgyen* (*Nor rgyan*) in the same year. For this project, Nyima Tso and I met several times online to read through the piece in Tibetan and then I drafted an English-language translation. Dhondup T. Rekjong then joined Nyima Tso and me to review the English translation and Tibetan text side by side. This prepared us for an online Zoom presentation (November 13, 2020) during which Nyima Tso read her poem in Tibetan followed by my recitation of its English translation.

ས་མཐའི་འཚོ་བ།

མུ་ཏིག[10]

ས་མཐའ་ནི་ལས་ཀྱིས་བསྐོས་པའི་གནས་ཚང་ཞིག་དང་འདྲ་ལ། ས་མཐའ་ནི་ཕྱུགས་
འདུན་སྐྱབ་སའི་ཁོར་ཡུག་ཅིག་དང་མཚུངས་པས། ཕ་ས་ཕ་ཡུལ་བོར་བའི་ཡུལ་གྱུར་བ་ཚོས།
ས་མཐའི་ངན་ངོན་གྱི་འཚོ་བའི་ཁྲོད། རང་ཉིད་ཀྱི་སེམས་ཤུགས་མི་ཏུ་སྦར་གྱིན་ཡོད།
ས་མཐའི་འཚོ་བ་ལ་སྐྱིད་སྣང་མེད་ཀྱང་། ས་མཐའ་ལ་ཡོང་བ་ནས་བཟུང་། སེམས་པའི་

8. The meeting was originally scheduled for April 2020, it moved online due to the COVID-19 pandemic and then met in person in April 2022.

9. Venuti (2000, 482–83; cf. 2017, xii) makes the case that when the translator chooses a text to translate, this act is one of the first steps of "inscribing and domesticating foreign texts" and is "densely motivated by the translator's choice."

10. Mutik is Nyima Tso's pen name. In the print version of the Tibetan text the title is given followed by her pen name as it is here. On the importance of pen names in the Tibetan context, see Pema Bhum 2008, 141–42.

ཡོལ་རས་ཀྱི་ངོས་སུ། བདེ་དྲོད་ཀྱི་ཚོར་བ་ཞིག་འཕྲོལ་ནས་ཡོང་བ་ལས། སུ་ཞིག་གིས་སྐྱལ་བའི་འཇིགས་སྣང་ཡོད་ཚད། འཇའ་ཚོན་བཞིན། རྒྱང་ནས་རྒྱང་དུ་ཡལ།

ས་མཐའ་ནི་དེ་སྔོན་རྒྱུས་མངའ་མེད་པ་ཞིག་ཡིན་ནའང་། ས་མཐའི་འཚོ་བ་ལ་དངོས་སུ་ཞུགས་པ་ནས་བཟུང་། དེའང་། ཕྲག་སྐྱེང་ན་རི་རབ་ལས་ལྗི་བའི་འགན་འཁྲི་ཡོད་པ་རྟོགས་ལ། སེམས་ཁོང་ན་རྒས་རྒྱུ་མེད་པའི་རྨི་ལམ་ཡོད་པ་ཚོར། འགན་འཁྲི་འདི་དང་རྨི་ལམ་འདི་དག་བསམས་ན། ས་མཐའ་ནས། ང་ལ་གཉིད་མི་འོངས་ལ། ས་མཐའ་ནས། ངའི་སེམས་མི་བདེ།

ས་མཐར་མ་སླེབས་པའི་ཡར་སྔོན་དུ། ས་མཐའ་ནི། ལྷའི་ཕོ་བྲང་བཞིན། ཟས་རང་གྲུབ་དང་གོས་རང་གྲུབ་ཡིན་པ་ཐོས་ལ། ས་མཐའ་ནི། གླུའི་བང་མཛོད་བཞིན། འཛད་མཐའ་མེད་པའི་ནོར་ལ་ལོངས་སྤྱོད་བྱེད་ས་ཞིག་ཏུ་སྙམ།

ས་མཐར་སླེབས་དུས། ས་མཐའ་ནི་གནའ་ཐོས་སུ་གྱུར་བའི་གཏམ་རྒྱུད་དེ་དག་དང་གཏན་ནས་མི་འདྲ་ལ། ས་མཐའ་ནི་ངས་བསམས་སྐྱོང་བའི་འཕྲུལ་སྣང་དེ་དག་དང་ཁྱོན་ནས་མི་མཚུངས། ས་མཐའ་ནི། བྲང་ཁོག་ན་མེ་རི་བཞིན་འཕྱུར་གྱིན་པའི་རེ་བ་ཞིག་སྒྲུབ་ས་རེད་འདུག ས་མཐའ་ནི། ཡུན་རིང་སེམས་ལ་རྨག་པའི་རྨ་ཁ་ཞིག་གསོ་ས་རེད་འདུག

ས་མཐའི་འཚོ་བ་ནི། ཕ་ཡུལ་གྱི་འཚོ་བ་དང་གཏན་ནས་མི་འདྲ་ལ། ས་མཐའི་དུས་ཚོད་ཀྱང་ཕ་ཡུལ་གྱི་དུས་ཚོད་དང་གང་ཡང་མི་གཅིག ས་མཐའ་ནས། བདེ་སྡུག་གི་ཚོར་བ་ཏ་ཙང་རྙོ་ལ། ས་མཐའ་ནས། དུས་ཚོད་ནི་རང་ཉིད་ཀྱི་མིག་མདུན་ནས། མངོན་སུམ་དུ་བཞུར་འགྲོ། འདི་ལྟར། ས་མཐའ་ནས་རྒས་སླ་ལ། ཤི་ཡང་མགྱོགས།

ས་མཐའི་འཚོ་བ་ལ་རོལ་བ་ནས། ལུས་ངག་ཡིད་གསུམ། རེ་བཞག་དང་ཡིད་སྨོན་ཞིག་ཏུ་འཐིམས་འགྲོ་ལ། ལང་ཚོ་དང་མཛེས་ཉམས་དེའང་། རིམ་གྱིས་རྒུད་འགྲོ། ཐ་ན་མཁུར་ཚོས་ཀྱི་དམར་མདངས་དེའང་རླུང་ཁ་ནས་ཟད་པ་ཇི་བཞིན། གང་ཞིག་ལ་ཡལ་འགྲོ། ཁ་ཤས་ཀྱིས་གནས་སྟངས་འདིར་འཁང་ར་དང་སུན་སྣང་བྱེད་བཞིན་ཡོད་ནའང་། ངས་ང་རྒྱལ་དང་སྤོབས་པ་སྐྱེས་བཞིན་ཡོད། རྒྱུ་མཚན། འདི་ལྟར་གྱུར་བ་ནས་བཟུང་། ངས་ང་ཉིད་ལམ་ཆེན་ཞིག་ཏུ་གོམ་པ་སྤོ་བཞིན་པ་ཤེས་ལ། ཨ་མའི་འབྲུམ་གྱི་བྱིས་པ་དེ་མ་ཡིན་པར། རང་རྐྱ་འཕེར་བའི་འཚོ་བ་ཞིག་མདུན་བསུ་བྱེད་བཞིན་པ་ཚོར།

ས་མཐའ་ན། མེད་ཐབས་མ་འདང་བའི་དུ་ཁ་ཤིན་ཏུ་མང་ནའང་། དེ་དག་གི་ཟུར་ཁ་རེ་རེ་ཡིས། ང་ཚོར་ཕུགས་བསམ་དང་སྤོབས་པ་སྟོལ་གྱི་ཡོད། བླ་ན་མེད་པའི་རྒྱབ་སྐྱོར་དང་སྐུལ་འདེད་བྱེད་ཀྱི་ཡོད། དེར་བརྟེན། ས་མཐའ་ནས། ང་ཚོ་དཔའ་ཞུམ་མི་ཉན་ལ། ས་མཐའ་ནས། ང་ཚོའི་མགོ་བོ་ཆེས་མཐོ་སར་འདེགས་དགོས།

ས་མཐར་འབྱམས་པ་ནས། ཡུལ་གྱུར་བའི་ཕྱི་ནང་གསང་གསུམ་འགྱུར་འགྲོ། ས་མཐར་འབྱམས་པ་ནས། ཡུལ་གྱུར་བ། སྐྱེ་འགྲོ་སྤྱིའི་བདེ་སྡུག་ལ་སེམས་ཁུར་གྱིས་རྒྱས་འགྲོ། ནམ་ཞིག་ཡུལ་གྱུར་བ་སྤྱིའི་དམིགས་ཡུལ་བཞིན། འཛམ་གླིང་རྒྱལ་པོ། སའི་གོ་ལའི་ཁྱིམ་གཞི་ཆེན་པོ་ཞིག་ཏུ་གྱུར་ན། ས་མཐའ་ཞེས་པའི་མིང་དེ་འཇིག་འགྲོ་ལ། ཡུལ་གྱུར་བ། གང་ལ་སོང་རུང་ཕ་ཡུལ་ཡོད།

ས་མཐའི་ནམ་མཁའ་ནི། ཕ་ཡུལ་གྱི་ནམ་མཁའ་དང་འདྲ་ལ། ས་མཐའི་ཉི་ཟླ་སྐར་གསུམ་ཡང་ཕ་ཡུལ་གྱི་དེ་དང་ཀུན་ནས་མཚུངས། འོན་ཀྱང་། ས་མཐའ་ན། ཚ་སོབ་སོབ་ཀྱི་ཁྱིམ་ཚང་མེད་ལ། ངག་འཇམ་འཇམ་གྱི་ཕ་མའང་མེད། ས་མཐའ་ན་ཡོད་པ་ནི། དྲན་གདུང་དང་རེ་སྒུག་འབབ་ཞིག་རེད།

Life in Samtha/Borderlands

Borderlands, a place to stay, determined by karma. Sort of.
Borderlands, a site for fulfilling future dreams. Kind of.
Having lost their *phayul*—homeland—
amid a pitiful life in exile, in *samtha*,
refugees lift their spirits, rising like flames.

Life in samtha lacks visible happiness.
But since coming to this borderland,
a warm feeling swirls on a screen of thoughts.
All threatening fears disappear into the distance like a rainbow.

Samtha. It was once unfamiliar.
But since being immersed in this borderland's life, I grapple with burdens on my shoulders heavy as mountains.
In my mind, I sense new dreams.
Thinking of these responsibilities and these dreams in samtha, sleep won't come to me.
In samtha, my mind is uneasy.

Prior to arriving in the borderlands, this samtha,
I heard it was like a heavenly palace where food and clothing appear instantaneously.
Samtha. I thought this place was like Naga's treasury with limitless wealth to be enjoyed.
Upon arriving in the borderlands, samtha was not at all like the fables I had heard before.

Samtha. This samtha was not at all like the illusion born in my
imagination.
In my chest, hope swells upward like a volcano. Borderlands, a place to
heal the long-festering wounds of my mind.

Life in samtha. Life in phayul. Never the same.
Samtha's time and phayul's time. Nothing is the same.
In the borderlands, feelings of happiness and suffering are intense.
In samtha, before my eyes, time rushes by so fast.
In samtha, one gets old and dies quickly.

In living this life in samtha, body, speech, and mind dissolve into hopes
and aspirations.
Youth and beauty gradually wane.
Similar to how wind wears down everything, even the redness of my
cheeks fades. In this situation, a few are resentful and frustrated,
but I find pride and encouragement in it, for this reason:
Since going through these changes, I know that I myself am taking
steps on a path where I am no longer the child near my Ama.
I know I am welcoming a life of self-sufficiency.

In samtha, despite wild cries of scarcity and despair,
some of those cries; each and every one
motivate us with endless encouragement to be brave and to think
about our dreams.
In the borderlands, we cannot lose courage; that's useless.
In samtha, we hold our heads high; that's necessary.

A wanderer in the borderlands becomes a refugee—inner, outer, and
secret.
A refugee in the borderlands grows old with weariness for the happiness
and suffering of all sentient beings.
One day, like the goal of all refugees, if the whole world becomes a large
family on planet earth, then the word *samtha* will die out.
Wherever refugees go, it will be homeland.

Samtha's sky. Phayul's sky. Similar.
Samtha's sun, moon, and stars resemble those of phayul and
everywhere.
But in the borderlands there is no warm, cozy home.

The soft voices of Ama and Apa are missing.
In samtha, there's something—homesickness and a longing to meet again.

In this translation, it felt vital to capture the cadence, repetition, and juxtaposition of *samtha* and *phayul*. Although the practice of reciting aloud Tibetan poetry prior to translation was instilled in me as a graduate student in classes with Gen-la Gedun Rabsal, the theoretical and ethical importance of approaching the English translation in a way that gives space for the foreign original, i.e., the Tibetan-language text, was inspired by Lama Jabb's keynote speech, "An Act of Bardo: Translating Tibetan Poetry," at the Lotsawa Translation Workshop (University of Colorado Boulder, October 5–8, 2018).[11]

In what was one of the first systematic attempts to theorize "translation practices"[12] for Tibetan studies, Lama Jabb brought attention to the violence that can be committed to Tibetan poetry due to the erasure of sound, cadence, and mood in English-language translations. To mitigate this, Lama Jabb recited poems in the original Tibetan followed by his own English translations. Maintaining key Tibetan terms throughout his translation and talk, this choice made visible the foreignness of the poems, thereby resisting the erasure of the Tibetan language which the act of translation itself threatens to enact. This move was cognizant of the perils of what translation theorist Lawrence Venuti refers to as the "invisibility" of the translator in creating domesticated translations.[13] According to Venuti, it is ethically imperative for translators to make explicit their role in either submitting to established norms and institutions of the receiving language and culture or resisting those by maintaining the foreignness of the original.

The Shape and Form of Translation

By way of self-reflection and a thought experiment, here I render visible and give shape and form to the otherwise invisible process that lies behind the above English translation.[14] When I met online with Nyima Tso, she recited

11. Tsadra Foundation Media Channel: https://www.youtube.com/watch?v=XZRJnPCP5Z8.

12. On translation practices, see Venuti 2017; Bassnett 2011; Bellos 2011.

13. See Venuti 2017.

14. I am grateful to Holly Gayley and Dominique Townsend for organizing the Lotsawa Translation Workshop, which encouraged dialogue between scholar-academic Tibetologists and professional translators of Buddhist texts prompting me to dive into translation theory and make connections with Tibetology. The field of analyzing acts of translation in the Tibetan context

"Life in Samtha," a free verse poem, in her native Amdo dialect several times. As I listened to her recitation of each stanza beginning with *samtha*, the cadence of that term became the focal point of my attention. The range of sounds starting from a voiceless, hissing *s-*, and moving into a voiced bilabial *m-* then to voiceless *t-*, all rounded with the short *a-* gave the poem a sonorous richness. This is one of the main reasons that I chose to leave *samtha* phonetically transcribed. This move counteracts the tendencies to neutralize the foreignness, or perhaps more precisely in this case the Tibetanness, of the text.[15] However, retaining the cadence of the original Tibetan was not my only goal.

To create a "foreignizing translation" is more than simply finding word-for-word equivalences or retaining foreign terms in the target language, it is also about ethical values. As Venuti articulates, "The 'foreign' in foreignizing translation is not a transparent representation of an essence that resides in the foreign text and is valuable in itself, but a strategic construction whose value is contingent on the current situation in the receiving culture."[16] It thereby resists the domesticating impulse and its ethical implication of "dominance over a text written in a different language and culture, assimilating its differences" and "reinforcing the asymmetry between cultures that is inherent in translation."[17] In retaining the Tibetanness of the poem, while considering the multilingual contexts of the global Anglophone literature, I chose to code-switch between the Tibetan term and its English translation of "borderlands," and in one instance "exile." This choice was informed by Nyima Tso herself, who stated that "Samtha is not always exile."

My choice was also inspired by the performative act of code-switching found in *Borderlands/La Frontera: The New Mestiza* by Gloria Anzaldúa, a feminist Chicana writer, whose semi-autobiographical account also gave rise to "borderlands theory." Anzaldúa's *Borderlands/La Frontera* expands on W.E. Dubois' ideas on double consciousness to theorize the border as a metaphorical space for addressing issues of gender, identity, race, and colonialism. In their

draws great interest as demonstrated by a well-attended session organized by Andrew Quintman and Kurtis Schaeffer at the American Academy of Religion in San Diego in November 2019.

15. The translator and translation theorist Antoine Berman crafted an analytic of translation around Heidegger's "trials of the foreign" in which he describes twelve common tendencies in domesticating translations. One such "negative analytic" is "qualitative impoverishment," whereby key terms and expressions are replaced with others that "lack their sonorous richness." Berman 2008, 278; 282). Berman argues and Venuti agrees that translators should be aware of these tendencies and take measures to counteract them.

16. Venuti 2017, 15.

17. Venuti 2017, 15.

introduction to the fourth edition of this inspirational work, feminist Chicana scholars Norma Élia Cantú and Aída Hurtado explain that for Anzaldúa, "living in the borderlands creates a third space between cultures and social systems" and "borderlands denotes the space in which antithetical elements mix, neither to obliterate each other nor to be subsumed by a larger whole, but rather to combine in unique and unexpected ways."[18] Unlike translation practices moving in bilateral directions from source to target languages, the space of language is one of hybridity, where growth is possible. Gloria Anzaldúa writes:

> The switching of "codes" in this book from English to Castilian Spanish to the North Mexican dialect to Tex-Mex to a sprinkling of Nahuatl to a mixture of all of these, reflects my language, a new language—the language of the Borderlands. There, at the juncture of cultures, languages cross-pollinate and are revitalized; they die and are born.[19]

Anzaldúa marshals code-switching as a practitioner, a writer, who does not translate but who moves between languages. This discursive space is where languages die and are reborn as intimated by Lama Jabb's approach to translation. Herein lies a creative potential that occurs in the space of the borderlands where languages and cultures meet: through the *bardo* comes rebirth.

Leaving the Tibetan phonetic rendering of *samtha* forces the English reader into articulating a term that has no linguistic reference—either semantic or phonetic—within the English language. The choice to allow the foreign term *samtha* to be the focal point of this poem has the effect of bringing the reader into a space shared by the author—a linguistic borderlands where she orientates herself through other means. Within this linguistic-cultural space, a reader chooses to either actively engage to understand *samtha* or to let the meaning go and enjoy the cadence of the sound. The author claims "a life of self-sufficiency" and encourages the reader to likewise find her own way. The orientation that an Anglophone reader needs can be found through code-switching.

As a thought experiment, we can also consider an argument against this type of code-switching to reflect on the validity of this choice. Some translators express anxiety about foreignization from a very practical standpoint. As Susan Bassnett highlights, "[translators] approach the question [of foreignization] very differently. They know about markets, they know what readers want and they know that most readers want a readable, accessible book that

18. Cantú and Hurtado 2012, 5–6.

19. Anzaldúa 2012, 20.

reads easily and fluently."[20] The problem is that if we were to translate *samtha* into English, we would automatically foreclose phonetic and semantic resonances found in the original Tibetan; but, say that for the sake of "readability," as Bassnett argues, we are willing to do that, then what term/s might we translators choose? *Samtha* literally means: (1) "another land" or (2) "borderland," i.e., "a remote region away from the center."[21] It could also be translated as "land's end,"[22] which, whether capitalized or not, for some readers may call to mind the eponymous British seaside village or the American clothing company. A case can be made for translating *samtha* as "exile," especially as the term is often juxtaposed with the term *phayul*, literally "fatherland," or "homeland." An example of this pairing can be found in the song "Phayul/Homeland" by contemporary lyricist, poet, and writer Menla Kyab:

ཕ་ཡུལ།

སྲིད་པའི་གངས་རི།
ས་ཆེན་མཁའ་ལ་འཕགས་པའི་གཞོགས་པ།
སུ་ཡི་རྨི་ལམ་གང་ལ་ཁྱེར་སོང་།
ག་རེ་ལུས་སོང་།

སུ་ཡི་ལྷམ་ཆུང་རླུང་གིས་ཟད་སོང་།
རང་ཡུལ་དྲན་སོང་།
གངས་རི།
སྐྱེས་དུས་མིག་ལ་ཐོགས་པའི་གངས་རི།
རྒས་དུས་ཞེ་ལ་ཐོགས་པའི་གངས་རི།

ཕ་ཡུལ།

ས་མཐའི་ཁ་བ་ཆར་དུ་གྱུར་སོང་།
ཆར་ཆུ་མིག་ལ་འཁྱིལ་སོང་།

20. Bassnett 2011, 39.

21. According to the bi-lingual Tibetan-English dictionary, *Bod rgya tshig mdzod chen mo*, "*sa mtha*" means (1) "*gzhan yul*, 外乡, 异地; (2) *dbus las ldogs pa'i sa mtha'*, 边区, 边地." It also has a third meaning in grammatical theory as the term for the *–sa* suffix. Zhang Yisun, ed. 1985, vol. 3, 2898.

22. Thanks to Lama Jabb for this eloquent suggestion during the Zoom presentation of this poem.

ཕ་མ་སྤུན་མཆེད་སྙིང་ནས་དྲན་བྱུང་།
ཡུལ་ལ་ལོག་ན་བསམས་སོང་།

Phayul/Homeland

Wings that ascend to the sky over the earth's
eternal snow mountains;
Whose dreams did you take with you?
What did you leave behind?

Whose baby shoes are worn down by the wind?
Remembering one's homeland
Snow Mountains
When I was born, those mountains met my eyes
As I get older, Snow Mountains meet my innermost feelings:

Phayul

Samtha's snows melt to water
as water gathers in my eyes.
I remember my beloved family
Thinking of returning home.[23]

The juxtaposition of *samtha* as "exile" with *phayul* as "homeland" is noticeable here as it is in Nyima Tso's poem. Note the first and last stanzas:

Having lost their *phayul*—homeland—
amid a pitiful life in exile, in *samtha*,
refugees lift their spirits, rising like flames

Samtha's sky. Phayul's sky. Similar.
Samtha's sun, moon, and stars resemble those of phayul and everywhere.
But in the borderlands there is no warm, cozy home.
The soft voices of Ama and Apa are missing.
In Samtha, there's something—homesickness and a longing to meet
again.

23. Thanks to Huatse Gyal and the rest of my classmates in Huatse's Amdo Tibetan lesson for our communal translation of this song and for Huatse who transcribed the lyrics from the YouTube video: https://www.youtube.com/watch?v=UI2n-tcRu5g&list=RDMM&start_radio=1

In these instances, when juxtaposed with *phayul*, *samtha* evokes "exile" and the longing for home associated with that experience. In this way, "Life in Samtha" fits within a larger movement by Tibetan contemporary lyricists and poets who focus on the exile experience. As Lama Jabb explains, "Exile thus plays an influential role in the formation of modern Tibetan national consciousness, as is evident from its impact upon contemporary Tibetan artistic output such as songs, poetry, and fictive narratives."[24] This sense of alienation, acute homesickness, and longing are evident themes in Nyima Tso's poem.

However, if *samtha* were simply translated and replaced by the term "exile," this act would foreclose other interpretative and poetic possibilities. For one, that act would, at minimum, ignore, or, at worst, violate the phonetic cadence of *samtha*, a sonorously rich word that gives the poem its auditory fullness as discussed above. Moreover, in the poem, *samtha* is not only the experience of exile, but also as a liminal space in which to wrestle with meaning-making about dreams and identity—"welcoming a life of self-sufficiency." I chose to code-switch between "borderlands," "samtha," and "exile" as "a place to heal the long-festering wounds of my mind." In my reading, this is a place to grow old, to feel confused, to be disillusioned, to be self-sufficient, to develop compassion, etc. "Borderlands" is a capacious choice because it can encompass the longing and homesickness of exile as well as the ambiguities of the life experiences expressed in the poem.

Further, the performative code-switching also discursively places Nyima Tso's poem within broader discourses on borderlands and the global reach of contemporary feminist literature. Although Nyima Tso's short poem is neither as radical nor as robust as that of Gloria Anzaldúa's *Borderlands,* nonetheless the notion of "borderlands" is relevant. It opens the possibility for a range of interpretations, evoking in particular a space in which identity, language, and the performativity of writing mix. Gloria Anzaldúa ties together language and identity to confront patriarchal structures and reject gendered norms, and thereby draws attention to oppressed and marginalized populations. Anzaldúa writes:

> As a refugee, she leaves the familiar and safe homeground to venture into unknown and possibly dangerous terrain.
> This is her home
> this thin edge of
> barbwire.[25]

24. Lama Jabb 2015, 48.

25. Anzaldúa 2012, 35.

Yet despite this ever-present danger, especially for women, Anzaldúa's borderlands are both home to the creative grounds of crosspollination and also a space in which she embraces confusing examples of what it means to be a woman:

> Through our mothers, the culture gave us mixed messages: *No voy a dejar que ningún pelado desgraciado maltrate a mis hijos*. And in the next breath, it would say, *La mujer tiene que hacer lo que le diga el hombre*. Which was it to be—strong, or submissive, rebellious or conforming?[26]

This prime example of Anzaldúa's code-switching shows how she claims her own mestiza heritage, but neither idealizes tradition nor submits to patriarchy, as she continues:

> In my culture, selfishness is condemned, especially in women; humility and selflessness, the absence of selfishness, is considered a virtue.[27]

I see parallels between Anzaldúa's candid voice and that of Nyima Tso's. They both address their heritage and the contradictory experiences of being a woman on the margins—in the liminal space of borderlands.

Although the space constraints of this essay do not allow a detailed analysis of the differences between these poems, let me note one of the main dissimilarities, which concerns the affective dimension of how each poet interprets the real political "borders" that gird their subject matter. Characterized by emotional rawness, Anzaldúa's *Frontera* shines a light on the bleak realities of life on the US-Mexican border, a border that she could cross with ease as an US citizen, unlike immigrants who illegally make the perilous journey across the border on foot. In contrast, Nyima Tso's "Life in Samtha" speaks to a longing for her homeland of Tibet on the other side of a border which is immensely difficult, if not at times impossible to cross. Yet, despite that obstacle, her poem is filled with hope:

> In the borderlands, we cannot lose courage; that's useless.
> In Samtha, we hold our heads high; that's necessary.
> [. . .]

26. Anzaldúa 2012, 40.

27. Anzaldúa 2012, 40.

> One day, like the goal of all refugees, if the whole world becomes a large
> family on planet earth, then the word *samtha* will die out.
> Wherever refugees go, it will be homeland.

This optimistic vision erases all borders and borderlands to create one common family that signifies a kind of universal compassion joining all sentient beings together.

Figure 2. Nyima Tso (left), Min Nangzey (right), and Janet Gyatso (front) at Harvard University in April 2022.

Conclusion

As one of only a handful of Tibetan women writers in exile who compose in Tibetan, Nyima Tso writes amid a patriarchal and at times misogynistic literary culture.[28] In choosing to find inspiration from Anzaldúa's *Borderlands* for my translation of Nyima Tso's "Life in Samtha," I self-consciously placed this poem within an established feminist discourse that addresses the positionality of marginalized peoples. This choice, motivated by a sensitivity to the receiving culture, is fundamentally an ethical act because as Venuti explains, "If any text can be interpreted in multiple and contradictory ways, evaluating interpretations is less a matter of truth as an accurate representation of the text than a matter of ethics, of how interpreters take responsibility for the forceful act that interpretation is . . . ."[29] At the end of the Zoom reading of her poem and the translation, Nyima Tso answered a query from Janet Gyatso (figure 2) on her experience as a female Tibetan writer as follows:

> As a writer, I don't see any gender discrimination. I think writers are writers. But then of course, when we look at Tibetan society there's always traditional restrictions, rules and norms that often try to discourage and often try to discriminate against Tibetan female writers. As a female writer, I have never had these experiences in my life personally. But in the last few years, there are emerging debates and discussions about women's rights and gender equality inside Tibet particularly among Tibetan female writers and intellectuals. I also notice that there are and were unwelcoming reactions to those issues of women's rights and gender equality. And often some Tibetan male writers use the traditional language, such as women are of lower birth (*skye dman*), to attack Tibetan female writers. These are not only ordinary Tibetan male writers; there are even university professors who are doing that as well. So when I see the discrimination, the unwelcoming reaction to the emergence of Tibetan female writers, and also the discussions around women's rights and gender equality, then I also feel the pain, and I also feel I have a responsibility to challenge and to respond to the discrimination that exists in society.[30]

28. Cf. Havnevik and Gyatso 2005, 7–11.

29. Venuti 2017, 12.

30. I transcribed and edited this based on Dhondup T. Rekjong's oral interpretation.

Works Cited

Anzaldúa, Gloria. 2012. *Borderlands/La Frontera: The New Mestiza*. Fourth edition. San Francisco: Aunt Lute Books.

Bassnett, Susan. 2011. *Reflections on Translation: Topics in Translation*. Bristol, Buffalo, Toronto: Multilingual Matters.

Bellos, David. 2011. *Is that a Fish in your Ear? Translation and the Meaning of Everything*. New York: Faber and Faber.

Benjamin, Walter. 1968 (1921). "The Task of the Translator" (Die Aufgabe des Übersetzers). In *Illuminations*, translated by Harry Zohn, 69–82. New York: Schocken Books.

Berman, Antoine. 2008 (reprint). "Translation and the Trials of the Foreign." In *The Translation Studies Reader*, translated by Lawrence Venuti, 276–89. New York and London: Routledge.

Bhum, Pema. 2008. "'Heartbeat of a New Generation' Revisited." In *Modern Tibetan Literature and Social Change*, translated by Lauran Hartley, 135–47. Durham and London: Duke University Press.

Cantú, Norma Élia, and Aída Hurtado. 2012. "Introduction to the Fourth Edition." In *Borderlands/La Frontera: The New Mestiza* by Gloria Anzaldúa, 3–13. San Francisco: Aunt Lute Books.

Diemberger, Hildegard. 2007. *When a Woman becomes a Religious Dynasty: The Samding Dorje Phagmo of Tibet*. New York: Columbia University Press.

Gayley, Holly. 2016. *Love Letters from Golok: A Tantric Couple in Modern Tibet*. New York: Columbia University Press.

Gyatso, Janet. 1989. "Down with the Demoness: Reflections on a Feminine Ground in Tibet." In *Feminine Ground: Essays on Women and Tibet*, edited by Janice Willis, 33–51. Boston: Snow Lion Imprint of Shambhala Publications.

———. 1999. *Apparitions of Self: The Secret Autobiographies of a Tibetan* Visionary. Princeton, NJ: Princeton University Press.

Gyatso, Janet, and Hanna Havnevik. 2005. *Women in Tibet*. New York: Columbia University Press.

Hartley, Lauran. 2003. *Contextually Speaking: Tibetan Literary Discourse and Social Change in the People's Republic of China (1980–2000)*. PhD Dissertation: Indiana University.

Hortsang Jigme. 2008. "Tibetan Literature in the Diaspora." In *Modern Tibetan Literature and Social Change*, edited by Lauran Hartley and Patricia Schiaffini-Vedani, 281–300. Durham and London: Duke University Press.

Lama Jabb. 2015. *Oral and Literary Continuities in Modern Tibetan Literature: The Inescapable Nation*. Lanham, Boulder, New York, London: Lexington Books.

Jacoby, Sarah, H. 2014. *Love and Liberation: Autobiographical Writings of the Tibetan Buddhist Visionary Sera Khandro*. New York: Columbia University Press.

Jampel Dronma ('jam dpal sgron ma) and Nyima Tso (Nyi ma mtsho). 2003. *Mi tshe 'di 'grul bzhud dang po* [First journey of this life]. Dharamsala: Archana.

Makley, Charlene. 2005. "The Body of a Nun: Nunhood and Gender in Contemporary

Amdo." In *Women in Tibet,* edited by Hanna Havnevik and Janet Gyatso, 259–84. New York: Columbia University Press.

Mackley, Charlene. 2007. *The Violence of Liberation: Gender and Tibetan Buddhist Revival in Post-Mao China*. Berkeley: University of California Press.

Nyima Tso (Nyi ma mtsho). 2007. *Zud tshig* [A fragment]. Dharamsala: Archana.

———. 2015. *Bod phyi nang gi mi rigs bsres lhad thad kyi snyan tho* ["A document on the minzu policy of Inner and Outer Tibet"]. Dharamsala: Tibetan Women's Association.

Schaeffer, Kurtis. 2004. *Himalayan Hermitess: The Life of a Tibetan Buddhist Nun*. Oxford: Oxford University Press.

Tseten Zhabdrung (Tshe tan zhabs drung). 2005. *Snyan ngag spyi don* [A general commentary on poetics]. Lanzhou: Gansu minzu chubanshe.

Venuti, Lawrence. 2000. "Translation, Community, Utopia." In *The Translation Studies Reader*, edited by Lawrence Venuti, 482–502. New York and London: Routledge.

———. 2017. *The Translator's Invisibility: A History of Translation*. New York and London: Routledge.

Zhang Yisun, ed. 1985. *Bod rgya tshig mdzod chen mo* (Ch. 藏汉大词典) [Tibetan-Chinese dictionary]. Beijing: Minzu chubanshe.

Sex, Part Two

Donald S. Lopez Jr.

Like his kinsman Prince Siddhārtha, Udāyin left his wife to become a monk. And like Yaśodharā, his wife Guptā followed him on the noble path, living in a nearby nunnery. They would often go on their alms round at the same time, eating their morning meal in his cell. Despite their efforts to destroy the passions, they were still very much in love. One morning as they ate from their begging bowls, Udāyin fell into a reverie, remembering their past pleasures. As he did so, he became aroused. Guptā noticed this but rather than avert her eyes, she opened her robe to reveal her vulva. Knowing that masturbation was a violation of the Vinaya, they did not touch other, or themselves. By the end of the meal, Udāyin had soiled his robe. Orgasm by eye contact. But now he was in serious trouble. It would soon be time for the morning assembly and his stain would be visible for all to see. He knew he had to wash his robe immediately. Guptā, who had always washed his clothes during their lay life, offered to help. Udāyin took off his robe and handed it to her. But instead of plunging it into the water pot in the corner of his cell, she rubbed the semen on her lips and licked them. Then she rubbed the semen on her vagina.

What is this? Perhaps it's a scene from a Sanskrit comic farce, along the lines of *Drunken Games* (*Mattavilāsa*), a seventh-century play in which a young Buddhist monk suspects that his elders have hidden the rules in which the Buddha allowed monks to have sex and drink alcohol.[1] Perhaps it's a passage from a Chinese pornographic novel from the Ming Dynasty, when Buddhist monks were often portrayed as lechers posing as celibates. Perhaps it comes from a pamphlet from Meiji Japan, part of the devastating *haibutsu kishaku* ("Abolish Buddhism, Destroy Śākyamuni") campaign of the late 1860s, portraying the Buddhist monastery as a den of depravity. Or perhaps it comes from that best forgotten New Age soft porn novel of the 1980s, *Love Lives of the Enlightened.*

1. For a translation, see Lorenzen 2000, 81–96. The passage occurs on p. 89.

In fact, it comes (with only slight embellishment) from the Vinaya, the Buddhist monastic code.[2]

When the Buddhism and Modernity series was launched by the University of Chicago Press in 2003, it was decided that the inaugural volume would be an edited collection entitled *Critical Terms for the Study of Buddhism*. Modeled on the successful *Critical Terms for Literary Study* (1990) and *Critical Terms for Art History* (1996), it would bring together leading scholars—not necessarily Buddhologists—who would be asked to write a provocative essay on a single term. In the case of Buddhism, there are 84,000 terms, far too many to choose from. Thus, as editor of the series, instead of selecting the terms, I selected the authors, inviting them to pick their own topic, feeling that for a book like this, the perspicacity of the author was more important than the particular term. Eve Sedgwick chose "Pedagogy," Timothy Barrett chose "History," Carl Bielefeldt chose "Practice," Janet Gyatso chose "Sex." The book was published in 2005. The present essay is inspired by her work.

In it, Janet makes the ostensibly shocking claim that in both the sūtras and the Vinaya, "sex epitomizes the central problematic of Buddhism,"[3] a claim that she convincingly defends with numerous instantiations from the canon. For example, she notes that in the development of monastic code, it is not murder or theft that is counted as the first of the *pārājika*, the "downfalls" that, at least in the Pāli version, entail permanent expulsion from the saṅgha.[4] Instead, the first such infraction is heterosexual intercourse, occasioned by a well-intentioned act of procreation, motivated not by lust but by filial piety, of the monk Sudinna. She argues that it is the first of the downfalls, not because having sex is more serious than committing murder, but because "sex is the most serious monastic transgression" and "the most difficult bodily transgression from which to refrain."[5]

Janet's essay opens by offering a number of possible readings of what she calls "the Pāli Vinaya's hyperanalysis of proscribed sex acts," noting that whatever reading one chooses, one should not miss the sense of humor. Here, however, I would like to consider one of the readings that Janet enumerates but does not pursue: what she calls "fantasies of an oversexed imagination." She argues that

2. See Thānissaro 1994, 209–10. For the Mūlasarvāstivāda story of the famous son resulting from this act, see Buswell and Lopez 2014, s.v. Kumāra-Kāśyapa.

3. Gyatso 2005, 274.

4. It is only in the Pāli Vinaya that having sexual intercourse (as specifically defined) definitely entails expulsion. All of the other extant vinayas provide provisions for monks who violate the rule to remain in the order. See Clarke 2009, 1–43.

5. Gyatso 2005, 276.

the monastic motivation for the description of all combinations and permutations of organs and orifices in the Vinaya is "to give the impression that the rule book is comprehensive, or to put it another way, that there are no ways to get around the rule. All possible misreadings and tricks have been anticipated by the elders, and none of them will succeed."[6] Although this is surely true, I would like to suggest another reason for the detailed discussions of sex in the Vinaya: the opportunity it provided to compose titillating tales, what we might call, for want of a better word, "dharma porn."

Before turning to the Vinaya, however, we might provide further evidence for Gyatso's claim that sex epitomizes the central problematic in Buddhism. Indeed, we might go further, suggesting that sex is the central problematic in Buddhism. We could begin at the beginning, the Buddhist account of the creation of our world, the *Agañña Sutta*, which provides so many of the creation myths of elements of human society. As we recall, the text describes the world as initially populated by ethereal beings, free from the markers of sex, able to fly, luminous, so free of worldly appetites that they do not require food. By consuming a foam on the surface of the waters of the newly formed world, they eventually came down to earth, their bodies becoming heavier and coarser, no longer able to fly, no longer luminous, causing the sun and moon to appear.

Through a process that is not explained, they then developed genitals, which led in turn to sexual intercourse. The fellow humans who witnessed this were so disgusted that they threw dirt, dung, and ashes at the coupling couples, driving the lovers into the woods. Reluctant to live there, they returned to the community where they built dwellings so that they could have sex without being pelted by their neighbors. As the text says, "And those beings who in those days indulged in sex were not allowed into a village or town for one or two months. Accordingly, those who indulged for an excessively long time in such immoral practices began to build themselves dwellings so as to indulge under cover."[7] Thus, the built environment was created so that humans could engage in unobserved sexual intercourse.

Such is the world of humans. To the perennial theological question, "Is there sex in heaven?" the Buddhists respond with an emphatic, "Yes." We recall that in Aśvaghoṣa's *Handsome Nanda* (*Saundarananda*)—one of the most misogynistic works in Buddhist literature (it contains an entire chapter entitled *Strīvighāta*, or "Attack on Women")—Nanda cannot stop thinking about his beautiful, and recently abandoned, bride Sundarī. To cure him of his longing and lust, the Buddha flies him to the Heaven of the Thirty-three on the

6. Gyatso 2005, 277.

7. "*Aggañña Sutta*: On Knowledge of Beginnings" in Walsh 1995, 412.

summit of Mount Meru, where he sees the forests and gardens filled with hosts of heavenly maidens called *apsaras*, seductively sporting with the inhabitants of the heaven, women so beautiful that the Buddha must create a kind of force field to prevent Nanda from dying of lust. Thus, there is sex, heavenly sex, in heaven.

But what good deed did these men perform in their former life in the realm of humans to win this reward? The text explains: "Eternally youthful and occupied solely with lovemaking, they were a communal enjoyment for heaven-dwellers who had earned merit. Taking these heavenly women as lovers was no fault, just an acceptance of the rewards of asceticism."[8] In other words, in yet another Buddhist example of deferred gratification, if you want great sex in the next life, practice celibacy in this life. Even more astounding is that this is what the Buddha (admittedly, using his skillful methods) counsels Nanda to do: "If you desire these women, practice asceticism in this life to pay the bride price. . . . Life here in heaven together with the gods, the delightful forests and these unaging women are the reward of one's own pure deeds."[9]

There is, therefore, sex in the Heaven of the Thirty-three and, presumably in the heaven below that, Four Heavenly Kings, located on the upper slopes of the mountain, the abode of the guardian kings of the four cardinal directions. But there are four more heavens in the Realm of Desire, all located in the sky above Mount Meru. Sex must certainly disappear in these ethereal abodes. It does not. As we read in Vasubandhu's *Treasury of Knowledge* (*Abhidharmakośa* III.69): "There are six gods who taste pleasure; they unite through coupling, an embrace, the touch of hands, a smile, and a look."[10] The commentary explains that, as we have seen, the gods of two terrestrial heavens engage in sex as humans do, they "unite through coupling." As one proceeds upward through the four celestial heavens, sexual pleasure does not require genital intercourse. In the heaven called Yāma (which Tibetans read as "Free from Combat"), sexual pleasure is derived from embracing (in the sense of hugging). In Tuṣita, the Joyous, the partners merely touch hands. In Nirmāṇarati (which Tibetans read as "Enjoying Emanation"), sexual pleasure requires no physical touch whatsoever; the partners merely smile at each other. The most subtle form of sexual intercourse occurs in the highest of the heavens of the Realm of Desire, called Paranirmāṇarati (which Tibetans read as "Controlling the Emanations of Others"), where it is "a look," as the text says. Orgasm by eye contact. There is much to say about this passage, including the uncanny fact that these five stages

8. Covill 2007, 203.

9. Covill 2007, 211.

10. De la Vallée Poussin 1989, 465.

in reverse order—eye contact, smiling, holding hands, embracing, and sexual intercourse—describe the mating rituals of the bourgeoisie of mid-twentieth-century America.[11] Sex in heaven differs from sex on earth in another way: in heaven the male gods ejaculate wind (*vayu*) instead of semen.

Just as there is sex in heaven, there is also sex in hell, depicted in ancient texts like the *Sūtra on the Establishment of Mindfulness of the True Dharma* (*Saddharmasmṛtyupasthāna Sūtra*) and in modern theme parks in Thailand.[12] Here, the experience of the damned is not so much sexual pleasure as sexual frustration, sexual frustration that lasts for millions of years in hell and then continues in future lives in the realm of humans. In her essay on sex, Gyatso asks, "What better place to mark the triumph of the law than in the body's successful subordination of sexual pleasure?"[13] Of course, there is none. But does the law also triumph over sexual pleasure in the mind?

According to the tradition, in the early years of the Buddha's teaching, there was no need for vows. Monks achieved one of the four stages of enlightenment (stream-enterer, once-returner, non-returner, and arhat) quickly, sometimes after simply hearing a single discourse; some sūtras conclude by reporting how many people attained which level. One of the attainments of the stream-enterer is abandonment of three fetters, the first of which is called, literally "holding [mistaken] codes of conduct and rituals to be superior" (*śīlavrataparāmarśa*), generally taken to mean the belief in non-Buddhist doctrines and practices. The attainment of the stream-enterer also destroys all causes for rebirth as an animal, a ghost, or a denizen of hell. Thus, the conduct of a monk who achieved even the first of the four stages is said to be naturally ethical, obviating a code of conduct.

As we read in a number of accounts, as the renown of the Buddha grew, so did the saṅgha, attracting those of less noble motivation and less rapid attainment. This was a problem that would persist long after the Buddha's passage into nirvāṇa. The Third Council, said to have been called by Aśoka, was occasioned by this problem. But it also occurred during the time of the Buddha, making it necessary to establish a system of rules to regulate his growing community. According to various traditions, this need first occurred five, twelve,

11. Vasubandhu notes in the autocommentary that according to the Vaibhāṣika, in a claim that calls out for Freudian interpretation, the four terms that describe sex in the upper realms—embracing, touching hands, smiling, looking—describe not the means of sexual pleasure but rather the length of time required for genital intercourse in each heaven. Thus, in Tuṣita, for example, sex lasts as long as it takes to hold hands. See La Vallée Poussin 1989, 465. For further canonical references, see Cabezón 2017, 34–42.

12. See Anderson 2012. See also Cabezón 2017, 43–69.

13. Gyatso 2005, 287.

or twenty years after the Buddha's enlightenment. Whenever it occurred, however, the Buddha did not set forth a complete and fully elaborated monastic code of two hundred (or more) rules. Instead, rules were added one by one. It was only after a particular transgression occurred that the Buddha would establish a rule against it. The monastic code is therefore presented as an organic document, growing and changing, being revised and refined over a period of many years, from the Buddha's harsh condemnation of Sudinna's night of love to the night of the Buddha's passage into nirvāṇa, immediately prior to which he told Ānanda that after his death the monks could ignore the minor vows. However, Ānanda neglected to ask the Buddha what constituted a minor vow and so the monks were required to keep them all. At the First Council, Ānanda was placed on trial for this and other crimes.

Thus, in the Vinaya, the Buddha is not portrayed as randomly announcing a rule or set of rules. Each rule is presented as a reaction by the Buddha, as if the event occasioned the rule—that is, as if something happened, causing the Buddha to make a rule ensuring that it did not happen again, or if it did, that there was a penalty imposed on the transgressor. We see, for example, that immediately after his grudging decision to ordain women, the Buddha is constantly being pestered to rule on this or that question concerning the proper comportment of the nun. Rules were added or amended as the situation required.

Despite the fact that the tradition portrays the monastic code as being formulated by the Buddha, according to the general scholarly consensus, the monastic code developed over a period of time extending far beyond the passing of the Buddha; Gregory Schopen has argued that the extant Vinayas were composed in the Middle Period between the fall of the Mauryan dynasty in 321 BCE and the founding of the Gupta dynasty in 275 CE. However, the Buddha, who had passed into nirvāṇa centuries before, had to be portrayed as establishing the rule. This meant that stories about the time of the Buddha had to be composed to justify new rules. Thus, rather than the story preceding the rule, the rule preceded the story. As the work of Schopen and others has shown, many of these rules dealt with "business matters," regulations for the receipt and distribution of the various forms of wealth that passed in and out of the monastery and among the inmates who lived within its walls. There is thus often a quotidian quality about these rules. When we read the stories of the events that occasioned a particular rule, we can sometimes imagine that such an event actually happened, or at least, might have happened.

This is often the case with stories of the "group of six" (not to be confused with the "group of five"), six mischievous monks whose antics provide the occasion for a large number of rules. Such antics are often more embarrassing than harmful, with the Buddha making a rule after the laity have complained about their bad behavior. Indeed, the Buddha displays a persistent concern to protect the reputation of the saṅgha and to avoid the condemnation of the laity. This is given as the motivation for many rules, including that establishing the rains retreat. In other cases, some dispute occurs in the monastery, requiring a rule to be established so that similar disputes can be avoided, and if not avoided, at least adjudicated in the future.

The rules regulating sex operate at a different register; it is often difficult to imagine the event that will eventually become a transgression actually having occurred. Some of the cases are, indeed, easily included in the category of "misreadings and tricks" to which Janet alludes. Two famous examples come to mind. We recall that a *pārājika* offense occurs when a monk inserts his penis into the orifice of a human, deity, or animal, living or dead, to the depth of a mustard seed. Some monk at some time seems to have wondered whether in order to be a violation, the rule required that those orifices belong to someone else. That is, is it a *pārājika* offense for a monk to penetrate one of his own orifices? The answer is "yes." However, as always, the Buddha does not make a rule against something that has not already been done. And so, of course, we have the story of the monk who performs what would seem to have the clinical name of autofellatio. Somewhat more surprising is the fact that there is a story of a monk who performs what might be called autosodomy. Such cases appear to be sheer fantasy, a situation imagined by a monk who should have had something better to do.

There is another type of transgression, however, one that seems to confound our sense of narrative, our sense of an ending. Here, we have a rule that seems entirely ordinary, even banal, without the slightest erotic content or suggestion. And yet the story of the event that occasioned the vow is all about sex. The story does not proceed in temporal and logical sequence to the conclusion. Instead, the conclusion comes first, requiring a plausible narrative to be constructed that would end in that conclusion. It would be like seeing the final scene in *Hamlet* where Fortinbras enters the great hall of Elsinore Castle to find Gertrude, Claudius, and Laertes dead on the floor, with Horatio cradling the dead Hamlet in his arms, and then concocting the plot that led to it. Fortunately for Fortinbras, Horatio promises to "speak to the yet unknowing world / How these things came about."

However, the unexpected rule that concludes these stories in the Buddhist Vinaya does not rise to the level of great literature, nor is it plausible. In his *Poetics*, Aristotle writes of *peripeteia*, literally "sudden change," an unexpected event or revelation that occurs near the end of a play that resolves elements of the plot; in the case of a tragedy, it causes pity and fear in the audience. It is described as "an unexpected yet logical shift in the events of the play."[14] Aristotle gives the example in *Oedipus Rex* in which a messenger informs the title character that Polybus and Merope are not his parents. In the case of comedy, the change in plot should cause the audience to smile or weep.

However, the conclusion to a Vinaya story about sex, that is, the Buddha's establishment of a rule, often has no dramatic connection to the deed that it occasions, no logical shift. Instead, it is like hearing the punchline and then having to concoct the joke, with the requirement that the joke be about sex. It is like watching a courtroom drama that begins with the verdict, one that, as it turns out, has nothing to do with the crime, with the requirement that it be a sex crime. There are many examples to choose from, examples that are found in both the bhikṣu and bhikṣunī Vinayas, both presumably composed by men.[15]

Buddhist monks were required by the monastic code to consume their last meal of the day by noon. They therefore often ate a large meal in the late morning and then took a nap. In one of the more fantastic sex stories in the Vinaya, a monk falls asleep in his cell. Lying on his back, he develops an involuntary erection, which becomes exposed when his robe falls open while he is sleeping. A large group of women who are returning home after gathering garlands of flowers notice this and take advantage of the situation, lining up outside the door to mount him. The monk, of course, remains fast asleep throughout. Other monks see what was happening and report it to the Buddha. The monk is summoned and questioned. He explains that he had been fast asleep and so could not confirm or deny that the event had taken place. In keeping with a general principle of sexual infractions in the monastic code, the monk is not charged with an offense because these multiple instances of intercourse had taken place, according to his testimony, without his intention and without any experience of pleasure. However, based on this event, the Buddha imposed a new rule. Henceforth, whenever a monk takes a nap, he must close his door.[16]

There have been attempts over the course of Gyatso's career to consider Buddhist texts not as religious scriptures or philosophical treatises but as literature. Janet herself was something of a pioneer in this endeavor, examining how Tibetan texts of the *rnam thar* genre did or did not map onto the European category of autobiography in *Apparitions of the Self*. We might ask, therefore, whether the sex stories found in the Buddhist Vinaya are literature and, if so,

14. See Else 1957, 344.

15. For a translation of passages that I.B. Horner bowdlerized from her own translations of the Vinaya, see Kieffer-Pülz 2001, 62–84.

16. Thānissaro, 1994, 50.

what genre. It may be the case that the most appropriate Western category for these stories is pornography, a term that is notoriously difficult to define. We recall the famous statement by Supreme Court Justice Potter Stewart (1915–85) in his opinion in the 1964 case *Jacobellis v. Ohio*, "I know it when I see it." Of greater relevance is the three-part test for obscenity set forth by Chief Justice Earl Warren in 1973 in *Miller v. California*: "Whether the average person, applying contemporary community standards, would find that the work taken as a whole, appeals to the prurient interest; whether the work depicts or describes, in a patently offensive way, sexual conduct specifically defined by the applicable state law; and whether the work, taken as a whole, lacks serious literary, artistic, political, or scientific value." Given this, do we want to claim that pornography is to be found in the Buddhist Vinaya?

There is much to ponder here. We note, for example, the great attention that the monastic code devotes to the topic of masturbation. Here, we find masturbation labeled as a transgression, yet one whose punishment was probation, not expulsion.[17] Why is this? Perhaps it is because when the Buddha makes the rule against it, one of his reasons is that it is unseemly to perform the act with the same hand with which one accepts food from the laity. With this rule established, the Vinaya seems obsessed with defining precisely what constitutes masturbation, each possibility, of course, accompanied by a story.[18] As Gendun Chopel (1903–51) writes in his *Treatise on Passion* (*'Dod pa'i bstan bcos*):

> When suitable deeds are prohibited in public,
> Unsuitable deeds will be done in private.
> How can religious and secular laws
> Suppress this natural desire of humans?[19]

Of perhaps greater interest to the question of pornography is the initially unexpected prominence in Buddhist literature of nocturnal emission. We recall, for example, that the question of whether an arhat could have a nocturnal emission was a point of controversy at the Second Council and listed among the five theses of Mahādeva. Indeed, the events of the nocturnal, including

17. Masturbation was placed in the second most grave category of violations, called *saṅghādisesa* in Pāli. For a description of the misdeeds that fall under this category and the punishment they entail, see Buswell and Lopez, 2014, s.v. saṃghāvaśeṣa.

18. For a discussion of masturbation, with references to additional studies, see Cabezón 2017, 184n486.

19. Gendun Chopel 2005, 19.

nocturnal emission, are a topic worthy of further research.[20] As Janet notes in her essay, nocturnal emission is not an offense. It is often said that what the Buddha added to Indian karma theory was the element of intention (*cetanā*). Vasubandhu begins his long chapter on karma in the *Abhidharmakośa* with the statement: "The variety of the world arises from karma. It is intention and that which is produced through intention."[21] Nocturnal emission therefore cannot constitute a transgression because there is no intention, or the intention occurs in a dream. We recall that in his commentary on the *Twenty Stanzas* (*Viṃśatika*), Vasubandhu (after his conversion to the Mahāyāna) gives nocturnal emission as one of the proofs that the external world does not exist; ejaculation can occur by merely dreaming of copulation.[22]

There is obviously much more to say. Perhaps it is best to simply end with a question. When dealing with matters of sexuality, the Buddhist Vinaya presents a minute analysis of the physical and mental elements of various sex acts, developed, at least ostensibly, to determine what is and is not an offense, and if an offense, of what gravity. Yet the stories that were concocted to justify these rules seem designed to arouse and titillate monks as much as they do to discipline and punish. Is it possible, then, that the writing and reading of the Vinaya served as a cause of nocturnal emission?

Before we close, we should answer the question that the reader must have been asking since the opening paragraph: What happened to Udāyin and Guptā? Did they get away with their touchless masturbation session? They would have, if Guptā had not rubbed Udāyin's semen-soaked robe on her vagina. She became pregnant, something that soon became impossible to hide from the order of nuns, who reported her to the Buddha, stating that this was clear evidence that she had committed the *pārājika* offense of engaging in sexual intercourse. As we know, however, she had not. Udāyin and Guptā therefore were not expelled. Nonetheless, the Buddha needed to do something to prevent such embarrassing events from occurring in the future. He therefore instituted a rule: Starting today, all monks and nuns must wash their own robes.

20. For a study based especially on the Dharmaguptaka Vinaya, see Heirman 2012, 427–44.

21. See La Vallée Poussin 1989, 551. In this passage, Leo Pruden translates *cetanā* as "volition."

22. For a translation, see Anacker 1984, 162. The original Sanskrit can be found on page 414, line 8.

Works Cited

Anacker, Stefan. 1984. *Seven Works of Vasubandhu*. Delhi: Motilal Banarsidass.

Anderson, Benedict. 2012. *The Fate of Rural Hell: Asceticism and Desire in Rural Thailand*. Chicago: The University of Chicago Press.

Buswell Jr., Robert E., and Donald S. Lopez Jr. 2014. *The Princeton Dictionary of Buddhism*. Princeton, NJ: Princeton University Press.

Cabezón, José Ignacio. 2017. *Sexuality in Classical South Asian Buddhism*. Somerville, MA: Wisdom Publications.

Clarke, Shayne. 2009. "Monks Who Have Sex: *Pārājika* Penance in Indian Buddhist Monasticisms." *Journal of Indian Philosophy* 37:1–43.

Covill, Linda, trans. 2007. *Handsome Nanda by Aśvaghoṣa*. New York: New York University Press and JJC Foundation.

Else, Gerald F. 1957. *Aristotle's Poetics: The Argument*. Cambridge: Harvard University Press.

Gendun Chopel. 2005. *The Passion Book: A Tibetan Guide to Love and Sex*. Translated by Thupten Jinpa and Donald S. Lopez Jr. Chicago: The University of Chicago Press.

Gyatso, Janet. 2005. "Sex." In *Critical Terms for the Study of Buddhism*, edited by Donald S. Lopez Jr., 271–90. Chicago: The University of Chicago Press.

Heirman, Anne. 2012. "Sleep well! Sleeping Practices in Buddhist Disciplinary Rules," *Acta Orientalia Academiae Scientiarum Hungaricae* 65.4 (December): 427–44.

Kieffer-Pülz, Petra. 2001. "Pārājika I and Saṅghādisesa I: Hitherto Untranslated Passages from the Vinayapiṭaka of the Theravādins," *Traditional South Asian Medicine* 6: 62–84.

La Vallée Poussin, Louis de. 1989. *Abhidharmakośabhāṣyam*, vol. 2. English translation by Leo M. Pruden. Berkeley, CA: Asian Humanities Press.

Lorenzen, David N. 2000. "A Parody of the Kāpālikas in the *Mattavilāsa*." In David Gordon White, ed., *Tantra in Practice*, 81–96. Princeton, NJ: Princeton University Press.

Thānissaro Bhikkhu, trans. 1994. *The Buddhist Monastic Code I*, rev. ed. Valley Center, CA: Metta Forest Academy.

Walsh, Maurice, trans. 1995. *The Long Discourses of the Buddha: A Translation of the Dīgha Nikāya*. Boston: Wisdom Publications.

The Possibilities of Emptiness and the Realities of (Trans) Gender[1]

Julie Regan

1+1=3?

WHILE JANET GYATSO may have abandoned a major in math to pursue Buddhist studies,[2] much of her work has continued to reflect a fascination with things that don't add up. Why are those who don't believe in a self so obsessed with autobiography?[3] Why would a community that has renounced sex produce such an outrageous and extensive catalogue of forbidden practices?[4] Why, in her most explicitly mathematical analysis, "One Plus One Makes Three: Buddhist Gender, Monasticism, and the Law of the Non-Excluded Middle," are the indeterminate boundaries of the third sex so essential in producing and reinforcing the male/female binary that is central to monasticism?[5] The questions Janet poses to address such problems are theoretical as well as practical. While they concern specific issues that arise in Buddhist texts and contexts, they often reveal useful insights for contemporary theoretical and ethical reflection about broader issues facing those in the Buddhist world and beyond.

Gender and sexuality have provided a rich site for such reflections, given the contradictions between Buddhist philosophical principles, which suggest that gender is empty in essence and that all human beings have the capacity for awakening, and the limitations which Buddhist institutions have placed on women. Janet has devoted much of her career to writing and teaching about

1. Thanks to Holly Gayley, Alexander Gardner, Julie Klein, and those at the fourth annual University of California Riverside Conference on Queer and Transgender Studies in Religion for valuable feedback in developing these ideas.

2. In an interview with Wisdom Publications in 2018, Gyatso explains that she connects her aptitude for mathematical ways of thinking with her interest in abstract thought.

3. Gyatso 1998.

4. Gyatso 2005.

5. Gyatso 2003.

women in Buddhism[6] and has lent her support as a scholar to efforts by Buddhist leaders, such as His Holiness the 14th Dalai Lama and Karmapa Orgyen Trinley Dorje, to provide access to full ordination, and all its benefits (education, leadership roles, cultural status), for women.[7] While she is herself informed by Western feminism, Janet has pointed out the ways in which the movement to ordain nuns draws its inspiration not only from such sources but from progressive Asian monastics across Buddhism, who draw their inspiration from Buddhist textual traditions and the historical precedents they establish.[8] Janet frequently teaches works that speak to this, such as the *Therīgāthā*, which paints a picture of fully ordained women's accomplishments in the same way as men's (in the *Theragāthā*), and the *Cullavagga*, which demonstrates not only Ānanda's intervention on behalf of Mahāprajāpatī and the women who join her, but also the women's agency in negotiating their own reforms and status.

While it may be more obvious in her reports on the events surrounding women's ordination,[9] Janet's most erudite scholarly writing, such as "One Plus One Makes Three," often seems motivated by an ethical impulse. While her role may not to be solve the problems faced by Buddhist women, much less resolve the contradictions in Buddhist traditions, her work as a scholar exposes the possibilities Buddhism presents for women both within and beyond Buddhist communities.

It is this broader ethical impulse in Janet's work, and in "One Plus One Makes Three" in particular, to which I pay tribute, and which I attempt to extend here. While the purpose of the textual and theoretical analysis of what she calls the "third sex" in "One Plus One Makes Three" is to gain a clearer understanding of "how the female is conceived in Buddhism," the ultimate goal of such an understanding, she suggests, is to address problems facing women in contemporary Buddhist communities, specifically ordination.[10] While Janet notes the impact early concepts of sex and gender have on others members of Buddhist communities,[11] "One Plus One Makes Three" is primarily focused on the discrimination faced by women in monastic contexts. Nevertheless, I believe Janet's analysis of how the third sex was conceived in the texts she explores is

6. Gyatso 2017, 90.

7. See Gyatso 2010 and 2017.

8. Gyatso 2017, 2.

9. Gyatso 2010 and 2017.

10. Gyatso 2003, 89.

11. Gyatso 2003, 89, mentions Buddhist communities more generally as well as those that specifically emphasize female deities and sexual yoga.

likewise useful in addressing the issues facing those identified as transgender[12] in Buddhist communities today.[13] My purpose is thus to extend Janet's reflection on the third sex by addressing the gap she notes, i.e., the missing evidence of "real people" described by terms such as *paṇḍaka* or *maning* (Tib: *ma ning*),[14] in order to consider the problems faced by those who fall under the restrictions defined by these ancient concepts today.

For those who have grown up in parts of the world dominated by Western science, where binary concepts of sex have been so strict that infants with genital variations were routinely "repaired" by surgery until recent years, the recognition of the reality of a third sex in early Buddhist traditions might feel affirming to some who identify as trans, intersex or nonbinary.[15] The possibilities of emptiness, or no self, as this is understood across Buddhist traditions, may even seem to open up a space for those who aren't defined as strictly male or female. Yet the realities of the "consistently negative profile" the third sex has received in "Buddhist paths of religious cultivation," as Janet points out, generally present a different picture.[16] Despite their more neutral descriptions in Indian and Tibetan medical literature, for example, the legacy of discrimination against the third sex endures for those identified as *hijra* in India today, While scientists have gradually come to understand that two sexes cannot adequately account for the variations of genetics, hormones, internal anatomy, and brain development in human beings,[17] such facts have little impact on legal and social realities. As the rise in anti-trans legislation and violence today demonstrates, acknowledging the reality of those who are intersex, nonbinary, or transgender in science and popular culture does not eradicate hate and exclusion.

12. The term "transgender" or "trans" is used here in the inclusive sense to designate anyone who identifies with being opposed to ("trans" or on the other side of) the sex they were designated at birth vs. in agreement with it ("cis" or on the same side). This includes those previously distinguished by terms now avoided, such as transsexual or transvestite, as well as those who may see themselves as nonbinary or genderqueer.

13. The fact that "One Plus One Makes Three" is highlighted on the *rainbodhi* webpage (Akāliko 2021) as a resource on "gender non-conforming people in early Buddhism" for contemporary LGBTQIA+ people (Lesbian, Gay, Bisexual, Trans or Transgender, Queer, Intersex, Asexual, or other, inclusive of Two-Spirit, Nonbinary, Genderqueer, or Pansexual) also demonstrates its relevance to those defined through the lens of the *paṇḍaka* in Buddhist communities today.

14. While there are other types of *paṇḍaka*, defined by other features, the focus here (and in Janet's work) is primarily on the third sex, including gender qualities in the Tibetan use of *maning*.

15. Michaelson 2018.

16. Gyatso 2015, 325.

17. Ainsworth 2018.

Just as Janet's concern in "One Plus One Makes Three" ultimately extends to non-monastic Buddhist women today, I am especially mindful of the need to consider the problems facing the broader community of lay Buddhists who identify as trans, especially given the general limits to their participation laid out in the early Buddhist literature Janet discusses. According to the *Mahavagga*, for example, anyone classified as *paṇḍaka* is forbidden from even the most basic lay practice of making donations to monks.[18] According to the *Lotus Sūtra*, they are not allowed to receive any sort of Buddhist teaching.[19] The *Questions of Milinda* suggests that *paṇḍaka*s can't understand the Buddhadharma at all,[20] and the *Visuddhimagga* claims they are unable to perform any kind of meditation.[21] While contemporary trans Buddhists in the West more often speak of the support Buddhism has provided to them in the process of transition, which some link to the transformative nature of Buddhist practice,[22] others have pointed to challenges they face in lay communities.[23] Buddhist liberation ultimately relies on the support of institutions, including teachers, communities, and texts, structurally informed by negative concepts of both the female and the *paṇḍaka* in Buddhist literature.

Janet's attention to these concept in "One Plus One Makes Three" is helpful in drawing attention to the way they operate, opening up the potential for further critique leading to structural change.[24] Unfortunately, as she points out, concepts of the third sex in particular may bear less resemblance to actual people than to Buddhist ideas about them, since the few stories of *paṇḍaka*s in early Buddhist literature, such as the *Mahavagga* and the *Therīgathā*, give us little sense of the "actual historical people" involved.[25] However, thanks to the recovery of the work of Michael Dillon,[26] the first person recognized to have completed gender transition through the use of hormones and surgery from

18. Gyatso 2003, 98n20.

19. Gyatso 2003, 98n21.

20. Gyatso 2003, 98n23.

21. Gyatso 2003, 98n22.

22. As Elizabeth Marston explains, "Buddhism gave me the tools to slip the shackles of identity, liberating me from within, so I could liberate myself from without." Marston 2019, 132.

23. See *Developing Trans* Competence: A Short Guide to Improving Transgender Experiences at Meditation and Retreat Centers* for details of discrimination and exclusion. Anonymous, 2014.

24. Gyatso 2003, 114–15.

25. Gyatso 2003, 93.

26. Jacob Lau and Cameron Partridge, two trans scholars of religion who encountered Dillon through Pagan Kennedy's account of him in *The First Man-Made Man* (2007), sought the posthumous publication of the autobiographical manuscript, *Out of the Ordinary*, completed just before his death in 1962, which Kennedy relies on, in addition to his published works on medi-

the late 1930s to 1940s,[27] as well as one of the first Europeans to be ordained as a novice Theravada monk and the first to be ordained in this way in the Tibetan tradition, we now have concrete evidence of how such ancient concepts of the third sex were applied to at least one, more recent, actual historical person. Dillon, or Lobsang Jivaka, who refers to himself in one work as "Imji Getsul" (Tib. *dbyin ji dge tshul*), the "English novice," is especially interesting to consider in relation to Janet, as his works reflect many of her interests (including Buddhism, medicine, theories of gender, and autobiography), though it is especially his focus on ordination I will explore here. As someone who identifies in distinct ways with the concept of *paṇḍaka*, he is not only subject to the rules of the Vinaya but also their critic, seeking to make Buddhist monastic traditions more inclusive for people like himself, much in the same way that Mahāpajāpatī and Ānanda advocate for reforms in the *Cullavagga*.

bumé + bu = mi?

As Janet observes, there is a close relationship between the third sex and the second sex in the Vinaya in that both are non-male (*napuṃsaka*) and objects of misogyny.[28] The possibilities for awakening presented by the human condition and the nature of the self as being always in process suggest that every human being has this potential and thus deserves support and training. This is the basis of the argument that Ānanda brings to the Buddha that ultimately allows women to become ordained.[29] And yet the Buddha's initial hesitance and

cine and Buddhism. See Lau and Partridge 2016. Lau and Partridge especially note their interest in making this work available as a resource for scholars of religion and of Buddhism in particular.

27. José Cabezón introduces the example of Michael Dillon in the epilogue to *Sexuality in Classical South Asian Buddhism* as "one of the most interesting contemporary test cases for the Buddhist rule against the ordination of queer men." Cabezón 2017, 532. I would argue for the use of the term trans in the broad sense as a more accurate translation of *paṇḍaka* in the case of Dillon and most of those whom we might now classify as "other" in the sense of third sex. While the term "queer" may likewise work to describe the sense of *paṇḍaka* as a broad category of people with a variety of divergent genders and sexualities, it is also problematic as a translation since contemporary usage of the term "queer" also includes those with same-sex orientations who are not gender non-conforming and therefore would not be excluded from the saṅgha. In short, the term includes too many people who are not *paṇḍaka*, suggesting it is roughly equivalent to homosexual, as some have suggested and which Janet rightly resists (Gyatso 2003, 97). Contemporary usage of the term "queer" further carries a sense of inclusivity which implies political solidarity between those included in its description. There is no evidence of community or solidarity among those classified as *paṇḍaka*.

28. Gyatso 2003, 95.

29. Horner 1997, 352.

the additional restriction he imposes clearly reflect the challenge of a social reality in which women, as well as *paṇḍaka*s, are not acknowledged to be as fully or universally human as men.

One of the ways Janet notes we can see that cisgender women are linked to *paṇḍaka*s is through the common term *bumé* (Tib. *bud med*) for "woman" in Tibetan literature, which literally means "lacking a bump," or penis. As she points out, the etymology in the history of medicine explains "*bu*" as a lump of flesh that developed in certain beings. When this phallic part fell off, or was missing, such beings became known as *bumé* or women.[30] This image of females as deformed or castrated males also suggests the notion of the "eunuch" with which the third sex is often associated.

But what if the *bu* in someone designated *bumé* might be restored as it was in Dillon? Laurence Michael Dillon, as he officially registered his name at the time of his transition, would have initially been designated *bumé* in Tibetan. However, as a young doctor being treated for gender dysphoria with testosterone and a double mastectomy, Dillon theorized a way to realize the *bu* that would express his masculity. After thirteen experimental phalloplasty procedures performed by a surgeon known for his expertise in repairing the wounded genitalia of soldiers, Dillon ultimately established that "lump of flesh" that meant he no longer lacked the *bu* that might prevent him from being seen as complete in his masculinity.[31]

Dillon's argument for his inclusion as a monk, together with others who fall under the category of *paṇḍaka*, follows the model Ānanda and Mahāprajāpatī present in the *Cullavagga*, approaching the monastic code not as a fixed text but as a set of norms that have been established and may be challenged on a case by case basis. His argument in *A Critical Study of the Vinaya* that those who might be banned due to deformity or mutilation could now be repaired by surgery,[32] appears to echo his own case for his "restored" masculine sexual organs.[33] While we don't know exactly what caused the Theravāda order to refuse his ordination, it is likely that he presented his case as one of restoration; since it was Dillon's understanding of himself as intersex that informed his doctor's decision

30. Gyatso 2015, 323.

31. Dillon's autobiographical account of this history is included in *Out of the Ordinary: A Life of Gender and Spiritual Transitions* in Jivaka/Dillon 2016, 201.

32. Jivaka 1960.

33. It should be noted that not all who are trans see hormones or surgery as essential parts of transition. Dillon's theories of gender identity in *Self* and his responses to questions in interviews suggest that he viewed himself as intersex (see Lau and Partridge, 2016, 21, n. 18 and 100–101, and Dillon 1946). It is in this sense that he may see his phalloplasties not as a change so much as a reparation.

that the surgeries performed upon him were warranted.[34] As he petitions in *A Critical Study of the Vinaya*:

> Should not each case be judged on its own merits so that victims of accidents, whether of man or of nature, may not be excluded if anyone feels he has a true vocation?[35]

Like Ānanda and Mahāprajāpatī, who don't ask so much as state that "it were well that women should obtain the going forth,"[36] Dillon simply suggests that it is time that he and others who might be classified as third sex were recognized as equally qualified to be included in the monastic community. While it may be true, as some note, that his concern for the reform of the monastic community's rules in light of modern technological advances reflects the tone of a European colonizer,[37] it also reflects the evolving dynamics of a monastic code that allowed reforms to include the participation of women.

If monasticism is itself a kind of gender, as Charlene Mackley suggests, it is essentially masculine.[38] When Mahāprajāpatī shows up with a shaved head and robes to join the monastic community, the ideal body she is embodying is a masculine one. While there is evidence in the *Therīgāthā* of nuns performing such a monastic gender while still being enlightened as women, it is also noteworthy that females, such as the Nāga princess in the *Lotus Sūtra*, must first develop masculine anatomy. Some might consider Dillon's medical transition to resemble this model, as his physical development as a man likewise enables him to progress along the path.

Judith Butler's description of gender resembles Buddhist descriptions of the self in that it is something that constitutes its reality through the repetition of actions. The performance of such actions become reiterated and reinforced by medical, legal, romantic, and religious discourses that make them appear natural or real. In that sense, gender is also an illusion, as the goddess in the *Vimalakīrtinirdeśa* makes clear when she swaps her female form with the male body of the Buddha's disciple, Śāriputra, who has denigrated it. Her display, which Vimalakīrti applauds, seems to "trouble gender" as Butler would describe it, by exposing the fictional dualities of "natural" or "real" men and

34. Jivaka/Dillon 2016, 100.

35. Jivaka 1960, 34.

36. Horner 1997, 352.

37. Lau and Partridge 2016, 19.

38. Mackley 2005.

women reinforced by Buddhist literature, such as the Vinaya, which Śāriputra strictly observes.[39]

Nevertheless, while the Buddha of the *Cullavagga* determines that women are capable of awakening, he only approves ordination to support this potential as long as the boundaries and special rules of these non-males are well defined.[40] Perhaps we see no actual person making the case for the ordination of the third sex in the Vinaya because they are not a group that's easily defined in such a way. As Janet explains:

> The third sex is a very porous and elastic category that in a sense does not stand as a proper category at all. Nor is it singular by any means. Rather, the third sex stands for all of the aberrations in between the two normative poles of male and female.[41]

While a woman such as a Mahāprajāpatī is able perform monastic (masculine) gender, within the boundaries of the special rules for women, the gender of someone classified as *paṇḍaka* has no clear boundaries that might be controlled in such a way. Those who can't perform normative gender convincingly, who are unintelligible as either male or female, are *undone* by gender, as Butler explains, with the result that others fail to perceive their full humanity.[42] Another possible reason that no one shows up to make the case for the ordination of the third sex in Vinaya literature is that no one sees them as fully human.

Imji Getsul

Dillon explored his own human existence in three distinct autobiographical accounts: *Out of the Ordinary*, his most complete description of his life, including reflections on the challenges of his trans experience; *Imji Getsul: An English Buddhist in a Tibetan Monastery*, a less-personal autobiography describing his experience at Rizong Monastery in Ladakh; and *Self: A Study in Ethics and Endocrinology* a crypto-autobiographical work that is widely credited with being the first theory of what is today described as transgender. *Self*,[43] which he wrote as a medical student in the process of transition in the mid-twentieth century, is a call for the ethical treatment of those who suffer from their inabil-

39. Butler 1991, 21.

40. Horner 1997, 354.

41. Gyatso 2015, 323.

42. Butler 2004, 2–3.

43. Dillon 1946.

ity to conform to gender norms. It echoes concerns that both Dillon and Janet raise in their critiques of the Vinaya.

Self presents the first evidence Dillon provides of how the gender binary harms those who resist its classifications. It demonstrates the real threats faced by those whose gender is unintelligible to "thoughtless persons who gaze after them and loudly voice the question, 'Is that a man or a girl?"[44] He argues that advances in medicine (including treatment with hormones) should be provided to gender non-conforming individuals to adapt their bodies to their actual experience of themselves. He claims it is easier to make the body fit the mind than to attempt to change the mind with psychoanalysis, as was the dominant approach in his day.[45] As Dillon's posthumous autobiography reveals, his experience as the first person to use hormones and surgery to adapt his own body in such a way informs his insights. After years of being taunted and threatened for his inability to conform to expectations about his gender, Dillon describes the great relief he felt in finally becoming recognizably male.

> How different was life now! I could walk past anyone and not fear to hear any comments for no one looked at me twice.[46]

Finally free to pursue what really mattered to him, Dillon devoted himself to what he describes as a search for truth that had begun in his undergraduate studies of theology and philosophy. Now able to turn his attention from body to mind, he became interested in the work on the self as proposed by the Russian thinker George Gurdjieff (1866–1949). The idea that "the purpose of man was to evolve, that he had no Self, as he fondly imagined he had, that I was not a unity but a multiplicity of moods"[47] eventually led to the study of Buddhism. Like many people in the 1950s, Dillon was initially introduced to Tibetan Buddhism through *The Third Eye* of Lobsang Rampa, whom he subsequently sought out for advice. Rampa suggested that he find a monastery in India and learn meditation. Eventually, Dillon made his way to more reputable teachers, texts, and scholars, including the renowned professor and pioneering translator of Tibetan Buddhist literature, Herbert Guenther.

Dillon read the same bowdlerized edition of the Vinaya texts translated by the Pali Text Society that Janet later supplemented with her translation of

44. Dillon 1946, 51.

45. Dillon 1946, 53.

46. Jivaka/Dillon, 2016, 88.

47. Jivaka 1962, 28–29.

the scandalous missing passages for her discussion in her article, "Sex."[48] Dillon's study was motivated by his intense personal interest in ordination, but like Janet, who as a student at UC Berkeley once insisted that her entire class, including the professor, receive the lung for the *Diamond Sūtra* from Kalu Rinpoche before studying it,[49] Dillon wanted to be sure he did things right.[50] Unfortunately, he immediately encountered obstacles. "The first thing noticeable in reading the Buddhist canon is the casual reference not to two but to the three sexes," Dillon notes, and the "many bans on various types of people from receiving the Higher Ordination, among them being anyone belonging to this 'third sex.'"[51] Dillon's alarm in recognizing himself among those who might be barred from full ordination in the Theravāda tradition is clear in his account of his life.

In some sense, there was no need for concern. He had already been ordained as a novice or *śrāmaṇera* and was arguably a man by the Vinaya's standards.[52] He was visibly male, had had a history of normative heterosexual desire, and had happily lived as a man among men for more than a decade without being challenged, even in the close quarters on the ship where he lived as a doctor. While he had (arguably) changed sex,[53] this change would have occurred only once, and so would not have made him a *paṇḍaka* according to the Vinaya. If Dillon had not been such a good student of Buddhism, it seems likely he would have been ordained without calling attention to his identity at all. And yet he, himself, clearly recognized a problem, as he explains:

> In Sarnath . . . one of the bhikshus there offered to give me the Higher Ordination and make me a bhikshu. At once I told him it

48. Gyatso 2005, is based on the "handy appendix containing the Pāli for many of these untranslated naughty bits," xxxvii.

49. Gyatso, personal correspondence, Jan. 20, 2022.

50. It should be noted that it was Dillon's concern with doing things properly, in having his name properly registered in British peerage records, that ultimately exposed his transition to the media and helped inspire the scandal around his ordination.

51. Jivaka/Dillon 2016, 228–29. Dillon took the name Jivaka, after the Buddha's doctor, and subsequently Lobzang Jivaka, when he ordained as a *getsul.* He published all his work under this name, though he also included the name Michael Dillon on the manuscript published posthumously as *Out of the Ordinary*.

52. Cabezón claims that there is no canonically valid reason for Dillon to have been denied ordination in 1959. Cabezón 2017, 536.

53. As I have previously suggested, Dillon sees himself not as changing so much as repairing or restoring his sex organs, as part of what would now be considered his transition.

> was not easy as I came under one of the bans and I even mentioned which. So for the present the matter was dropped.[54]

While Dillon doesn't mention which ban this was, the points on which he focuses his critique of the Vinaya suggest it related to anatomy. In *A Critical Study of the Vinaya*, he is especially concerned about bodily defects considered obstacles to ordination, arguing that modern medicine could now repair such conditions. It is noteworthy that this was Dillon's own solution to what he perceived as his problem. He notes that even those punished by violence or misfortune are not themselves immoral, pointing out there is no "correlation between the physical state and the morals of the person" in general,[55] a point Janet subsequently makes in "One Plus One Makes Three":

> At the very least it seems unfortunate for the Vinaya to allow anatomy to become so determinative of spiritual value, to assume simplistically that someone whose sexual organ was ambiguous would themselves be of ambiguous or changing or unreliable moral worth, incapable of taking vows or even practicing the dharma at all.[56]

While Dillon has no access to the more extreme examples of sexual indulgence that have been censored from this work (which Janet's essay, "Sex," provides), he is also struck by what he describes as the "horrifying list of perversions indulged in by 'normal' monks in the Vinaya." Dillon argues that such rules seem more likely to produce perversions in these so-called "normal" (or what might be described today as cisgender) monks than in someone like himself, who clearly understood the value of discipline for transformation.[57]

3 = 1+1+1?

The calculation 1+1=3, which Janet highlights, suggests a variety of potential problems that arise as a result of a monasticism "that wants to define everything" by reinforcing the male/female binary on the basis of an undefinable third term.[58] But perhaps there is another way of framing this equation where the third gender has a role to play in undermining dualistic and hierarchal ways

54. Jivaka/Dillon 2016, 229.
55. Jivaka 1960, 33.
56. Gyatso 2003, 106.
57. Jivaka 1960, 334.
58. Gyatso 2003, 108.

of thinking about gender. As Janet explains, from a more theoretical perspective, the very nature of this nonduality embodied by the third sex would seem "to undermine its own exclusion" and "call into question any strict separation of the other two." Indeed, she notes this concept of a third sex might be even more effective in subverting gender essentialism than the teaching the goddess performs in the *Vimalakīrtinirdeśa*.[59] A way to represent this reorganized view might be 3=1+1+1. If each of the three sexes, established in the more neutral medical sense, is not viewed in the context of a hierarchy of first, second, and third, but rather acknowledged to each contribute an equal, independent part (i.e., 1+1+1) of that greater sum (3) we call humanity, the calculation makes a lot more sense.

In fact, Janet points out there is support for a more neutral and positive description of the third sex in the Tibetan concept of *maning*. In Tibetan medicine, for example, attributes that are described as *maning* are said to reflect a kind of balance that results from an equal contribution of the parents' male and female seeds.[60] Janet notes that in Tibetan medicine the *maning* pulse is valorized as the "bodhisattva pulse," which is described as more even or steady than either the male or female pulse and is associated with good health, long life, and is therefore appreciated by those in power.[61]

Given the negative depiction of the third sex in Buddhist literature, the notion of male, female, and "bodhisattva" pulses may seem surprising, but the way that bodhisattvas are said to operate in Buddhist traditions provides further reasons to associate them with the variability of the third sex. In Tibetan contexts, for example, there is the exceptional flexibility of a bodhisattva such as Yeshe Tsogyal who is likewise flexible in her performance of gender. Unlike the goddess who transforms her sex to teach wisdom or the Nāga princess who becomes male in order to achieve enlightenment, Yeshe Tsogyal claims the ability to become whatever sex others desire or need as a manifestation of selfless compassion. As she explains:

> To those who craved a woman, I became a lovely girl and thus their joy.
> To those who sought a lover, I was a handsome youth and thus their joy.[62]

The ability to change sex at any time in this way is clearly a power in the service of bodhisattva activity, not the threat of instability that the Vinaya sees

59. Gyatso 2003, 104.

60. Gyatso 2003, 95.

61. Gyatso 2015, 329.

62. Changchub, Nyingpo, and Yeshe Tsogyal 2002, 161.

in the similar capacity of a *paṇḍaka*. Tibetan tantric practices likewise encourage transformations which one repeats imaginatively in order to develop the potential for awakening. Such practices often unproblematically include gender crossing, as for example when male practitioners seek to embody the female deity Vajrayoginī. The effect of such reiterated acts performed successfully is not unlike the effect of the "realness" achieved by performers in the Harlem drag balls, documented in the film *Paris Is Burning* and the television series *Pose*,[63] who demonstrate their power to go out into everyday life in the embodiment of their ideal.[64]

While Tibetan monks do not literally perform (or visualize themselves performing) drag, Janet tells a story of being ushered into the room where Kalu Rinpoche was ostensibly meditating, after a day of classes at UC Berkeley, only to have him turn around to flash long red-painted fingernails and a lipstick grin.[65] Since performing gender is something one *does*, gender can also become *undone* in such ways to point to its lack of essence, whether by Kalu Rinpoche or *Vimalakī*'s goddess. Such a teaching suggests the fundamental reason gender can change in Buddhism, which is that gender, like self, is empty of essence. While the realities of gender may make such possibilities hard to see, they also point out the skillful means by which the unique raw materials of human lives provide opportunities for liberation.

Works Cited

Ainsworth, Claire. 2018. "Sex Redefined: The Idea of 2 Sexes Is Overly Simplistic." *Scientific American*. https://www.scientificamerican.com/article/sex-redefined-the-idea-of-2-sexes-is-overly-simplistic1/. Accessed February 2, 2022.

Akāliko, Bhante. 2021. Welcoming the Rainbow: A Guide to LGBTQIA+ Inclusion for Buddhists. https://rainbodhi.org/resources/. Accessed January 24, 2022.

Anonymous. 2014. *Developing Trans* Competence: A Short Guide to Improving Transgender Experiences at Meditation and Retreat Centers*. https://transbuddhists.org/retreat-guide/. Accessed February 2, 2022.

Bettcher, Talia. 2014. "Feminist Perspectives on Trans Issues," *The Stanford Encyclopedia of Philosophy*, Edward N. Zalta (ed.), https://plato.stanford.edu/archives/fall2020/entries/feminism-trans/. Accessed December 11, 2021.

63. Livingston 1997 and Pose 2018–2021.

64. One might compare this concept of "realness" to the manifestation of the reality of the *Samayasattva* in Vajrayāna practices, which seeks to train the practitioner to embody the deity in post-meditation.

65. Gyatso 2018 and personal correspondence, January 18, 2022.

Butler, Judith. 1991. "Imitation and Gender Insubordination." In *Inside/Out, Lesbian Theories, Gay Theories.* New York: Routledge.

———. 2004. *Undoing Gender.* New York: Routledge.

Cabezón, José Ignacio. 2017. *Sexuality in Classical South Asian Buddhism.* Studies in Indian and Tibetan Buddhism. Somerville, MA: Wisdom Publications.

Changchub, Gyalwa, Namkhai Nyingpo, and Yeshe Tsogyal. 2002. *Lady of the Lotus Born*, translated by the Padmakara Translation Group. Boston: Shambhala Publications.

Dillon, Michael. 1946. *Self: A Study in Ethics and Endocrinology.* London: Butterworth-Heinemann.

Gyatso, Janet. 1998. *Apparitions of the Self: The Secret Autobiographies of a Tibetan Visionary.* Princeton, N.J: Princeton University Press.

———. 2003. "One Plus One Makes Three: Buddhist Gender, Monasticism, and the Law of the Non-Excluded Middle." *History of Religions* 43.2: 89–115.

———. 2005. "Sex." In *Critical Terms for the Study of Buddhism*, edited by Donald S. Lopez Jr., 271–90. Chicago: University of Chicago Press.

———. 2010. "Female Ordination in Buddhism: Looking Into a Crystal Ball, Making a Future." In *Dignity and Discipline: Reviving Full Ordination for Buddhist Nuns*, edited by Mohr, Thea, and Venerable Jampa Tsedroen, 1–21. Boston: Wisdom Publications.

———. 2015. *Being Human in a Buddhist World: An Intellectual History of Medicine in Early Modern Tibet.* New York: Columbia University Press.

———. 2017. "Recently, Under the Bodhi Tree." *Tricycle: The Buddhist Review.* Accessed July 18, 2022. https://tricycle.org/magazine/recently-bodhi-tree/.

———. 2018. Interview with Daniel Aitken. "Janet Gyatso: Tibetan Buddhism, Animal Ethics and Compassion." 2018. The Wisdom Experience. Podcast audio. Accessed January 21, 2022. https://wisdomexperience.org/wisdom-podcast/janet-gyatso/.

Horner, I. B. 1997. *The Book of Discipline (Vinaya-Piṭaka).* Vol. V (*Cullavagga*). Oxford: The Pali Text Society.

Jivaka, Lobzang. 1962. *Imji Getsul: An English Buddhist in a Tibetan Monastery.* London: Routledge & Kegan Paul.

Jivaka/Dillon, Lobzang/Michael. 2016. *Out of the Ordinary: A Life of Gender and Spiritual Transitions.* Edited by Jacob Lau and Cameron Partridge. New York: Fordham University Press.

Jivaka, Sramanera. 1960. *A Critical Study of the Vinaya.* Sarnath: Maha Bodhi Society.

Kennedy, Pagan. 2007. *The First Man-Made Man: The Story of Two Sex Changes, One Love Affair, and a Twentieth-Century Medical Revolution.* New York: Bloomsbury.

Lau, Jacob, and Cameron Partridge. 2016. "'In His Own Way, In His Own Time': An Introduction to *Out of the Ordinary.*" In Jivaka/Dillon. *Out of the Ordinary: A Life of Gender and Spiritual Transitions.* Edited by Jacob Lau and Cameron Partridge. New York: Fordham University Press, 2016.

Livingston, Jennie. 1990. *Paris Is Burning.* San Francisco: The Criterion Collection.

Mackley, Charlene E. 2005. "The Body of a Nun: Nunhood and Gender in Contemporary Amdo." In *Women in Tibet: Past and Present,* edited by Hanna Havnevik and Janet Gyatso. New York: Columbia University Press.

Marston, Elizabeth. 2019. "Working with Nothing: Being Trans and Buddhist in North America." *Transcending: Trans Buddhist Voices*. Berkeley, California: North Atlantic Books.

Michaelson, Jay. 2018. "We're Queer and We've Been Here." *Tricycle: The Buddhist Review*. https://tricycle.org/trikedaily/buddhisms-lgbt-history/. Accessed Jan. 24, 2022.

Pose. 2018–2021. Fox 21 Studios and FX Productions.

II.
Biography and Autobiography

How I Fell into Tulkuship: A Childhood Memoir from Northeastern Tibet

Matthew T. Kapstein

Introduction

LET ME BEGIN with my own memoir, but one from Berkeley and not northeastern Tibet: I first met Janet Gyatso, then Janet Frank, just over a half century ago, when we were both undergraduates at the University of California. We were studying Sanskrit with Robert Goldman, with whom we read Aśvaghoṣa and Andersen's *Pali Reader*, and Barend van Nooten, who introduced us to Buddhist Hybrid Sanskrit and Apabhraṃśa. Our Classical Tibetan lessons were with the doyen of Mongolian studies, James Bosson, in whose classes we delved into the *Testament of Ba* and *Milarepa*. Lewis Lancaster, in Buddhist studies, guided polyglot readings of the *Diamond Sutra* and the *Sutra of the Ten Stages*, while Frits Staal devoted seminars to Buddhist logic and epistemology. Janet and I, together with Robert Kritzer and other comrades, would sometimes meet for bag lunches at my small apartment near campus, where we pored over our dictionaries and crammed before dashing off to Dwinelle Hall or Durant to prove ourselves before our exacting mentors. The first year in which we were classmates, 1971, was the last in which Edward Conze taught at Berkeley as a visitor and just preceded the arrival of Padmanabh Jaini, a key figure for Buddhist studies there in the decades that followed. Given such beginnings, Janet is surely my closest lineage sister in the field.

In the fifty odd years (!) that have since passed, our paths and our interests have often intersected. A prominent cluster of themes, to which both of us have periodically returned, hovers around the nexus of literary personae, particularly as disclosed in life-writing and visionary, or revelatory, experience, so that my present offering to this collection falls appropriately within this broad area. It completes an earlier piece that I presented at the International Association for Tibetan Studies Seminar held in Leiden in 2000, where Janet was among those in attendance (and where she would be elected president of the association). Her pathbreaking book, *Apparitions of the Self*,[1] had appeared not long before,

1. Gyatso 1998.

and Tibetan autobiography was very much on her mind. Janet immediately expressed her interest in the account I presented of a tulku who not only gave voice to doubts about his status but who seems to have reacted to it with sufficient vehemence to have actually left it behind, quitting a Geluk sinecure in his native Amdo to enter Dzogchen Monastery in Kham, where he immersed himself in the Nyingma tradition before becoming a "treasure finder" (*gter ston*) in his own right. Although the paper that I delivered on the subject was published some two decades ago,[2] recollecting now one of Janet's talks, in which she urged her colleagues to undertake more translations of Tibetan autobiographies, I offer here my rendering of the text I summarized there, the nineteenth-century adept Düjom Dorjé Rölpatsel's remarkable account of his childhood as an unwilling tulku, entitled "How I Fell into Tulkuship" (*sprul sku'i go sar lhung tshul*). Before presenting the translation, however, it may be useful to briefly review the background.

In the Tibetan religious world, during the period of the dominance of the Ganden Phodrang (1642–1959) and beginning in some religious orders even earlier,[3] the upper echelons of monastic hierarchies were dominated by those who had been recognized during childhood as tulkus, "emanational embodiments" thought to be the rebirths of past masters. The institution required in most cases that the children so recognized—who with only a small number of exceptions were boys[4]—be separated from their parents at an early age to receive an intensive religious education. The most famous, and the highest in rank, of tulkus under the Ganden Phodrang regime was of course the Dalai Lama,[5] but many hundreds of others were known. Some occupied only modest positions in smaller religious establishments, while great centers such as Labrang Tashikhyil, in the Sino-Tibetan marches in Gansu, were home to dozens of such incarnations, representing the tentacular extension of Labrang's dominion among Tibetans and Mongols throughout Amdo and adjacent regions.[6] Whatever their precise rank, such figures were widely revered and were among the major recipients of the offerings of devotees, as merit was believed to accrue above all from gifts to worthy recipients. Because even a minor tulku might come to have considerable local prestige, various regional powers, both eccle-

2. Kapstein 2002.

3. The Karma Kagyü is generally considered to have been the first order to have adopted the tulku system. See now Gamble 2018.

4. For a study of the best-known exception, see Diemberger 2007.

5. Schwieger 2015 surveys the history and institution of the Dalai Lama, together with the origins and development of reincarnate hierarchy in Tibet.

6. Refer to Nietupski 2011. Labrang was one of the six leading centers of the Gelukpa order.

siastical and familial, sometimes felt it in their interest to establish and then control such positions. The religious ideals that provided the ideological underpinnings of the system were thus in reality often subordinate to a variety of social, political, and economic forces, making the position of the tulku sometimes a conflicted, uncomfortable one. Despite this, traditional Tibetan writings only rarely include critical remarks reflecting upon the less savory aspects of the institution of the tulku itself.[7]

Among the available examples of such criticism, one of the most interesting that has come to my attention is surely the passage translated here. A native of Repkong (Tongren in modern Qinghai), Düjom Dorjé Rölpatsel (1845–1921)[8] was designated by his family in early childhood to become an ordinary monk after the suspicion was raised that he had been conceived in an incestuous relationship.[9] He was therefore sent to live with an uncle, who was an administrator at Labrang. In the excerpt from his memoirs presented here, he recounts the circumstances of his recognition as a tulku when he was eight and the trials that followed, his none-too-positive view of the matter being clearly signaled by the acerbic title he chose for this part of his life story.

Although Düjom Dorjé eventually did abandon his position as a tulku, leaving his monastery and the Geluk order when he was in his mid-twenties,[10] he did not by any means leave the religious life. Instead, he became an adept of esoteric, tantric Buddhism in the Nyingmapa order, the ancient school that claims to represent the Buddhism introduced into Tibet during the eighth and ninth centuries. In later life, he returned to his native district of Repkong, where he became known as Khagyé tergen (*kha rgya'i gter rgan*), or "the old treasure finder of Khagya,"[11] whose teachings were believed to be revelations of

7. Kapstein 2002 includes further remarks on traditional expressions of criticism, though the subject remains very far from being exhausted.

8. Hūṃ chen 2010, 1, gives the birth year as 1857, but this is impossible if, as Düjom Dorjé relates in the passage translated here, he was about seven or eight when recognized by Detri Jamyang Tubten Nyima (1779–1862) and received the Kālacakra initiation from the same master when he was in or just past his fifteenth year. If his birth is pushed back by one duodecennial cycle, however, the chronology is readily reconciled with the lifetime of the Detri Rinpoché.

9. Bkra shis rab brtan 1991, 6–10.

10. His departure seems not to have been so abrupt or dramatic as it appears here but was rather a more gradual reorientation—first seeking out Nyingmapa associates in regions familiar to him in Amdo and only later traveling to Khams—as is recounted in the sections of the autography immediately following the selection translated below.

11. His major revelatory cycle, entitled the *Chos nyid rig pa'i klong sgrom*, is published in Hūṃ chen 2010. I am grateful to the editor, Humchen Chenaktsang, for presenting me with this volume and for informing me, too, that the transmission of Düjom Dorjé's terma was revived not long ago in Repkong.

instructions and prophecies inspired by Padmasambhava. Düjom Dorjé's critical view of his experiences as a tulku, therefore, should not be taken as a rejection of the Tibetan religious system but only of what he believed to have been specific abuses. Though his critique of his tulkuship and especially his rejection of it may be regarded as departures from traditional norms within the Tibetan religious milieu, the way he expressed and channeled his rebellion in fact reflected well-defined facets of the same tradition overall.

The translation that follows adheres closely to the original text but simplifies a small number of technical or highly ornate expressions that do not lend themselves to very literal renderings. Many concepts pertaining to Tibetan Buddhism are mentioned; though these will be familiar to most readers of this volume, I have explained them concisely in the notes on behalf of those who may not be accustomed to them. Parts of the text provide humdrum accounts of teachings received during what seems the normal upbringing of a tulku, but they are punctuated with expressions of deep misgiving and narratives of dreams in which Düjom Dorjé begins to awake to his own potential for spiritual self-discovery.

Translation[12]

You may wonder, how was it that I amassed "karma and dispositions" by falling into the status of a tulku when infallible karmic conditions struck like lightning?[13] From what I can recall, and according to the rumors that circulate all about, here's what happened:

In the region of Tsö,[14] there was formerly a hidden adept named Lama Khetel (Khe thal). After he passed into peace, his relations, who hankered to find his reincarnation, decided the matter based only on their desires and so came before my uncle with their request. Considering this elevation of rank to be flawed, my uncle did not wish to give me up, but because it was impossible for him to resist the order of the venerable Rinpoché, he accepted to do so.[15] Before long, although offering-scarves, robes, the enthronement ceremony, and such

12. The present translation follows the text as given in Bkra shis rab brtan 1991, 11–24. The text may be also found in Hūṃ chen 2010.

13. The references to karma here are full of irony, the author suggesting that his recognition was the product of former misdeeds and that it served only to reinforce evil predispositions.

14. Tsö (*gtsos*) is in the southern part of Gansu province in China and is now called Hezuo.

15. This no doubt refers to Detri Jamyang Tubten Nyima (1779–1862), a prominent Labrang hierarch who was the superior of the author's uncle. His biography is summarized in Ko shul and Rgyal ba 1992, 912–13.

Figure 1. Düjom Dorjé Rölpatsel as an iconic *ngakpa*. After the frontispiece of Hūṃ chen 2010.

had to be prepared, because the lama (Khetel) had been of low rank and miserable, his relations were destitute of means and made only symbolic offerings. When the time came for my investiture, it was therefore my uncle who had to furnish the robes and ecclesiastical accoutrements, and thus, when I was in my ninth year,[16] I was installed at Ganden Chöling in Tsö. In the commotion of the feasting that followed, sheep were butchered, and we were supposed to relish their flesh and blood. Beginning then, I fell under the influence of sinful deeds. But just after I arrived at my monastery, when the eating and drinking were done and I ventured outside, a vajra made of meteoric iron came into my

16. That is to say, he was eight according to our way of reckoning age.

hands; it was a self-fulfilling omen of my future course.[17] One of my relatives, called Rabjampa, stayed on as my companion, so that after the other relations had returned to their homes, I had no pangs of despair.

A holy mentor named Akhu Sherab was assigned as my tutor, and continuing from what I had learned earlier, I memorized and practiced the funerary ritual of the All-Knowing, the liturgies of the monastic college, together with the prayers, rites of purification, and the *Ornament of Realization* and *Introduction to the Middle Way*.[18] Because I had a strongly childish character, my tutor scolded me and slapped me so much that I was sometimes brought to grief. During my twelfth year, I received the vows of the novitiate before the Dungtruk tulku, Losang Jamyang Giteng Rinpoché (Dung phrug sprul sku Blo bzang 'jam dbyangs Sgi steng rin po che), and he additionally bestowed the instructions of *powa*, which I practiced for about a week.[19] Except for being a means to consume the wealth of the deceased, there was nothing at all here of ultimately meaningful practice, which makes this free occasion [of human birth] valuable—for instance, the exercise of the virtues, the stages of creation and perfection,[20] or meditation and mantra recitation. Like one sitting astride a horse but boxed into a pen with no freedom of movement, I was solely occupied with bringing in offerings of the riches of the living and the dead, the best of the harvest. Though some trifling wealth was gathered in this way—let's not talk about moving even so far as a sesame grain in the direction of the Precious Jewels' field!—I was without any power to do more than to bring to waste the food and clothing of patrons and to receive payment for

17. Just how he obtained the vajra is left somewhat mysterious, but Düjom Dorjé is here affirming it to have been a prophetic indication of his future destiny as a "treasure-finder," or tertön.

18. The "funeral ritual of the All-Knowing" (*Kun rig*, i.e., Sarvavid Vairocana) is derived from an important tantra called the *Purification of All Evil Destinies* (*Sarvadurgatipariṣodhanatantra*) and is widely practiced throughout Tibet. The two texts mentioned at the end of this sentence are the *Abhisamayālaṃkāra* of the bodhisattva Maitreya and the *Madhyamakāvatāra* of the philosopher Candrakīrti, two fundamental treatises of Indian Mahāyāna Buddhism that figure prominently in the obligatory curriculum in all Tibetan monastic colleges. For background on the system of monastic education, see Dreyfus 2003.

19. As will emerge below, the Giteng Rinpoché appears to have been an important figure at Ganden Chöling in Tsö, where Düjom Dorjé was recognized. *Powa* (*'pho ba*) is a tantric technique that is believed to project the consciousness at death directly into a pure rebirth, for which reason Tibetan lamas are frequently asked to perform the ritual on behalf of those on their deathbeds or recently deceased. In some cases, this became (as it did here) an important source of monastic income. For further detail regarding the rite of *powa* itself, refer to Kapstein 1998.

20. The two main phases of advanced tantric practiced, focusing respectively upon the imaginative creation of the divine realm of the maṇḍala and upon techniques of esoteric yoga through which the energies of the subtle body are believed to be mastered.

their debts.[21] My patrons, moreover, were coarse people of bad character who took no care of me and, though I was but a child, they cursed me, bestowing titles but [at the same time] finding faults. Though they called me "tulku," I was in fact more like their servant. Nevertheless, because this situation arose from my former malice and avarice, for the while I had no recourse except to remain equanimous. As for my own food, clothing, provisions, and items of worship, including the symbols of the Buddha's body, speech, and mind,[22] it was the fruit of past karma that my uncle alone, in a timely manner, provided them unstintingly, so that I could just manage to present myself in public.

On entering the monastic college, I studied the *Abbreviated Logic Course*, the way of reason. Because I didn't even understand the general application of the reason or consequence, I was rejected by my companions and despairingly scolded by my teachers, who took to beating me harshly, though it did no good at all.[23]

In my fifteenth year, my tutor resided in a meditation retreat, and I joined him. During this retreat, at dawn on the fifteenth of the lunar month,[24] I dreamed that I arrived at a great shrine full of offerings where there was a performance of sacred dance. When the male and female servants of the Lord of Death entered the stage, I met them briefly, and then, when I took my leave, I saw a mountain behind that was splendid, lofty, and bluish, seeming to reach the heavens. Before it, men and women were assembled who all held offering-scarves, lamps, incense, and flowers. With their prayers resounding they approached the cliff face as a place of pilgrimage. It appeared to me that on the summit of that adamant peak, the full moon formed a mansion of light, arising as a glowing orb. Just then a pathway appeared, and after setting out on it, I arrived before the opening of a meditation cave. Entering, I saw a naked yogin

21. This may have a double meaning. In traditional Tibet, where there was no banking system, the monasteries frequently acted as lenders, though administrative officers, such as Düjom Dorjé's uncle, and not tulkus, would typically be occupied with this aspect of monastic affairs. On the other hand, past misdeeds were frequently conceived as involving a kind of "karmic debt," which must be paid off either through expiation or the suffering one experiences when the unexpunged "debt" comes due.

22. That is, paintings and images as symbols of body, books as those of speech, and ritual implements such as vajras as those of mind.

23. The *Abbreviated Logic Course* is taught through debate, one of the mainstays of education in the Geluk colleges. See Dreyfus 2003. The system of reasoning employed in monastic debates stresses the assessment of propositions taken as consequences of reasons thought to entail them, expressed in the form, "It is implied that *q*, because *p*" (*der thal de'i phyir*). Düjom Dorjé is saying here that he had little idea of how the formula was supposed to work.

24. That is, during the full moon.

seated upon a platform of stone, his legs crossed, palms resting evenly in his lap, his locks reaching the floor with the remainder piled in a topknot. Coming before him, who was seated in absorption, I prostrated and circumambulated, asking to meet with him.

At that he laughed a bit and, looking right at me, asked, "So you've come here?"

"So I have," I answered.

"Now's not the time. But later, when the time is right, there's a land to which you must go. Will you go there?"

"Now I will certainly go, far though it be." As I said this, I experienced limitless joy and while in that state started to dance.

He then held up a pure crystal in his hand and said, "Look here! All that will be, you'll clearly see." I looked, and all at once there was an amazing land, with a magnificent snow peak adorned with forests where I heard the songs of various birds. The whole mountain had caves and ravines and was dotted with snow; seeing this inspired my mind in the Dharma, and I was left alone for a moment, with a limitless sentiment of renunciation. He spoke again: "Up in that valley is the lord of your family,[25] one called Crystal Vajra. If you approach him in the twelfth year hence, all purposes, your own and those of others, will certainly be fulfilled." When he said this, I became absorbed as before in the expanse of his thought and then woke up.

Figure 2. The cover illustration of Hūṃ chen 2010, perhaps inspired by Düjom Dorjé's dream of a yogin in a mountain cave.

25. The "lord of the family" in this context means one's main teacher, the root guru.

[Returning to my studies,] I was instructed in the eight chapters and seventy topics of the vehicle of the perfection of wisdom, according to the eleven "mother and son" scriptures and their commentaries, the doctrines of Maitreya, and so on.[26] On occasions when we practiced debates concerning the scriptural basis and reasoning of the text, though I gained a rough understanding of the boundaries and ascertainments of the vehicles of śrāvakas, pratyekabuddhas, and bodhisattvas, I did not give myself airs and maintained only an aspirant's demeanor, for which reason my teachers were content and all praised me, saying that my studies were going well. Nonetheless, my own motivations were so weak that I couldn't get my head around even a bit of the sense of the stages, paths, and results of the three vehicles, not to mention the very entranceway to the Dharma, the instructions and vow of refuge, which I could never take to heart. This really depressed me.

At about that time I began to encounter the accounts of the lives of past holy masters—the eighty gnostics of India, the conqueror Padma, and Tilopa, Nāropa, Marpa, Milarepa, and so on[27]—who had realized the intentions of all the Buddha's sūtras and tantras and so cleansed themselves of all saṃsāra's flaws and mastered all the qualities of nirvāṇa. These irresistibly captured my imagination so that I gained such an irreversible faith that my hairs stood on end; I shed tears and prayed devotedly, with uncontrived aspirations. Owing to this I was inspired to make efforts to amass the virtues whereby my spirit might merge somewhat with the Dharma, such as by sponsoring images or making offerings, but my tutor took no account of it; it was but a personal enthusiasm and most certainly not tending to perfect enlightenment!

One time, on being summoned to the Evaṃ Sungjuk College (*e waṃ zung 'jug*) of Labrang Tashikhyil, I obtained the great consecration of the glorious Kālacakra before Venerable Detri Rinpoché Jamyang Tubten Nyima (Sde khri rin po che rje 'Jam dbyangs thub bstan nyi ma), who conferred it in full over one week together with the ceremony of feast offerings and dedications of merit.[28]

26. The "eight chapters and seventy topics" are taught in the *Abhisamayālaṃkāra* (note 18 above) and pertain to the interpretation of the Perfection of Wisdom sūtras, referred to here as the eleven mother and son scriptures, the "mother" being the longest version in 100,000 lines and the ten "sons" being the several abridged versions.

27. "Eighty gnostics" (*rig 'dzin brgyad bcu*) refers to the eighty-four *mahāsiddhas*, or great adepts, of India. The "conqueror Padma" is Padmasambhava, and the names last mentioned are, of course, those of the Indian and Tibetan teachers revered as the fountainheads of the Kagyü traditions.

28. Kālacakra, the "wheel of time," is considered the most exalted of Buddhist tantric teachings and is the object of advanced study and practice at the specialized Kālacakra College (*dus 'khor grwa tshang*) of Labrang Monastery.

In this way, a seed of beatitude was well planted within me, and I formed a genuine connection with the aspiration for rebirth in Shambhala, the mission field of the original Buddha Kālacakra. Appearances were transformed so as to be as the dance steps and cosmic chant of the precious nondual *Kālacakra Tantra*, the culmination of all the inconceivable tantras pronounced by the Buddha, the master of all teachings, who had arisen in the form of the body of rapture.[29]

With my mind thus inspired by faith, wishing to establish good dispositions, I practiced the three rites of visualization, the self-consecration, and so on, memorizing them and learning their chants. At all times, relying upon the nine-deity rite, I always made ten thousand recitations of the heart mantra and recited the abbreviated tantra. Not slipping into my selfish desires, but motivated with a pure and positive intention, I commissioned paintings of the deity and his maṇḍala. I collected the sacramental accoutrements of the creation stage, including a *ḍamaru* drum, bell, skull-bone rosary, armbands, *khaṭvāṅga* staff, meditation support and cushion, wig, skull head-ornaments and garlands, a corpse seat, and so on—all the wrathful stuff.[30] And I gathered also those of the perfection stage, the exercises of vital energy, including the meditation straps and belts.[31] Although I wasn't really clear about the sequence of visualizations involved in the methods for purifying rebirth—the means for training on the stages and paths of purification, cleansing the taints of the subtle channels, vital energies, and seminal essences—the dispositions of my former lifetimes had been reawakened.[32] So I stripped myself naked, donned the wig, did myself up with the armbands and so on, and sat in the sevenfold posture of Vairocana.[33] I performed the ritual down to the dissolution of the elements and birth from the womb of the goddess, until the vision of the deity according to the

29. The *Kālacakra Tantra* is thought to have been taught by the Buddha Śākyamuni himself in southern India in the divine form of buddhahood known as the "body of rapture" (*sambhogakāya*).

30. The *ḍamaru* is a small two-sided hand-drum, sometimes made of monkey skulls. The *khaṭvāṅga* is a mendicant's staff with a skull at the top. Tibetan ritual implements did often make use of real bone but also represented skulls and the like in wood, metal, or other materials. The wig represents the long, flowing locks of the adept of yoga.

31. The special techniques of the yogas of the subtle energies require very long periods of intense practice, during which the adept literally binds himself in the correct posture.

32. The positive affinity one feels for a particular religious teaching, as here, in Düjom Dorjé's youthful enthusiasm for the Kālacakra tantra, is often understood in Tibet as signifying a connection with that teaching in a former lifetime.

33. The sevenfold posture of the buddha Vairocana is the standard position for Buddhist meditation: legs folded, hands evenly resting in one's lap, shoulders level, spine erect, chin tucked in, tongue touching the hard palate, and eyes gazing into the space before the nose.

"path practice of the triple embodiment" was clear and the play of conceptual thought had merged into nonduality, in which I became absorbed.[34]

At all times, whenever I saw a painting of my favored deity, I pressed my palms together and repeatedly made devoted prayers. Above all, on seeing images of the great Orgyen,[35] unbroken faith continually arose, and from beholding representations of the gnostics and siddhas, I wished to obtain all the consecrations and accomplishments of inborn gnosis, the union of bliss and emptiness that is the culminating heart of the secret mantras, by relying upon the wisdom woman's secret maṇḍala.[36] I was certain that, without renouncing sensory objects but enjoying them as adornments, I would mature within my consort's encompassing embrace, traversing the stages and paths, and so I drew pictures of various naked gnostic women, smiling and coquettish, and commissioned images of Tilopa, Nāropa, and the other mystical heroes who, by these supreme means, had obtained the highest accomplishment of coalescent ecstasy.

When all this came to be seen and heard, those who had some thought for the qualities of monks said, "Just what's this tulku up to? Who's to say? We shouldn't rush to judgment." But some faultfinders did judge me, saying, "If he isn't cut down to size, the fabrications of his imagination will wind up as a con man's tales of divine and demonic visions. What use is it to discuss it any further?"

One time at Labrang Tashikhyil, I was among thirty Labrang, Repkong, and mostly Mongol monks who received the vows of celibate *bhikṣus* before the great benefactor Venerable [Akhu] Sherab Gyatso Rinpoché.[37] But the precepts, all the details of the vows for disciplining body, speech, and mind, didn't enter my spirit, and so I played make-believe in the company of Buddhist *bhikṣus*, insomuch as I always wore the three religious robes.

Then one night, in my dreams as I slept before dawn, I arrived at a great plain heading off toward the east. On the horizon, where everything was covered in black obscurity, many men and women were crying and wailing. Here and there were square and triangular fortresses of molten iron, before which

34. The triple embodiment refers to the three "bodies" of the Buddha: emanation body (*nirmāṇakāya*), body of rapture (*sambhogakāya*), and body of reality (*dharmakāya*), the last being equivalent to the omnipresent absolute reality itself. The tantric Buddhist adept is expected to practice in constant recollection of these.

35. An alternative name of Padmasambhava.

36. Düjom Dorjé alludes here to the practices of sexual yoga. Though this was the object of widespread religious symbolism in Tibet, the suggestion that one might actually undertake such practices was frequently regarded as scandalous.

37. A khu chin Shes rab rgya mtsho (1803–75).

men and women were lined up in rows, and all the beings there reeked of burnt hair—I saw them falling over one another. I too went there, but no harm came to me at all. A little bit farther beyond was a great ravine in which, in the midst of a reddish whirlwind, many folks were crying out in anguish. I entered their midst but remained cool and proceeded on my way at ease. Thinking, "It's not right that I do that," I turned back. At the center of the aforementioned plain was a thumb-sized golden elephant in reclining position, and I picked it up and tucked it into my belt. At that, two men arrived, one bull-headed and the other stag-headed, and they led me to a circular grassy enclosure with a palanquin throne in the middle. On it sat a beautiful prince, pleasing to behold, his orange hair tied up in a topknot, his body wrapped in a blue robe. He held a mirror in his right hand and a divination board in his left and sat in a posture of ease. Coming before him, he said, "You must have made a mistake coming here! Go back to your own country, where you can be of some use to yourself and others. That's what you must do! A son of the gods will show you the way."

As soon as he said this, a seven-year-old youth wearing white silk became my guide, and we ascended the slopes of a tall mountain. At some point there was a well-appointed temple, in which there were many assembled *bhikṣus* who performed prostrations and recited the *Prayer of Excellent Conduct*.[38] Just when we arrived among them, I woke up in my bed.

At my own monastery, thanks to the kindness of the lord of refuges, the supreme precious emanation, Losang Jamyang Giteng, I well obtained early on, from the Vajradhara of Sé, Losang Tashi Rabgyé Rinpoché (Bse rdo rje 'chang Blo bzang bkra shis rab rgyas rin po che, 1814–79), the consecrations of Cakrasamvara, Guhyasamāja, and Vajrabhairava, Sarvavid and the nine-deity maṇḍala of the most secret Hayagrīva, and the five consecrations of the protectors of the teaching, including the heart mantras of Rahula, the Lion-Headed Goddess, and Bektsé.[39] And later on, I had the good fortune to obtain a great many consecrations and authorizations of the ancient and modern traditions before Venerable Vajradhara Ngawang Chöpel (Ngag dbang chos 'phel), together

38. The *Bhadracaryāpraṇidhānarāja*, one of the most popular Mahāyāna prayers and known by almost all Tibetan monks (and many laypersons) by heart.

39. In the context of formal consecration in tantric teachings, the master who confers the consecration is considered equivalent to the Buddha and so called by the name of the tantric Buddha Vajradhara. The divinities mentioned are the major tutelaries of the Geluk order, while the three protectors who are named are the planetary divinity Rahula, who is associated with eclipse, the Lion-Headed Goddess Siṃhavaktrā, who protects from obstacles, and Bektsé, originally a Mongolian warrior-divinity, representing the coat of mail, who became one of the special protectors of the Dalai Lama.

with the whole college including the supreme precious emanation [Losang Jamyang Giteng] first and foremost: the consecrations of various tantric collections such as the Vajra Garland, the Hundred Deities of Mitrayogin, and so on; and before that holy supreme emanation himself, with just a few others, the Jewel Mine of Sādhana, the Excellent Wish-Granting Vase, the Lion-Headed Goddess according to Nyidrak and her red form according to Matiratna, as well as the authorizations of the thirteen testaments of the Lord and those of Gaṇapati.[40]

At intervals, it often happened that I gazed into the space of the completely clear sky or just let myself fall into a natural relaxation of body, speech, and mind. Nevertheless, I was unable to recognize the expansive nature, in the disposition of suchness, of limitless awareness.[41]

Owing to the power of past evil karma, I had knowingly, even while recognizing the poison, squandered the wealth of the living and dead without restraint. I helplessly amassed the terrible karma of killing by enjoying the flesh and blood of goats, sheep, and pigs slaughtered for funerals, or for protective rites for the living, such as appeasements, exorcisms, and severance.[42] I indulged in lying in violation of religious principles, by engaging in divinations, prophecies, and dream auguries; divisiveness by chattering without forethought; coarseness by whining narcissistically in order to fill my belly with religious wealth; and prattle by speaking carelessly out of attachment and anger. I was given to avarice, hoping to receive offerings and services for village rites on behalf of the living and the dead; to harmfulness, rejoicing in the bad fortune of those for whom I felt enmity, owing to apparent discrepancies of karma [between us]; and hence false views, for clearly, I did not really have confidence in karmic causation and so indulged in all sorts of unvirtuous thoughts and practices. I was subject to insatiable desire for food, clothing, riches, and things; burning anger that raged unbearably for even small reasons; stupidity with no thought for cause and effect, or for what was to be undertaken or avoided; envy that led me

40. The textual collections mentioned are all famous compilations of diverse tantric teachings, though a curious feature of this list is the inclusion of the Excellent Wish-Granting Vase (*'Dod 'jo'i bum bzang*), a Nyingma collection that one would not expect to see in a Geluk context. The "Lord" here is Mahākāla, an important protector of Indian origin. Gaṇapati is the well-known elephant-headed Hindu god Ganesh, serving also as a Buddhist tantric protector.

41. The references to gazing at the empty sky and resting in a naturally relaxed state evoke the Great Perfection (*rdzogs chen*) teaching, the highest instructions of the Nyingma tradition with which Düjom Dorjé would be later affiliated. The "limitless awareness" that is the goal of that teaching, however, remained beyond his grasp at this time.

42. The rites of "severance" (*gcod*), involving visualized self-sacrifice, do not usually require actual animal slaughter, though offerings of meat were customary in some versions of the ritual.

to rival and slander my betters; stinginess so that I tried to gather, hoard, and increase whatever desirable possessions I had; and great pride, flattering myself for even the most trivial aptitude in the arts and crafts. All my thoughts were afflicted. All my deeds were pervaded by suffering. Because nothing surpassed that, I had no prospects beyond the ripening of karma in saṃsāra's three lower realms. That I came to see this was solely because the blessing of the Great Guru [Padmasambhava] entered my heart.

Works Cited

Bkra shis rab brtan, ed. 1991. *Rig 'dzin bdud 'joms rdo rje rol pa rtsal gyi rnam thar.* Xining: Mtsho sngon mi rigs dpe skrun khang.

Diemberger, Hildegard. 2007. *When a Woman Becomes a Religious Dynasty: The Samding Dorje Phagmo of Tibet.* New York: Columbia University Press.

Dreyfus, Georges B. J. 2003. *The Sound of Two Hands Clapping: The Education of a Tibetan Buddhist Monk.* Berkeley: University of California Press.

Gamble, Ruth. 2018. *Reincarnation in Tibet: The Third Karma pa and the Invention of a Tradition.* New York: Oxford University Press.

Gyatso, Janet. 1998. *Apparitions of the Self.* Princeton, NJ: Princeton University Press.

Hūṃ chen He ru ka [= Humchen Chenaktsang] et al., eds. 2010. *Kha rgya'i gter rgan rig 'dzin bdud 'joms rdo rje'i gsung 'bum.* Sngags mang dpe tshogs 16. Beijing: Mi rigs dpe skrun khang.

Kapstein, Matthew T. 1998. "A Tibetan Festival of Rebirth Reborn: The 1992 Revival of the Drigung Powa Chenmo." In *Buddhism in Contemporary Tibet: Religious Revival and Cultural Identity*, edited by Melvyn C. Goldstein and Matthew T. Kapstein, 95–119. Berkeley: University of California Press.

———. 2002. "The Sprul-sku's Miserable Lot: Critical Voices from Eastern Tibet." In *Proceedings of the Ninth Seminar of the International Association for Tibetan Studies: Amdo Studies,* edited by Toni Huber, 99–111. Leiden: Brill.

Ko shul Grags pa 'byung gnas and Rgyal ba Blo bzang mkhas grub. 1992. *Gangs can mkhas grub rim byon ming mdzod.* Lanzhou: Kan su'u mi rigs dpe skrun khang.

Nietupski, Paul Kocot. 2011. *Labrang Monastery: A Tibetan Buddhist Community on the Inner Asian Borderlands, 1709–1958.* Lanham, MD: Lexington Books.

Schwieger, Peter. 2015. *The Dalai Lama and the Emperor of China.* New York: Columbia University Press.

Auto/Biography for the End of the World: A Treasure Theory of Reading Revealed Life Stories

Elizabeth Angowski

I considered, too, how aptly Dickens had identified the strange potency of a great book—the way a book can insert itself into a reader's own history, into a reader's own life story, until it's hard to know what one would be without it.
—REBECCA MEAD, *My Life in Middlemarch*, 16

RECALLING A BIBLIOMEMOIR on *Middlemarch*, George Eliot's Victorian-era masterwork, might seem a curious way to begin an essay on treasure revelation and biographical writing in Tibet. But when I read Rebecca Mead's words above, I thought immediately of *Apparitions of the Self*, Janet Gyatso's landmark study on these topics and an enduring force in my life. Granted, *Apparitions* is a work of scholarship, not a novel, as Mead would no doubt expect her readers to envision when prompted to think of "a great book." Still, *Apparitions* is a great book, and it would be hard for me to know what I would be without it, or the author behind it. A future in which I wouldn't continue to feel the influence of both seems to me, moreover, hardly imaginable. It certainly isn't desirable. After all, what kind of uninspired life would that be to lead?

What follows will not be my own bibliomemoir, however much joy it would bring me to write one. Nevertheless, it will have everything to do with the potentially transformative effects of great works. More precisely, it will consider how certain Tibetan Buddhist life stories might become—or, at least, *aspire* to become—integral to a reader's own biographical thinking and being. In light of this volume's call to be creative, broadly accessible, and theoretically oriented, I present a *terma* (*gter ma*), or "treasure," theory of reading, one trained on revealed auto/biographies. My hope is that this approach—grounded in emic understandings of terma and informed by Euro-American literary theory—will demonstrate a productive way to think with the premises underlying treasure discovery, whatever one makes of the phenomenon as a whole or the claims of any treasure revealer (*gter ston*) in particular.

Reading Treasures, in Theory

Studies of treasure revelation in Tibet to date have taught us much about the making (or expanding) of religious histories, scriptural canons, and visionary careers. There is still a great deal more to learn about how the ideological mechanisms animating terma support the recognition of treasures and authenticate their discoverers.[1] Here, though, my goal is to see what, if anything, a theoretical consideration of treasure as a whole can tell us,[2] first and foremost, about the realization of literary worlds and the cultivation of readers in front of religious texts. In essence, I wonder what new avenues of inquiry open up if we shift our focus from the text-revealer relationship to the text-reader (or hearer) relationship.

At the broadest level, I am motivated by questions of textual agency. To wit: How does terma imagine a world for itself and its texts? What, or who, is supposed to populate that world? And what makes an ideal treasure-reader? The answers that revealed auto/biographies, as a subset of treasure texts, have for these questions interest me for a couple of reasons. First, and not least, I find such texts compelling because they are often richer in description than the more abundant pedagogic and practice-oriented texts.[3] Life stories are not the majority of texts rediscovered, yet such works often provide the reader with more information about what terma is and how it ought to be perceived.

But, beyond being troves of treasure-related information, revealed life stories are fascinating because *as treasures themselves*, they offer the literary analyst unique interpretive challenges, puzzles not only of form and classification but also of function—how religious texts work. In addition to questions like "Is this account an autobiography, a biography, or something in between?" or "What is a life story anyway, and when might it be told? What should it say? Who is it for?"[4] such rediscovered narratives urge us to ask, "When an instance of life writing is also a divinely inspired text, how should a reader engage with it?" Or, alternatively, "When a life story is a scripture—whatever that means—what then?"

1. On this topic, see especially Gyatso 1993.

2. To say "treasure as a whole" is to indicate that this essay will think alongside the logics underlying presentations of treasure revelation as a coherent phenomenon. Of course, the idea of treasure revelation as a unified tradition is just that, an idea. (On this point, see Hirshberg 2016, particularly 28–30.) Yet the effort here will be to see where the very ideas supporting and animating treasure can lead us.

3. Gyatso 1996, 149, and Thondup 1986, 186.

4. This series of questions is adapted from Cavell 2010, 186.

Typically, one sees the term *scripture* applied to treasures in ways that evoke the generic (as in classificatory), not necessarily the phenomenological, sense of the term.[5] That is, treasure texts are called *scriptures* for being written artifacts recognized by religious communities as sanctified or authoritative,[6] and the designation is certainly fitting insofar as they meet these criteria. Yet what it is to be or to act as a scripture in a three-dimensional sense is often only implied. In a word, generic senses of the term usually tell us little about texts' potential or actual roles in people's lives.

For this reason, a thorough exposition of what treasure thinks its texts can and should *do*—in tandem with what they actually do—strikes me as worth undertaking. In the long run, such a project could augment comparative studies of scripture as a global phenomenon. More immediately, though, we will see how, when one takes up the premises of treasure revelation as keys to reading and interpreting certain treasure texts, a revealed auto/biography can quickly become much more than a story of a single remarkable life.

Entering the Past's Future, An Ever-Degenerate Present

In narratives that depict Tibet's imperial period (seventh–ninth century) as a "golden age" during which Buddhism suffused the plateau, one finds powerful, idealized figures anticipating a far less halcyon future. Whatever else these story worlds convey, a degenerate age (*snyigs ma'i dus*) looms on the horizon. Soon, there will be widespread civil unrest. Monastery abbots will become army generals, epidemics will rage, and famine will lay waste to whole populations.[7] But all accounts agree that the most appalling thing imminent is the loss of authentic Dharma. During the end times (*dus mtha'*), Buddhist teachings, once so abundant, will have all but disappeared—unless larger-than-life heroes find some way to intervene.

For Padmasambhava, the eighth-century Indian Buddhist tantric adept popularly credited with converting Tibet, the answer to this problem of Dharma's wane is always clear. To curtail catastrophe and mitigate moral iniquity, Tibet's "Precious Guru" and his immediate disciples will conceal treasures, many in

5. See, e.g., Kunsang 2004, 3 and 4, and Thondup 1986, 61, 72, and 83. Doctor (2013, 43–44) notably cites Smith (1993) on "scripture as a human activity" where he discusses the processes by which treasures become perceived as valid scriptures. His point in that instance is about authentication practices, not readerly engagement, however. On readerly engagement with scriptures more broadly, see especially Hallisey 2004.

6. See Graham 2005.

7. Prophesies of what will happen during the degenerate age abound. For one example in translation, see Kunsang 2004, 138–39.

the form of texts.[8] Upon their rediscovery by qualified treasure revealers, these texts would subsequently ensure the propagation of the Dharma in perpetuity. Even if, as it happened, authentic teachings could no longer be imported directly from the Indian subcontinent—whether this was because some gurus were disinclined to trans-Himalayan travel or because they proved to be in short supply—wisdom from a bygone era of religious fervency could still come to light. With that, future generations might be spared the misfortunes certain to accompany widespread ignorance of the Buddha's teachings.

Since written accounts of Padmasambhava's efforts to conceal treasures did not appear in earnest until several centuries after the imperial period, narratives of treasure concealment do more to construct a past in retrospect—and a present *for* the present—than they do to represent historical events.[9] Still, imagining the guru mapping out his concealment plans in some detail is a useful exercise for outlining treasure's underlying terms. And so, as if by design, treasure could be characterized in the following way:

First, under the assumption that the Dharma would otherwise disappear, tantric Buddhist texts—broadly understood and construed, which is to say, various in content and form—would be hidden across the Tibetan plateau. Some might be physically concealed, buried in the ground or interred in rocks or pillars as "earth treasures" (*sa gter*); others could be mentally concealed in the mind streams of individuals as "mind treasures" (*dgongs gter*); and still more could be revealed when, during a "pure vision" (*dag snang*), a deity or guru offered a teaching.[10] Then, aided by various technologies of augury, treasure revealers would later rediscover teachings in specific places at precisely the right moment in time.[11] Finally, confidence-engendering and self-legitimating strategies would be embedded in the texts themselves.[12] A teaching's charge (to address a time of degeneracy) as well as its authority (conferred by Padmasambhava or another enlightened being) could, in other words, be referred to explicitly by a treasure text or corpus as part of its own account of what it is, where it came from, when it was discovered, and so on. Texts might not merely convey much-needed teachings, in other words. They could also express their own authority and establish that of their revealer in one and the same stroke.

8. Scholars writing about terma are often careful to note that treasures are not limited to texts and objects. On the "taxonomic richness of Treasure hermeneutics," see, e.g., Doctor 2013, 23.

9. On terma and constructions of the past, see Gayley 2007.

10. Thondup 1986, 60–62. On the matter of this tripartite rubric of earth, mind, and pure vision treasures as the now standard typology, see Hirshberg 2016, 28–31.

11. Thondup 1986, 63–64.

12. Gyatso 1993, 110, and Gyatso 1998, 153.

Particularly germane to our purposes in thinking about revealed auto/biographies is the fact that treasures rhetorically construct their relevance in time. The era in which an authentic treasure is discovered is, by the genre's definition, a time in need of that treasure, and an ideal reader should view their time—and themselves—as effectively impoverished, lacking in what is essential. Depending upon whom one asks, of course, this time-in-need could be a moment amid an age that is degenerate overall, or it could be an age degenerate only in certain regards. Basically, however, things are not going as they ought to whenever a treasure enters the scene. In fact, based on traditional theories of treasure concealment, one could even say that things are downright *unwell* when treasures appear. Without the Dharma, physical illnesses may tear through one's community. Epidemics may rage. But so, too, will spiritual disorders, such that a treasure receiver would be apt to consider themself, in every sense, living in disease.[13] With that, they might regard the Dharma, in the form of treasures, as a protective or even curative force.

Seeing Dharma as therapeutic or medicinal is a familiar trope. Dharma is frequently described as the medicine that the Buddha (likened to a doctor) administers to his disciples, who, as patients, incorporate it into their being. But we also see the analogy directly applied to treasure, particularly in contemporary introductions of treasure to Western audiences. For example, after citing the famed treasure revealer Jigmé Lingpa (1730–98) on the reasons for concealing treasures, Tulku Thondup (b. 1939) explains that treasure revealers reveal many different treasures "just as different medicine is given for different sicknesses."[14] More broadly, one could say treasure, as the force intent on saving defenseless beings,[15] provides a form of emergency services.

If one views treasure in this way, rhetorics of moral precarity, urgency, immediacy, and specificity ring out time and again as one reads treasure texts alongside broader discussions of treasure revelation as a phenomenon. Invariably, an authentic treasure will be revealed by the *right* person at *exactly* the *right* (*ergo* degenerate, diseased) time, and each treasure is *precisely* what is needed *straightaway* at the moment of discovery.[16] To be in that moment—i.e., to see a treasure appear in one's time, or retain access to it post-rediscovery—is to be susceptible to spiritual disease. It is to need the medicine that is the treasure's immediate—as in swift but also direct—relief.

13. Hallisey (2004, 35–36) observes and analyzes the call to view oneself as sick (and scripture as the remedy) in Patrul Rinpoché's *Words of My Perfect Teacher*.

14. Thondup 1986, 150.

15. Thondup 1986, 150.

16. See, e.g., Gyatso 1998, 151 and 154.

Whether a reader accepts the perils of their time, the threat to the Dharma's endurance, as their burden to bear, this remains treasure's claim. If one does take up that burden, however, one winds up with something more to ponder: the texts destined to be rediscovered in or sustained as relevant to your time were, at least in theory, destined for you.

A Clash of Subjectivities, or Corpora and Incorporation

It is not difficult to imagine how texts that present instructions for religious practice stand to meet needs—needs that, in treasure's case, a text might simultaneously anticipate and construct. A ritual manual tells the reader how to perform a ritual that will somehow mark or make a difference in the status quo. (By implication, a difference is required.) A text that instructs one in meditation offers the opportunity to obtain new, liberative insight. (Therefore new or more refined levels of insight are necessary.) The inscribed mantra, when recited, could provide protection from a malicious force. (Protection is vital.) And I think it is also fairly easy to imagine how philosophical and doctrinally focused texts could meet needs. In order to right the sinking ship of Dharma, knowledge might need to be (re)gained, nuanced, clarified; current norms and values might need to be upheld, revised, or contested, and so on. Less clear—or, better, more open to interpretation—is how an instance of life writing could prove essential, especially in the corrective or curative sense. How or why might someone *need* the life story of another?

Many good responses to this question are possible. Some obvious answers advanced in treasure texts have to do with "proof" (of both provenance and power) and with the generation of faith and inspiration. Stories that richly elaborate the imperial past and celebrate the personalities at its helm seek to bolster confidence in the vitality and authority of those personalities. Similarly, audiences might benefit from seeing doctrinal ideals brought to life. Reading how an extraordinary life was lived in light of the Dharma, one's faith might increase; one might experience joy in knowing that someone lived that way; one might even be moved to live accordingly.

The list could certainly go on, but apart from whatever attitudes or actions a source may encourage, treasure first and foremost has the readers see themselves as vulnerable. Remarkably, the solution to overcoming vulnerability (i.e., defenselessness in the face of Dharma's wane) is to embrace susceptibility to whatever treasures may appear. Imagine, for a moment, that an ideal reader accepts that she is mired in her degenerate age, and she acknowledges that a revealed life story can potentially remedy her situation. "But how exactly could this be so?" she wonders. "What are my circumstances such that this story can help *me*?" Turning to the text for insight, she continues: "Well, what does it say? What speaks to me readily and what doesn't? Where I don't immediately hear myself and my circumstances addressed, shouldn't I? Let me take another look."

If a reader approaches a life story with treasure's premises in mind, then the process of interpretation stands to become dialogic. In practice, it might also be recurring and mutually illuminating. If she looks again, the reader might find fresh cause for self-evaluation in light of the text, or in light of her life's changing circumstances, she might find the impetus to revisit and reinterpret the text. Whatever the case, the cyclical process could bring text and reader not just into proximity but into an intimate relationship. One not only encounters the text but attempts to integrate it into oneself, as one takes the right medicine dose after dose. And as time and subjectivities are bridged, we notice, too, that transmissions indeed become direct—so close that the reader's guiding question might be revised along transpersonal lines: "What if the key to understanding and interpreting my life was yours?"

Without a Refuge in the World?

An instance of this process is modeled in the *Testimonial Record of Padmasambhava* (*Pad ma bka' thang*), perhaps the most well-known account of Padmasambhava's life and teaching-related activities in Tibet.[17] Tradition attributes the discovery of this 108-chapter text to the fourteenth-century treasure revealer Orgyen Lingpa (b. 1323), while its recording and concealment are attributed to Yeshé Tsogyal (eighth century), Padmasambhava's disciple and consort, who, having obtained the power to recall everything she had ever seen and heard, preserved her guru's life story for the sake of future generations.

The *Testimony* is traditionally understood to be an auto/biography hybrid, though it is relayed primarily in the biographical mode. It is one teacher's story as he told it to, and lived it in front of, a disciple, who now retells it and elaborates upon it. That is, in her role as narrator, Yeshé Tsogyal is moved to weave some of her own autobiographical details into the story.

At the end of the *Testimony* we find a précis of her life. Several of Padmasambhava's disciples are lingering together in sorrow and disbelief following their guru's departure from Tibet. A collective sense of abandonment charges the scene, and Yeshé Tsogyal speaks to the grief-stricken crowd, expressing her profound sense of loss but amplifying the significance of Padmasambhava's departure in the grander scheme. "E ma ho!" she begins, calling out to her absent guru as if he were still within earshot, and then utters an anguished soliloquy:

17. O rgyan gling pa 2006.

O Lotus-Born festooned with many good qualities,
you have for countless eons upheld the ways of the buddhas
and passed among manifestations over many births.
Born as Mārirāja prior to his birth here,
the king of Jambudvīpa, Tri Songdetsen,
an emanation of Mañjuśrī, invited you here to his pure land.
So, you came to Tibet. After thirteen years had passed,
to a father named Drakpa Namkha Yeshé
and a mother named Nupmo Gewabum,
in a wood-hen year, I, Tsogyal, was born.
In a fire-hen year, I met you, O Lord.
I obtained the *dhāraṇī* of total recall, and all the things required of a disciple.
Until I was eighty-five, I lived a life of service to you.
I had no children, neither sons nor daughters;
I was a nun, untainted by worldly imperfections.
Three-bodied lama, Pema Jungné:
You gazed upon the whole Tibetan landscape and suffused it with compassion.
You were extremely gracious to the king and all his subjects.
You blessed every rocky hermitage.
You showered Dharma upon every fortunate being.
To the wise you taught every vehicle,
to every vessel you conferred instructions thoroughly.
Upon the devout you made blessings shine like the sun,
and to those with felicitous karma, you foretold the future.
O Lotus-Born, whose compassion is unbiased,
you departed for Ngayab Ling to tame its demons
on the tenth day, when the heroes and *ḍākas* gather.
Like a cloud or a rainbow, you vanished into the sky.
What distance have you created from your devoted Tsogyal?
The refuge and protector of the degenerate age, Pema Jungné, has gone!
Without a refuge in the world, sentient beings have been abandoned.
The Second Buddha, Pema Jungné, has departed;
faithful Tsogyal is left behind![18]

Two aspects of this passage bear analysis: its tone and its shifts in narrative focus. As to tone, it is worth noting that the chapter's title deems its contents

18. O rgyan gling pa 2006, 576–77, my translation.

"an expression of devotion" (*mos gus brjed byang*). Overall, this is an accurate description, but readers expecting a joyful hymn or paean will find the chapter rather melancholy. From the outset, Yeshé Tsogyal's words create an atmosphere that is mournful and palpably tense. As she calls to Padmasambhava, her lines build with increasing desperation. At times, we also find her so vexed by her circumstances she becomes openly accusatory. While above, Yeshé Tsogyal states that she and all others have been "abandoned" (*shul du bzhag*) by their guru, later in the chapter, she will describe Tibetans as "fatherless orphans" (*pha med dwa phrug*) in the wake of his departure.[19] Across the eulogy, the message is that with Padmasambhava gone, sentient beings have not only lost a beloved teacher, they are also in imminent danger. Deprived of the refuge of the "Second Buddha," who can deny that the degenerate age has come?

To the degree that the reader finds themself aligned with Yeshé Tsogyal throughout this chapter—that is, insofar as they also inhabit this vulnerable position, shot through with grief at a loss of refuge—they might begin to recognize themself as similarly bereft, likewise stranded in an era awaiting a resurgence of hope. We can imagine the *Testimony* not only seeking to inform readers about Padmasambhava and his miraculous deeds, then, but also encouraging self-reflection and an emotional response: "If the guru's immediate disciples felt so distraught without him, how much more distraught should I be given that I stand at an even greater remove?" Whatever other thoughts and sentiments arise, the space that Yeshé Tsogyal's words open is one where Padmasambhava's absence is acutely felt. Fortunately for the bereft, it is also the space that treasures, like life stories, promise to fill.

As to shifts in focus, what I mean primarily is how and when Yeshé Tsogyal inserts herself within the context of evoking her teacher. Prior to introducing herself, she addresses the physically absent Padmasambhava as if he were present, and notably, she begins by conjuring him as he exists in a cosmic, ahistorical capacity. (Padmasambhava is not only a guru possessed of many good qualities but an enlightened being—an upholder of the buddhas' ways—born many times over countless eons.) Next, we see Yeshé Tsogyal situate Padmasambhava in history within Tibet. Via the invitation of emperor Tri Songdetsen (742–ca. 800), a figure also depicted as largely otherworldly, Padmasambhava, a being seemingly outside of time, touched down within it. Before narrating any of his deeds in Tibet, however, Yeshé Tsogyal cuts from his arrival to the specific, conspicuously mundane details of her parentage and birth. From there, she outlines her life of discipleship and devotion. Only after this does she proclaim Padmasambhava's compassionate acts in service of all Tibetans.

19. O rgyan gling pa 2006, 579.

It seems as if—from the depths of her despair and in an effort to capture the full extent of her loss—Yeshé Tsogyal cannot help but make her beloved guru's departure about herself.

Plotted in this way, the shift from cosmic guru to individual disciple might seem abrupt or surprising. The lines leading up to Yeshé Tsogyal's statement about her birth and parentage could have easily proceeded seamlessly onward with the *alls* and *everys* that emphasize the pervasiveness and impartiality of Padmasambhava's compassionate deeds. Instead, Yeshé Tsogyal inserts her own story. The reader is not treated to even a single line about what might have transpired during the thirteen years Padmasambhava spent in Tibet before she was born.

How can we make sense of Yeshé Tsogyal's move from the transhistorical to her own vitae? Perhaps she simply does not see the need to review Padmasambhava's early days in Tibet in summary. After all, the previous chapters of the *Testimony* covered that. And maybe in her grief, she feels bewildered. A jump in her narration could mimetically suggest disorientation and scattered thinking. Or perhaps the start of the last chapter is simply a good place to remind the reader who the narrator is, how close a devotee of the story's subject she was, how flawless her memory is (such that she could tell his story accurately), and how committed to him and his teachings she remains. In a word, one could say that by including her life when and where she does, Yeshé Tsogyal offers up her story as an especially personal testimony within the larger *Testimony* to Padmasambhava's greatness. All that she, an utterly devoted adept, has seen and felt and accomplished is submitted in evidence for the power of her guru and the profundity of his loss.

The latter reading is an especially compelling argument, well supported in various ways by the text. Still, in our analysis, I think we might do better not to leave the reader in despair.

Let's say, then, that the reader should not be at all surprised by the way the passage shifts from the evocation of a cosmic guru to the details of Yeshé Tsogyal's own life. One could simply accept the structure as a natural, intentional progression *for her*. That is, Yeshé Tsogyal has the important points follow one another in what she takes to be their proper succession. Perhaps this is how she always tells her own story from the start; her life with her guru begins in earnest well before her birth, eons ago. Perhaps a cradle-to-grave account would not convey nearly enough. Or maybe the shift from the emperor's invitation to Yeshé Tsogyal's life indicates for the reader just how intimate the relationship between guru and disciple should be. At this particular moment, deep in her mourning, perhaps Yeshé Tsogyal feels like Padmasambhava might as well have bided his time before she became his disciple. As far as she is concerned, his arrival in Tibet was for her sake alone.

Conclusion

This passage marks the only time in the 108 chapters of the *Testimony* that Yeshé Tsogyal speaks at length about who she is and how she understands her situation. Of course, readers already familiar with Padmasambhava's exploits might bring some knowledge of her life to the text, and so one could argue that the information Yeshé Tsogyal provides here functions mnemonically to encourage recollection of her larger backstory, not to present anything new or noteworthy.

Still, why here? Why now, at the end of this life of Padmasambhava, does Yeshé Tsogyal feel compelled to throw into relief who she is? Reminding the reader of her commitment to her guru and the profundity of her devotion might make Padmasambhava's abandonment seem all the more egregious. But along with that, it strikes me that the point of underscoring that she was an exemplary disciple might be just that. That is, the important thing could be to emphasize that she can serve as an example—one who now, with the object of her devotion gone, models above all how to grieve. If this is the case, and if a reader, aligned with Yeshé Tsogyal in both her devotion and her grief, also sees fit to align themself with her in terms of her thoughts and actions upon Padmasambhava's departure, they could be moved to reevaluate—or to reread—their own life in terms of his. "Padmasambhava came to Tibet out of compassion for all sentient beings," one might agree, "but like Yeshé Tsogyal, I should consider what that means for me."

What, exactly, it does mean will no doubt vary based on the person, time, place, and so on. But the treasure would have Padmasambhava's revealed life story mean something for every individual. As to what, if anything, the *Testimony* encourages its readers to do, for starters, they might embrace Padmasambhava's biography, as a whole or in parts, as not merely relevant to them but also integral to how they imagine their own trajectory. Ideally, as in the case of Yeshé Tsogyal, it should someday be hard to know what one would be without it. For even if we do not always read as if our lives (or *Life*) depended on it, or as if the world were ending, treasure would have its readers recognize that great books, or great *Lives*, are nothing if not potent opportunities for revision, or transformation, where stories and subjectivities converge.

Works Cited

Cavell, Stanley. 2010. *Little Did I Know: Excerpts from Memory*. Stanford, CA: Stanford University Press.

Doctor, Andreas. 2013. *Tibetan Treasure Literature: Revelation, Tradition, and Accomplishment in Visionary Buddhism*. Boston: Snow Lion Publications.

Gayley, Holly. 2007. "Ontology of the Past and Its Materialization in Tibetan Treasures." In *The Invention of Sacred Tradition*, edited by James R. Lewis and Olav Hammer, 213–40. Cambridge: Cambridge University Press.

Graham, William A. 2005. "Scripture." In *Encyclopedia of Religion*, 2nd ed., edited by Lindsay Jones, 12: 8194–8205. Detroit: MacMillan Reference.

Gyatso, Janet. 1993. "The Logic of Legitimation in the Tibetan Treasure Tradition." *History of Religions* 33.2: 97–134.

———. 1996. "Drawn from the Tibetan Treasury: The gTer Ma Literature." In *Tibetan Literature: Studies in Genre*, edited by Jose Ignacio Cabezon and Roger R. Jackson, 147–69. Ithaca, N.Y: Snow Lion.

———. 1998. *Apparitions of the Self: The Secret Autobiographies of a Tibetan Visionary*. Princeton, NJ: Princeton University Press.

———. 2006. "A Partial Genealogy of the Lifestory of Ye shes mtsho rgyal." *Journal of the International Association of Tibetan Studies* 2 (August): 1–27.

Hallisey, Charles. 2004. "The Surprise of Scripture's Advice." In *Religious Identity and the Problem of Historical Foundation: The Foundational Character of Authoritative Sources in the History of Christianity and Judaism*, edited by Judith Frishman, Willemien Otten, and Gerard Rouwhorst, 28–44. Leiden and Boston: Brill.

Hirshberg, Daniel. 2016. *Remembering the Lotus-Born: Padmasambhava in the History of Tibet's Golden Age*. Somerville, MA: Wisdom Publications.

Kunsang, Erik Pema, trans. 2004. *The Lotus-Born: The Life Story of Padmasambhava*. 3rd ed. Hong Kong: Rangjung Yeshe Publications.

Mead, Rebecca. 2015. *My Life in Middlemarch*. New York: Broadway Books.

O rgyan gling pa. 2006. *Testimonial Record of Padmasambhava* (*Pad ma bka' thang*). Chengdu: Si khron mi rigs dpe skrun khang.

Smith, Wilfred Cantwell. 1993. *What Is Scripture? A Comparative Approach*. Minneapolis: Fortress Press.

Thondup, Tulku. 1986. *Hidden Teachings of Tibet: An Explanation of the Terma Tradition of the Nyingma School of Buddhism*. London: Wisdom Publications.

A Biography of Zur Chöying Rangdröl by the Fifth Dalai Lama

Samten G. Karmay

THE FIFTH DALAI LAMA (1617–82), hereafter Losang Gyatso, was one of the most prolific writers of biographies in the seventeenth century. His collected works contain twelve biographies. The subjects of these biographies are mostly his contemporary religious masters of the Nyingma (Rnying ma), Sakya (Sa skya), and Geluk (Dge lugs) schools as well as those of his two predecessors, the Third and Fourth Dalai Lamas. He also wrote an account of his own life, commonly known as the *Dukula*.[1]

Here I would like to focus on the *namthar* (*rnam thar*) by Losang Gyatso of Zur Chöying Rangdröl (1604–57), *Chariot of the Supreme Vehicle* (*Theg mchog bstan pa'i shing rta*), and particularly on Zur's activities as a painter of thangkas (thang ka) and as a specialist in tantric rites. Zur was a Nyingma monk highly skilled in painting and performing Buddhist rituals. He was also the head lama of the monastery at Tsal Gungthang, which was originally, of course, a Kagyü (Bka' rgyud) establishment. It was founded by Lama Zhang (1123–93), who Losang Gyatso regarded as one of Zur's former births.

Losang Gyatso considered Nyingma rituals indispensable in dealing with opponents in his time. However, the Geluk school in general looked upon the Nyingma ritual practices as unacceptable. In his youth, Losang Gyatso was often asked to perform rituals to avert calamities such as war, but his knowledge of how to perform rites was slight, and he struggled to find rites in his own tradition appropriate to a given situation. When he turned to the Nyingma masters, Desi Sönam Rabten (1595–1658), his treasurer, would disapprove of it. Here I quote a passage from his autobiography that reveals his frustration with this hindrance:

> Zhal-ngo [i.e., the future Desi] never liked me performing violent rites. He would not allow me to meet a lama I wished to take as a master. I thought that for the time being it would be hard to find

1. For the full title see the references.

> someone from whom I could get a complete teaching of tantric initiations and rites, but I never gave up hope. I really thought I would be [for the time being] nothing but a preceptor of verbosity.[2]

This was when the Dalai Lama was twenty-one and was simply the abbot of Drepung Monastery. It was in this context that Losang Gyatso tells a story. In a dream, he was receiving teachings from Nyingma masters, and some Geluk monks including the Desi were glaring at him from outside a window, looking shocked. At that moment Changdak Tashi Topgyal (1550–1603), a great Nyingma master, handed him a ritual dagger, and with it he frightened off the Geluk monks.[3] Losang Gyatso tells this story to explain why he had kept a ritual dagger in his belt since the age of twenty-six, when he had this dream. The anecdote illustrates the sectarian wariness of the Geluk.

The position of Zur was delicate. Losang Gyatso laments: "Zur knew that Desi Sönam Rabten profoundly disliked him because he belonged to a different school and would never do him any favors beyond mere civility. Despite this, Zur performed rituals for the benefit of the Desi's strategies whenever there were conflicts. Zur did so over a long period and also performed rituals that would help the Desi remove obstacles in his life and gave him protective amulets."[4]

Losang Gyatso was both a master and a pupil of Zur and was therefore well acquainted with him. Beyond the connection around Nyingma rituals, he obviously had firsthand knowledge of the life of Zur through personal contact and collaboration on various projects. His biography of Zur is unlike those of the Third and Fourth Dalai Lamas, which are perhaps inevitably rather sketchy. He wrote Zur's biography at the Potala and finished writing it in 1676, nineteen years after Zur's death. Several people urged him to do it. Among these were Zur's chief disciple, Losang Pema Trinlé (1640–1718), the second head lama of Dorjé Drak Monastery, and particularly Agur and his brother Ngakben Ngawang Trinlé of Zhikashar House. (Of these two we have more below.) Losang Gyatso states that he had already intended to compose the biography well before the requests came. He also states that his account was mainly based

2. *Dukula* (174): *zhal ngo drag las la mi mnyes shing bla ma gang 'dod kyang bsten chog rigs min 'dug pas/ da cha sngags phyogs kyi smin grol las tshogs sogs mtha' chod pa tshang mar zhus rnyed dka' snyam re ba bskyangs te tha snyad mkhan po rang zhig byed pa'i blo rtse bstad/.*

3. Karmay 1998, 15.

4. Gang shar, *Zur gyi rnam thar*, 206b: *mi dbang bsod nams rab brtan grub mtha'i dbang gis zhal mdzes tsam las gting nas ye mi dgyes pas sha tshar (tsha) bcar ba'i thugs 'dogs mi gnang ba mkhyen rung bde gzar snga phyi bar gsum tshang mar las sbyor gyi sku rim dang sde ba'i sku tshe bar chad sel byed kyi srung 'khor 'bul ba.*

on a manuscript scroll containing records of Zur's life kept by Agur and Ngawang Trinlé. The tantrist Trogyal Palgön, another close disciple of Zur, had brought it up to date.

Nevertheless, Losang Gyatso follows the traditional pattern of Tibetan life-writing. He starts with an account of the old Zur clan and its family lineage in considerable detail. Before beginning his account of Zur's life, he also gives a stereotypical enumeration of the supposed previous births of Zur, beginning with a disciple of the Buddha, continuing through famous Tibetan figures of the imperial period, and including prestigious clerics of later centuries.

Zur Chöying Rangdröl was born into the Zur family, whose contribution to the development of the Nyingma tradition was seminal, but at the same time he spent his youth in Tsethang Monastery, studying the Buddhist philosophy of the monastic tradition. In spite of this Geluk education, he remained a staunchly Nyingma practitioner and had deep knowledge of the magic rituals of the Nyingma tradition, which he had learned mainly from his father in his youth. It was this knowledge that attracted Losang Gyatso when the latter was young and under pressure from Desi Sönam Rabten, who was unfairly pushing him to demonstrate whatever magic skill he might have to defeat their political opponents. This was in the period of the conflict in 1641 and 1642.

The biography is special in many ways. It largely employs Nyingma terminology such as *khorling* (see below) to describe the activities of Zur as an artist, an astrologer, and an adept in ritual magic. Elsewhere Losang Gyatso reproaches Geluk writers who ignore the specialized Nyingma vocabulary when dealing with Nyingma material. The chronology in this biography is less rigorous than in his autobiography, but the work is set within a framework of dates that helps us to track the timeline fairly precisely. The text notes both the successes and failures of Zur's projects, so that Losang Gyatso does not seem to be very selective, in contrast to the uniformly triumphal accounts that are a distinctive feature of Tibetan *namthar*. Inevitably, there are gaps and events not recorded, but because Losang Gyatso was both a disciple and master of Zur, he was uniquely well situated to make observations about Zur's life.

Apart from being a Nyingma master, Zur was also, as mentioned above, the head of Tsal Gungthang, a monastery originally of the Kagyü school. He became the head of the monastery in 1633, but the process of this accession is unclear in the biography. He remained its head until his death in 1657 and carried out much of the renovation of the monastery. At the same time, he was almost continuously involved in Losang Gyatso's artistic and ritual projects that invariably required him spend much of his time in residence at Gaden Phodrang in Drepung, and hence in a Geluk monastery. Zur, like Losang Gyatso, was a disciple of Khöntön Paljor Lhundrup (1561–1637), a great Nyingma master who was the head of the Phabongkha hermitage near Sera Monastery and had a teaching duty in this Geluk monastery. It was in the presence of this lama that Losang Gyatso first met Zur, in 1629, when Losang Gyatso was only twelve. In 1631 Zur was invited to Drepung to draw amulets that the young Losang Gyatso was supposed to wear. Zur was often called in to carry out the rituals that Losang Gyatso himself presided over. The rituals they performed mostly belonged to the tradition established by Changdak Tashi Topgyal (1550–1603). In 1640, during the New Year celebration, Zur performed a magic ritual at Gaden Phodrang in Drepung that Losang Gyatso describes: "For the New Year celebration, the lama carried out the Molten Metal Lord of Death (*gshin rje khro chu*) ritual for seven days. When it came time to hurl the *torma* (*gtor ma*), his complexion changed from its usual aspect to dark brown and looked magnificent."[5] This is the only place in the entire biography where a sort of description of Zur is given; there is no other remark whatsoever on his physical characteristics.

Zur had taken to drawing from the age of six.[6] Losang Gyatso states that at the age of seventeen, Zur had vowed to paint a thangka with a hundred figures of Amitāyus and another with a hundred figures of Tārā every year until his death. There is no mention in the biography of whether he fulfilled this resolution. However, he certainly painted thangkas of the life of Padmasambhava,[7] and the biography is full of references to his other artistic activities. I should mention that Zur was certainly the inspirational source of the paintings—especially the magic circles (*cakra*) and the human effigies (*liṅga*)—in the Gold Manuscript of the Lionel Fournier Collection, which I had the good fortune to publish in 1988 (e.g., Karmay 1988, plates 22–24). These magic circles and effigies are known as *khorling* (*'khor ling*), an abbreviation of the words *'khor lo* and *liṅga*.[8] The artist of the paintings in the Gold Manuscript was the aforementioned Agur of Zhikashar House, who is also known as Guru Tamdrin. He and his younger brother Ngakben Ngawang Trinlé were both tantrists connected with the Zur clan.

Their home, Zhikashar House, was a kind of workshop for painting thangkas in Lhasa in the seventeenth century. The house is not mentioned in the Gold Manuscript, but the *namthar* indicates that the paintings in the Gold Man-

5. Gang shar, *Zur gyi rnam thar*, 124a: *lo gsar dus rim la gshin rje khro chu'i sgrub zhag bdun dang bcas te zor las gnang ba'i tshe sku mdog kyang rgyun dang mi 'dra bar smug nag tu 'gyur zhing lta bar mi bzod pa'i gzi byin dang bcas.*

6. Gang shar, *Zur gyi rnam thar*, 113a.

7. Gang shar, *Zur gyi rnam thar*, 84a.

8. Gang shar, *Zur gyi rnam thar*, 132a.

uscript were painted in 1673 by Agur of Zhikashar House. The two brothers were both highly skilled painters and prominent disciples of Zur. Their home in Lhasa also served as a guesthouse for lamas visiting from far away, especially Nyingma lamas such as Yölmo Tulku Tenzin Norbu (1589–1644) and Gamnyön Tulku Chakdor Norbu.[9] It was the place where Zur painted many thangkas and often stopped when he passed through Lhasa. This house remained intact until the 1940s, as shown on the map of Lhasa made in 1948 by Peter Aufschnaiter, where it is marked as Ga no. 26.[10]

The official residence of Losang Gyatso in Lhasa was Gaden Khangsar which was built by the noble family Gaden in the sixteenth century. He would also sometimes stay in the Zhikashar House. Gaden Khangsar House is also shown on Peter Aufschnaiter's map as Cha no. 106, just south of the Ramoché Temple.[11] Zur would often meet Losang Gyatso in Gaden Khangsar when the latter was in Lhasa.

Zur's participation as the ritual master when the construction work on the Potala Palace began was regarded as crucial. Losang Gyatso states:

> Construction of the palace on Red Hill (Dmar po ri) began in 1645. First, the lama came to Drepung and stayed there for a few days. Then we both, master and pupil, went together to pacify the ground for the construction. Every morning the lord made offerings to the eight kinds of gods and demons so that they would be harmoniously disposed. On the twenty-eight of the third month (April 24), he performed the ritual of the soil master to mark the lines on the ground (for the construction work) in accordance with the tantras.[12]

Concurrently the Lokeśvara image, which was carried away from Marpori first to Amdo and then to Kham, was finally returned from its wanderings thanks to the efforts of Dalai Kunchi Gyalmo, the senior wife of Gushri Khan (1582–1654). However, there were signs that ghosts might have come with it. Losang Gyatso states: "Zur, adorning himself with the fierce apparel of the

9. Gang shar, *Zur gyi rnam thar*, 178a.

10. Larsen and Sinding-Larson 2001, 29.

11. Larsen and Sinding-Larsen 2001, 29.

12. Gang shar, *Zur gyi rnam thar*, 144a–144b: *shing mo bya lo dmar po rir pho brang gsar bzheng sgo dod pa'i thog mar rje bla ma 'bras spungs su phebs zhag shas bzhugs nas nged dpon slob phyogs mtshungs su sa 'dul la po ta lar byon/ rje nyid kyis lha srin sde brgyad cha mnyam pa'i ched du rgyags rngan gyi cho ga zhogs star dang/ hor zla gsum pa'i nyer brgyad kyi nyin phyag bstar nas rgyud sde'i dgongs don bzhin sa bdag lto 'phye'i thig 'debs gnang/.*

deity Blood Drinker (*khrag 'thung*), performed rituals to exorcise nonhumans beyond the oceans, to suppress obnoxious spirits down below, to hide the treasure vase, and to effect hail protection in the higher ground, and he performed many other activities that brought blessing and luck to the great palace."[13]

In 1657, Zur came to Drepung and stayed there for two months, giving teachings to Losang Gyatso. He also began to draw a map of Tibet based on a manuscript that had been "revealed" for clarity by Ogyen Lingpa (b. 1323). Losang Gyatso states that it was a very large painting, showing Tibet as a she-demon lying on her back.[14] In the same year, 1657, Zur died at Gaden Phodrang in Drepung. His remains were cremated in Chimphu, near Samyé.

Figure 1. Master Chöying Rangdröl. Paris, Musée Guimet, MA5244. Photo © MNAAG, Paris, Dist. RMN-Grand Palais / Michel Urtado

13. Gang shar, *Zur gyi rnam thar*, 145a: *dpal chen khrag 'thung drag por khros pa'i chas su zhugs te bgegs skrod gnang bas mi ma yin gyi tshogs rgya mtsho' pha mthar bskrad/ rmang zhabs su dgra 'dre gnon pa/ stod du bum gter dang sel (ser) srung 'jug pa sogs pho brang chen po bkra shis dge legs kyis khyab pa'i phrin las mang du gnang'/.*

14. Gang shar, *Zur gyi rnam thar*, 208a.

Works Cited

Western Language Sources

Karmay, Samten G. 1988. *Secret Visions of the Fifth Dalai Lama*. London: Serindia Publications. Reprint edition 1998.

———. 2014. *The Illusive Play: The Autobiography of the Fifth Dalai Lama*. Chicago: Serindia Publications.

Larsen, Knud, and Amund Sinding-Larsen. 2001. *The Lhasa Atlas*. London: Serindia Publications.

Tibetan Language Sources

Gang shar rang grol (aka Ngag dbang blo bzang rgya mtsho). *Zur thams cad mkhyen pa chos dbyings rang grol gyi rnam thar theg mchog bstan pa'i shing rta*. I used a Bhutanese edition that indicates neither the name of the publisher nor the name of the place where it is published. However, a reproduction of the Lhasa blockprint can be found at BDRC.io: *The Collected Works (Gsung-'bum) of Vth Dalai Lama, Ngag-dbang blo-bzang rgya-mtsho*, vol. 9, text no. II (W294-1814-eBook.pdf). Gangtok: Sikkim Research Institute of Tibetology, 1992.

Ngag dbang blo bzang rgya mtsho. *Dukula—Ngag dbang blo bzang rgya mtsho'i rnam thar, Za hor gyi ban de ngag dbang blo bzang rgya mtsho'i 'di snang 'khrul ba'i rol rtsed rtogs brjod kyi tshul du bkod pa duku la'i gos bzang*, vols. 1–3. Lhasa: Bod ljongs mi dmangs dpe skrun khang, 1989.

The Eleven Acts of Padmasambhava

Kurtis R. Schaeffer

"[I]t is difficult to compose his complete life story. . ."
—GURU CHÖWANG

Introduction: Opening Anecdote

RATNA LINGPA (1403–78), in his *Great History of Treasure*, tells us a story about the *Eleven Acts of Padmasambhava*:

> Once when I was twenty-seven years old, on the morning of the tenth day of the summer month (around the year 1429), I was on the north end of my village taking care of the cows in the green pasture. And I was making a copy of the *Eleven Acts of Orgyen Rinpoché*. I had drunk a lot of beer in the archery competition the night before. I was feeling bad! And in the midst of copying out the text, I fell asleep. I awoke to find that an old Khampa beggar had approached me. From his hat to his boots, he was clothed only in yellow cotton. He glanced at my unfinished copy of the text. "This story is the treasure of Guru Chöwang," he said. "Do you have singular faith in Padmasambhava?"
>
> "I do have singular faith in Padmasambhava!" I replied.

This encounter with the yellow-clad beggar from Kham leads to Ratna Lingpa's first treasure discovery.[1] The scene also points us to an important text in the history of Padmasambhava narratives that has until recently been inaccessible or unnoticed. This is none other than the *Eleven Acts of Orgyen Rinpoché*, a text attributed by tradition and contemporary scholarship to Guru Chöwang (1212–70). The eleven acts of Padmasambhava are a variation on the twelve acts of Śākyamuni Buddha,[2] tailored to meet the distinctive powers, career, and

1. Ratna gling pa, *Gter 'byung chen mo*, 69–70. This passage is mentioned in Blondeau 1992.

2. See Doney 2019a, 1203, for more remarks on the eleven acts, and the article more generally for an overview of narrative and liturgical literature about Padmasambhava.

charisma of Padmasambhava. While the twelve acts of the Buddha became a popular structure for Tibetan narratives of the Buddha's life, the *Eleven Acts of Guru Rinpoché* is one of only a few narratives of Padmasambhava that relies heavily on them, there being other rubrics to choose from to organize a treatment of Guru Rinpoché's story. Like the twelve acts of the Buddha, Padmasambhava's eleven acts appear to have been popular in liturgical and devotional verse.

In brief, the eleven acts are, according to Guru Chöwang's work:

1. The intention to civilize living beings
2. Entry into the lotus womb—that is, gestation
3. Spontaneous birth in Danakośa
4. Playing as a prince
5. Ordination in Zahor and completion of mental purifications
6. Mental and physical training in snowy mountains and retreats
7. Taming gods and demons
8. Enlightenment
9. Using all paths to turn the wheel of Dharma everywhere
10. Undergoing extreme spiritual practices of all sorts
11. Hiding treasures of the Buddhist teachings[3]

The opening verses of the *Eleven Acts* place these deeds in context of the reader or listener's soteriological goals:

> Guru of Orgyen, Padmasambhava—child of every victor throughout all space and time, in whom every enlightened quality and action of body, speech, and mind, are combined, a lord eternally without equal in this worldly realm—is indisputably known from the Buddha's scriptures to be an enlightened emanation. So it is difficult to compose his complete life story. Nevertheless, were I to briefly describe his life and enlightenment for learning purposes, there are these eleven acts, after the fashion of the acts of the victor's children: (1) the intention to civilize living beings, (2) entry into the lotus womb, (3) spontaneous birth, (4) play as a prince, (5) ordination, (6) austerities, (7) defeating demons, (8) enlightenment and

3. Gu ru Chos kyi dbang phyug, *Mdzad pa bcu gcig ma* B, chapter titles: (1) *'gro 'dul dgongs pa*; (2) *padma'i snying por lhum su zhugs pa*; (3) *dri med ko sha'i mtsho gling du rang byung du sku bltams pa*; (4) *rgyal sras rol rtsed*; (5) *za hor yul du rab tu byung nas blo sbyangs rdzogs pa*; (6) *gangs dang ri khrod du dka' thub sna tshogs*; (7) *lha srin dregs pa can bdud sde dpung bcas btul ba*; (8) *mngon par byang chub*; (9) *theg pa mtha' yas kyis chos 'khor phyogs bcur bskor ba*; (10) *brtul zhugs kyi spyod pa phyogs med du mdzad pa*; (11) *sangs rgyas kyi bstan pa mtha' rgyas gter sbed kyi phrin las.*

> buddhahood, (9) turning the wheel of Dharma, (10) yogic practice, (11) hiding treasure to extend the life of the teaching. If the story of Orgyen is summarized in this way, whoever writes it, sees it, hears it, or teaches it to others will be reborn from this world into the Pure Land. Whoever has faith in this story and takes up its charge will doubtless achieve unsurpassed enlightenment as a buddha. Therefore, through the composition of these eleven acts, all the hopes for fortunate karma will be fulfilled.[4]

While there are variations in the order and scenes that make up the eleven acts throughout the total corpus of narrative and devotional literature using the rubric,[5] the *Eleven Acts of Guru Rinpoché* shares its list with that included within Orgyen Lingpa's (b. 1323) *Minister's Testament* (*Blon po'i bka' thang*) a part of the larger anthology of imperial history and lore the *Five Testaments* (*Bka' thang sde lnga*), which quotes this verse passage almost verbatim.[6]

The Work

In broadest terms, the themes of the *Eleven Acts* are good versus evil, the establishment of cosmic order, and the embodiment of that order in both the deeds of Padmasambhava and the mythic landscape in which he works. The setting

4. Gu ru Chos kyi dbang phyug, *Mdzad pa bcu gcig ma* B, 1b–2a: *phyogs bcu dus bzhi rgyal ba thams cad kyis <kyi>/ sku gsung thugs yon 'phrin las thams cad 'dus pa'i sras/ u rgyan gu ru padma 'byung gnas te/ dus gsum 'jig rten khams* [2a] *'dir mtshungs med rje/ rgyal ba'i bka' las rtsod bral sprul skur grags/ de phyir rnam thar yongs rdzogs bkod dka' yang/ thos pas <pa'i> byang chub rnam thar mdo bshad na/ rgyal sras mdzad tshul bcu gcig 'di lta ste/ 'gro 'dul dgongs mdzad pad ma'i lhums zhugs mdzad/ rang byung ltams mdzad rgyal sras rol brtsed mdzad/ rab tu byung mdzad* <version C is missing two verse lines in an apparent paralepsis, while B rightly includes: *dka' thub sna tshogs mdzad// bdud dpung 'joms mdzad sangs rgyas byang chub mdzad// chos 'khor bskor mdzad> brtul zhugs spyod pa mdzad/ bstan pa 'thar <mtha'> rgyas gter sbed 'phrin las mdzad/ u rgyan rnam thar mdo bsdus bshad pa 'dir// sus bris pa dang 'thong thos gzhan la ston// de dag 'jig rten bde ba can du skye// 'di la dad mos rnam thar don spyod tshad// bla med byang chub sangs rgyas the tshom med// de phyir mdzad pa bcu gcig 'di bkod pas// las 'phro can gyi re ba kun bkongs <skong> 'gyur//.*

5. See Doney 2019a, 143–44.

6. O rgyan gling pa, *Bka' thang sde lnga*, 505–6: *de phyir rnam thar yongs rdzogs brjod dka' yang/ thos pas byang chub rnam thar mdor bshad na// rgyal sras mdzad pa bcu gcig 'di lta ste// 'gro 'dul dgongs mdzad padma lhums zhugs mdzad// rang byung bltams mdzad rgyal sras rol rtsed mdzad// rab tu byung mdzad dka'* [506] *thub sna tshogs mdzad/ bdud dpung 'joms mdzad sangs rgyas byang chub mdzad// chos 'khor bskor mdzad rtul zhugs spyod pa mdzad// bstan pa mthar rgyas mi nub gter sbe mdzad// u rgyan rnam thar mdor bsdus mdzad pa 'di// sus bris pa dang mthong thos gzhan la ston// de dag 'jig rten bde ba can du skye// 'di la dad mos rnam thar don spyod tshad// bla med byang chub sangs rgyas the tshom med// de phyir mdzad pa bcu gcig 'di bkod do//.*

for the *Eleven Acts* is largely "India," both mythical and real. Like Orgyen Lingpa's *Testament of Padmasambhava*, the eleven acts map a landscape of enlightened beings and their domains upon a more prosaic geography of South Asia. It is this mythic setting in which the bulk of the action takes place; only about 15 percent of the story takes place in Tibet. Contrast this to the setting of Nyangral Nyima Öser's (1124–92) more famous *Copper Isle* (*Zangs gling ma*) story of Padmasambhava, where the relative time in the two general locales, Tibet and India, is reversed; less than 10 percent of Nyangral's work is set in India. Orgyen Lingpa's *Testament of Padmasambhava* situates its hero in Tibet for approximately 60 percent of the book and in India for 40 percent. This suggests that the author of the *Eleven Acts* was particularly concerned to portray the epic beginnings of Padmasambhava's career, in part through relying on the fantastic settings and landscape afforded by a mythologized India.

The tempo of the *Eleven Acts* is mid-paced; there are no extensive poetic foretellings or recapitulations of the action, as in the case of the *Testament of Padmasambhava* or the *Living out of the Game Sūtra* (*Lalitavistara Sūtra*). Where the *Testament* is entirely in verse, and the *Copper Isle* about half in verse, the *Eleven Acts* is mostly prose, with verse punctuating the chapter conclusions. Prose thus moves the story along, rarely interrupted by verse elaboration. Padmasambhava moves from location to location, from episode to episode, with relative brevity. Yet neither does the action feel quick or fast-paced, as it does in the *Copper Isle* or as does Milarepa's story in Tsangnyön Heruka's (1452–1507) *Life of Milarepa*. This is owing in great part to one of the key features of the *Eleven Acts*: the extensive delineation of elaborate names given to Padmasambhava upon his completion of a certain task or deed. In the latter chapters in particular, the work begins to feel like liturgy, with staccato narrative vignettes separating the dozens of names for the master that he accrues as he goes about his work.

Yet not all of the work takes this form. The earlier chapters elaborate on the formative moments in Padmasambhava's life and its cosmic importance for both human and divine recipients of his benevolence. Early scenes make great use of dialogue as well. A good example of the work's style may be found in chapter 2, which tells of Padmasmbhava's entry into his mother's womb. The chapter begins with Buddha Amitābha, Padmasambhava's "actual" identity, making contact with Earth:

> Then Buddha Amitābha emitted a single red light ray from his tongue, which fired out like a shooting star. On the northwest bank of the City of Glory, a square plain of gold arose, surrounded by various items. And in the center was a cave called Serpent Pool Cave.

Dhanakośa Lake, a vast lake, formed a clear, spinning circle. And in its center fell the red ray of light.

No sooner had that happened, a turquoise spring shot up in the center of that lake. And upon the surface of that spring emerged a lotus blossom stalk, with an elevated throne with four wheels, and an elegant and dazzling rainbow. Above that sat a lotus with sun and moon discs in the womb of a flower. Above that the letter *hrīḥ* upon a five-pointed vajra descended from Buddha Amitābha's heart.

Then all the gods made offerings such as music from the sky. All the ḍākinīs danced in space. The eight classes of gods and demons circled the shoreline of the land three times. A great rain of flowers fell day and night. The eight great *nāga* serpents circled the lotus stalk and cast precious jewels. The great land quaked, and a rain of nectar fell.

At the same time, King Indrabodhi had a dream: In a western land of great peace, a golden vajra with five points fell into the king's right hand. He beheld a diamond light pervade the billionfold cosmos. And there a prophesy by the gods resounded from the lotus stalk [on] the jewel-lake island:

"This Gone to Bliss One emanated and was actually born as a human. He will become a buddha while he acts as the son of the king."

At this the king was overjoyed. He awoke from his sleep and sent three people to ascertain if the prophecy were true or false. He paid great reverence to the supreme jewels and produced a magnificent feast of offerings. The entire palace blazed with light. The savage gods and demons were pacified, and the gods and demons circled the palace.

Many good signs, such as a thousand blazing suns and moons, appeared in the dreams of all the Buddhist scholars. And a prince was born to the queens of each king in the realms of Orgyen. In every land bloomed flowers of great variety that had never before blossomed. Lions, elephants, and tigers encircled the palace. All sorts of birds circled overhead as well. The non-Buddhist scholars became pale. Overcome, they fell to the ground. A great rain of flowers fell upon every land. The entire sky shimmered with a lattice of rainbow clouds.

In front of the palace, in a bathing pond, a stūpa of lotus steps with nine stories made of five precious jewels, including *padmāraga*, spontaneously emerged. When the king circled round, the gods

> emerged from the rainbow clouds to pay homage to the king . . . in a single voice: "O Great King, please do not show disfavor to us gods and demons; the son of the king will be an emanated sugata, one gone to bliss."
>
> As soon as he heard this prophecy, the king was overjoyed. He gave orders for making offerings to the Buddhist teachers, giving thanks to the scholars, and hosting a festival. The scholars undid the seals, and thereby the nonhuman spirits departed and returned to their own realms.
>
> The people whom the king had sent earlier had beheld the prince and now returned. Then the ḍākinīs of Orgyen assembled and encircled the sea of Dhanakośa. Vajrayoginī, first among the ḍākinīs, offered praise, saying, "The identity of *hrīḥ* power, blazing splendor, the best of lotuses: His compassion is pervasive; it provides for living beings like a wish-fulfilling gem. He is endowed with a diamond-like contemplation that overcomes all demon armies. Bow down to the great Padmavajra."

The chapters immediately following this rely on dialogue to move the action forward. The latter chapters of the *Eleven Acts* tend toward a clipped presentation of action followed by the name Padmasambhava is known for in relation to that action. In this it bears some structural similarity to the *Copper Isle*, with its many concluding chapters of verses to specific social groups. Each work, Nyangral's and Guru Chöwang's, begins with a strong emphasis on narrative and ends with a move toward presenting ritual and doctrinal material using nonnarrative structure. Neither of these, however, maintains the epic combination of prose and verse that Orgyen Lingpa's *Testament of Padmasambhava* musters throughout its many chapters, though in the *Eleven Acts* the setting of Lake Dhanakośa provides the text with a fantastical character that foreshadows Ogyen Lingpa's longer work.

Many narrative elements in the *Eleven Acts* are found in almost every currently known Padmasambhava narrative. Some, however, are shared only by a few and thus mark out distinctive constructions of the narrative within the Padmasambhava tradition. Padmasambhava's birth is the most well known such element. Is Padmasambhava born in human-like fashion, from the womb? Or is he miraculously born from a lotus? Both elements can be found in the tradition, though they appear never to be mixed and therefore suggest divergent storylines.[7]

Another element that exists in different versions is Padmasambhava's

7. Blondeau 1980.

marriage. The *Eleven Acts* would have Padmasambhava married to two princesses, Nyima Özer and Dawai Özer Men. These two were but the finest among five hundred noblewomen that Padmasambhava married. It is possible that the *Eleven Acts* is the source of this marriage account, for there are no known earlier examples of it. Chapter 4, "Playing as a Prince," portrays this polygyny so:

> Now the prince was thirteen years old, and the time had come for him to have a wife. He was then called King Pema. The daughter of Nyima Ö, the king of southern Orgyen was named Nyima Özer. She was the most beautiful among an excellent lineage. The daughter of Dawa, the king of northern Orgyen, was named Dawai Özer Men. She was the most radiant of complexion among an excellent lineage. These two were foremost among five hundred of the most beautiful royal, noble, brahmin, and householding young women. The prince took them all as his queens at a single time. A palace of jewels with seven treasuries, and jewels as well, were offered to the prince. He was surrounded by youthful amusements, diversions such as singing, dancing, and shows. He enjoyed himself passing the time in such pleasures. Then he was called Prince Yimön Nyingpo.[8]

If we wish to sketch the history of the Padmasambhava narrative, scenes such as this are useful, for we can readily see which versions of the story are included, and which are not. The early *Copper Isle* contains no marriage scene at all. Orgyen Lingpa's *Testament of Padmasambhava* presents his marriage to Ö Changma, which would eventually become the more common account. However, at least three versions use both narratives, such that he is married first to Ö Changma and then to Nyima Özer, Dawai Özer Men, and the five hundred noblewomen.[9] The latter marriage episode seems to have fallen out of favor with writers after that.

Scholarship on the Work

The *Eleven Acts* is a compelling work in its own right, deserving full translation and study. Initial questions toward this effort might include: Where are manuscripts of the work located? What did the tradition know of it? How is it related to the larger corpus of Padmasambhava narratives? And what has Western

8. Gu ru Chos kyi dbang phyug, *Mdzad pa bcu gcig ma* C, 10a.

9. These include, Sangs rgyas gling pa (1340–96), Ratna shri/Rin chen dpal bzang po (16th century), and 'Jam dbyangs bsod nams dbang po (1559–1620).

scholarship known of the work up to this point? Beyond that, we might use this recent addition to the available versions of Padmasambhava stories to ask how this tradition relates to other major narrative traditions in Tibet, such as the life of Milarepa or the life of the Buddha. And, finally, we might ask a simple question from the perspective of literary criticism: Is it interesting? Let's start with Western scholarship's knowledge of the *Eleven Acts*.

While Anne-Marie Blondeau's benchmark essay on the narratives dedicated to Padmasambhava has oriented much work on the corpus since its publication in 1980, scholarship on the narrative tradition goes back well over a century. Blondeau's brief but historically provocative and evaluative comments on the literary tradition also appear to have animated interest in the *Eleven Acts* for contemporary scholarship; while dividing Tibetan stories of Padmasambhava into two basic categories, Blondeau laments (in 1980) that we are missing certain key works: "[W]e lack certain milestones such as the rNam-thar mdzad-pa bcu-gcig-ma by Gu-ru chos dbang (1212–70/73) and many others."[10] In the 1990s we could say much the same thing, as Sørensen laments: "Guru Chos-dbang is e.g. famous for having executed an important biography of Padmasambhava titled rNam-thar mdzad-pa bcu-gcig-pa. Unfortunately, this important chain in the history and dissemination of the biographical tradition of Padmasambhava has not come down to us. This makes it far from easy to attempt to sketch out the history of the mutual relationship between the numerous Padma-Vitas."[11] This was true until very recently, yet knowledge of the *Eleven Acts*, if not access to it, was available in the early twentieth century. European scholars did know of the work, or at least of its impact on the later narrative tradition, as early as Gründwedel's 1913[12] mention of an important blockprint from the Waddell collection in the Berlin State Library, namely the large narrative work by Ratna Shri/Rinchen Palsangpo, likely dating from the late sixteenth or early seventeenth century.[13] This important compendium of Padmasambhava stories is, as Vostrikov noted in the 1930s, based upon a number of earlier works, including Guru Chöwang's *Eleven Acts*.[14]

It would not be until second decade of the twenty-first century that intensive work on the Padmasambhava corpus would approach the challenge set forth

10. Blondeau 1980, 48.

11. Sørensen 1994, 12n29.

12. Gründwedel 1913, 3.

13. See Ehrhard 2015, 171n35, for historical remarks on this work.

14. See Vostrikov 1994, 34, 33–49, on narrative literature dedicated to Padmasambhava more generally. Vostrikov offers a critical evaluation of Gründwedel, basing his knowledge of the work on an examination of the same blockprint.

by Vostrikov, Blondeau, and others both to produce textual scholarship on the early full-fledged narratives and to piece together a literary history of the narrative from its beginning as an independent tradition of narrative writing in the twelfth century up through the nineteenth century, when major versions were still being written. Lewis Doney has done more than anyone to bring this field forward beyond Blondeau's 1980 article, such that we now have a robust framework within which to begin to understand the creative transformations that author and redactors wrought throughout the centuries.[15] Guru Chöwang's *Eleven Acts* remained a work that was, by all accounts, important to the tradition yet unavailable to contemporary scholarship outside China.[16]

In China and Bhutan the situation was different. In 2012 scholar Lodrö Gyatso published an edition of the *Eleven Acts* in Tibet. This was in an early volume in an important multi-volume set collecting narrative works dedicated to Padmasambhava.[17] Lodrö Gyatso's edition was the first publication of Guru Chöwang's *Eleven Acts*. It appears to be an edition based on a manuscript from a private collection in Kham that was subsequently scanned in 2016 by the Buddhist Digital Resource Center.[18] Just a few years earlier, another manuscript of the work was being scanned in Bhutan. This manuscript was, and by all accounts remains, located in Phurdrup Monastery, just south of Thimphu, in Bhutan.[19] It was scanned as part of the British Library's Endangered Archives Programme (EAP). Dan Martin seems to be the first person to have mentioned

15. See Doney 2014 and 2019b.

16. See Ehrhard 2015, 172n35: "The biography structure along the 'Eleven Outstanding Acts' of Padmasambhava, a treasure of Gu ru Chos kyi dbang phyug, is up to now unavailable," and Doney 2019b, 1210: "Some extant works speak of earlier Rnying ma sources . . . that have not yet come to light. These include . . . Gu ru chos dbang's Padmasambhava biography structured around his 11 deeds."

17. The *Slob dpon padma 'byung gnas kyi rnam thar dpe tshogs* series, now comprising at least seven volumes.

18. This can be found in volume 9 of: *Bla ma nyi 'bum gyis nyar tshags mdzad pa'i dpe rnying dpe dkon*. Buddhist Digital Resource Center (BDRC), purl.bdrc.io/resource/W4PD973. Accessed July 27, 2021. [BDRC bdr:W4PD973].

19. This manuscript was filmed under the direction of Dr. Karma Phuntso. According to local digital records at the Bhutan National Library, digital images of Guru Chöwang's *Mdzad pa bcu gcig ma* is in the "thorbu" (thor bu) group, as deemed by the digitization team. Digital images of the work are located on local storage at the Bhutan National Library. The thorbu group is included within the online holdings of the EAP: https://eap.bl.uk/collection/EAP310-3-3/search. This collection largely accords with the list of contents at the Bhutan National Library. However, as of July 2021, the *Mdzad pa bcu bcig ma* is not among the works cataloged and made available through the EAP's online portal.

this manuscript, in 2014.[20] There are thus now available two manuscripts of the work, one from Bhutan and one from Kham, and one edition in modern print.

Traditional Knowledge of the Work and Comparisons

What did Tibetan tradition know of it? Quite a bit, it turns out. The colophon of the Bhutanese manuscript version of the work attributes the authorship of the work somewhat cryptically to both Mandarava and Yeshé Tsogyal: "Queen Metok Mandarava heard this great chronicle of Orgyen [Padmasambhava] directly from Orgyen and wrote it down. Tsogyal heard the Tibetan [portion of the] chronicle directly from him and wrote down. When he was 3,500 years old, he went to Tibet. He stayed at Samyé for between twenty-three and twenty-five years. The lineage for this [work is]: Dharma Body Samantabhadra; Enjoyment Body Great Mahākaruṇika, Emanation Body Padmasambhava; Ḍākinī Yeshé Tsogyal; Dharma King Tri Songdetsen; Guru Chökyi Wangchuk."[21] In this account of the work's pedigree, Guru Chöwang is in the place of the treasure discoverer. Be that as it may, Ratna Lingpa's anecdote above says more plainly that the work belongs to Guru Chöwang.

If the *Eleven Acts* is indeed the work of Guru Chöwang,[22] either in the form of treasure or authorship, then it stands as the second oldest of the major narrative works about Padmasambhava, for it would have been created in the midthirteenth century. Only Nyangral's *Copper Isle* predates it, albeit by a century or so. The two works do not, at cursory glance, appear to have much to do with each other, suggesting distinctive traditions of narrative forming within the period. It is when we look forward to the next major period in the Padmasambhava corpus that we begin to see the place of Guru Chöwang's *Eleven Acts*,

20. Martin 2014.

21. Colophon, Gu ru Chos kyi dbang phyug, *Mdzad pa bcu gcig ma* B, 74a3: *o rgyan gyi lo rgyus chen mo/ lha lcam me tog maṇḍa ra bas u rgyan nyid la zhus nas yi ger rigs su bkod pa'o/ bod kyi lor rgyus mtsho rgyal gyis/ nyid la zhus ste yi ger bkod/ nyid kyi lo gsum stong lnga brgya zhes pa gcig bod du byon/ bsam yas su lo nyer gsum lnga bzhugs so/ 'd'i rgyud pa ni/ chos sku kun tu bzang po/ longs sku rdo thugs rje chen po/ sprul sku padma 'byung gnas/ mkha' 'gro ye shes mtsho rgyal/ chos rgyal khri srong lde btsan/ 'gu ru chos kyi dbang phyug/ sras padma dbang chen/ mtshan ldan chos kyi rgyal mtshan/ chos kyi rdo rje 'chang/ don yod rgyal mtshan/ 'gu ru bshes gnyen nor bu/ 'gu ru bshes gnyen chos rgyal/ 'gu ru bsam 'phel nor bu/ chos kyi rgyal po/ ras chen blo gros dpal ldan/ sprul sku sna tshogs rang grol/ dge'o/.*

22. The authorship of the work, like most every other aspect of it, requires further research now that it is available. Initial attempts to corroborate at least the title in Guru Chöwang's corpus have proved unsuccessful; there does not appear to be any mention of the work in his autobiography or in his Great History of Treasure (*Gter 'byung chen mo*, contained in Guru Chos kyi dbang phyug, *The Autobiography*).

for the same set of eleven acts is included in both his work and the work of Orgyen Lingpa, as we have seen above. It is tempting to say that Orgyen Lingpa's *Five Testaments* was quoting Guru Chöwang's *Eleven Acts*, though this is not certain (there could have been a tertiary source, for instance). If this represents a shared tradition, would readers of the *Five Testaments* have recognized this as a quote, or at least as referring to Guru Chöwang's work? At any rate, other than the work itself, this shared passage from the *Five Testaments* constitutes the earliest circumstantial evidence for the text of the *Eleven Acts*. It is not until the fifteenth century, when Ratna Lingpa tells the story with which we began, that the *Eleven Acts* is explicitly mentioned and is attributed to Guru Chöwang.

The colophon to the Bhutan manuscript (*Mdzad pa bcu gcig ma* B) offers its own history of the work from Guru Chöwang forward:

- 'Gu ru Chos kyi dbang phyug (1212–70)
- Sras Padma dbang chen (13th cent.) P7173
- Mtshan ldan Chos kyi rgyal mtshan
- Chos kyi rdo rje 'chang
- Don yod rgyal mtshan
- 'Gu ru Bshes gnyen nor bu
- 'Gu ru Bshes gnyen chos rgyal
- 'Gu ru Bsam 'phel nor bu
- Chos kyi rgyal po
- Ras chen Blo gros dpal ldan
- Sprul sku Sna tshogs rang grol

Most names in the Bhutan manuscript's colophon are not confidently identifiable at this point, beyond pointing out similarities between this list and other lineage lists. Yet when cross-referenced with Mönben Palden Zangpo's (1447–1507) list of the teachings he received, the possibility emerges that this lineage ends in the mid- to late fifteenth century or the early sixteenth century, if we accept that the Guru Norbu Samphel in the *Eleven Acts*' list is the same as Norbu Samphel in Mönben's list. If, as his list states, Norbu Samphel was a teacher of Mönben, he would have lived in the mid-fifteenth century. The three generations beyond him in the *Eleven Acts*' list might put the colophon in the early sixteenth century.[23] This suggests that the manuscript is no earlier than that.

23. Mon ban Dpal ldan bzang po's *thob yig* for certain teachings of Gu ru Chos dbang suggests that this list ends in the sixteenth century. (See p. 67.) Underlined names are found, in nearly the

Regardless of when the manuscripts date from, Guru Chöwang's work was cited and used as a source, as we have seen, by other writers, including the Sakya hierarch Jamyang Sönam Wangpo (1559–1620) in his 1611 work[24] and Rinchen Palsangpo not long before him.[25] And by the mid- to late seventeenth century, Guru Chöwang's work was "well known" according to the Fifth Dalai Lama (1617–82), who received the work from a teacher in the Northern Treasure tradition, Tratsang Lochok Dorjé (1595–1671).[26] In the late seventeenth or early eighteenth century, Pema Trinlé (1641–1718) wrote the *Lives of the Lineage Masters of the Kama Dowang*, which includes a section entitled "The Eleven Acts of the Second Buddha, or the Dharma King of Orgyan, Pema Jungné." This section utilized Guru Chöwang's eleven acts in order to structure a brief account of Padmasambhava.[27] Finally, later writers such as the Third Dodrupchen Jigmé Tenpai Nyima (1825–1926) mention Guru Chöwang's work as a source for teaching the birth of Padmasambhava.[28] The full literary history of this work remains to be written, yet it is clear even from a cursory glance that within the Tibetan tradition Guru Chöwang's *Eleven Acts* deserves to be called, as Sørensen and others have, "famous" throughout its eight-hundred-year life.

---

same order, in the Bhutanese manuscript of *The Eleven Acts*: *chos sku snang ba mtha' yas / longs sku thugs rje chen po / sprul sku o rgyan padma / mkha' 'gro ye shes mtsho rgyal / 'gro mgon chos kyi dbang phyug / rgyal sras pad ma dbang chen / mtshan ldan chos kyi rgyal mtshan / drin can sangs rgyas kun 'grol / gu ru chos kyi rdo rje / gu ru mi 'gyur rdo rje / gu ru don yod rgyal mtshan / gu ru shes snyen nor bu / gu ru chos rgyal shes snyen / bsam gtan ling pa nor bu bsam 'phel / des bdag dpal ldan bzang po la'o //*.

24. See Ehrhard 2015 for dating and authorship.

25. See Padma 'phrin las, *Bka' ma*, 23–46.

26. Ngag dbang blo bzang rgya mtsho, *Zab pa*, 2:635.4-.6: *gter kha 'di la o rgyan chen po'i rnam thar rgyas 'bring bsdus gsum yod ces skal ldan yar klungs sprul sku mi bskyod rdo rje gsung yang deng sang yongs su grags pa'i rgyas sras padma 'byung gnas kyi mdzad pa bcu gcig pa zhes bya ba'i lung gi brgyud pa ni/ dpal o rgyan chen po/ lha lcam mandha ra ba/ mkhar chen bza'/ gter ston chos dbang / sman lung sha'aka 'od/ dwags ston pa/ gnyan ston pa/ se sdings pa yab sras/ chos sku 'od zer/ dpal 'byor dbang phyug / chos kyi dbang po/ karma gu ru/ chos dbang bstan 'dzin nyi ma/ khra tshang pa chen po/ des bdag la'o//*.

27. The numbered sections of this portion of Padma 'phrin las' work are familiar by now: (1) *rang cag kha ba can pa rnams la dgongs pa*, (2) *lhum su zhugs pa*, (3) *bltams pa*, (4) *rol rtsed*, (5) *rab tu byung ba*, (6) *dka' thub sna tshogs*, (7) *bdud dpung 'joms pa*, (8) *sangs rgyas byang chub*, (9) *chos 'khor bskor ba*, (10) *brtul zhugs kyi spyod pa*, (11) *bstan pa mthar rgyas mi nub gter shed*.

28. Rdo grub chen, *Brjed tho*, 162.

Comparisons

The eleven acts of Padmasambhava's life in India and, to a limited extent, in Tibet will be familiar to those acquainted with the twelve acts of Śākyamuni Buddha.[29] Pema Trinlé made this comparison explicit in his history of the Nyingma *bka' ma* tradition, which he begins with back-to-back stories of Śākyamuni and Padmasambhava—the Buddha's story told in twelve acts and Guru Rinpoché's told in eleven. Pema Trinlé characterizes the notion of an "act" (*mdzad pa*) as a heuristic device that is useful when attempting to convey the infinite richness of the founders' lives with some brevity so that learners with ordinary human faculties might gain something of practical value from such narratives. The Buddha, Padmasambhava, the masters of India and Tibet of the old and new schools—their activities are inconceivable, too numerous to count, and resist being set down in any form of human communication. The "act" then is, among other things, a literary device intended to bring structure and concision to topics—the lives of enlightened beings—that resist structure and boundary.[30] For those of us interested in literary history, the acts form a powerful basis for comparing narratives, both within and across distinctive traditions. With the *Eleven Acts of Padmasambhava* now available, work on the literary history of Padmasambhava narratives can proceed with constant reference to another of the key early works. How, we can now ask, for instance, were the twin founding narratives of the *Copper Isle* and the *Eleven Acts* treated, integrated, adapted, or ignored by later writers?

Beyond this, the availability of the *Eleven Acts* for contemporary global scholars can serve as a prompt to engage more fully in the comparative literary history of Tibetan narratives. The Buddha, Padmasambhava, Milarepa—narrative traditions for each of these figures utilize some form of eleven- or twelve-act rubric to structure what in theological terms are topics of impossibly infinite scope, and in literary terms are still so rich and varied as to present any writer wishing to contribute to those traditions with more choices than are practical. And beyond these three major narratives, what of others? Shenrab? Tsongkhapa? The Dalai Lamas? Gesar? Vessantara? Each boasts a rich narrative tradition, each of which employs "acts" to a greater or lesser extent, and can thus be efficiently compared in order to enhance our understanding and appreciation of Tibetan narrative writing broadly. Contemporary scholarship now has enough to engage in such comparative work.

29. See Tenzin Chögyel 2015, for a summary of the twelve acts, and a brief narrative of Shakyamuni Buddha's life organized into the twelve acts.

30. Padma 'phrin las, *Bka' ma*, 22–23.

Works Cited

Tibetan Language Texts

Gu ru Chos kyi dbang phyug. *Mdzad pa bcu gcig ma* A: *Sprul pa'i sku thams cad las khyad par lngas 'phags pa / mthu dang rdu 'phrul dus mas 'gro ba'i don mdzad pa/ u rgyan gyi slob dpon pad ma 'byung gnas kyi rnam par thar pa/ mdzad pa bcu gcig*. In *Bka' thang phyogs bsgrigs snyigs ma'i rgud 'joms rdo rje'i me char*, edited by Blo gros rgya mtshos, 96–144. Beijing: Bod ljongs mi dmangs dpe skrun khang, 2012.

———. *Mdzad pa bcu gcig ma* B: *Rgyal dbang padma'i rnam thar mdzad pa bcu gcig ma*. Manuscript located at Phurdrup Gonpa / Phur grub dgon pa, Bhutan. 74 folios.

———. *Mdzad pa bcu gcig ma* C: *Sprul pa'i sku thams cad las khyad par lngas 'phags pa / mthu dang rdu 'phrul dus mas 'gro ba'i don mdzad pa/ u rgyan gyi slob dpon pad ma 'byung gnas kyi rnam par thar pa/ mdzad pa bcu gcig*. Manuscript located in private collection, Sichuan. 55 folios.

———. *The Autobiography and Instructions of Gu-ru Chos-kyi-dbaṅ-phyug*. 2 vols. Paro: Ugyen Tempai Gyaltsen, 1979.

Mon ban Dpal ldan bzang po. *Mon ban dpal ldan bzang po'i thob yig thos pa rgya mtsho*. Thimphu: Dorji Namgyal, 1985. BDRC W21495.

Ngag dbang blo bzang rgya mtsho. *Zab pa dang rgya che'i dam pa'i chos kyi thob yig gangg'a'i chu rgyun*. In *Record of Teachings Received: The Gsan-yig of the Fifth Dalai Lama Nag-dban-blo-bzan-rgya-mtsho*. 1970. Delhi: Lelung and Lhakhar.

O rgyan gling pa. *Bka' thang sde lnga*. Beijing: Mi rigs dpe skrun khang, 1990.

Padma 'phrin las. *Bka' ma mdo dbang gi bla ma brgyud pa'i rnam thar*. Leh: S.W. Tashigangpa, 1972. BDRC W21523.

Ratna gling pa. *Gu ru ratna gling pa'i gter 'byung chen mo gsal ba'i sgron me*. In *Gter chen ratna gling pa'i gsung 'bum mun sel sgron me*, 2:1–232. Gser rta: Snga 'gyur rnying ma dpal bla med gsang chen gnubs zur dgon. 2014. BDRC W3PD1003.

Ratna shri/ Rin chen dpal bzang po. *O rgyan padma 'byung gnas kyi rnam par thar pa/ gter ston chen po o rgyan gling/ mnga' bdag nyang ral/ gu ru chos dbang bcas nas gdan drangs pa'i bka' thang gter kha gsum bsgrigs mthong ba don ldan*. BDRC W1KG3713: dbu med manuscript, 263 folios. Berlin State Library, Waddell Collection 36a: blockprint, 275 folios.

Rdo grub chen 03 'Jigs med bstan pa'i nyi ma. *Brjed tho sna tshogs*. In *Rdo grub chen 'jigs med bstan pa'i nyi ma'i gsung 'bum*, 7:131–94. Sichuan: Si khron mi rigs dpe skrun khang, 2006.

European Language Sources

Blondeau, Anne-Marie. 1980. "Analysis of the Biographies Padmasambhava According to Tibetan Tradition: Classification of Sources." In *Tibetan Studies in Honour of Hugh Richardson*, edited by Michael Aris and Aung San Suu Kyi, 45–52. Warminster: Aris & Phillips.

———. 1992. "Conférence de Mme Anne-Marie Blondeau." *École Pratique des Hautes Études, Section des sciences religieuses* 101: 67–72.

Doney, Lewis. 2014. *The Zangs gling ma: The First Padmasambhava Biography*. Andiast: IITBS GmbH.

———. 2019a. "Life and Devotion: The Biography of Padmasambhava in Two Works of A mes zhabs." In *Unearthing Himalayan Treasures: Festschrift for Franz-Karl Ehrhard*, edited by Volker Caumanns, Marta Sernesi, and Nikolai Solmsdorf, 143–64. Marburg: Indica et Tibetica Verlag.

———. 2019b. "Padmasambhava in Tibetan Buddhism." In *Brill's Encyclopedia of Buddhism: Volume II: Lives*, edited by Jonathan Silk, 1197–1231. Leiden: Brill.

Ehrhard, Franz-Karl. 2015. "'An Ocean of Marvelous Perfections': A 17th-Century *Padma'i thang yig* from the Sa skya pa School." In *Tibetan Literary Genres, Texts, and Text Types: From Genre Classification to Transformation*, edited by Jim Rheingans, 139–81. Leiden: Brill.

Gründwedel, Albert. 1913. "Padmasambhava und Verwandtes." *Baessler-Archiv, Band III*, 1–37. Leipzig and Berlin: B. G. Teubner.

Martin, Dan. 2014. "Name Dropping, It Happens." *Tibeto-Logic*, August 8, 2014. https://tibeto-logic.blogspot.com/2014/08/name-dropping-it-happens.html. Accessed November 10, 2020.

Sørensen, Per K. 1994. *Tibetan Buddhist Historiography: The Mirror Illuminating the Royal Genealogies: An Annotated Translation of the XIVth Century Tibetan Chronicle rGyal-rabs gsal-ba'i me-long*. Asiatische Forschungen 128. Wiesbaden: Harrassowitz Verlag.

Tenzin Chögyel. 2015. *The Life of the Buddha*. Translated by Kurtis R. Schaeffer. New York: Penguin Classics.

Vostrikov, A. I. 1994. *Tibetan Historical Literature*. Translated by Harish Chandra Gupta. Surrey: Curzon Press.

III.
The Nyingma Imaginaire

"Karma and Aspirations Converge": On Tendrel, Tsok, and Two Portraits of Jigmé Lingpa

Benjamin Bogin

While there is no direct correlate for Festschrift in Tibetan, connections between feasting, festivals, and scholarship are well known. Perhaps the closest resemblance is the "festival for the learned" (*mkhas pa'i dga' ston*), best known as the title of Pawo Tsuklak Trengwa's (1504–66) history of Buddhism but appearing in other titles as well. This fits well, as the term for "festival" (*dga' ston*) may be applied to a variety of contexts, including a broad range of celebratory events. In this Festschrift contribution, however, beyond invoking the "festival for the learned" as a model, I would like to turn our attention to another kind of feast—the *tsok* (*tshogs, gaṇacakra*). The editors of this volume invited me to contribute a brief essay on the topic of "the Nyingma imaginaire," and I cannot imagine a ritual more central to Nyingma communities than the tsok feast offering. Janet Gyatso's many publications on the treasure (*gter ma*) tradition, culminating in her masterful translation and study of the secret autobiographies of Jigmé Lingpa (1730–98), mapped the world of Nyingma religiosity as a dynamic network of texts, individuals, and communities all orbiting around the timeless presence of Padmasambhava. One of the places where Jigmé Lingpa's influence may be observed is in the popularity of his songs in the standard liturgy of Nyingma ritual, including his famous "feast song" (*tshogs glu*) commonly referred to by its first few words: "Karma and Aspirations Converge" (*las smon rten 'brel*).

"Converge," or *tendrel* (*rten 'brel*), points to another fundamental aspect of the Nyingma imaginaire brilliantly explored in Janet Gyatso's writings on the treasure tradition. The workings of tendrel are a central theme of her study of Jigmé Lingpa's secret autobiographies, where she defines the term thus:

> "Tendrel" abbreviates the Tibetan rendering of the famous Buddhist concept of "interdependent origination" (*rten cing 'brel bar 'byung gnas*; Skt. *pratītyasamutpāda*). It is the principal characterization of Buddhist causality and ontology. Everything is constituted by the coming together of multiple causes and conditions; everything is

> dependent for its existence upon something else . . . In colloquial Tibetan usage, tendrel concerns matters of auspiciousness and fortune. When the right conditions connect, it augurs that something good will happen.[1]

The course of my own academic life would be unimaginable without the tendrel I have been so fortunate to enjoy with Janet Gyatso—first as a reader of her work, then as her student during the Spring 1999 semester at the University of Michigan, and eventually (through her generous mentorship) as a colleague in the guild of Tibetan Buddhist scholars and, most valuably, as a friend. With a profound sense of gratitude and admiration, I offer here a new translation of Jigmé Lingpa's feast song. Before getting to that translation, however, I would like to share an anecdote far removed from Tibet that illustrates an aspect of performance that connects the worlds of tendrel and tsok. My reading of Jigmé Lingpa's song will focus on the ways in which these touchstones of the Nyingma imaginaire intersect in its verses. The translation itself will be followed by a brief consideration of another, more esoteric, reading of the song. Finally, I will share the story of an unexpected connection between two portraits of Jigmé Lingpa that demonstrates yet another aspect of tendrel.

The performative and communal context of the feast song resonates with a particular force in the context of this Festschrift offering to Janet Gyatso because our shared appreciation of musical performance was one of the keys to our own connection. During her semester at the University of Michigan, I had the good fortune to become Janet's unofficial guide to the musical treasures of Ann Arbor. One of the many memorable performances that we attended was by the Roscoe Mitchell Quartet at a tiny little venue called the Kerrytown Concert House. That night, the convergence of the beauty of the compositions, the extraordinary skill and creativity of the musicians, the acoustic qualities of the space, the technical precision of the sound engineer, and the focused appreciation of the audience created a mutual experience of transcendent power. I recall vividly the ways that the sounds of the clicking of the saxophone keys and the drummer's occasional grunts added further texture to the music. Many in the crowd had clearly been listening to Roscoe Mitchell's avant-garde jazz for decades, and there was a joyous sense of celebratory reverence in the entire room, made audible with every outburst of applause. This personal anecdote may take us far from the worlds of tendrel and tsok that I intend to describe, but the celebratory sense of coming together in a shared performance that Jigmé

1. Gyatso 1998, 179.

Lingpa evokes in his feast song is difficult (if not impossible) to convey in the abstract.

The tsok feast may help us to better understand tendrel by encompassing both usages described in Gyatso's definition: the philosophical sense of tendrel (encompassing the twelve links of interdependent origination detailed in the Sūtra and Abhidharma traditions and the Madhyamaka presentation of tendrel as the inverse of emptiness) and the colloquial sense of tendrel where it refers to good fortune or serendipity. Similarly, Gyatso's exploration of tendrel in the secret autobiographies of Jigmé Lingpa demonstrates that it is much more than either of those characterizations and that these two different aspects of tendrel are themselves interconnected. The entire process of treasure revelation enacts an understanding of tendrel that includes both the philosophical and colloquial meanings of the term. Key to Gyatso's analysis is the question of agency. For example, when Jigmé Lingpa writes in his secret autobiography that his vision of Terdak Lingpa (1646–1714) had created the auspicious connections leading to his obtaining a ritual dagger that had belonged to Terdak Lingpa, one might take this to mean that Jigmé Lingpa is a passive recipient of forces and events beyond his control. Gyatso argues against this reading, pointing out that ". . . even in these instances, Jigme Lingpa is not a mere passive recipient, for one has to actively participate in an initiation, one has to impose an interpretation upon a vision."[2] The active participation of the treasure revealer is merely one factor necessary for the successful revelation of a treasure: Padmasambhava's intention, the timing, the place, the support of the protectors, the pacification of obstructors, and the outer and inner purity of the audience must all converge harmoniously. Jigmé Lingpa's secret autobiographies are replete with examples of his own vacillation between doubt and confidence in his ability to perform his role in this elaborate ensemble. Gyatso's readings of Jigmé Lingpa's autobiographies clearly demonstrate the links between the philosophical view of interdependent origination and the more mundane sense of serendipitous circumstances as they are embodied in the treasure tradition's particular instantiation of tendrel. In considering the feast song "Karma and Aspirations Converge," I intend to look at one of the ways in which this particular understanding of tendrel infuses Nyingma ritual life in contexts somewhat more mundane than treasure revelation.

As mentioned above, the song lacks a proper title but is frequently referred to by its first three words: karma (*las*), aspirations (*smon*), and convergence, or tendrel. These three words offer a powerfully concise glimpse of the intersections of philosophical view and ritual practice in the Nyingma tradition.

2. Gyatso 1998, 179.

Following Gyatso's exploration of the agency of an egoless subject, we can see karma and aspirations as two different expressions of tendrel. *Karma*, here, denotes the past actions that planted the seeds for one's present circumstances and experiences; the inconceivably vast complex of causal factors that led to the subject's presence at a particular gathering at a particular time in a particular physical, mental, and emotional state. All of this is the result of previous actions, and the recognition of that might engender a sense of gratitude for positive circumstances or acceptance and determination in the face of challenging ones. *Aspirations*, on the other hand, are the wishes and motivations born from such reflections, which chart a course for future actions to follow. The agency of the egoless subject is emphatically present in the act of making aspirations. Unlike ego-driven goal setting, where the determination and will of the subject are isolated as the ultimate causal factor, making aspirations recognizes the limitations of the self by expressing a determination to strive for transformation in a way that remains open to unseen connections and causes by eschewing attachment to self-centered outcomes. In this sense, karma is the tendrel of the past and aspirations are the tendrel of the future. When these two aspects of tendrel are in harmony, as Jigmé Lingpa sings, they become a wish-fulfilling tree.

It is a fortuitous accident that, in English, the word *aspiration* carries meanings related to both hope and breath. Although the Tibetan word *smon* does not share this etymological connection to breath, the act of making aspirations is often understood as a voiced act thus often rendered as "prayer." Internal resolve and determination are activated through the voicing of that intention. Ideally, this voiced aspiration is made in the presence of representatives of the Buddhist teaching, whether those be in the form of a teacher, fellow aspirants, texts and images, visualized buddhas and deities, or all of the above. It is not only the act of making an internal commitment public that makes it an aspiration but also the way in which it is voiced. To sing one's aspirations requires a willingness to amplify a voice of intention unimpeded by timidity, doubt, and self-consciousness. The very act of singing one's aspirations provides the singer with a confidence and determination qualitatively distinct from what one might muster in silent contemplation. This voiced aspect of aspiration is particularly relevant in considering Jigmé Lingpa's "Karma and Aspirations Converge," which was spontaneously composed as part of a tsok ritual and remains one of the most popular songs for such occasions in the Nyingma tradition.

Recent research on the development of tantric ritual in India and Tibet has underscored the importance of *gaṇacakra/tsok* in this history.[3] Jigmé Lingpa himself composed a detailed presentation of the theory and practice of the tsok

3. See, for example, Shizuka 2008, Szántó and Griffiths 2015, and Szántó 2019.

ritual in his *Commentary on the "Embodiment of the Guru's Intention"* (*Dgongs 'dus rnam bshad*).[4] Jigmé Lingpa's feast song must be understood within these historical and theoretical contexts. Here, I wish to focus attention on tsok practice in contemporary Nyingma communities as a way of recovering essential aspects of the tradition that are often obscured by academic studies. First and foremost, a consideration of Jigmé Lingpa's song offers us an opportunity to reflect on the performative and communal nature of tsok. In the Nyingma ritual calendar, the tenth and twenty-fifth days of the lunar month require tsok offerings devoted to Padmasambhava and the ḍākinīs, respectively. These may take the shape of a gathering of thousands at a large monastic institution, a small gathering of family and neighbors in a household shrine, or a solitary retreatant performing the ritual with an assembly of visualized guests.

In any of these cases, song plays a central role in the performance. "Karma and Aspirations Converge" is beloved not only because of the poetry of its words but also for the beautiful melody that allows a talented singer or ensemble to demonstrate their vocal abilities. Although the words of the song are fixed, there are significant differences in the performance, ranging from variations in melody and harmonic accompaniment in *a cappella* performances to the arrangements of different percussion and wind instruments. Today, it is possible to gain an appreciation for some of these variations in the performance of the song through recorded examples available online.[5] The widespread popularity of the song is attested to in an essay on "Dharma in Poetry" by the contemporary teacher Anam Thubten Rinpoche (b. 1968): "One of the most recited poems in the Tibetan Buddhist tradition is a *tsok lu* (song of feast) by Jigme Lingpa. Even today, many monasteries and communities sing this during sacred feasts. It's beautifully written. People sing it with various melodies, which are often exquisite. It has the power to invoke bliss immediately upon hearing it."[6] These "various melodies" often mark a singer as part of a particular lineage of practice. On numerous occasions in Tibet, I encountered a well-traveled *ngakpa* (*sngags pa*) or lama who could identify the lineage of a feast-song singer based on the melody. Recognizing a familiar melody in a distant region of Tibet (or beyond) as one's own brings a visceral sense of

4. Jigmé Lingpa, *A Hundred Rays of Light, The Mirror of Compassion and Wisdom: A Commentary on the "Embodiment of the Guru's Intention."*

5. There are at least a dozen versions of Las smon rten 'brel on YouTube. See, for example, https://www.youtube.com/watch?v=BLA7O7jvGro, https://www.youtube.com/watch?v=whToyfopXvA, and https://www.youtube.com/watch?v=FroKdURuD3I.

6. Anam Thubten 2020.

connection that may tell us as much about tendrel in the Nyingma imaginaire as a philosophical treatise in the scholastic curriculum could.

For the most part, questions of melody, voice, and performance in Tibetan studies have been left to musicologists, leaving the study of texts such as "Karma and Aspirations Converge" rather flat and decontextualized.[7] Jigmé Lingpa's feast song has its roots in a specific performance that is recorded in his "outer" autobiography. At a large gathering, the author reports that he was "requested to offer a melodious song of great joy"[8] and spontaneously sang the words now famous as his feast song. The song does not appear to have been included in any of the collections of various songs and prayers found within Jigmé Lingpa's *Collected Works*,[9] but it became far more popular than many of the songs that did find their way into that collection. The immediate impact of the song is exemplified by the reaction of the requesting lama, who touches his forehead to Jigmé Lingpa's with tears streaming down his face.[10] With these untranslatable contexts in mind, let us turn to the translation of the song:

> Karma and aspirations converge as a wish-fulfilling tree
> upon which the young peacock of eastern India alights.
> When the peacock's twirling parasol guides us toward the holy teachings,
> we young ones are set on the path of liberation.
>
> Merit, the sweet song of the cuckoo from the Mön forests in the south,
> has arrived on the chariot of the queen of spring.
> A song sweeter than the flutes of the heavenly musicians
> augurs auspicious conditions for the three warm months of summer.
>
> Vajra kin, whose karma and aspirations are aligned, gather here.
> Let us go to the Dharma assembly where our lama resides.
> At this festival where we drink the nectar of ripening and liberation,
> I have the honor of singing a joyous song.

7. There are, of course, notable exceptions to this generalization. See, for example, Sujata 2004.

8. *Fruit from the Wish-Fulfilling Tree of Virtuous Deeds*, 187: *mgur dbyangs la dgyes che bas bskul bar mdzad pa bzhin.*

9. For a scholarly analysis of this collection, see van Schaik 2014.

10. *Fruit from the Wish-Fulfilling Tree of Virtuous Deeds*, 188: *ngos la dbu gtugs nas spyan chab bsil bar 'dug/.*

Within these rows where we sit in unchanging great bliss,
even without meditating, we see the faces of the lama and yidam.
Through the vehicle of luminous clarity, heart essence of the mother
and ḍākinīs,
please grant us the attainment of the rainbow body, the dharmakaya![11]

In these four stanzas, Jigmé Lingpa evokes the image and mood of a perfect tsok gathering. The physical beauty of the gathered assembly is compared to the magnificent display of the peacock's tail and the beauty of melodious song is evoked through the voice of the cuckoo. These two birds from south of the Himalayas are both frequently conjured in Tibetan literature for their symbolic associations with aspects of Buddhist teaching. Here, although those allusions remain active, the emphasis is more on the physical and musical characteristics of the peacock and the cuckoo. The latter, in particular, also serves to mark a moment in time, as the cuckoo is well known to return to Tibet from the south in the spring, just before the beginning of three months of summer retreat. Singers of this feast song simultaneously connect their own tsok with the late eighteenth-century assembly where Jigmé Lingpa first sang it and with the timeless perfect tsok gathering evoked in those lines. It is perhaps important to recollect that for many Nyingmapas, this song would be one of many performed at least twice a month over a lifetime. There are inevitably instances when the song is performed with a sense of ritual obligation lacking any depth of feeling. However, there are also occasions when the song resonates powerfully with Jigmé Lingpa's own melodious voice and transforms a mundane space into a perfect realm of practice and realization. Here, we encounter again the rich understanding of tendrel that animates the treasure tradition—the karma of the tsok participants converges with their aspirations to create the environment in which Jigmé Lingpa's aspirations are fulfilled, and he is able to sing through and with them.

There is a danger of reducing the notion of tendrel to a form of "magical

11. *Fruit from the Wish-Fulfilling Tree of Virtuous Deeds*, 187–88: *las smon rten 'brel dpag bsam ljon shing gi steng du/ rgya gar shar gyi rma bya gzhon nu yang phebs byung/ rma bya'i gdugs skor dam pa'i chos phyogs la bsgyur dang/ gzhon pa nga tshos thar pa'i lam sna zhig zin yong/ bsod nams dpyid kyi rgyal mo'i shing rta la phebs pa'i/ lho mon shing lo'i tshal gyi khu byug gi gsung snyan/ ya gi dri za'i bu mo'i gling bu las snyan pa/ dbyar gsum nam zla bsro ba'i rten 'brel la yag byung/ 'dir 'dus las smon mthun pa'i rdo rje'i dang spun sgrogs/ nga tsho'i bla ma bzhugs pa'i chos ra la phebs dang/ smin grol bdud rtsi 'thung ba'i dga' ston gyi ngang nas/ nyams dga' glu ru len pa'i khyad chos shig yod do/ bde chen 'pho 'gyur med pa'i bzhugs gral gyi dbus nas/ lha dang bla ma'i zhal ras ma bsgoms kyang mthong byung/ ma dang mkha' 'gro'i snying tig 'od gsal gyi theg pas/ 'ja' lus chos skur bsgrub pa'i dngos grub cing zhu'o/*. I would like to acknowledge my debt to previous translations of this song by Erik Pema Kunsang (2004) and Thinley Norbu Rinpoche (n.d.).

thinking," wherein simply believing something to be true is sufficient cause to make it so.[12] It is true that the conception of tendrel outlined above suggests that causality is far more complex and subtle than our rational minds are able to fathom and that aspirations have causal efficacy. However, the idea that an aspiration alone is sufficient cause for its realization is anathema to the Tibetan Buddhist understanding of tendrel for several reasons. First of all, the entire point of tendrel is the recognition of how many causal factors are at play in every phenomenon—nothing is caused solely by itself. Secondly, tendrel operates within metaphysical and ethical systems governed by inviolable laws of cause and effect. For an aspiration to be efficacious, it must be in harmony with these laws of karma. Third, and perhaps most importantly, all of this takes place within a system of esoteric contemplative practice in which the aspirant's mastery of the mind and subtle body is the key factor in realizing the potential voiced in the aspiration.

One of the foremost masters of Jigmé Lingpa's teaching and incarnation lineages, Dilgo Khyentse Rinpoche (1910–91), composed a brief commentary on his previous incarnation's feast song that reads the entire text as a secret teaching on aspects of these practices: *Illuminating Awareness-Emptiness: A Clarification of the Hidden Meaning of the Feast Song Called "Karma and Aspirations Converge."* To give an example of how this commentary interprets the song, here is the word for word explanation of the first two lines: "Karma and aspirations converge as a wish-fulfilling tree/ upon which the young peacock of eastern India alights."

> Therefore, conventionally, the direct result of both the good *karma* that ripens from the power of a propensity for virtue and the *aspiration* prayer of positive intentions and actions is the *auspicious coincidence* [*tendrel*] of the human body (endowed with six elements), which is more than flesh and bone—the channels, winds, and essences that are the wisdom of the vajra body. Through ripening in the direction of the good, all the desired qualities of the grounds and paths of the inner vajra arise in the central channel, which is referred to in many tantras as a *wish-fulfilling tree*. Because of the need to join the mind-energy with the essence in the [central channel], it says *upon which*. Here, because *India* is [2b] the central region of

12. The most notable recent example would be Rhonda Byrne's *The Secret* (2006), which has sold over 30 million copies and has been translated into fifty languages. Byrne's work bears many similarities to predecessors ranging from Madame Blavatsky to Norman Vincent Peale.

> Jambudvīpa and a land where heat naturally intensifies, it designates the fire of *caṇḍālī*.[13]

Without attempting to explain the practices referred to in this commentary in any detail, we can simply observe the way in which the tendrel from the first line of the song is here interpreted as referring specifically to the channels, winds, and essences that comprise the human body and create the arena for the manifestation of buddhahood. The very existence of this body is described as the convergence of karma and aspirations and the terms that follow—wish-fulfilling tree, upon which, India—are then interpreted with reference to that body. The wish-fulfilling tree is the central channel. The heat of India refers to *caṇḍālī*, the inner heat of the subtle body. For Dilgo Khyentse Rinpoche, singing Jigmé Lingpa's feast song is not merely about poetically evoking the ideal setting for a feast offering, it is a profound and concise instruction on the channels and winds (*rtsa rlung*) at the heart of Nyingma perfection-stage practice.

This esoteric reading of "Karma and Aspirations Converge" coexists with readings focused on the lyrical content or on the ritual context of the tsok. In the secret autobiographies that Janet Gyatso translated, Jigmé Lingpa similarly represents himself in many different registers—both as an aspiring practitioner wrestling with self-doubt and uncertainty and as a realized master who has received the direct blessing and empowerment of Padmasambhava, Longchen Rabjampa (1308–64), and other luminaries of the Nyingma tradition. In many ways, it is precisely this tension between pride and humility that renders Jigmé Lingpa so human and relatable in his secret autobiographies. Compared to some of the more one-dimensional representations of Tibetan Buddhist masters found in hagiographies composed by disciples engaged in the practice of viewing their guru as a buddha, Jigmé Lingpa's autobiographies present a multifaceted subject whose awakening is embodied within the complex vicissitudes of human life. Similarly, the two portraits of Jigmé Lingpa that I wish to consider in the final section of this essay evoke a comparable quality of lifelike individuality. These two portraits, one sculpted and one painted, are connected by an unusual story that returns us to the topic of tendrel in yet another mode.

The first portrait is an exquisite bronze sculpture from the collection of

13. Dilgo Khyentse Rinpoche, 707–8: des na kun rdzob rnam dkar gyi bag chags mthu brtas pa'i las dge ba dang bsam sbyor rnam dag gi smon lam gnyis kyi rang 'bras lha bas lhag pa'i khams drug ldan gyi rdo rje'i lus kyi ye shes kyi rtsa rlung thig le'i rten 'brel legs phyogs su smin pas rdo rje nang gis lam gyi yon tan 'dod rgu 'byung ba'i dbu ma la dpag bsam ljon shing gi sgras rgyud sde du ma nas gsungs la/ de'i dbyings su rlung sems thig le dang bcas pa dag dgos pas steng na zhes gsungs shing/ rgya gar 'di 'dzam gling gi yul dbus drod tshad rang bzhin gyis 'phel ba'i nas su gyur pas gtum mo'i me mtshon zhing/.

the Rubin Museum of Art (see figure 1). Compared with much Tibetan Buddhist sculpture, this work contains far more naturalistic detail: the wrinkles around the eyes and on the brow, the shape of the nose and mouth, the style of the beard and top knot. Over the years, I visited this sculpture at the Rubin Museum many times and was thrilled when it was included in an exhibition devoted to Padmasambhava called *The Second Buddha: Master of Time*,[14] which was installed at the Rubin Museum in 2018 and then traveled in spring 2019 to the Tang Teaching Museum at Skidmore College where I teach. I had the great honor of organizing a series of public lectures connected to the works in the show. The fact that it was the twentieth anniversary of the publication of *Apparitions of the Self* made it a particularly auspicious time to invite Janet Gyatso to speak about her work on Jigmé Lingpa.

Figure 1. Detail of Jigmé Lingpa (Rubin Museum of Art, acc. #C2002.29.2)

A few days before Janet's arrival, I was standing in the lobby of the museum with the painter Pema Namdol Thaye (b. 1966). One of his thangka paintings, depicting the wrathful form of Padmasambhava known as Dorjé Drolö (*rdo*

14. See Pakhoutova and Seligman 2018.

rje gro lod), was included in the exhibition, and he had kindly agreed to spend a week in residence on campus, visiting classes in Asian studies and art, delivering a public lecture on *The Second Buddha*, and engaging in a public conversation with a geoscience professor on the topic of minerals and pigments used in Tibetan painting. His first morning on campus, we toured the exhibition together while the museum remained closed to the public. Viewing the paintings and sculptures in the exhibition with an artist of such extraordinary knowledge and ability was an amazing gift, and his observations deepened my appreciation of every work. However, Pema Namdol Thaye's response to the bronze sculpture of Jigmé Lingpa stands out in my memory. It was his first encounter with the statue, and it truly stopped him in his tracks. Most of the other works we had seen inspired an impromptu mini-lecture on aspects of Tibetan painting styles and techniques, the attributes of certain materials, and astute observations of details I had overlooked till then. The Jigmé Lingpa statue, however, left Pema Namdol Thaye speechless for a long time as he gazed upward with his head lowered reverently and his hands joined before him. Eventually, Pema explained that the statue gave him the feeling that he was in the presence of Jigmé Lingpa himself and that he "felt as if he was receiving a raw, primordial blessing accompanied by a very unique smell."[15] That extraordinary feeling was compounded by the sculpture's uncanny resemblance to a ngakpa he had known well during his childhood in Kalimpong. Pema shared some stories about this ngakpa's eccentric behavior and renowned healing powers and mentioned that the most unusual thing about him was the strong scent that emanated from his body regardless of how well he bathed. Pema had been told by his uncle, the renowned master artist Lama Gonpo Tenzing Rinpoche (1920–2015), that this odor was a sign of the siddhis passed through his familial ngakpa lineage.

A few days later, Pema Namdol Thaye attended Janet Gyatso's lecture. Near the end of her lecture, Janet showed an image of the bronze Jigmé Lingpa sculpture from the exhibition and remarked upon the naturalistic representation of the subject's features. She noted that the sculpture was very likely made near the end of his life by someone who knew him well. She then showed the portrait of Jigmé Lingpa from the cover of *Apparitions of the Self*. The cover for the paperback edition is an enlarged detail of a black-and-white photograph of a painted portrait of Jigmé Lingpa (See figure 2). Janet explained her initial resistance to the cover design and her eventual embrace of the somewhat fuzzy image as an appropriate face for a book that celebrates indeterminacy, ambiguity, and empty appearances. In passing, she mentioned that the photograph had been

15. Pema Namdol Thaye, email to the author, August 15, 2021.

given to her by Tashi Tsering of Amnye Machen Institute, who reported that it had been taken in Tibet and that the original painting itself was probably lost. Janet said she had spent almost ten years trying to locate the original painting before the photo was used as her book cover and that now, thirty years later, it seemed unlikely that it would ever be found.

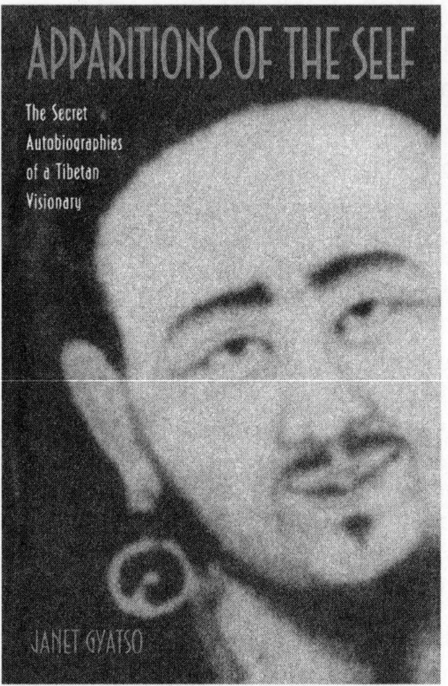

Figure 2. Cover of *Apparitions of the Self* (paperback edition)

There was a lively question-and-answer period, lengthy applause, and when I approached the lectern to thank Janet, I saw Pema Namdol Thaye introducing himself. Then he pointed to the frontispiece of *Apparitions of the Self*—a black-and-white photo of the complete Jigmé Lingpa portrait from which the detail on the cover was taken—and said, "I know this painting." He explained that the painting was not lost; he had seen it with his own eyes. As Janet started asking him more questions and suggesting that perhaps the painting he had seen was another (perhaps similar) portrait of Jigmé Lingpa, Pema Namdol Thaye calmly but forcefully said, "No. There is absolutely no question. This is the exact painting." He then went on to explain that one day in his childhood, he was in the home of a ngakpa in Kalimpong and happened to look at the shelf of a cabinet where the ngakpa kept torma and other ritual objects, and there was this small, extraordinary portrait of Jigmé Lingpa. The painting was right at eye-level for a child, in the back of a cabinet and without the traditional brocade frame. Pema Namdol Thaye said he would look at that painting again and again, studying the precise tiny brushstrokes and the lifelike detail of Jigmé Lingpa's smiling face. He said that it was this painting that made him want to become a thangka painter, that he immediately knew he wanted to learn how to paint like that.

Stunned by this strange coincidence, I started to question Pema further and asked if the ngakpa who owned the painting might still be in Kalimpong. Then he explained that he had passed away around 2005 and said, "Actually, Ben, this ngakpa is the same one I told you about the other day, the one with the very strong scent." What had already seemed to be an inexplicably lucky coincidence now seemed like something even more unfathomable. The ngakpa who looked so much like the bronze Jigmé Lingpa from the Rubin Museum of Art that Pema Namdol Thaye smelled his characteristic scent in its presence was also the owner of the "lost" original painting of Jigmé Lingpa that became the slightly out of focus black-and-white picture on the cover of Janet's book? And it was that very painting that inspired Pema Namdol Thaye to become a thangka painter? As we unraveled all these layers of connections over dinner at a restaurant in Saratoga Springs with stories and laughter, we all took delight in the shared experience of tendrel. The aspirations voiced in Jigmé Lingpa's song converged with the aspirations of the artists who sculpted the Rubin Museum's bronze image and Lama Drakden's painting, these converged with Pema Namdrol Thaye's childhood aspiration to become a thangka painter and with Janet Gyatso's aspiration to translate Jigmé Lingpa's secret autobiographies into English. That night, I made my own aspiration to locate Lama Drakden's painting and offer Janet a color print as a small token of my heartfelt gratitude for her mentorship and friendship and through the generous efforts of Venerable Sean Price and Changling Rinpoche (both of Shechen Monastery in Nepal), that aspiration was also fulfilled, and the color image of Jigmé Lingpa's "lost" portrait is included in this Festschrift (plate 5).

Postscript

Shortly before this volume went to press, I was astonished to discover that Janet Gyatso had previously published her own translation of Jigme Lingpa's "Feast Song." The realization that my *festschrift* offering was unwittingly constructed around a text that the recipient had already translated caused an immediate panic. When I confessed the oversight to Janet, after much good-natured laughter, she insisted that I proceed with publishing my version. If nothing else, having labored over my own translation of this song before discovering

Janet Gyatso's version has enhanced both my own humility and the depth of my admiration for Janet's skill as a translator of Tibetan poetry.

Works Cited

Tibetan Sources

Dilgo Khyentse Rinpoche, Rabsal Dawa (Dil mgo mkhyen brtse rin po che, Rab gsal zla ba). *Illuminating Awareness-Emptiness: A Clarification of the Hidden Meaning of the Feast Song Called "Karma and Aspirations Converge." Tshogs glu las smon rten 'brel gyi bas don rnam par gsal ba rig stong dgongs pa'i snang byed.* In *The Collected Writings of Skyabs-rje Dil-mgo Mkhyen-brtse Rin-po-che*, 13:707–14. New Delhi: Shechen Publications, 1994.

Jigmé Lingpa ('Jigs med gling pa). *Fruit from the Wish-Fulfilling Tree of Virtuous Deeds. Yul lho rgyud du byung ba'i rdzogs chen pa rang byung rdo rje mkhyen brtse'i 'od zer gyi rnam par thar pa legs byas yongs 'du'i snye ma.* Chengdu: Si khron mi rigs dpe skrun khang, 1998.

———. *A Hundred Rays of Light, The Mirror of Compassion and Wisdom: A Commentary on the "Embodiment of the Guru's Intention." Dgongs 'dus rnam bshad mkhyen brtse'i me long 'od zer brgya pa.* In *The Collected Works of Kun-mkhyen 'Jigs-med-gling-pa*, 4:7–378. Gangtok, Sikkim: Sonam T. Kazi, 1970–75.

English-Language Sources

Anam Thubten Rinpoche. 2020. "Dharma in Poetry." *buddhistdoor global*, August 12, 2020. https://www.buddhistdoor.net/features/dharma-in-poetry.

Byrne, Rhonda. 2006. *The Secret.* New York: Atria Books.

Gyatso, Janet, tr. 1997. "From the Autobiography of a Visionary." In *Religions of Tibet in Practice*, edited by Donald S. Lopez, Jr., 369–75. Princeton, NJ: Princeton University Press.

Gyatso, Janet. 1998. *Apparitions of the Self: The Secret Autobiographies of a Tibetan Visionary.* Princeton, NJ: Princeton University Press.

Kunsang, Erik Pema, tr. 2004. "Feast Song by Kunkhyen Jigmey Lingpa." In *Dzogchen Essentials*, edited by Marcia Binder Schmidt, 249–50. Boudhanath: Rangjung Yeshe Publications.

Pakhoutova, Elena, and Rachel Seligman, eds. 2018. *The Second Buddha: Master of Time.* New York: Prestel.

Schaik, Sam van. 2014. "A Tibetan Catalogue of the Works of 'Jigs-med gling-pa." *Revue d'Études Tibétaines* 29 (April): 39–63.

Shizuka, Haruki. 2008. "An Interim Report on the Study of Gaṇacakra: Vajrayāna's New Horizon in Indian Buddhism." In *Esoteric Buddhist Studies: Identity in Diversity*, edited by the Editorial Board, ICEBS, 185–98. Koyasan: Koyasan University.

Sujata, Victoria. 2004. *Tibetan Songs of Realization: Echoes from a Seventeenth-Century Scholar and Siddha in Amdo*. Leiden: Brill.

Szántó, Péter-Dániel. 2019. "Minor Vajrayāna texts V: The Gaṇacakravidhi attributed to Ratnākaraśānti." In *Tantric Communities in Context*, edited by Nina Mirnig, Marion Rastelli, and Vincent Eltschinger, 275–314. Vienna: Austrian Academy of Sciences Press.

Szántó Péter-Dániel, and Arlo Griffiths. 2015. "Sarvabuddhasamāyogaḍākinījālaśaṃvara." In *Brill Encyclopedia of Buddhism, Vol. I Literature and Languages*, edited by Oskar Von Hinuber, Vincent Eltschinger, and Jonathan Silk, 365–72. Leiden: Brill.

Thinley Norbu Rinpoche, tr. n.d. *Lay Mön Ten Drel by Rigdzin Jigmé Lingpa*. Watsonville, CA: Bero Jeydren Publications.

Jigmé Lingpa's Theology of Absence

Willa B. Baker

WITH HER ANTHOLOGY *In the Mirror of Memory* (1992), Janet Gyatso left an indelible mark on Buddhist studies by drawing attention to the role of memory in the Buddhist literary tradition, not merely as remembrance of the past but as mnemonic textuality, the attention of mindfulness (*smṛti*), devotion to historical thinking, and the construction of the narrative self.[1] Her dive into memory was deep, leaving its mark on the field of religion. Later, her seminal *Apparitions of the Self* (1998) again explored the role of memory in the construction of the narrative self, embracing the irony that a tradition centered on the doctrine of no-self (or emptiness of self) so fully embraces the complexities and subtleties of identity.[2]

In a memoir of Jigmé Lingpa (1730–98) that recently surfaced from a cache of texts in Central Tibet, memory figures as a prominent theme. *Turning the Wheel of Diligent Practice in the Forest Where Maheśvara Plays*, a "testament of realization" (*rtogs brjod*) in seventy-four calligraphed folios,[3] unfolds a detailed narrative of recollected conversations, personal impressions, insights, wanderings, and events during the pivotal thirtieth year of the author's life, between his first and second three-year retreats. While the autobiographical nature of this text bears the hallmark of Jigmé Lingpa's impulse to process personal memories as a mode of constructing the narrative self, it also celebrates memory as a transpersonal and collective phenomenon.

What I want to explore briefly here in this essay is a particular sort of remembering operative in Jigmé Lingpa's testament that highlights a dimension of Tibetan historical consciousness connected not to factuality but rather to affect. In the testament, Jigmé Lingpa maps an indelible overlay of the past onto the present, so that collective memory for events long past and people long gone blends with the present reality of the natural landscape of the trees, rocks, and caves of Samyé Chimphu. This mapping repeatedly yields a sentiment

1. Gyatso 1992.

2. Gyatso 1998.

3. 'Jigs med gling pa, n.d. This work is abbreviated "Testament" in notes to follow.

blended with the act of remembering that could be best described as nostalgia, memory tinged with longing for an idealized past that is partially retrieved in the act of remembering.

Nostalgia, heralding from the Greek *nostos*, meaning "homecoming," and *algos*, meaning "ache," is a yearning to return home to a past that is at once alive in memory but otherwise inaccessible in the present time. Nostalgia for Jigmé Lingpa manifests as a "remembering" (*dran*) that carries a shadow of absence. The sentiment carried in his acts of remembering is conditional, always ignited by place (*gnas*), by memory of a specific person or persons who once wandered there, and by the reality of their *absence* from the place. Remembering, for Jigmé Lingpa, is an act of recognition that what once was is no longer. The result is a theology of absence (sentimental remembering, nostalgia) that becomes a driving force of the memoir.

Jigmé Lingpa's nostalgia emerges gradually as a religious experience, seated in the context of his abnegation of his role as a ritual specialist with which the memoir begins. The year is 1759, when Jigmé Lingpa emerges from his first three-year retreat at Palri Thekchen Ling Monastery in Chongyé in south-central Tibet. At first, the fresh graduate begins teaching a small group of disciples and offering them empowerments, but he is soon overwhelmed with a wave of aversion to the busyness and stickiness of ministry. As he ruminates, "Although I meditate in the middle of the village, the only transference I master is that of funds of the living and dead."[4]

Eschewing his ministerial duties, he withdraws from this social circle and travels fifty kilometers overland with two of his students, crosses the Tsangpo River, and finds refuge at Chimphu, the cave complex above Samyé Monastery. At first, he seems to find his solace and joy in reclaiming an identity outside the confines of temporality: "I am a non-doing yogi who realizes the unborn great perfection. In the nature of spontaneously arising awareness, there is no transcendence or change."[5] But this refrain of a timeless present, which recurs throughout the memoir, soon is challenged by the overlapping temporal narrative of his own pilgrimage and his ongoing mythic memory of Padmasambhava,[6] Yeshé Tsogyal, and the so-called twenty-five disciples extending into the narrative past, which draw him into the ache of homecoming.

4. Testament, fol. 3.4.

5. Testament, fol. 8.4.

6. Padmasambhava (referred to by his alternate names Guru Rinpoché, Padma, and Orgyen below), Yeshe Tsogyal, and the twenty-five disciples are the eighth-century progenitors of Jigmé Lingpa's Nyingma lineage.

Soon after arriving at Samyé Chimphu, Jigmé Lingpa settles into a cave to escape a rainstorm, and looking out from there he reflects on the natural features of the mountain via a "Long Vajra Song Praising the Glorious Samyé Chimphu."

> On the king of practice mountains,
> indivisible from all the ḍākinī sites of India and Tibet,
> those sacred places that bless whoever visits,
> is Chimphu, with its forest of Maheśvara,
> rising from a valley shaped like the face of a blooming lotus.
> The regal grassy meadows of its upper slopes reach into the sky,
> culminating with the precious treasure at its summit,
> the holy cave of Guru Rinpoché, like a great open pavilion
> surrounded by the practice caves of the twenty-five retinue disciples.
> Below, summer mists drift through the valleys where ḍākinīs gather.
> On its slopes, young antelope gambol playfully
> remote) from the snare of human dramas. . . .
> Just by arriving in this place, perception changes.[7]

The power of the wild, dynamic features of the mountain, intertwining with the collective memory of Nyingma mythos, change perception (*snang ba 'gyur*). This power of sacred place (*gnas*) to transform perception becomes an ongoing refrain in the poetry throughout the memoir: that the key ingredients of Jigmé Lingpa's transformation are not merely practice, reading, or Dharma per se but rather the sacred geography, the traces of collective memory invoked there, and a poignant nostalgia for the past that propels Jigmé Lingpa to reconfigure time.

In what way is Jigmé Lingpa's perception changed by place? As the song unfolds, the nature of transformation becomes intertwined with his realization of absence:

> When I see this amazing, wonderous place
> in light of the power of self-arisen Padma's blessings,
> I miss (*dran*) Orgyen from the bottom of my heart.
> When I reflect in the morning, I miss him in the morning.
> When I reflect in the evening, I miss him in the evening.[8]

7. Testament, fol. 11b.6–12.4.

8. Testament, fol. 12.6–12b.1.

As he evolves from seeing the geography of the mountain to reflection on the significance of place, he considers that the people who passed through it are no longer there, and his perception opens to sense the shadow of absence. For Jigmé Lingpa, to remember is to miss, to know absence, to become aware that the present is *amiss*. (It is important to remark here that *dran*, which is so often translated as "to remember," has an alternate meaning of "to miss.")[9] To encounter the place of pilgrimage is to grapple with the extent of one's distance from that which one wishes to unite, the unrequited love of missing. This absence is tinged with sorrow but is not without purpose in terms of his overall salvific aims, as becomes apparent as the memoir unfolds.

Later in the same long song, he extensively extols the qualities of "The Little Nest" of Kiu Tsang, another cave on the mountain, where Nyang Tingdzin Zangbo (eighth–ninth century), a student of Vimalamitra and one of Padmasambhava's twenty-five disciples, meditated, culminating with:

> The qualities of "The Little Nest" are inconceivable!
> I miss, miss, miss you Tingdzin Zangpo!
> From my heart, I supplicate:
> Bless me right now to completely cut the root of grasping,
> to ripen into the essence of authentic awareness (*rig pa*),
> to train in luminosity throughout the day and night.[10]

In this passage too we see an immediate connection between the qualities of the place—qualities that unfold as a poetic praise of the natural features of the cave and its catalytic power for meditation practice—and the theology of absence, an absence that begins with unrequited yearning: "I miss you!" But rather than collapsing into sorrow, this encourages Jigmé Lingpa to invoke what actually is present, his own potential to fulfill the aim of Dzogchen practice by recognizing primordially present awareness (*rig pa*) and training in luminosity, a sharpening of attention to the cognizant luminous nature through formal yogic practice. The link between the felt absence of this beloved mortal ancestor and the felt presence of Jigmé Lingpa's own timeless awareness is supplication, activating blessings that remain as traces latent in the place. The steppingstone from the ordinary to the salvific is the absence, which encourages invocation into being.

9. My sources Kelsang Lhamo and Anam Thubten underscore that the meaning of dran here is aligned with the sentiment of absence, to the extent that dran becomes not "remember" but rather "miss" in the sense of feeling the lack of embodied presence.

10. Testament, fol. 16b.4–5.

In a later passage, his theology of absence is unpacked with even greater specificity:

> Just seeing [this place], my hair stands up with faith.
> Missing the teacher and students, my eyes fill with tears.
> Their absence moves my heart to sadness.
> Describing the history of these sacred sites makes me remember impermanence.
> Reflect in such a way, you of future generations![11]

This passage explicitly frames Jigmé Lingpa's historical project and his nostalgia as a salvific act, a literary pilgrimage undertaken for the sake of faith and acknowledgment that the objects of faith lie just out of reach, an unrequited love that requires an invocation of presence to heal. The religious nature of this project is underscored by his encouragement to future generations not only to record history but to continue to link place to narrative with the requisite sentiments.

Jigmé Lingpa's "Long Vajra Song Praising the Glorious Samyé Chimphu" culminates in a resolution of the tension of nostalgia, this uncomfortable yearning to reunite with presences long gone. The resolution takes the form of two realizations: first is that even though the guru and his disciples are deceased, their Dharma is still being taught *by the mountain itself* and second is that impermanence is enfolded in the stable ground of awareness. As he prepares to conclude his long song, the song pivots back to the natural features of the mountain:

> Sometimes this place is enveloped by a thick fog,
> revealing the nature of saṃsāra and nirvāṇa.
> Although the arrangement of the mountain's features is intact,
> everything is rendered unclear.[12]
> This natural phenomenon is a symbol of how the ground for the arising of both saṃsāra and nirvāṇa
> is complete within the nature of awareness.[13]

11. Testament, fol. 17b.2.

12. Something can be actually present but seem to be absent; appearances of saṃsāra and nirvāṇa are like the fog obscuring the presence of awareness.

13. The verses leading up to this passage indicate a second implicit valence: the lineage masters' residual blessings are present on the mountain, even though the people themselves are long deceased (another presence that is seemingly absent).

Sometimes the waist of the mountain is ringed with a fringe of mist,
a symbol that all people who enter the path
are under the unconscious influence of the two habitual
obscurations.

Sometimes when the sky is clear, with a buffeting wind,
the mountain's features are as crisp and clear as the palm of your hand,
a symbol of the perfection of the inherent energy of the fruitional
three kāyas
that follows from the mastery of the wisdom that knows things
as they are and as many as they are.[14]

Jigmé Lingpa's nostalgia propels him into reunion, not with the human but with the natural features of the mountain, and with its sacred geography arising as a teacher of the Dharma that is both fully present and adequate for his practice of Dzogchen. This provides resolution of Jigmé Lingpa's longing. While the masters have passed on, their Dharma continues to unfold as the thick fog, the mists, the buffeting wind. The mountain draws the yogi into meditation, a phenomenon that we suddenly realize has been happening from the very first few words of the song ("On the king of practice mountains, indivisible from all the ḍākinī sites of India and Tibet, those sacred places bless whoever visits").

The resolution continues with a more far-reaching insight, namely that healing the sorrow of absence is not found in restoration of presence but rather in the dissolution of grasping to a permanence that has always been elusive:

All phenomena express the interdependence of skillful means and
wisdom.
Yet there is not an atom's worth of reality to anything.
Everything is the miraculous display of mind alone.
Eternal permanence is a confused meditation.
The idea is there in order to inspire seekers,
but from an ultimate perspective, it is just a convention.
By knowing how to relax in the great unconstrained self-awareness,
fixation, grasping, and miserliness are liberated in their own place.
From the overflowing of the secret treasure that is the intention of
Longchenpa,
outer appearing objects arise as symbols and text.[15]

14. Testament, fol. 18b.2–5.

15. Jigmé Lingpa is referring here to his lineage predecessor and great essentializer of the

> And this awareness, free from beliefs and reference points,
> ceases to chase after appearing objects.[16]

Jigmé Lingpa, in this final passage, sums up the final salvific stage of his theology of absence. The shadow of nostalgia ultimately draws the pilgrim into a state of sorrow that is healed by the wisdom of realizing that persons never were *truly* present ("there is not an atom's worth of reality to anything"), but they were always existing in the mind of the observer ("the miraculous display of mind alone"). The ultimate encounter with presence is not found in the grasping but rather in the act of relaxing into the nondual field ("in the great unconstrained self-awareness") in which every appearance becomes the Dharma ("outer appearing objects arise as symbols and text"). This is where Jigmé Lingpa finds himself coextensive with the mountain. When the mountain arises as text, he can finally "cease to chase after appearing objects," including the gurus of his reveries.

The question of absence and presence is, of course, a long-standing one in Buddhism going back to the parinirvāṇa of Śākyamuni, and it has been addressed in the scholarship of Buddhist studies over the years.[17] However, Jigmé Lingpa poses a quintessentially Tibetan answer to the problem of absence, through devotion to the Tibetan landscape, the sentiment of nostalgia, and ultimately through the Dzogchen emphasis on the primordial presence of awareness. In her introduction to *In the Mirror of Memory*, Janet Gyatso observes that "Even if the Buddha needed to remember in order to forget, many Buddhists want to remember in order to remember."[18] Such seems to be the case with Jigmé Lingpa, who seeks to remember (*dran*) in order to miss (*dran*), and finally miss in order to become mindful (*dran*) of awareness.

Works Cited

Eckel, Malcolm David. 1994. *To See the Buddha: A Philosopher's Quest for the Meaning of Emptiness*. Princeton, NJ: Princeton University Press.

Gyatso, Janet, ed. 1992. *In the Mirror of Memory: Reflections on Mindfulness and Remembrance in Indian and Tibetan Buddhism*. Albany: State University of New York Press.

Nyingma teachings Longchenpa (1308–64), whose works encourage perception of all of reality as the Dharma (hence "outer appearing objects arising as symbols and text").

16. Testament, fol. 18b.5–19.2.

17. For example, see Eckel 1994.

18. Gyatso 1992, 16.

———. 1998. *Apparitions of the Self: The Secret Autobiographies of a Tibetan Visionary.* Princeton, NJ: Princeton University Press.

Heim, Maria. "Buddhism." 2008. In *The Oxford Handbook of Religion and Emotion*, edited by John Corrigan, 17–34. New York: Oxford University Press.

'Jigs med gling pa, Kun mkyhen. *Dbang chen rol pa'i nags khrod du bsgrub pa nan tan gyi 'khor lo la gzhol ba'i rtogs pa brjod pa* [*Turning the Wheel of Diligent Practice in the Forest Where Maheśvara Plays,* abbreviated "Testament"]. Buddhist Digital Resource Center (W4CZ302350), unpublished manuscript accessed as scan, n.d.

Introductions in Order and Matter Out of Place: Entangled Epiphanies Between Mind and Matter

James Gentry

Without becoming a system, the site of semiotics, where models and theories are developed, is a place of dispute and self-questioning, a "circle" that remains open. Its "end" does not rejoin its "beginning," but, on the contrary, rejects and rocks it, opening up the way to another discourse, that is, another subject and another method; or rather, there is no more end than beginning, the end is the beginning and vice versa. No form of semiotics, therefore, can exist other than as a critique of semiotics.
JULIA KRISTEVA[1]

JANET GYATSO has perhaps done more than any other scholar in Tibetan studies to introduce us to the roles of signs and their interpretation in the history of Tibetan religion.[2] Janet's ruminations about signs are indicative of her careful thinking about how immediacy, opacity, and mediation have figured rhetorically, and materially, in the lives and writings of Tibet's greatest Buddhist visionaries and intellectuals. This paper is an initial step onto one of the paths opened by Janet's pioneering work—a tentative venture into the uncharted territories of how signs connect with materiality to bring about effects in Tibetan Buddhist contemplative and ritual practice. My thoughts on this theme represent only a small token of my inestimable gratitude for Janet's tremendous contributions to the fields of Tibetan studies, Buddhist studies, and humanistic and post-humanistic studies at large, which she continues to shape in important ways.

This foray specifically examines the relationships struck between mind and matter in the semiotics of the mind-nature "introduction" (*ngo sprod*), an interactive process by which Buddhist teachers in Tibet have sought to elicit in students an epiphany of nondual cognition. Rather than narrate a history of the semiotics of mind-nature introduction, I describe its general features and touch

1. Kristeva 1986, 78.

2. Gyatso 1986, 1992, 1993, 1998, 1999.

on a few examples before juxtaposing it to two other partially connected semiotic contexts—the ritualized consumption of flesh-relic pills and large-scale initiation rites, both of which also aim ultimately to elicit epiphanies of nondual cognition. Each of these three contexts aims through enacting its semiotic operations to point out the entanglements between mind and matter, subject and object, signifier and signified, and all other dualities in the interest of collapsing their boundaries.

But in the spirit of Julia Kristeva, my selection of these three examples is not to suggest that they partake of a unified or closed semiotic system. Rather, this juxtaposition is inspired by Janet Gyatso's evocation of Kristeva to suggest "the *ḍākinī*'s style of thinking and using language" as "working within language to subvert it, drawing attention to its own (dualistic) structures while never retreating outside its realm."[3] The following discussion thus seeks to question how drawing partial connections among disparate semiotic settings can open new interpretative possibilities for understanding how Buddhists in Tibet have related mind with matter in attempting to communicate the ineffable.[4] How, in other words, might relating the entanglements between mind and matter enacted in these different semiotic settings suggest unexplored entanglements between these different settings as well? And what, for that matter, might these relationships tell us more broadly about the repertoire of semiotic sensibilities operative in tantric Buddhist practice in Tibet?[5]

The Mattering of Mind

In the Great Perfection tradition of the Nyingma School of Tibetan Buddhism we encounter a tripartite semiotic operation through which Buddhist teachers have sought to evoke breakthrough epiphanies in others of their own intrinsic nondual cognition. This semiotic operation appears in abbreviated form as "the

3. Gyatso 1998, 251.

4. This methodology of drawing "partial connections," rather than seeking to draw identities, holistic organicisms, antagonisms, and so forth, is inspired by Marilyn Strathern (2005, 36–40), as inspired in turn by Donna Haraway (1985).

5. By "semiotic sensibility" I aim to sensitize to the tantric Buddhist performative context Webb Keane's (2003, 419) usage of the term *semiotic ideology*. Keane describes semiotic ideology as "basic assumptions about what signs are and how they function in the world. It determines, for instance, what people will consider the role that intentions play in signification to be, what kinds of possible agent (humans only? animals? spirits?) exist to which acts of signification might be imputed, whether signs are arbitrary or necessarily linked to their objects, and so forth." The sensory, material, and performative contexts of the semiotic frameworks under consideration in this essay suggest a more embodied "sensibility" than the overwhelmingly discursive emphasis implied in "ideology."

triad of example, actuality, and sign" (*dpe don rtags gsum*). It formally structures the dynamics by which such "introductions" to nondual cognition, as these evocative techniques came to be called, purport to do their work.

In mediating the paradoxical mechanics of how conditioned methods might lead to unconditioned nonduality, introductions occupy a paramount position in Great Perfection theory and practice. Only when Great Perfection students have been so "introduced" to their intrinsic nondual cognition are they sufficiently equipped to practice repeated re-recognizing of this experience as the basis of their path of practice, whose aim, the full awakening of buddhahood, is claimed to be nothing more or less than the full development, stabilization, and integration of this initial introduction into every facet of life.

The tripartite semiotic typology for framing introductions makes its first appearances in texts held to be the scriptural foundations of the Great Perfection tradition. The typology is enlisted repeatedly throughout the *Sūtra of the All-Creating Sovereign*, one of the primary scriptures of what came to be called the *mind section* of the Great Perfection's threefold division into mind, space, and pith instructions (*sems klong man ngag sde gsum*).[6] Here "example, actuality, and sign" form an aesthetic approach toward conveying and apprehending the inconceivable and inexpressible nature of mind and reality. The *example* that appears throughout is the sky, or space.[7] Its *actuality*—that is, what this example signifies—is the unborn nature of reality, also referred to in the text as the all-pervading essence of the mind of awakening. The *sign*, or evidence for this, is the readily observable glimpses into the all-pervading mind of awakening from the perspective of the untrained or partially trained observer, such as the unimpeded functioning of cognition. These evidential "signs" serve to thread together space with reality—example with actuality—in the service of evoking path-blazing, breakthrough epiphanies.

The typology of example, actuality, and sign appears with greater regularity in the scriptural sources of the Heart Essence (*Snying thig*), which likely first developed in Tibet in the eleventh century and came eventually to form the *pith instruction* class of Great Perfection theory and practice.[8] In the Heart

6. *Chos thams cad rdzogs pa chen po byang chub kyi sems kun byed rgyal po*, in *Bka' 'gyur dpe bsdur ma* 2006–2009, 101:3–189. For traditional discussions of the Great Perfection tradition's transmission history and subdivisions, see Dudjom 1991, 1:319–45, and Nyoshul Khenpo 2005.

7. For examples see chapters 5 and 15 of the *Sūtra of the All-Creating Sovereign*, 13 and 55. For English translation of these passages, see Neumaier-Dargyay 1992, 57 and 97, respectively. However, the translator has in both instances failed to recognize the significance of the term *sign* (*rtags*) in this typology, rendering it in the first instance as "main characteristic" and in the second as "investigation." For more on this sūtra, see also Namkhai Norbu et al. 1999.

8. Germano 1992.

Essence and its offshoots we witness the use of this tripartite semiotic typology taking a marked turn toward the material and the luminous. Rather than focus on the image of the sky, as in the *Sūtra of the All-Creating Sovereign*, the Heart Essence literature anchors the threefold typology to a series of material objects, like crystals, lamps, and mirrors, among others; these are its "examples" for introducing nondual cognition. Moreover, instead of emphasizing the unobjectifiable and empty essence of mind and reality, as the example of the sky does, the Heart Essence literature extends the semiotic typology of example, actuality, and sign to illustrate the mind's intrinsically radiant and luminous nature.

An important source for this turn toward the material and the luminous in Great Perfection semiotics is the *Tantra that Reveals the Pure Land from Conferring the Precious Introduction*.[9] This tantra, one of the Heart Essence tradition's foundational Seventeen Tantras, outlines a sequence of twenty-one techniques for introducing nondual cognition. Here, nonduality does not just entail the nonduality of apprehended object and apprehending subject but also, in the language of the tantra, the nonduality of emptiness and phenomenal content, the nonduality of the emptiness and radiance of cognition, and along similar lines, the nonduality of the open expanse of ultimate reality and intrinsic cognition.[10]

Key in all these senses of nonduality is that basic cognition is not simply empty of intrinsic existence. It is also radiant or luminous by nature, a feature evident foremost in the immediacy of phenomenal experience and the ongoing optical perception of light and color. Each introduction in the tantra thus aims to elicit its epiphany of nonduality—a dynamic it calls "finally resolving the ultimate nature of the buddhas"—through staging optical experiments with light and its colorful refraction and/or strategic obscuration vis-à-vis the "examples" of material objects like crystals and other gemstones, water surfaces, lamps, mirrors, porous walls, fabrics, peacock feathers, sticks, masks, silhouettes, statues, and flower bouquets, among others.[11] Here is where the triad of example, actuality, and sign figures: the tantra states that it is through the choreography of this triad in its performative introductions that "the fruition of the intrinsic nature is attained."[12]

After enumerating a series of such introductions, the tantra stipulates that introductory optical experiments can alternatively assume the form of provoking visual experiences of light and color by pressing the fingers to the eyes at

9. *Ngo sprod rin po che spras pa'i zhing khams bstan pa'i rgyud*.

10. *Ngo sprod rin po che spras pa'i zhing khams bstan pa'i rgyud*, 107.5–6.

11. *Ngo sprod rin po che spras pa'i zhing khams bstan pa'i rgyud*, 83.3–91.1.

12. *Ngo sprod rin po che spras pa'i zhing khams bstan pa'i rgyud*, 94.5–6.

their corners or directly on their lids, or by pressing the nerves at the neck that connect to the optic nerves, while also gazing obliquely at the sun, manipulating light sources, or depriving oneself of light entirely.[13]

Interlinear notes that appear in several versions of the tantra frame the material bases of all these optical experiments—light and its material sources and manipulations—as "examples" for the "actuality" of the empty and radiant nondual cognition or primordial knowing (*ye shes*) present in the hearts of all beings.[14] These notes, moreover, construe the "signs" or evidence that links examples with their actuality as none other than the lights and colors that these optical experiments aim to produce in the visual field.[15] In this, the semiotic typology of example, actuality, and sign is made to reflect broader Heart Essence theory linking cosmology, embryology, physiology, thanatology, and contemplative practice to frame intrinsic nondual cognition as the dynamically radiant, but intrinsically empty, generative matrix of body, mind, and world.[16] In keeping with this holistic conception of nonduality, the tantra also categorizes intrinsic nondual cognition itself according to the levels of example, actuality, and sign, depending on the degree to which epiphanies remain mediated by substance, language, and concepts.[17] This notion of an "exemplary nondual cognition" also appears in broader Indian Buddhist *yoganiruttaratantra* or *yoginītantra* contexts to explain the role of the introductory epiphany triggered in initiations and to distinguish it from the "actual nondual cognition" of complete awakening.[18] Here we can see that this distinction also plays a foundational role in the Great Perfection.[19]

A short manual instructing Buddhist teachers how to confer such introductions, composed by the Nyingma scholar Sokdokpa Lodrö Gyaltsen (1552–1624), offers clues into how such introductions and their semiotic typology were integrated into initiation rituals centuries later. Sokdokpa's manual *Clarifying the Symbolic Meaning: An Exposition on the Separately Concealed Meaning of the Supreme Initiation* is written according to the Great Perfection tradition

13. *Ngo sprod rin po che spras pa'i zhing khams bstan pa'i rgyud*, 92.1–93.1.

14. *Ngo sprod rin po che spras pa'i zhing khams bstan pa'i rgyud*, 94.5–6.

15. *Ngo sprod rin po che spras pa'i zhing khams bstan pa'i rgyud*, 96.6.

16. Germano 1992.

17. *Ngo sprod rin po che spras pa'i zhing khams bstan pa'i rgyud*, 96.1–2.

18. Isaacson 1998, 9; Tomlinson 2018, 14.

19. This contradicts Kapstein (2000, 117–18), who refers to the distinction between such levels of mediation as specific to the New Translation tantras of the *yoganiruttaratantra* class. This feature merits consideration as a possible Indian Buddhist influence on the Great Perfection tradition.

of the Black Quintessence (*Yang ti nag po*), revealed by the fifteenth-century visionary Dungtso Repa.[20] This revelation, which presents itself as a continuation of the Heart Essence revelation, structures its "supreme initiation" in terms of a series of five introductions to nondual cognition.[21] Similar to the Heart Essence tantra introduced above, the explicit aim of these introductions is to sequentially evoke the epiphanies that the ultimate nature of perfectly awakened body, speech, mind, qualities, and activities is no different from the pure, gnostic dimension of one's own intrinsic awareness, as reflected in phenomenal perceptual experience.

In keeping with Heart Essence style, each of the initiation's introductions opens with injunctions for the master of ceremonies to show initiates an object—a crystal, drum or bell, lamp, mirror, fan, and so on—and perform an action associated with that object—refract light, sound the instrument, reflect the initiate's face in the mirror, wave the fan, and so on.[22] In elucidating the dynamics involved, Sokdokpa goes beyond explicating the meanings of the objects presented to also offer meta-statements that lend insights into the logic of signification, the interpretative work involved in the process of introduction.

For instance, in the third initiation, where the master of ceremonies introduces the nature of mind based on the example of a butter lamp, Sokdokpa provides a script for the master of ceremonies to use in elucidating the relationship between signifier and signified:

> The awakened mind of all *sugata*s is lucid and radiant, but free of conceptuality. Through having cracked open the sheath of ignorance, the self-effulgence of primordial knowing, which has been present from the beginning in its naturally radiant state, shines forth, and is devoid of conceptuality, like the example of a butter lamp. Understand the meaning of this![23]...
>
> Like a butter lamp unmoved by wind, the primordial knowing of awareness neither brightens nor dims. This intrinsically present self-effulgence of primordial knowing, the indivisibility of aware-

20. *Dbang gong ma gud du sbas pa'i don bshad pa brda don gsal ba*, in Sog bzlog pa 1976–80.

21. Dung mtso ras pa 1979. The Heart Essence connection is evident in its emphasis on contemplative evocation of visionary experience otherwise known as the *direct-crossing* practices and a number of other distinctive themes held in common with the Heart Essence's Seventeen Tantras.

22. Sog bzlog pa 1976–80.

23. Sog bzlog pa 1976–80, 150.6–151.1.

> ness and emptiness, is the primordial knowing of the pristine awakened mind of all conquerors, called "the mind of awakening."[24] . . .
>
> In this way, the support for the initiation, this butter lamp, which is radiant, yet free of conceptuality, is demonstrated to be an illustration for mind.[25]

Sokdokpa follows this with a reflection on the mediation process of signification itself. He begins with a citation from Ngorchen Könchok Lhundrup's (1497–1557) mid-sixteenth-century manual on the *Hevajratantra* contemplative/ritual practice, only to conclude with explicit reference to the framework of "the triad of example, actuality, and sign" as what distinguishes the Great Perfection as superior to *yoginītantra*s like the *Hevajratantra*:

> That which the example gnosis illustrates
> is the unerring, nonconceptual gnosis of one's own awareness.
>
> Like a reflection in a mirror when looking at your face,
> it is not the actual gnosis, but it is similar to the actual.[26]
>
> In this way, the actuality is introduced based on an example. This is unlike the foolish talk of some who might say, "There is a tiger in the middle of the jungle because such a thing exists there." Since it can be directly shown right now, it is superior to others, for the "introduction through the triad of example, actuality, and sign" is a special feature of the Great Perfection.[27]

As illustrated by Sokdokpa's presentation, introduction initiations are premised on the observation that the basic nature of consciousness shares features with lamps, mirrors, fans, crystals, and so on—that is, luminosity, reflexivity, motility, insubstantiality, nonconceptuality, and so on. It is precisely because of such commonalities that these objects can function as iconic signifiers for pointing out the properties of nondual cognition.

The signified "example gnosis" (*dpe yi ye shes*) that Sokdokpa invokes in his explanation pivots precisely on this iconic reflexivity between material examples and the actuality of mind. Through the given material examples, nondual

24. Sog bzlog pa 1976–80, 151.3–4.

25. Sog bzlog pa 1976–80, 152.1.

26. Ngor chen Kun mchog lhun grub 2000, 56.2–3.

27. Sog bzlog pa 1976–80, 152.3–6.

cognition is "directly shown" (*mngon sum du ston*). Yet, at the same time, what is revealed is still not actual unmediated experience of nondual cognition. Truly unmediated participation must still be inferred, even as its example is given directly to experience for the first time. In this, "example gnosis" skirts the fuzzy edges of materiality, discursivity, and nondual cognition. It is itself signified by the material attributes of the examples, but once experienced, it pivots to signify actual nondual cognition in a way that is neither divorced from nor identical with it. The "example gnosis" revealed in introductions thus functions primarily as evidence for actual nondual cognition—it threads together through experience the signifier of material examples and the signified of nondual cognition. This dynamic allows the exemplary epiphany to serve as the experiential guarantor for the path of contemplative practice, as long as the guru's exegesis helps fill the gap.

Toward this end, Sokdokpa is resolute that explanation of the significance of each example is paramount for a successful introduction initiation. After the fifth sequence of the ritual, which rounds out the traditional set of awakened body, speech, mind, qualities, and activities, Sokdokpa explains that he was moved to write his short text because even the great lamas of his day "just place the crystal, bell, and the rest on the head and do not perform the introduction."[28] More important, he critically adds, is introducing the *significance* of each object. In this way, Sokdokpa is careful to delineate the role of material examples in introductions as iconic props for exegesis. That he contrasts this exegetical role of material objects to just touching them to the head of initiates suggests to my mind not a rejection of this tactile operation, so integral to the performance of tantric initiations, but a reckoning with overemphasis on physical touch at the exclusion of accompanying explanations in triggering breakthrough epiphanies.

The Minding of Matter

The misgivings voiced by Sokdokpa about whether discursive or physical contact ought to figure more prominently when introducing nondual cognition are flipped on their head when we turn our attention to how a similar semiotic dynamic between mind and matter plays out in the ritual preparation and consumption of flesh-relic pills (*skye bdun ril bu*). The tantric Buddhist consumption of antinomian substances—human flesh foremost—came to signal above all else the recognition of nondual cognition through the sudden transcendence of the most binding social strictures of purity and pollution, precept and

28. Sog bzlog pa 1976–80, 156.4–5.

prohibition.[29] Nonetheless, tantric Buddhist literature also treats human flesh as a powerful substance in its own right, promising the acquisition of flight, longevity, physical transmutation, control of the spirit world, and other effects to whomever incorporates through ingestion its nutritional and magical potencies.[30] Human flesh consumption has thus gathered a wide range of theories and practices in tantric Buddhism, combining soteriological, medical, alchemical, and other registers.[31]

Prescriptions found throughout several Indian Buddhist tantras and commentaries to consume the flesh of a man born for seven consecutive lifetimes as a human being, or as a male brahman, stand out as a particularly colorful development of this tradition. Such prescriptions are often accompanied by descriptions of how to identify such a person, how to best acquire their flesh, how to ritually prepare it into pills, and the many benefits of consuming it.[32]

Based on Indian Buddhist precedents, the visionary Treasure tradition of the Nyingma school came to regard this kind of flesh to derive specifically from human emanations of Avalokiteśvara, the bodhisattva of compassion, who is said to have intentionally materialized as seven-times-born humans to "liberate through tasting" (*myong grol*) all who ingest or otherwise come into contact with their flesh.[33] Despite this shift from pollution to purity—from a forbidden antinomian substance to an intrinsically efficacious materialization of pure altruism—the flesh has nonetheless retained its earlier transgressive ritual valence, along with its other medical and alchemical values.[34] Most importantly, the flesh's connection with epiphanies of nondual cognition has remained paramount, whether this is understood in terms of the cognitive dissonance of consuming a forbidden and repulsive substance, in terms of the liberating impact of ingesting a materialization of awakened intentionality, or both.

In a flesh-pill accomplishment initiation liturgy composed by the

29. Gray 2005, 67; Snellgrove 2010, 71–72.

30. Snellgrove 2010, 71–73 and 86–87; Gray 2007, 206–9 and 367–69.

31. Gray 2005.

32. Snellgrove 2010, 71–73 and 86–87; Gray 2007, 206–9 and 367–69; and Gray 2005.

33. For details on human-flesh pills claimed to "liberate through tasting" and other material objects with similar claims of sensory efficacy, see Gayley 2007, Gentry 2017, and Gentry 2019. For an introduction to the literature of the Tibetan Treasure tradition, see Gyatso 1996.

34. That this shift was already well underway in Indian Buddhist circles and not just a creative adaptation of Tibetans is demonstrated by the twelfth-century Indian Buddhist scholar Abhayākaragupta's understanding of the flesh of "one born seven times" as that of bodhisattvas, ripened through seven successive lifetimes and given in fulfillment of their altruistic intention to benefit beings. This appears in his famous *Āmnāyamañjarī* commentary on the *Sampuṭatantra* (2015, 886–87).

nineteenth-century luminary Jamyang Khyentsé Wangpo (1820–92), we find an attempt to organize these multiple senses of human-flesh consumption according to a semiotic typology that bears a striking resemblance to the tripartite schema of example, actuality, and sign considered above.[35] Khyentsé Wangpo draws this fleshly iteration of the typology from the *Great Tantra of the Tamer of Beings Who Churns Up the Lower Realms from the Depths*, part of the visionary revelations of the nineteenth-century Treasure revealer Chokgyur Lingpa (1829–70).[36] This typology likewise invokes three registers but applies them to the layered meanings reflecting the nature of material flesh pills rather than to material objects reflecting the nature of mind. According to this typology, the flesh should simultaneously be construed according to (1) the level of actuality (*don*), "the unborn" nature of ultimate reality; (2) the level of sign, or evidence (*rtags*), the material elixir of the seven-times-born flesh itself; and (3) the level of phenomenal mark (*mtshan ma*), the flesh as formed into pills whose efficacious power has been "accomplished" through ritual proceedings.[37]

As the liturgy makes clear, the triad of actuality, sign, and phenomenal mark organizes the substance along a spectrum of signification—from the actual level, in which signifier and signified have collapsed in the realization of emptiness, phrased in terms of a playful inversion of the seven-times-born flesh as "unborn"; to the evidential level, in which the substance indexes the potent flesh of a past buddha, bodhisattva, or accomplished being who once realized the actual; down to the material level, in which concrete pills are produced from traces of flesh along with other materials, and their power is augmented through the intensive group ritual action of "great accomplishment" (*sgrub chen*) and its accompanying initiation rite, ideally performed until manifesting its own "signs of success" (*rtags mtshan*). Such signs include sensory evidence such as the flesh-pill concoction's boiling over, wafting smoke, emitting light and sound, and taking flight, among other indicators that the ritual has maximally empowered the already potent flesh.

It is in fact within the context of precisely this ritual that the threefold typology figures. Khyentsé Wangpo enlists the scriptural citation with this typology in his liturgy as the scriptural passage for initiates to recite while they receive the final initiation, or "empowerment" (*dbang*), from the flesh pills that have been ritually treated through the "great accomplishment" outlined in the liturgy. In this way, the threefold typology presents itself as the discursive frame-

35. *Ngan song dong sprug 'gro ba 'dul ba'i rgyud chen po*. 'Jam dbyangs mkhyen brtse'i dbang po 1975–80.

36. 'Jam dbyangs mkhyen brtse'i dbang po 1975–80, 58.3–59.4.

37. 'Jam dbyangs mkhyen brtse'i dbang po 1975–80, 58.4–5.

work for receiving and consuming the flesh in the context of its empowerment and the transfer of its potency to others. The typology thus serves to mediate flesh consumption discursively in tandem with its ritual accomplishment, which mediates flesh consumption performatively.

What Matters More

The final semiotic framework I will briefly consider here involves not a typology per se but a few particularly telling remarks present throughout the narrative writings of the Fifth Dalai Lama Ngawang Losang Gyatso (1617–82). The Tibetan leader offers his opinion about what constitutes the most efficacious element in large-scale tantric rituals—the personal realization of the master of ceremonies or the material orthopraxy of ritual itself. These remarks appear in the Fifth Dalai Lama's autobiography and in his biography of the Nyingma hierarch Nyangtön Tratsangwa Lodrö Choki Dorjé (1595–1671), where the Great Fifth criticizes some of his contemporaries for not properly observing exacting ritual protocol with respect to ritual materials when performing tantric rites. Critical passages pointing out the faults of specific Tibetan figures, past and present, appear throughout the Fifth Dalai Lama's writings, reflecting the Tibetan leader's attempts to publicly discredit his political and sectarian foes. In this case they also give voice to a perspective prevalent among Buddhist ritualists of his day on the relative roles of mind and matter in conveying ineffable nondual cognition.

The Fifth Dalai Lama's critical remarks target Gongra Shenphen Dorjé (1594–1654).[38] The Great Fifth specifically charges Shenphen Dorjé with not properly observing the material specifications for large-scale tantric rites, calling him out for "not at all performing proper accomplishment offering rites," an important ritual akin to the lengthier great-accomplishment rite considered above, and for "not following any iconometric procedures with the maṇḍala but just drawing whatever is easiest, like an ordinary thread-cross maṇḍala."[39] Elsewhere, the Great Fifth extends this allegation to Shenphen Dorjé's style of conferring initiations, claiming that he "engages in the activity of initiation based upon a drawn maṇḍala without first doing any of the iconometric

38. The Fifth Dalai Lama dismissively calls him Gongrawa, "the One from Gongra." This figure happens to have been Sokdokpa's most high-profile student and abbot of Ngesang Dorjé Ling Monastery in Gongra, Central Tibet, before the Great Fifth appointed Nyangtön Tratsangwa as abbot on the occasion of Gongra Shenphen Dorjé's passing. For more on this figure and his relationships with Sokdokpa and the Great Fifth, see Gentry 2017, 384–408.

39. Ngag dbang Blo bzang rgya mtsho 1991–95b, 290.3.

procedures or preparations at all."[40] The Great Fifth couches this charge within a broader concern about the tendency among tantric masters of his day to just "visually show the initiation substances" to initiates, forcing them to "construe each as objects" from afar, rather than make the rounds through the aisles and personally bring the substances into direct physical contact with initiates.[41] Such improprieties around the improper treatment of substances and material protocol, the Great Fifth contends, "will become a basis for the extinction of all ritual practices."[42]

The Great Fifth chalks up all of these indiscretions to the arrogant misconception, common to Shenphen Dorjé and other masters of his ilk, that "they are coming from the expanse of the Great Perfection view," through which they wrongly presume to possess the requisite personal power to dispense with the material specifications that otherwise ensure ritual efficacy.[43] Rather than posture as a ritual specialist of great personal realization, the Great Fifth counters, "I, being of meager intellect, follow the protocol of an ordinary vajra master conferring initiation upon ordinary students."[44] On this note, adds the Great Fifth, he is simply observing the "tradition of not disrespecting the scriptures of Abhayākaragupta and Darpaṇācārya," two authoritative Indian scholars of tantric Buddhist ritual.[45]

In this way, the Fifth Dalai Lama writes that the efficacy of initiation rites hinges on observing the exacting protocol for ritual practice; he calls special attention to observing the proper iconographic preparations and to staging physical interactions between the masters of ceremonies and the initiates through the mediation of material initiation props. For the Great Fifth, it would seem, following an initiation ritual's protocol of material and aesthetic presentation and performing it interactively with the audience according to traditional guidelines is more likely to elicit an epiphany of nondual cognition than assuming the posture of a realized being and thereby dispensing with such material protocol in favor of direct mind-to-mind transmission.

40. Ngag dbang Blo bzang rgya mtsho 1991–95a, 5:313.1.

41. Ngag dbang Blo bzang rgya mtsho 1991–95a, 312.2–312.3

42. Ngag dbang Blo bzang rgya mtsho 1991–95a, 312.3.

43. Ngag dbang Blo bzang rgya mtsho 1991–95b, 290.3.

44. Ngag dbang Blo bzang rgya mtsho 1991–95a, 5:313.3. The Great Fifth extends this particular charge to the Sixth Shamar Garwang Chökyi Wangchuk (Gar dbang Chos kyi dbang phyug, 1584–1630).

45. Ngag dbang Blo bzang rgya mtsho 1991–95a, 5:313.3. For an English translation of this passage, see Karmay 2014, 237–38. Here the Fifth Dalai Lama is likely referring specifically to the tantric ritual compendia of Abhayākaragupta's (ca. 12th cent.) *Vajrāvalī* and Jagaddarpaṇa's (ca. 13th cent.) *Kriyāsamuccaya* based on it.

Closing Remarks

This exercise in drawing partial connections has juxtaposed three interrelated ways of triggering epiphanies of nondual cognition. To briefly retrace our steps, we started out by considering the Great Perfection semiotic typology of example, actuality, and sign in introductions to nondual cognition, specifically the use of exemplary material objects and experiential evidence to signify and trigger transformative experiences. After examining the pivotal role of "example gnosis" as both the signified experience of introduction epiphanies and the signifying example for the contemplative path of practice, we briefly considered Sokdokpa's critique of an overreliance on touch at the expense of exegesis in the successful performance of such introductions. This served as segue into Khyentsé Wangpo's semiotic treatment of flesh-relic pill production and consumption in his liturgical citation of the very similar semiotic framework of actuality, sign, and phenomenal mark. From this we turned to consider the Fifth Dalai Lama's insistence on material ritual protocol in his critique of masters of ceremonies who emphasize their own personal realization of nondual cognition at the expense of protocol.

In this way, we are presented with three different approaches to striking the proper relationship between mind and matter, person and object, in eliciting transformations, each steeped in distinct but overlapping semiotic sensibilities concerning what counts for immediacy, mediation, opacity, and signification. The first foregrounds the substance of the semiotics of mind and its principles, eschewing exclusive reliance on physical touch in its performance. The second explicates the semiotics of substance, thinking through the transgressive viscera of human-flesh consumption to theorize its significance and efficacy. And the third extols the power of traditional orthopraxy, performance, and touch within its critique of charismatic leaders and their personal realization as an adequate mediator of experience.

This foray has thus demonstrated that there are multiple semiotic sensibilities operative in tantric Buddhist practice in Tibet, which relate mind, matter, and sensory experience in different but entangled ways. It has also shown that the points of inflection of these different sensibilities have periodically been contested among Tibet's leading tantric experts. Fundamentally at issue are competing models of efficacy—different conceptions of what constitutes the essential active ingredients, the most effective mediators, for rendering the performance of introduction, ingestion, and initiation most effective. All this suffices to suggest that efforts to understand how dualistic semiotic operations can be used to gesture toward nondual cognition will be rewarded by attending to the mind-matter juxtapositions, aesthetics, and language of specific instances, together with the broader reflections about these voiced by ritual experts.

Viewed together, however, these three approaches also bring to the surface key connections that might be part and parcel of any attempt at collapsing the boundaries between dualistic constructs. Even as each approach calls for the enactment of slightly different configurations of mind and matter, sign and substance, in eliciting recognition of nondual cognition, the fact that each approach hinges on striking its own perfect balance—the ideal entanglement—suggests another, more fundamental entanglement, endemic perhaps to any attempt at enlisting semiotics to undo its dualistic structure. I refer here to the relationship between signifier and signified, whose entanglement in these approaches poses a critique of semiotics from within semiotics, in a way reminiscent of the words of Kristeva and Gyatso that open this essay.

Notwithstanding this suggestion regarding the possible entanglement of all such approaches, the present discussion only scratches the surface of the full range of semiotic sensibilities operative in Tibetan religion and is therefore certain to raise more questions than it answers. For instance, although each approach examined here is aimed ultimately at eliciting an immediate experience of nondual cognition, left only partially addressed is whether one must *necessarily* experience a transformative epiphany for these operations to take effect. Is it enough to have a transformative *aesthetic* experience through ritual performance? Or is this another way of saying the same thing? For that matter, is it possible to simply be present at a ritual performance, remaining relatively unmoved even by its aesthetics of physical touch, for effects to take hold at the edge of conscious awareness and ripen as epiphanies only later? What role then, if any, would there be for gradual cultivation, when it is an unmediated breakthrough experience of unfabricated nondual cognition that is sought? A more detailed look into how the potentially captivating aesthetic impact of ritualized semiotic procedures relates to epiphanies of nondual cognition must be a matter for another discussion. The aim of this reflection has been limited to tracing a few partial connections, and the entanglements they begin to outline, as a modest contribution toward such future considerations.

Works Cited

Abhayākaragupta. 2015. *Dpal yang dag par sbyor ba'i rgyud kyi rgyal po'i rgya cher 'grel paman ngag gi snye ma, Śrī Sampuṭatantrarājaṭīkāmnāyamañjarī* (Tōh. 1198). Rare and ancient Tibetan texts collected in Tibetan regions series, vol. 1. Chengdu: Sichuan Nationalities Publishing House.

Chos thams cad rdzogs pa chen po byang chub kyi sems kun byed rgyal po (Tōh. 828). 2006–09. In *Bka' 'gyur dpe bsdur ma*, vol. 101 (Ka, Rying rgyud), 3–189. Beijing: Krung go'i bod rig pa'i dpe skrun khang.

Dudjom Rinpoche, Jikdrel Yeshe Dorje (1904–87). 1991. *The Nyingma School of Tibetan Buddhism: Its Fundamentals and History*. 2 vols. Translated and edited by Gyurme Dorje and Matthew Kapstein. Boston: Wisdom.

Dung mtsho ras pa (15th cent.). 1979. *Yang tig nag po gser gyi 'bru gcig pa'i chos skor*. 3 vols. Dalhousie: Damchoe Sangpo.

Gayley, Holly. 2007. "Soteriology of the Senses in Tibetan Buddhism." *Numen* 54: 459–99.

Gentry, James. 2017. *Power Objects in Tibetan Buddhism*. Boston and Leiden: Brill.

———. 2019. "Liberation through Sensory Encounters in Tibetan Buddhist Practice." *Revue d'Études Tibétaines* 50 (June): 73–131.

Germano, David. 1992. *Poetic Thought, the Intelligent Universe, and the Mystery of the Self: The Tantric Synthesis of rDzogs chen in Fourteenth-Century Tibet*. PhD dissertation, University of Wisconsin, Madison.

Gray, David. 2005. "Eating the Heart of the Brahmin: Representations of Alterity and the Formation of Identity in Tantric Buddhist Discourse." *History of Religions* 45.1: 45–69.

———. 2007. *The Cakrasamvara Tantra (The Discourse of Śrī Heruka) (Śrīherukābhidhāna): A Study and Annotated Translation*. New York: The American Institute of Buddhist Studies at Columbia University in New York, co-published with Columbia University's Center for Buddhist Studies and Tibet House US.

Gyatso, Janet. 1986. "Signs, Memory and History: A Tantric Buddhist Theory of Scriptural Transmission." *Journal of the International Association of Buddhist Studies* 9.2: 7–35.

———. 1992. "Letter Magic: Peircean Meditations on the Semiotics of Rdo Grubchen's Dharani Memory." In *In the Mirror of Memory: Reflections on Mindfulness and Remembrance in Indian and Tibetan Buddhism*, edited by Janet Gyatso, 173–214. Albany: State University of New York Press.

———. 1993. "The Logic of Legitimation in the Tibetan Treasure Tradition." *History of Religions* 33.2 (Nov.): 97–134.

———. 1996. "Drawn from the Tibetan Treasury: The Gter-ma Literature." In *Tibetan Literature*, edited by José Ignacio Cabezón and Roger Jackson, 147–69. Ithaca, NY: Snow Lion.

———. 1998. *Apparitions of the Self: The Secret Biographies of a Tibetan Visionary*. Princeton, NJ: Princeton University Press.

———. 1999. "Healing Burns with Fire: The Facilitations of Experience in Tibetan Buddhism." *Journal of the American Academy of Religion* 67.1: 113–47.

Haraway, Donna. 1985. "A Manifesto for Cyborgs: Science, Technology, and Socialist Feminism in the 1980s." *Socialist Review* 80: 65–107.

Isaacson, Harunaga. 1998. "Tantric Buddhism in India (from c. AD 800 to c. AD 1200)." In *Buddhismus in Geschichte und Gegenwart*, 23–49. Hamburg: Hamburg University.

'Jam dbyangs mkhyen brtse'i dbang po (1820–92). 1975–80. *Thugs rje chen po padma gtsug gtor gyi myong grol ril bu'i sgrub thabs gzhan phan bdud rtsi*. In gTer chos / mChog gyur gling pa, vol. 9 (Ta), 27–62. New Delhi: Patshang Lama Sonam Gyaltsen.

Kapstein, Matthew. 2000. "We Are All Gzhan stong pas." *Journal of Buddhist Ethics* 7: 105–25.

Karmay, Samten G. 2014. *The Illusive Play: The Autobiography of the Fifth Dalai Lama*. Chicago: Serindia Publications.

Keane, Webb. 2003. "Semiotics and the Social Analysis of Material Things." *Language & Communication* 23: 409–25.

Kristeva, Julia. 1986. *The Kristeva Reader*, edited by Toril Moi. New York: Columbia University Press.

Namkhai Norbu, Adriano Clemente, and Andrew Lukianowicz. 1999. *The Supreme Source: The Kunjed Gyalpo, the Fundamental Tantra of Dzogchen Semde*. Ithaca, NY: Snow Lion Publications.

Neumaier-Dargyay, E. K. 1992. *The Sovereign All-Creating Mind, the Motherly Buddha*. Albany: State University of New York Press.

Ngag dbang Blo bzang rgya mtsho (1617–82). 1991–95a. *Za hor gyi bande ngag dbang blo bzang rgya mtsho'i 'di snang 'khrul pa'i rol rtsed rtogs brjod kyi tshul du bkod pa du kū la'i gos bzang (Dukūla)*. In *The Collected Works (gsung 'bum) of the Vth Dalai Lama Ngag-dbang-blo-bzang-rgya-mtsho*, vols. 5, 6, and 7 (Ca, Cha, Ja). Gangtok, Sikkim, India: Sikkim Research Institute of Tibetology.

———. 1991–95b. *Nyang ston khra tshang ba blo gros mchog gi rdo rje'i rtogs pa brjod pa nyung ngu rnam gsal*. In *The Collected Works (gsung 'bum) of the Vth Dalai Lama Ngag-dbang-blo-bzang-rgya-mtsho*, vol. 9 (Ta), 243–368. Gangtok, Sikkim, India: Sikkim Research Institute of Tibetology.

Ngo sprod rin po che spras pa'i zhing khams bstan pa'i rgyud. 1973–77. In *Rnying ma'i rgyud bcu bdun*, 3 vols., vol. 2, 77–109. New Delhi: Sanje Dorje.

Ngor chen Kun mchog lhun grub (1497–1557). 2000. *Rgyud kyi mngon par rtogs pa'i don nyung ngu'i ngag gis gtan la 'bebs pa'i bstan bcos ljon shing mdzes par byed pa'i rgyan*. In *Rgyud sde khag gcig phyogs bsgrigs*, 1:29–88. Kathmandu, Nepal: Sachen International, Guru Lama.

Nyoshul Khenpo Jamyang Dorjé (1931–99). 2005. *A Marvelous Garland of Rare Gems: Biographies of Masters of Awareness in the Dzogchen Lineage*. Translated by Richard Barron. Junction City, CA: Padma Publishing.

Snellgrove, David. 2010. *The Hevajra Tantra: A Critical Study*. Hong Kong: Orchid.

Sog bzlog pa Blo gros rgyal mtshan (1552–1624). 1976–80. *Dbang gong ma gud du sbas pa'i don bshad pa brda don gsal ba*. In *Rin chen gter mdzod chen mo*, vol. 91 (Mi), Hi, 143–63. Paro, Bhutan: Ngodrup and Sherap Drimay.

Strathern, Marilyn. 2005. *Partial Connections*. Updated Edition. Walnut Creek, CA: Altamira Press.

Tomlinson, Davey K. 2018. "The Tantric Context of Ratnākaraśānti's Philosophy of Mind." *Journal of Indian Philosophy* 46.2 (March): 355–72.

Divine Creation and Pure Lands in Renaissance Tibet[1]

David Germano

Pure Lands, Buddha Nature, and Divine Creation

The Great Perfection (*rdzogs chen*) traditions are amongst the most innovative forms of Buddhism to develop in Tibet in terms of theory and practice from its eighth-century origins to contemporary times.[2] While characterized by extreme rhetorics of negation and effortlessness that have historically often been misunderstood as entailing little ritual or contemplative content, the Great Perfection's transformation within the broader eleventh-century religious renaissance in Tibet[3] produced new movements that incorporated

1. I am very happy to be part of this volume, since Janet Gyatso is one of my earliest and most inspiring friends in the field of Tibetan studies. In addition to being a wonderfully warm and supportive presence during the early days of fashioning a career in the Academy, Janet was intellectually inspiring for me in the graceful and often brilliant ways she integrated equally deep commitments to the densities and intricacies of Tibetan texts, practices, and systems of thought, on the one hand, and to nuanced and theoretically engaged interpretative reflection on their significance on the other hand.

2. The Great Perfection traditions in their Buddhist form claim Indian origins, but the vast majority of texts clearly emerged in Tibetan language in Tibet through largely anonymous processes in the ninth and tenth centuries and then increasingly from the eleventh century through the revelatory processes of the Treasure (*gter ma*) tradition. The Treasure tradition in general was based on the claim that later generations of Tibetans from the eleventh century forward were generally excavating eighth- and ninth-century Tibetan translations of Indian scriptures and compositions concealed in Tibet, and for Tibetans, by such figures as the Indian masters Vimalamitra and Padmasambhava during those later days of the Tibetan Empire. The specific narrative and colophonic claims of the vast majority of Great Perfection texts and traditions appearing in this way from the tenth through the fourteenth centuries in the Buddhist "Ancients" (*rnying ma*) lineages clearly indicate that, if taken at face value, they had Indian origins in the eighth and ninth centuries, either as compositions of the time or scriptures of divine origins that were translated into Tibetan at that time. However, it is clear on linguistic and content grounds that the key scriptures were in fact born in the fertile soil of Tibetan language, experience, and imagination. See Davidson 2005, 210–43, for an excellent overview of the early Treasure tradition and its relationship to the Great Perfection; see Thondup Rinpoche (1986) for an excellent study of the Treasure tradition overall.

3. See Davidson 2005 for an outstanding history of the Tibetan Renaissance.

adapted tantric praxis into their very core and created an intensely philosophical discourse out of late Buddhist tantra in India. The most elaborate and influential of these movements was the Seminal Heart (*snying thig*) tradition, which originated in a two- or three-volume collection of *The Seventeen Tantras* and culminated in many ways with the fourteenth-century corpus of Longchenpa (1308–64), who both systematized and reshaped the tradition. While often portrayed as reflecting external influences from a variety of quarters, the Seminal Heart's multiple innovations are best understood as deeply embedded critiques and reimaginings of the Indian Buddhist traditions inherited from Tibet's Imperial past and flooding up into Tibet in new translations and lineages within the eleventh- and twelfth-century Renaissance. At the core of these innovations is an explicit model of divine creation by buddhas and their gnosis, which serves as the unifying thread of comprehensive accounts of reality, being, and human existence as driven from beginning to end by the agency and dynamics of buddhas. I will explore these accounts of radical divine agency in the eleventh through fourteenth-century corpus of *The Seventeen Tantras* and Longchenpa's writings across nine different contexts of knowledge production: cosmogony, cosmology, embryology, physiology, psychology, epistemology, soteriology, thanatology, and eschatology.

Buddhism is famous for its early rejection of creator gods and its central focus on a founder—Śākyamuni Buddha—who realizes fundamental truths about reality and existence by dint of his philosophical quest and contemplative practices. A fundamental component of the ensuing philosophical and contemplative traditions is that the world as we experience it can be accounted for in terms of the creative character of the interdependent actions (*las*, Skt. *karma*) of sentient life and their entailments. However, the long Indian history of Buddhism is also pervaded by theologies, narratives, and religious practices that point to a long and complex development of figurations of a buddha, or buddhas, their divinity and transcendent character, and their capacity in diverse forms to engage in acts of creation that exceed ordinary karmic models of how creation takes place. For example, within exoteric Mahāyāna doctrinal and narrative traditions, we find interior buddhas said to inhabit all living beings' deep interiority, vast cosmological buddhas said to hold galaxies within the pores of their skin, buddhas creating and sustaining special worlds called "pure lands" as paradigmatic acts, and buddhas inhabiting and manifesting a variety of Bodily Presences (*sku*, Skt. *kāya*) most famously theorized as "three Bodies"—Reality, Enjoyment, and Emanational—with an extraordinary array of capacities.[4] All of these themes are further radicalized and centralized within

4. See Radich 2015a and 2015b on buddha nature; Howard 1986 and 2018 and Howard and

Vajrayāna or esoteric Buddhism, which also adds the thematization of pure lands into esoteric maṇḍalas representing buddha-centered divine communities, the representation of bodily interiors in terms of such maṇḍalas as part of a tripartite subtle physiology of channels, winds, and nuclei,[5] and a plethora of contemplative and ritual practices centered upon these buddhas and their relationships with self, community, and world.[6] These are all core strands woven together by the Seminal Heart tradition into a striking model of divine creation portraying body, mind, and world as articulated and sustained by diverse buddhas operating from within and without the human self with a variety of gnostic processes.

At the level of being and its matrix, an exclusively divine vision is thus offered in which all manifestation without exception ultimately derives from the primordial knowing (*ye shes*, Skt. *jñāna*), or gnosis, of buddhas.[7] This divine

---

Vignato 2014, as well as Granoff 1998 and Sadakata 1997, 143–58, on cosmological buddhas; Halkias 2012 and Kapstein 2004 on pure lands; and Makransky 1997, Williams 2008, 172–86, and Radich 2007 on the three bodies of a buddha (*sku gsum*, Skt. *trikāya*)—the Reality Body (*chos sku*, Skt. *dharmakāya*), Enjoyment Body (*longs spyod rdzogs pa'i sku*, Skt. *saṃbhogakāya*), and the Emanational Body (*sprul sku*, Skt. *nirmāṇakāya*).

5. *Nuclei*, or *nucleus* in the singular, translates the Tibetan *thig le*, itself a translation of the Sanskrit *bindu*. Variably translated in other sources as drop, seminal points, dots, essences, information input, and so forth, the term is the third constituent of the subtle body, along with channels and winds. Together, these are termed the "adamantine body" (*rdo rje'i lus*) which represents the body's interior structures and processes in ways amenable to using for contemplative practice focused on the body. In the Seminal Heart tradition, channels are the structural pathways in the body/mind through which diverse types of energy flow, winds are the currents impelling energy through those pathways, and nuclei are the dynamic essences carried by those currents and which organize (*bkod pa*) and shape our physical, psychological, and spiritual processes. All three operate at various levels ranging from the material to the immaterial, while nuclei also play an important role in visionary meditations as concentric circles of color that ultimately become the locus of manifestations of buddhas. In this context, at least, I find *drop* to be a very poor translation and prefer *nucleus* to convey the dynamic organizational function of the *thig le*.

6. See Davidson 2002 for an overview of the Indian Buddhist tantric tradition.

7. The majority of Tibetan neologisms created for rendering Buddhist technical vocabulary into a freshly minted Tibetan literary language in the eighth and ninth centuries have the same number of syllables as the corresponding Sanskrit term. While Tibetan is not a syllabic language, the etymological roots of most syllables in multisyllabic terms are readily understood, in marked contrast to, for example, English. It appears clear that in many if not most cases, Tibetans tried to understand the original Sanskrit term in an etymological way syllable-by-syllable, whether from literary sources or on the spot folk etymologies delivered by obliging Indian consultants. While the resulting etymologies are often factually very clear, the explanations of what each syllable signifies can be widely divergent—even in one passage. Certainly in later discourse these etymological renderings might be largely neglected, but within classical Great Perfection writings they are of fundamental importance and passage after passage plays off the syllablic meanings in explicit ways. Thus, in this case, *ye shes*, rendering the Sanskrit *jñā-na*, very much means

ontology is complemented by a bifurcated epistemology, which accounts for the problem of suffering and impurity by delineating two contrasting modalities in which being and non-being are interpreted and experienced—*gnostic* and *karmic* epistemologies respectively. The Seminal Heart understands traditional Buddhist exoteric thought to be centered on a model of karmic creation—which accounts for the creation of body, mind, and world on the basis of emotionally infused volitional actions (*karma*) committed by living beings. For the Seminal Heart, however, karmic creation is repositioned as a *secondary* process, which is more hermeneutical in character than ontological—it is how we interpret the world rather than how the world fundamentally is in its creative processes. The ordinary mind (*sems*, Skt. *citta*) is portrayed as an epiphenomenon with a specific moment of origin as driven by karmic causes and conditions rooted in non-awareness (*ma rig pa,* Skt. *avidyā*), and is viewed as definitively fading away upon enlightenment. In other words, it only affects the experiential quality of the world, not its basic character, which continues to be articulated and sustained by a perpetual efflorescence of gnosis (*primordial knowing*) referred to most typically as spontaneity (*lhun grub*, Skt. *anābhoga*). Thus gnostic creation and gnostic idealism—the notion that the external world is a manifestation of what is literally the Buddha's *primordial knowing*—account for being, while karmic creation describes particular tendencies toward interpretation and the feedback mechanisms through which those types of interpretations are expressed, proliferate, and are sustained. These models of creation are also bound up with distinct visions of the nature of relatedness. Karmic creation is portrayed as linear sequences of causes and effects (*rgyu 'bras*) associated with manipulation, exertion, rigidity, restriction, and otherness that are part and parcel of the traditional model of interdependent origination (*rten 'brel*, Skt. *pratītyasamutpāda*). Gnostic creation is described in contrast as a "magical web of emanation" (*sgyu 'phrul drwa ba, Skt. māyājāla*), complex self-organizing systems of coordinated expanding and collapsing hierarchies or arrays, and characterized as involving naturalness, ease, release, freedom, and self.

The Seminal Heart presents this complex system through an innovative coalescence of various strands of Mahāyāna and Vajrayāna Buddhism with a particular focus on encounters with buddhas. In particular, the Mahāyāna

---

how it is literally translated, namely "primordial (*ye*) knowing (*shes*)." I strongly suspect that its origins were in an Indian etymologizing, whether linguistically appropriate or highly creative of its two syllables as pointing in these two directions respectively. It is a type of knowing or cognition that precedes cosmogenesis itself, and that is also coterminous with the emergence of consciousness itself, prior to the ordinary existence (*saṃsāra*) or transcendence (*nirvāṇa*). I will thus translate it and other key terms quite literally, though I will use "gnostic" at times because of the need for a short-hand adjective.

notion of an indwelling buddha—the "womb, embryo, or nucleus of the Buddha" (*de bzhin gshegs pa'i snying po*, Skt. *tathāgatagarbha*) and most commonly rendered in English as buddha nature—is integrated with the Mahāyāna motif of cosmological buddhas, buddhas that bodily create and sustain worlds to create a complex vision of reality that is woven together across interior and exterior registers with a common thread of gnostic creation. The crucial bridge between these visions of vast and intimate buddhas (the cosmological and the interior forms they take both containing life and inhabiting life's innermost recesses), as well as the central dynamic in world creation by buddhas and the underlying structure of all ensuing worlds and communities, lies in a buddha's creations of pure lands (*dag pa'i zhing*, Skt. *buddhakṣetra*), another lynchpin of Mahāyāna literature. The proliferation of buddhas in Mahāyāna went hand in hand with an evolution of a new figuration of buddhas that came to include as a central defining element the creation of worlds for the salvific rebirth of followers, worlds that were known as "pure lands." This formed the background for the evolution of cosmological buddhas, the most splendid of which is no doubt the vision of Mahāvairocana, "Great Illuminator," a buddha whose vast body has galaxies literally pouring out of the pores of his skin. At the same time, these accounts defined a creative process that offered a competing model to the older models of creation as karmic in character. These divine creative processes eventually were transferred to human practitioners themselves in ritual developments of Mahāyāna that blossomed eventually into tantric practice, as formalized miniaturizations of pure lands known as maṇḍalas became the subject of visualized evocation. Whether in iconographic depictions in paintings, murals, or sculptures, contemplative variants evoked within the body, around the body, in front of the body, or in social formations of a local culture forming around a guru, maṇḍalas and training in their iconographic, ritual, and contemplative creation came to represent an extension to practitioners of creative processes originally limited to the depiction of buddhas and their creation of pure lands.[8]

Another fertile area of divine creation in Mahāyāna was the evolving "yoga practice" (Skt. *yogācāra*) school of thought's theology of the "three Spiritual Bodies" of a buddha (*sku gsum*, Skt. *trikāya*), which described a buddha's protean capacity to create not worlds, but multiple bodies. These somatic processes intersect with the creation of pure lands, since the divine bodies emitted in this fashion both articulate and are situated within these pure lands as their creators and grounding centers. The two present a joint account of the creation of divine bodies or identities, which then fashion broader worlds around

8. See Davidson 2002, 113–68, and Bentor and Dorjee 2019.

them, and cultures that reside within those worlds. The great narrative introductory frames (*gleng gzhi*, Skt. *nidāna*) of Buddhist sūtras and tantras themselves are thus important resources for understanding these issues, as they are dedicated to narratively describing the encounters with buddhas, their cultures, and their worlds that form the conditions for the oral speech constituting the bulk of Buddhist scriptures. These encounters came to be described in terms of five sublime facets (*phun sum tshogs pa lnga*)—namely, teacher, retinue, location, place, and teaching. While initially focused on the historical founder of Buddhism and his primary sites of activity located in northern India, increasingly over time locations in various pure lands came to predominate. A distinct pedigree of development, however, lies in the sūtras articulating the notion of a "nucleus of a Buddha" coded within the bodies of all living beings, thereby at least implicitly raising the possibility of a gnostic process of creativity at work *within* beings, and not simply *without* them. While cosmological buddhas and their pure lands may generally have an explicit or implicit origin story grounded in human actions leading to enlightenment as the buddha in question, the image and discourse of a buddha within ordinary beings lacks such human narratives explaining the generation of such internal buddhas, thereby freeing the language of a buddha and their gnosis from the confines of precedent human agency. Vajrayāna then conjoined these distinct processes with an elaborate contemplative physiology portraying divine buddhas seething with activity within the very flesh and blood of embodied existence, thereby building upon the Mahāyāna motifs but extending them in important ways. It is true that the maṇḍalas of buddhas located within the body, and for the Seminal Heart particularly within the heart (serene maṇḍala) and brain (fierce maṇḍala), consist of recognizable figures that in other contexts do have associated human narratives of liberation, but there is no clear correlation of those narratives with their intimate presence within individual living beings, nor the agency they exhibit therein.

This forms the background for post-tantra, a rubric of my own invention that clearly correlates to particular Tibetan texts' rhetoric of traditions that are beyond Mahāyāna and Vajrayāna, and which expresses the indebtedness to, and yet fundamental divergence from, Buddhist tantra that characterize the Seminal Heart and the Great Perfection overall. The Seminal Heart is dominated by issues pertaining to the multiple encounters with interior and exterior buddhas, with a socio-epistemological focus on "encounter," "(non-)recognition," and "introduction." Buddha nature, pure lands, and cosmological buddhas function to integrate embryology, psychology, physiology, cosmogony, and so forth into a complex philosophical architecture, leading to it often being characterized as an instance of philosophical Vajrayāna in contrast to the more ritually focused strands of mainstream Vajrayāna. Using this gnostic vantage point, the tradition can be understood as a wide-ranging reinterpretation of Indian Buddhism that reveals how the intersection of buddha nature and pure lands serves as a base to reinterpret contemplative praxis, birth and death, psychology, and other dimensions. It is perhaps best understood as an innovative response to one of the great questions haunting earlier buddha nature literature in India, literature centered on the assertion of a primordial "nucleus" or "womb" of the Buddhas as present within all life: how does buddha nature actually function in the lives and worlds of living beings who are manifestly not buddhas? Or is it simply a vague potential that remains wholly inert in the present? The tradition responds to this problematic by looking to standard descriptions of how buddhas function in the world, and in particular, how they create worlds, or pure lands. These same processes of creation, or creative processes embodying the expressiveness of buddhas, are then redeployed to account for the generation of physical form with embryos, human sensation, individual creativity/imagination, death, and so forth in relationship to ordinary life processes.

These creative processes are thus described in terms of the three bodies of a buddha: the Reality Body (*chos sku*, Skt. *dharmakāya*), the Enjoyment Body (*longs spyod rdzogs pa'i sku*, Skt. *saṃbhogakāya*), and the Emanational Body (*sprul sku*, Skt. *nirmāṇakāya*). Most importantly, a buddha's transition from the Reality Body to the Enjoyment Body became a site of intense philosophical speculation about how form comes into being from non-form/emptiness, and thus the nature of creativity and creation. Buddhology, buddha nature, and cosmology are all combined together in this inquiry into creation, the stepping into being of form, and the gnostic or karmic character of agency therein, as well as its personal or impersonal character. The Seminal Heart is also distinctive for how a wide variety of issues often not viewed in Indian Buddhism as central philosophical issues—relegated to issues of narrative, lay/popular concerns, or practices falling outside of philosophical inquiry—are instead deeply interwoven as central themes into a broader and complex philosophical system. These include pure land, relics, post-death intermediate states, and yogic practices. The overarching architecture of this philosophical and yogic system lies in the linkage of cosmology to the human interior, with the paradigmatic instance of each being pure lands and buddha nature respectively. Thus the movement across, exchanges between, and interrelation of exteriority and interiority get expressed preeminently as the explosion of Enjoyment Bodies out of the Reality Body and the withdrawal of Enjoyment Bodies back within the Reality Body. For instance, cosmology begins with a cosmogonic account of the explosive growth of Enjoyment Bodies and their pure lands across an expanding universe, which is immediately followed by either an enlightened withdrawal back into a thoroughly reflexive and dynamic Reality Body (*nirvāṇa*) or an unenlightened withdrawal back into an embodied buddha nature (*saṃsāra*). Across these fluctuating rhythms of creation and dissolution that constitute, interpenetrate, dissolve, and reconstitute boundaries of exterior and interior, all these other elements—relics, pure lands, yogic contemplations, physiology, and so on—are employed in ongoing inquiry into questions of self and other. Thus, for example, there are the controversies over whether a given pure land is "manifest only to self" (*rang snang*) or "manifest to others" (*gzhan snang*), a controversy that revolves around issues of the relationship of buddhas to sentient beings and the status of external reality in relationship to knowing.

Scholarship on East Asian Buddhism generally uses the rubric of "pure land" to identify and emphasize the central importance of sectarian movements focusing on devotional prayer and contemplation centered around a particular buddha and rebirth in his/her pure land.[9] While not exclusively so, the cultic focus of these movements is generally the Buddha Immeasurable Light (*'Od dpag med*, Skt. *Amitābha*), and his western Buddha field named Blissful (*bde ba can*, Skt. *sukhāvatī*). Their practices stress recitation of the buddha's name and/or simply prayers focused on them, as well as the aspiration to be reborn within their pure field. In contrast, despite the pervasive importance of pure lands, corresponding belief systems, and similar practices in Tibet, there is scarce scholarship on any parallel movements therein, or attempts to contrast the configuration of religious literature, practices, and beliefs relating to pure lands in Tibet to those in East Asia.[10] I believe this is in part because of the profoundly tantric character of Tibetan Buddhism, which tended to subsume devotionalism and pure lands into the broader trajectories of tantric practice with its maṇḍalas and devotion to the guru principle. The present essay offers the beginning outlines of how at least one distinctive tantric system arose in Tibet centrally based, however, upon pure lands and their formation.

Gnostic Buddhism

The Seminal Heart tradition can thus best be understood as a creative blend of Mahāyāna and Vajrayāna traditions focused on buddhas and the interconnection of luminosity and emptiness. Within Mahāyāna, it concentrates on a configuration of materials focusing on buddhas, their cultures, and their visionary encounter: the pure land literature, the vision quests,[11] the cosmological bud-

9. See Jones 2021.

10. See Kapstein 2004 and Halkias 2012 for exceptions.

11. See Harrison 1978 and 1990.

dhas whose bodies contain cosmos, the ritual evocations of buddhas, and the buddha nature literature with its buddhas contained within ordinary bodies. This is reinforced by certain elements drawn from the yoga practice school—an innately luminous mind contained below conscious awareness, idealism or mentalist rhetoric often interpreted as idealism, and the three-Bodies theory of Buddhahood. Within Vajrayāna, the tradition concentrates on key tantric elements, such as deity yoga and the basic notion of a subtle body within the physical body, as well as spontaneous light images flowing out of subtle-body yogas. These various elements are bound together by a common concern with the figure of the buddha in terms of their ongoing presence and divine creativity and the way in which ordinary individuals encounter and participate in both.

While a Tibetan equivalent is not used adjectivally in this way, the use of the English "gnostic" for this configuration of elements is drawn directly from the Seminal Heart's own central defining contrast of gnosis to karma. The term *primordial knowing* refers to a wisdom or gnosis of a buddha, and I thus use *gnostic* to refer to Buddhist scriptural traditions presenting a buddha's gnosis as *the* critical and preexistent agency in the primordial generation of a world, cosmos, individual body, and individual subjectivity.[12] The Seminal Heart contrasts this to its own portrayal of a normative Buddhist tendency to begin with the problem of impure cyclical existence (*'khor ba*, Skt. *saṃsāra*) and human action (*karma*), and thus view the buddha as a type of telos arrived at only by a long and arduous path of religious practice. In that view, gnosis represents insight into reality as an end product of such practices, rather than a generative force or creative matrix that precedes human actions. In the gnostic view,

12. In the present context, I am simply using the term *gnostic* to highlight the distinctive way an eleventh- through fourteenth-century Tibetan movement reinterprets Indian Buddhism and the manner in which it links together disparate sources. I disavow any suggestions of a historical or thematic connection to "gnosticism" as it is typically used in relation to Western religious traditions, a subject that would lead us too far afield in the present context. For example, many of the stereotypical associations pertaining to the use of *gnostic* as a rubric identifying a number of early Christian movements—perverting orthodox doctrine, hatred of the body, anti-cosmic motifs, orientation towards protest, and so forth—do not apply to the Seminal Heart or even polemical representations of it. In addition, we have a divinization of the human body, not its rejection, though certainly there are strong similarities in the idea of a "divine spark" within men and women. The notion that Western gnosticism is above all else an orientation towards esoteric knowledge is a characteristic that applies to the whole of later Indian Buddhist tantra. However, Merkur 1993 has suggested using gnostic to refer to historical movements involving "an esoteric practice of visionary and unitive mysticism," which is of more relevance since the Seminal Heart reiterates the old Great Perfection emphasis on unitive contemplative experiences with a new visionary focus on the manifestation of buddhas out of the body's interior. Obviously the model of gnostic creativity outlined herein could be fruitfully compared to other religious traditions across region and time, though this falls outside of the current essay's scope.

however, buddha nature is understood as a radically active agent that is operative primordially in constituting world, body, and mind. Its activity is modeled after the explosion of Enjoyment Body pure lands out of the Reality Body, a process that is located in many contexts in which we do not generally think of the buddhas as active agents. This innovative reinterpretation of Indian Buddhism blends ritual, yogic, and philosophical elements; in particular, the Seminal Heart needs to be considered as a systematic philosophical discourse that ranges over such classical Buddhist philosophical topics as the ontological status of external objects, the nature of emptiness, the nature of the mind, epistemology, and so forth.

Nine Contexts for Divine Creation

In order to explore this model of gnostic creativity, I will discuss nine key contexts in which its agency and priority are exemplified and demonstrate how together they constitute an intricate portrayal of primordial buddhas possessed of radical and primary agency in almost every conceivable cosmic and human process. I have organized these nine contexts into a temporal sequence to evoke the way these primordial buddhas' activities constitute temporal arcs spanning the origins to the ends of the universe, as well as spatial expanses across myriads of galaxies, bodies of self and other, interior and exterior spaces, and life and death. They include a triad of origins—cosmogony, cosmology, embryology; a triad of endurance as life—physiology, psychology, epistemology; and a triad of ends—soteriology, thanatology, eschatology.

While I have utilized terms from the modern international academy with European and often Christian pedigree for these nine contexts, each is clearly identified in the Tibetan literature within the context of the famous "eleven adamantine topics" (*rdo rje'i gnas bcu gcig*), a highly influential organizing framework for the classical Seminal Heart tradition.[13] All eleven apply to primordial knowing, with the first and eleventh representing the primordial *ground* (*gzhi*) of reality's pure potential and the *fruit* (*'bras bu*) of a buddha's self-conscious understanding of that ground, while the second through tenth signify different aspects of primordial knowing within human existence in regards to the path (*lam*), or the journey that happens between the ground and fruit. The second topic is thus *the process of straying* (*'khrul tshul*) marking the inception of cyclic existence when sentient awareness fails to recog-

13. This framework is most famously used by Longchenpa in *The Treasury of Words and Meanings*, in which each of its eleven chapters precisely correspond to these eleven topics.

nize the manifestations of primordial knowing as self,[14] while the third topic addresses *the process of pervading* (*khyab tshul*) of human existence by divine buddha nature, and then explores this pervasion in more detail in topics four through seven in terms of that buddha nature's respective *locations* (*gnas*), *paths* (*lam*), *gateways* (*sgo*), and *object spheres* (*yul*) within human existence and experience. The eighth through tenth then explicitly focus on contemplative pathways to realization first with *taking (primordial knowing) into one's experience* (*nyams len*) through contemplative practices, monitoring *signs and measures* (*rtags tshad*) that indicate deepening contemplative realization as primordial knowing comes to the fore, and navigating *the intermediate phases* (*bar do*) of dying, death, and rebirth to move towards enlightenment.

Each of the present nine contexts in which I explore the tradition's focus on divine creation can be correlated directly to one of these traditional eleven topics, whether as a whole or with one of the topics' high-level subdivisions. Thus (1) **cosmogony** is a subtopic of the first topic of the primordial *ground* of reality's pure potential—namely "the presencing of the ground" (*gzhi snang*) that constitutes a divine flow from the ground that initiates existence. (2) **Cosmology** is a combination of the third subtopic of the *ground*—namely, *the manner in which* [the primordial Buddha] *All Good is freed* (*kun tu bzang po'i grol lugs*)—and the final topic of the *fruit* of Buddhahood with a focus on the first of his "dynamic qualities" (*yon tan*)—namely, Enlightened Bodies (*sku*) and primordial knowing (*ye shes*). (3) **Embryology** is a subtopic of the second topic of the straying process, which is expressed as "the formation of the body" (*lus grub*). (4) **Physiology** corresponds to fifth topic of *pathways*, which is presented in terms of the channels, winds, and nuclei of the "adamantine body" (*rdo rje'i lus*) portrayed as the deep infrastructure of the human body through which primordial knowing pervades it. (5) **Psychology** is the fourth topic of *location*, which is exemplified in terms of the systematic differentiation of a buddha's "Reality Body" (*chos sku*, Skt. *dharmakāya*) and the ordinary "universal ground" (*kun gzhi*, Skt. *alayavijñāna*), and primordial knowing and the mind (*sems*, Skt. *citta*). (6) **Epistemology** is the fifth topic of the *gateways* of primordial knowing, using a standard Buddhist term for the senses, here reimagined in terms of luminous projecting *lamps* (*sgron ma*) of illuminating visions, rather than the exoteric philosophical term often rendered as epistemology (*tshad ma*, Skt. *pramāṇa*). (7) **Soteriology** is first and foremost referred

14. While this may seem provocative from the point of view of certain mainstream Buddhist philosophical traditions to speak of beginningless cyclic existence as having a beginning, it is a core premise of the Seminal Heart tradition. For example, it is classically expressed in Longchenpa's *The Treasury of Words and Meanings*, 187.3–190.4.

to as the *path* (*lam*) from ordinary cyclic existence to transcendent enlightenment, here represented as the eighth topic of *taking into experience* as the standard term for contemplative practice, or *the process of becoming free* (*grol tshul*). (8) **Thanatology** is the tenth topic of the *intermediate phases* focusing on the events of dying, death, and rebirth. (9) Finally, **eschatology** points to the eleventh topic of the *fruit* of Buddhahood and the "process of freedom" (*grol tshul*) it involves, though I will stress more unusual passages about the final collective enlightenment of the entire cosmos.

1. Cosmogony: The Origins of Existence

The first three contexts emphasize beginnings: the origins of being (*cosmogony*), world (*cosmology*), and human life (*embryology*). In each case we find a buddha's gnosis presented as the key creative agent. To begin at the most fundamental beginnings, the Seminal Heart frames its entire system with a cosmogonic account of the beginnings of the universe, which it presents in both a philosophical and abstract account of the ground of being *and* a narrative account of buddhas such as All Good (*Kun bzang*, Skt. *Samantabhadra*), Vajra Holder (*Rdo rje 'chang*, Skt. *Vajradhara*), and Illuminator (*Rnam par snang mdzad*, Skt. *Vairocana*). Both types of presentations share a description of the unfolding of Bodily Displays (*sku*) out of a buddha, the former involving more generic pure land displays and the latter more particularized accounts of specific buddhas. Since the narrative account proceeds to a detailed cosmology of the consequent structure of the universe detailing its plural worlds, I will discuss it subsequently under the heading of cosmology.

The philosophical cosmogony begins with a ground (*gzhi*) of pure potentiality devoid of exteriorized manifestation; it is subsequently identified with the buddha's Reality Body as well as buddha nature due to its unmanifest character. It is imaged as "a Youthful Enlightened Body in a Vase" (*gzhon nu bum pa'i sku*)—that is, a luminous body contained within a vase such that it is only internally radiant.[15] This ground has three qualities described as empty in essence,

15. This image of "a Youthful Enlightened Body within a Vase" clearly aligns with Tibetan metaphors for the "instantaneous enlightenment," such as Jackson 1992 outlines with special birds in the egg and newborn lion cubs which "were thought to be born already possessing extraordinary qualities" and conveyed either "the idea of the instantaneous actualization of remarkable potentialities" or "the delayed manifestation of enlightened qualities" (95). While these images are found in the Great Perfection literature, the body within a vase image has a quite distinct semantic profile focused on cosmogenesis rather than the manifestation of a yogi or buddha and their qualities. It is an image intended to depict the nature of reality as inherently dynamic and vibrant in potential prior to manifestation, while the breaking of the vase's seal then images how divine manifestation floods out from within its deep interiorities *prior* to the very existence of

radiant in nature, and all-pervasive in compassion, which clearly correspond to the three Bodies of a buddha. *The Tantra of Self-Arising Awareness* describes it thus:[16]

> The ground is termed "a great original purity" and abides in terms of the triad of essence, nature, and compassion. [That] essence is unobstructedly radiant as unchanging primordial knowing, and as such is termed "the abiding condition of the Youthful Body in a Vase." Its nature is the unobstructed presencing of the five lights, while the presencing of its compassion is like a cloudless [sky]. That [triune ground] is termed "the abiding reality of original purity," and is utterly devoid of any fragmentation or lapsing into partiality.

The Tantra of Exquisite Auspiciousness offers a similar description:[17]

> Prior to the emergence of awakened buddhas in consequence of realization, and the emergence of sentient beings in consequence of non-realization, awareness's self-emergent primordial knowing does not waver from the ground, and dwells together with its unconditioned triune presencing. Then again Awareness's Primordial Knowing itself taught this abiding reality of its own manner of being:
>
> "Hey! This vast matrix of great presencing abides as the great expansive awakening of a buddha that never strays from the great unwavering Reality Body. The Essence Body (*ngo bo'i sku*) abides unobstructedly: [its] essence is unchanging and [its] means secret; it has never wavered, it is unwavering, and it is without agitation; therein all appearances are simultaneously perfectly complete;

buddhas and sentient beings, though thereby setting the conditions for their emergence by the consequent self-recognition or failure to recognize. Thus its relevance is not in the context of realized buddhas and soteriology, but rather in the context of theorizations of reality in regards to appearances first emerging out of emptiness, something from nothing. It is true that the same language of the ground (pure potential) and ground-presencing (the first movement into divine manifestation) is applied to a living being's own deep interiority within the heart, but I am not familiar in that context either with uses of the "body in a vase" image as applied to the development of a visionary or buddha, much less in relationship to instantaneous models of enlightenment. It would seem relevant to this distinction that the first set of images are profoundly biological as they evoke animals with their eggs or wombs, while the present image is based upon a generic "Enlightened Body" being present with an inorganic vase.

16. Chapter thirty (Tb11 435.1 and Ab1 529.5). See Smith 2018 for a different translation of the passage.

17. Chapter one (Tb12 174.3 and Ab1 210.1); it is also cited by Tcd1 285.2.

> all primordial knowings are instantaneously perfectly complete; all Spiritual Bodies are present in ripened form; and all luminous appearances and visions are radiantly clear without obscuration. This abiding reality's presencing is unobscured by its modes of presencing and is a total Great Perfection with its essence, nature, and compassion devoid of fragmentation."

This state of pre-cosmic hyper-interiority is ruptured (*rgya ral*) when a gnostic wind (*ye shes rlung*) stirs, such that the agent of manifestation is a buddha's primordial knowing. It impels an exteriorization referred to as the ground-presencing (*gzhi snang*), which is described explicitly as the flowing out of pure lands rather than as an emanation of phonemes, generic lights, or some other phenomena used in other South Asian or Tibetan religious accounts of cosmogenesis. These pure lands are described as a vertical array with the Reality Body's open sky at the uppermost apex, and trailing off down below into the impure lands of cyclic existence. Dominant, however, are the intermediate pure land arrays of the Enjoyment Body, which are centered on the five buddhas—Vairocana, Akṣobhya, Ratnasambhava, Amitābha, and Amoghasiddhi—in their serene and fierce forms. The full maṇḍala is of one hundred deities, a set drawn from the eighth-century *Guhyagarbha Tantra* which is closely intertwined with the Great Perfection's origins.[18] The phased manifestation of these arrays of buddhas is clearly based upon standard descriptions of a buddha's post-enlightenment manifestations as Enjoyment Bodies emerge out of the Reality Body, and Emanational Bodies out of them in turn. Karma has no presence or role whatsoever in the primordial ground, nor in the initial raising of awareness and manifestation of spontaneous presence. The following passage from Longchenpa's *The Treasury of Words and Meanings* is typical:[19]

> The seal of the Youthful Body in a Vase, the primordial ground of the originally pure internal expanse, is rent open, and the winds of primordial knowing's impulsion raise awareness up from the ground. As [its] self-presencing thus dawns in the eight gateways of spontaneous presence, above the originally pure Reality Body's presencing [is] like a cloudless sky, while directly in front the Enjoy-

18. The tantra and key commentaries have been translated into English by Dorje 1987, Chönam and Kandro 2011, Chönam and Kandro 2010a, Chönam and Kandro 2010b, and Dharmacakra Translation Committee 2009. In addition, Guenther 1984 has published a highly interpretative study of it with a focus on Longchenpa's Great Perfection-slanted interpretation of it.

19. Chapter one (Tdd 178–9).

> ment Body's luminously radiant pure lands' presencing pervades the sky's expanse. Through its dynamism below [is] the great ground-presencing, while through its dynamism [in turn] below [it is] the Enjoyment Body's presencing and in [its] interstices [are] the natural Emanational Bodies' pure land presencings. Further down below [are] the measureless world systems of the sixfold living beings' self-presencing through the gate of cyclic existence. Because all of this naturally arises from the presencing of spontaneous presence's eight gateways, it is termed "the simultaneous dawning of cyclic existence and transcendence's great presencing." As these appearances arise in external radiance from within internal radiance, essence's presencing is an inherently radiant unobstructed clearing-space; nature's presencing is primordial effulgence in five[-hued] light; and compassion's presencing is an opening up resembling a cloudless sky.

Thus instead of the typical Buddhist cosmogonic accounts where world generation is driven by the impure karmic residue of beings from a former eon, here we find a buddha's gnosis igniting and impelling the process, and that the Bodies of a buddha constitute the initial manifestation of the process itself. Thus not only is gnosis primordial, but it also has prior agency in the generation of worlds and being, while the primary act of creation in the universe is that of pure lands. The "buddha" here is understood to be indeterminate, in that it can yield both cyclic existence dominated by suffering (*saṃsāra*) *and* the realization's transcendence (*nirvāṇa*). Thus despite the use of all the classic descriptive terms for a buddha, their knowing, and their bodily displays, there is a crucial lack of reflexivity that yields a bifurcation based upon the interpretative response: the incipient cognitive capacity deriving from primordial knowing either self-recognizes (*rang ngo shes pa*) the display, or it fails to do so. The former yields transcendence, and primordial knowing goes into the reflexive ascendancy, while in the latter eventuality, mundane human action (*karma*) goes into the ascendancy as primordial knowing retreats into the background. This dualism is persistent throughout the system, and in the present context constitutes the seventh and eighth gateways of spontaneous presence, the interpretative reactions to the ground's manifestation which trigger cyclic existence or transcendence respectively.

2. Cosmology: The Origins of World

Against this background, which accounts for the emergence of being from nonbeing, the narrative literature describes a secondary cosmogony involving the creation of precise worlds in a type of historical space beyond the generic emergence of being outlined in those philosophical accounts. Drawing heavily upon Mahāyāna sūtras, especially the *Avataṃsaka sūtra*, these narratives begin with beings and arrays of pure lands shining forth from the impersonal buddhaground's deep interiority as ignited by the stirring of gnostic winds, and within all of this manifestation one being becomes primordially awakened right in the moment of emergence. He is "All Good," the primordial buddha and the emblematic embodiment of the Reality Body for the Great Perfection tradition. Longchenpa's *The Treasury of the Supreme Vehicle* describes the process in the following:[20]

> The first topic is that prior to everything—cyclic existence and transcendence of misery not divided, not dividing, nor to be divided—All Good himself, the teacher whose dominion is perfectly complete, arose in the ground-presencing from the primeval ground, the expanse that is self-emerging primordial knowing, the enlightened nucleus of the ones gone to bliss.[21] In that instant as he elevates from the ground, he recognized [everything] as self-presencing, such that through the triune self-emerging principle he took hold of the imperial citadel within the sheath of precious spontaneity, the great original purity of the primeval site of exhaustion, the field of the youthful body in a vase. Having perfected the enlightened qualities in renunciation and realization, he was expansively awakened into buddhahood within the nature of the Reality Body and abided within its internal radiance. His dynamism or inspiring blessings [gave rise to] the dense array of spontaneous self-presencing[22] pure land permeated with the five primordial knowings. Its maṇḍala as endless as the sky, the individual buddhas corresponding to the five affinities arrayed in self-presencing fashion and resided there beyond the scope of anyone requiring training [i.e., ordinary living beings].
>
> Then after a long time, he saw fluctuations out of the dynamism arising within the ground-presencing from the ground, as living beings appeared like one errs without any cause of error, such as in a dream. He thus felt a caring compassion stir and he arrayed cos-

20. Chapter one (Tcd1 5.2–6.2).

21. "The enlightened nucleus of the ones gone to bliss" is a literal translation of the Tibetan translation of one of the main terms for buddha nature (*bde bar gshegs pa'i snying po*, Skt. *sugatagarbha*).

22. Tibetan *rang snang lhun grub stug po bkod pa*.

> mic fields for the welfare of these beings. Out of this presencing of self-presencing Perfect Enjoyment Bodies, he arrayed the *overflowing oceans* (*gangs chen mtsho*) Bodies of the victors of the five affinities in an extent as endless as the sky itself. Lotuses were born from within the interior of the appearance of their [respective] precious hand-held seals—a wheel, vajra, jewel, lotus, and double vajra. Atop [those lotuses] are twenty-five cosmic fields, while in the expanse of the flowing *overflowing oceans* of incense-infused water streaming from the pores of their skin, there are minute particles of earth, water, fire, and wind.
>
> In all [those particles'] spaces to their full extent, [these buddhas] make present the different cosmic fields [stemming from] the buddhas' blessings and the actions of ordinary living beings in an inconceivably limitless [variety] of forms and arrays such as spherical, square, elongated, and half-moon shaped.

All Good's gradual awareness of less fortunate newly emergent beings thus elicits a response in the form of the creation of pure lands. The most significant is his manifestation as fivefold massive Enjoyment Body buddhas known as "glacial oceans" or "overflowing oceans" buddhas.[23] They are so named because the pores of their skins overflow with perfumed oceans, within which originate galaxies. Their cosmological bodies literally overflow with worlds, which constitute a web of billionfold galaxies. The most important is the overflowing oceanic form of Vairocana, since he constitutes the matrix for our own world. These further manifest emanatory reflexes, or Emanational Bodies, which permeate the vast universes that they bodily constitute, such as the twelve emanations of Vajra Holder (*rdo rje 'chang*, Skt. *Vajradhara*) or the three sources of the teachings—a vajra, statue, and book—that spin around the universe emanating out enlightened activities.

The description of the process is—barring the narrative details—a straightforward description of the sequential manifestation of Enjoyment Body buddhas out of the Reality Body, and Emanational Body buddhas in turn out of them. It is conjoined to the Mahāyāna notion of understanding the creation of pure lands as a paradigmatic act of a buddha following enlightenment, which is here seen as entailing that primordial knowing is the constitutive agent in the external worlds of the universe. A buddha is a world creator, and hence

23. The texts oscillate between two spellings that have the same sound but very different meanings, which can be translated as "glacial oceans" (*gangs mtsho*) or "overflowing oceans" (*gangs chen mtsho*) respectively.

our world environments are contained within, and fabricated out of, massive buddhas.

3. Embryology: The Origins of Life

From these cosmic processes of beginnings, we now turn to a more intimate space, namely the process of embryogeny taking place within a mother's womb, the creation of a human body. Within the unfolding of the ground in the ground-presencing, two pathways are possible—the aforementioned path to transcendence with All Good and his self-recognition *and* the path to cyclic existence triggered by the failure to achieve such self-recognition. In the latter path, this lack of awareness gradually deepens and proliferates into the evolution of sentient beings and their reactive patterns of emotionally infused actions, which emerge newly from the unfolding consequences of the lack of recognition. As cyclic existence is now established and its karmic mechanisms of causation go into the ascendancy, primordial knowing recedes to the background but, despite not achieving reflexive self-knowledge, continues to act as the primary agent in human existence in radically active ways. Thus, in considering the development of the embryo, while mainstream Buddhist accounts view the karma of the reincarnating individual as the driving force, Longchenpa describes the process in *The Treasury of Words and Meanings* as instead driven by primordial knowing:[24]

> On the fourteenth day, the embryo's [elemental] space [energy] opens up space, whereby in the middle of these four channels' developing from the navel's channel-knot at the body's center, like the stretching out of ropes, two small "eyes"—the Eye of the Lamps and the Eye of the Elements—become much more clearly manifest than previously. Within these small eyes, the extremely subtle and difficult to analyze essence of primordial knowing is also present.

He is more explicit in *The Treasury of the Supreme Vehicle,* where he makes clear these "Eyes" (*spyan*) organize the entire human existence, both of our physical body and our capacity for vision:[25]

> At the time of the body first developing, within the channel-knot of the generativity wheel [i.e., the navel] which previously devel-

24. Chapter two (Tdd 201.6–202.1).

25. Chapter thirteen (Tcd2 1.2–4).

> oped in dependence upon the water [element], the pair of the Eye of the Lamps and the Eye of the Elements develop first off. [The subsequent manner in which] the physical body [constituted] of the four elements takes form [in embryogeny] from the Eye of the Elements has been previously explained. From the Eye of the Lamps, two channels resembling the horns of a buffalo with a narrow base and opening wide at their tips in the middle of the two eye balls originate as the foundation of the ultimate transcendence of misery (nirvāṇa), which has the nature of primordial knowing's manifestation in terms of lights, nuclei, the Spiritual Bodies, and so on. That is called the far ranging lasso water lamp, and in dependence upon it there is the empty nuclei lamp, the self-emergent insight lamp, and the thoroughly pure expanse lamp.

Thus the physical and mental generation of a human embryo is guided by two "Eyes" (*spyan*), which are undoubtedly the Eyes of a buddha located within the human body as signified by the use of the honorific term. The Eye of the Elements (*'byung ba'i spyan*) is of material existence—earth, water, fire, and wind—and the Eye of the Lamps (*sgron ma'i spyan*) points to the luminosity of the buddha nature that constantly spills out of its interior state, whether at the cosmos's beginning or the heart of the human body, into external fields of perception. The use of the term *lamps* is based upon the common description of the Buddhist teachings as lamps which buddhas array to illuminate the ten directions of the cosmos. The Eye of the Elements thus acts to impel and organize the embryo's physical development, while the Eye of the Lamps impels and organizes its mental and spiritual development. The embryo is in this way from its conception to birth impelled first and foremost by gnostic forces, even as karmic forces constantly modify and redirect the final result under the conditions of non-recognition.

4. Physiology: Our Human Bodies

The second triad of contexts then turns from origins to persistence in the form of human existence. They range over body (*physiology*), mind (*psychology*), and perception (*epistemology*) respectively, and in each case, primordial knowing is the primary agent creating and animating human being and experience, while karmic processes are secondary and derivative processes that come into existence under the conditions of unawareness. When recognition is achieved, the karmic processes dissolve without residue, leaving only primordial knowing, but within cyclic existence, the karmic processes dominate one's experience.

When we turn to the adult human body, we find a significant alteration of tantric physiology that begins with the primacy of divine maṇḍalas located at the heart and brain interwoven by a network of pure light channels, which are also linked to the sensory systems. Thus against the backdrop of the ordinary Buddhist esoteric body within a body—the three vertical channels, which have central nexuses or wheels (*'khor lo*, Skt. *cakra*) at the crown, throat, heart, navel, and sometimes genitals—we find a more primary network of light channels (*'od rtsa*), such that the ordinary subtle body is depicted as a coarse subsidiary manifestation formed by ignorance and karma. In addition, the buddha nature is represented by maṇḍalas of forty-two serene buddhas in the heart—called a Mind palace[26]—and fifty-eight fierce buddhas in the skull—called a conch shell chamber (*dung khang*). The light channels are thus called transcendent[27] channels permeating the body, with the most important branch running from the heart to the two eyes in a "crystal channel" (*shel sbug can*). The eyes are then termed the "gateway" by which buddhas exit and enter the body. *The Tantra of Unimpeded Sound*:[28]

> The gateways of primordial knowing's shining forth
> involves [it] issuing forth through the gateways called *Eyes*[29]
> that comprise all the vibrant energies, the body's elixir,

26. "Mind" translates *tsitta*, which is the Tibetan transliteration of the Sanskrit *citta*, the standard word for mind. In this context, the use of the Sanskrit clearly is intended to point to a numinous or hidden dimension of the phenomena in question, in contrast to its ordinary mundane functioning or significance. Thus it evokes a divine Mind in contrast to the ordinary mind signified by the standard Tibetan translation (*sems*) of *citta*. I have thus tried to evoke this through capitalizing Mind.

27. Transcendent renders the Tibetan translation (*myang 'das*) of the Sanksrit *nirvāṇa*, which is most typically just given as "transcendence" (*'das pa*), though its fuller expression is the "transcendence of suffering" (*myang/mya ngan las 'das pa*).

28. Question and answer seven of chapter two (Tb12 94.4 and Ab1 113.5). The commentary on it is found in Vimalamitra, *The Secret Tantra of the Illuminating Lamp's Blazing* (*sgron ma snang byed 'bar ba'i gsang rgyud*) (Kt.2 186.5–193.3, Lg, Li.2 54.8–59.14, and Nx.2 61.13–67.21; it is cited by Tcd2 71.3, Knt1 457.2, and partially by Kyt2 371.4). In my translation, I have followed the commentarial readings and exegesis.

29. "Eyes" translates *tsakShu*, which is a Tibetan transliteration of *cakṣu*, the standard Sanskrit term for "eye," and which is used in passages in the Seminal Heart even when the standard Tibetan translations (*mig*, *spyan*) are also used. Just as with *tsitta*, this renders the term numinous and points to its divine dimensions, which I have rendered by capitalizing Eye. In general, Tibetan itself has two common words for eye—the standard common form *mig* and the honorific form *spyan*, the latter which is also used when referring to the eyes of a buddha and which I have discussed in the section on embryology. In general I use capitalization in English to indicate such a difference in Tibetan—ordinary being's *eyes* and the *Eyes* of a buddha—which does entail

such that the twofold dimensions [of cyclic existence and transcendence] are apprehended, and appearances displayed.

It develops [from the navel] and emerges linked [to the eyes] via the [navel's] channel
and via becoming a single [channel] at the [body's] summit (the head),
that single [channel] enabling the shining forth via the sensory objects
has five branches manifesting
at and as the respective gateways of the five sensory faculties;
in particular, the illuminating faculty of defective and holistic qualities [channel]
winds around like a buffalo's horns,
and thus at the "eye orb," half black and half white,
there is awareness in which visible forms are apprehended,
and cognition's inherent dynamism is displayed in perfect completeness.

Through this [lamp], the real primordial knowing emerges.
By virtue of its immediacy and its own key points,
the objective dimension of pure reality's self-manifestation
is present with all that involves conceptuality in a state of cessation.

In Longchenpa's *Introduction to the Presencing of the Expanse* found within his *Seminal Quintessence of the Ḍākinīs*:[30]

> In this body of ripened karmic propensities during the straying [into cyclic existence], the principal channels [are as follows]. White quintessence descends through the channel-petals in which fierce winds flow via the right flavor [channel] (*ro ma*, Skt. *rasanā*). Red quintessence descends from the channel petals in which gentle winds flow via the left solitary [channel] (*kyang ma*, Skt. *lalanā*). The great intense quintessence descends by means of the neuter winds via the middle central [channel], and acts as support for the channel petals in which flows the element of primordial knowing

---

that the English for *spyan* and *tsakShu* is the same (*Eyes*), just as the English for *thugs* (enlightened mind) and *tsitta* is the same (*Mind*).

30. Kyt3 118.3–119.2. I have translated the names of the right (*ro ma*) and left (*rkyang ma*) channels in conjunction with the repeated clear etymological unpacking of these names within the Seminal Heart tradition.

> that is beyond the coarse. The [three channels] support the three [emotional] poisons, and thus are termed "the channels of cyclic existence" . . . The ordinary tantras explain these three channels as the three buddha Bodies, the three gateways, the three emotional poisons, and the (contemplative triad of generation, perfection, and [great perfection], but since they are not ultimate, they are termed the "channel-petals of cyclic existence." [In contrast], the primordial channel-petals of the great transcendence of misery are also termed the "channel of self-emergent primordial knowing," "the channel of the spontaneous presencing within the ground," and the "pure crystal tube". . .

This body within the body in fact is the residue of the primordial divine cosmogony, since the two maṇḍalas of buddhas are the interiorized remains of the original pure land displays that began the universe. The heart is described as the "ground," and the light channels are explicitly portrayed as the cosmogonic overflowing of that ground into the luminous display of the ground-presencing. The original cosmogonic scenario is thus reinscribed within the body's interior as a perpetual event occurring and reoccurring in the background of all life. Thus "three thousand buddhas" permeate the body's channels as fragments of this ongoing explosion of Enjoyment arrays, while the entirety of pure lands lies encoded within fragments of light floating across the eyes evocatively termed "linked lambs" (*lu gu rgyud*) that ultimately transform into buddhas within direct transcendence (*thod rgal*) visionary contemplation.[31] And the same recognition scenario with its interpretative bifurcation also endlessly repeats itself.

5. Psychology: Our Human Minds

However, to describe these internal buddhas as static, inert residues or dormant seeds would be inaccurate, since in fact these buddhas and their gnostic overflow are depicted as the primary agents in the ongoing generation of the human body *and* mind. In the eventuality of non-self-recognition, the luminosity of the central channel is sequentially converted in an ongoing fashion into ordinary psycho-physical processes. In psychological terms, there is a strict duality between two types of cognitive process: primordial knowing (*ye shes*) and

31. See Garab Dorjé's *A Secret Commentary on The Single Son of the Teachings as a Liberation through Wearing*, Vnti 112.1 and 112.6, for references to the three thousand buddhas, and Longchenpa's *The Lamp of the Key Points of Contemplatively Taking it into Experience*, Lyt2 40.6, for the connection to the linked lambs.

ordinary mind (*sems*).[32] The primary activity is the primordial knowing stirring out of these internal buddhas, but under the conditions of lack of awareness its effects get diluted and distorted into ordinary mental processes, which are thus an epiphenomenon. Longchenpa's *Treasury of Words and Meanings* describes the relationship of ordinary mind and primordial knowing thus:[33]

> In this way, the cloud-like mind obscures primordial knowing and there is no way it can be identified with the sun-like primordial knowing—they are distinct from each other as "the obscured" [i.e., primordial knowing] and "the agent of obscuration" [i.e., the mind]. Thus when one understands how the ordinary mind and the appearances it perceives are distorted, one realizes that these externally appearing objects and the mind that apprehends them are adventitious and groundless. When one understands that primordial knowing and the presencing of primordial knowing are undistorted, one attains mastery over the maṇḍala of awareness's Reality Body. Thus the mind and primordial knowing must be differentiated from each other. Their non-differentiation entails the defect of primordial knowing's continuing obscuration by one's mind, such that its own essence (which links [one back to reality]) cannot manifest.

The somatic character of primordial knowing is made clear in *The Tantra of the Adamantine Hero's Heart-Mirror* where it addresses how the ground, identified as buddha nature, is present in ordinary living beings:[34]

> The wonder of it! Listen up you great mistresses of space!
>
> The enlightened nucleus of Realized Ones[35] integrally resides within all sentient beings in the worldly realms. Moreover, it is present like oil pervades a sesame seed. Furthermore, its support is based upon the aggregate of [their] physical form.
>
> Its residence is to abide in the maṇḍalic center of their heart. This also is termed "the wisdom of the closed amulet of All Good," which is present analogically like a closed amulet of red-gold enamel.

32. See Higgins 2013.

33. Chapter four (Tdd 242.6–243.1).

34. Chapter 3 (Tb11 207.1 and Ab1 334.1); it is also cited by Tcd2 68.4 and partially cited by Lyt1 463–64.

35. "The enlightened nucleus of the realized ones" translates the Tibetan translation of one of the main terms for buddha nature (*de bzhin gshegs pa'i snying po*, Skt. *tathāgatagarbha*).

> Within it is five-colored light, in the center of which the mustard seed-sized Serene Spiritual Bodies reside, with [the lights] present in the manner of a luminous home. That is the residence of awareness, analogically like a Body in a vase.
>
> The primordial knowing that emerges from that [i.e., its effulgence shining out from the heart] resides in the site of the brain, the conch shell house. To expand on this, it is present as mustard seed-sized fierce Bodies, with proportionately sized eyes. They are also present in the manner of light rays. The light emerging from them is radiant and lucent like the center of a mirror-disc, or it can be said that it is present amidst light rays, analogically like the eyes of a fish.
>
> In the connection between this and awareness, up from the heart's tip a mere thread of white silk channel rises from the proximity of the vertebrae. [Awareness's radiation] emerging on [its] pathway through this, enters into the head. This channel proceeds upwards from the left via the "small extremities" [channels in the throat] and thus links up with the brain. That also is linked to the eyes via the right and left areas.
>
> Moroever, having upturned [your] eyes towards the sky and applied pressure to this channel, the presencing of primordial knowing will arise, and come to fill the sky.

Thus primordial knowing is not a refinement of the mind, or its enhancement, but rather a deeply somatic process constantly active within the body's interior independent of the ordinary mind. These activities remain in the background of human awareness, but they still retain the primary agency in human awareness. This is imaged as the action of sun rays (*primordial knowing*) giving rise to clouds (*karma*), but the sun itself remaining primordially active and generative behind their screen.

6. Epistemology: Our Human Knowing

Epistemology, how human perception takes place, is also accounted for in primarily gnostic terms and only secondarily in terms of karmic processes. The body's transcendent light channels project out into the eyes "like water buffalo horns," and the visual objects flow out from within as derived from the ongoing unfolding of primordial knowing from the heart in the ground-presencing. Vision is thus understood to be radically projective, and not just receptive. The same character is explicitly attributed to the ears, also a "gateway" to primordial knowing via these light channels, and thus to hearing. In either case, the principal example of this projective nature of sensation—a fluid and nondual process in contrast to the constructive and dichotomizing projections of karmic sensation—is that of the manifestation of pure lands. From Longchenpa's *The Treasury of Words and Meanings*:[36]

> The actual gateway for the shining forth of primordial knowing's presencing in external radiance is the two eyes. To expand on that, the vibrant quintessences of the four elements [earth, water, fire, and wind] develop as two Eyes in the channel knot of the navel wheel. The three channels link [them to the other wheels thus]: from the navel [they] are connected to the heart; then [they] are connected to the throat; and then to the brain, the conch chamber. Therein, from the four channels spiraling to the right, the channel which brings about the shining forth of the sensory faculties' objects divides into five tips from a single root, and thus acts as the support of the five individual sensory gateways. From [these five tips,] in particular the channel that acts as the support for the vision of forms is named "the sensory faculty illuminating defective and positive qualities." With narrow root and large tips, two channels like buffalo horns run to the vibrant quintessence of the two eyeballs. Within the vision of manifest forms in dependence upon these channels, there are two visual processes: the vision of earth, stones, mountains, rocks and so forth, which are the distorted appearances of impure cyclic existence; and the vision of the presencing of radiant light, the empty forms of the pure transcendence of misery.

This aspect of sensation thus becomes an important site for the discussion of idealism: are appearances "projections of the self" (*rang snang*) or "projections of an other" (*gzhan snang*)? The central place these issues are raised is the manifestation of pure lands in cosmogony and in contemplative vision: are these visions "self" or "other"? For example, a text may ask the practitioner to close their eyes, only to discover that the visions persist. This is offered as clear evidence that the visions are self-projections and not independently existent external objects. Finally, there is the theme of the five senses being the site of liberation: "liberation upon seeing" (*mthong grol*), "liberation upon hearing" (*thos grol*), and so forth. In this sense also, sensation leads directly to liberation, and epistemology thus becomes the study of soteriology.

36. Chapter six (Tdd 259.5–260.1).

7. Soteriology: The Path to Enlightenment

The final three contexts shift to questions of ends: liberation (*soteriology*), personal death (*thanatology*), and collective salvation (*eschatology*). The accounts of each are dominated, again, by the preexistent and spontaneous dynamics of primordial knowing. Liberation is generated by the central contemplative process, known as direct transcendence (*thod rgal*), which constitutes a cultivation of spontaneous but phased visions of pure lands or maṇḍalas. The practice is prefaced by the cultivation of perfectly fluid awareness through "breakthrough" (*khregs chod*) contemplation, which itself meditatively reiterates the primordial ground of pure potential. Longchenpa's *The Treasury of Words and Meanings* describes the initial stages of practice:[37]

> In accordance with the three postures and three gazes, [focus] on the sky twelve fingerwidths in distance from the spot between the eye brows. [This is done] in accordance with the key points of the triad of the eyes not wavering, the mind not being distracted, and the winds being thoroughly quiet . . . With respect to that, at first one sees forms like smoke, white clouds billowing, a mirage, stars, fire sparks, a butter lamp, and the great pervading blue's light in the form of a black figure like a [(Tibetan)] naro [vowel]. Light rays, nuclei, and immeasurable empty forms of the expanse/awareness thus shine forth.

Direct transcendence consists of using external light sources—such as the sun, moon, or a lamp—or complete darkness within a specially prepared house, to cultivate a spontaneous flow of visual images through simple postures, breathing, and gazes. One is not supposed to intentionally modify this flow of images, but rather allow them to develop of their own accord. The driving force behind this imaginal flow is believed to primarily be the internal buddhas, especially those located within the heart and skull as the iconic manifestations of the internal buddha nature. The practice creates an opening for their self-expression into one's sensory experience, and they flow via the body's light channels to permeate the exterior visual field through the gateway of the eyes. The other agent—both of manifestation and influence—is that of the emotional distortions (*nyon mongs*, Skt. *kleśa*), and thus the practice also involves techniques for eliding their manifestation and instead encouraging the expression of the buddhas' agency.

37. Chapter seven (Tdd 283.2–4).

Through a developmental process summed up overall into four visionary sequences (*snang ba bzhi*), the imaginal flow slowly self-shapes itself into maṇḍalas of serene and fierce buddhas that constitute a massive pure land pervading the entire sky. *The Tantra of Unimpeded Sound* describes the later phases of the practice, all of which are claimed to spontaneously occur beyond intentional mental processes:[38]

> In [awareness's] optimization, the body as well becomes thus:
> Having divested oneself of the body's material atoms,
> windows of light appear in [the resultant] spaces,
> and from them light rays shaped as iron hooks
> project and wind [into one], thereby taking hold of the appearances.
>
> The body's corporeality having ceased in and of itself,
> becomes a stainless transparent body of light
> and its center is marked by an "A" [syllable].
>
> Light rays a full fathom long shine from one's hair-ringlet [between the eyebrows][39]
> while [one's] winds elevate a top knot [of hair],
> (one's own body as) a Serene (Buddha) Body, garlands of light
> gather densely from the fingers of one's hands.
>
> Without sounds, experiences of the mind,
> the fierce Heruka[40] (buddhas) come to the fore
> from the immeasurable mansion of one's skull.
>
> At this time one's own body is optimized,
> and, in its unimpeded transparency, encapsulates the three Spiritual Bodies.

38. Question and answer twelve of chapter four (Tb12 143.1 and Ab1 170.4). The commentary on it is found in Vimalamitra, *The Secret Tantra of the Illuminating Lamp's Blazing* (*sgron ma snang byed 'bar ba'i gsang rgyud*) (Kt.2 474.6–476.5, Lg 279b.1–9, Li.2 303.6–304.15, and Nx.2 341.19–343.10; it is cited by Tdd, Tcd2 233.5, and Lyt1 479.4). In my translation, I have followed the commentarial readings and exegesis.

39. This ringlet of hair between the eyebrows is said to be a physical characteristic of the Buddha and some sutras will depict him projecting rays of light from it.

40. This Sanskrit term *heruka*, translated into Tibetan as "blood drinkers" (*khrag 'thung*), is the standard term for fierce forms of buddhas.

The entire array of interior buddhas has been fully exteriorized at this point, particularly the key Enjoyment Body images. The pure land then begins to collapse within itself back to the dark blue expanse, identified as emptiness and the Reality Body, which marks the attainment of enlightenment. The practice thus involves an autonomous, self-organizing process driven by the active agency of buddhas outside of intentional plans or programs, and deeply intertwined with the practitioner's embodied sensory system. Agency is explicitly understood as pertaining to these interior buddhas generally hidden away in the deep intimate recesses of the practitioner's body and is not attributed to the mind of the practitioner, which accounts for their effortless character. This revision of late tantric contemplative procedures questions the necessary centrality of ritualized deity yoga practices in classical tantric Buddhist systems and the priority of internally mastered interior spaces in subtle body practice. The pairing of breakthrough and direct transcendence brings the process of gnostic efflorescence into reflexive self-awareness, directly echoing the primordial cosmogony of the ground, its presencing, and All Good's liberation.

8. Thanatology: The Process of Death

We now shift from liberation—the end of ordinary existence—to the more common endings of death. The Seminal Heart literature is the original matrix in which the innovative post-deaths scenarios of the so-called *Tibetan Book of the Dead* were actually worked out.[41] In contrast to earlier forms of the Great Perfection, the literature is very thanocentric, with a pervasive interest in corpses, dying, and post-death intermediate processes (*bar do*, Skt. *antarābhava*). This interest is one of the most important fault lines between the various sub-traditions of the Great Perfection.

For our present purposes, it is the tradition's innovations in Buddhist postmortem theory that are most relevant. Earlier Indian Buddhist literature often referred to a type of intermediate existence between death and rebirth. However, this phase is dominated by karmic experiences of the past life, and in particular portents of one's impending rebirth back in cyclic existence. Buddhas are only involved in this process in two specialized contexts: (1) they can appear as escorts to lead a devotee to a pure land, and (2) masters of tantric contemplations are said to be able to emerge within the post-death state in the form of their chosen personal deity (*yi dam*), by force of their sustained visualization during life of themselves as that deity.

The Seminal Heart is innovative in its creation of a new phase of post-death

41. See Germano 2005.

existence that pushes the earlier postmortem phase into a secondary and subsequent role. It thus presents all of life, death, and rebirth in terms of four intermediate phases—the *natural* phase of this life between birth and dying, the *dying* phase, the new postmortem *reality* phase, and the older model now presented as pre-birth *existence/becoming* phase. *The Tantra of Unimpeded Sound* presents the reality phase:[42]

> Through the spread of the propelling winds
> the five colored light and rays
> manifest in rainbow-colored designs in indeterminate ways.
>
> Via the engaging and ripening winds, also,
> [those visions of awareness] become present throughout the four quarters, zenith and nadir,
> and by force of the directions' light gathering therein
> the Spiritual Bodies of the five spiritual families appear manifestly as well—
> deep blue, white, yellow, red, and green,
> each [buddha] appearing with its respective consort.
>
> If one understands the spread and apprehension in relation to these [visions],
> the buddhas' spiritual qualities will be perfectly complete,
> and one will not enter the three realms [of cyclic existence].
>
> Their characteristics are like this:
> since they are beyond dependence upon the coarse elements,
> nuclei blaze in rays from the light,
> and nuclei linked in groups of five [show] single buddha bodies,
> and then from [initial] half Bodies [from the navel up] their form is complete.
>
> Thus from Bodies [with] only half form, [there] are [the Father-Mother] pairs in sets of five,

42. The last part of the question and answer twenty of chapter four and the entirety of the twenty first question and answer in the same chapter (Tb12 146.7 and Ab1 175.1). The commentary on it is found in Vimalamitra's *Secret Tantra of the Illuminating Lamp's Blazing* (*sgron ma snang byed 'bar ba'i gsang rgyud*) (Kt.2 488.6–497.4, Lg 283b.1–285b.7, Li.2 315.9–322.15, and Nx.2 355.10–363.12; it is cited by Tdd and Tcd2 444.4). In my translation, I have followed the commentarial readings and exegesis.

and the individual clusters become complete
[first] in fives, [then] tens, hundreds,
thousands of clusters, and hundred thousands—
they presence naturally pure of intellectual perspectives,
and in inexpressibly infinite numbers.

This new phase, most commonly termed *the reality intermediate phase* (*chos nyid bar do*), is driven by the spontaneous agency of internal buddhas. The serene and fierce buddhas of the body's interior are released through the rupture of physical embodiment and unfold out of death's empty radiant light (*stong pa'i 'od gsal*) in postmortem experience. These visions of radiant light (*snang ba'i 'od gsal*) flow out through the deceased's eyes to temporarily pervade the visual field. This exteriorization of pure lands in death explicitly reiterates the depiction of cosmogony and the core contemplative process of direct transcendence. In all three processes we find the same encounter scenario with interior buddhas—the womb/embryo of a buddha—confronting one in an exterior field of vision. In addition, these buddhas are primarily portrayed as Enjoyment Body buddhas flowing out of the interior Reality Body, and constituting pure lands, spontaneously without any explicit human actions or guiding of the event. In all three cases there is a bifurcated response expressed as recognizing these buddhas as self (*rang ngo shes pa*) or failing to do so, which results in the dissolution into the transcendence of nirvāṇa or the reconsolidation of the cyclic existence of saṃsāra respectively. Finally, these spontaneous events also exist in the scripted ritual system famous as *The Tibetan Book of the Dead* (a Seminal Heart cycle), in which a lama uses name cards and so forth to ritually lead the deceased person's consciousness sequentially through these pure lands.

In summation, in death also we find buddhas as invariably an active and primary agent in the central processes that constitute the event in spontaneous irruptions. In contrast to the ordinary Indian Buddhist depiction of death as a process dominated by karmic processes, we instead find effulgent buddhas pervading postmortem experience. This divine encounter scenario precisely reiterates the original divine cosmogony and the self-organizing visions dominating the contemplative process.

9. Eschatology: The Final Destination

Our account ends with eschatology, the collective end that mirrors the personal end of death. The Seminal Heart developed a complex set of prophetic histories tracing the past and future, and this includes the projection of a future moment when all sentient beings without exception throughout the universe will be enlightened through the activities of these webs of buddhas both within and without. Longchenpa's *Oceanic Clouds of Profound Meaning*:[43]

> Those Realized Ones pervade everywhere in the limitless reaches of the sky's expanse pervaded by the realms of sentient beings. Abiding everywhere right up to its outer limits with a teacher taming as appropriate, retinue, teachings, and so forth, this is a single Great Eon of the Great Brahmā. It is spontaneously present as a single great taming field of the glorious All Good who is enlightened directly within the ground. Thus he remains right up until all sentient beings are freed from cyclic existence, the gyration of inexhaustible beauty in his Enlightened Body, Speech, and Mind emanating in those worlds and great eons in the form of buddhas taming as appropriate, teachings, religious communities, sages, brahmins, Brahmā, Indra, and so forth. Thus, acting naturally, he [eventually] empties out cyclic existence [as follows]. A thoroughly pure taming teacher called World Based on Great Brahmā acts for the welfare of sentient beings in piecemeal fashion . . . Finally he sets forth the Vehicle of the Adamantine Nucleus, and when not even one sentient being remains [as all] are expansively awakened into Buddhahood, the activities of All Good are finally completed. That is known as "emptying out The Great Eon of the Great Brahmā."

Similar comments are made in Longchenpa's *Treasury of the Supreme Vehicle*:[44]

> After that, all the beings in that field—as well as those in all the fields present in The Great Brahmā Eon [cosmos] arrayed by the Vajra Holder—will be freed within the primeval site. The Great Brahmā Eon arrayed by the Vajra Holder together with its material environments and life forms will thus be emptied out. Becoming the same as space, it abides for eighty-five eons. The three sources of the teachings naturally vanish within the expanse of reality's serenity and no longer manifest, once the Vajra Holder has completed this great activity. Then living beings again manifest from the expanse and the great Brahmā land is arrayed with emanations.

43. Kyt2 44.6–46.1.

44. Chapter five (Tcd1 170.13).

Finally, Longchenpa's *Introduction to the Precious Secret Path* is more explicit on how the three buddha Bodies gradually dissolve back into one another:[45]

> [He] remains without transmutation or change across the three times in a state like the moon of the empty sky, the Reality Body's sheath of precious spontaneity. The fields of the Enjoyment Body [manifest] without wavering from the Reality Body for the sake of those requiring taming, and from them, immeasurably many Emanational Bodies act in uninterrupted spontaneity for the sake of living beings. Later again the Emanational Bodies dissolve into the Enjoyment Bodies, and the Enjoyment Bodies dissolve into the Reality Body. Thus there is no transmutation or change within the primordial knowing of the four times' sameness, such that it abides in the single flavor of the expanse and primordial knowing.

Not surprisingly, this collective enlightenment is understood as a collective non-manifestation, such that the universe is literally empty, just as for Longchenpa direct transcendence contemplation culminates in the perfect emptiness of the sky's dark blue expanse. Left with no further rationale for being, the Emanational Body buddhas withdraw back into their Enjoyment Body matrix, which in turn retreat into the Reality Body, which itself swirls back into the expanse (*dbyings*, Skt. *dhātu*). Here, it is said, even the buddhas no longer see each other. And hence we find, in the end, primordial knowing alone (*'ba' zhig*), the same active agent that initiated the beginning.

Conclusion

Certain orthodox readings of Indian Buddhist thought may find the Seminal Heart's focus on gnostic creation and agency to be highly irregular, which over time has raised scholarly questions as to what possible external influences may be at work, whether Chinese Daoism, Kashmiri Shaivism, Indigenous tradi-

45. Kyt 3 160.2–5. See related comments on Kyt1 306.5–307.3 and Kyt3 91.5–92.2. In Kyt3 92.1, Longchenpa appears to be explicit that the Reality Body dissolves into the expanse, and then subsequently straying into cyclic existence remerges. The image of a sheath conveys that the Reality Body is a self-contained interiority devoid of external manifestation or dynamic changes, just like the empty sky of the thirtieth of the lunar month when the moon no longer manifests at all. However, just as the empty sky contains the moon—even if hidden for the moment in the "sheath" of the sky, on the first of the new month it always reemerges—the Reality Body is brimming with precious spontaneity that emerges in the form of the other Buddha Bodies when there is need.

tions, Manichaeism, Zoroastrianism, or some other tradition.[46] While some of these traditions may very well have been pertinent historical influences, the present essay attempts to present the Seminal Heart as a highly innovative interpretation of Mahāyāna Buddhism in India, against the backdrop of later Vajrayāna movements, with Indian Buddhist precedents for all of its key components. Admittedly, many of its key insights appear only in germinal fashion in these earlier materials, while in other cases its elaborate systematizations point to the significance of explicit doctrines or motifs that have often been marginalized in contemporary discussions of the philosophical significance of Mahāyāna literature. It is in fact a complex, architectonic philosophical and contemplative system ranging over such classical Buddhist philosophical topics as the ontological status of external objects, the nature of emptiness, the nature of the mind, cosmology, and so forth. It is as much based on sūtras and their exegetical literature as it is on tantras and their exegetical literature, such that it must be considered a central dialogical pole when evaluating Tibetan philosophical speculation from the eleventh to fourteenth centuries. One of its most distinctive achievements is to articulate a sophisticated philosophical discourse out of innovative treatments of central and implicit motifs of earlier Indian sūtras and tantras, though this process was perhaps only fully realized in the later fourteenth-century corpus of Longchenpa. Its integration of tantric concepts and Mahāyāna doctrines involves a creative reinterpretation of the latter and not simply a mere ritualization of earlier concepts and/or a sterile concordance that hermeneutically retrieves shocking tantric images, rhetorics, and practices back into a normative doctrinal framework.

I have outlined an innovative and gnostic orientation in the Seminal Heart tradition that is eclectic in its ranging over a wide variety of Indian Buddhist materials, tantric and non-tantric. What binds them all together into a single integrated system is the radical emphasis on the prior, primary, and ongoing agency of primordial knowing and buddhas as constitutive of being, world, body, mind, and development in general in the beginnings, middles, and ends of these same processes. This polyvalent focus on divine creation interweaves cosmogony, cosmology, embryology, physiology, psychology, epistemology, soteriology, thanatology, and eschatology into a powerful blend operating on multiple interior and exterior registers, with the semantic fields of each doctrine in constant transformation mirroring the protean nature of its own

46. For example, when I presented this work at a panel during the annual meeting of the American Academy of Religion, I recall a senior colleague in Indian and Tibetan Buddhism exclaiming, "What's next?!!" The context made it quite clear that he felt the doctrines being discussed were far outside of what he considered to be boundaries of Buddhist thought in these traditions.

primordial ground. Much more can and should be inquired into as to its pedigree in Indian Buddhism (the clear and deep influence of the *Kālacakra Tantra* in particular) and possible external influences, as well as its interpretative significance, but this will have to wait a later venue.

Works Cited

Tibetan Works

Short alpha-numerical codes are used in footnotes to point to the source of a given citation of a Tibetan text. The alphabetic segment signifies a unique id for a collection of texts or an individual text title, while the numerical segment indicates the volume number. The following table provides an easy way to decode the references.

Ab	The A 'dzoms edition of ***The Seventeen Tantras***
Knt	*The Seminal Heart of the Ḍākinīs* by Padmasambhava and other authors
Kt	The Bka' ma edition of *The Secret Tantra of the Illuminating Lamp's Blazing* by Vimalamitra
Kyt	*The Seminal Quintessence of the Ḍākinīs* by Longchenpa
Lg	The Lhasa edition of *The Secret Tantra of the Illuminating Lamp's Blazing* by Vimalamitra
Li	The Namkhai Norbu input of the Lhasa edition of *The Secret Tantra of the Illuminating Lamp's Blazing* by Vimalamitra
Lyt	*The Seminal Quintessence of the Spiritual Mentor* by Longchenpa
Nx	The Namkha Norbu critical edition of *The Secret Tantra of the Illuminating Lamp's Blazing* by Vimalamitra
Tb	The Mtshams brag edition of ***The Seventeen Tantras***
Tcd	*The Treasury of the Supreme Vehicle* by Longchenpa
Tdd	*The Treasury of Words and Meanings* by Longchenpa
Vnt	*The Seminal Essence of Vimalamitra* by Vimalamitra (editor)

The Seventeen Tantras. *Rgyud bcu bdun*. Of transcendental authorship. This collection of tantras is located in most editions of *The Collected Tantras of the Ancient* (*Rnying ma rgyud 'bum*), from which I have used the Mtshams brag edition in volumes 11 and 12 (referred to herein by the abbreviation Tb11–12, depending upon the volume). The edition was printed in forty-six volumes in Bhutan by the National Library (Thimphu: Royal government of Bhutan, 1982). I have also used the separately published three-volume edition based on the A 'dzom 'brug pa blocks (New Delhi: Sanje Dorje, 1973), referred to herein by the abbreviation Ab1–3, depending upon the volume. The individual titles are as follows.

The Tantra of Unimpeded Sound (*Rin po che 'byung bar byed pa sgra thal 'gyur chen po'i rgyud*). See *The Seventeen Tantras* for full bibliographical reference. Tb12 1–173, Ab1 1–205.

The Tantra of Exquisite Auspiciousness. (*Bkra shis mdzes ldan chen po'i rgyud*). See *The Seventeen Tantras* for full bibliographical reference. Tb12 173–193, Ab1 207–232.

The Tantra of the Adamantine Hero's Heart-Mirror (*Rdo rje sems dpa' snying gi me long gi rgyud*). See *The Seventeen Tantras* for full bibliographical reference. Tb12 193–245, Ab1 315–388.

The Tantra of Self-Arising Awareness (*Rig pa rang shar chen po'i rgyud*). See *The Seventeen Tantras* for full bibliographical reference. Tb11 323–696, Ab1 389–855. See Smith 2018 for a translation.

Garab Dorjé (dga' rab rdo rje). *A Secret Commentary on The Single Son of the Teachings as a Liberation through Wearing* (*Btags pas grol bar bstan pa bu gcig gi gsang 'brel*). See Vimalamitra's *The Seminal Essence of Vimalamitra*, vol 2, 73–271.3.

Longchenpa (Klong chen pa). *Introduction to the Precious Secret Path* (*Gsang lam rin po che'i ngo sprod*). See Longchenpa's *The Seminal Quintessence of the Ḍākinīs*, vol. 3, 154.3–162.5.

———. *Introduction to the Presencing of the Expanse* (*Dbyings snang ngo sprod*). This text is located in Longchenpa's *The Seminal Quintessence of the Ḍākinīs*, vol. 3, 116–125).

———. *The Lamp of the Key Points of Contemplatively Taking it into Experience* (*Nyams len gnad kyi sgron me*). See Longchenpa's *The Seminal Quintessence of the Spiritual Mentor*, vol 2, 35–74.

———. *The Oceanic Clouds of Profound Meaning* (*Zab don rgya mtsho'i sprin*). See Longchenpa's *The Seminal Quintessence of the Ḍākinīs*, vol 2, 1–488.

———. *The Seminal Quintessence of the Ḍākinīs* (*Mkha' 'gro yang tig*, Kyt1–3, depending upon the volume). See vols. 4–6 of *The Seminal Heart in Four Parts* (*Snying thig ya bzhi*). New Delhi: Trulku Tsewang, Jamyang and L. Tashi, 1971.

———. *The Seminal Quintessence of the Spiritual Mentor* (*Bla ma yang tig*, Lyt1–2, depending upon the part—"E" indicated by Lt1 and "Wam" indicated by Lyt2). See vol. 1 of *The Seminal Heart in Four Parts* (*Snying thig ya bzhi*). New Delhi: Trulku Tsewang, Jamyang and L. Tashi, 1971.

———. *The Treasury of the Supreme Vehicle* (*Theg mchog mdzod*, Tcd1–2, depending on volume). This is published within the six-volume *The Seven Treasuries* (*Mdzod chen bdun*) by Longchenpa. Gangtok, Sikkim: Sherab Gyaltsen and Khyentse Labrang, 1983.

———. *The Treasury of Words and Meanings* (*Tshig don mdzod*, Tdd). This is published within the six-volume *The Seven Treasuries* (*Mdzod chen bdun*) by Longchenpa. Gangtok, Sikkim: Sherab Gyaltsen and Khyentse Labrang, 1983.

Padmasambhava and other authors. *The Seminal Heart of the Ḍākinīs* (*Mkha' 'gro snying thig*, Knt1–3, depending upon the volume). See vols. 2–3 of *The Seminal Heart in Four Parts* (*Snying thig ya bzhi*). New Delhi: Trulku Tsewang, Jamyang and L. Tashi, 1971.

Vimalamitra. *The Secret Tantra of the Illuminating Lamp's Blazing* (*Sgron ma snang byed 'bar ba'i gsang rgyud*). Four different editions are cited (1) Kt.1-2: Volumes 107–8 of the *Snga 'gyur bka' ma shin tu rgyas pa* published in 2009 as edited by Tshe ring rgya mtsho; Chengdu: Si khron mi rigs dpe skrun khang; BDRC #MW1PD100944. (2) Lg: Images made by myself of a manuscript cursive version kept in Lhasa; an inferior quality image of this can be found in the seventh volume of the seven volume edition published in 2009 as edited by Chos rgyal nam mkha'i nor bu; Australia: Publisher unknown; BDRC #MW3CN647. (3) Li.1–2: a flawed but useful input version of the Lhasa manuscript published in volumes one and two of the Nam mkha'i nor bu edition. (4) Nx.1–2: a problematic critical edition published in volumes five and six of the Nam mkha'i nor bu edition.

Vimalamitra (editor). *The Seminal Heart of Vimalamitra* by Vimalamitra and other early Great Perfection Masters (*Bi ma snying thig*, referred to herein by the abbreviation Vnt1–3 depending on the volume). See volumes 7–9 of *The Seminal Heart in Four Parts* (*Snying thig ya bzhi*). New Delhi: Trulku Tsewang, Jamyang and L. Tashi, 1971.

Non-Tibetan Works

Bentor, Yael, and Penpa Dorjee. 2019. *Essence of the Ocean of Attainments: The Creation Stage of the Guhyasamaja Tantra according to Panchen Losang Chökyi Gyaltsen.* Somerville, MA: Wisdom Publications.

Chönam, Lama and Sangye Kandro. *Essence of Clear Light.* 2010a. Ithaca, NY: Snow Lion Publications.

———. 2010b. *Key to the Precious Treasury.* Ithaca, NY: Snow Lion Publications.

———. 2011. *The Guhyagarbha Tantra: Secret Essence Definitive Nature Just As It Is with commentary by Longchen Rabjam.* Ithaca, NY: Snow Lion Publications.

Davidson, Ronald M. 2002. *Indian Esoteric Buddhism: A Social History of the Tantric Movement.* New York: Columbia University Press.

———. 2005. *Tibetan Renaissance: Tantric Buddhism in the Rebirth of Tibetan Culture.* New York: Columbia University Press.

Dharmachakra Translation Commitee. 2009. *Luminous Essence: A Guide to the Guhyagarbha Tantra by Jamgön Mipham.* Ithaca, NY: Snow Lion Publications.

Dorje, Gyurme. 1987. *The Guhyagarbhatattvaviniścayamahātantra and its XIVth Century Tibetan Commentary Phyogs bCu Mun Sel.* Unpublished Ph.D. thesis. The School of Oriental and African Studies at the University of London.

Germano, David F. 2005. "The Funerary Transformation of the Great Perfection (*rDzogs chen*)." *Journal of the International Association of Tibetan Studies* 1: 1–54.

Granoff, Phyllis. 1998. "Maitreya's Jewelled World: Some Remarks on Gems and Visions in Buddhist Texts." *Journal of Indian Philosophy*, 26.4: 347–71.

Guenther, Herbert. 1984. *Matrix of Mystery: Scientific and Humanistic Aspects of rDzogs-chen Thought.* Boulder & London: Shambhala.

Halkias, Georgios T. 2012. *Luminous Bliss: A Religious History of Pure Land Literature in Tibet.* Honolulu: University of Hawai'i Press.

Harrison, Paul M. 1978. "Buddhānusmṛti in the Pratyutpanna-Buddha Saṃmukhāvasthita-Samādhi-Sūtra." *Journal of Indian Philosophy* 6.1, 35–57.

———. 1990. *The Samādhi of Direct Encounter with the Buddhas of the Present: An Annotated English translation of the Tibetan version of the Pratyutpanna-Buddha-Saṃmukhāvasthita-Samādhi Sūtra with Several Appendices Relating to the History of the Text.* Tokyo: International Institute for Buddhist Studies.

Howard, Angela Falco. 1986. *The Imagery of the Cosmological Buddha.* Leiden: E. J. Brill.

———. 2018. "A case of identity: who is the Cosmological Buddha?" *Rivista degli studi orientali* XCI, 1/4:181–209.

Howard, Angela, and Guiseppe Vignato. 2014. *Archaeological and Visual Sources of Meditation in the Ancient Monasteries of Kuča.* Leiden: E. J. Brill.

Higgins, David. 2013. *The Philosophical Foundations of Classical Rdzogs Chen in Tibet: Investigating the Distinction Between Dualistic Mind (Sems) and Primordial Knowing (Ye Shes).* Wien: Arbeitskreis für Tibetische und Buddhistische Studien, Universität Wien.

Jackson, David. 1992. "Birds in the Egg and Newborn Lion Cubs: Metaphors for the Potentialities and Limitations of 'All-at-once' Enlightenment." In *Tibetan Studies: Proceedings of the 5th Seminar of the International Association of Tibetan Studies, Narita 1989,* edited by Ihara Shōren and Yamaguchi Zuihō, 95–114. Narita: Naritasan Shinshoji.

Jones, Charles B. 2021. *Pure Land: History, Tradition, and Practice.* Boulder, CO: Shambhala.

Kapstein, Matthew. 2004. "Pure Land Buddhism in Tibet? From Sukhāvatī to the Field of Great Bliss." In *Approaching the Land of Bliss: Religious Praxis in the Cult of Amitābha* edited by Richard K. Payne and Kenneth K. Tanaka, 16–51. Honolulu: University of Hawai'i Press.

Makransky, John J. 1997. *Buddhahood Embodied: Sources of Controversy in India and Tibet.* Albany, NY: State University of New York Press.

Merkur, Dan. 1993. *Gnosis: An Esoteric Tradition of Mystical Visions and Unions.* Albany, NY: State University of New York Press.

Radich, Michael. 2007. "Problems and Opportunities in the Study of the Buddha's Bodies." *New Zealand Journal of Asian Studies* 9.1: 162–85.

———. 2015a. "Tathāgatagarbha Scriptures." In *Brill's Encyclopedia of Buddhism,* Volume One: Literature and Languages, edited by Jonathan Silk, Oskar von Hinüber, and Vincent Eltschinger, 261–73. Leiden: Brill.

———. 2015b. *The Mahāparinirvāṇa-mahāsūtra and the Emergence of Tathāgatagarbha Doctrine.* Hamburg Buddhist Studies 5. Edited by Michael Zimmermann. Hamburg: Hamburg University Press.

Sadakata, Akira. 1997. *Buddhist Cosmology: Philosophy and Origins.* Tokyo: Kōsei Publishing Co.

Smith, Ācārya Malcom. 2018. *The Self-Arisen Vidyā Tantra: A Translation of the Rigpa Rangshar.* Somerville, MA: Wisdom Publications.

Thondup Rinpoche, Tulku. 1986. *Hidden Teachings of Tibet: an Explanation of the Terma Tradition of the Nyingma School of Buddhism.* Edited by Harold Talbott. London: Wisdom Publications.

Williams, Paul. 2008. *Mahāyāna Buddhism: The Doctrinal Foundations.* 2nd Edition. Abingdon: Routledge.

Evoking the Divine Human:
An Appearance of Suchness: Ornament of the Sacred

Jacob P. Dalton

OVER THE SPAN of Janet Gyatso's career, Tibetan Buddhist studies has come into its own as a field of study in its own right. Throughout this advance, Gyatso has led the way, incisively identifying much of what is most interesting about Tibetan history and culture. From terma to autobiography, Tibetan medicine to Tibetan adaptations of Indian literary forms, she has done much to define the field of Tibetan studies and bring Tibetan voices into contemporary conversations on autobiography, gender, modernity studies, the history of science, and more. Her work has been particularly remarkable for its focus on Tibetans *as human beings*—not just fonts of Buddhist doctrine, but people negotiating their places in the world. She has brought to scholars' attention previously ignored genres of Tibetan literature while setting a new standard for the ethics of scholarship by consulting regularly with native Tibetan readers.

On a more personal note, Janet has been a teacher and a dear friend to me since the very beginning of my studies. From my sophomore year at Amherst College, when she first arrived there, through our travels in Central Tibet in the 1990s, to our laughter-filled evenings at conferences around the world, her wit, curiosity, and creativity have been constant inspirations. I have found her interest in close readings of Tibetan writings particularly stimulating, and I offer this paper as a small thank you for all she has given me and the wider field.

The rise of tantric Buddhism in the seventh and eighth centuries did more than just introduce some new ritual forms; it brought new ways of engaging with the Buddhist tradition, even new ways of being in the world. Before this, most Buddhists could only aspire to glimpse the Buddha, gazing up at his distant feet from their benighted worldly existences. Thus, early ritual manuals for Buddhist image worship, which gained widespread popularity in the fifth and sixth centuries C.E., instructed their readers to construct a maṇḍala altar and carefully purify it before placing a buddha statue at its center, making offerings and reciting prayers and dhāraṇī in its presence. With the rise of the yogatantras and tantra proper, the Buddhist reader of *vidhis* and sādhanas "entered" the maṇḍala to take up residence as the buddha at its center. This ascent marked something of a shift in Buddhist thought and practice. No longer were the all-too-human experiences of the meditator roundly dismissed as worldly distractions or, at best, signs of progress; now those same emotional (desire, anger, envy, etc.) and aesthetic (laughter, disgust, surprise, etc.) experiences were the expressions of a buddha and part of the path to awakening. Tantric Buddhism was, in this sense, at once a raising up of the human to the level of a buddha and a drawing down (sometimes even with hook, noose, and shackles) of the buddha into our world as an imminent presence.

All this was mirrored, and furthered, by significant changes within the genre of ritual manuals. As the line between Buddhist and buddha blurred, so did that between the explicitly human-authored ritual manuals and the ostensibly buddha-authored tantras. Ritual manuals began to be gathered into and repackaged as tantras, and soon tantras, with all their markings of *buddhavacana*, began to reshape ritual manuals. Thus, a generic change unfolded across the eighth century, a shift from the prosaic language of the dhāraṇī-based *vidhi* (Tib. *cho ga*) and even some early yogatantra manuals to the increasingly evocative and poetic forms of the Mahāyoga sādhana. By the mid-eighth century, sādhanas were regularly composed and read, in part, for the inward visionary, aesthetic, and transcendent experiences they evoked. Their concomitant use of poetic forms for expressing and ritually engendering tastes of awakening was just one of the ways the Vajrayāna transformed Buddhism. In sutras and the like, the words of the Buddha (or buddhas) had long been written in verse; now human-authored sādhanas too began to be framed as emanations out of the luminous space of sādhana and marked as such by verse and poetic devices.

An Appearance of Suchness: Ornament of the Sacred (*De kho sādhana snang ba dam pa rgyan*) offers a good example of this blurring between human authorship and *buddhavacana*. A Mahāyoga sādhana written entirely in verse (consisting of seven-syllable lines in its Tibetan translation), the work consists mostly of a weave of quotations carefully selected from the *Guhyagarbhatantra*. It is an important work for our understanding of early tantric ritual development, and as it remains largely unstudied, it is translated below, following these brief introductory comments.

While several versions of the Tibetan text are extant, *An Appearance of Suchness* was rare enough in Tibet not to have been included in the Dergé Tengyur. It does appear, however, in some other editions of the Tengyur, including the Narthang and Peking. The version used herein is that of the Narthang. Unfortunately, the canonical versions lack any colophon, but another recently published version from Nyarong closes with the statement that it was "written by the master Buddhagupta" (Gsang rgyas gsang ba).[1] Were this true, it would date the work to the second half of the eighth century. Such an early date is supported by the existence of still another version of the sādhana among the Dunhuang manuscripts.[2] (As I have explained elsewhere, the tantric materials from Dunhuang generally reflect a period in Indian ritual development of the late eighth century.)[3]

The Dunhuang version is found in IOL Tib J 332/1, a well-preserved *poti*-style manuscript penned in a careful hand that itself almost certainly dates to the tenth century.[4] The text is immediately followed in the manuscript (18v.4) by a manual for a tantric feast (gaṇacakra). Aside from occasional differences in wording or verse order, compared to the canonical, the Dunhuang version of our text is unique in having considerable commentarial notes interspersed inline between the original verses, notes that introduce each part of the proceedings with a prose summary that regularly ends with, "this is expressed in these words:" after which the root verses continue. Before the commentarial notes settle into this reliable pattern, they take slightly different forms at the outset of the text. Thus, the whole sādhana is introduced with these words: "Now, what follows are the practices. The wrathful maṇḍala will be generated. By means of this maṇḍala for taming beings, the marvelous activities will be enacted." Following this opening note, no further comments are made on the sādhana's introductory section, a section that includes the homage, promise to compose (*rtsom par dam bca'*), advice on maintaining secrecy, a statement on the siddhis that will result, and a verse on the ideal ritual location. This introduction then ends with a double-*shad* and a gap in the line before the text continues with a further commentarial note on the meditation proper.

Often, the inline comments add little in the way of substantive explanation, even repeating much of the wording that follows, but occasionally important information is imparted. The initial three comments on the meditation section

1. *De kho na nyid snang ba* B, 6b.2. For some comments on Buddhagupta's (a.k.a. Buddhaguhya) possible involvements with the *Guhyagarbha*, and the *Māyājāla* tantras more generally, see Karmay 1988, 63. It is also notable that the Peking Tengyur includes our sādhana (Q. 4735) in a section of volume *bu* (83) containing several other Buddhagupta-attributed works.

2. Kenneth Eastman (1983) was the first to identify the Dunhuang text as a Guhyagarbha-based sādhana, though he did not notice its similarity to the modern canonical version. Nor, it should be admitted, did Dalton and van Schaik notice the presence of the canonical version in their 2006 catalogue. Only more recently did Yi Ding make this significant identification in his 2020 Ph.D. thesis.

3. See Dalton 2011, 221n14.

4. The manuscript bears the Stein site number of Ch.73.III, which Takeuchi (2012, 209–11) has identified as a bundle consisting almost entirely of tenth-century manuscripts.

are examples, as they read the three samādhis of the generation stage onto the first three verses of the meditation section.[5] Given the popularity of the three samādhis at Dunhuang, we may begin to suspect a Tibetan hand behind these interspersed comments.[6]

The author of the Dunhuang comments was well aware of the fact that the sādhana's verses were drawn from the *Guhyagarbhatantra*. The comment that introduces the first samādhi ends not with the usual, "This is expressed in these words:" but with, "Where is this evident? In that same great tantra, these words appear:" The word "same" (*nyid*) here is probably a reference to the immediately preceding line, which references the *Māyājāla* by name (the *Guhyagarbha* being the main tantra of the *Māyājāla* cycle and often referred to by that name in early Tibetan writings). In many sources, Tibetan and Indian, the *Guhyagarbha* and other tantras of the Mahāyoga class are framed as partial manifestations of a larger mythic *ur*-tantra, often supposed to contain 100,000 verses or chapters. In being cobbled out of such a manifestation, our adhana in effect partook of this mythic origin and its worldly manifestations. In this sense, the adhana is itself a piece of that emanatory process, as its title already suggests: *An Appearance of Suchness: Ornament of the Sacred*. Human authored, perhaps by Buddhagupta, but also sacred scripture in its own right. The claiming of such high status for Buddhist ritual manuals was a recent development within the genre.

The Dunhuang version's commentarial notes exhibit a further significant stylistic difference (beyond their being prosaic): the root sādhana's verses with parallels in the tantra are mostly either narrative or evocative in style, with their ritual purposes left almost entirely implicit. The narrative aspects may be explained by the fact that the verses are drawn from the *Guhyagarbha*'s mythic narrative of the buddhas' original performance of the rites. Thus, for example, our sādhana's verse 56 reads: "In that way, having luminously displayed the maṇḍala,/ throughout the ten directions of the six realms,/ the blazing maṇḍala luminously manifests." One might expect here that the final verb, "manifests," would be in the past tense, since the same verse in the *Guhyagarbha* describes the original event that took place in the mythic past, and indeed, in the tantra itself, the final verb is "became" (*gyur*). Yet in our sādhana it reads "manifests" (*snang*). Elsewhere again, in verse 22, our sādhana reads: "Throughout the

5. The three samādhis, which appear throughout the Dunhuang Mahāyoga materials, are usually listed as the thusness, all-illuminating, and causal samādhis, though here the first samādhi is termed the equilibrium samādhi (*mnyam ba nyid kyi ting nge 'dzin*).

6. The Dunhuang comments also, quite helpfully, divide the proceedings into sections, marked in the present English translation in square brackets.

ten directions of the six realms,/ pervading infinite space, wrathful/ maṇḍalas the size of the billionfold world-system emerge,/ as numerous as the atoms [in the universe], throughout the ten directions."[7] The parallel verse in the tantra includes two verbs, corresponding to "pervading" and "emerge," respectively, and both are in the past tense, ending with *gyur*.[8] In our sādhana, however, the first ("pervading") functions adverbially with the final verb, "emerge" (with a *par* instead of a *gyur*), while the final verb's tense is future, or perhaps present (*'gyur*). Our author, then, assuming the Tibetan translation is faithful to the Sanskrit original's verb tenses, was sensitive to the linguistic implications of transferring verse narrative from tantra to ritual manual.

The verses' more evocative aspects (and some verses are both narrative and evocative) sit more easily in both generic contexts, evoking images or experiences of either the original mythic performance or of the sādhana's present reenactment. Verse 12 reads: "Emaho! These fantastic and marvelous phenomena/ are the secrets of all the perfected buddhas;/ all is born from the birthless./ Even in birth itself, they are birthless." This verse is used to evoke the sense of emptiness that constitutes the thusness (or "equilibrium") samādhi that opens the generation stage. Because the verse's description is less one of specific events in the past or present than of the very nature of all phenomena, its grammar more easily moves between *buddhavacana* and human-authored sādhana.

In fact, the lack of explanation regarding the ritual significance of such evocative verses is specifically what the Dunhuang version's commentarial notes seek to remedy. The notes are far more directive than the sādhana's verses themselves, explaining what should be done before reproducing the verse that evokes the experience of its being done. Thus, the Dunhuang notes introduce the above-cited verse on the birthless nature of phenomena by explaining: "one should first cultivate the equilibrium samādhi." Likewise, where the sādhana may simply insert a mantra at the appropriate point in its proceedings, the notes explain that it "should be recited," what its result is, and so on. The Dunhuang commentarial notes therefore suggest that the evocative verses of our sādhana were obscure enough for some readers to require further instruction, explanations written in more mundane prose that could help bring the tantra's verses more fully into the realm of human experience.

This said, it is important to recognize that not all our sādhana's verses have parallels in the *Guhyagarbha*. Some were probably composed by the sādhana's

7. *'jig rten drug gi phyogs bcu dag/ mtha' yas khyab par khro bo yi/ dkyil 'khor stong gsum 'jig rten tsam/ phyogs bcu'i rdul snyed 'thon par 'gyur/* (846.3–4).

8. *'jig rten drug gi phyogs bcu mtha' yas pa khyab par gyur to/ khro bo'i dkyil 'khor gyi tshogs stong gsum gyi 'jig rten tsam phyogs bcu'i rdul phra mo snyed 'thon par gyur pas* (125b.5–6).

author, especially the opening and closing verses, but perhaps too others describing key points in the proceedings such as the absorption of oneself into the buddha's heart and the subsequent descent down the vajra path in verses 37–38, or the beginning of the sexual yoga in verses 42–44. Several verses not found in the *Guhyagarbha* do appear in another sādhana preserved in the modern Tengyur.[9] The *Sādhana that Distinguishes the Stages of the Seven Maṇḍalas from the* Vajra Array Tantra (*Rdo rje bkod pa'i rgyud las dkyil 'khor bdun pa'i rim pa rnam par phyed ba'i sgrub thabs*), apparently based on the Anuyoga tantra better known as the *Gathering of Intentions Sutra* (*Dgongs pa 'dus pa'i mdo*), is attributed to the Ācārya *Bhāskarāṅkura (Slob dpon Snang mdzad myu gu), who apparently looked to one Mahācārya Sthiramati (presumably not the sixth-century Abhidharma and Yogācāra scholar) for inspiration.[10] There is some overlap between those verses found in the *Guhyagarbhatantra* and those in the *Vajra Array Sādhana*, but a number appear only in the latter. It remains unclear whether the verses with parallels in the *Vajra Array* were copied from that other work or simply enjoyed a wide enough circulation around the late eighth and ninth centuries to be included in both works.

Before turning to the translation, a brief overview of its rites may be in order. The *Appearance of Suchness* is foremost an early Mahāyoga sādhana for sexual yoga. It remains unclear whether the visualized union it describes was meant to be performed in conjunction with an actual physical act. The work stands apart from other translations of Indic sādhanas from Dunhuang because of its layering of buddhas—the initial "outer" buddha, with his consort and surrounding maṇḍala of deities, and a further inner buddha that is generated at the point of union of the previous "outer" buddha and his consort. Thus, following some opening advice, the reader is to begin, in verse 12, with the three samādhis (if we are to accept the Dunhuang notes' reading), which result in oneself as a heruka at the center of a wrathful maṇḍala palace (described in vv. 14–18). The heruka then generates his consort, with whom he enters into union to produce a cloud of bodhicitta within her lotus (vv. 19–21). From this cloud spread forth (presumably via light rays) infinite buddhas who fill the universe, then return to become the herukas of the other four families immediately surrounding oneself as the central vajraheruka (vv. 22–26). Next, the remaining deities of the maṇḍala are produced by reciting a series of seed-syllables (vv. 27–33). At this point, one returns to one's ordinary form and prays before the central deity of

9. For these parallels and others, see Yi Ding 2020, appendix 26.

10. *Rdo rje bkod pa'i rgyud las sgrub thabs*, 100a.6. The full colophon reads: *slob dpon chen po stir ma tis dgongs pa las rdo rje bkod pa'i rgyud bstan pa bsrung ba rnal 'byor yongs kyi mgon po legs ldan nag po'i sgrub thabs dkyil 'khor bdun gyi rim pa rnam par phye ba slob spon snang mdzad myu gus mdzad pa.*

the maṇḍala just created. In response, the buddha emits light rays that incinerate one, leaving only a string of three syllables (*oṃ, āṃ, hūṃ*) that are the purified forms of one's body, speech, and mind, which are then drawn into the buddha's heart and descend to the tip of his vajra within the consort's lotus, "dwelling there as the dharmakāya-bodhicitta" (34–37). Next, the *hṛdaya* of the surrounding deities resound, light rays emanate and regather, and one is transformed into the "inner" buddha together with his consort. A further emanation and regathering of light rays, together with a series of mantras consecrates this inner buddha (38–41). ITJ332/1 introduces the two buddhas in reproductive terms, highlighting the shift from one being created at the "outer" deity's point of union to one creating a buddha at the "inner" deity's point of union: "Up to this point has been the generation of oneself as a son of the conqueror. Having in that way generated pride with the nature of the five wisdoms, now from here on, the conqueror is to be generated as one's own son." Now one commences the practice of sexual union proper. One retains the drop of bodhicitta at the tip of the vajra, binding and shackling it in place and forcefully singing, until emission occurs and the bodhicitta emerges as a luminous maṇḍala (vv. 42–45). The jñānasattvas, or wisdom beings, then consecrate this "inner" maṇḍala (vv. 46–51), and a series of verses describing the resulting maṇḍala follows (vv. 52–56). It is possible that the last verse of the consecration (v. 50), the "song of accomplishment," would have been accompanied by the self-bestowal of the "supreme sacrament" (*dam tshig mchog*), which is mentioned in the last line of verse 48—that is, a drop of the bodhicitta—but the rite is not made explicit. If so, it is significant that consecration with the jñānasattva (or samaya) is tied to the bestowal of the sacrament.[11] Now the reader recites praises to the central deity of the maṇḍala (vv. 57–62). Finally, the sādhana ends with the dissolution of the visualization (vv. 63–65), some closing instructions on continuing to consider oneself as the deity (vv. 66–68), and a dedication of merit (v. 70).

Notes on the translation: I have organized my translation into numbered verses but doing so was difficult and often rather arbitrary. Further work is required to map the verse breaks to those in the *Guhyagarbha* and other parallel sources. Page numbers for the Narthang edition, upon which my translation is based, are provided in [square brackets]. The root verses of the sādhana itself are represented in bold, while the Dunhuang comments are not.

11. For more on the developmental continuities between consecration with the jñānasattva and the self-bestowal of the bodhicitta sacrament, see Dalton 2023, chapter 4.

Translation[12]

[Introduction:]

Now, what follows are the practices. The wrathful maṇḍala will be generated. By means of this maṇḍala for taming beings, the marvelous activities will be enacted:

[844.4] To the body that is the essential equality of all,
to the body, speech, and mind of the lord of the dance of great bliss,
to the wheel of inexhaustible ornaments,
to the heruka, I pay homage. (1)

In the Māyājāla-tantras,
one must cultivate the deity yoga.[13]
So that sentient beings may generate gnosis,
I will teach, carefully compiling [this work].

If the master has not been pleased, or
the initiations have not been received,
then those who undertake to study and so on
will gain no results and be brought to ruin.[14]

[The teachings are] well represented using words that rely
on groupings of letters, labels, and names.
From within those, the concealed, hidden meaning is extracted
and abides in the vajra mind of the teacher.[15]

This is the definite great secret,
the result that becomes path.
For the maṇḍalas of the conquerors without exception,
there is no secret definitive meaning apart from that.[16] **(5)**

12. The Narthang provides no title at the beginning of the text.

13. ITJ332/1, 1r.3 prefers: "one must perform the stages of deity yoga" (*lha'i rnal 'byor rim pa zhig*).

14. Compare *Gsang ba'i snying po*, ch. 10, 121b.6–7.

15. Compare *Gsang ba'i snying po*, ch. 13, 123b.6. The lines immediately follow the passage that interpreters take as a doxography (on which see Dalton 2005, 128), so the "teachings" referenced here are all those of the preceding doxography.

16. The tantra appends a fifth line to this four-line verse that is for some reason represented in neither our sādhana nor the Dunhuang version (ITJ332/1, 1v.1). The line reads: "Though sought,

Supreme among the mahāmudrās of all [the buddhas],
by those who have trained in study, contemplation, and cultivation,
who are endowed with the wisdom eye, it is apprehended.

It should be taught to worthy vessels of good disposition, [845]
given to those who offer their bodies and possessions;
it should not be given to others.

If it is given to the ignorant or the derisive,
one's life will come to an untimely end,
and one will be alternately roasted then frozen for a long time.[17]

Having tamed with meditative equipoise
the mind that is like a rutting elephant,
if one is taught in the mantras and mudrās,
one will gain the amazing great siddhi.[18]

In a great charnel ground or an isolated place,
surrounded by mountains and
ornamented with vines and garlands of flowers,
or in a comfortable place, be seated.[19] (10)

In order to display the great pride
that pacifies suffering powered by grasping,
and tames the cruel and the three worlds,
The māyājāla concentration is cultivated:

[Generation of the "Outer" Deity at the Center of the Palace:]
Completing the *no pyi ka* [i.e., sādhana] for the wrathful maṇḍala [referred to] above, toward that end, one should first cultivate the equilibrium samādhi. Within the expanse of all phenomena being primordially unborn and unceasing, the miraculous appearances that emerge, no matter how they are revealed, are thought to be without even the slightest speck of wavering from the expanse

none is found by the conquerors" (*btsal kyang rgyal bas mi bsnyes so*). The line is present in the *Spar khab* commentary to the *Guhyagarbha* (*Dpe bsdur ma* edition, 389–90).

17. Reading *bsribs* as *sbreb*, which is seen in other versions and a *brda rnying* for *'khyag pa*.

18. Compare *Gsang ba'i snying po*, ch. 5, 115b.5–6.

19. This last line is missing from ITJ332/1, IV.4, which reads instead: *ri bo bskor ba'i lcug ma dang/ men tog 'phreng bas brgyan pa'i/ dben ba'i gnas su khyad bar du/*.

that is ultimately without birth or cessation. Where is this evident? In that same great tantra, these words appear:[20]

Emaho! These fantastic and marvelous phenomena
are the secrets of all the perfected buddhas;
all is born from the birthless.
Even in birth itself, they are birthless.[21]

Thereby, the equilibrium samādhi is cultivated for a moment. Now one should cultivate the all-illuminating great compassion samādhi. This is expressed in these words:[22]

Fully lucid within emptiness,
the compassionate mother should be cultivated:
within that ascertainment is the great vajra.

By reciting *ma sūrya maṇḍala ma*, out of the expanse which is the cultivation of the identity's great equilibrium samādhi, within the mother, a sun maṇḍala that is all the universes is cultivated as rich red and pervaded by fire. In the center of that, by reciting *hūṃ*, clearly imagine the blazing red sprout of a *hūṃ* syllable. By reciting *hūṃ spharaṇa jāḥ*, light rays emanate in the ten directions, exhorting the oaths of the sugatas. Having performed the purposes of the oceans of beings, as one recites again *saṃharaṇa hūṃ*, they dissolve back into the earlier *hūṃ*, melting into and enriching the *hūṃ*, whereby, reciting *vajratiṣṭhatiṣṭha*, one imagines it becomes a five-spoked vajra. One recites *oṃ buddha śrī heruka hūṃ*, whereby one clearly cultivates that, out of the vajra, there comes oneself as the Bhagavan Buddhaheruka, endowed with the nine dances of great blazing in the moods of erotic, heroic, terrifying, as well as laughing, disgusted, surprised, compassionate, ferocious, and the ultimately tranquil, [that are danced] without wavering from the reality body, terrifying like the time of the universe's destruction. This is expressed in these words:[23]

20. Here, ITJ332/1, 1v.5–2r.2, introduces the following passage in terms of the three concentrations (*ting nge 'dzin gsum*). That the equilibrium samādhi (*mnyam ba nyid kyi ting nge 'dzin*) is another name for the thusness samādhi (*de bzhin nyid kyi ting nge 'dzin*) is confirmed by the Dunhuang text's comments below.

21. Compare *Gsang ba'i snying po*, ch. 2, 112a.4.

22. ITJ332/1, 2r.3–4.

23. Here, ITJ332/1, 2r.4–2v.4, introduces the next verse as the beginning of the third, causal samādhi.

From that, the great Śrī Heruka:
with the nine dances of great blazing,
ferocious like the time of the apocalypse:[24]
Bhruṃ hūṃ viśva viśuddhe.[25]

By reciting *ra ra*, from a luminous safflower-red *ra* syllable like the color of polished coral, by reciting *ra rakta ra rakta* a massive whirlpool of blood is cultivated. A surge of waves swirling from east to south, waves swirling from south to west, and waves from west to north, all at once. By reciting *keng keng*, at the center of that, from a white *keng* syllable comes a pile of fresh and decomposed skeletons like Mount Meru. By reciting *ba ba*, from a dark blue *ba* syllable comes a palace of skulls, with neither outside nor inside, everywhere remaining inward. Imagine clearly that its immensity is unbounded throughout the ten directions. That is expressed in these words:[26]

A horrifying great charnel ground,
amid a turbulent whirlpool of blood.
Upon a great Mount Meru of skeletons,
at the center of a mass of blazing flames:[27] (15)

An inestimable palace of blazing gnosis,
is immensity unbounded throughout the ten directions,[28]
with neither outside nor inside, everywhere within.[29]

Thus it is clear, and what is at the center of that palace? By reciting *bhruṃ viśvaviśuddhe*, four gnosis lines are laid: Focus! Focus! (*preng preng*). Thus there comes to be a four-cornered hall upon a four-spoked blazing wheel. Each of its four doors has a double blazing veranda, with various ornaments of great horror—skulls, snakes, a sun and a moon, fresh and rotting corpses, and the

24. ITJ332/1, 2v.4 lacks our sādhana's final mantra.

25. Correcting *bam* to *bhruṃ*, in accordance with the parallel in *Rdo rje bkod pa'i rgyud las sgrub thabs* (see n. 22). More or less the same mantra (*'brung viśva viśuddha brung*) is used in ITJ552, 3v.4, also to generate the maṇḍala palace at a similar point, i.e., toward the end of the three *samādhis*.

26. ITJ332/1, 2v.4–3r.1, introducing the emergence of the maṇḍala palace.

27. Compare *Gsang ba'i snying po*, ch. 15, 126a.2–3.

28. Compare just these two lines to *Gsang ba'i snying po*, ch. 1, 110b.3.

29. Compare just this one line to *Gsang ba'i snying po*, ch. 1, 110b.7. Though the foregoing verses are thus cobbled together out of the tantra, the entire passage, with the initial mantra, appears in the *Rdo rje bkod pa'i rgyud las sgrub thabs*, 92a.5–6.

like. In every direction, it is alive with many blazing garlands. On the eastern spoke of the wheel, atop interlaced male and female *gandharvas*, [is a throne] held up by the hoofs of a great bull. On the southern spoke of the wheel, atop interlaced male and female *yakṣasas*, [is a throne] held up on the hooves of a gray, long-horned buffalo. On the western spoke of the wheel, atop interlaced male and female *rakṣasas*, [is a throne] held up by the claws of a leopard. On the northern spoke of the wheel, atop interlaced male and female *yamarājas*, [is a throne] held up by the claws of a tiger. That is also expressed in these words from the tantra:[30]

Upon a blazing wheel with four spokes,
adorned with a four-cornered [foundation].
A square [hall] with four entryways,

each decorated by two verandas,
resplendent with various skulls and snakes and a sun and a moon,
and alive with many proliferating blazing flames. [846]

[The thrones are held aloft] in the claws of a ferocious bear,
a great bull, a buffalo, a leopard, and a tiger,
atop Maheśvara and other gods in embrace.[31]

[Generation of the Remaining Deities of the Maṇḍala:]
Thus it is clear, and oneself (*bdag nyid*) is also the identity (*bdag nyid*) of the vajra body, speech, and mind of all the tathāgatas of the three times, which is also the wrathful king, though one never wavers from the equilibrium of the ultimate reality. From the expanse of the father, with the radiance of extreme pleasure, *hi hi* is recited, whereby the mother, Krodiśvarī, with ornaments and implements just like the main deity, uncrowned, sits on his left side upon a base of interlaced human corpses. Recite *jaḥ hūṃ vaṃ hoḥ*, whereby, within the samādhi of no lust, imagine one's mind is moved by lust. *Jaḥ* captures with a hook, *hūṃ* ties with a lasso, *vaṃ* binds with shackles, and *hoḥ* pleasantly arouses with a bell. Thereby the bodhicitta descends into the space of the mother, as expressed in these words:[32]

30. ITJ332/1, 3r.2–3v.1. The lines that follow open with a *hūṃ* in ITJ332/1 that is missing from the canonical version.

31. Compare *Gsang ba'i snying po*, chapter 17, 129a.3–4, and *Rdo rje bkod pa'i rgyud las sgrub thabs*, 92a.6–7.

32. ITJ332/1, 3v.3–7.

The lord of the vajra body, speech, and mind
of all the buddhas is oneself,
because one is primordially the wrathful king.

From the expanse of thusness,
the wrathful goddess emerges.
***Hi! Hi!* Through the radiation of pleasure, (20)**

His jewel is expanded by her lotus,
and through the pleasure of their nondual embrace, he dissolves.
A cloud of bodhicitta is emitted, from which:
Hūṃ hūṃ hūṃ viśvakrodha jvalamaṇḍala phaṭ phaṭ phaṭ halāhala hūṃ.

Imagine that light rays spread forth, scintillating, from that bodhicitta, and all ten directions within the six realms are entirely filled with nothing but the great wrathful ones, as numerous as the atoms in the universe, wielding weapons as numerous as the atoms in the universe. Imagine that in the east are as many *vajraherukas* as there are grains of sand in the river Ganges. Imagine that in the south are as many *ratnaherukas* as there are grains of sand in the river Ganges. Imagine that in the west are as many *padmaherukas* as there are grains of sand in the river Ganges. Imagine that in the west are as many *karmaherukas* as there are grains of sand in the river Ganges. This is expressed in these words:[33]

Throughout the ten directions of the six realms,
pervading infinite space, wrathful
maṇḍalas the size of the billionfold world-system emerge,
as numerous as the atoms [in the universe], throughout the ten directions.[34]

Then imagine the great joyous Bhagavan, his heads, arms, and legs as numerous as the atoms in the thousandfold universe and bearing weapons also as numerous as the atoms in the universe, all of which stand in a pose with one leg stretched out and the other bent, upon a throne of couples that include Maheśvara, the Lord of the Charnel Grounds, and the Great Haughty Demon. That is expressed in these words:[35]

33. ITJ332/1, 4r.3–6.

34. Compare *Gsang ba'i snying po*, ch. 15, 125b.4–6.

35. ITJ332/1, 4r.6–4v.2.

Then the great delighting Bhagavan,
his head, arms, and legs as numerous as the atoms
in the thousandfold universe and holding weapons,
stands in a pose with one leg stretched out and the other bent, upon a base of the couple—
Maheśvara, the haughty Lord of the Charnel Grounds.[36]

Imagine that all those assemblies, those heaping clouds of wrathful deities, emerge in the eastern direction as numerous as the grains of sand in the Ganges River, gathering as noble blood-drinker *vajraherukas*. Imagine that the wrathful ones of the southern direction emerge as numerous as the grains of sand in the Ganges River, becoming noble blood-drinker *ratnaherukas*. Imagine that the wrathful ones of the western direction emerge as numerous as the grains of sand in the Ganges River, becoming noble blood-drinker *padmaherukas*. Imagine that the wrathful ones of the northern direction emerge as numerous as the grains of sand in the Ganges River, becoming noble blood-drinker *karmaherukas*. That is expressed in these words:[37]

All those heaping clouds of wrathful ones
become the noble Great Blood-Drinker [i.e., the heruka of the vajra family],
and of the jewel, the lotus, and
the karma [families]—residing in their four directions.

Imagine that every one of all of those, moreover, with horrifying regalia and roaring savagely, at the center of a blazing mass of apocalyptic fire, having transformed into [a form with] three heads, six arms, and four legs, stand in a pose with one leg stretched out and the other bent, atop a base of interlaced males and females including *gandharvas*, *yakṣasas*, *rakṣasas*, and *yāmarājas*. That is expressed in these words:[38]

All of those are mahābhairavas,
with the regalia, and roaring savagely,

36. Compare *Gsang ba'i snying po*, ch. 15, 126a.2–3, though with some significant differences, as with *Rdo rje bkod pa'i rgyud las sgrub thabs*, 92b.2–3. ITJ332/1 switches the order of the next two and a half verses so that our next verse (v. 24) comes after vv. 25 & 26ab. Thus ITJ332/1's introductory comments on these verses are also switched. In what follows, I reproduce them to fit with our canonical order, so we read this summary for our next verse (v. 24) and 26cd.

37. ITJ332/1, 4v.7–5r.3.

38. ITJ332/1, 4v.3–5, introducing only the following verse and a half (25 & 26ab).

amidst a swirling blaze, three headed,
six arms, four heads, (25)

standing upon a throne of entwined couples of
gandharvas, yakṣasas, rakṣasas,* and *yāmarājas,
their queens, the great blood-drinking women
arrayed embracing their respective [mates'] bodies.[39]

Imagine that by reciting *krodhīśvarī jāḥ hūṃ vaṃ hoḥ*, the four consorts of each of the main wrathful deities are embracing them on their left sides. Then imagine that, from the delighted clouds of bodhicitta of the nondual father and mother, by means of reciting *ha ha ha ha ha ha ha ha*, come the host of Gaurī, the host of Caurī, the host of Pukkāsī, the host of Caṇḍālī, the host of Ghasmarī, the host of Smaśānī, and many others, surrounding them with magnificence starting from the east of the blazing wheel, standing upon seats of stretched-out corpses. This is expressed in these words:[40] [847]

Then, delighting, *ha* is expressed,
whereby, from the pure clouds of bodhicitta:
the host of Gaurī and the host of Caurī,
the host of Pramohā and the host of Vetālī,
the host of Pukkasī and the host of Caṇḍālī,
the host of Smaśānī and the host of Ghasmarī,

each with its own implements,
and miraculous attire, awesomely emerge.
From the east of the great blazing wheel,
they are arrayed with horrifying forms as the retinue.[41]

Then from the clouds of bodhicitta of the nondual father and mother, by reciting *he he he he he he he he*, the assembly of Siṃhamukhī, the assembly of Vyāghrīmukhī, the assembly of Śṛgāmukhī, the assembly of Śvānamukhī, the assembly of Gṛdhramukhī, the assembly of Kaṅkamukhī, the assembly of Kākamukhī, the assembly of Ulūkamukhī, the assembly of the Crow-Faced

39. Compare the foregoing two verses to *Gsang ba'i snying po*, ch. 15, 126a.5–6, and (less the first two lines and the last two lines) *Rdo rje bkod pa'i rgyud las sgrub thabs*, 92b.6–7.

40. ITJ332/1, 5r.5–5v.1.

41. Compare *Gsang ba'i snying po*, ch. 15, 127a.5–7, and *Rdo rje bkod pa'i rgyud las sgrub thabs*, 92b.7–93a.1.

One, and so on stand upon seats of stretched-out corpses, variously and terrifyingly adorned, surrounding with extreme magnificence starting from the east. This is expressed in these words:[42]

Then, delighting, *he* is expressed,
whereby the assemblies of Siṃhamukhī and
the assemblies of the great Vyāghrīmukhī, Śṛgāmukhī, Śvānamukhī, Gṛdhramukhī,
of Kaṅkamukhī, Kākamukhī, and Ulūkamukhī,

Each with its own implements
and miraculous attire, emerge.
Surrounding the great blazing wheel,
on the outside, starting from the east,
they are arrayed in their magnificence.[43] (30)

Then imagine that the great delighting Bhagavan, from the delighting clouds of bodhicitta of the nondual father and mother, recites *phaṭ phaṭ phaṭ phaṭ*, whereby the assembly of Vajratejasī, the assembly of Vajrāmoghā, the assembly of Vajrālokā, the assembly of Vajravetālī, and so on are arranged in splendor upon bases of stretched-out corpses, each with their own implements, at the four gates of the maṇḍala. This is expressed in these words:[44]

Then, delighting, he expressed *phaṭ*,
whereby the hosts of Vajratejasī,
of Vajrāmoghā, Vajrālokā, and Vajravetālī,

each with its own implements
and miraculous attire, horrifically emerge.
They reside at the four gates to the maṇḍala in their awesome forms.[45]

42. ITJ332/1, 5v.3–6r.1.

43. Compare *Gsang ba'i snying po*, ch. 15, 127a.7–127b.2, and *Rdo rje bkod pa'i rgyud las sgrub thabs*, 92b.7–93a.1. ITJ332/1, 6r.2, has the deities described here in the intermediate directions.

44. ITJ332/1, 6r.3–6.

45. Compare *Gsang ba'i snying po*, ch. 15, 127b.2–4, and *Rdo rje bkod pa'i rgyud las sgrub thabs*, 93a.1–2. Note, however, that here our sādhana seems to follow the *Guhyagarbha* more closely than the *Rdo rje bkod pa'i rgyud las sgrub thabs*, which has just listed the deities in a more minimal fashion.

Then imagine that, from the delighting clouds of bodhicitta of the nondual father and mother, *phaṭ* is recited, whereby all those assemblies of heaping clouds of wrathful ones become extremely wrathful in a manner that is like suddenly alarmed black vultures. Then, in order to spontaneously accomplish oneself and join in equality with the body, speech, and mind of the tathāgatas of the three times, imagine oneself in the nature of Śakra and the consort in the nature of a *piśāca* (*sha tsa ma*). This is expressed in these words:[46]

In the ten directions within the delighting clouds,
shouting *phaṭ*, all [of the above-described deities] become wrathful.[47]

[Generation of "Inner" Deity at the Point of Union:]
Then, to spontaneously accomplish
the family of the great noble wrathful one,
having apprehended one's own condition,[48]
these words of exhortation are expressed:

Oṃ. Great spiritual pledge (*thugs dam*) of previous times:
so that every one of all the worlds without exception
may be united in the field of the conqueror,
may I be united with the mahāmudrā [i.e., the form of the buddha]. (35)

Thereby, from the bodhicitta of the nondual father and mother, gnostic light rays purify the concepts of one's body, speech, and mind. One becomes bodhicitta, like refined gold. Recite *oṃ āṃ hūṃ*, whereby from the syllables *oṃ āṃ hūṃ*, strung together in the manner of a chain (*lu gu rgyud*), dissolves into [the deity's] heart. From his heart, it emerges through his vajra-path. Dissolving into the sky of the mother, it transforms into the reality bodhicitta. Imagine that, out of her expanse, the mantras, *hṛdaya*, and so forth of the various deities arise. This is expressed in these words:[49]

46. ITJ332/1, 6v.1–5.

47. Compare *Gsang ba'i snying po*, ch. 15, 127b.4. *de nas dgyes pa'i sprin las phyogs bcu nas phaTa ces bsgrags pas thams cad khros nas.*

48. Compare ITJ331/2, 3r.3–4. This means one returns to one's ordinary form and stands before the buddha just generated, as made more explicit in ITJ554, 3v.2. All three manuscripts may have been scribed by the same hand.

49. ITJ332/1, 7r.1–5, introducing the next two and a half verses. Again, ITJ554, 2v and ITJ331/2, 4r.1, probably written in the same hand, clarify that these light rays incinerate the concepts, leaving only one's mind in the form of bodhicitta, "like refined gold."

The body and concepts are purified by the rays of the gnosis
of nondual means and wisdom.
The pure mind that is like refined gold [takes the form of]
luminous seed[-syllables] that are consecrations of the three [i.e., body, speech, and mind].

Having dissolved into the heart, the treasury body
arises through the vajra-path into the space of the mother,
dwelling there as the dharmkāya-bodhicitta.

The sounds of the *hṛdaya* of the various deities
arises: *Hūṃ ha ha phaṭ!*
Then they dissolve as one into the bodhicitta.[50] **[848]**

Then, just by remembering the *hṛdaya*,
the two mudrās of speech are perfected,
whereupon, through the yoga of emanating and regathering,
the mudrā of mind blazes up.

Then one emanates and regathers the subtle body,
perfecting the two bodies of the mahāmudrā. (40)

In order to become the mudrā of means:[51]

Oṃ mahāśūnyatājñāna vajrasvabhāvātmako'ham.
Oṃ mahādarśajñāna vajrasvabhāvātmako'ham.
Oṃ mahāpratyavekṣaṇājñāna vajrasvabhāvātmako'ham.
Oṃ mahāsamatājñāna vajrasvabhāvātmako'ham.
Oṃ mahākṛtyupasthānajñāna vajrasvabhāvātmako'ham.
Oṃ sarvatathāgata mahākāya vajrasvabhāvātmako'ham.
Oṃ sarvatathāgata mahāvāg vajrasvabhāvātmako'ham.
Oṃ sarvatathāgata mahācitta vajrasvabhāvātmako'ham.

50. The preceding two verses appear only in our sādhana; I have been unable to locate them anywhere else.

51. ITJ332/1, 7v.1. This single phrase (*thabs kyi phyag rgyar gyurd pa'i phyir*) appears in *Gsang ba'i snying po*, chapter 9, 120b.6, in a discussion of how the maṇḍala emanates out of nonconceptual wisdom. ITJ332/1 also provides Tibetan translations for each of the mantras listed, though it reverses its translations of the third and fourth. I have also corrected a few of the mantras to make them match their appearance in the *Guhyagarbha*; see *Gsang ba'i snying po*, chapter 7, 117b.3–5.

Oṃ sarvatathāgata mahānurāgana mahāvajrasvabhāvātmako'ham.
Oṃ sarvatathāgata mahāpūjā mahāvajrasvabhāvātmako'ham.

[Sexual Yoga Performed by "Inner" Deity:]
Up to this point has been the generation of oneself as a son of the conqueror. Having in that way generated pride with the nature of the five wisdoms, now from here on, the conqueror is to be generated as one's own son. Atop a five-spoked vajra [at the point of union] between the father and the mother, the single syllable [*hūṃ*] is cultivated. At the center of the mother's space, upon an eight-petaled lotus, imagine that from the mother there comes a sun disc: *jaḥ hūṃ vaṃ hōḥ!* The father's mudrā [i.e., drop of semen] is held with the hook, bound with the lasso, restrained with the shackles. Moved with pleasure by the bell, imagine the bodhicitta within the space of the mother. This is expressed in these words:[52]

The vajra that consecrates the lotus
is a five-spoked vajra from a *hūṃ*[-syllable].
At the center of the lotus that comes from a *ba*[-syllable],
imagine a sun maṇḍala from a *ma*[-syllable].

By means of the *sādava* [melody] and so forth,
the exhortations should be properly performed.

One recites in that way, and at the mother's four secret places, the four branches of propitiation should be set forth. This is expressed in these words:[53]

Propitiation and near propitiation,
accomplishment and great accomplishment—
in the maṇḍala of the mother's lotus,
the blissful maṇḍala of [awakened] mind emanates forth.

Into all the assembled clouds of buddhas,
it dissolves, through this supreme bestowal of ecstatic equality.[54]
Out of that, the maṇḍala is luminously displayed:
oṃ oṃ sarvatathāgata mahāśrīheruka...[55] **(45)**

52. ITJ332/1, 8r.4–8v.1.

53. ITJ332/1, 8v.2–3.

54. Compare the previous six lines to *Gsang ba'i snying po*, ch. 11, 122a.5–6.

55. There follows a long series of mantras that matches that found in *Gsang ba'i snying po*, chapter

[Summoning the jñānasattvas:]
Furthermore, suppose one asks, what manifests? In the that same tantra, it is expressed in these words:[56]

If the mudrās are created on the ground and so on,
the stages of liberation will be attained.
If they are refined with the gnosis of purity,
what need is there to speak of this?!

The great lord of the maṇḍala of directions and times,
from the nonreferential maṇḍala of [awakened] mind,
invites all the maṇḍalas.[57]

By joining with the characteristic of engaging
in the self-appearing indivisible maṇḍala,
he perfects the maṇḍala of propitiation
which arises in all directions and times.
This is the supreme sacrament of the imminent:[58]

Oṃ rulurulu hūṃ bhyo hūṃ/ ehyehi anayavajra/ jaḥ hūṃ vaṃ hoḥ hoṃ raṃ/ oṃ vajrakrodha samaya hūṃ!

Oṃ.[59] **The wrathful ones who pacify the wrathful,**
awesome assembly of those who are noble in compassionate wrath,
may you grant me right now
the great wonderous blazing consecration. (50)

16, 128b.2–6, and (more roughly) *Rdo rje bkod pa'i rgyud las sgrub thabs,* 93a.2–7. In the interest of space, I have not reproduced them here. Following the same maṇḍala-producing mantra used above (*bhrūṃ viśvaviśudde*), ITJ332/1, 8v.6–16v.1, spreads the mantras across numerous pages, interspersing them with iconographic descriptions of each deity and its position within the maṇḍala. Again, in the interest of space, I have not translated this portion of the text. The section ends on 849.4 in the Snar thang.

56. ITJ332/1, 16v.1.

57. The foregoing two verses correspond to ITJ332/1, 16v.1–3, while the next verse in our text is missing from ITJ332/1, though the mantra that follows it does appear in a slightly different form.

58. Compare all the foregoing three verses to *Gsang ba'i snying po,* ch. 9, 120b.3–5. *Rdo rje bkod pa'i rgyud las sgrub thabs,* 93b.1, contains the first verse, followed soon after by a similar mantra.

59. ITJ332/1, 16v.4, refers to this verse as the "song of accomplishment" (*grub pa'i glu*), though it opens it with a *hūṃ* rather than our *oṃ*. It also adds a final fifth line: "Please bestow on me the mahāmudrā" (*phyag rgya' chen po bdag la stsol*).

Oṃ vajrakrodha samayastvaṃ/ oṃ vajrakrodha samaya phaṭ/ oṃ vajrakrodha samaya hoḥ/ ali uli tala tapali/ traṃ staṃ kho go na/ rauti kharaṃ yoginī kha hi hūṃ ha hi phaṭ.[60] [850]

Dark brown, dark blue, dark yellow,
dark red, and dark green: the terrifying bodies,
with three heads, six arms, and six legs extended.

Wearing a variety of fresh skins,
resounding with terrifying, great awesome roars,
with snakes, fresh skulls, and the sun and moon,
with the trichiliocosm encircling.

They hold their various respective implements—
vajras, skull-cups filled [with blood],
swords, axes, ploughs, and so on,
and embrace their terrifying assembly of queens.

Made beautiful by the mudrās of places and objects,
and by the mudrās of the four gates,
and made beautiful by the twenty-eight-fold
assembly of attendants, courtesans, and maids,
each with her own seat and implement,
in servant's attire, they stand ready.[61] (55)

In that way, having luminously displayed the maṇḍala,
throughout the ten directions of the six realms,
the blazing maṇḍala luminously manifests.[62]

[Praises to the Wrathful Ones:]
Hūṃ! Great Ferocity, blazing like the conflagration at the end of time,
splendid with the light rays of a hundred thousand suns,

60. For the last two mantras and the intervening verse, compare *Gsang ba'i snying po*, ch. 17, 128b.6–129a.1.

61. Compare foregoing four verses to *Gsang ba'i snying po*, ch. 17, 129a.4–6, and ITJ332/1, 17r.1–5, though the latter has the four verses *after* the single verse that follows ours.

62. Compare *Gsang ba'i snying po*, ch. 17, 129a.6–7, and ITJ332/1, 16v.7, though as stated in the previous note, the latter has this verse *before* the previous four verses (and also includes an additional line).

flashing angry frowns like a thousand lightning bolts,
a great devouring with a billion fangs: *Hoḥ!*

Hūṃ! Thundering with the awesome roars of a thousand dragons,
great anger, resounding like 100,000 Mount Merus,
a massive laughter: *A! A! Hala!*
The great quaking of a sweeping hurricane: *Hoḥ!*

Hūṃ! Great light of wrathful wisdom,
illuminating everywhere the gnosis maṇḍala,
a blazing gnosis that completely defeats,
the great seminal drop of diverse gnoses: *Hoḥ!*

Hūṃ! Great clouds of wrathful conquerors,
a great rain of wrathful conquerors descends,
the maṇḍala, a treasury that arises to fulfill wishes:
a great seminal drop of diverse wrathful ones: *Hoḥ!* (60)

Hūṃ! Great demon of all demons,
the demon of demons that defeats the demons,
terrifying even the hosts of terrors,
the great seminal drop of Mahābhairava: *Hoḥ!*

Hūṃ! Great vajra-rock that is incorruptible,
vajra-water that is a subsuming,
vajra-fire that is a great blazing everywhere,
vajra-wind that is a great hurricane: *Hoḥ!*[63]

[Dissolution of the Maṇḍala:]
[851] One who does not deteriorate in the branches, who possesses the ritual necessities,
and thoroughly understands the rites,
such a yogin, by means of the feast maṇḍala,
will definitely accomplish their excellent aims.[64]

63. These verses comprise the bulk of chapter twenty-one of the *Guhyagarbha*; compare *Gsang ba'i snying po*, 131b.5–132a.2, and *Rdo rje bkod pa'i rgyud las sgrub thabs*, 94a.3–6, as well as ITJ332/1, 17v.1–7, though once again the last switches the verses with the single verse that closes them in our sādhana.

64. Compare *Gsang ba'i snying po*, ch. 11, 122b.2, and ITJ332/1, 17r.6–7, though the latter has the

By means of the great assembly of wrathful gods and goddesses
and the assembled ambassadors, helpers, attendants—
their assemblies of servants and so forth—
the siddhis and activities are perfected.[65]

The all the entire maṇḍala
regathers into one's heart:
reciting *hūṃ hūṃ*,
that regathering may be performed as one prefers. (65)

[Closing Instructions:]
And, having in that way regathered,
the great yogin who is oneself
should never allow his conduct to deteriorate
and ever cultivate himself as the deity.

Now the great blazing maṇḍala should be gathered into one's own *skandhas*, *dhātus*, and *āyatanas*. Regarding that, this verse on cultivating the continuous samādhi is expressed in these words:[66]

The five *skandhas* themselves are the principal deity, the wrathful conqueror.
The five great [elements] themselves are the mother goddesses.
All the *āyatanas* and *dhātus* without exception
are the maṇḍala assembly of awesome compassion.[67]

By means of these four—
the methods of the single cause, the seed-syllables,
consecration, and direct realization—
all becomes the manifest, perfect great conqueror.[68]

---

verse *after* the six verses of praise above. It also ends with the final line of the next verse in our sādhana, i.e., "Will perfect the siddhis and activities."

65. Compare *Gsang ba'i snying po*, ch. 11, 122b.4–5.

66. ITJ332/1, 17v.7–8.

67. Compare ITJ332/1, 18r.1–2, which offers a slightly different wording: *phung po lnga nyid 'khro rgyal 'tshogs/ chen po rigs kyi de bzhin yum/ skye mched kh+'ams rnams mang po kun/ thugs rje rngam ba'i dkyil 'kh+'or 'tshogs.*

68. Compare *Gsang ba'i snying po*, ch. 11, 122a.2–3, and ITJ332/1, 18r.2–3. The final two verses of our sādhana translated below are absent from ITJ332/1. Instead, the Dunhuang version describes

Perfect in the ten directions and four times,
the body, speech, qualities, activities, and mind
are all seen as one's own face:
such is the excellent, supreme mastery itself.[69]

Through any merit I may obtain
by compiling this sādhana,
may all sentient beings attain
the body, speech, and mind of great noble Samantabhadra. (70)

***An Appearance of Suchness, Ornament of the Sacred* is complete.**

Works Cited

Dunhuang Manuscripts Referenced

IOL Tib J 331, 332, 552, 553, 554
Pelliot tibétain 321

Other Primary Sources

De kho na nyid snang ba dam pa rgya A. Full title: *Sgyu 'phrul drwa ba khro bo bsdus pa'i sgrub thabs de nyid snang ba dam pa rgyan*. Attributed to Buddhagupta (*Sangs rgyas gsang ba*). Snar thang Bstan 'gyur, *rgyud*, vol. *bu*, 844–851 (422b.3–426a.6).

De kho na nyid snang ba dam pa rgyan B. In *Nyag klu mo a bse dgon du bzhugs pa'i dpe rnying dpe dkon*, 18 vols., No publication information (BDRC W3PD888): vol. *nya*, 519–530.

Gsang ba'i snying po. Full title: *Dpal gsang ba'i snying po de kho nan yid rnam par nges pa* (*Śrī-Guhyagarbhatattvaviniścaya*). Toh. 832. Vol. *kha*, 110b.1–132a.7.

Rdo rje bkod pa'i rgyud las dkyil 'khor bdun pa'i rim pa rnam par phyed pa'i sgrub thabs. Toh. 3755, *rgyud*, vol. *tshu*, 90b.7–100a.6.

Sarvabuddhasamāyogaḍākinījālasaṃvara-nāma-uttaratantra. Toh. 366, *rgyud*, vol. *ka*, 151b–193a.

Spar khab. Asc. Vilāsavajra. Full title: *Rgyud kyi rgyal po chen po dpal gsang ba snying po'i 'grel pa. Dpe bsdur ma Bstan 'gyur, rgyud*, vol. *zu*, 267–428.

---

a gradual dissolution of the visualization into the central *hūṃ*-syllable and then of the *hūṃ* itself, piece-by-piece from the bottom up.

69. Compare *Gsang ba'i snying po*, ch. 13, 124a.2–3.

Secondary Sources

Dalton, Jacob P. 2011. *Taming of the Demons: Violence and Liberation in Tibetan Buddhism.* New Haven: Yale University Press.

———. 2023. *Conjuring the Buddha: Ritual Manuals in Early Tantric Buddhism.* New York: Columbia University Press.

Dalton, Jacob, and Sam van Schaik. 2006. *Tibetan Tantric Manuscripts from Dunhuang: A Descriptive Catalogue of the Stein Collection at the British Library.* Leiden: Brill.

Davidson, Ronald. 2005. *Tibetan Renaissance: Tantric Buddhism in the Rebirth of Tibetan Culture.* New York: Columbia University Press.

Eastman, K. W. 1983. "Mahāyoga Texts at Tun-Huang," *Institute of Buddhist Cultural Studies* 22: 42–60. Kyoto: Ryukoku University.

Gray, David B. 2012. "Imprints of the 'Great Seal': On the Expanding Semantic Range of the Term Mudrā in Eighth through Eleventh Century Indian Buddhist Literature," *Journal of the International Association of Buddhist Studies* 34.1–2: 421–81.

Karmay, Samten. 1988. *The Great Perfection.* Leiden: E. J. Brill.

Takeuchi, Tsuguhito. 2012. "Old Tibetan Buddhist Texts from the Post-Tibetan Imperial Period (Mid-9 c. to Late 10 C.)." In *Old Tibetan Studies*, edited by Cristina Scherrer-Schaub, 205–14. Leiden: Brill.

Yi Ding. 2020. *Divine Transactions: The Transformation of Buddhist Communal Liturgies at Dunhuang (8th–10th Centuries).* Unpublished PhD dissertation, Stanford University.

IV.
Literature, Art, and Poetry

What Did Śāntideva Learn from Lovers?

Sonam Kachru

"What is Desire (*kāma*)?"
"Imagination (*saṅkalpaḥ*)."
—Daṇḍin, *What Ten Young Men Did.*[1]

"Do you think, if you look into yourself, that there is an incompatibility between the literary mind and the philosophical mind?" Etienne Borne set this question for a young Jacques Derrida in the spring of 1952 when the latter attended the preparatory school Louis-le-Grand.[2] It is a question to which Janet Gyatso's oeuvre—beginning with her famous book on what she aptly described as "philosophical literature"[3]—can serve as a particularly eloquent response.

Mindful of this question, I wish to invite a distinct (though related) one: Is there an incompatibility between the mind of the connoisseur of beauty and desire who disciplines mind and body in pursuit of pleasure and the mind of an ascetic? More directly, Can the ascetic learn anything from one who takes up an aesthetic approach to life?

My question takes its bearings from premodern South Asian categories and a South Asian provocation. In premodern South Asia, particularly in the world as imagined in Sanskrit literary culture, the aesthete can claim as his or her own a principled way of life, consisting in demanding regimens of training,[4] oriented by pleasures of sense—including, though not confined to, sexual pleasure—in a cultured world centering desire, love, and the experience of beauty.[5] If the pursuit of literature in Sanskrit as a way of life (replete with its own virtues and values) falls within this scope,[6] it is one to which the (classical) Buddhist ascetic's

1. Onians 2005, 417.
2. Peeters 2013, 53.
3. Gyatso 2001, xvii.
4. Doniger 2007, 72–3.
5. Ali 2011; Desmond 2011.
6. Ollett 2019.

life, as some defined it, could stand almost in antithesis. The Buddha states the opposition (with courtly culture in mind) in the *Majjhima Nikāya*, for example.[7] And Śāntideva suggests it in his *Introduction to the Practice of Awakening* (circa late seventh–early eighth century C.E.): "Those in love are entranced by filth."[8] The *kāmin*—the impassioned, the amorous, the enamored—is sometimes presented as being everything the ascetic is not.

Of course, thus stated the opposition can be misleading. Like so many of his co-religionists, Śāntideva can entertain the continuity of beauty and felicity, as he does when enacting "the unexcelled worship" at the beginning of his work, imagining "sweet-smelling bath-houses, where canopies gleam with pearls, over delightful pillars, brilliant with gems, rising up from the mosaic floors of clear, brilliant crystal, from many pots, encrusted with gems, filled with exquisitely fragrant water and flowers."[9] The enjoyment of beauty and beautiful things, evidently, even as defined and valued by the aesthetic standards of Sanskrit literary culture, can come apart from the gratification of censorable desires. But as long as the Buddhist ascetic's way of life is defined by exclusion of sexual relations and characterized by principled suspicion of the gratification of desires indexed to sensory pleasure, it can seem to be incongruent with an aesthete's form of life.[10] Or so it appears to be in much of Śāntideva's work.

And yet, in verse 62 of the seventh chapter, Śāntideva says that,

> One ought to be addicted
> solely to the task one begins;
> one ought to be intoxicated

7. See, for example, his comments to Aggivessana about Prince Jayasena in Ñāṇamoli and Bodhi 1995, 990, §7.

8. Verse 8.50 in Crosby and Skilton 2008, 92.

9. Verses 2.10–2.11 in Crosby and Skilton 2008, 15. (See also verses 2.2–2.6.) A role for the aesthetic enactment of utopic felicities in imagination returns at the conclusion. See verse 10.8 for example (Crosby and Skilton 2008, 138), where even the crystal mosaic is recapitulated.

10. See Collins 1997; Gyatso 2005. Though the elective affinities between these two disciplines of the body and the patterns of attention and feelings they (can) foster was noticed early enough by Buddhists themselves. See the translator's remarks (and those of Martin Wickramasinghe) on Ambapālī's poem in Hallisey 2015, xvi–xvii. Within South Asia, the tension between eroticism and asceticism can be evaluated and enacted very differently, as in medieval Śaiva materials (Doniger O'Flaherty 1973). Outside of South Asia, as in the context of early (Latin) Christianity, the paradox between eros and asceticism may be only apparent. It has certainly proven difficult to convincingly reconstruct, as Karl Shuve notes, given the many meanings (and experiential resonances) eros (as distinct from carnality) can involve, and the many sociological functions of sexuality (Shuve 2016, 5–12).

by that task, insatiable—
as one given over
to the thrills of amorous play.

Some translators mince no words when presenting the analogy: one should be "as one hankering for the pleasure and the fruit of love-play."[11] Therein lies our provocation.

What's the Problem?

To say, as Śāntideva's wonderfully learned translators Kate Crosby and Andrew Skilton do, that "his description of delight in one's spiritual practice borders upon the profane"[12] is to put things accurately but mildly. Why, to adapt Śāntideva's commentator Prajñākaramati, is it necessary to soak in the savor or taste of addictive behavior? Or, why, to speak with Crosby and Skilton, is it necessary "to savor [actions] as does a lover his carnal pleasures, or the gambler the game"?[13] How shall we understand this: In the service of awakening oneself and liberating beings from suffering, the savor of agency approaches the thrills of erotic delight.[14]

To be sure, the orders of asceticism and the aesthete's way of life in South Asia can be seen to be continuous in that they each involve disciplines of self-control.[15] But here the affinity between these lifeways is expressed in quite the opposite terms: One ought to be addicted! Intoxicated! Insatiable! At the edge of control.

Śāntideva's injunctions befit the stereotypical lover of literary culture and those invested in sensory pleasure; the person of leisure, rather than learning; the aesthete, rather than the monk. (In case we were in any doubt, Prajñākaramati uses the word *lampaṭaḥ*, "greedy, dissolute libertine," and so

11. Crosby and Skilton 2008, 73.

12. Crosby and Skilton 2008, 65.

13. Crosby and Skilton 2008, 65.

14. Prajñākaramati glosses Śāntideva's phrase "one passionately addicted to the action [one has begun] (*tat-karma-vyasanī*)" as "*tat-kriyā-rasa-nimagna-cittaḥ*," or, "one whose mind is completely soaked in the savor of that activity." See comment on 7.62 in Vaidya 1988, 137.

15. As Lorraine Daston persuasively argues on the basis of a common investment in control of the senses and the necessity of a calculative investment in postponement of gratification. Quoted in Doniger 2018, 45. On the twinning of disciplinary technologies of self in courtly and monastic disciplinary cultures—down to the level of patterns of controlled attention to inventories of signs—see Ali 1998.

on, to gloss *śauṇḍa*,[16] which is elsewhere used to emphasize censorable addiction by Śāntideva.) And if Prajñākaramati also thinks that Śāntideva uses "play" to indicate the thrills of gambling,[17] we should recall that while not directly erotic, such games were nevertheless part of the world of leisure and calculated loss of control that Śāntideva, a celibate ascetic, has shunned. He explicitly tells us that intoxication commits one to imprudent courses of action beyond what one has any reason to believe feasible;[18] and talk of thrills of chasing anything like a gambler's high seems to pull against his recommendation for an order of cognitive felicities quite distinct from strictly sensory modes of gratification.[19]

So much for the provocation at the level of content. There is also the matter of style. The provocative injunctions are reinforced by the invocation of a distinctively urban literary imaginaire, one that in Sanskrit invokes an aestheticized register of sexuality, violence, and danger. Śāntideva sounds like he's reveling in the suggested taste: "So even at the conclusion of one task, one should straight away plunge into the next, as does a tusker inflamed by midday heat on coming upon a pool of water."[20] The danger and vigor, given an only imperfectly tamed creature of nobility and power provoked to thrillingly instinctive and vigorous movements, are palpable; as is the animating and ungovernable force of heat and "thirst," so often metaphorically indexed in Buddhist texts to the confounding power of desire.[21]

Consider, then, the irony. Kings are embodiments of power and erotic energy in late medieval poetry and in works of political self-fashioning popular in Śāntideva's time. Yet such works could use the image of the elephant as one imagines ascetics should, recommending self-control against the vanishing satisfactions of indulging the desires of senses: "Like an elephant falling in a trap," the *Nītisāra* advises, "a king falls in danger whenever his heart is ensnared by the beautiful objects of enjoyment, the charm of which vanishes as the enjoyment is over."[22] Why promote the opposite in a work celebrating effortful and vigilant self-governance?

16. In verse 7.62; see Vaidya 1988, 137; for further criticism of libertines, see verses 8.50–51 in Crosby and Skilton 2008, 92. For the negative use of *śauṇḍa*, see verse 8.57.

17. He glosses *krīḍā* in verse 7.62 as *dyūtādi* (Vaidya 1988, 137).

18. Verse 4.42 in Crosby and Skilton 2008, 28.

19. See verses 7.15 and 7.28–30 in Crosby and Skilton 2008, 68–69. For antecedents for such imagery, see Ñāṇamoli and Bodhi 1995, 187.

20. Verse 7.65 in Crosby and Skilton 2008, 73.

21. Later the image becomes that of skill and training in martial and violent arts. See verses 7.67–70 in Crosby and Skilton 2008, 73.

22. Verse 1.38 in Dutt 1896, 10. I was unable to access Jesse Knutson's recent translation of this seminal work, published as *The Essence of Politics* as part of the Murty Classical Library of India.

A Lust to Do Good?

As if given over to the thrills of amorous play—Were he being literal, we would be in the realm of the now familiar transgressive rhetoric of tantra and esoteric Buddhism. In time, the ritual transgression of monastic commitments came to entail the invocation of erotic literary moods theorized by Sanskrit literary culture, offering us the spiritualization of the erotic and eroticization of ritual in what Ronald Davidson calls "the aestheticization of the [Buddhist] esoteric scriptures."[23] Is this the secret to what the translators discuss as a variety of alchemy of desire on the part of Śāntideva?[24]

Note, however, that what matters to Śāntideva is the affinity of disciplines of pleasure and asceticism, not their identity. And it is expressed with the help of an analogy, in Sanskrit a mode of thought implying a partial and contextual likeness. We must be "as" one given over to love play. The question is what provides the basis here for the aptness of "as"? To find answers we will need to make room for a distinctive acknowledgment of the nature of desire, given a reappraisal of the hermeneutics of action.

By speaking of "hermeneutics of action" I intend to go beyond talk of the causes of action to consider the meaningfulness of patterns of activity. I mean this: We should go beyond questions concerned with identifying which antecedent states may serve as ethical motivations to action. Śāntideva's enjoining addiction on us as a model and unsatisfiable desire, for example, goes far beyond the exculpation of desire in the *Bodhisattvabhūmi* and the invocation of passion in Dharmakīrti.

In the *Bodhisattvabhūmi* we find the recognition that actions deriving from attachment to (in the sense of affection for) sentient beings are appropriate for an awakening being to carry out because what is censorable is, for the most part, brought about by hatred, not desire.[25] And memorably, in the *Pramāṇavārttika* Dharmakīrti concedes that one can describe the moral concern and compassion motivating a buddha to act as an instance of *rāga*, or as (typically, for Buddhists, censorable) passion.[26] But while such discussions may indeed contextualize what Śāntideva (basing himself on a long tradition) means by a normatively valuable variety of righteous desire (*dharmacchanda*), and which he

23. Davidson 2002, 197. Davidson has the *Guhyasamāja* in mind when speaking of the ritualization of desire, and the *Sarvabuddhasamāyoga* when speaking of eroticization of ritual. On poetics associated with esoteric Buddhism, see Campbell 2009, 230–42.

24. Crosby and Skilton 2008, 65.

25. Engle 2016, 303. Śāntideva relies on the *Upāli-paripṛcchā* to make the same point (Bendall and Rouse 1922, 161).

26. Dunne 1996, 535–37.

believes no one can rationally reject,[27] this set of issues will not get at the affinity between the ethical task of awakening others and urban cultures of sexuality and sensuality.

We need to think of the intelligibility of entire ways of life. In the context of saving living beings, Śāntideva outlines the conditions for success in exertion and practical effort. These involve "the capacity for desire (*chanda*), perseverance (*sthāma*), delight (*rati*), and the ability to put down a task (*mukti*) and pick it up again when appropriate."[28] The injunction to be "as one given over to the thrills of amorous play" is offered after a discussion of the power to begin and maintain action and in the context of a discussion of the power of delight (*rati*). Most dictionaries will tell us that *rati* connotes taking pleasure and enjoyment in something, or has the sense of "to delight in," frequently (though not exclusively) apposite in erotic contexts. Elsewhere, Śāntideva says that we should move from seeking *rati* in the ostensible satisfactions of desire in sensory experience (*kāma*) to *rati* for Dharma.[29] Is that what is happening here: Does *rati* primarily signify something like a sublimated delight in what ought to be done?

Not quite. The temptation is to think of *rati* as designating *merely* an experiential savor. When glossing the word here, however, Prajñākaramati calls it *satkarma-āsakti*, which means something more like being wholly and uninterruptedly devoted to, and sticking with, a course of action that is good: it refers, then, not only (or not even principally) to experiential qualities but also to an orientation to action and to the dispositions actualized in it. Moreover, this describes a praxis with an eye on its structure of intelligibility and articulates praxis in connection with a particular form of life. To explain the analogy, Prajñākaramati says that to be one desirous of the satisfactions of amorous play is to be someone who wishes to obtain the kind of satisfaction afforded as the goal of certain forms of play, such as gambling and the like.[30] That's the clue.

Play, generally, involves a hermeneutic structure by way of exhibiting a par-

27. Verse 7.39 in Crosby and Skilton 2008, 70. *Cf.* verse 7.31 in Crosby and Skilton 2008, 69. For the roots of this in Buddhist discussions of wholesome desire (and desire for wholesome things [*kuśalo-dharma-cchanda*]), see the note in Anālayo 2011, 2:589n15.

28. Verse 7.31 in Crosby and Skilton 2008, 69. On problems with finding this typology in the chapter, see Crosby and Skilton 2008, 65. A study of the background for this way of thinking might begin with Śāntideva's use of the *Sāgaramatisūtra* and its discussion of *kṣānti*. See Bendall and Rouse 1922, 180.

29. Or, "Sweeping away of all desire for lusts, establishing a desire for all righteousness," in Bendall and Rouse 1922, 179.

30. "*krīḍā-phala-sukhepsuvat dyūtādi-krīḍāyā yat-phalaṁ sukhaṃ tad-āptum icchur iva.*" See Prajñākaramati on verse 7.62 in Vaidya 1988, 137.

ticular way of having a goal. Beginning with the observation that in games, unlike in ordinary activity, we do not do X in order to attain a goal,[31] C. Thi Nguyen infers the following: in play we may, instead, take on an end for the sake of the activity of pursuing that end.[32] When D. H. Lawrence said that "there is no point in work / unless it absorbs you / like an absorbing game,"[33] he too had in mind by absorption in agency the way a goal can recede from view. But Prajñākaramati is not speaking of just any form of play: he is speaking of gambling. For Śāntideva, that involves a model of addiction and the unrealizability of the goal which brings the experience of agency to the fore in a distinctive way.

Not every form of life will do. Earlier, when Śāntideva says that with "their minds set only on their own livelihood, fisherman, cāṇḍālas, ploughmen, and the like withstand their distress as extreme heat and cold,"[34] he had in mind to use these forms of life to exemplify endurance, a relevant factor in the context of activities when the goal is not attractive. The texture of action involved in such enterprise is entirely different from the context of the ethical art of liberating being where the goal is not unattractive. On the contrary: "One cannot get enough of the sensual pleasures in samsara, that are like honey on a razor's edge. How can one get enough of the benign, ambrosial acts of merit, sweet in their result?"[35]

Again and Again

We are faced with the prospect of not getting enough of a good thing. And with the prospect of not getting enough *as* a good thing—we are dealing with a particular order of action, as indicated by the way that Prajñākaramati glosses Śāntideva's compound phrase *atṛpta-ātmā*, translated above as "insatiable" (though I also like "one made of thirst"): "One who is linked to desire (*abhilāṣa*) again and again (*punaḥ-punar-abhilāṣa-yuktaḥ*)."[36] This is an emphasis that echoes Śāntideva's theme:

31. An observation important to other medieval South Asian philosophers for whom the distinctive structure of agency in play (at leisure)—and with particular reference to courtly culture—was apposite. See, for example, Śaṅkara on *Brahmasūtrabhāṣya* I.i.33 in Thibaut 1890, 2:356–357.

32. Nguyen 2019.

33. Lawrence 1994, 367.

34. Verse 4.40 in Crosby and Skilton 2008, 28.

35. Verse 7.64 in Crosby and Skilton 2008, 73.

36. In his comments on verse 7.62 in Vaidya 1988, 137.

So even at the conclusion
of one task, one should
straight away plunge
into the next, as does a tusker
inflamed by midday heat
on coming upon a pool of water
and, when it is completely finished,
one should let it go with a thirst
for the next, and the next . . . [37]

Note the invocation of interminability, and the rejection thereby of closure. We are, as it were, invited to embrace the ellipsis—"for the next, and the next"—and not the full stop.

There is, very possibly, a subtle difference between "for the next, and the next (*uttara-uttara*)" and "again and again (*punaḥ-punar*)." Both involve interminability; but the latter also involves a kind of possibly infelicitous (attempted) repetition. In fact, animating "again and again" is a long (and as yet unwritten) history.[38] Consider the *Therīgāthā*:

samsara is long
for those born again
and again, killed
again and again.[39]

Sumedha here makes the point that there is no end to pain—"samsara," as she puts it later, being "long for fools and for those who cry again and again (*punappuna*)"[40]—suggesting thereby the fact that interminability *is* a kind of pain, a point (reputedly) made explicit by the Buddha in a verse recorded in

37. Verses 7.65–66 in Crosby and Skilton 2008, 73.

38. Even as there is a history of eroticism and practical exhortation. Earlier, I had occasion to cite the *Nītisāra*'s advice that kings ought to emulate ascetics. Note also the (sadly utterly misogynistic) way it recommends energetic striving in verses 13.9–10: "By constant activity he should add to his everything, even as fire is added to by adding fuel in it. Even a weak king, if he is ever energetic, reaps nothing but prosperity. For enjoying prosperity, which is like a faithless woman, a king should ever, with all his manliness desire activity, and should not behave like one impotent" (Dutt 1896, 194). The fire, of course, is linked to the interminability of sensory gratification: see verse 9.43 in Covill 2007, 187.

39. Verse 477 (*cf.* Hallisey 2015, 223).

40. Verse 498 in Hallisey 2015, 229.

the *Dhammapada*: "birth again and again is pain (*dukkhā jāti punappunaṃ*)."[41] Many centuries later, Prajñākaramati explains the word *saṃsāra* as deriving from having "to wander on through again and again (*saṃsarati punaḥ punaḥ*)."[42]

The connection between existential discontent and interminability is sometimes also made by thinking of sensory experience and gratification in the context of different styles of agency and the conditions for practical success. Poets in Sanskrit often stylize love-play—scaled to gestures, such as looking at one another again and again, or at the level of longer sequences of activity—as involving the virtues of mutuality and (aspirational) interminability. In *Beautiful Nanda*, Aśvaghoṣa describes Nanda and Sundarī as bringing bliss to one another through the quickening of their shared passion, punctuated by intervals of exhaustion in which the couple playfully turn one another on.[43] In Śrīharṣa's *Man from Niṣadha*, where the lovers look on one another (as lovers in Sanskrit do) again and again, kissing one another again and again.[44] Their love for each other, even in the moment of satiety and post-coital tenderness, is propulsive: described as an elixir, the hunger they feel for one another (*saṃbubhukṣurmanasau*) makes them "[seek] to love each other *again* [*punaḥ*]."[45]

What does this have to do with action? A philosopher in *Beautiful Nanda* claims that there is a parallel to be drawn between interminability, the desire for gratification in sensory experience, and a mind chasing after the fruit of action (*dravat phalebhyo . . . mano*):[46] There is no end to activity, for no goal ever fully accomplishes what it seeks to do in that it either generates desire for the next thing or gives rise to a new situation that will entail further activity: either way, there is always some further goal. So too, there is no closure, satiety, or rest in sensory gratification. And no closure in doing things for the sake of extrinsic ends to gratify desire.[47]

41. Verse 153 in Norman 2000, 22.

42. On verse 7.64 in Vaidya 1988, 167.

43. Verse 4.11 (*cf.* Covill 2007, 83).

44. See verse 18.106 in Ram-Prasad 2018, 173; see also (the model of) the repetitively coupling birds in 18.16 in Ram-Prasad 2018, 159, with the emphasis on "again" being mine.

45. 18.141 in Ram-Prasad 2018, 178. Note that the adjective used here, *bubhukṣu*, meaning "hungry," fittingly enough, is a desiderative form, involving the reduplication of the root *bhuj-*, "to eat" or "to enjoy."

46. Verse 9.42c in Covill 2007, 187.

47. Verse 9.44 in Covill 2007, 187.

The monk, offering the argument as therapeutic intervention in the life of Nanda, an aesthete, draws an analytic distinction: he distinguishes between interminability involving recurrence from interminability as irrevocable change: "[T]he seasons pass and return again; the moon waxes and wanes again / but gone, gone, never to return: the waters of a river and the youth of a man."[48] There are periodic and recurring structures, like seasons and the moon's phases; and there are directed processes, flows of intrinsic change which do not involve recurrence. The cultures of desire, and desire itself, the monk teaches, would have us imagine ourselves in terms of recurrent structural patterns instead of flows: "Imagining that green youth is integral to you, your mind turns homeword in the expectation of finding pleasurable sensations. Stop it, for youth, like a coursing mountain stream, flows swiftly and does not return."[49] On such a view, the interminability entailed by desire and our efforts at acting for extrinsic ends would not be a problem were we otherwise than we are.[50] But we do seem to be more like flows than periodic seasons.

Śāntideva identifies another problem with what Aśvaghoṣa's monk called chasing after ends:

> An infant cannot make money.
> With what will he secure his happiness,
> comfort, and ease when in his teens?
> His youth is spent earning. What's an old man
> to do with things young men desire?[51]

Note the language here of desire and the invocation of ends as a calculative rational order imposed on an otherwise possibly irrational sequence exhibited by our variable selves. (Variable with respect to our changing capacities and changing preference sets that we cannot subsume entirely under a means/end involving calculative rational order.) The verse inaugurates a brief narrative of disenchantment with a life shaped by the pursuit of material ends, a lyrical and contemplative enactment, at the same time, of disenchantment with a certain

48. Verse 9.28 in Covill 2007, 181. It is intriguing that the Buddha, as Walpola Rahula once noted, attributes a similar view—that human life is like a mountain river, and that there is no moment when it ceases its ongoing flow—to a past teacher named Araka who was free from desire (Rahula 1974, 26n1).

49. *Cf.* Covill 2007, 181.

50. Verse 9.9 in Covill, 2007, 177.

51. This is the first verse of a longer (if still miniature) narrative arc. See verses 8.74–8.77 in Crosby and Skilton 2008, 94.

kind of narrative order: there is no X the doing of which could bring action to a close and provide meaning to the sequence that preceded it.

But what if we don't run on after the ends of action? "A task," Śāntideva argues in the context of discussing the conditions of praxis, "is performed for the sake of satisfaction, notwithstanding that there may or may not be satisfaction. But how can one, for whom the task itself is satisfaction, be satisfied without a task?"[52] This is the argument that councils a reorientation to action, and that brings amorous play into view as a more fitting model of ethical activity; more, at any rate, than is provided by the calculative order of thinking in terms of means and ends: "Therefore (*tasmāt*)," says Śāntideva, "even at the conclusion of a task, one ought to plunge into the next. . . ."[53] And this is what sophisticated connoisseurs of aesthetic culture know: in the case of certain tasks—tasks undertaken not so much for the ends they bring about but because of their expressing who, in part, one is—one may orient to activity differently: foregrounding agency through the beginnings (rather than ends) of action and absorption into the experience of such foregrounded agency. Given which, interminability may mean something else. We can go from "again and again" to "and the next, and the next"—taking up our endless task not with the heaviness of the true addict, but with the lightness and ludic artistry of the aesthete.

Conclusion

When Śāntideva, in the context of speaking of pain and hardship, says that "there is nothing that remains difficult if it is practiced" or that "through practice with minor discomforts, even major discomfort becomes bearable,"[54] he had in mind the plasticity of emotions and the supervenience of their experiential texture—their very nature, for that matter, and their meaning and value—on praxis. We watch him learn something about pain as he finds something to admire even in the frenzied prospect of violent and (to his own mind) irrational religious practices: "In Karṇāṭa, the devotees of Durgā willingly endure to no purpose the pain of burns, and cuts, and worse."[55]

What do we learn about desire overhearing Śāntideva enjoin on himself the virtues of amorous play? Here's my hypothesis. We may learn from moments like this that there is more to the relevance of desire and literature to Buddhism

52. *Cf.* verse 7.63 in Crosby and Skilton 2008, 73.

53. Verse 7.65a; cf. Crosby and Skilton 2008, 73.

54. Verse 6.14a–b in Crosby and Skilton 2008, 51.

55. Verse 6.13 in Crosby and Skilton 2008, 51.

in South Asia than "the synonymity of pleasure and guilt,"[56] more too than what histories of hypocrisy or transgression can show us. We must learn to acknowledge something else about the hermeneutics of agency in connection with desire, as Śāntideva suggests: Desiring bodhisattvas, given the infinite task at which they are engaged, are as if lovers excelling in a game not entirely unlike erotic love as thematized in literary cultures of pleasure. Why? Because their practices exhibit isomorphic structures and require similar orientations for success.

Let me contextualize the significance of this. As the epigraph to this essay suggests, the true nature of desire can seem a mystery. And its link to cognitivity and structure can come as a revelation. After being shipwrecked on an island of fabulous colored rocks in the course of a journey on a Greek ship, Mitragupta answers a demon's desire to know what desire is: it is imagination, he says—*saṅkalpa*—thus inviting us to consider the proleptic dimensions of thought as well as its constructive and structuring dimensions (associated with the verbal root *kḷp-*).[57] The story that Mitragupta adduces as an epistemic source (*pramāṇa*) for the identity of desire and imagination involves a variant on comedies of mistaken identity beloved of Sanskrit romances (as well as Hollywood comedies of remarriage).[58] He shows that desiring someone cannot be a cognitively "blind" affair, nor a mere mechanical motive force in the generation of action. For if one can fall out of love with X one moment only to unknowingly desire them again while mistaking them for Y, then desire must be a condition suffused with cognitivity, with thought structuring the contents and character of experience and action.

Buddhist philosophers might agree. At least, they often claimed that desire was grounded in cognitivity by virtue of *arising from* proleptic or imaginative thought (*saṃkalpa*; *kalpanā*), even if they did not, like Mitragupta, identify desire with thought.[59] But whereas Buddhists (for the most part) could disavow (most forms of) desire for this reason, the cultures of beauty and pleasure of which literature is a part may have made of desire something more than either cognitively inert satisfactions of the senses or cognitive illusion. Desire in

56. To borrow Edward Gibbon's characterization of the history of early Christian monasticism (Gibbon 1950, 2:356). For accounts of hypocritical monks in Indian Buddhism, see Schopen 2007.

57. See Shulman 2012, 112–17.

58. Mitragupta thus sees what Stanley Cavell and Wendy Doniger in our own time do, that such stories turn on the acknowledgment of desire and the nature of desire. See the discussion of Cavell in Doniger 2005, 76; Onians 2005, 417; 433–41.

59. See the sources gathered in Lang 1986, 79n2n–3, to explain Āryadeva's thesis that "desire . . . is not found apart from conceptual constructs (*kalpanā*)."

Sanskrit literature testifies to more than just our (problematic) incompleteness (to adapt a phrase from the *Bṛhadāraṇyaka-Upaniṣad*[60]). Involving more than fantasies and frustrations of consummation, desire in South Asian literature—emphasizing the virtues of repetition, interminability, and a valuable variety of incompleteness—can provide a style of thought no less than entertainment, an example of attention to the structural conditions for the meaningfulness of experiences, action, and possible forms of life. My conjecture is that this hermeneutic link between eroticism and agency at the level of structure is something to which Śāntideva was attuned, and to which he attunes us in his provocative injunctions to be insatiable, to give ourselves over as if engaged in amorous play.

Much, much more needs to be said. I offer this essay as a humble move made in a longer conversational game. At the root of this essay is a mere detail, a humble simile, the partial and contextual likeness—the workhorse of imagination in Sanskrit and Pāli. It is what lies at the root of my relationship with Janet Gyatso. For the first thing I wrote for her, my first pukka attempt at a paper in Buddhist studies, touched on what I believed to be a concealed simile (or an aberrant literalization) in the contemplative exercises of the *Visuddhimagga*. It was for a class in which we read with her (in translation) those monuments of fifth-century Buddhist scholasticism, the *Visuddhimagga* and the *Abhidharmakośa*. Yes. Both. (Isn't that forbiddingly marvelous?) I'll be honest. That class was an event and a revelation for me. And the experience of watching her read in that class influences me to this day.

To adapt Nietzsche,[61] as with light from distant sources, it can take time for the experiences that shape one to come into view as such. I continue to learn from her the necessity of moving texts from the realm of esoteric ethnic, area-bound significance and into what she has called "broadly based discourse." She's right. I'm sure of it. We need to bring Buddhist texts into thematic view on a par with other cultural objects of study in the humanities, thereby to realize their possibilities, as well as our own.[62]

If you think that this could mean many things, perhaps too many things, listen to this—"It simply means that I am taking them seriously,"[63] she once wrote of Jigme Linpa's autobiographies. The same could be said of nearly everything

60. Olivelle 1996, 17.

61. Nietzsche 2002, 171.

62. Gyatso 2001, xiv.

63. Gyatso 2001, xvii.

she has written. But there's more. "Taking them seriously, and," she went on to say, "I hope, encouraging other readers to the same." I offer this essay as proof of having been so encouraged, and in acknowledgment of the many times she has made it possible for me to stick with and to begin again this interminable task we find ourselves in, as instructive and as earnest as any true game.

Works Cited

Ali, Daud. 1998. "Technologies of the Self: Courtly Artifice and Monastic Discipline in Early India." *Journal of the Economic and Social History of the Orient* 41.2: 159–84.

———. 2011. "Rethinking the History of the Kāma World in Early India." *Journal of Indian Philosophy* 39.1:1–13.

Anālayo (Bhikkhu). 2011. *A Comparative Study of the Majjhima-nikāya*. 2 vols. Taipei: Dharma Drum Publishing Corporation.

Bendall, Cecil, and W. H. D. Rouse, trans. 1922. *Śikshā-samuccaya: A Compendium of Buddhist Doctrine*. London: Murray.

Campbell, John R. B. 2009. "Vajra Hermeneutics: A Study of Vajrayāna Scholasticism in the Pradīpoddyotana." PhD Dissertation, Columbia University.

Collins, Steven. 1997. "The Body in Theravāda Buddhist Monasticism." In *Religion and the Body*, edited by Sara Coakeley, 185–204. Cambridge: Cambridge University Press.

Covill, Linda, trans. 2007. *Handsome Nanda by Aśvaghoṣa*. New York: New York University Press.

Crosby, Kate, and Andrew Skilton, trans. 2008. *Śāntideva: The Bodhicaryāvatāra*. Oxford: Oxford University Press.

Davidson, Ronald M. 2002. *Indian Esoteric Buddhism: A Social History of the Tantric Movement*. New York: Columbia University Press.

Desmond, Laura. 2011. "The Pleasure Is Mine: The Changing Subject of Erotic Science." *Journal of Indian Philosophy* 39: 15–39.

Doniger, Wendy. 2005. *The Woman Who Pretended to Be Who She Was: Myths of Self-Imitation*. New York: Oxford University Press.

———. 2007. "Reading the 'Kamasutra': The Strange and the Familiar." *Daedalus* 136.2: 66–78.

———. 2018. *Beyond Dharma: Dissent in the Ancient Indian Sciences of Sex and Politics*. New Delhi: Speaking Tiger.

Doniger O'Flaherty, Wendy. 1973. *The Erotic Ascetic*. Oxford: Oxford University Press.

Dunne, John D. 1996. "Thoughtless Buddha, Passionate Buddha." *Journal of the American Academy of Religion* 64.3: 525–56.

Dutt, Manmatha Nath, trans. 1896. *Kamandakiya Nitisara: Or The Elements of Polity*. Calcutta: H. C. Dass.

Engle, Artemus B., trans. 2016. *The Bodhisattva Path to Unsurpassed Enlightenment: A Complete Translation of the Bodhisattvabhūmi*. Boulder, CO: Snow Lion.

Gibbon, Edward. 1950. *Decline and Fall*. 3 vols. New York: Modern Library Edition.

Gyatso, Janet. 2001. *Apparitions of the Self: The Secret Autobiographies of a Tibetan Visionary*. Delhi: Motilal Banarsidass Publishers.

———. 2005. "Sex." In *Critical Terms for the Study of Buddhism*, edited by Donald S. Lopez Jr., 271–91. Chicago: University of Chicago Press.

Hallisey, Charlies, trans. 2015. *Therigatha: Poems of the First Buddhist Women*. Cambridge, MA: Harvard University Press.

Lang, Karen. 1986. *Āryadeva's Catuḥśataka: On the Bodhisattva's Cultivation of Merit and Knowledge*. Copenhagen: Akademisk Forlag.

Lawrence, D. H. 1994. *The Complete Poems*. London: Wordsworth Editions.

Ñāṇamoli, Bhikkhu, and Bhikkhu Bodhi, trans. 1995. *The Middle Length Discourses of the Buddha: A New Translation of the Majjhima Nikāya*. Boston: Wisdom Publications.

Nguyen, C. Thi. 2019. "Games and the Art of Agency." *Philosophical Review* 128.4: 423–62.

Nietzsche, Friedrich. 2002. *Beyond Good and Evil*. Edited by Rolf-Peter Horstmann and Judith Norman. Translated by Judith Norman. Cambridge: Cambridge University Press.

Norman, K. R., trans. 2000. *The Word of the Doctrine (Dhammapada)*. Oxford: Pali Text Society.

Olivelle, Patrick, trans. 1996. *Upaniṣads*. Oxford: Oxford University Press.

Ollett, Andrew. 2019. "Making It Nice: Kāvya in the Second Century." *Journal of Indian Philosophy* 47: 269–87.

Onians, Isabelle, trans. 2005. *Dandin: What Ten Young Men Did*. New York: New York University Press and JJC Foundation.

Peeters, Benoît. 2013. *Derrida: A Biography*. Translated by Andrew Brown. Cambridge: Polity Press.

Rahula, Walpola. 1974. *What the Buddha Taught*. New York: Grove Press.

Ram-Prasad, Chakravarthi. 2018. *Human Being, Bodily Being: Phenomenology from Classical India*. Oxford: Oxford University Press.

Schopen, Gregory. 2007. "The Learned Monk as a Comic Figure: On Reading a Buddhist Vinaya as Indian Literature." *Journal of Indian Philosophy* 35: 201–26.

Shulman, David. 2012. *More Than Real: A History of the Imagination in South India*. Cambridge, MA: Harvard University Press.

Shuve, Karl. 2016. *The Song of Songs and the Fashioning of Identity in Early Latin Christianity*. Oxford: Oxford University Press.

Thibaut, George, trans. 1890. *Vedānta-sūtras with the Commentary of Saṅkarācārya*. 2 vols. Oxford: Clarendon Press.

Vaidya, P. L. 1988. *Bodhicaryāvatāra of Śāntideva with Pañjikā of Prajñākaramati*. Darbhanga: Mithila Institute.

On Gutsiness: The Courageous Eloquence of *Pöpa Chenpo*

Dominique Townsend

"Is there a courage which can conquer the anxiety
of meaninglessness and doubt?"
—Paul Tillich and Peter Gomes[1]

In reflecting on how to contribute to this Festschrift I thought about the many ways Janet Gyatso has shaped me and recalled a seminar at Harvard Divinity School with her in the spring of 2005. The term *pöpa chenpo* (*spobs pa chen po*) came up in a text we were reading together. This term is often translated as "self-confidence." It can also be "eloquence." Someone who embodies this characteristic (*spobs pa can*) might be called "bold" and "daring." This was in my first year of studying with Janet, and her energy in the classroom was so exciting and energizing—confident, eloquent, and bold. And I quickly noted, as my grandmother used to say, Janet doesn't suffer fools. That day, eager to give us the full sense of the word, she gesticulated, elucidating. Her gestures suggested a courageous energy, forceful expression, *chutzpah*, and guts. This last term sums up the impression that stayed with me—I think of *pöpa chenpo* as a kind of brilliant gutsiness. The physical sense of confidence in what it means to "have guts" strikes me as apt here.

And at the same time, the Tibetan term connotes something more abstract and more refined about an elevated style of communication. It suggests rhetorical eloquence—the ability to express oneself clearly, convincingly, courageously. The flavor it evokes might be a cousin to *vīrarasa* or heroism,[2] as both express the capacity to meet challenges head on. But more than a flavor of aesthetic experience to enjoy, *pöpa chenpo* is a quality to be cultivated through practice.

On a literary level, the Tibetan acrostic or abecedarian form (*ka rtsom* or *ka bshad*) seems to me to be an evocation of the quality of courageous eloquence.

1. Tillich and Peter Gomes 2000, 174.

2. Higgins 2007.

To play this out, I analyze a translation of an acrostic poem by the eminent seventeenth-century Nyingma master Terdak Lingpa (1646–1714) in which he grants permission for a disciple to begin Dzogchen (*rdzogs chen*) or Great Perfection practice. This example illustrates the gutsy mood of *pöpa chenpo* through a challenging Tibetan poetic form, and it displays a bit of a critical and provocative edge.

In that regard, at least colloquially in modern Central Tibetan Lhasa dialect, an agonistic aspect can sometimes outweigh the positive valence of the term. Such a colloquial variation of the term *pöpa chenpo* can lean toward the negative aspects of confidence—self-importance, argumentativeness, haughtiness, or arrogance.[3] Similar to the Yiddish *chutzpah*, the Tibetan term can have these undertones in colloquial contexts, but most often it refers to an admirable quality of self-confidence. I focus here on the positive connotations since those are predominant in the Buddhist literary contexts I'm concerned with. (In fact, I'm not aware of any written examples of the negative usage in Buddhist sources.)

With that semantic range in mind, in order to approach the expression of *pöpa chenpo* in English, it is necessary first to ask how to translate this particular Tibetan Buddhist expression of "courageous eloquence." Is there a single word for this phase in English? If not, is there an equivalent or nearly equivalent concept or phrase? My first impression is that the concept resonates most vibrantly in scenarios of protest, and especially in speaking truth to power, for example in social justice or civil rights work. It is easy to think of Dr. Martin Luther King Jr. when reflecting on the words "courageous eloquence" in a modern American context, but I have yet to find a single English term for that quality Dr. King so nobly exemplifies. In the following few pages I consider a range of possibilities of how *pöpa chenpo* might be translated based on a brief sketch of the scope of the term in Tibetan Buddhist contexts. I propose that the term that applies to the boldness, courage, and clarity of Buddhist adepts can fruitfully be applied to poetic examples such as the acrostic. In the process I reflect on the courage and eloquence that are the foundation of good translation since after all, it takes guts to translate, especially if you want to get inside the experience of the source text's author to convey something of the feeling of their work. I see this quality in Janet's translations and scholarship.

3. Thanks to Riga Shakya for reminding me of this negative colloquial valence.

Encountering Janet Gyatso

Prior to the evocative lesson on the term *pöpa chenpo* and the many other pleasurable hours I spent in Janet's classrooms, I read *In the Mirror of Memory: Reflections on Mindfulness and Remembrance in Indian and Tibetan Buddhism,* while staying with friends in Kathmandu, Nepal, in 2000. Janet edited the volume and contributed the introduction and a chapter. Then in 2003, as an applicant to Harvard Divinity School, I rode the train from New York to Boston to meet Janet for the first time in person. I finished her transformative book *Apparitions of the Self: The Secret Autobiographies of a Tibetan Visionary* on the journey. For years I used the train ticket as the bookmark for the pages I read and re-read countless times, always finding new details to appreciate.

What do I like about her writing? Her exquisitely close reading of Tibetan sources, respect for and collaboration with Tibetan and Himalayan scholars and practitioners, artful translations, humor, sparkling prose, theoretical fluency, and sheer eloquence. Her work has a sense of immediacy, and her voice is clear and confident. She is playful and humorous, and she cares about the details, not just in her research but in the quality of her writing. The transitions are graceful. I like the way she is able to interweave diverse theories with Tibetan sources, fluidly at ease in multiple intellectual spheres. In brief, gutsy is the word that comes to mind when I think of Janet's translations and insights. She has guts, and she goes right for the guts of the matter. That means getting the meaning right, of course, through careful close reading, study, comparison, engagement with native Tibetan speakers and Buddhists. It also means being bold enough to play with the literary qualities and the voice of the source text while rendering the translation into the target language. In that way, maybe good translation is always gutsy, since it demands a leap into the impossible.

All those years ago on the quiet car of Amtrak's Acela service, reading her work sealed my determination to study with her, and I was fortunate to be able to do so. After finishing my MTS at Harvard, I shifted to Columbia to pursue my doctoral studies under the direction of Gray Tuttle. Janet and I kept in touch, and she continued to mentor me. When I was preparing for my qualifying examinations in 2009, she offered to speak on the phone with me every Saturday to grill me on my progress. I was so nervous before these meetings that my partner developed a ritual of placing a glass of tequila on the desk next to me for "courage" during the conversations. I never touched the tequila, but somehow this offering helped me face my fears of Janet's brilliance. I still recall many details of those phone calls. In particular, I remember her response to a nascent idea I was exploring for my dissertation. Janet reflected back to me on the delicate balance of discovery and creativity that makes up good scholarship.

This made a massive impression on me; I continue to try to find that balance. It requires a certain self-confidence and eloquence, too. In more recent years, Janet has graced me with an even more precious blessing than mentorship—her friendship. This brief piece is a homage to her courage, eloquence, creativity, and guts.

Self-Confidence & Eloquence in Buddhist Literature

What is the relationship between self-confidence, eloquence, and, at the margins, audacity and haughtiness, all resonant in the Tibetan term *pöpa chenpo*? When is someone self-confident, and when are they audacious? Are the negative and positive valences all part of the capacity to meet the challenges that arise, even though the negative valence is off-putting? The answer lies in context and attitude, and in a cursory survey of Buddhist literary sources, the vast majority of written examples focus on the valor of *pöpa chenpo*.

To approach these questions, I'll start by asking when and where the term appears. The following overview gives a sense of the range of ways the term is used. The negative connotations are limited to colloquial usage and seem to be restricted to the Lhasa region, but the term can also be positive in a modern colloquial context. In one example of a positive colloquial expression, Françoise Robin documents a Tibetan woman impressed by another woman's willingness to address a large crowd of people as *pöpa chenpo* which Robin translates as "really brave."[4]

In Buddhist canonical sources, the Tibetan term *spobs pa* translates the Sanskrit *pratibhāna*. This is what Conze referred to as "ready speech," which is named as one of the four types of analytical knowledge (*so so yang dag par rig pa*) of the Abhidharma literature.[5] In the context of the four types of knowledge the term might also be translated as "the perfect understanding of confidence."[6] The root term appears in bodhisattva names such as Pratibhānakūta,[7] as well as in the name of the questioner Pratibhānamati in the Mahāyāna sūtra *Pratibhānamatiparipṛcchā*.

In other Mahāyāna sources where it connotes the eloquence of bodhisattvas, it is the twin quality of memory. In this context the *Lalitavistara Sūtra* presents it as a necessary step towards awakening that allows one to express the Buddha's teachings pleasantly and expertly: "Attaining pratibhāna is an entrance

4. Robin 2015, 162.

5. Conze 1975, 37.

6. Tsepak Rigdzin 2008.

7. Braarvig 1985, 17.

into the light of Dharma, as it functions so as to please all living beings with good sayings."[8] This is in keeping with Braarvig's equation of the Tibetan *spobs pa* with the Sanskrit *pratibhāna*, which he argues means "eloquence" in the context where it is paired with memory as the "two principal parts of rhetoric."[9] In some Mahāyāna contexts the term is translated as "coherent and free speech."[10] The quality it denotes is central to the configuration of the eight treasures of confidence (*spobs pa'i gter brgyad*) delimited in the *Lalitavistara*. In Mipham Gyatso's (1846–1912) *The Sword of Wisdom for Thoroughly Ascertaining Reality*, a response to the *Lalitavistara*, he states: "Satisfying all beings with excellent explanations—This is the treasure of confidence."[11] What would such braveness, courage, and eloquence look like in literary form? From a literary perspective, the Tibetan form of acrostic or abecedarian poetry presents an enticing possibility.

An Abecedarian Song of Courageous Eloquence

Having established this range of contexts for the term, I experiment with it as way of conceptualizing a Buddhist literary style. The Tibetan abecedarian form is adapted from the Sanskrit *citrakāvya* and *śabdacitra*. These playful poetic forms are associated with wonder, play, and virtuosity, and work on the visual as well as the sonic level since the play with form can be observed visually on the page (as with a-b-c poems in English) more readily than it can be heard when the poem is recited or read aloud. Similar to the way that gutsiness can be seen in a positive (courageous) or negative (arrogant and showy) light, the playful visual forms are sometimes deemed a "lower" category of Sanskrit poetics.[12] In Tibetan, the form requires training, cultivation, and practice. Yet the question arises whether this is a good use of one's time and energy as a practitioner. The Tibetan abecedarian form is showy and expresses a kind of bravado that matches the sense of *pöpa chenpo* as courageous eloquence, and perhaps as haughtiness or superiority, depending on the perception and attitude of the reader. For instance, the piece translated below might be read as a sharp critique of a certain aristocratic style of dress associated with materialism and superficiality. I propose that this literary form is a perfect vehicle for the mood of courageous eloquence.

8. Braarvig 1985, 18.

9. Braarvig 1985, 24.

10. Braarvig 1985, 18.

11. Pearcey 2004.

12. Jhā 1986, 112.

To demonstrate, take an example by Terdak Lingpa, a famous visionary and founder of Mindröling, a major Nyingma monastery in south-central Tibet.[13] While Terdak Lingpa is best known as a revealer of concealed Treasure (*gter ma*), he was also a skilled and celebrated writer who was adept at a wide range of poetic genres including *kāvya* (*snyan ngag*), such as the acrostic form, and poem-songs known as *gur* (*mgur*). Terdak Lingpa's oeuvre demonstrates a facility and I think a great pleasure in working with different meters and formal devices to communicate with his readers. He composed these verses for a student he calls Namka Wangjor. The tone is complex—there is a clear foundation of respect for the Dzogchen teachings and a sense of decorum in addressing the recipient, but there is also some sense of humor and perhaps even subtle mockery in the choice selections the author makes as he addresses Namka Wangjor. I've bolded the first letter of each line to highlight the visual aspect, and translated this in nine-syllable lines to approximate the Tibetan line length.[14] (I return to A when I run out of letters.)

> **A**ttention that expands lily-like—
> **B**est intentioned for us Tibetans—
> **C**ompassion that soothes like cool camphor—
> **D**ear Guru Rinpoche, think of me.
>
> **E**ver watchful, even from afar,
> **F**orget about what doesn't matter.
> **G**ive up thinking only of money,
> **H**old motivation like the full moon.
>
> **I**n lonely places, like groves of palms,
> **J**ust forget all that's distracting you.
> **K**eep at it and you'll achieve freedom,
> **L**et it be today you reach your aim.
>
> **M**astering the six pāramitās,
> **N**ow you know the path of transcendence.
> **O**bstinate cattle are hard to tame.
> **P**ersevere and you'll liberate them.

13. On the early history of Mindröling as a site of cultural production, see Townsend 2021.

14. A different translation of the same poem, in which I maintained the initial letter but did not use equal number of syllables for each line, is in Townsend 2021, 114–15.

Quite a small spark, a mere sesame,
Really can ignite a scorching heat.
Stave off wild careless behaviors—
Take up vividness and memory.

Undue concern with fashions like hats &
Vainly collecting brocades wastes time.
Why not forget your biases; even
Extremely rich people can be free.

Your courtyard can't keep out Death's army.
Zipping about, you cannot escape.
Abandon the body as a corpse—
Bits of mere stone and dirt—don't you see?

Cast off laziness and idleness.
Dzogchen is the right path for you now.
Extreme in your effort, marshal strength—
Fantastic! The meaning of this life!

These are the rousing words Terdak Lingpa wrote for Namka Wangjor. In the following section I briefly consider the content and context of the verses and then indicate the ways in which the poem resonates with courageous eloquence.

How Is Courageous Eloquence Expressed?

Through this carefully cultivated form, Terdak Lingpa is calling on the recipient to abandon many of the trappings of worldly existence. The recipient, Namka Wangjor, appears to be a member of the ruling class. He appears to be ready to begin Dzogchen practice, but he faces the significant obstacles of everyday distractions and preoccupations. He needs courage and boldness to take his teacher's advice. Since the initial recipient was a member of the nobility, there is a degree of social critique implied in these lines. On the one hand, the visually striking alphabetic verses give him permission to engage in advanced Dzogchen practice, but on the other hand, the verses call other practitioners mentioned in the poem "obstinate cattle" and suggest the recipient himself is prone to wasting time on fancy hats and brocades.

The first verse is an invocation to Guru Rinpoche, or Padmasambhava, and a homage to him for caring for Tibetan Buddhists. The convention in the first verse of imploring the teacher to "think of me" is common in Tibetan literature, and that can make it easy to overlook, but there is a boldness inherent in calling the teacher's attention to the verses, especially not just any teacher, but Padmasambhava himself. The poet seems to say, "listen to me, this is going to be good!" He also speaks to some extent for all Tibetans, whom he refers to as people of the Snowland (*kha ba can gyi'gro la*).

The second verse seems to conclude the reflection on Padmasambhava and then moves to the importance of focusing on the things that matter and cultivating a state of mind—"like the full moon"—which suggests effortless, nondiscriminatory, regular, dependable, egoless. The speaker shifts focus to address the recipient of the verses as the reader. Here is a clear argument—that the recipient is overly concerned with wealth and material benefit, and that he should instead cultivate the bodhisattva's motivation, like the full moon shining for the benefit of all.

The third verse encourages solitude and concentration as necessary steps leading to liberation. The images evoke a place far from Tibet—the Indic environment of palm trees—as the speaker invites the recipient to shift attention from his ordinary concerns to the prospect of solitary practice. By developing the right kind of attention as opposed to distraction and mundane concerns, the promise is that enlightenment is possible, not just in this lifetime broadly, but *today*.

The fourth verse evokes the pāramitās as the Mahāyāna basis for tantric practice. The emphasis here shifts to all those who need to be trained, in particular those students of Buddhism who lack discipline. It is not clear here whether the speaker is including the recipient in this group, or whether, more likely, he is encouraging the recipient to focus on training others. At this point the recipient should be ready to guide others. But how? Through the *confidence* to keep at it.

The fifth verse suggests how this might be accomplished. If a spark the size of a sesame seed can ignite a great flame, likewise even a glimmer of the motivation to liberate others can have a potent effect. The spark might be the spark that leads to awakening. Conversely, this spark might lead to wildness and carelessness if it is not tended to properly through "vividness and true memory," which suggests a kind of alert watchfulness and attention to what really matters. What follows concerns the sixth verse, where the distinction is made between good aesthetics (careful vividness) and bad aesthetics (stylish hats and collecting brocades). The latter just wastes time. The former leads to bias, which must be abandoned for the purpose of awakening, in the meantime proving that members of the noble class are capable of being freed. This seems to be a dig at the privileged students of the ruling class who might be inclined to get distracted by the trappings of material rather than cultivating the senses and attention for enlightenment.

This sixth stanza conveys the clearest critique when the author strongly warns against wasting time on hats and brocades, things that might very well be seen as reasonable daily preoccupations for an early modern Tibetan nobleperson. What might the recipient's "bias" have to do with the ideal of *pöpa chenpo*? Crucially, holding prejudice through bias, for instance clinging to preferences around such superficial concerns, is from the author's point of view a significant obstacle to awakening. It takes confidence and courage, as well as clarity of expression, to face one's biases and to abandon them—this might antagonize one's loved ones and allies, and in extreme cases even reorient one to one's supposed enemies. This is a daunting challenge coming from one's Buddhist teacher. What is at stake seems to be not only the recipient's potential awakening; the speaker also calls the recipient to demonstrate boldly and unequivocally that members of the nobility can actually become enlightened, despite the pitfalls of wealth and position in pursuing a Buddhist path.

In the seventh stanza, the larger context in these verses is made clear: the ubiquitous Buddhist reminder that death is inevitable and that its arrival is unpredictable. Again, it takes confidence and courage to face reality. Only by facing it boldly can one cast off laziness and idleness in the final stanza to achieve awakening.

This brief string of verses demonstrates bold eloquence joined in form and content. The form itself is a show of confidence verging on bravado—a Tibetan literary *chutzpah*. The alphabetic form is visually engaging and draws the reader to look closely at the verses. It is a difficult form to write well, and in that sense, it requires both guts and eloquence, making it an apt vehicle for the quality of *pöpa chenpo.*

Braving the Act of Translation

The elephant in the room with my translation and all translations is whether a translated poem can convey the original *as poetry*. And more specifically, can a translation convey the style of the original—bold, playful, balancing the valorization of the practices and a warning about going astray—without jeopardizing the accuracy of the original meaning? What does it require to translate a string of alphabetic verses that calls the reader to achieve awakening by means of Dzogchen from Tibetan to English? Here my effort has been to weigh form and content equally, or as nearly as I am able, as a way to test the relationship in the original between confidence and eloquence.

In thinking about the possibilities of translation, Ricoeur's work on "linguistic hospitality" has been my mainstay these past few years.[15] Reflecting on his theories, how can I make a space for the Tibetan source and the English target to meet and enjoy each other's company? How can I introduce the author to the reader across time, space, language, and religious and cultural contexts? I've attempted to show this by focusing on courage as the content and eloquence as the form. *Pöpa chenpo* is an ideal rooted in the Tibetan Buddhist cultural world that might compel us as translators and scholars of Tibetan literature to take risks, for instance by experimenting freely with meter, line length, sound, and visual elements of Tibetan literature as equally important to content as I have attempted in the translation above.

Janet Gyatso's work as a teacher, scholar, translator all conveys the quality of courageous eloquence expressed by the Tibetan *pöpa chenpo*. This characteristic, which in Buddhist literature is associated with enlightenment, is also embodied in the literary form of Terdak Lingpa's playful yet weighty verses. The demands of the form as well as the content call the reader to abandon laziness and bias, even when it is not necessary to do so from a worldly point of view. To express the work compellingly in translation demands eloquence and the courage to try.

15. Ricoeur 2006.

Works Cited

Braarvig, Jens. 1985. "Dhāranī and Pratibhāna: Memory and Eloquence of the Bodhisattvas." *The Journal of the International Association of Buddhist Studies* 8, no. 1: 17–30.

Conze, Edward. 1975. "List of Buddhist Terms." *The Tibet Journal* 1, no. 1: 36–62. Accessed June 15, 2021. http://www.jstor.org/stable/43299782.

Dharmachakra Translation Committee, trans. 2013. *The Play in Full: Lalitavistara.* 84000.

Higgins, Kathleen Marie. 2007. "An Alchemy of Emotion: Rasa and Aesthetic Breakthroughs." *The Journal of Aesthetics and Art Criticism* 65, no. 1: 43–54. Accessed June 29, 2021. http://www.jstor.org/stable/4622209.

Jhā, Kalānāth. 1986. "Sanskrit *Citrakāvyas* and the Western Pattern Poem: A Critical Appraisal." *Visible Language* XX 1 (Winter), 109–120.

Mi nyag mgon po, editor. 2006. "'Phags pa spobs pa'i blo gros kyis zhus pa'i mdo." *mDo sde spyi'i rnam bzhag*, Par gzhi dang po, Mi rigs dpe skrun khang. pp. 472–472. *Buddhist Digital Resource Center (BDRC)*, purl.bdrc.io/resource/MW1PD76588_9773EF. [BDRC bdr:MW1PD76588_9773EF]. Accessed June 30, 2021.

Pearcey, Adam, trans. 2004. *The Sword of Wisdom for Throroughly Ascertaining Reality.* Lotsawa House. https://www.lotsawahouse.org/tibetan-masters/mipham/sword-of-wisdom. Accessed June 30, 2021.

Ricoeur, Paul. 2006. *On Translation (Thinking in Action).* New York: Routledge.

Robin, Françoise. 2015. "Caring for Women's Words and Women's Bodies. A Field Note on Palmo and her 'Demoness Welfare Association for Women.'" *Revue d'Etudes Tibétaines* 34, 153–69.

Tillich, Paul, and Peter J. Gomes. 2000. *The Courage to Be: Second Edition*. Yale University Press.

Townsend, Dominique. 2021. *A Buddhist Sensibility: Aesthetic Education at Tibet's Mindröling Monastery*. Columbia University Press.

Tsepak Rigdzin. 2008. *Tibetan-English Dictionary of Buddhist Terminology*. Library of Tibetan Works and Archives.

The First Tibetan Orthographical Dictionary: *Dag yig nyer mkho bsdus pa (Précis of Essential Orthography)*

Pema Bhum

THE ELEVENTH CENTURY was a foundational period for the centering of Buddhism in Tibetan culture. Under the leadership and patronage of the kings of Gugé in the western Tibetan region of Ngari, Tibetan Buddhist clerics (*chos pa*) and translators during that time actively undertook projects to newly translate Dharma texts from India that were not yet in Tibetan and to revise earlier translations. These religious scholars also sought to expose heresies (*chos log*) and perverse mantras (*sngags log*). Meanwhile, the four main schools of Tibet's own Dharma transmission lineages had formed or were forming.

For several centuries, the translation of canonical texts from Sanskrit into Tibetan was a major component of Buddhist cultural activity. Tibetan scholars have counted 273 translators, beginning with Thönmi Sambhoṭa, arguably the very first Tibetan translator, in the seventh century, up through and including Gendün Chöphel (1903–51).[1] Among these, a full one hundred lived during the eleventh century. Ngok Loden Sherab (1059–1109), who is the author of the *Précis of Essential Orthography* (*Dag yig nyer mkho bsdus pa*) and our focus here, was one of the leading translators from this period.

While Tibetan religious and other histories detail the proliferation of the teaching and study of Dharma in the eleventh century, there is little mention of how the teaching and study of Tibetan grammar and orthography spread during this time. Furthermore, since woodblock printing was not yet in use, manuscripts were the only means for disseminating translations and other writings. We can imagine the reliance on manuscript copies led to many grammatical errors and inconsistent spellings.

Tibetan scholars have long acknowledged words that are "incorrect but widespread" (*ma dag rgyun 'byams*) referring to the expectation that even

1. Dbang 'dus tshe ring and 'Phrin las rgya mtsho, 2001, as cited in Sgo me Tshe dbang rnam rgyal, 2019.

when the spelling of a word is knowingly mistaken, it will anyway be relayed or copied per the original. For such terms, amendments are not an option; they are accepted "as is" by convention. In all likelihood, if these misspellings were traced back in time, a good many would predate the advent of Tibetan orthographies (*dag yig*), such as the one we shall now discuss.

It is reasonable to assume that Tibetan language writing and reading flourished without precedent in the eleventh century. The great translator Ngok alone translated seventy-two Buddhist works and wrote more than forty of his own works. He and others like him would have needed a system for uniform spelling to avoid common errors and to standardize terms with variant spellings. We can imagine that Ngok Lotsāwa composed the *Précis of Essential Orthography* with this need in mind: to clarify correct spellings for commonly misspelled words.

Précis of Essential Orthography *and Language Reform (*skad gsar bcad*)*

Traditional Tibetan histories identify three major reform periods for the Tibetan language, referring to them collectively as the three *skad gsar bcad* (lit. decisions [stipulating] new terminology). The first *skad gsar bcad* is described as occurring in the Tibetan imperial period during the reign of the *tsenpo* (*btsan po*) Tri Songdetsen (r. 755–97), the second during the reign of Tri Ralpachen (r. 815–38), and the third during the period of the later diffusion of Buddhism (*phyi dar*). The *skad gsar bcad* are sometimes referred to as the *bkas bcad* in these histories—that is, decided or stipulated by decree—reasoning that when scholars coined new terms in Tibetan, they were not allowed to transgress what had been authorized by the *tsenpo* or monarch. If so, it is difficult to apply the term *bkas bcad* beyond the first and second *skad gsar bcad*, because during the third reform the Tibetan empire had already disintegrated and there was no king with such vast power.

The first and second language reform periods lasted for just part of the reign period of each ruling *tsenpo*, Tri Songdetsen and Tri Ralpachen, at most for twenty or thirty years per ruler. The third reform period, by contrast, is generally recognized by most scholars of Tibetan history and language to have continued for a period of some three hundred years, beginning in the late tenth century with the translator Rinchen Zangpo (Rin chen bzang po, 958–1055) and lasting until Pang Lotsāwa Lodrö Tenpa (1276–1342).

If asked to identify the specific works and achievements of this long period, many scholars would point to the *Clove Pavilion*: *Well-Spoken Instruction on the Distinctions Between New and Old Terms in the Tibetan Language* (*Bod kyi skad las gsar rnying brda'i khyad par ston pa legs par bshad pa li shi'i gur khang*), written in the fifteenth century by Kyok Lotsāwa Rinchen Tashi (fl. 15th century), in which he mentions the third reform (he uses the term *bkas bcad gsum pa*) but only briefly. To illustrate the reform, Kyok Lotsāwa lists only ten or so archaisms, noting that they were given new spellings by Rinchen Zangpo. His list includes, for example, *gnyi zla*, *bstan chos*, and *dkon cog*, which were changed to *nyi zla*, *bstan bcos*, and *dkon mchog*, respectively. Otherwise, the main text of his orthography *Clove Pavilion* is not to reform, but to define some one thousand old terms so that they could be understood by his contemporaries. But, if we then seek details about the specific projects of the third *skad gsar bcad*, the *Clove Pavilion* offers no additional information.

While Tibetan historians and linguists concur that there was a third *skad gsar bcad* and on when it happened, we do not find in religious and other histories much mention of language reform projects, certainly not enough to understand a three-hundred-year period. We must look instead to the grammars and orthographies written during these centuries. They reveal that the formation of sentences and the spelling of certain words then differed considerably from past practices. In effect, it is these individual works, written by various scholars in succession, which we can identify as comprising the third *skad gsar bcad* when viewed collectively. Those same scholars made the language lighter or more concise by discarding extraneous elements, making the unintelligible more accessible, standardizing the application of previously irregular or inconsistent particles (e.g., genitive or ablative markers), and disseminating these newly established conventions widely.

According to his biography, on one occasion when Ngok Lotsāwa was to give teachings at the Kadam monastery Sangphu, more than twenty-three thousand monks attended. They are referred to in the text as *dpe 'grems kyi grwa pa*. In modern Tibetan, this can be understood as either "monks who distribute books" or "monks to whom books were distributed."[2] It is unlikely, however, that twenty thousand copies of anything were distributed at that time. Rather, the phrase more likely refers to their being literate. For the price of a cow they could get housing and were allowed to attend the teaching. I mention this incident in order to highlight the possibility that Ngok Lotsāwa, while teaching Buddhist philosophy, was probably also commenting on, if not propagating, his views on spellings and grammar conventions as well.

By my count, we find a total of only eight grammars and orthographies written during the three-hundred-year period between the great translator Rinchen Zangpo and Pang Lotsāwa Lodrö Tenpa. Of these, the first was *Entryway to*

2. Paṇ chen Shākya mchog ldan, 2018, 3:344.

Speech: A Weapon (*Smra sgo mtshon cha*) written by the Tibetan-fluent Indian scholar Smṛtijñānakīrti, who was active in Tibet during the eleventh century and who served as the Sanskrit-grammar teacher of Dromtönpa (1004–64). The last work was Pang Lotsāwa's own *Clarification of the Three Gatherings* (*Tshogs gsum gsal ba*), which gave instruction on how to form syllables (*yi ge*), words (*ming*), and sentences (*tshig*).

The contemporary scholar Ācārya Aklö notes how the third *skad gsar bcad* differs from the first two in that the third round of reforms were not done primarily for translating the Dharma, but rather to accord with Tibetans' *own* language, without concern for the rendering of Sanskrit terms. Aklö points out that the third *skad gsar bcad* focused mainly on the characteristics of Tibetan language and sought to make the writing system more concise—for example, discarding the post-suffix letter *-d*, as well as the final letter *'a* which until then was often applied as a post-suffix to a given syllable.[3]

We do not need to search hard for additional proof to back Aklö's observation. Powerful evidence can be found in Ngok Lotsāwa's *Précis of Essential Orthography* itself. First, in its very title, where the element "*nyer mkho*" signifies that the words in this orthography are essential—terms necessary for everyday life, not just on occasion. Second, the body of the text demonstrates that this work aims to instruct on the spellings of terms that average people use in daily life but which due to their similar pronunciations are easy to mistake. For the homonyms *gcin* (urine) and *spyin* (glue), Ngok Lotsāwa clarifies with this verse:[4]

> "G" for *gcin*, "s-p" for *spyin*.
> One is dirty, the other fastens.

Buddhist terms are very few in his speller. Ngok himself clearly states in the colophon: "Although this [orthography] may accord only slightly with the language applied in earlier translations, most of the terms follow the New [Language] Reforms."[5] In other words, the entries in his orthography differ considerably from the terminology of the imperial period, which preceded him by three to four hundred years and during which translation work was focused on

3. Ācārya Ag lod, 2017.

4. *Ga gcin sa la pa btags spyin / / mi gtsang ba dang 'byar byed do /*. Rngog Blo ldan shes rab, 2006a, 1:103 (folio 6r).

5. *'Di ni sngon gyi sgra bsgyur rnams / / sbyor tshul mthun pa'i brda la ni / / cung zad phal cher ma mthun na'ang / / phal cher gsar bcad dbang du byas /*. Rngog Blo ldan shes rab, 2006a, 1:109 (folio 9r).

Buddhism. Ngok clarifies that in compiling his own orthographical dictionary, he avoided the religious terminology of the first two periods, and instead followed the *gsar bcad*—that is, the *skad gsar bcad* of the third reform period.

No one has yet drawn a connection between the oft-cited third *skad gsar bcad* and efforts to compile orthographies during the long period it comprised. However, if we ignore the latter, then any sense of a third *skad gsar bcad* is void of much meaning. Instead, by examining several of the orthographical dictionaries at that time, including their grammatical treatises, the pronunciation of vowels and consonants, the method of applying word particles, and clarifying the unique spellings of words that sound the same, we see a structure that was rather complete and systematic—and, at least 95 percent of that system continues to be used by us today. The very first orthography in the history of Tibetan language to offer such a comprehensive structure was Ngok Loden Sherab's *Précis of Essential Orthography*—which we shall now examine more closely.

Précis of Essential Orthography *and* Kāvya *Poetry*

The single most influential Indic text for the writing of Tibetan belles-lettres from the thirteenth through early twentieth century is arguably the *Kāvyādarśa* (*Mirror of Poetry*), by the poet Daṇḍin (ca. 700). Janet Gyatso is among those scholars to have paid special attention to its influence in Tibet.[6] It is widely accepted that a full translation of this work into Tibetan was completed only in the thirteenth century by Shong Lotsāwa (fl. 13th century)—more than two hundred years after the lifetime of Ngok Loden Sherab. We would think it was not available to him during his lifetime, and yet with an ever-growing number of Tibetan translations of canonical texts and active exchange with Indic scholars, Sanskrit rhetorical or literary techniques were beginning to affect Tibetan literary content and writing structure. One easily visible inspiration is the practice of opening a text with a benediction (*mchod brjod*) followed by an introduction, typically one stanza, to what the author will write about (*bshad par dam bca' ba*). When composing their own texts, many later writers often point to the *Kāvyādarśa* to explain the need for these two structural elements. During the eleventh century, however, many authors of Tibetan were already adopting these practices, including Ngok Lotsāwa himself.

Tibetan scholars were also beginning to apply *alaṃkāra* (*rgyan*), the ornamental or poetic figures of speech prescribed in classical Indian literary theory. A clear example of this is the "Drop of Nectar: An Epistle to Gatön Sherabdrak and Other Members of the Buddhist Community of Tsongkharusum" (*Rga*

6. Bhum and Gyatso, forthcoming.

ston Shes rab grags la sogs pa Gtsong kha ru gsum gyi dge 'dun la springs pa'i yi ge bdud rtsi thig le), written by Ngok Lotsāwa. This letter, addressed to the monks of Tsongkharusum Monastery (unknown location), is composed entirely in verse and contains some forty stanzas. In terms of content, it does not refer to any specific business or concern. It is merely to express the author's Buddhist philosophical views to the monks. From start to finish, the lines of verse again and again employ Sanskrit *kāvya* figures, including similes (*dpe rgyan*) and metaphor (*gzugs rgyan*). For example, Ngok opens his letter with the following stanza:[7]

> You, grove of noble trees, in the stable earth of faith, your excellent roots of aspiration,
> your nature of mind is beautiful with the trunks of thought,
> with your flowers of practice in full bloom and cool shade for gathering [the faithful],
> sweet with the fruit of your work for the benefit of others.

In the Tibetan original, the stanza contains four lines, with each line composed of eleven syllables. The qualities of the monk congregation who were the recipient of this letter—their faith, aspiration, thought, practice, gathering, and concern for others—are transferred or instantiated (*gzugs su bkod pa*) one by one to the respective metaphors: earth, roots, trunk, flowers, the gathering of followers, and fruit. Element by element, the author ultimately addresses the monks as a whole: "You, grove of trees." It is a clear example of the literary technique of the "all elements form-ornament" (*mtha dag gzugs rgyan*), one of the twenty different form-based *alaṃkāra*. He then greets them using the same technique in the subsequent stanza:[8]

> I hope you have not been struck by the blazing thunderbolts of wrongdoing that issue forth from the rumbling thunder of hatred,
> with lightning streaks of desire in the clouds of ignorance, conjured by the nāgas of improper thought who dwell in the sky of true nature.

7. *Dad pa'i gzhi brtan 'dun pa'i rtsa ba bzang po can / / sems pa'i rang bzhin bsam pa'i ldong [sdong] pos rnam mdzes shing / / bsgrub pa'i me tog rab rgyas bsdu ba'i grib bsil can / / gzhan don 'bras bus mngar ldan 'phags pa'i ljon tshogs khyed / /*. Rngog Blo ldan shes rab, 2006b, 1:708.

8. Tib. */ rang bzhin mkhar gnas tshul min yid byed klus sprul ba / / gti mug sprin tshogs chags pa'i glog gi phreng ba can / / zhe sdang 'brug sgra chem chem sgrogs pa las 'thon pa / / nyes spyod gnam lcags 'bar bas phog par ma gyur cig /*. Rngog Blo ldan shes rab 2006b, 1:708.

Anyone familiar with *kāvya* writing conventions, but who did not know the author of these two verses nor the time of their composition, would in all likelihood identify them as written by someone who had studied the *Kāvyādarśa*. However, since Daṇḍin's work was translated into Tibetan long after, we can be fairly certain that Ngok Lotsāwa did not study *kāvya* through a Tibetan translation of Daṇḍin's text. Even so, we see from these examples that during his lifetime, while the text of the *Kāvyādarśa* had not yet spread in Tibet, its techniques were already influencing literary composition in Tibet. The writings of Ngok Lotsāwa are just one example. We find other instances of translators and writers from this period who were also skilled in the writing methods specific to the *Kāvyādarśa*, or at least certain *alaṃkāra*.[9]

Ngok Lotsāwa's *Précis of Essential Orthography* was neither a treatise on poetry nor a poetic composition per se. Rather it was a text to offer instruction on grammar and the correct spelling of words. In the grammar books that appeared in subsequent centuries each individual word is simply listed, as a means to show how to combine vowels and consonants, or how to apply superscribed letters or subscribed letters. They drew no connection between the separate entries. While Ngok Lotsāwa's primary goal was also to relay such instruction, he composed his text completely in verse, expressing a unified meaning with several lines while demonstrating the grammatical points or the correct practices to combine letters.

We generally now follow the tradition of simply listing the consonants—similar to "a, b, c" but more meaningfully grouped. Ngok Lotsāwa went much further—he composed a four-line verse that includes all thirty consonants and links them semantically:[10]

> *a pha kho ni ja chang sha / / gcig pu za 'dzu de la he / / nye wa tsho ni ti ka re / / thob tsam zhu zhes bya ba yin /*

This verse includes some vernacular language. Its meaning is not entirely clear, but it describes a father who is unkind towards his family, appearing tough, powerful, and rather selfish. The verse roughly says the following: The father selfishly enjoys tea, alcohol, and meat alone. It is as if his family members are

9. For discussion of a conversation between Dromtönpa and his Bengali teacher Jowo Atiśa (982–1054) in which the latter references *kāvya* techniques, see Bhum and Gyatso, forthcoming. A likely path of transmission by which our Ngok Loden Sherab may have learned *kāvya* techniques might lie in the fact that his uncle Ngok Lekpai Sherab (Rngog Legs pa'i shes rab) was one of the three famous disciples of Atiśa. This connection merits additional research.

10. Rngog Blo ldan shes rab, 2006a, 1:94 (folio 1v).

asking for a small share. To this day, serious students of calligraphy write this verse as a method for practicing all thirty consonants in relation to each other. While Ngok's technique of including all of the consonants and still conveying some meaning is not among the "difficult ornaments" (*bya dka ba'i rgyan*) described in *Kāvyādarśa*, nevertheless the verse resembles and must be recognized as a Tibetan example on par with later advanced exemplary verses of *kāvya*.

Although Tibet itself did not originally have the exact term or concept of "difficult ornaments," we can find many instances of verses—both in writing and in oral literature—that are abecedarian poems or engage in wordplay that accords with the Tibetan language. The *Précis of Essential Orthography*, for example, contains one stanza that demonstrates "placing the prefix *g-* in front of eleven root letters":[11]

gtan du gdan sar gnas pa'i tshe //
lan grangs gcig dang gnyis min par //
gtsug lag gzhung rnam blo la bzungs //
g.yel me bde gshegs gsung rab bltas //

While residing permanently in the monastery,
not just once or twice,
he memorized the texts of the classical sciences,
and read the Buddhas teachings without distraction.

It does not appear that Ngok Lotsāwa was intentionally setting out in the poem above to write an exemplary verse to illustrate the "difficult ornament." The scholar primarily wants to explain that there are eleven consonants before which the prefix *g-* can be placed. Still, his literary skill is evident. If this were a grammatical text written at a later date, it would be sufficient to list words illustrating the eleven letters before which the prefix *g-* can be placed. However, Ngok Lotsāwa does not list them separately, rather he combines all of the words in one stanza and is able to express a coherent meaning. We can guess that this might be for mnemonic purposes. Although the "difficult ornament" techniques prescribed in the *Kāvyādarśa* do not include a "same prefix ornament," again Ngok Lotsāwa's clever verse would fit right in as an exemplary verse for this category of phonetic-based figures of speech.

Another verse in his *Orthography* also illustrates how to combine consonants and vowels, while employing a figure of speech that is in the *Kāvyādarśa*:

11. Rngog Blo ldan shes rab 2006a, 1:96 (folio 2v).

the "difficult ornament of fixed vowels" (*dbyangs nges pa'i bya dka' ba'i rgyan*). Although Ngok did not set out intentionally to compose the *kāvya* phonetic *alaṃkāra* (*sgra rgyan*) when writing a verse that employs the rather difficult device of attaching vowels to consonants, he was effectively using the *alaṃkāra* of "fixing a certain vowel to each of the four lines" (*dbyangs kyi yi ge rkang pa bzhir nges pa*)—exactly as described in the *Kāvyādarśa*.[12]

> *Tshig 'di yid kyis 'dris bgyi'i phyir*
> *bu tshur myur du zung du zungs*
> *g.yel med bshes gnyen nyer bsten te*
> *chos nor longs spyod yongs thob mdzod*
>
> In order to become familiar with this word
> son/boy, draw near quickly and regard [them] as a pair[?].
> Adhere closely without distraction to the teacher, and
> obtain fully the Dharma, wealth, and enjoyment.

While the second line is difficult to understand, still the stanza expresses a coherent meaning. Note the order: the first line contains only the vowel *i*, the second *u*, the third line is *e*, and the fourth line is *o*. This accords exactly with what we today still consider the standard order for listing the vowels.

The Influence of the Précis of Essential Orthography

The influence of the *Précis of Essential Orthography* is clearly visible in three aspects to date. Its first impact lies in the very term "orthographical dictionary" (*dag yig*). Nearly one thousand years have passed since Ngok Lotsāwa, to the best of our knowledge, coined the term. This is not to say that other terms have not appeared over the centuries. Scholars have applied a variety of others, including but not limited to *brda dag*, *brda yi bye brag*, *brda'i bstan bcos*, and *brda sprod*. (While these terms today are more associated with grammars proper, this was not always the case.) It must anyway be recognized that for hundreds of years, the term most widely used and accepted to refer to orthographies and dictionaries has been *dag yig*. Even the compilation of an orthography that began in 1973 during the Cultural Revolution was entitled *Newly Compiled Orthography* (*Dag yig gsar bsgrigs*). It was published in three separate editions, the third as late as 2012, and still the title remains unchanged.

12. Rngog Blo ldan shes rab 2006a, 1:95 (folio 2r).

Although the term *tshig mdzod* is now becoming more prevalent, the term *dag yig* cannot be altogether dismissed.

The second impact of Ngok's famous orthography is on the method of compiling an orthographical dictionary. The main function of such a work is commonly considered to be for instruction on the spelling, meaning, and usage of terms. One might think metered verse is an ill-suited writing style for such purposes. Nevertheless, Ngok Lotsāwa composed his *Orthography* entirely in verse, and by my count most of the forty-plus texts written since then and explicitly titled *dag yig* (including woodblock prints and modern-format publications) are written completely in verse. The most famous exception is the *Clove Pavilion*.

From a chronological view, the first modern-era dictionary *not* written in verse is mostly likely the dictionary (*tshig mdzod*) compiled by the Kinnaur-born editor Gegen Dorjé Tharchin (1890–1976), famous for his publishing projects in Kalimpong, India, during the mid-twentieth century. The manuscript of his dictionary can be found online through Columbia University Libraries, but the work was never formally published. The first published orthographical dictionary not written in verse is that of Geshé Chodrak (1898–1972). Completed in 1946, this important work was published by Horkhang Sonam Pelbar in 1949 via woodblock printing with the title *Clarification of Orthography and Terms* (*Brda dag ming tshigs gsal ba*) and remains actively used to this day.

Still, the practice of writing orthographical dictionaries using verse was not entirely halted. One orthography written in verse, the *Dictionary for Elementary Students* (*Slob chung dag yig*), was compiled by the Textbook Compilation and Translation Office of the Tibet Autonomous Region (TAR) Education Bureau and published in 1987 by the TAR People's Publishing House. Aside from that, I have also seen some examples composed by individuals but never formally published.

The third influence concerns the relative role of grammar (*brda sprod*). By common understanding today, the function of a Tibetan orthographical dictionary is to explain spelling, as well the meaning and usage of terms. Most modern examples do not include a section on grammar. Ngok Lotsāwa, however, included a section on grammar in his *Orthography*. This approach was adopted by Sakya Paṇḍita Kunga Gyaltsen (Sa skya paṇ ḍi ta Kun dga rgyal mtshan, 1182–1251) and continued by at least some scholars up until the twentieth century. Sakya Paṇḍita's orthography, *Précis of Essential Orthography: Wish-Fulfilling Gem of Composition* (*Dag yig nyer mkho bsdus pa sdeb sbyor yid bzhin nor bu*) also includes a separate section for grammar. Except for the subtitle, the main title of Sakya Paṇḍita's work is identical to that of the orthographical work by Ngok Lotsāwa. Moreover, about 90 percent of the entire body of Sakya Paṇḍita's text—aside from the benediction, colophon, and subheadings—is also identical to Ngok Lotsāwa's work, down to the exact wording. From the contemporary perspective of copyright, Sakya Paṇḍita's blatant plagiarism might be seen as a scholarly defect. Viewed otherwise, it is a clear illustration of the enormous influence of Ngok Lotsāwa even on the great scholar Sakya Paṇḍita, who himself was renowned for opening a new chapter of Tibetan learning.

The practice of including grammar in orthographies did not completely disappear. In the twentieth century, for example, we find the *Abridged Orthography: White-Lotus Bouquet: Ear Ornament to Delight Children* (*Dag yig mdor bsdus pad dkar chun po byis pa dga' ba'i rna rgyan*), a concise orthography written for younger learners in 1932 by Dudjom Rinpoche (1904–85). This work too contains a section on orthography and one on grammar.

Above all, Ngok's *Orthography* influenced Tibetan grammar itself. These days, Tibetan grammar includes two main texts: the *Thirty Verses* (*Sum cu ba*), which instructs on how to form sentences, and the *Usage of Gendered Markers* (*Rtags kyi 'jug pa*), which mainly instructs on how to form nominal stems (*ming*) and verbs (*bya tshig*). The application of rules discussed in the *Thirty Verses* involves two types: grammatical particles that depend on the preceding suffix letter (*phrad gzhan dbang can*) and particles formed independently of the preceding letter (*phrad rang dbang can*). Ngok Lotsāwa's *Orthography* discusses only the former, which he refers to as "dependent particles" (*tshig phrad gzhan dbang can*). But this is the primary part of Tibetan grammar, even today. His instructions there are precisely what is still followed today. Dudjom Rinpoche's *Orthography* was written eight hundred years after Ngok Lotsāwa composed his. Tibetan society and culture have transformed greatly over these many centuries, yet the application of grammatical particles has not changed. Dudjom's *Orthography* offers new examples for illustration, but the number and delineation of particles, as well as his system for applying them, are exactly those prescribed by Ngok Lotsāwa.

While scholars dispute the authorship of the *Thirty Verses* and the *Usage of Gendered Markers*, these two texts are considered to have served as pillars for Tibetan language instruction since the imperial period. There is reason to question this assumption. Importantly, Thupten Jinpa has observed, "Ngok Lotsāwa was well-read. If the *Thirty Verses* and the *Usage of Gendered Markers* had existed at the time, he would have at least mentioned these titles in his own discussion of grammar, but he did not."[13] Thupten Jinpa here offers

13. Thub bstan sbyin pa 2013, xxv.

clear grounds for doubting that a Thönmi Sambhoṭa in the seventh century authored these foundational texts. The "Grammar" to which Thupten Jinpa refers must be the section on grammatical particles (*tshig phrad*) in Ngok's *Orthography*. Nor did Thupten Jinpa find reference to these two works in the writings of Ngok's contemporaries. If we cannot find evidence for the existence of the *Thirty Verses* and the *Usage of Gendered Markers* during Ngok Lotsāwa's time, then his section on particles (*tshig phrad*) may well be the very first indigenous Tibetan grammar text. Unless other sources are found, there is good reason to believe that the scholar who established the method of applying particles in relation to the preceding suffix letter—the rules we still follow today—was most probably Ngok Lotsāwa.

Translated by Lauran R. Hartley

Works Cited

Ācārya Ag lod. 2017. "Skad gsar bcad gsum dang bdag gi bsam gzhigs kyi yo lang," *Khabda*. September 6, 2017. Accessed March 4, 2021. https://www.khabdha.org/?p=91041.

Bhum, Pema, and Janet Gyatso. Forthcoming. "*Kāvyādarśa* on Fire: An Ardent Reception in Tibet and Mongolia." In *A Lasting Vision: Dandin's Mirror in the World of Asian Letters*. Oxford University Press.

Dbang 'dus tshe ring and 'Phrin las rgya mtsho. 2001. *Bod kyi sgra 'gyur lo rgyus dang lo tsā ba rim byon gyi mdzad rnam gsal ba'i me long*. Beijing: Mi rigs dpe skrun khang.

Paṇ chen Shākya mchog ldan. 2018. "Rngog lo tsā ba chen pos bstan pa ji ltar bskyangs pa'i tshul mdo tsam bya ba ngo mtshar gtam gyi rol mo zhes bya ba bzhugs so." In *Lo paṇ gyi rnam thar phyogs bsgrigs*, edited by Dhiḥ Lha ldan, 3:341–53. Hong Kong: Krung go'i shes rig dpe skrun khang.

Rngog Blo ldan shes rab. 2006a. "Dag yig nye mkho bsdus pa Shākya'i dge slong Blo ldan shes rab kyis mdzad pa bzhug so." In *Bka' gdams gsung 'bum phyogs bsgrigs*, 1:93–110. Chengdu: Si khron dpe skrun tshogs pa, Si khron mi rigs dpe skrun khang.

Rngog Blo ldan shes rab. 2006b. "Rngog Blo ldan shes rab kyis mdzad pa'i springs yig bdud rtsi'i thig pa." In *Bka' gdams gsung 'bum phyogs bsgrigs*, 1:707–12. Chengdu: Si khron dpe skrun tshogs pa, Si khron mi rigs dpe skrun khang.

Sgo me Tshe dbang rnam rgyal. 2019. "Bod brgyud nang bstan phyi dar gyi skabs su byon pa'i Bod kyi lo tsā ba'i dpyad gleng," *Bod ljongs nyi gzhon*, July 4, 2019. Accessed March 14, 2021. http://ti.zangdiyg.com/article/detail/id/14417.html.

Thub bstan sbyin pa. 2013. *Brda dag snyan ngag sogs tha snyad rig gnas kyi gzhung gces btus*. New Delhi: Bod kyi gtsug lag zhib dpyod khang.

What Language We Dare Learn and Speak: Decolonizing the Study of Tibetan Poetry[1]

Nancy G. Lin

MORE THAN thirty years ago bell hooks wrote:

> Language is also a place of struggle. I was just a girl coming slowly into womanhood when I read Adrienne Rich's words "this is the oppressor's language, yet I need it to talk to you." This language that enabled me to attend graduate school, to write a dissertation, to speak at job interviews carries the scent of oppression.[2]

English, Rich and hooks remind us, is a language of imperialism. It was American postwar imperialism in Taiwan that brought my parents to the United States, that has made it possible for me to learn proper English, educated English, tasteful English, to speak and write as I do. *Language is also a place of struggle.*

Yet as both authors recognize, English is also a language of poets. Poets stretch the boundaries of what language can do, to speak truth and remember, to name and recognize, to break silence "where language needed to be and was prevented," to imagine what is possible.[3] As hooks asks: "Dare I speak to you in

1. I thank Natalie Avalos for organizing a 2019 AAR roundtable on "Decolonial/Anti-Racist Interventions in Tibetan/Buddhist Studies" where I first presented the ideas in this essay, along with fellow roundtable participants for our shared conversations: Sarah Jacoby, Matt King, Dawa Lokyitsang, Karin Meyers, Annabella Pitkin, Riga Shakya, and Sangseraima Ujeed. I am grateful to Rebekah Linh Collins, Linda Lin, Roy Tzohar, and Nicole Willock for their insightful comments on drafts of this essay.

In this essay "Tibetan poetry" refers to Tibetan-language poetry; similarly, "Tibetan literature" refers to Tibetan-language literature. It is important to note that *snyan ngag* and other forms of Tibetan-language literature have been and continue to be composed and circulated beyond Tibetan borders, e.g., in Bhutan, Mongolia, and so forth.

2. hooks 1989, 16.

3. Rich 1997, 322.

a language that will move beyond the boundaries of domination—a language that will not bind you, fence you in, or hold you?" Such language, she tells us, is made possible "by remembrance of the past, which includes recollections of broken tongues giving us ways to speak that decolonise our minds, our very beings."[4]

I want to think with you about how we remember the past through language. Language can limit and oppress, yet language can also offer possibilities for learning, being, creating, and emancipating. How we approach language is crucial to how we produce knowledge, which in turn can redress harmful legacies of imperialism, colonialism, and other forms of power and inequity by helping to dismantle their structures, methods, and presumptions. What may be less obvious is how tastes we call our own may obstruct our ability to recognize the capacities of language and the possibilities they afford.

In this essay I examine how scholars in Europe and North America have largely neglected *nyenngak* (*snyan ngag*), the classical tradition of Tibetan-language poetry, belletristic prose, and poetics.[5] A major factor is the ongoing lack of institutional support in these regions for the study of Tibetan-language literature as such: very few specialists in this subject hold positions in literature departments, while the lion's share of faculty positions in Tibetan, Himalayan, and Inner Asian studies are occupied by specialists of Tibetan Buddhism. But this alone cannot entirely explain the lacuna, because much Tibetan Buddhist writing bears the stylistic imprint of *nyenngak*, and many Tibetan Buddhist texts have been studied and interpreted in great detail. This general lack of attention exists in stark contrast with voluminous Tibetan-language scholarship on *nyenngak*; moreover, a significant proportion of English-language publications dealing with *nyenngak* are authored or co-authored by Tibetans.[6] I argue that we have too often regarded *nyenngak* through certain Romantic, modern, and mysticist notions—filtered through flawed and ambivalent Orientalist perspectives—of what counts as "good literature" and "authentic religion." My work repurposes Pierre Bourdieu's social theory of taste and builds on Donald Lopez's critical genealogies of Tibetan/Buddhist studies. I suggest how attending to *nyenngak* can help decolonize our own assumptions, while pointing us to key Tibetan/Buddhist epistemologies.[7]

4. hooks 1989, 16, 21.

5. By "poetics" I refer broadly to literary techniques and principles.

6. Bhum 1999; Rabsal 2016; Bhum and Gyatso 2017, forthcoming; Jabb 2015, 10–17, 193–205. Limited studies of *snyan ngag* have begun to ramp up only recently, with other contributions including those of van der Kuijp 1996; Kapstein 2003, 776–94; Gold 2007, chap. 6; Lin 2008; Martin 2014; Townsend 2021, chap. 3, 152–63; Willock 2021, *passim*.

7. I gratefully acknowledge Geshe Lozang Jamspal, Tenzin Norbu, Lauran Hartley, Pema Bhum,

The fields of Tibetan and Buddhist studies have been subjected to critiques of Orientalism, especially during a period from the mid-1990s to the early 2000s.[8] Yet if we have moved on since then, it is often unclear whether that entails progress or abandonment. On balance have we seen major, widespread, and continuing changes to our theories and methods as a result of these critiques or rather, a lack of deliberate and concerted effort to rebuild collectively and self-reflexively in their wake? As scholars in these fields, are we heeding Charles Hallisey's call to "restructure our understandings . . . in a manner that will enable us to overcome the distortions of our scholarly inheritance," e.g., by valorizing the production of knowledge in local, historical contexts and their possible translocal, "transhistorical value to those who produce and receive those meanings?"[9] If we are, it is incumbent on us to scrutinize whatever received ideas may persist in our particular areas of inquiry and in our subjectivities as scholars. Otherwise we risk not only distorting the objects we choose to study, but missing or failing to include others altogether. With the space I have here, I sketch a genealogy of the European and American reception of *nyenngak*, critique its persistent assumptions, and end by suggesting a way forward.

In this task I am inspired by and indebted to the work and career of Janet Gyatso. Janet has been a model of a fearless woman scholar who dares to open new fields within Tibetan and Buddhist studies in exciting and rigorous ways, challenging us to engage broadly with the humanities even as we strive to do justice to our sources. *Nyenngak* is but the latest in a succession of topical inquiries she has taken up with vitality and aplomb. Since an early stage of my graduate work and throughout my career, she has encouraged my intellectual interests and given invaluable advice. For all this I thank her and offer this essay as a small token of gratitude.

Michael Hahn, Gedun Rabsal, and others for their instruction in Tibetan poetry and poetics over the years.

8. Lopez 1995; Lopez 1998. See also studies of Western images of Tibet such as Dodin and Räther 2001. Such genealogical scholarship can be uneven, unwittingly reproducing a "latent Orientalism" when it fails to directly refer to, or convey the voices of, people and places from which such accounts are imagined to emanate (Hallisey 1995, 31–32). My use of "Orientalism" refers to Western cultural/ideological formations that work to dominate, restructure, and assert authority over the Orient (Said 1979, 3).

9. Hallisey 1995, 52. Recent publications that have explicitly grappled with this challenge in Tibetan and Mongolian studies include Avalos Cisneros 2015; Lokyitsang 2016; Lokyitsang 2017; King 2019. For case studies that investigate Tibetan knowledge production in the early modern period on the topics of ornament and personhood respectively, see Lin 2021; Chou and Lin 2021.

Decolonizing Taste

In the landmark 1996 publication in honor of Geshe Lhundup Sopa, *Tibetan Literature: Studies in Genre*, Leonard van der Kuijp remarked that *nyenngak* was "among the least developed areas in modern Tibetology."[10] More than two decades later this remains true among scholars based in Europe and North America, despite a modest uptick of activity in recent years. Why this lack of interest? Over the years I have observed certain reactions when Tibetologists and Buddhologists (none of them native Tibetan speakers) hear I study *nyenngak*. They often start with a facial expression of distaste, followed by something along the lines of, "Ugh, you like that stuff? I can't stand it. It's so contrived, so artificial."[11] Ornate, contrived, baroque, pedantic, derivative: such adjectives imply that this is not good poetry. This is not to our taste.

Such responses don't come out of thin air, nor from some timeless universal standard. Taste, as Bourdieu demonstrated in *Distinction*, is produced by social conditions; in turn, art and cultural consumption serve to legitimate social differences. Mastering the cultural codes that dictate taste marks our belonging in a socioeconomic class. Our educational capital and social origin correlate to our aesthetic tastes and values in music, photography, and other forms of art. The trick of taste is that groups distinguish themselves from others hierarchically through particular codes that define and reinforce "legitimate culture." For those immersed in this so-called "legitimate culture," taste is ingrained as part of one's habitus. Nonchalantly exercising one's taste seems as natural as breathing air.[12] This ingrained embodiment may foster the illusion that taste is somehow innate, but Bourdieu takes pains to demonstrate how aesthetic tastes are historically formulated, tracing cultural ideas and practices in 1960s France to seventeenth-century developments.

European and North American tastes in Tibetan poetry have likewise followed recognizable codes, with favor bestowed on song-poetry (*mgur*, *glu*), especially collections attributed to Milarepa (1028/1040–1111/1123) and the Sixth Dalai Lama Tsangyang Gyatso (1683–1706). In his 1906 publication the British scholar and missionary Graham Sandberg opined that the works attributed to Milarepa demonstrated "the faculties of a true poet," who "had not only an eye for the beauties of nature but also words at his command wherewith to record the feelings which such beauties inspired." Sandberg preferred Milare-

10. van der Kuijp 1996, 394.

11. A second, related response is to insinuate that *nyenngak* is not truly and authentically Tibetan because it is derived from Sanskrit *kāvya*. I plan to address this issue in future work.

12. Bourdieu 1984, 91.

pa's use of vernacular language—although he incorrectly asserted that his song-poetry had "no particular metre whatsoever"—to "the stilted artificial style of the Kangyur treatises" of the Tibetan Buddhist canon.[13] He found the poet-saint "full of interest and novelty not only for the frequent depth of feeling displayed, but also as setting forth the recondite philosophy and mysticism of the northern cult of Buddhism."[14]

While Sandberg's scholarship has been largely superseded by that of later generations, the tastes he expressed in Tibetan poetry have lingered. In *Tibetan Painted Scrolls* (1949), Giuseppe Tucci commends Milarepa's poetry whenever, in his view, it breaks loose from "esoteric abstruseness" and "the technicalities of yoga" and "soars in perfect purity on the wings of fancy." Tucci further praises Milarepa's "earnestness" and "genius," his ability to bring "a personal touch" to his verses.[15] Elsewhere he rhapsodizes about the Sixth Dalai Lama's poetry:

> They are simple songs, fresh and artless, imbued with a great feeling for nature: the author calls upon plants and animals to sympathize and feel compassion for the fire burning in his heart . . . They breathe the fragrance of a free and simple life, hence they often touch the noble heights of real poetry.[16]

Tucci deems such poetry far superior to *nyenngak*, which he refers to as *kāvya*, using the name of the Sanskrit poetic tradition from which *nyenngak* was adapted. He prefers Tibetan poetry where "the style is simple and direct, there is nothing stilted or artificial about it, no pretentious imitation of Kāvya's elaborate subtleties." This simple, direct style was allegedly ruined by the influence of *nyenngak*, which Tucci narrates in the language of infectious disease: the "first symptom" of *nyenngak* appears in the writings of Pakpa Lodrö Gyaltsen (1235–80), spreads to other authors and genres, and is full-blown in the Fifth Dalai Lama's (1617–82) writings. The Fifth Dalai Lama, in Tucci's estimation, composes "in the most artificial manner prose and poetry, both extremely florid and refined."[17]

To anyone acquainted with key strands of European Romanticism and its

13. On the use of metrics in *mgur*, including work attributed to Mi la ras pa, see Sujata 2005, 112–38.

14. Sandberg 1906, 253, 250. For a survey of Western interest in Mi la ras pa see Quintman 2014, 11–17.

15. Tucci (1949) 1999, 1:98.

16. Tucci (1949) 1999, 1:138.

17. Tucci (1949) 1999, 1:104, 135.

American offshoot, Transcendentalism, such aesthetic tastes and values should ring familiar. Wordsworth famously asserted that "all good poetry is the spontaneous overflow of powerful feelings," promoting an aesthetic of lyric expression that valorized personal experience, especially exalted states of mind, passionate emotions, and the voice of the individual self.[18] Romantic and Transcendentalist poets often celebrated visionary insights and pastoral beauty, and many, like Wordsworth, sought to capture this in plain language they attributed to rustic folk. They idealized originality, creative imagination, and apparent naturalness and artlessness. As if traditional forms could not contain their spontaneous overflows of feeling, poets keenly revised or exceeded the strictures of rhyme, meter, and stanza; Walt Whitman is widely considered the American father of free verse.[19] Modern poet-theorists like Ezra Pound went even further in rejecting literary ornament and the appearance of artifice. In 1917 he called for twentieth century poetry to be "'nearer the bone' . . . as much like granite as it can be, its force will lie in its truth, its interpretative power . . . it will not try to seem forcible by rhetorical din, and luxurious riot. We will have fewer painted adjectives impeding the shock and stroke of it."[20] The turn to subjectivity, emphasis on the natural, rejection of apparent artifice, freedom from traditional verse conventions: these became hallmarks of "good" poetry that have shaped and continue to shape tastes among European-language readers.

These movements were largely built on a fascination with bygone Eastern mysticism and the literature from which they sought to recover it. The view of ancient India as a primordial paradise, purer and more innocent than a supposedly advanced Europe, was popularized by Johann Gottfried Herder and persisted among German intellectuals and Romantics. Herder's engagement with India largely stemmed from his captivation with *Śākuntala*, Kālidāsa's classical Sanskrit play, and with the *Bhagavad Gītā*.[21] Friedrich Schlegel proclaimed that India was "the source of all languages, all ideas and poetry of the human spirit: *everything, everything comes from India* without exception."[22] While Samuel Taylor Coleridge fluctuated between enthusiasm for and criticism of

18. Wordsworth 1800, xiv.

19. The diversity of Romanticism, e.g., the antinaturisms of Blake and Byron or the range of experimentation and engagement with traditional forms, should make us wary of synthetic generalizations about a set of cultural/ideological formations. What concerns me here, however, are features of the poetical economy that were tapped by Western arbiters of Tibetan poetry. O'Neill 2005, Sheats 2005, Packer 2004, McGann 1992.

20. Pound quoted in Ferrall 2001, 43.

21. Herling 2006, 58–69, 86–93, 96–112.

22. Herling 2006, 127.

Hindu thought, many of his own writings express intuitions of the infinite that he claimed to find troubling in Hinduism.[23] Ralph Waldo Emerson sought "a religion founded on immanence and intuitive certainty" in such works as the *Bhagavad Gītā*, the *Kaṭha Upaniṣad*, and the *Viṣṇu Purāṇa*; his poem "Brahma," which caused a literary sensation in 1857 with its Hindu-inspired pantheism, contains parallels with these texts in translation.[24] As Richard King has observed, Western intellectuals singled out such texts as allegedly containing the "grand mysteries" of Hinduism, finding them amenable to their own emphasis on interiority and non-institutionalized forms of spirituality. Prominent Romantic and Transcendentalist figures strongly associated Sanskrit and other Asian literatures with the mystical notion that genuine religion lay in extraordinary experiences of the divine, often through direct personal encounters, and in a return to primitive, natural origins.[25]

In the process of selecting, translating, and appreciating Sanskrit literature, translators and intellectuals focused on the elements that reflected their own desires, perceptions, and tastes. Regarding his popular translation of the *Gītā Govinda* (1792), William Jones stated outright that he had eliminated passages "too luxuriant and too bold for a *European* taste."[26] Similarly, Jones's rendering of *Śākuntala* into English omitted vivid descriptive and figurative language that is stock-in-trade for *kāvya*, privileging a pastoral aesthetic while undermining the erotic (*śṛṇgāra*) mode by which Sanskrit poetics classify Kālidāsa's play.[27] Jones's watershed rendering of *Śākuntala* into English, which engendered forty-six translations in twelve different languages, was blithely praised as a translation of "utmost fidelity" by Schlegel.[28] Yet even where Schlegel still detected "a profusion of imagery and poetic ornament," he was willing to overlook it as "only the adornment of innocence" that reflected "the fondness for an indolent solitude, [and] the delight excited by the beauty of nature." More importantly, he affirmed, "tenderness of feeling, genial grace, artless beauty pervade the whole" of the text.[29]

Tibetan-language texts were mostly neglected by Europeans and Americans during the nineteenth century, except as translations that could shed light on Indic Buddhism. Yet there are striking parallels between Romantic

23. Harries 2013, Vallins 2013.

24. Packer 2004, 92; Carpenter 1968, 110–19.

25. King 1999, 7, chap. 6.

26. Jones quoted in Rangarajan 2014, 133.

27. Culp 2018b, 138–139.

28. Figueira 1991, 12; Schlegel quoted in Culp 2018a, 100.

29. Schlegel quoted in Culp 2018a, 100.

and Transcendentalist receptions of Sanskrit poetic and aphoristic literature, and later English-language receptions of Tibetan literature. Like Sandberg and Tucci before them, scholars, translators, and publishers echo a shared zest for artless simplicity, natural imagery, depth of personal feeling, and spiritual profundity and purity in Tibetan song-poetry, coupled with distaste for artifice and a perceived lack of originality in *nyenggak*. In his publisher's foreword to Garma C. C. Chang's 1962 translation of *The Hundred Thousand Songs of Milarepa*, Peter Gruber asserts that it was "immeasurably easier" for Tibetans "to contact the spiritual verities and to lead devotional lives" because "*they had much simpler minds and they led much simpler lives.*" For Gruber Milarepa's collection is "a personal favorite . . . an inexhaustible fountainhead of inspiration," where "the profoundest ideas and teachings of Buddhism are revealed . . . in simple language."[30] Aurel Stein, who in the same year published much more nuanced and sophisticated studies of Tibetan culture, nevertheless dismisses *nyenngak* as "an exercise in Indian style" and declines to discuss it despite recognizing that is has been "certainly very popular with Tibetan men of learning." Instead, Stein praises the "poetic creativity" exercised by those with a "lack of pedantry or learned imitation of Indian patterns," who enjoy "rapture or 'madman-like' inspiration" and "keep in touch with the living indigenous tradition."[31] Introducing his 1998 translation of the Sixth Dalai Lama's song-poetry, Rick Fields muses that the poems are "plain and unadorned, without much recourse to literary artifice. But as we look closer, the poems split open to reveal hidden depths." Fields concludes by praising "the heart-to-heart, mind-to-mind genius of the poems," which "speak and sing for themselves."[32] The fact that Milarepa and the Sixth Dalai Lama remain the most widely read Tibetan-language poets in English translation is due not only to their literary styles, which apparently concord with Western tastes in poetry. It is also based on Western notions that authentic religion is rooted in personal, direct encounters with the divine or the true face of reality, and that poetry is an outlet for expressing visionary encounters.

But at what cost do we bring our own tastes, socially conditioned by European and American history, to our representations and reception of Tibetan poetry? When these are unwittingly dictated by such "personal" inclinations, it obscures what Tibetans and others have made of their own literature. The song-poems of Milarepa and the Sixth Dalai Lama have been and remain immensely

30. Gruber 1962, x, xi. Cf. Tucci, who characterized Tibetans as having the ingenuous serenity of children (Benavides 1995, 164).

31. Stein 1972, 264–65, 250–51, 272, 275, 276.

32. Fields and Cutillo 1998, 25, 27.

popular among Tibetans. That these and other examples of the genre deserve scholarly attention is not at issue, given their literary qualities and historical significance.[33] Yet *nyenngak* has also been highly regarded by Tibetan-language readers, evidenced not only by its voluminous production and commentary by eminent authors since at least the thirteenth century to the present day, but also by the adoption of *nyenngak* elements in other genres, including song-poetry. And as we would expect, Tibetans have debated, expressed preferences for, and critiqued different genres and styles of poetry and literature.[34] All this is obscured if, unaware of how our tastes have been conditioned by non-Tibetan histories, we fail to pay attention to *nyenngak* as a major part of Tibetan literary history and what it may offer us through the process of interpretation. If "imperialism is the export of identity," as Said pithily observed, we ignore at our peril which representations of Tibetan literature, or any topic for that matter, collectively get exported and consumed through our individual and institutionally supported decisions—and how much that says about European and American tastes, preoccupations, and structures of knowledge rather than Tibetan ones.[35]

Transformative Language

Tibetans since the second half of the twentieth century including Dungkar Losang Trinlé (1927–97), Alak Tseten Shabdrung (1910–85), and Döndrup Gyal (1953–85) have created space for learning and writing *nyenngak* in the face of repeated destruction of their language, culture, and religion. I wish to honor their work by returning to bell hooks's call to decolonize through language. How can *nyenngak* "create space where there is unlimited access to the pleasure and power of knowing, where transformation is possible"?[36] How have Tibetan-language poets experimented with form and content within the strictures of meter, figuration, and other elements afforded by *nyenngak* to explore such possibilities, different as their poetry may appear from what Wordsworth or any European-language poet since has envisioned?[37]

33. For examples of rigorous scholarship and excellent translations, see Sørensen 1990; Quintman 2010, 2014.

34. See for example Lin 2008; Martin 2014, 569–70; Rabsal 2016; Bhum and Gyatso forthcoming, "Tibetan Resistance to the *Mirror*," section 6.7 in "*Mirror* on Fire."

35. Said 1990, 38; Mufti 2010.

36. hooks 1989, 15.

37. Wordsworth emphatically launched his manifesto by referring to *Lyrical Ballads* as an "experiment" (Wordsworth 1800, v). On Buddhist poets experimenting with our sense of what is possible, I am indebted to Kachru 2017.

A verse by Shuchen Tsultrim Rinchen (1697–1774) speaks to these very questions:

tshangs dbyangs 'bum sde'i khrod nas nyer 'phos dri za'i rgyud stong rnam par 'khrol ba'i glu dbyangs dang//
mnyam par bsres nas bcu phrag rig pa'i gtsug lag rab 'byams sgra don sbas pa'i rgyan nyid du//
ches cher song ba'i legs bshad snyan dgu thos pa 'dzin pa'i bcud du 'dzad pa med 'jo bas//
yid can thams cad gzigs pa'i sar 'khrid rgyal kun skyed ma dbyangs kyi rgyal mo mgrin par rol//

Dally in my throat, queen of song, mother of all buddhas who leads sentient beings to the all-seeing state
by inexhaustibly yielding nectar for the ears—many sweet turns of phrase that have become
the very ornaments of sound, sense, and riddles—the vast ten fields of learning,
modulating melody as you play the thousand-stringed gandharva lute that sprang from the multitudes of Brahmā's voice.[38]

This is a manifestly virtuosic composition, underscored by nineteen-syllable metrical lines, the sophisticated use of poetic figures (*rgyan*, Skt. *alaṃkāra*), and mythic allusions. Praising Yangchenma (Skt. Sarasvatī), patron goddess of *nyenngak*, the verse intertwines notions of wisdom and eloquence. Yangchenma is capable of leading sentient beings to the omniscient state of buddhahood. She does this by "yielding nectar for the ears" with her "sweet turns of phrase" that take the ornamental forms of recognized poetic figures. Her phrases collectively constitute the ten fields of learning (*rig gnas*, Skt. *vidyāsthāna*), that is, everything worth knowing. All of this is governed by the metaphor of Yangchenma playing her polyvocal lute. Here aesthetics are integral to the endeavors of knowledge and liberation. The ten fields of learning are characterized not by their content but by their style. And Yangchenma leads beings to omniscience through the musical methods of poetry and song.

Shuchen's words suggest the versatility, range of influence, and efficaciousness of this kind of poetry for producing knowledge and for liberation. Given the ubiquitous praises of Yangchenma by Tibetan-language poets and the vast production of *nyenngak* in general, surely we can find much more material that

38. Zhu chen Tshul khrims rin chen 1971, 284.4–284.5.

comments on the transformative potential of this tradition of poetic language, or models it in some form.[39] If we learn how to listen we may recognize some of the ingenuity, subtlety, knowledge, wit, and vision at play, and ourselves find new ways to speak, to think, and to be.

Works Cited

Avalos Cisneros, Natalie. 2015. "Interdependence as a Lifeway: Decolonization and Resistance in Transnational Native American and Tibetan Communities." Ph.D. dissertation, University of California, Santa Barbara.

Benavides, Gustavo. 1995. "Giuseppe Tucci, or Buddhology in the Age of Fascism." In *Curators of the Buddha: The Study of Buddhism under Colonialism*, edited by Donald S. Lopez Jr., 161–96. Chicago: University of Chicago Press.

Bhum, Pema. 1999. "The Heart-beat of a New Generation: A Discussion of the New Poetry" [Mi rabs gsar pa'i snying khams kyi 'phar lding/ snyan ngag gsar pa'i skor gleng ba]. Translated by Ronald Schwartz. *Lungta* (Summer): 2–16.

Bhum, Pema, and Janet Gyatso. 2017. "Condensed Tibetan Allusions." *Rivista degli Studi Orientali* 90: 169–82.

———. Forthcoming. "*Mirror* on Fire: An Ardent Reception in Tibet and Mongolia." In *A Lasting Vision: Daṇḍin's Mirror in the World of Asian Letters*, edited by Yigal Bronner. South Asia Research Series. Oxford: Oxford University Press.

Bourdieu, Pierre. 1984. *Distinction: A Social Critique of the Judgement of Taste*. Translated by Richard Nice. Cambridge: Harvard University Press. Originally published as *La Distinction: Critique sociale du jugement* (Paris: Les Éditions de Minuit, 1979).

Carpenter, Frederic Ives. 1968. *Emerson and Asia*. New York: Haskell House.

Chou, Wen-shing, and Nancy G. Lin. 2021. "Karmic Affinities: Rethinking Relations Among Tibetan Lamas and the Qing Emperor." In *Water Moon Reflections: Essays in Honor of Patricia Berger*, edited by Ellen Huang, Nancy G. Lin, Michelle McCoy, and Michelle H. Wang. China Research Monographs 77. Berkeley: IEAS Publications.

Culp, Amanda. 2018a. "Searching for Shakuntala: Sanskrit Drama and Theatrical Modernity in Europe and India, 1789–Present." Ph.D. diss., Columbia University.

———. 2018b. "Shakuntala's Storytellers: Translation and Performance in the Age of World Literature (1789–1912)." *Theatre Journal* 70, no. 2 (June): 133–52.

Dodin, Thierry, and Heinz Räther, eds. 2001. *Imagining Tibet: Perceptions, Projections, and Fantasies*. Boston: Wisdom Publications.

Ferrall, Charles. 2001. *Modernist Writing and Reactionary Politics*. Cambridge: Cambridge University Press.

39. On the kinds of Buddhist work that *snyan ngag* can do, see Bhum and Gyatso 2017, 172–74; Lin 2017, 137–44; Townsend 2021, chap. 3. On the kinds of Buddhist work that Sanskrit *kāvya* can do, see Langenberg 2013, 216–22; Kachru 2019a, 2019b, 2020; Tzohar 2019, 2021.

Fields, Rick, and Brian Cutillo, trans. 1998. *The Turquoise Bee: The Lovesongs of the Sixth Dalai Lama*. San Francisco: HarperCollins.

Figueira, Dorothy Matilda. 1991. *Translating the Orient: The Reception of Śākuntala in Nineteenth-Century Europe*. Albany: State University of New York Press.

Gold, Jonathan C. 2007. *The Dharma's Gatekeepers: Sakya Paṇḍita on Buddhist Scholarship in Tibet*. Albany: State University of New York Press.

Gruber, Peter. 1962. Foreword to *The Hundred Thousand Songs of Milarepa*. Translated and annotated by Garma C. C. Chang. New York: Oriental Studies Foundation.

Hallisey, Charles. 1995. "Roads Taken and Not Taken in the Study of Theravāda Buddhism." In *Curators of the Buddha: The Study of Buddhism under Colonialism*, edited by Donald S. Lopez Jr., 31–61. Chicago: University of Chicago Press.

Harries, Natalie Tal. 2013. "'The One Life Within Us and Abroad': Coleridge and Hinduism." In *Coleridge, Romanticism, and the Orient: Cultural Negotiations*, edited by David Vallins, Kaz Oishi, and Seamus Perry, 131–44. New York: Bloomsbury Academic.

Herling, Bradley L. 2006. *The German Gītā: Hermeneutics and Discipline in the German Reception of Indian Thought, 1778–1831*. New York: Routledge.

hooks, bell. 1989. "Choosing the Margin as a Space of Radical Openness." *Framework* 36: 15–23.

Jabb, Lama. 2015. *Oral and Literary Continuities in Modern Tibetan Literature: The Inescapable Nation*. Lanham: Lexington Books.

Kachru, Sonam. 2017. "Of Poets, Their Lies, and the Savage Fruits Thereof: Four Brief Vignettes on the Imagination in Buddhism." Paper presented at the Annual Meeting of the American Academy of Religion, Boston, MA, November 2017.

———. 2019a. "After the Unsilence of the Birds: Remembering Aśvaghoṣa's Sundarī." *Journal of Indian Philosophy* 47: 289–312.

———. 2019b. "On Learning to Overhear the 'Vanishing Poet.'" In *Readings of Śāntideva's Guide to Bodhisattva Practice*, edited by Jonathan C. Gold, Douglas S. Duckworth, and Stephen Teiser. New York: Columbia University Press.

———. 2020. "Of Doctors, Poets, and the Minds of Men: Aesthetics and Wisdom in Aśvaghoṣa's *Beautiful Nanda*." In *Buddhist Literature as Philosophy, Buddhist Philosophy as Literature*, edited by Rafal Stepien, 113–44. Albany: State University of New York Press.

Kapstein, Matthew T. 2003. "The Indian Literary Identity in Tibet." In *Literary Cultures in History: Reconstructions from South Asia*, edited by Sheldon Pollock, 747–802. Berkeley: University of California Press.

King, Matthew. 2019. *Ocean of Milk, Ocean of Blood: A Mongolian Monk in the Ruins of the Qing Empire*. New York: Columbia University Press.

King, Richard. 1999. *Orientalism and Religion: Post-Colonial Theory, India and 'The Mystic East.'* New York: Routledge.

Langenberg, Amy Paris. 2013. "Evangelizing the Happily Married Man Through Low Talk: On Sexual and Scatological Language in the Buddhist Tale of Nanda." In *Family in Buddhism*, edited by Liz Wilson, 205–35. Albany: State University of New York Press.

Lin, Nancy G. 2008. "Döndrup Gyel and the Remaking of the Tibetan Ramayana." In *Modern Tibetan Literature and Social Change*, edited by Lauran R. Hartley and Patricia Schiaffini-Vedani, 86–111. Durham: Duke University Press.

———. 2017. "Recounting the Fifth Dalai Lama's Rebirth Lineage." *Revue d'Etudes Tibétaines* 38: 119–56.

———. 2021. "Ornaments of This World: Materiality and Poetics of the Fifth Dalai Lama's Reliquary Stūpa." In *Jewels, Jewelry, and Other Shiny Things in the Buddhist Imaginary*, edited by Vanessa R. Sasson. Honolulu: University of Hawai'i Press.

Lokyitsang, Dawa. 2016. "Decolonizing Ethnographic 'Responsibility': Towards a Decolonized Praxis." *Lhakar Diaries*, October 5. Accessed July 5, 2021. https://lhakardiaries.com/2016/10/05/decolonizing-ethnographic-responsibility-towards-a-decolonized-praxis/.

———. 2017. "Are Tibetans Indigenous?" *Lhakar Diaries*, 27 December. Accessed July 5, 2021. https://lhakardiaries.com/2017/12/27/are-tibetans-indigenous/.

Lopez, Donald S., Jr., ed. 1995. *Curators of the Buddha: The Study of Buddhism Under Colonialism*. Chicago: University of Chicago Press.

———. 1998. *Prisoners of Shangri-La: Tibetan Buddhism and the West*. Chicago: University of Chicago Press.

Martin, Dan. 2014. "Indian Kāvya Poetry on the Far Side of the Himālayas: Translation, Transmission, Adaptation, Originality." In *Innovations and Turning Points: Toward a History of Kāvya Literature*, edited by Yigal Bronner, David Shulman, and Gary Tubb, 563–608. Oxford: Oxford University Press.

McGann, Jerome. 1992. "Rethinking Romanticism." *ELH* 59.3 (Autumn): 735–54.

Mufti, Aamir R. 2010. "Orientalism and the Institution of World Literatures." *Critical Inquiry* 36, no. 3 (Spring): 458–93.

O'Neill, Michael. 2005. "Romantic forms: an introduction." In *Romanticism: An Oxford Guide*, edited by Nicholas Roe, 275–91. Oxford: Oxford University Press.

Packer, Barbara. 2004. "Transcendentalism." In *Nineteenth-Century Poetry, 1800–1910*, edited by Sacvan Bercovitch, 87–136. Vol. 4 of *The Cambridge History of American Literature*. Cambridge: Cambridge University Press.

Quintman, Andrew. 2010. *The Life of Milarepa*. New York: Penguin Books.

———. 2014. *The Yogin and the Madman: Reading the Biographical Corpus of Tibet's Great Saint Milarepa*. South Asia Across the Disciplines. New York: Columbia University Press.

Rabsal, Gedun. 2016. "Vajra Melodies: Approaching the Tenth Karmapa's (1604–74) Songs (*mgur*), Poetry, and Poetics from a Tibetan Perspective." In *The Tenth Karmapa & Tibet's Turbulent Seventeenth Century*, edited by Karl Debreczeny and Gray Tuttle, 69–94. Chicago: Serindia Publications.

Rangarajan, Padma. 2014. *Imperial Babel: Translation, Exoticism, and the Long Nineteenth Century*. New York: Fordham University Press.

Rich, Adrienne. 1997. "Arts of the Possible." *The Massachusetts Review* 38.3 (Autumn): 319–37.

Said, Edward W. 1979. *Orientalism*. New York: Vintage Books. First published 1978.

———. 1990. "On Jean Genet's Late Works." *Grand Street* 36: 26–42.

Sandberg, Graham. 1906. *Tibet and the Tibetans*. London: Society for Promoting Christian Knowledge.

Sheats, Paul D. 2005. "Lyric." In *Romanticism: An Oxford Guide*, edited by Nicholas Roe, 310–31. Oxford: Oxford University Press.

Sørensen, Per K. 1990. *Divinity Secularized: An Inquiry into the Nature and Form of the Songs Ascribed to the Sixth Dalai Lama*. Vienna: Arbeitskreis für Tibetische und Buddhistische Studien, Universität Wien.

Stein, R. A. 1972. *Tibetan Civilization*. Translated by J. E. Stapleton Driver. Stanford: Stanford University Press. Originally published as *La Civilisation tibétaine* (Paris: Dunod Editeur, 1962).

Sujata, Victoria. 2005. *Tibetan Songs of Realization: Echoes from a Seventeenth-Century Scholar and Siddha in Amdo*. Leiden: Brill.

Townsend, Dominique. 2021. *A Buddhist Sensibility: Aesthetic Education at Tibet's Mindröling Monastery*. Studies of the Weatherhead East Asian Institute, Columbia University. New York: Columbia University Press.

Tucci, Giuseppe. (1949) 1999. *Tibetan Painted Scrolls*. 2 vols. Reprint, Bangkok: SDI Publications.

Tzohar, Roy. 2019. "A Tree in Bloom or a Tree Stripped Bare: Ways of Seeing in Aśvaghoṣa's *Life of the Buddha*." *Journal of Indian Philosophy* 47: 313–26.

———. 2021. "How Does It Feel to Be on Your Own: Solitude (*viveka*) in Aśvaghoṣa's *Saundarananda*." In *The Bloomsbury Research Handbook of Emotions in Classical Indian Philosophy*, edited by Maria Heim, Chakravarthi Ram-Prasad, and Roy Tzohar, 277–302. New York: Bloomsbury Academic.

Vallins, David. 2013. "Immanence and Transcendence in Coleridge's Orient." In *Coleridge, Romanticism, and the Orient: Cultural Negotiations*, edited by David Vallins, Kaz Oishi, and Seamus Perry, 119–30. New York: Bloomsbury Academic.

van der Kuijp, Leonard W. J. 1996. "Tibetan Belles-Lettres: The Influence of Daṇḍin and Kṣemendra." In *Tibetan Literature: Studies in Genre; Essays in Honor of Geshe Lhundup Sopa*, edited by José Ignacio Cabezón and Roger R. Jackson, 393–410. Ithaca: Snow Lion Publications.

Willock, Nicole. 2021. *Lineages of the Literary: Tibetan Buddhist Polymaths of Socialist China*. New York: Columbia University Press.

Wordsworth, William. 1800. Preface to *Lyrical Ballads, with Other Poems*, v–xlvi. 2nd ed. 2 vols. London: T. N. Longman and O. Rees.

Zhu chen Tshul khrims rin chen. 1971. *The Autobiography of Tshul-khrims-rin-chen of Sde-dge and Other of His Selected Writings*. Delhi: N. Lungtok & N. Gyaltsan.

The Immortal Ring of Love, Karma, and Poetry

Lama Jabb

DURING A LIFETIME of thinking, teaching, and writing Janet Gyatso has subjected a multiplicity of themes and issues concerning Tibet to critical scholarly investigation. Respecting and employing Tibetan language as the key to the Tibetan world and wisdom, she has enlightened many with her novel explorations of topics ranging from Tibetan religion, history, literature, and art to medicine and gender. Because of her long and deep immersion in Tibetan language, the central themes of her many books, articles, and talks engage consummately with the complex nervous system of Tibetan identity.

I had the karmic fortune to meet Janet Gyatso for the first time at the Tenth Seminar of the International Association for Tibetan Studies (IATS) at the University of Oxford in 2003. This was the first time ever that a relatively large cohort of Tibetan scholars from Tibet and China could attend an IATS conference. Then Janet Gyatso was the IATS president, and I particularly recall her speech to the Tibetan attendees from Tibet and the diaspora at one lunch break. She expressed unaffected delight in seeing so many Tibetan faces at the conference and enthused about the unprecedented opportunity for intellectual exchange between Tibetan and non-Tibetan scholars from around the world. She spoke of the indispensable role of Tibetan language scholarship and the paramount importance of academic freedom for the advancement of the field in general and for Tibetans in particular. Like many, I was struck and heartened by her nuanced understanding of Tibet and deep sympathy with the Tibetans.

Janet Gyatso and I have crossed paths at many intellectual gatherings since then, and we have engaged in stimulating conversations about all things Tibetan. The recurrent themes we mull over every time we meet are Tibetan literature, the role and status of Tibetan women in history and society, and female agency and representation in Tibetan creative writing. In fall 2018 at the Rubin Museum–convened *Perspectives on Padmasambhava* seminar, Janet Gyatso, Jue Liang, and I concurred that it was high time that an international conference on Tibetan women's literature was organized and reached a decision to act upon it promptly. Our discussion resulted in the *Tibetan Women Writing Symposium* organized by Erin Burke, Tashi Dekyid, Eben Yonnetti, and Andrew Taylor at the University of Virginia on April 8–10, 2022. In July 2020, I had the pleasure to present a paper on a poem of Chimay (a.k.a. Pema Tso) called "The Ring," including a translation of it, at the inaugural session held online due to the COVID-19 pandemic. Janet Gyatso and all the attendees showed genuine appreciation of the poem and the poet and spurred me to translate and comment on more of Chimay's poetry. In our subsequent meetings Janet Gyatso reiterated her strong desire to see more of Chimay's work in English.

As a result of this warm reception and encouragement, I have turned the workshop paper into an article and have translated two more famous poems by Chimay in their entirety. To my knowledge this is the first time that the work of this acclaimed modern Tibetan writer has been rendered into English. With humility and admiration, I would like to dedicate these original English translations and my short commentary to Janet Gyatso. It is wished that they honor and echo her enduring scholarship on Tibet, including her concern for the condition of Tibetan women and her love of Tibetan poetry. My English translations of "Love and Karmic Destiny" (1994), "The Tibetan Mastiff" (2009), and "The Ring" (2017) are presented chronologically, in accordance with their publication dates, in the first part of this essay. This is followed by a commentary that employs "The Ring" to explore some principal themes of Chimay's poetry, and then the Tibetan original.

Love and Karmic Destiny

Two fragmented little red heart-minds
Revived in the moonlight driven by years and months.
The pledge of faith that does not wax and wane
Leapt from the first entwining of two hands and seeped into the moon.
In those moments
Slowly parting the veil of water-laden clouds the moon flaunted its
  whiteness.
For the soul of poetry beat once again
My bloodstream gushed out of your pen nib.
However,
The heart-minds of tight secret knots of love
Borrowed a cozy abode of moonlight,
And the sweet ambrosiac wine turned to tears.
Each droplet of white light sprinkled from the moon
Might also have been the bitterness stored in our hearts.
Still, only the lasso of others' power

Bound the karmic destiny of our love.
Since that time,
Searching for those ineffaceable footprints in the moonlight,
I've hoped to gain some comfort within the expanse of nostalgia.
The story of mingled joy and woe snatched away by tyranny
Has always
Been vivid deep inside the unhazy chronicle of the heart,
Yet now I can only recite it with lamentations of anguish and woe.
Though the moon that revived in the sky got wounded in the west,
And each petal of water-laden clouds swirling over the peaks of
    earth-loaded mountains
Finished pulling the final curtain over the moon's bed,
I've never forgotten that realm wrapped in mists,
Indeed, I've never.

Tibetan Mastiff

I am a Tibetan mastiff, and I too have a life of my own.
In essence, I too am born of the union of two consciousnesses,
And am a real sentient being consciously complete with flesh, blood,
    and mass.

My bark vibrated inside the circle of snow-mountains
Amid the cold wind that made the stars shiver,
The beauty of my hair upon which the sleek dark light played
Made dim the light of the moon on the winter landscape.

When the fierce roar of blizzards devoured entire mountains and valleys
My majesty—to meet head-on and cut through the sharp cold and wind,
My ambition—to pull the stars down to earth with a single leap,
My arrogance—to run in hot pursuit of the fast-blowing wind.

Ah, Ah! Since I knew that only in my homeland was I that prince free
    from birth and death,
And that only my homeland was the realm of Shambhala,
I never gave thought to my karmic fate of the future.

That year—that master who descended like gods with compassion
    and altruism,
Who entered like bandits by cunning and coercion,

Depriving my summer of the freedom to meditate upon beauty
And depriving my stars of the freedom to talk about the sky,
Deceived all with a hurt like that.

For the door of reason is now sealed shut,
The curtain of a story hard to capture in memory spontaneously opens.

Since that time, since the unbearably heavy ring of black steel was put around my neck
Sticks and slender whips have been the reward of each mealtime.
However, for a pure and immaculate primordial nature
Permeates the essence of the trinity of my blood, flesh, and bones.
Ah, my master! Through what means can I then make myself clear inside out?

A common language spreading from the four directions pains the ear,
And many strange faces with thieving eyes shifting and shifting,
And still more, those terrifying and untrustworthy bright smiles. . .

Isn't it so? That *gongkhug*[1] of yours that wouldn't be sated even by swallowing whole the round world
Might strip and tear into pieces the trinity of my skin, flesh, and bones,
Even before my consciousness leaves my body and four elements crumble into themselves.

Inside this cage of tempered steel and concrete
My years and months have aged like that, and my tears have dried up like this.
Even so, who can put a lock on my subtle mind?
I'm always meditating upon the trinity of homeland mountains, rivers, and plains.
No one can rob my beautiful dream,
For my heart-mind is nursing the distant homeland—
The immaculate sky, the expansive earth,

1. The unique Tibetan term *gongkhug* (*'gong khug*) is retained here, but it could be unsatisfactorily translated into English as "demon bag," or even "devil's bag." It is an unfillable and impoverishing bag (*khug ma*) carried by a type of ruinous evil spirits known as *gongpo* (*'gong po*). Just as in this poem it also symbolizes insatiable and destructive greed and terrifying hatred.

Pure and bright air, cool rock mountain rivers murmuring and flowing with ease,
All things of that land where the earth and sky intersect are already fixed in my memory.

For the heart-mind of mingled hatred and hope has suffered
The gateless iron fortress on earth—
The heat and the cold of the eighteen realms of hell,
My vital organs and innards are already rotten.

Ah homeland! Would I get a chance to rest in your lap
And dream that long-cherished green dream?

It would definitely be enough to let the chill wind carry
The echo of my earth- and sky-tearing bark
And mount it just once upon the snow-mountain peaks.
Yet, my master!
Might you one day also end up smothering my door of speech?

The Ring

Though gone over are the years and come back the months,
Though the distance be just within and over that distance,
These years and months of longing and long separation
Are the ring of steel, the saṃsāra of oscillating joy and woe.

Though the mind and the mind-met heap of feelings
Are written on the pages of a mountainous book
Inside the little house ripened in karma and body,
The ring of home wears not out, be it written for a lifetime.

The little dance stage of quivering strings of music
Amid the joyous play of strobing lights, white and red,
The sudden awakening from this very dream of a song
With no lyrics is the ring of illusion in bed.

The sheer beauty of shimmering flowers has no bounds,
Bliss imbues the mind when little bees imbibe with their lips.
To be fatigued, seeking there the container and the contained,
Yet remain without home and in solitude is the ring of exhaustion.

In the expansive landscape formed with ease and grace,
When I think and reflect in tranquillity and solitude
And fold each finger inward counting the joys and woes,
The ring of past sufferings remains incalculable.

Hidden thoughts and the green garden of love,
Indelible pictures of the mind when displayed for view,
Recalling the uncoloured and natural state of youth,
To the saturated mind is the ring of emptiness.

To cast aside tales that narrate unchanging love due to
The karmic burden of hope and fear, loss, gain, and discord,
To scatter life and *lungta* soaked in muddled visions,
To the winds on the mountaintop is the ring of hope.

Consorting with the sun and the moon circling in the sky
Ends in utter despair, for the body possesses no wings.
Though little feet might gain a hold in the thin, thin clouds,
To perish on encountering the wind is the ring of karma.

How happy I would be if the ground was higher than this,
I would still reach the mountaintop even lying down.
How joyous I would be if the water was clearer than this,
The desire to bathe in the open is the ring of swaying.

In that land where the sun shines upon the snow,
The blue meadow has gathered me up into its lap.
To scramble on herding the thirty-four consonants and vowels
Imprinting footsteps in the meadow is the ring of life.

When I furiously stroke the oars roaming aimlessly
Into the sweep of the sea that blankets the earth,
To be fleetingly dazed in the abrupt fissure
Of the earth and the sky is the ring of confusion.

Should human life bound by ever-binding customs
Be wiped out by the free and untampered imagination,
Only then in a perishable world of purity would I, myself,
Fulfil every single necessary reality, the ring of desire.

The grey years and months of my solitary wandering,
Seeing no blissful worldly revels on this single visit
Are winding pictures on the surface of the earth and moon.
To not reconcile myself to that is the ring of imagination.

It is no obstacle to be merely troubled by cold winds,
Do you not think, you whose mind-core is mingled with mine?
To cocoon each other without betrayal in the warmth of the heart
And hold each other's hands tightly is the ring of promise.

During that hour when dawn and dusk take turns to arrive,
Putting on a show of all the comings and goings from inside and out,
The aimless wayward conduct of my mind running wild
Cannot be captured by limitless intellect, the ring of speech.

The Immortal Ring of Saṃsāra and Poetry[2]

Chimay (*'Chi med* or "Immortality") is the pen name of one of the most esteemed and prolific contemporary Tibetan female poets. Her real name is Palma Tso, but she is popularly known by her nom de plume. Her brooding, subjective, lyrical poetry is often concerned with life, loss, survival, and memory, and at its heart looms a profound sense of suffering. She was born in Sakyil village in Rebkong, northeastern Tibet, in 1967 and as such was tempered in the fires of the Cultural Revolution. Her father Wandi Tashi was accused of taking part in "the Revolt" during the 1950s and sentenced to ten years' imprisonment. He passed away several years after his release, when Chimay was six years old, due to injuries he had sustained in prison. Her mother Khamo Gyal was a victim of "class struggle" and suffered incessant public humiliation and torture in "struggle sessions" during the 1960s and 1970s. Chimay went to primary and secondary school in Rebkong and graduated from the Tsongon College for Nationalities in 1987. She has been teaching Tibetan language and literature ever since. She is an award-winning poet and has published numerous

2. The first draft of this article was presented online at the University of Virginia–run *Tibetan Women Writing Workshop* on 22 July 2020. I would like to extend my gratitude to the organizers—Janet Gyatso, Jue Liang, and Tashi Dekyid—and attendees for their warm reception, encouragement, and stimulating feedback, and a huge thanks to Jane Caple for her constructive insights and editorial input. This is a revised version of the article first published in the inaugural issue of *Yeshe: A Journal of Tibetan Literature, Arts and Humanities* in 2021: https://yeshe.org/the-immortal-ring-of-samsara-and-poetry/.

poems and prose pieces in literary journals and on online platforms. She has also released two books of her collected poems, *The Dreams of the Moon* (*Zla ba'i rmi lam*) in 2012 and *The Youth of Water* (*Chu'i lang tsho*) in 2016. The former was awarded the Wild Yak Prize for Literature in 2015.

Here I present my translation of Chimay's famed poem "The Ring" (*A long*), in its entirety, as an aperture onto her brilliant poetry.[3] I will make a few brief remarks about its content and form, which are seamlessly bound and charged with emotion and thought. It goes without saying that readers who are literate in Tibetan should consult the original, given at the end of the essay, for a true appreciation of the poem's arresting rhythm, haunting lyricism, and salient as well as subtle repetition of unique Tibetan words and sounds that escape translation.

The Ringed

"The Ring" is a splendid autobiographical poem characterized by technical brilliance, striking lyricism, emotional intensity, deep reflection, and intriguing abstraction. It first appeared in the Tibetan language edition of *The Journal of Nationalities Literature* (*Mi rig rtsom rig dus deb*) in 2017, a bimonthly literary magazine published by the China Writers' Association. The following year it won a literary award named after that journal. Since then it has reached a much wider audience on social media, transcending the limits of the print media and nation-state boundaries. While assisted by this new communication technology, the popular reception of the poem has ultimately been driven by its emotional and intellectual charge and the attraction of its meticulously crafted Tibetan language. Special features consciously devised by the poet appeal to the ear and the heart alike, rendering the poem striking on first encounter and triggering an urge to read it over and over again that makes it endure in the mind.

Among a multitude of other things, poetry is about remembering and being remembered through imaginative marshalling of language. John Carey states that poetry is "language made special, so that it will be remembered and valued."[4] Chimay's "The Ring" is valued and remembered through its wide circulation and repeated reading, but it is also itself an expressive mode of communication that recalls. It is a store of memories about and reflections on suffering,

3. My translation is based on a version preferred by the poet which differs slightly from the published version listed in the works cited. This can be found online at the Great Tibetan Recitation Platform (*Bod kyi gyer 'don spyi stegs chen mo*): https://mp.weixin.qq.com/s/7zuFifXN2uckBIMukcnaqA.

4. Carey 2020, 1.

strife, loneliness, love, hope, death, and poetry, recording all of this for the present and posterity. It also appears to be constituted of what Toni Morrison in her 1987 novel *Beloved* calls "rememories"—one's identity reconstructed or rediscovered through recollecting layers of often painful memories. In short, "The Ring" is a remembrance of and a meditation on the various iterations of what Tibetans call *khorwa* (*'khor ba*): *khorwa* as in saṃsāra that is diametrically opposed to Nirvana; *khorwa* as in the human condition that is, to echo William Blake, woven fine of joy and woe; and *khorwa* as in domesticity—the arduous management of family life that runs counter to the life of the religious renunciate. Chimay's poem is about her unique experience of this multivalent *khorwa*—a ring of unbroken, endless mental and physical activities that revolve around life, struggle, death, and rebirth.

Commenting on his own poetry W. B. Yeats states: "I must leave my myths and symbols to explain themselves as the years go by and one poem lights up another."[5] When we read Chimay's poetic work, each poem also brightens and sets ablaze the others with their interlaced content, imagery, and language. In her poetry one often comes across reflections on love, loss, separation, remembering, and a profound sense of suffering. There is a complex private and public dimension to this deep agony, which is often indivisibly subjective and collective. Like an old, open wound that refuses to heal, its causes and underlying conditions are never explicitly stated. Many seem unspeakable and as such remain unnamed. Given that all things—including texts—are the mere products of dependent origination (*rten 'brel gyi ngo bo tsam*), we need to appreciate Chimay's other poems and prose writing for a more nuanced understanding of "The Ring." One informative piece of writing that commands special attention is Chimay's autobiographical essay "Tibetan Women on Tibetan Women's Literature" (*Bod mos bod mo'i rtsom rig gleng ba*).[6] This candid account of her life and creative intellectual journey sheds vital light on her poetry. There is no space here to undertake even a cursory review of that and Chimay's other literary output, but reference to two of her other poems will go some way to contextualising the poem under review. Even a fleeting appreciation of these acclaimed works can help to illuminate "The Ring."

"Love and Karmic Destiny" (*Brtse dungs dang las dbang*) is Chimay's first ever published poem. As can be seen in the translation above it is in free verse

5. As quoted in Parkinson 2001, 122.

6. 'Chi med 2017, 41–84. Although I have relied on the version published by Mtsho sngon mi rigs dpe skrun khang (Tsongon People's Press), a more recent edited version of this essay can be accessed online via the *Amnye Machen Messaging Platform* (*A myes rma chen 'phrin stegs*): https://mp.weixin.qq.com/s/FZHNbfR2jhVTTjNokS9IVg.

form. It was published in the literary magazine *Drangchar* (*Sbrang char*) in 1994 and awarded the Drangchar Prize for Literature in 1997. It is a tragic love poem that begins promisingly with the resuscitation of two broken hearts ("two fragmented little red heart-minds") in the moonlight thanks to the long passage of time. This restoration reaffirms and deepens enduring love and gives new life to poetry: "For the soul of poetry beat once again/ My bloodstream gushed out of your pen nib." The unclouded moon reignites thwarted love and poetry utters it. These are two cathartic sites of nature and culture—both non-corporeal—where the two long-separated lovers can meet. However, the lack of freedom and the tyranny of the other make actual reunion in the flesh impossible. This turns their love into a bitter tale of happiness and suffering that the poet is compelled to read with anguish and lamentation. As the poem draws to a close even the moon whose light first revived the lovers is fatally wounded in the west. Swirling clouds on the mountaintop draw the final curtain over the fallen moon. Only the poet's refusal to forget keeps alive this record of love and karmic destiny.

These themes of love, hurt, loss of freedom, violence, and remembrance resonate with redoubled force in another of Chimay's award-winning free verse poems, "The Tibetan Mastiff" (*'Brog khyi*). This lauded poem, for which Chimay won the Gangjen Metok Prize for Literature in 2012, was first published in the Tibetan poetry magazine *Gangjen Metok* (*Gangs rgyan me tog*) in 2009. It is a powerful work about the rise, fall, ongoing plight, and undying spirit of the proud, independent, and fearsome Tibetan mastiff. The measured tone with which it starts immediately crescendos into a loud bark as the mastiff starts narrating its tragic tale:

> I am a Tibetan mastiff, and I too have a life of my own.
> In essence, I too am born of the union of two consciousnesses,
> And am a real sentient being consciously complete with flesh, blood, and mass.
>
> My bark vibrated inside the circle of snow-mountains
> Amid the cold wind that made the stars shiver,
> The beauty of my hair upon which the sleek dark light played
> Made dim the light of the moon on the winter landscape.
>
> When the fierce roar of blizzards devoured entire mountains and valleys
> My majesty—to meet head-on and cut through the sharp cold and wind,
> My ambition—to pull the stars down to earth with a single leap,
> My arrogance—to run in hot pursuit of the fast-blowing wind.

The poem goes on to announce the arrival of a cunning and coercive master, resulting in the subjugation and exiling of this once almighty Tibetan guardian and the loss of its homeland. Its tone decreases back to a steady, dignified pace as this story of hurt, repression, and mental resilience unfolds. The Tibetan mastiff whose awesome bark resonated within the ring of snow-mountains is stripped of its freedom, independence, and wild habitat. It is driven into exile to a distant urbanized landscape that contrasts sharply with its pristine mountainous home. Now it remains chained with an "unbearably heavy ring of black steel" around its neck and is subjected to relentless torture. As it grows old inside a "cage of tempered steel and concrete," its tears dry up and it unfailingly meditates upon the "homeland mountains, rivers and plains." The Tibetan mastiff fights off mind control ("Who can put a lock on my subtle mind?"), embraces homeland within the mind, and refuses to give up its dreams even though it suffers hell on earth. The poem ends with a potent mix of imagery depicting an infernal scene, longing for home, and hope and horror. The Tibetan mastiff fears that one day its master might completely silence its voice, but then expresses the ultimate satisfaction it would feel were the wind—just once—to carry its "earth- and sky-tearing bark" and mount it upon the snow-mountain peaks. In her autobiographical essay Chimay reveals that Toni Morrison's writings on the hardship and suffering of Black people in the United States inspired "The Tibetan Mastiff," which is a metonym (*bsdus gzugs*) for her own reawakened pain.[7]

In polished formal verse "The Ring" continues Chimay's treatment of the intermingled aspects of individual and collective tragedy. Although taking a more personal turn, it addresses the same themes of love, loss, strife, and the strong poetic will to remember what she has experienced in her life. In one of her illuminating review articles, Chimay opines that to capture and express one's true self with transparency is the function and soul of poetry. She believes that "it is to lose the life and soul of poetry when one writes poetry without prioritizing oneself as the subject and looks for subjects and feelings in other things unconnected to oneself."[8] This notion of poetry informs "The Ring"

7. 'Chi med 2017, 74.

8. 'Chi med 2017, 107: *rang nyid brjod byar bya rgyu gtso gnad du mi 'jog par snyan ngag 'bri skabs rang nyid dang 'brel ba med pa'i bya dngos gzhan kyi steng nas brjod bya dang tshor ba 'tshol bar byas na snyan ngag gyi bla dang srog stor pa red.* In her autobiographical essay Chimay also touches on this proclivity for frank personal accounts of life in poetry often revealing inner torments. She was influenced by the confessional poetry of Sylvia Plath. After reading Plath's "Daddy" Chimay composed many poems including "Dear Mother, Why Were You in Such a Hurry to Leave?" (*A ma lags/ khyed rang phebs par de 'dra'i brel don ci/*). See 'Chi med 2017, 72–74. Chimay's central belief that good poetry must capture real life is also vividly evident

which focuses on the poet herself and reveals a life born of hardship, loneliness, and suffering ("The ring of past sufferings remains incalculable"), and a life dedicated to learning and teaching Tibetan language and writing Tibetan poetry ("To scramble on herding the thirty-four consonants and vowels/ Imprinting footsteps in the meadow is the ring of life"). Through a mixture of directness and abstraction "The Ring" also exposes stifling aspects of domesticity, challenges of married life, and the juggling of family, work, and writing ("The ring of home wears not out, be it written for a lifetime . . . Yet remain without home and in solitude is the ring of exhaustion").

Through a cluster of metaphors "The Ring" reveals aspects of Chimay's lived experiences "by flashes of lightning."[9] Each metaphor pegged to the recurrent image of the ring is an intense illumination in distilled brevity. The reader's encounter with this set of images carries them on a journey through the poet's life into the deep interior of the poem. Ultimately "The Ring" seems to concern Chimay's inner life tempered with pain. Just as in Emily Dickinson's work, "The Ring" and similarly themed poems appear to communicate "some irremediable shock" that Chimay has endured.[10] Like many of Chimay's poems "The Ring" is written for those who Shakespeare's Hamlet unforgettably calls "wonder-wounded hearers" (*Hamlet* 5.1).[11] Her "phrase of sorrow," recollection

---

in her moving appraisal of Naro's (Na ro) free verse poem "Mother and Her Life Wisdom" (*A ma dang mo'i 'tsho ba'i shes rab*). Her high esteem of this poem lies in its true to life portrayal of an ordinary mother in a farming village forged by fruitful yet relentless physical labor. Triggered by this poem Chimay recalls her own mother as a woman of strength, independence, and indomitable spirit who comes to epitomize all hardworking Tibetan farmers. See 'Chi med 2018, 149–63.

9. In 1842 Samuel Taylor Coleridge described the great Shakespearean actor Edmund Kean in these immortal words: "To see him act, is like reading Shakespeare by flashes of lightning." See Coleridge 1917, 44.

10. Detecting the "irremediable shock" conveyed by Emily Dickinson's poetry, the cultural critic and libertarian thinker Isabel Paterson stated: "There are poems also which indicate that Emily endured some irremediable shock, more profound than a parting in life." See Pohl 1933, 480. Chimay acknowledges the influence of Emily Dickinson on her poetry. As a young poet she wrote several love poems inspired by Dickinson's poetic treatment of love and life including "Love and Karmic Destiny." See 'Chi med 2017, 71–72.

11. The verse in full reads:

What is he whose grief
Bears such an emphasis, whose phrase of sorrow
Conjures the wand'ring stars, and makes them stand
Like wonder-wounded hearers? This is I,
Hamlet the Dane.

of often painful memories and self-reflection both engage and further sting the already wounded readers.[12]

The Ring Itself

One could be forgiven for overlooking the arduous crafting that goes into the composition of a fine poem like "The Ring." Its lyrical beauty and seemingly natural fluidity might make the reader take this aspect of laborious devising for granted. If we reread the poem closely with a consideration of its style, Chimay's conscious verbal inventiveness becomes apparent. Language is manipulated in a deliberately creative way to simultaneously communicate meaning and draw attention to itself. Unlike Chimay's early poems that are mostly in free verse, "The Ring" and many of her later poems are predominantly metrical compositions. This reflects her esteem for the varied and rich Tibetan literary tradition and deliberate turn to the practice of sophisticated formal verse informed by it.[13] With regards to meter, "The Ring" features fifteen adroitly worked out stanzas, each consisting of four ten-syllabled lines. Each syllable is a pronounced beat. For scansion the syllables are read in pairs and in most cases each pair is a single word that forms the basic metrical unit. This measured flow of two-syllabled words makes up the rhythmical backbone of the poem:

ཕར་སོང་ ལོ་དང་ ཚུར་འོང་ ཟླ་བ་ ཡིན་ཡང་།།
བར་ཐག་ བར་ཐག་ དེ་ཡི་ ཕར་ཚུར་ ཡིན་ཡང་།།
དྲན་བཞིན་ རིང་དུ་ གྱེས་པའི་ ལོ་ཟླ་ འདི་དག།
རེས་སྐྱིད་ རེས་སྡུག་ འཁོར་བ་ ལུགས་ཀྱི་ ཨ་ལོང་།།

Depending on one's preferred reading style, individual lines can be read in one breath or with a slight pause immediately after the third syllable pair. Such choice is determined by the tempo, tone, and mood one senses in the poem and the elements one wishes to emphasise when reciting. The introduction of a short pause after the sixth syllable (which is frequently the last phoneme of the third word) makes the flow of sounds smoother and more effortless. While

12. For examples of Chimay's introspective poems characterized by reflection on love, longing, and inner torment see "I Long in This Way in the Last Month of Spring" (*Dpyid zla tha mar ngas 'di ltar dran*) in 'Chi med 2018, 148–51; "Lama Tsongkhapa who Longed for his Mother on the Summit of Gandan Mountain" (*Dga' ldan ri bo'i rtse nas A ma dran myong ba'i bla ma tsonag kha pa*) in 'Chi med 2019; "One Thousand Years of Yearning" (*Lo ngo stong gi re sgug*) in 'Chi med 2017, 20–21; and "The Crystal Stamen" (*Shel gyi ze'u 'bru*) in 'Chi med 2016, 15–17.

13. 'Chi med 2017, 83–84.

drawing attention to the four remaining syllables and placing particular stress on the fourth word, it also allows the reader to finish the line in a more relaxed and unhurried manner. The number of such pauses and their specific placement within the metrical line is not set in stone. To a certain degree it is dictated by which aspects of the overall rhythmic pattern one wishes to stress.

Another distinct feature of "The Ring" is the frequent use of an incredibly contracted and distilled form of Tibetan collocation. More often than not these collocations are two-syllabled words made up of two different terms. Their use is an integral part of the ten-syllabled poetic sound pattern of "The Ring" and its chiselled diction. As the two constituting units of these compound words are often semantic opposites, they might convey either one single meaning or two or more separate denotations within a given context. Their specific placement might even inject contradictory meanings. This sematic flexibility and multivalence enhance the poem by deepening and complicating it:

ཕར་ཚུར།	ཕོ་ཁྲ།	དཀར་དམར།	སྣོད་བཅུད།
དགའ་སྡུག	རེ་དོགས།	འགལ་འདུ།	ཐོབ་ཤོར།
ཕན་ཚུན།	ཞོགས་སྲོད།	ཕྱི་ནང་།	འགྲོ་འདུག

The employment of such collocations enriches "The Ring" in several ways. First, as they are mostly constituted of two monosyllabic words and are in common currency, they furnish the poem with a steady rhythm and, like healthy heartbeats, infuse it with a sense of security or comfort. Most of these collocations have high frequency usage and this linguistic familiarity—for the Tibetan reader—endows the poem with a quality of intimacy even though it is quite abstract in parts. Second, the multivalence of such collocations creates ambiguity, that attribute celebrated by William Empson as a salient feature of poetic richness. This display of ambiguity introduces indeterminacies, suggests various meanings, opens up multiple readings, and also sometimes unites the seemingly disparate elements of a complex whole. Third, the frequent use of these multivalent collocations provides the poem with unfathomable depth. Their ambiguities and their pairings and juxtapositions of words, images, ideas, and emotions allow us to dig deep into the poem, thus ferrying us closer and closer to the inner world of the poet.

Chimay's poem also contains pairings and juxtapositions of distinct entities that are not overtly demonstrated through actual collocations but are arranged in pairs within a single line or separate lines and stanzas. They are sometimes just hinted at. As matches and correlated or contrasted entities that are obvious to the Tibetan reader they can often be overlooked. For instance, *phar song lo, tshur 'ong dza ba, sa 'di, chu 'di, gangs, spang, sa gzhi,* and *nyi zla* are scattered throughout the poem forming a repeat pattern. Like the compound words these pairings and juxtapositions underline both disunity and fusion of separate entities. Another juxtaposition that is not made explicit but that pervades the poem like breath is that of life and death.

Conclusion—Translation Escapees

Repetition is a prominent formal feature of Chimay's poem. The overall rhythmic pattern and the unique collocations are both forms of repetition. There is also a pervasive and arresting alliterative presence in the Tibetan original which my translation attempts to mimic but does not necessarily succeed in doing justice to it.[14] The ring (*A long*) is a motif reiterated in each stanza mirroring its referent, saṃsāra—that perpetual cycle of recurrent joy, woe, life, death, and rebirth. John Hoskyns, a seventeenth-century British scholar of rhetoric, states that "in speech there is no repetition without importance."[15] The repetitions in Chimay's poem are not just there for stylistic reasons but also for hammering home the content, thereby confirming the Tibetan saying, "One must emphatically repeat what is urgent" (*gal po che la nan bshad*).

These diverse forms of repetition are one of several aspects of Chimay's poem that do not easily lend themselves to translation. Besides the untranslatability of the Tibetan meter, sound patterns, and cadence, there are many words and phrases that have multiple meanings and which are jammed with visual and symbolic significances that escape translation. To cite a few of these fugitives:

འཁོར་བ།　　སྣོད་བཅུད།　　ལན་ཆགས།　　རླུང་རྟ།
ཁང་བགྲོད་ལག་བགྲོད།　　ཅི་བསམ་འདི་དྲན་མེད་པ།
སྣང་བ།　　གནས་ལུགས།

Although I have rendered all these terms into English bar one, there are neither singular "accurate" ways of translating them nor exact English equivalents. The context of the poem in its original and target languages and the assumed degree of multicultural sensibility and knowledge of the audience affect the

14. For my tentative reflections on the challenges and rewards entailed in the translation of Tibetan poetry see my keynote lecture given at the Lotsawa Translation Workshop in October 2018, available at https://conference.tsadra.org/session/an-act-of-bardo-translating-tibetan-poetry.

15. See Kermode 2000, 19.

translator's judgement. For instance, I have left *lungta* (*rlung rta*) untranslated for the readers of Janet Gyato's Festschrift but might translate it as "fortune" for an audience assumed to be unfamiliar with the term and unlikely to explore its significance even when prompted by a footnote. *Lungta* can be translated literally as "windhorse" or liberally as "fortune." It signifies more than just a thin piece of paper or stretches of material or other artifacts imprinted with holy images and prayers used in a range of private and public rituals. In its common usage it denotes fortune, fame, deeds, and the capricious success and failure of us mortals. It is left untranslated here due to its multivalence and complex cultural associations and with a view to letting it act as a doorway to another translation escapee, the Tibetan cultural world that supplies the bloodstream of Chimay's poem. In concordance with Arthur Schopenhauer's misgivings about the translatability of poetry, I hope that I have managed to transpose "The Ring" into English albeit "awkwardly."[16]

For a more nuanced understanding of the poem and a fuller appreciation of Chimay's imaginative deployment of Tibetan language and her immersion in the Tibetan literary tradition, I recommend the reader to savour "The Ring" in the Tibetan original. This is not just to offset the limitations of translation but also, most importantly, for the simple fact that Chimay has composed "The Ring" through a painstaking exploration of the resourcefulness of the Tibetan language. For her the making of Tibetan poetry is shaped by one's real life and the ability to mine the Tibetan language with dogged determination as encapsulated by this Tibetan epigram, which Chimay uses to close her autobiographical essay:

ཕ་སྐད་རུས་པ་ཡིན་ཡང་དམུར་དགོས།།
མ་ཡིག་ས་རྟོད་ཡིན་ཡང་རྨོ་དགོས།།

Though the father tongue is a bone, one must gnaw at it.
Though the mother letter is a wilderness, one must plough it.[17]

16. Schopenhauer (1992, 33) states: "Poems cannot be translated; they can only be transposed, and that is always awkward."

17. 'Chi med 2017, 84.

The Poems in the Original Tibetan

བཅོ་དུངས་དང་ལས་དབང་།

ཆག་གྲུམ་ཤོར་བའི་དམར་ཆུང་གི་ཡིད་སེམས་གཉིས།
ལོ་ཟླས་དེད་པའི་ཟླ་ངོགས་ནས་སླར་ཡང་སོས།
བྲི་གང་མེད་པའི་ཡིད་ཆས་ཀྱི་དམ་བཅའ་དེ།
ཐོག་མའི་ལག་ཟུང་བསྣོལ་བ་ལས་འཕོས་ཏེ་ཟླ་བར་འཐིམ།
སྐབས་དེ་དག་ལ།
ཆུ་འཛིན་གྱི་སེང་རས་དཔལ་གྱིས་སྤྱི་ཞིང་ཟླ་བས་དཀར་ཉམས་ངོམ།
སྙན་ངག་གི་བླ་སྲོག་སླར་ལྷང་བས།
ཁྱེད་ཀྱི་སྨྱུག་རྩེ་ནས་བདག་གི་ཁྲག་རྒྱུན་ལུད།
ཡིན་ན་ཡང་།
བཅོ་དུངས་ཀྱི་མདུད་རྒྱ་དམ་པའི་ཡིད་སེམས་ཀྱིས།
རྫོད་སྙིད་ཀྱི་ཁང་བཟང་ཟླ་ངོགས་ལ་གཡར་ཞིང་།
ཞིམ་མངར་གྱི་མདུད་རྩེ་མིག་ཆུ་རུ་གྲུབ།
ཟླ་བ་ལས་གཏོར་བའི་འོད་དཀར་གྱི་ཟེགས་མ་རེ་རེ།
ངེད་ཅག་སེམས་ཁོང་ན་ཉར་བའི་འཁང་སེམས་ཡིན་ཡང་སྲིད་དེ།
གཞན་དབང་གི་འཆིང་ཞགས་ཁོ་ནས།
ང་ཚོའི་བཅོ་དུངས་ཀྱི་ལས་དབང་བསྡམས།
དུས་དེ་ནས།
ཟླ་ངོགས་ཀྱི་བསུབ་ཏུ་མེད་པའི་རྐང་རྗེས་དེ་འཚོལ་བཞིན།
ཕྱིར་དྲན་གྱི་གློང་ནས་བདེ་བ་ཞིག་འཐོབ་པར་རེ།
བཙན་དབང་གིས་ཁྱེར་བའི་སྙིད་སྡུག་འདྲེས་མའི་གཏམ་རྒྱུད།
ནམ་ཡིན་ཡང་།
མོག་མོག་མ་ཡིན་པའི་སྙིང་ཁོང་གི་དེབ་ཐེར་དུ་གསལ་ནའང་།
ད་ལྟ་སྐྱོ་སྡུག་གི་སྨྲེ་སྔགས་ཁོ་ནས་གློག་འཇོན་བྱེད་དགོས་བྱུང་།
བར་སྣང་ནས་སོས་པའི་ཟླ་བ་ནུབ་ཕྱོགས་ནས་རྨུས་ཤིང་།
ས་འཛིན་གྱི་རྩེ་ན་འཁྲིགས་པའི་ཆུ་འཛིན་གྱི་འདབ་མ་རེ་རེས།
ཟླ་བའི་མནལ་སར་མཐའ་མཇུག་གི་ཡོལ་རས་འཐེན་ཟིན་ན་ཡང་།
ངས་སྨྱུག་ལོང་གིས་གཡོགས་པའི་ཞིང་ཁམས་དེ་བརྗེད་མ་མྱོང་།
ང་མ་མ་མྱོང་།

འབྲོག་ཁྱི།

ང་ནི་འབྲོག་ཁྱི་ཞིག་སྟེ། ང་ལའང་རང་ཉིད་ཕོ་ནར་དབང་བའི་འཚོ་སྟངས་ཤིག་ཡོད།
མ་གཞི་ནས། ང་རང་ཡང་རྣམ་ཤེས་གཉིས་ཀྱི་འཕྲད་སྦྱོར་ལས་བྱུང་ཞིང་།
ཤ་ཁྲག་གདོས་བཅས་ཀྱི་ཀུན་གཞི་ཚང་བའི་སེམས་ཅན་རྣལ་མ་ཞིག་ཡིན།

བདག་གི་ཟུག་སྐད་ནི་གངས་ཀྱི་ར་བ་ན་གཡོ་ཞིང་།
སྐར་མར་ཕོང་འདར་སློང་བའི་གྲང་རླུང་གི་ཁྲོད་དུ།
གནག་རྫུམ་འོད་ཀྱིས་རྩེན་པའི་སྤྱུ་ཁ་ཡི་མཛེས་ཉམས་ཀྱིས།
དགུན་ལྗོངས་ཟླ་བའི་འོད་སྣང་མོག་པོར་བསྒྱུར།

བུ་ཡུག་གི་གད་རྒྱངས་དྲག་པོས་རི་ཀླུང་ཧྲིལ་གྱིས་འགེམས་དུས།
ཅག་དང་བསེར་བུ་ཐོད་ལ་བླངས་ཤིང་ཐད་ཀྱིས་གཤགས་པའི་ངའི་ཟིལ་ཤུགས།
མཚོང་ཐེངས་གཅིག་གིས་སྐར་ཚོགས་ས་ལ་འདྲུད་སྙིང་འདོད་པའི་ངའི་ཧམ་སེམས།
བསེར་མ་རླུང་གི་རྒྱུ་ཕྱོགས་ལའང་རྩོལ་གྱིས་རྗེས་འདེད་གཏོང་བའི་ངའི་ང་རྒྱལ།

ཨ་ཨ། ཕ་ཡུལ་ཕོ་ན་ནས་རང་ཉིད་ད་གཟོད་སྐྱེ་འཆི་མི་མངའ་བའི་རྒྱལ་སྲས་དེ་ཡིན་ཞིང་།
རང་གི་ཕ་ཡུལ་ཕོ་ན་ནི་ད་གཟོད་ཤམ་བྷ་ལའི་ཞིང་དུ་ངེས་པས།
ངས་འབྱུང་འགྱུར་གྱི་ལས་སྐལ་ལ་བསམ་གཞིག་བཏང་མ་མྱོང་ཨང་།

ལོ་དེར། ལྷ་ཚོགས་བཞིན་སྙིང་རྗེ་དང་གཞན་དོན་གྱིས་བབས་ཤིང་།
ཧག་རྒྱུན་བཞིན་གཡོ་སྒྱུ་དང་བཙན་ཤུགས་ཀྱིས་འཛུལ་བའི་བདག་པོ་དེས།
ངའི་དབྱར་གཞུང་ལ་མཛེས་སྡུག་སྒོམ་དབང་མེད་ཅིང་།
ངའི་སྐར་ཚོགས་ལ་ནམ་མཁའ་གླིང་དབང་མེད་པར།
ཡོད་ཚད་ན་ཟུག་ཅིག་གིས་དེ་ལྟར་བསླུས།

ད་ནི་གནས་ལུགས་ཀྱི་སྒོ་མོར་རྒྱ་བཏབ་པས།
དྲན་ཡུལ་དུ་འདུ་དཀའ་བའི་གཏམ་རྒྱུད་ཅིག་གི་ཡོལ་རས་ངང་གིས་ཕྱེས།

དུས་དེ་ནས། ཐེག་དཀའ་བའི་ལྕགས་ནག་གི་ཨ་ལོང་དེ་བདག་གི་མགུལ་དུ་བསྒྲོན་པ་ནས།
དབྱུག་པ་དང་ལྕག་ཚན་ཕྲ་མོ་ཇ་ཚན་རེའི་གཏང་རག་ཡིན་ཡང་།
ལྷོད་མེད་ཅིང་གཡའ་བྲལ་བའི་གདོད་མའི་རང་གཤིས་ཤིག
ངའི་ཤ་ཁྲག་རུས་གསུམ་གྱི་བཅུད་དུ་སིམ་ཡོད་པས།

ང་ཡི་བདག་པོ་ཨ། ཐབས་ཅི་ཞིག་གིས་ད་གཟོད་ངས་རང་ཉིད་ཕྱི་གསལ་ནང་གསལ་ཞིག་བྱ་ཐུབ་བམ།

ཡུལ་མི་རང་བཞིན་པའི་སྐད་རིགས་ཤིག་ཕྱོགས་བཞི་ནས་མཆེད་པ་རྣར་གཟན་ཞིང་།
ཀུན་མིག་ལིང་ལིང་བསྒྱུར་ཅིང་རྒྱུས་མེད་པའི་ངོ་གདོང་མང་པོ་དང་།

ད་དུང་། ཞེད་སྣང་སློང་ཞིང་ཡིད་རྗེན་བྲལ་བའི་འཛུམ་མདངས་དེ་དག……
མ་ཡིན་ནམ། ཁྱོད་ཀྱི་འཇིག་རྟེན་རིལ་མོ་ཁྱུར་མིད་བཏང་ཡང་ཚིམ་པ་མེད་པའི་འགོང་ཁུག་དེས།
རྣམ་ཤེས་བེམ་པོར་མ་བྲལ་ཞིང་འབྱུང་བཞི་རང་སར་མ་འཐོར་གོང་ལ།
ངའི་ཤ་རུས་པགས་གསུམ་སོ་སོར་དབྲལ་ཚོད་རེད།

རྡོ་ལྕགས་དང་ཨར་འདམ་གྱི་གཟེབ་དྲ་འདི་ནས།
ངའི་ལོ་ཟླ་དེ་ལྟར་རྒས་ཤིང་ངའི་མིག་ཆུ་འདི་ལྟར་བསྐམས།
ཡིན་ནའང་། ངའི་སེམས་པ་ཕྲ་མོར་སྔོ་ཟླ་རྒྱག་ཐུབ་མཁན་སུ་ཞིག་ཡོད།
དུས་ནམ་ཡང་། ཕ་ཡུལ་གྱི་རི་ཆུ་ཐང་གསུམ་བསྒོམས་ནས་ཡོད།
ངའི་མཛེས་སྡུག་གི་རྨི་ལམ་སུས་ཀྱང་འཕྲོག་ནུས་མིན་ཏེ།
ཡིད་སེམས་ཀྱིས་རྒྱང་རིང་གི་ཕ་ཡུལ་འཚོས་ནས་ཡོད།
གཡའ་དག་པའི་ནམ་མཁའ། ཁོད་ཡངས་པའི་ས་གཞི།
དྭངས་གཙང་གི་མཁའ་དབུགས། ལྷུང་ལྷུང་ལྡོད་ཀྱིས་འབབ་པའི་ཟ་ཆུ་བསིལ་མ།
གནམ་ས་བསྡོལ་མཚམས་ཀྱི་གནས་དེའི་ཡོད་ཚད། ངའི་དྲན་ཡུལ་ལ་འཐས་ནས་ཡོད།

མི་ཡུལ་གྱི་ལྕགས་མཁར་སྒོ་མེད།
དམྱལ་ཁམས་བཅོ་བརྒྱད་ཀྱི་ཚ་གྲང་།
ཞེ་འཁོན་དང་རེ་སྨོན་འདྲེས་མའི་ཡིད་སེམས་ཀྱིས་མྱངས་པས།
ང་ཡི་དོན་ལྷ་སྟོད་དྲུག་རུལ་ནས་ཡོད།

ཕ་ཡུལ་ཨ། ང་རང་ཁྱོད་ཀྱི་པང་དུ་བསྙེས་ཏེ།
ཡུན་རིང་ཉར་བའི་རྨི་ལམ་ལྡང་གུ་དེ་རྨི་བའི་སྐལ་བ་ཞིག་ལྡན་ཨེ་སྲིད།

གནམ་ས་རལ་བར་བྱེད་པའི་བདག་གི་ཟུག་སྐད་ཀྱི་བྲག་ཅ་གང་།
སྐྱི་བསེར་རླུང་གིས་བསྣམས་ཏེ།
གངས་རྩེར་ལན་གཅིག་བསྐྱོན་དབང་ཡོད་ན་ཅིས་ཀྱང་ཆོག་སྟེ།

ང་ཡི་བདག་པོ་ལགས། ནམ་ཞིག་གི་དུས་ན།
ཁྱོད་ཀྱིས་ངའི་ངག་སྙོའང་བསྡམ་ཨེ་འགྲོ།

ཨ་ལོང་།

ཕར་སོང་ལོ་དང་ཚུར་འོང་ཟླ་བ་ཡིན་ཡང་།།
བར་ཐག་བར་ཐག་དེ་ཡི་ཕར་ཚུར་ཡིན་ཡང་།།
དྲན་བཞིན་རིང་དུ་གྱེས་པའི་ལོ་ཟླ་འདི་དག།
རེས་སྐྱིད་རེས་སྡུག་འཁོར་བ་ལྟུགས་ཀྱི་ཨ་ལོང་།།

སེམས་དང་སེམས་ཀྱིས་མྱངས་པའི་ཚོར་བའི་ཕུང་པོ།།
ལས་དང་ལུས་ལ་སྨིན་པའི་ཁང་ཆུང་ཕུ་ན།།
ཤོག་ངོར་བྲིས་པའི་སྒླིགས་བུ་རི་ལ་བསླམས་ཀྱང་།།
ཚེ་གང་བྲིས་པས་མི་ཟད་ཁྲིམ་གྱི་ཨ་ལོང་།།

རོལ་མོའི་རྒྱུད་སྐུད་འདར་བའི་གར་གྱི་སྙིགས་བུ།།
དཀར་དམར་སྒྲོག་འོད་འཁྱུགས་པའི་རོལ་རྩེད་ངོགས་ན།།
གཞས་ལ་ཚིག་འབྲུ་མེད་པའི་རྨི་ལམ་དེ་ག།
ཧོལ་གྱིས་སད་པ་མལ་གྱི་འཁྲུལ་བའི་ཨ་ལོང་།།

མི་རྟོག་ཁྲ་ཆིལ་མཛེས་ལ་ཚོད་ཅིག་མི་འདུག།
སྤྲང་ཆུང་མཆུ་རྩེས་འཛིབ་ན་རང་སེམས་བདེ་ཡོང་།།
སྟོད་བཅུད་ཕར་ལ་བཅལ་བས་ཨ་ཐང་ཆད་དེ།།
གཞི་མེད་གཅིག་པུར་གནས་པ་ངལ་བའི་ཨ་ལོང་།།

ལྟོད་མོ་ལྟོད་ཀྱིས་གྲུབ་པའི་ཡུལ་ལྗོངས་ཡངས་པོར།།
གླིང་འཛགས་སྟོང་བའི་ངང་ནས་མཉེ་བསམ་འཁོར་ཏེ།།
དཀའ་སྡུག་བགྱང་བའི་མཛུབ་མོ་རིམ་གྱིས་བཀུག་ན།།
གྲངས་ཀྱིས་མི་ལང་འདས་སོང་སྐྱོ་བའི་ཨ་ལོང་།།

གབ་པའི་སེམས་འགྱུ་དྭངས་པའི་གླིང་ག་ལྷང་གུ།
བཤམས་ཏེ་བལྟས་ན་བསྲུབས་མེད་སེམས་ཀྱི་རི་མོ།།

ཁ་དོག་ལང་ཚོ་མ་བྲིས་རང་བྱུང་ཉམས་ཀྱིས།།
སེམས་པའི་ཡིད་ལ་དྲན་པ་སྟོང་བའི་ཨ་ལོང་།།

རེ་དོགས་འགལ་འདུ་ཐོབ་ཤོར་ལན་ཆགས་ཀླུ་མོས།།
མི་ཕྱེད་དུངས་པ་བརྗོད་པའི་གཏམ་རྒྱུད་པོར་ནས།།
རང་སྣང་རྟོག་མས་བརྟན་པའི་ཚེ་དང་རླུང་རྟ།།
རི་རྩེའི་རླུང་ལ་ཕྱུར་བ་རེ་བའི་ཨ་ལོང་།།

ནམ་མཁའི་དབྱིངས་ལ་འཁོར་བའི་ཉི་ཟླར་འགྲོགས་ན།།
ལུས་ལ་གཤོག་པ་མེད་འདིས་རེ་ཐག་ཆད་འགྲོ།།
སྤྲིན་པ་སྲབ་སྲབ་རྐང་ཚུང་སྟེགས་ལ་ལོན་ཀྱང་།།
རླུང་བུ་གར་འཕྲུད་འཛིག་པ་ལས་ཀྱི་ཨ་ལོང་།།

ས་འདི་འདི་ལས་མཐོ་ན་ཅི་འདྲའི་སྐྱིད་ཨང་།།
ང་རང་ཉལ་ཏེ་བསྡད་ཀྱང་རི་རྩེར་སླེབས་འགྲོ།།
ཆུ་འདི་འདི་ལས་དྭངས་ན་ཅི་འདྲའི་སྤྲོ་ཨང་།།
སྒྲིབ་ཡོལ་མེད་པར་འབྲུད་འདོད་སྐོམ་པའི་ཨ་ལོང་།།

གངས་ལ་ཉི་ཟེར་འཕྲོས་པའི་ཡུལ་གྲུ་དེ་ན།།
སྟོན་མོ་སྤྱང་གིས་ང་རང་པང་དུ་བླངས་ཡོད།།
དབྱངས་གསལ་སོ་བཞིའི་ཐེ་བོར་རྐང་བསྒྲོད་ལག་བསྒྲོད།།
གོམ་པ་སྤྱང་ལ་བཏབ་པ་མི་ཚེའི་ཨ་ལོང་།།

ས་གཞི་ཁེབ་ཀྱིས་གནོན་པའི་མཚོ་མོའི་གློང་དུ།།
སྐྱ་བ་ཤུགས་ཀྱིས་བསྐོར་ཏེ་ངེས་མེད་ཡན་ན།།
རེ་ཞིག་གནམ་ས་ཧར་གྱིས་གས་པའི་བར་ནས།།
ཅི་བསམ་འདི་དྲན་མེད་པ་འཐོམས་པའི་ཨ་ལོང་།།

སྒྲོལ་ཞེས་བསྡམས་ཤིང་སྡོམ་པའི་མི་ཡི་མི་ཚོ།།
མ་བཅོས་གང་དྲན་སྣང་བས་ཤུལ་མེད་གཏོར་ན།།
ད་གཟོད་རང་ཉིད་དག་པའི་འཇིག་རྟེན་ཞིག་ཏུ།།
མགོ་དགུའི་གནས་ལུགས་འཛོ་བ་འདོད་པའི་ཨ་ལོང་།།

ལན་ཅིག་ཡོང་བའི་འཛིག་རྟེན་སྒྲོ་དགའི་འདུ་འགོད།།
མ་མཐོང་གཅིག་པུར་འཕྲུན་པའི་ལོ་ཟླ་སྐྱ་བོ།།
ས་གཞི་ཟླ་བའི་ངོས་ན་རི་མོ་གྱུ་གྱུ།།
དེ་ལ་རང་སྙོམས་མ་བྱས་སྣང་བའི་ཨ་ལོང་།།

ལྷགས་པས་འཚོ་བ་ཙམ་ཞིག་བར་ཆད་མ་ཡིན།།
སེམས་དང་སེམས་རྩ་འབྲིས་པའི་ཁྱེད་ཀྱིས་སོམས་དང་།།
ཕན་ཚུན་སྨུ་མེད་སྙིང་གི་དྲོད་ལ་ཧུམ་སྟེ།།
ལག་པས་ལག་པ་བསྣམས་པ་དམ་བཅའི་ཨ་ལོང་།།

ཞོགས་སྲོད་རེས་མོས་ཡོང་བའི་དུས་ཚོད་དེ་ལ།།
ཕྱི་ནང་ཕར་ཚུར་འགྲོ་འདུག་ལྷོད་མོ་སྟོན་དུས།།
རང་སེམས་རྒྱ་ཡན་ཤོར་པའི་ངེས་མེད་ཐོ་སྒྱུད།།
མཐའ་མེད་ཀློ་ཡིས་མི་ཟིན་ངག་གི་ཨ་ལོང་།།

Works Cited

Tibetan Sources

འཆི་མེད། ['Chi med, Chimay]. 2012. འབྲོག་ཁྱི། ["The Tibetan Mastiff"]. ༼ཟླ་བའི་རྨི་ལམ།༽ [*The Dreams of the Moon*], མཚོ་སྔོན་མི་རིགས་དཔེ་སྐྲུན་ཁང་། ཤོག་ངོས་༡༢༩ནས་༡༣༣།

———. 2012. བརྩེ་དུང་དང་ལས་དབང་། ["Love and Karmic Destiny"]. ༼ཟླ་བའི་རྨི་ལམ།༽ [*The Dreams of the Moon*], མཚོ་སྔོན་མི་རིགས་དཔེ་སྐྲུན་ཁང་། ཤོག་ངོས་༢༠༡ནས་༢༠༢།

———. 2012. ༼ཟླ་བའི་རྨི་ལམ།༽ [*The Dreams of the Moon*]. མཚོ་སྔོན་མི་རིགས་དཔེ་སྐྲུན་ཁང་།།

———. 2016. ཤེལ་གྱི་ཟེའུ་འབྲུ། [The Crystal Stamen]. ༼ཆུའི་ལང་ཚོ།༽ [*The Youth of Water*], སི་ཁྲོན་མི་རིགས་དཔེ་སྐྲུན་ཁང་། ཤོག་ངོས་༡༥ནས་༡༧།

———. 2016. ༼ཆུའི་ལང་ཚོ།༽ [*The Youth of Water*]. སི་ཁྲོན་མི་རིགས་དཔེ་སྐྲུན་ཁང་།

———. 2017. བོད་མོས་བོད་མོའི་རྩོམ་རིག་གླེང་བ། ["Tibetan Women On Tibetan Women's Literature"]. ལྷུགས་རྫོར་རྒྱལ་དང་། གོ་ཤུལ་གྲགས་པ་འབྱུང་གནས་གཉིས་ཀྱིས་བསྒྲིགས་པའི་ ༼བུད་མེད་རྩོམ་པ་པོས་གསར་རྩོམ་གླེང་བ།༽ [*Women Writers On Creative Writing*], མཚོ་སྔོན་མི་རིགས་དཔེ་སྐྲུན་ཁང་། ཤོག་ངོས་༩༡ནས་༩༥།

———. 2017. ང་རང་དགའ་བའི་ལྷུག་རྩོམ་ཞིག ["A Piece of Prose I Love"]. ༼གངས་རྒྱན་མེ་ཏོག༽ དེབ་བཞི་བ། ཤོག་ངོས་༡༠༡ནས་༡༠༤།

———. 2017. ལོ་རྡོ་སྟོང་གི་རེ་སྨུག ["One Thousand Years of Yearning"]. ༼མི་རིགས་རྩོམ་རིག༽ དེབ་དང་པོ། ཤོག་ངོས་༢༠ནས་༢༡།

———. 2017. ཨ་ལོང་། ["The Ring"]. ༼མི་རིགས་རྩོམ་རིག༽ དེབ་དང་པོ། ༢༠༡༧། ཤོག་ངོས་༢༢ནས་༢༣།

———. 2018. ཞིང་ཁ་ན་འཛད་ཀྱིན་པའི་སླེ་བོ། ["The Withering Away Basket at the Edge of the Field"]. ༢༠༡༨ལོའི་༼སྦྲང་ཆར།༽ དེབ་བཞི་བ། ཤོག་ངོས་༡༦༩ནས་༡༨༣།

———. 2019. དགའ་ལྡན་རི་བོའི་རྩེ་ནས་ཨ་མ་དྲན་སྐྱོང་པའི་བླ་མ་ཙོང་ཁ་པ། ["Lama Tsongkhapa Who Longed for his Mother on the Summit of Gandan Mountain"]. བོད་ཀྱི་ཅེར་འདོན་ཀྱི་སྒྲིགས་ཆེན་མོ། https://mp.weixin.qq.com/s/fFgMZSri9-uwvi9dRx7OAA

English Works Cited

Blake, William. 1979. "Auguries of Innocence." *Blake's Poetry and Designs*. Edited by Mary Lynn Johnson and John E. Grant, 209–12. New York and London: Norton Critical Edition.

Carey, John. 2020. *A Little History of Poetry*. New Haven and London: Yale University Press.

Coleridge, Samuel Taylor. 1917. *The Table Talk and Omniana of Samuel Taylor Coleridge*. Oxford: Oxford University Press.

Empson, William. 1995 (1930). *Seven Types of Ambiguity*. London: Penguin Books.

Kermode, Frank. 2000. *Shakespeare's Language*. London: Allen Lane and The Penguin Press.

Lama Jabb. 2018. "An Act of Bardo: Translating Tibetan Poetry." Keynote lecture, Lotsawa Translation Workshop, University of Colorado, October 4–8. Available at: https://conference.tsadra.org/session/an-act-of-bardo-translating-tibetan-poetry/.

Morrison, Toni. *Beloved*. 1997 (1987). London: Vintage.

Parkinson, Thomas. 2001. *W. B. Yeats: The Later Poetry*. Berkeley: University of California Press.

Pohl, Frederick J. 1933. "The Emily Dickinson Controversy." *The Sewanee Review*, vol. 41, no. 4 (Oct.–Dec.): 467–82.

Schopenhauer, Arthur. 1992 (1800). "On Language and Words." Translated by Peter Mollenhauer. *Theories of Translation: An Anthology of Essays from Dryden to Derrida*, edited by Rainer Schulte and John Biguenet, 32–35. Chicago: University of Chicago Press.

Shakespeare, William. 2007. *The Tragedy of Hamlet, Prince of Denmark*. In *William Shakespeare: The Complete Works* (The RSC Shakespeare), edited by Jonathan Bate and Eric Rasmussen, 1924–1999. Basingstoke: Macmillan.

A Sad Song of Jonang

Andrew Quintman

Emotions are not mere icing on the cake—at best a pleasurable distraction, at worst a mystifying spell to be broken so that the work of hard-nosed analysis can begin. Rather, affective engagement is the very means by which literary works are able to reach, reorient, and even reconfigure their readers.
—Rita Felski, *The Limits of Critique*[1]

There is nothing but sadness,
We are never happy.
—Yolmo sad song.[2]

It was spring 1989 when I entered Janet Gyatso's undergraduate class on Buddhist psychology. The lectures began, as I remember, with a survey of *kleśa* theory, an introduction to "main minds" (*citta*) and "mental factors" (*caitasika*), and the attendant catalogues of primary and secondary afflictive mental states. As a college senior awaiting graduation, I could relate to inattentiveness (*asaṃprajanya*) and laziness (*kauśīdya*). Still, I wasn't certain how these abstruse lists—including categories such as wrong view (*dṛṣti*) and lack of faith (*āśraddhya*)—shaped my experience of human existence. Indeed, such questions underlay much of our classroom discussion throughout the semester. This was my first recollection of Janet's discussion of emotions (afflictive) and mental states (affective), topics that would come to inhabit much of her work.

This essay is a brief exploration of Tibetan expressions of sadness and the ways in which they not only reflect subjective states of experience, or even

1. Felski 2015, 177. Thanks to Robert Barnett, Tenzin Dickie, Gedun Rabsal, Françoise Robin, and Michael Sheehy for their comments and suggestions. I would also like to thank my students in the School for International Training Tibetan Studies program during the spring 1993, spring 1997, and spring 1998 semesters, as well as program assistant Karma Namgyal. Finally, thanks are due to my co-academic director and dear friend, the inimitable Hubert Decleer, who passed away shortly after this essay was completed.

2. Desjarlais 1991, 391.

objects of experience, but also critiques human experience in the face of social, cultural, religious, and political forces. It draws, if somewhat indirectly, on Janet's work on poetry, literature, Buddhist philosophy, and her explorations of what it means to be fully human in the world. While the latter certainly includes the broad spectrum of emotions—the carefree nature of the yoginī meditating in the mountain, the pain of losing a loved one, the perplexity of one's own true nature—this essay focuses mainly on sadness, especially songs of sadness often referred to as *kyolü* (*skyo glu*). In a way, it also serves as my own song of sadness, reflecting on the decline of a once prominent religious institution, offered in gratitude for Janet's expertise as an undergraduate instructor and advisor, her clarity as a graduate mentor, and her brilliance as a colleague.

I.

We arrived at the Jonang Kumbum stūpa shortly before nightfall. It was spring 1993, and the day's bus ride from Shigatse had worn us down with its standard array of obstacles. Muddy ruts and irrigation ditches stranded our vehicle until a team of local farmers came to the rescue, wielding an arsenal of antique shovels and pickaxes. Together with my fifteen students, I clambered on to the bed of our support truck and we rode the last hour in the open air, squeezed between equipment duffels and petrol drums. The truck labored along a track washed away by recent storms until, cresting the final hill, our destination came into view.

Dolpopa Sherab Gyaltsen (1292–1361) laid foundations for the Great Kumbum Stūpa of Jonang in 1329 as an homage to his master Yonten Gyatso (1260–1327).[3] It was an ambitious feat of engineering, constructed on a massive scale and consisting of some 108 interior chapels. Dolpopa likened it to the raising of Mount Meru at the center of the universe. It was no surprise that the work required scores of laborers and artisans assembled from across the region, including Newars from Kathmandu. The structure's consecration four years later marked a turning point in Dolpopa's career as a Buddhist teacher. It coincided with his first public exposition of the *shentong* (*gzhan stong*) or "extrinsic emptiness" philosophical view for which he would become famous.[4]

In 1621, Dolpopa's successor Tāranātha Kunga Nyingpo (1575–1634)

3. For a description and photographs of the Jonang Kubum prior to its destruction, see Tucci 1949, 189–96, and 1973. Vitali 1990 likewise published a photograph of the stūpa. Henss 2014 (2:705–8) surveys the site and includes photographs taken shortly after restoration efforts in 1990.

4. Stearns 1999, 19.

Figure 1. Jonang Stūpa. (Photo: Andrew Quintman 1997.)

restored the monument, which had deteriorated a good deal. By the mid-twentieth century the structure was once again in ruins, through the slow march of time and the quicker pace of the People's Liberation Army. Dolpopa is said to have justified plans for such a massive undertaking in this way: "There is no doubt that anyone who even sees, hears, or touches this stūpa will be freed, that the seed of liberation will be planted, and that vast benefit for others will occur. Those who oppose it will later be regretful."[5] With the ravages of the Cultural Revolution in mind, these words suggest an ill fate for those who would desecrate the site.

Standing in the shadow of towering cliffs, and flanked by a row of apple trees, the stūpa assumed an unexpected grandeur. Through conversation that evening with the young *khenpo* in charge, we learned that the newly reactivated site housed nearly forty monks, all originally from Amdo and now divided between a monastic college (*bshad grwa*) and a retreat center (*sgrub grwa*), where young novices were completing their preliminary practices. The community paid special attention to restoring the Kumbum stūpa: the exterior was finished with plans underway for work on the statuary that would inhabit the shrines within. After several days spent visiting the renovated stūpa, the monastic complex, and the pilgrim's circuit (*ri skor*) around the mountain ridge above, we were happily

5. Translated in Stearns 1999, 19.

Figure 2. Dolpopa Seated in the Stūpa of Jonang. ('Dzam thang mkhan po blo gros grags pa. *Jo nang chos 'byung gsal byed zla ba'i sgron me*. Library of Tibetan Works and Archives, 1993. 1:215.)

surprised to have found an active religious center keenly aware of its unique cultural heritage. That would soon change.

In 1997, I returned to Jonang to find the site overtaken by a Communist Party cadre and the community forced into a program of "patriotic re-education." During the previous spring, re-education teams began conducting a series of three-month residencies at monasteries across Central Tibet, operating under the slogan "Love the Country, Love Religion" with an intention to "totally smash the separatist scheme to divide the motherland."[6] This program of nationalist indoctrination followed on the so-called Strike Hard anticrime campaign through which Chinese authorities purported to target "political splitists." Such activity was, as Tibetan Autonomous Region (TAR) Party Secretary Chen Kuiyuan put it, "a fundamental constituent of the basic Party line."[7] As part of their patriotic re-education, monks and nuns were forced to memorize a four-part admonishment of the Dalai Lama: that he is "the head of the serpent and the chieftain of the separatist organization conspiring for independence for Tibet, an unmistakable tool of international forces opposed to China, the root cause of social instability in Tibet, and the biggest obstacle to

6. Tibet Information Network 1998, 24.

7. Tibet Information Network 1998, 24. The most complete assessment of the Strike Hard campaign is Barnett et al, 1996. See also International Campaign for Tibet 2001.

the establishment of normal order in Tibetan Buddhism."[8] Monastic residents were then compelled to "sign a declaration agreeing to reject independence for Tibet; reject the boy recognized by the Dalai Lama as the 11th reincarnation of the Panchen Lama; reject and denounce the Dalai Lama; recognize the unity of China and Tibet; and not listen to the Voice of America."[9]

We met the monastery's elderly cook who informed us the re-education work team consisted of ten individuals (both Chinese and Tibetans) in residence for three months, holding indoctrination sessions each day for eight to ten hours with barely a break. "They force the monks to write letters denouncing the Dalai Lama," he said. "How can we denounce the Dalai Lama? He is all we have left. Without him, what will we have? Nearly half the resident monks had already left or been taken away." None, he added, would sign the letter.

After reminding us to "refrain from any political discussion with the residents of Jonang," members of the local Public Security Bureau reluctantly allowed us to spend a few hours visiting the stūpa and the hillside meditation caves, watching us carefully through binoculars the entire time.

Figure 3. Police Watching. (Photo: Andrew Quintman, 1997.)

8. Tibet Information Network 1998, 25.

9. U.S. Congress, Committee on Foreign Affairs and Committee on Foreign Relations, *Country Reports on Human Rights Practices for 1999*–Volume 1, 106th Cong., 2d sess. p. 1069. Website accessed 1/10/2021. https://1997-2001.state.gov/global/human_rights/1999_hrp_report/china.html.

As we drove back down the mountain, a police jeep passed us struggling its way up the pitted track from the village below. The jeep pulled into the monastery courtyard and two uniformed officials stepped forward. From its rear, they lifted several boxes of Chinese beer, which they carried into the drab olive tent that served as their headquarters.

When I returned once more the following year, in the spring 1998, the monastic complex was shuttered, locked, and completely empty. Later in the day I encountered an elderly woman from the village below. She confirmed that no one remained at Jonang. Since the re-education committee had arrived the previous year, all the monks had been taken to prison or forcibly expelled. Even the few lay people who stayed there were compelled to return to the village. The U.S. State Department corroborated these observations in its report that, "Monks at the Jonang Kumbum monastery in Shigatse . . . reportedly were dispersed in 1998 after they refused to accept conditions laid out by the Government's patriotic education teams including renouncing the Dalai Lama and Gendun Choekyi Nyima, the boy recognized by the Dalai Lama as the Panchen Lama."[10] "When I was a young girl," the elderly woman said, "I remember watching Chinese soldiers tear apart the monastery and the stūpa. Now they have done it again."

Following the circumambulation path around the stūpa's inner courtyard, filled with straw and animal dung, I came upon a box piled with wood printing blocks. Each one had been meticulously shaved so that only a faint impression of the letters remained. Another box held a collection of printing blocks burned beyond recognition. From this pile, a student pulled out a small worn booklet of typeset Tibetan text, its cover long since torn off. The first page of text began:

Lesson One

1. The Industriousness of Marx[11]

It was a textbook on Communist theory and propaganda, no doubt used by the re-education work team the previous year. Flipping through the booklet, a page of handwritten Tibetan hastily penned in blue ink caught my eye, as did the word inscribed in tall letters at the top of the page:

Sorrow (*skyo ba*)

10. U.S. Congress, Committee on Foreign Affairs and Committee on Foreign Relations, *Country Reports on Human Rights Practices for 1999*–Volume 1, 106th Cong., 2d sess. p. 1069. Website accessed 1/10/2021. https://1997-2001.state.gov/global/human_rights/1999_hrp_report/china.html.

11. *slob tshan dang po/ mar ke si'i brtson sems/.*

Figure 4. Shaved Wood Blocks. (Photo: Andrew Quintman, 1998.)

II.

Sadness, as an expressive emotion, is ubiquitous in Tibetan literature, especially as a form of religious sentiment. Following Gary Kuchar's observations about the medieval European world, Tibetan formulations of religious sadness might be seen "not simply [as] one or another affective state" but rather as "a set of discursive resources which allow writers to express the implications that theological commitments have on the lived experience of faith."[12] Sadness is prevalent, for example, in the lives of Buddhist masters (*rnam thar*), where terms of sorrow express dissatisfaction with the state of the ordinary world, grief at the separation from one's religious teacher, or distress about the nature of saṃsāra and the suffering that beings endure. These sentiments are exemplified in the visionary autobiographical writing of Jigmé Lingpa (1729/30–98) explored in Gyatso's groundbreaking *Apparitions of the Self*. In one poem he writes "I awoke from sleep, absorbed in a state of sadness./ As a result of that,/ . . . unbearable compassion arose/ for sentient beings experiencing that sort of karma./ Uncontrollably, a rain of tears fell."[13] Later, following a visionary encounter with Yeshe Tsogyal (8th c.), he proclaims, "I recall that lordly

12. Kuchar 2008, 2.

13. This appears in the text translated as *Dancing Moon in the Water*. See Gyatso 1998, 26–27.

father-mother in my heart intensely,/ and my sadness was such/ that there was no way to bear the longing."[14] In Gyatso's reading, such exclamations suggest that treasure revealers like Jigmé Lingpa "were obsessed with sadness at their Father's [i.e. Padmasambhava's] absence and longed incessantly for reunification with him."[15] Such emotional outpourings also led to a powerful sense of compassion for sentient beings, inspiring the treasure revealer to gird himself "like the Prajñāpāramitā bodhisattva 'armed with great armor'" and work for their benefit, even if both the suffering and the beings who experience it are ultimately illusory in nature.[16] Sadness, then, underscores Jigmé Lingpa's most basic religious aspirations. His sorrow reveals what it means to be a Buddhist and, more fundamentally, a human deeply concerned with the lives of others.

It may be, as Kuchar suggests, that this kind of sorrow—"religious sorrow"—is "less an emotional state than it is a language—a grammar of tears."[17] Tibetan literature incorporates this language to communicate the full range of tearful expression: dejection, depression, despondency, gloominess, grief, heartache, heartbreak, melancholy, misery, mournfulness, sadness, and of course sorrow—each of which illuminate complex networks of religiosity. But Tibetan writing is not limited to this kind of sadness—that is, to religious sadness rooted in dissatisfaction with the mundane world or longing for an absent guru. Sadness also expresses nostalgia for a distant homeland, yearning for a return to the familiar, despair in response to lived or remembered political events. Sorrow bears witness to the trauma of occupation, to powerlessness in the face of intimidation, to dashed dreams and smothered aspirations. Kuchar's observation notwithstanding, sadness remains a deeply human response to forces beyond one's immediate control.

Rather than compile an extended Tibetan "grammar of tears" (a task I hope to explore elsewhere), the remainder of this essay will track just a few impressionistic examples that illustrate the range of implications for the word *sorrow* (*skyo ba*) penned in the Jonang re-education pamphlet, with the aim of disambiguating "sad songs" as they appear in both religious and largely non-religious contexts.

Buddhism, it might be said, begins with sadness—or rather, suffering, with which it is deeply enmeshed. Suffering forms one of the three "marks of exis-

14. Gyatso 1998, 32.

15. Gyatso 1998, 154. Compare 'Jigs med gling pa's response to Xuanzang's lament at the Buddha's absence discussed in Eckel 2004 and Eckel 2005.

16. Gyatso 1998, 213.

17. Kuchar 2008, 2. On religious weeping, see Patton and Hawley 2005.

tence" (*trilakṣana*), together with impermanence and non-self, said to characterize all things. It is the first of the four truths of the noble ones, stipulating that birth, aging, sickness, and death are all suffering, as are separation from the desired and union with the unpleasant. The term *duḥkha* (Pali, *dukkha*), ubiquitously translated as "suffering," has a broad semantic range including uneasiness, pain, trouble, difficulty, and sorrow.[18] Buddhaghosa expands the Buddhist definition to include not only birth, aging, and death but also lamentation, grief, and despair.[19] The Tibetan translation of *duḥkha* into the compound *dukngal* (*sdug bsngal*) is defined in the *Great Tibetan Dictionary* as *nyangen* (*smya ngan*), "misery, unhappiness, pain" but then qualified by every sort of mental and physical discomfort. Sadness is thus both the cause for and the result of suffering, even as it is a defining characteristic of suffering more broadly.

Tibetan Buddhist literature lacks a single term that neatly translates the English word *emotion*, although *tsorwa* (*tshor ba*, Skt. *vedanā*), often rendered "feeling," offers an approximation, while *nyonmong* (*snyon mongs*, Skt. *kleśa*) is occasionally translated as "afflictive emotion."[20] Classical Indian thinking about emotions and emotional states often appeared in the context of *rasa* theory, an approach to aesthetics dating back Bharata's *Treatise on Drama* (*Nāṭyaśāstra*), composed at least as early as the fourth century CE.[21] This work outlined systematic correspondences between the so-called eight "stable" or "primary" emotions (Skt, *bhāva*: sexual attraction, amusement, grief, anger, determination, fear, revulsion, and amazement) and the aesthetic states (*rasa*, literally "taste") they engender in the context of artistic practice (the erotic, comic, tragic, violent, heroic, fearful, macabre, and fantastic).

Sakya Pandita's (1182–1251) treatment of *rasa* theory, as Matthew Kapstein noted, "cast a mold for the treatment of Indian literary theory that has endured in Tibet to the present day," in which the focus shifted from aesthetic considerations of art to the somewhat more straightforward "classification of harmonious and conflicting sentiments."[22] The innovation produced a list of dyads in which eight internal emotions (literally "movement [of mind]," rendered *'gyur ba* in Tibetan) are paired with eight corresponding external "manifestations

18. Monier-Williams, 1899, s.v. *duḥkha*, 483.

19. Buddhaghosa 2010, 510.

20. Maria Heim 2021 offers an extended exploration of *vedanā* from Pali sources. On the cross-cultural examination of emotions, including sadness, see Lutz 1988 and Lutz and Abu-Lughod 1990.

21. See Pollock 2003, 2016.

22. Kapstein 2003, 780–81.

[of movements of mind]," (Tib. *nyams* [*'gyur*]).[23] According to this scheme, the emotion of misery (*mya ngan*) is paired with the manifestation of compassion (*snying rje*): underscoring the Mahāyāna Buddhist framework for religious sadness in which one's sorrow at the suffering of others becomes a powerful motivational force and natural primer for generating compassion. While representations of sadness in Tibetan traditions of *kāvya* and belles-lettres (*snyan ngag*) deserve greater attention, examples below mainly reflect the indigenous forms of songs (*glu*) and songs of realization (*mgur*).[24]

Tibetan terms suggesting sadness and sorrow are widespread. A non-exhaustive list stemming from the root *skyo ba* (sadness) includes *skyo chad de ba* (desperation), *skyo ting nge ba* (deep sadness), *skyo shas* (intense sadness or strong dislike), *sems skyo/yid skyo* (mental unease), and *skyo mun ne ba* (debilitating sadness).[25] Sadness also appears in onomatopoetic expressions such as Milarepa's lament "Alas, alas, ay me, ay me, how sad" (*kye ma, kye ma, kyi hud, kyi hud, ang*) uttered upon discovering the bones of mother.[26] Widely attested terms for literary forms expressing sadness include "sad story" (*skyo ba'i gtam*), "lament" (*gdung dbyangs*), and "sad song" (*skyo glu*).

III.

On the blank half-page of the Jonang re-education booklet, just below the word "sorrow," a brief poem was inscribed in quick cursive letters. These fourteen lines of verse, set in a six-syllable meter, is headed by the simple title "Sad Song" (*skyo glu*).[27]

Sad Song

Setting out from my family home
I was offered this advice from my parents:

23. See Henrion-Dourcy 2017.

24. See the essay by Nancy Lin in this volume for a discussion of scholarly approaches to Tibetan *snyan ngag* traditions.

25. For an example of the last term, see the poem by 'Jam dbyangs chos kyi blo gros referred to as a "lament composed in a state of debilitating sadness." *Rgyal zla'i tshes nyer brgyad nyin snang ba skyo mun ne ba'i ngang bris pa'i gdung dbyangs* in 'Jam dbyangs chos kyi blo gros kyi gsung 'bum. Bir: Khyentse Labrang, 2012, 8: 480–81, and translation at https://www.lotsawahouse.org/tibetan-masters/jamyang-khyentse-chokyi-lodro/lament-to-loter-wangpo. See also the list of associated terms for suffering and sadness in Schaeffer 2004, 194n2.

26. Quintman 2010, 122.

27. A transliteration is provided at the end of this essay.

"Complete your studies and learning and then
Come back home bearing good news."
Among the great community of virtuous monks
I'm no more foolish than others.
But then the Work Team Committee[28] stormed in
And there was nothing at all to be done.
So now the monks, one and all,
Have gone to their lands in Amdo.
My dear father and mother,
Please stay well and be happy.
The young son, Kunzang Tenzin
Will come in one month's time.

We know little of the author Kunzang Tenzin beyond what he wrote in this short autobiographical poem. He was born in the eastern Tibetan region of Amdo, perhaps near Dzamthang, a constellation of monastic institutions and religious sites that have formed a center for the Jonang tradition with foundations dating to the fourteenth century.[29] He was ordained as a monk, and he appears strong willed, aspiring to fulfill the wishes of his parents. He is literate, and although the short poem is rife with spelling errors, he appears dedicated to his studies and considered himself equal to those in his cohort. He was, perhaps, a pupil of the *khenpo* who had reinvigorated the monastic college of Jonang back in the early 1990s. These lines, composed shortly before his departure, swell with melancholy and the resignation of dreams unfulfilled. Perhaps he intentionally left behind the poem, where it serves as testament to the desolation of his religious home: a sad song to fill the silence of an emptied monastery courtyard.

28. *Las don tshogs chung*. On the translation of this term, see Lawasia Human Rights Committee et al. 1991, 63, where such groups are described as committees of the larger Work Teams (*las don ru khag*, Ch. *gong zuo dui*). The work team committee has been further defined as "trusted government employees considered to have persuasive characters and be well versed in political doctrine. They hold regular jobs and are periodically formed into ad hoc mobile teams that undertake specific assignments, in lieu of their normal work, to investigate suspected criminal activity. . . . Work teams have been the key weapon in the extra-judicial attack on politically active monasteries and nunneries" (63). Schwartz (1994, 115) has "sub-committee."

29. See Gruschke 2001, 2:72ff.

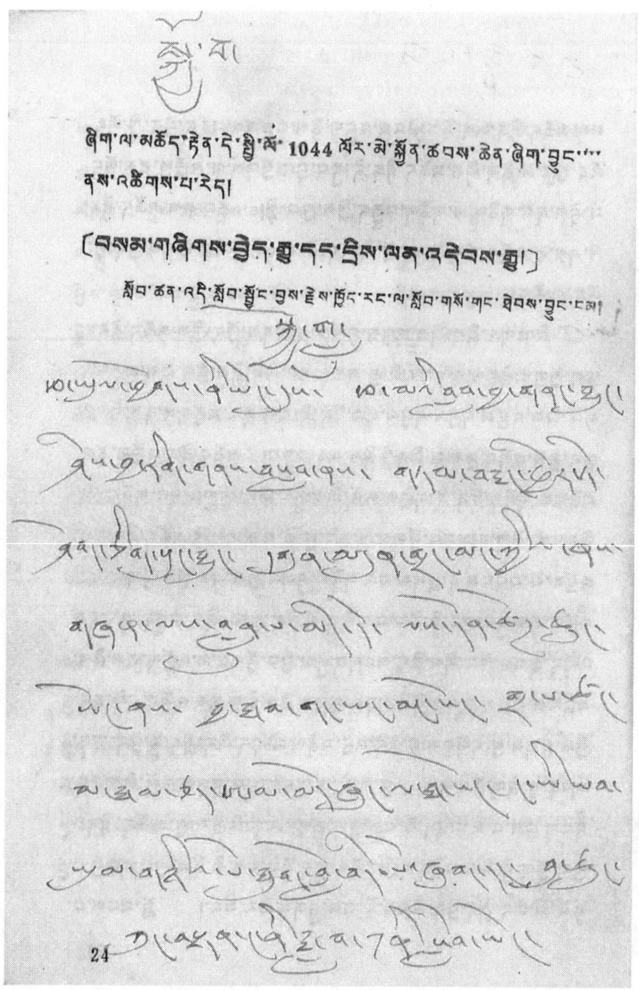
ཞིག་ལ་མཆོད་རྟེན་དེ་སྤྱི་ལོ་ 1044 ལོར་མི་སྐྱོན་ཆབས་ཅན་ཞིག་བྱུང་…
ནས་འཚིགས་པ་རེད།

[བསམ་གཞིགས་བྱེད་རྒྱུ་དང་དྲིས་ལན་འདེབས་རྒྱུ།]

སློབ་ཚན་འདི་སློབ་སྦྱོང་བྱས་རྗེས་ཁྱོད་རང་ལ་སློབ་གསོ་གང་ཐེབས་བྱུང་ངམ།

24

Figure 5. Jonang Sad Song

IV.

One paradigm for religious sadness in Buddhism is the bodhisattva "Ever Weeping" (Sadāparudita, Rtag tu ngu) known primarily through his descriptions in the perfection of wisdom literature. Narratives of his travails spread widely across India, Central Asia, China, and Tibet, where they surfaced in literature as varied as Candrakīrti's *Prasannapadā* and Śāntideva's *Śikṣāsamuccaya*. These accounts describe the bodhisattva's repeated struggles to seek a teacher and attain perfect wisdom, resulting in a form of religious sadness expressed by his ever-present tears. In one famous embellishment of the story, Tsongkhapa (1357–1419) describes the bodhisattva's attitude in this way:

> Though there is no firewood in one's heart
> The great bonfire of suffering still blazes.
> Though there are no clouds in the sky of one's eyes
> A rain of tears still falls.[30]

Milarepa, whose own life story famously provoked tears in the most stoic reader, is said to have read Ever Weeping's tale following his first painful encounter with Marpa, after which he mustered the resolve to return to his teacher.

In 1254, Phakpa Lodro Gyaltsen (1235–80) composed the short treatise entitled *Sad Story in Thirty-Five Verses* (*Sko ba'i gtam tshigs su bcad pa sum cu rtsa lnga pa*), referring to himself in the colophon as "The one named Phakpa with the sad mind. . . ."[31] The composition surveys what he considers to be the pitiful status of religious engagement and practice at the time, such as this early passage: "[People] don't rely on the teachings of the protectors / and assiduously perform faulty actions. / This makes me sad."[32] Short works with similar titles are also found in the writings of Tsongkapa, the Third Dodrupchen Jigmé Tenpé Nyima (1865–1926), and the previous abbot of Drakar Taso Monastery Tenzin Norbu (1899–1959). The last begins with the author recognizing his "unbearable anguish upon simply calling the lord guru to mind."[33]

Tibet's illustrious narrative, *The Life of Milarepa*, is suffused with the theme of religious sadness. The best-known version of the story, composed in the late fifteenth century, famously begins with the yogin's declaration, "Were I to explain these events [of my life] at length, some would be reason for laughter, others would be reason for tears."[34] There are undoubtedly genuine moments of humor: his crafting of a penis sheath from a gift of woolen cloth and his final written testament that proclaimed, "Whoever says that Milarepa possessed gold, fill his mouth with shit" represent just two of many examples.[35] But

30. After Pema Gyatso and Bailey 2013, 23.

31. 'Gro mgon chos rgyal 'Phags pa 2007, 287.

32. 'Gro mgon chos rgyal 'Phags pa 2007, 284. *skyob pa'i gsung la yid kyang mi rton zhing// skyon ldan bya ba brtun nas sgrub byed pas// bdag yid skyo ba brten par bskyed par 'gyur//.*

33. Brag dkar Bstan 'dzin nor bu 1996, 138: *rje bla ma yid la dran tsam gyis// sems gdung ba'i tshul la bzod blag med//.*

34. Quintman 2010, 15.

35. Quintman 2010, 160, 263.

Milarepa's tale is largely framed by sorrow and tears: the boy's stolen patrimony, the mother driven to madness, the acolyte pushed to the brink of suicide. The story's most poignant scene occurs when Milarepa returns to his family estate, now in disrepair. Walking through the ruins, he pulls out a heap of rags. He recounts, "When I gathered them up, a number of human bones, bleached white, slipped out. When I realized they were the bones of my mother, I was so overcome with grief that I could hardly stand it. I couldn't think, I couldn't speak, and an overwhelming sense of longing and sadness swept over me. I was on the verge of fainting."[36] Then, "bursting into tears," he uttered the song,

> Alas, alas. Ay me, ay me. How sad!
> People invested in things of life's round—
> I reflect and reflect, and again and again I despair.
> They act and they act and stir up from their depths so much torment.
> They spin and they spin and are cast in the depths of life's round.[37]

Later in the narrative Milarepa describes this as a "sad melody of my weariness with the world," while one woman in his small audience "sat there with tears streaming from her eyes."[38]

A song attributed to Milarepa's acclaimed female disciple Salé Ö (Sa le 'od) similarly expresses sadness at the suffering of saṃsāra. One stanza reads:

> My whole being is filled with despair,
> And thinking about what can be done,
> I remember impermanence and death, deep within.
> From the time I was born to my mother 'till now,
> I've seen many die, both the old and the young.
> Life is impermanent like a dewdrop on grass. . . .
> I know that there's no place anywhere
> That death does not come.[39]

36. Quintman 2010, 119.

37. Gtsang smyon Heruka, 1981, 137. *kye ma kye ma kyi hud kyi hud ang// 'khor ba'i chos la blo gtad byed pa rnams// bsam zhing bsam zhing yi mug yang yang ldang// spyad cing spyad cing sdug bsngal gring nas 'khrug/ bskor zhing bskor zhing 'khor ba'i gting la 'phen//*. Cf. Quintman 2010, 122.

38. Quintman 2010, 123.

39. Gtsang smyon Heruka, 1981, 569. *rang la rang nyid yi mug che// ci drag sems kyi bsam mno la// mi rtag 'chi ba gting nas dran// rang ma la skyes nas da bar la// rgan gzhon mang po zhi ba mthong// tshe mi rtag rtswa kha'i zil pa 'dra//. . . sa phyogs gang na'ang med par go// bdag la nges par 'chi dgos shing//*. Cf. Stagg 2017, 435.

In this context, sorrow is not simply an expressive emotion but rather the underlying motivation for religious practice, as suggested in the refrain "Thinking this, sadness has welled up inside,/ so this girl will practice sublime Dharma./"[40] Salé Ö's sadness (reflected in the third person's "this girl") is also explicitly gendered. Subsequent stanzas express a sentiment attuned to the sorrows of Tibetan womanhood that include marriage to an abusive husband:

> You leave your kind parents behind.
> You are yoked, and then taken to an unkind man.
> It's a foundation laid out near the three lower realms. . . .
> He carries away your parents' food and wealth,
> And meaninglessly, you work as his slave. . . .
> First, he's a divine prince with a sweet smile.
> Next, he's a demon with an angry black face.
> Finally, he's a young bull, always ready to beat you.[41]

We see echoed in these words what Steven Hopkins has referred to as the "work of tears," in which "the bitter and devastatingly eloquent laments of bereaved women do to memorialize and bear witness to, but also to critique, blame, shame, resist, curse, demand, disrupt, and subvert the brutalities of celebrated male heroism."[42]

This kind of gendered religious sorrow is mirrored in the autobiography of Orgyan Chokyi (1675–1729), the nun from Dolpo writing some six centuries later. She laments the misery of samsaric existence, but also the mundane cruelties of her mother and the hardships of menial labor, drawing on her experience as a Himalayan woman named Kyilo ("Happiness Dashed") by parents who had hoped instead for a son. Her sadness reflects the sorrows of a Buddhist nun who aspired to meditation retreat but was repeatedly forced into the kitchen. She also expresses a special kind of sadness for the pain inflicted upon animals, as in this poem from her youth as a goatherd,

> Alas, the hand of this girl's body.
> Virtue is not in this hand. Sin is in this hand.

40. Gtsang smyon Heruka 1981, 570–71. *bsam shing skyo ba nang nas skyes// de na bu mo lha chos byed/.*

41. Gtsang smyon Heruka 1981, 569–70. *pha ma drin can rgyab tu bur// rang gnya' drin med mi la bskyal// ngan song gsum gyi 'gram gzhi bting// . . . pha ma'i zas nor khur nas su// don med mi yi g.yog la brtson// . . . dang po lha bu 'dzum bag can// bar du bdud po ngo nag po// tha mar glang bu brdung snying can//.* Cf. Stagg 2017, 435–36.

42. Hopkins 2021, 14.

Taking mother's milk from the mouth of her kid,
My mind is sad, though I do need the milk.
In this human body, I need milk.[43]

V.

These few examples have depicted typical Buddhist expressions of sadness, framed by despair at the fate of beings trapped in saṃsāra and the resultant feelings of renunciation. Where they reflect sadness at the limitations of the human body or the shortcomings of social conventions, they often do so within the context karma theory within a Buddhist cosmos. But the lament in the Jonang sad song is not the sorrow of saṃsāra writ large—at least not explicitly so. Toward the booklet's end, Kunzang Tenzin inscribed a final line in the upper margin, confirming the picture of what had happened the preceding year, and offering a final rationale for the poem's title. In the same blue pen, he wrote, "Destroyed by the Jonang Work Team Committee."[44] This suggests a different emotional tenor: a sadness inflected by themes of political oppression and domination, directed at the agents of governmental power against which "there was nothing to be done." Kunzang Tenzin's words suggest a longing for a happier past, a world that has been forcibly stripped away.

One parallel in thematic content if not poetic styling is the well-known early-twentieth-century poem known as "Song of Lhasa Memories" (*Lha sa dran glu*) composed by Shelkar Lingpa (1876–1913) in 1911–1912, while in the service of the Thirteenth Dalai Lama during his period of forced exile in Darjeeling. The primary tones are nostalgia and longing for a homeland then under threat by the Qing, and the work is remarkable, in Lauran Hartley's view, for "how the contemporary is made tangible in the poet's expression of longing for Lhasa."[45] Equally remarkable, however, is the way in which its verses have remained poignant for contemporary Tibetan readers facing a land still under threat, as it "invokes longings for a Tibet that most students have seen only in their mind's eye: the Tibet of traditional Lhasa" through a poem that "effectively conveys the very object whose absence is being mourned."[46] Verse 8 captures this mood:

43. Schaeffer 2004, 138.

44. *jo nang las don tshogs chung gyis gtor*.

45. See Hartley 2008 and Upton 1999. The poem in Tibetan was originally published by G. Tharchin at the Tibet Mirror Press, Kalimpong in 1936.

46. Upton 1999, 19, also cited in Hartley 2008, 14. The poem inspired a theatrical performance at the Tibetan Institute of Performing Arts in 1985 (Jamyang Norbu 2014, 239n4). In May 1989, following the Barkhor demonstrations in Lhasa, the contemporary Tibetan poet Jangbu com-

> I miss Lhasa: its careful and dependable ways,
> Not awhirl with busyness like here;
> Its casual folks' calm dispositions,
> Mulling over their meals and doing honest work.[47]

And the political overtones in a concluding verse would likely have rung true to Kunzang Tenzin nearly a century later:

> We were surrounded by the Chinese army.
> The body, taxed by running, torments the mind.
> Since the Chinese kill for voicing even a little criticism,
> Now, even for the region of the gods, my longing is little.[48]

In the early twentieth century, "Tibetan modernist" Gendun Chopel composed another noteworthy lament. The final stanza refers to the poem as "A sad song recalling fleeting appearances, my mother's changing frowns and smiles,/ And my own experiences, sometimes happy, sometimes painful."[49] On one level, the composition reads like a traditional religious commentary, its images evoking Buddhist notions of ephemerality. Some editions of the poem add the title "A Song Recollecting Impermanence." But as with much of Gendun Chopel's writing, the piece incorporates complex layers of meaning, subject to interpretation on multiple levels. Two middle stanzas, for example, suggest a scathing attack directed toward an unnamed individual, stemming from personal slights and perceived disrespect that seem to have little to do with fundamental Buddhist truths.[50]

---

posed a poem about Shelkar Lingpa entitled "The Poet" that begins "On that long night when snow fell/ A poet was born from turmoil and from wandering./ With a sharp knife he carved "Song of Lhasa Memories, O City of the Dharma"/ On the hearts of those at home and abroad who had lost their way,/ Incising the deep suffering that accompanies decline" (Ljang bu and Stoddard 2010, 4).

47. After Epstein and Nornang. *brel brel 'tshub 'tshub de 'dra ma yin par// lhod lhod mi rnams ngang rgyud chis ring zhing// mur mur kha zas zhing drang po'i las// tan tan tig tig byed pa'i lha sa dran//*

48. After Epstein and Nornang. *ngar ngar rgya mi'i dmag gis mtha' nas bskor// shog shog rgyugs rgyugs khral gyis lus sems mnar// lab lab tshig gi mtho dmar srog 'dor bas// da lta lha ldan khul la'ang thags zhen chung//.*

49. Lopez 2009, 71.

50. For a review of theories identifying this individual as either Rahula Sankrityayana or Georges Roerich, see Bogin and Decleer 1997.

When you are rich, they slink up close;
When you are poor, they scorn you from afar with pointing fingers.
The nature of bad friends who do not know kindness as kindness;
I think of this; tears and laughter rise up in me.

The talents of a humble scholar, seeking only knowledge
Are crushed by the tyranny of a fool, bent by the weight of his wealth.
The proper order is upside down.
How sad, the lion made servant to the dog.[51]

Yet Gendun Chopel retains a keen self-reflexiveness, steering the poem from what might read as doleful regret for unobtained status to a more profound, and deeply Buddhist, commentary on the very nature of sadness itself:

When looked at, the marvels of the world seem pleasing.
When attained, each has its own suffering.
After moments of brief happiness become but a dream,
There is always something that makes me sad.[52]

Sad songs remain a potent genre in contemporary Tibetan performance. The influential Tibetan singer Dubhe (1968–2016), described by Lama Jabb as a "unifying and revered Tibetan national hero" who "discovered a new language to sing the contemporary Tibet that had just experienced unprecedented socio-cultural traumas,"[53] has extend the themes of *kyolü* (rendered "dirge" by Lama Jabb) in powerful new ways. *Dirge of the Deer* (*ri dwags skyo glu*, 1993) and *Dirge of the Ewe* (*ma mo'i skyo glu*, 1993), for example, recount tragic tales of animal cruelty and reflect the greedy and abusive sides of human nature.[54] For some listeners, these songs, which call to mind Orgyen Chokyi's compositions, serve as allegories for the "fate of contemporary Tibet," even as they inspired a heightened awareness about the harms of animal hunting and slaughter.[55]

Sad songs likewise retain a psychological potency in contemporary Tibetan Buddhist communities. In the Himalayan region of Yolmo in Nepal, sad songs, known as *tserlu* (*tser lu*), form couplets that describe a form of distress called *tsera* (*tser ra*), "an unwanted sentiment which 'falls' on the heart when a person

51. Lopez 2009, 69.

52. Lopez 2009, 71.

53. Jabb 2020, 387, 397.

54. Jabb 2020, 402.

55. Jabb 2020, 402.

separates, for a lasting period of time, from friends and family."[56] They are sung individually or in small groups as forms of "'structuring structures,' [after Bordieu] to express, shape, comment upon, and transform emotional distress."[57] Such poetry, Desjarlais suggests, both constructs and transforms cultural worlds.

VI.

Kunzang Tenzin's sad song of Jonang articulates sorrow that is grounded in Buddhist sentiment but not limited to it. We sense an exhaustion with the ebbs and flows of the mundane world, in line with Jigmé Lingpa's laments. But his words also resonate with Shelkar Lingpa's nostalgic longing and Gendun Chopel's barbed attacks. The poem hints at a suspicion of personal defeat in the face of implacable colonial power. The Jonang *kyolü* thus suggests that sadness may form a grammar of tears even as it offers a language of resistance, expressing sentiment from (and in) the margins but forbidden in the public square. There is a parallel here to the sorrow that some Buddhist authors expressed in the face of a perceived waning of the Dharma during the degenerate age. Mahāyāna narratives record accounts of the Dharma's decline at the hand of evil kings who will "destroy stūpas, ruin the temples and monasteries, and massacre communities of monks and nuns. Neither scholar nor regular practitioner will escape them. They will burn the holy texts and nothing will remain of them."[58] Those of us who read, study, and translate such words must not only grapple with their emotional valences, but also find ways to express those emotions in writing. Much like Kunzang Tenzin himself.

Tibetan Transcription

Suggested corrections: <x>
skyo glu
pha yul phyogs ni <nas> yong dus/
pha ma'i blab <bslab> bya gnang byung/
shes bya rig gnas bslab nas/
gdam bzang khyer te shog cig sung <gsungs> byung/
dgun mdun <dge 'dun> grang <grwa> mang kyil <dkyil> nas/
gzhan las blun pa med de/

56. Desjarlais 1991, 389.

57. Desjarlais, 1991, 390.

58. Translation after a slight paraphrasing of Lamotte 1988, 199.

las don tshogs chung yong nas/
bya thabs gang yang mang <ma> song/
gra pa tsang ma tham <thams> cad/
a mdo zhung <gzhung> la tha <thal> song/
nga yi yab yum gnyis po
thug <thugs> blo bde po zhug <bzhugs> dang
bu chung kun bstan nga ni
zla ba 1 ni <nas> sleb yong/

Works Cited

Barnett, Robert, Tibet Information Network, and Human Rights Watch. 1996. *Cutting off the Serpent's Head: Tightening Control in Tibet, 1994–1995*. New York: Human Rights Watch.

Bogin, Benjamin, and Hubert Decleer. 1997. "Who Was 'This Evil Friend' ('the Dog', the 'Fool', 'the Tyrant') in Gedün Chöphel's Sad Song?" *The Tibet Journal* 22 (3): 67–78.

Brag dkar Bstan 'dzin nor bu. 1996. "Rang byung la skyo ba'i gtam nges 'byung 'gugs pa'i pho nya" in *The Collected Works of Dkar-Brgyud Bstan-'dzin Nor-bu*, 137–42. Leh, Ladakh: D. I. Tashigang.

Buddhaghosa. 1991. *Visuddhimagga: The Path of Purification*. Translated by Bhikkhu Ñāṇamoli. 5th edition. Kandy: Buddhist Publication Society.

Desjarlais, Robert R. 1991. "Poetic Transformations of Yolmo 'Sadness.'" *Culture, Medicine and Psychiatry* 15 (4): 387–420.

Eckel, Malcolm David. 2004. *To See the Buddha: A Philosopher's Quest for the Meaning of Emptiness*. Princeton, NJ: Princeton University Press.

———. 2005. "Hsüan-Tsang's Encounter with the Buddha: A Cloud of Philosophy in a Drop of Tears." In *Holy Tears: Weeping in the Religious Imagination*, edited by Kimberley Christine Patton and John Stratton Hawley, 112–31. Princeton, NJ: Princeton University Press.

Epstein, Lawrence, and Geshe Ngawang Nornang. "Song of Lhasa Dreams." Unpublished translation.

Felski, Rita. 2015. *The Limits of Critique*. Chicago: Chicago University Press.

'Gro mgon chos rgyal 'Phags pa. 2007. *Skyo ba'i gtam*. In *'Gro mgon chos rgyal 'phags pa'i gsung 'bum*, vol. 4, 283–87. Bejing: Krung go'i bod rig pa dpe skrun khang.

Gruschke, Andreas. 2001. *The Cultural Momuments of Tibet's Outer Provinces. Amdo Volume 2. The Gansu and Sichuan Parts of Amdo*. Bangkok: White Lotus Press.

Gtsang smyon Heruka. 1981. *Mi la'i rnam mgur. Rnal 'byor gyi dbang phyug chen po mi la ras pa'i rnam mgur*. Zi ling: Mtsho sngon mi rigs dpe skrun khang.

Gyatso, Janet. 1998. *Apparitions of the Self: The Secret Autobiographies of a Tibetan Visionary*. Princeton, NJ: Princeton University Press.

Hartley, Lauran R. 2008. "Heterodox Views and the New Orthodox Poems: Tibetan Writers in the Early and Mid-Twentieth Century" in *Modern Tibetan Literature and Social Change*, edited by Lauran R. Hartley and Patricia Schiaffini-Vedani, 3–31. Durham, NC: Duke University Press.

Heim, Maria. 2021. "Some Analysis of Feeling." In *The Bloomsbury Research Handbook of Emotions in Classical Indian Philosophy*, edited by Maria Heim, Chakravarthi Ram-Prasad, and Roy Tzohar, 87–106. London: Bloomsbury Academic.

Henrion-Dourcy, Isabelle. 2017. "The Art of the Tibetan Actor: A Lce Lha Mo in the Gaze of Western Performance Theories." *Revue d'Etudes Tibétaines*, no. 40 (Juillet): 179–215.

Henss, Michael. 2014. *Cultural Monuments of Tibet*. Munich: Prestel Verlag.

Hopkins, Steven P. 2021. "Lament and the Work of Tears: Andromache, Sītā, and Yaśodharā." In *The Bloomsbury Research Handbook of Emotions in Classical Indian Philosophy*, edited by Maria Heim, Chakravarthi Ram-Prasad, and Roy Tzohar, 107–30. London: Bloomsbury Academic.

International Campaign for Tibet. 2001. *When the Sky Fell to Earth: The New Crackdown on Buddhism in Tibet*. Washington, DC: International Campaign for Tibet.

Jabb, Lama. 2020. "The Wandering Voice of Tibet: Life and Songs of Dubhe." *Life Writing* 17 (3): 387–409.

Jamyang Norbu. 2014. "The Lhasa Ripper: A Preliminary Investigation into the 'Dark Underbelly' of Social Life in the Holy City." Special Volume: *Trials of the Tibetan Tradition: Papers for Elliot Sperling. Revue d'Etudes Tibétaines* 31 (Février) 233–50.

Kapstein, Matthew. 2003. "The Indian Literary Identity in Tibet." In *Literary Cultures in History: Reconstructions from South Asia*, edited by Sheldon Pollock, 747–802. Berkeley: University of California Press.

Kuchar, Gary. 2008. *The Poetry of Religious Sorrow in Early Modern England*. Cambridge: Cambridge University Press.

Lamotte, Étienne. 1988 *History of Indian Buddhism from the Origins to the Śaka Era*. Translated by Sara Webb-Boin. Louvain: Institut Orientaliste.

Lawasia Human Rights Committee, Law Association for Asia and the Pacific, and Tibet Information Network. 1991. *Defying the Dragon: China and Human Rights in Tibet*. Lawasia Human Rights Report. Manila: Lawasia Human Rights Committee.

Ljang bu and Heather Stoddard. 2010. *The Nine-eyed Agate: Poems and Stories*. Lanham, MD: Lexington Books.

Lopez, Donald S. Jr. 2009. *In the Forest of Faded Wisdom: 104 Poems by Gendun Chopel*. Chicago: University of Chicago Press.

Lutz, Catherine A. 1988 *Unnatural Emotions: Everyday Sentiments on a Micronesian Atoll and Their Challenge to Western Theory*. Chicago: University of Chicago Press.

Lutz, Catherine A., and Lila Abu-Lughod. 1990. *Language and the Politics of Emotion*. Cambridge: Cambridge University Press.

Monier-Williams, Monier. 1899. *A Sanskrit-English Dictionary*. Oxford: Oxford University Press.

Patton, Kimberley Christine, and John Stratton Hawley. 2005. *Holy Tears: Weeping in the Religious Imagination*. Princeton, NJ: Princeton University Press.

Pema Gyatso and Geoff Bailey. 2013. *Byang chub sems dpa' rtag tu ngu'i rtogs brjod*. Lhasa: Bod ljong mi dmangs dpe skrun khang.

Pollock, Sheldon, ed. 2003. *Literary Cultures in History: Reconstructions from South* Asia. Berkeley: University of California Press.

———. 2016. *A Rasa Reader: Classical Indian Aesthetics*. New York: Columbia University Press.

Quintman, Andrew, translator. 2010. *The Life of Milarepa*. New York: Penguin Classics.

Schaeffer, Kurtis. 2004. *Himalayan Hermitess: The Life of a Tibetan Buddhist Nun*. New York: Oxford University Press.

Schwartz, Ronald David. 1994. *Circle of Protest: Political Ritual in the Tibetan Uprising, 1987–92*. New York: Columbia University Press.

Stagg, Christopher, translator. 2017. *The Hundred Thousand Songs of Milarepa*. Boulder, CO: Shambhala Publications.

Stearns, Cyrus. 1999. *The Buddha from Dolpo: A Study of the Life and Thought of the Tibetan Master Dolpopa Sherab Gyaltsen*. Albany: State University of New York Press.

Tucci, Giuseppe. 1949. *Tibetan Painted Scrolls*. Rome: La Libreria Della Stato.

———. 1973. *Transhimalaya*. Geneva: Nagel Publishers.

Upton, Janet. 1999. "Cascades of Change: Modern and Contemporary Literature in the PRC's Junior-Secondary Tibetan Language and Literature Curriculum." *Lungta* 12:17–28.

Vitali, Roberto. 1990. *Early Temples of Central Tibet*. London: Serindia Publications.

Two Sculpture-Portraits of the Fifth Dalai Lama, His Dedications, and the People to Whom He Bestowed Them[1]

Amy Heller

In a spirit of homage and esteem for Janet Gyatso's outstanding scholarship on Tibetan Buddhism and the cultural history of Tibet, I offer this small contribution as inklings of probing questions my dear friend of forty years has raised in her writings, presentations, and in private conversations. In her pioneering study of the Fifth Dalai Lama and codifications of medical and Buddhist science and ethics during his lifetime, her focus turned toward intellectual history. Janet demonstrated that those medical texts and practices reflect epistemic shifts and their constraints, far broader than and lasting long beyond the span of the Great Fifth's life. Earlier, Janet's research and translations raised questions about biography and autobiographies, how individuals see themselves, how the texts reflect the nature of an individual's identity, and how the individual's vision shapes the autobiographical truths. In these portrait sculptures of the Fifth Dalai Lama as an embodiment of Avalokiteśvara, we may observe literally, here invoking the title of Janet's grand opus, the portrayal of what is meant by "being human in a divine world."

The Fifth Dalai Lama qualified such sculptures as "self-portraits" (*nged rang gi 'dra 'bag*), but this is idiosyncratic as there is no indication that he was the artist. Instead it is understood that these are portraits in sculpture, made in Lhasa during the lifetime of the Fifth Dalai Lama, which allow appreciation of his vision of how to portray his physicality, his bodily form. The dedication inscriptions offer an opportunity to glimpse a level of personal interaction with two distinguished Lhasa gentlemen, both participants in aspects of the Fifth Dalai Lama's private life as well as specific official events.

The two sculptures are cast in gilt brass alloy with cold gold (matte) on the faces as well as pigment for the wide-open eyes, thin eyebrows, and the closed

1. I gratefully acknowledge criticisms, clarifications, and suggestions offered by Samten Karmay and Christoph Cüppers in the writing of this essay; the errors and shortcomings are mine alone.

lips of his mouth. Both sculptures portray a portly, middle-aged man, seated in *vajraparyaṅkāsana* on a square cushion, the right hand raised in *vitarka mudrā* or the gesture of religious exposition, the left hand in the lap, a small prong in the middle of the palm, which formerly held a small volume of scripture. Both sculptures portray him wearing richly decorated inner and outer monastic robes, with a *phurbu* dagger prominently displayed on his chest, inserted within the folds of the inner robe. One sculpture portrays him with a paṇḍita hat (plate 6), the other has no hat, thus dark pigment indicates the hair on the head as well as his moustache (plate 8).[2] The robes have incised motifs which distinguish the two sculptures. Plate 6 has floral and vegetal motifs for the robes, and cushions; there is a four-line inscription on the back of the throne cushion (plate 7). Plate 8 has robes with triple gem, dragon, and foliate motifs, also with a four-line inscription at verso (plate 9). The cushions that form the bases of the sculptures are decorated with incised carvings—in the inscription of plate 6, the *viśvavajra* is prominently displayed at the center of the cushion and partially visible at both edges. In plate 8, the *viśvavajra* is also at center and at the two edges but the scale of the *viśvavajra* is completely enlarged, surrounded by diamond-shaped geometric motifs. The visual impact of the two bolsters is very different. In terms of the back, there are no embellishments in the two inscriptions. Both inscriptions are carefully incised in print (*dbu can*) letters (see below) as offerings personally dedicated and consecrated by the Fifth Dalai Lama himself, and providing the name of the recipient of the sculpture.

The portrait of the Fifth Dalai Lama wearing the paṇḍita hat was commissioned as a present for a member of the Fifth Dalai Lama's entourage, named in the inscription as Sölpön Gerawa Losang Majentsé (Gsol dpon Ge ra ba blo bzang ma byan brtse). In comparison with the Fifth Dalai Lama's autobiography and his records of dedications known as the *Smon lam* and *Tham phud*, it is possible to learn more about this person and identify his presence at specific times during the life of the Fifth Dalai Lama.[3] The role of *solpön* (*gsol dpon*) has sometimes been translated as "master of ceremonies."[4] Dictionaries are more precise: head cook, master cook, a household official, butler, kitchen

2. Plate 6 was previously published as plate 23 in Tibet, in Nor bu don grub and Snying lcags rgyal 2019, 50–51. Plate 8 was previously published by Sotheby's auction catalogue, September 2016. https://www.sothebys.com/en/auctions/ecatalogue/2016/important-chinese-art-n09541/lot.161.html?locale=en. As the catalogue author misunderstood the name of the donor, it was initially listed as eighteenth-century Sino-Tibetan; the website now has corrected this to Central Tibet, seventeenth century. It was further analyzed by Jacqueline Dennis (2016).

3. See Ngag dbang blo bzang rgya mtsho 2009a and 2009b.

4. Kossak and Casey Singer 1998, 174.

steward, chief food steward; or *sölpön khenpo* (*gsol dpon mkhan po*), steward in charge of grand lama's tea and food.[5] In 1977, Ariane Macdonald, Dvags-po Rinpoche, and Yonten Gyatso studied two historic dedication inscriptions of portraits of the Fifth Dalai Lama, in which the Fifth Dalai Lama personally participated. One of these was requested by a member of his close entourage, the *chöpön* (*mchod dpon*), "chief of offerings." In order to contextualize his role, Macdonald, Dvags-po Rinpoche, and Yonten Gyatso discussed the hierarchy of his close entourage composed of some thirty-five members. Among the most important they list "*gsol dpon*, literally, 'chief of the meals,' a title which corresponds better to 'Majordomo' because, for a person of importance of the Dalai Lama, the person in charge of organization of meals for the Dalai Lama and his guests was certainly a high dignitary. . . ."[6] Furthermore, according to their analysis, in addition to the chöpön, and the sölpön, there were "two 'incense holders' (*spos 'dzin*) and all in all, not more than a dozen (people) were really significant."[7] This greatly clarifies the importance inside the household of the person designated by this title of sölpön. Samten Karmay has more recently adopted the term "kitchen steward" to refer to sölpön, which translation is also perfectly appropriate, however the sentence does not elaborate at all upon the official context of the role.[8]

Curiously, in the inscription as written on the sculpture, the person named Gerawa (Ge ra ba) is qualified as *ma byan*, literally, the cook, but this appears to be a spelling error. It is far more logical to consider that the vowel (*dreng bu*) was misunderstood, as in the writings of the Fifth Dalai Lama, both spellings are encountered: Ge re ba and Ge ra ba. However, "Ge ra ba" is far more frequent. In the inscription, the reading of *ma byan* should be corrected to *mkhyen* (with the missing *dreng bu* added to the word *mkhyen*) followed by *brtse*, which is then logical in the construction *mkhyen brtse*. His full name is written this way in the *Tham phud* dedication (see below). That said, this Sölpön Gerawa was in fact linked to cooking—he was responsible as cook for the Fifth Dalai Lama's trip to Beijing in 1652–53! In a document recording aspects of the trip to China, thanks to Christoph Cüppers, and his great acumen for historic and administrative documents and his long familiarity with obscure administrative terms, we know that the individual Gerawa is qualified as *bzhes spro ba*, which

5. Nitartha, citing JV: http://nitartha.pythonanywhere.com/search?csrf_token=202105251440 24%23%23376b0c1e4720a15658 02ee266b7de4b443bb5e3d&search_term=gsol+dpon.

6. Macdonald et al. 1977, 131.

7. Macdonald et al. 1977, 131.

8. Karmay 2014, 507.

is a term not found in dictionaries.[9] Cüppers interprets this specific term as "the confectioner, the one taking care of the sweets," as indeed the term *bzhes spro* means "cakes, biscuits."[10] Cüppers considered that Gerawa must have been sölpön in the Potala when the Dalai Lama moved there upon completion of the construction in 1649. At this time Gerawa was sölpön with the obligation to be constantly present (*gsol dpon sdod rtag cing*).[11] Further, Cüppers has encountered elsewhere the full name of Gerawa, often addressed as Phodrang Gerawa (Pho brang Ge ra ba) in the Fifth Dalai Lama's writings: in fact he is a scion of Yarlung Phodrang (Yar klung pho brang).[12]

Further confirmation of his presence in the entourage during the Fifth Dalai Lama's trip to China is given by a later passage in the autobiography known as *Du kū la gos bzang*, referring to circa 1664, where the Fifth Dalai Lama records Gerawa as the person who requests composition of an abridged text of *guru pūjā* because the one the Fifth Dalai Lama had composed during his trip to China was too long.[13]

The Dedication Inscription of Gerawa's Portrait of Fifth Dalai Lama

This inscription does not specify a year, or circumstances leading to the request for a portrait by Gerawa. It shows intimate devotion in the sense that Gerawa hopes to never be separated from his personal protector, the Fifth Dalai Lama, who is referred to by his pen name, the Monk of Zahor:

> bsod nams nyer bsags grangs mang skye ba'i mtshor// mgon khyod thugs rje'i zla gzugs rtag shar te/ byang chub bar du 'bral med rjes 'dzin par// smon pa'i re ba ji bzhin 'grub gyur cig/ ces pa 'di yang gsol dpon ge re ba blo bzang ma byan brtses rang gi 'dra 'bag bzhengs pa'i

9. See Blo bzang rnam rgyal and Brag g.yab blo bzang, 2017, 2:1, line 17. Thanks to Christoph Cüppers for pointing out this reference (personal communication, 2019). That text reads: *rgyal dbang thams cad mkhyen pa chen po rgya nag tu chibs [kyi kha lo bsgyur ska]bs las tshan bkod bzhag gi tho / bzhes spro ba do dam pho brang dge ra ba.*

10. Das 1983, s.v. "*bzhes spro.*"

11. Personal communication, 2021. See Ngag dbang blo bzang rgya mtsho, *Dū ku la* 2:111.

12. Personal communication, Christoph Cüppers, 2021. See Cüppers 2017.

13. Karmay 2014, 507. See Ngag dbang blo bzang rgya mtsho 1989, 1:348r line 1–2: *bla ma mchod sngar rgya nag tu 'gro skabs 'bris pa de tshigs don gnyis ka legs po yod pas de'i ,gro don la gnod pa 'dug kyang gsol dpon ge ra ba go sla zhing 'dzin bde la tshigs nyung ba zhig byung ba ltar bla ma mchod pa dngos grub 'dod 'jo bris//.*

kha byang skye bar rjes 'dzin gyi smon lam rab gnas brgya rtsa dang bcas dgos tshul byung ba ltar za hor gyi bandes bris///

The Monk of Zahor wrote (this dedication) in order to perform the hundred prayers and consecrations for the next life for the inventory of portraits at the request of Sölpön Gerawa Losang Khyentse (Gsol dpon ge re ba Blo bzang mkhyen brtse), "In the ocean of countless rebirths accumulating good merits, the great protector Avalokiteśvara arising like the moon of compassion, may the great vow accordingly be accomplished to never be separated until reaching the state of bodhicitta!"[14]

In addition to the dedication inscription inscribed on this portrait, the Fifth Dalai Lama included discussion of the offering of the sculpture to his faithful sölpön again named Gerawa Losang Khyentse in his book of dedications known as the *Smon lam*, where he also named the scribe responsible for the inscription on the sculpture. Here he wrote:

skye bar dal brgyad 'byor bcu'i rten bzang thob/ dam pa'i mgon gyis rtag tu rjes bzung nas/ zab rgyas chos kyi bdud rtsir longs spyod cing/ ma rgan 'gro rnams byang chub thob phyir bsngo/ zhes gsol dpon ge re ba blo bzang mkhyen brtses 'dra 'bag bzhengs pa'i tshe 'di bzhin dgos tshul ltar za hor gyi bandes sbyar ba'i ye ge pa ni sngags rams pa ngag dbang dge legs so//

The scribe Ngakrampa Ngagwang Gelek (Sngags rams pa Ngag dbang dge legs) wrote according to instructions by the Monk of Zahor at the time of making the portrait (requested) by Sölpön Gerawa Losang Khyentsé: May all beings obtain bodhi and enjoy the nectar of the profound Dharma, as the holy protector constantly protects with this favorable support for rebirth with the ten riches and the eight freedoms.[15]

Did the Fifth Dalai Lama take the time to review the work of Ngawang Gelek and realize the error of *ma byan* instead of *mkhyen* on the base of the sculpture? Was the scribe Ngawang Gelek aware of the cooking activities of

14. I thank Roberto Vitali for discussion of this inscription with me.

15. Ngag dbang blo bzang rgya mtsho 2009a, 246.

Gerawa if both were members of the personal entourage of the Fifth Dalai Lama? We cannot know for certain.

We can pinpoint the year of the portrait thanks to the *Du kū la Gos bzang*, which records the writing of the back inscription of a portrait commissioned by Sölpön Gerawa.

One may glean a few other facts about Gerawa thanks to the Fifth Dalai Lama's detailed writings. There are many brief passages in the autobiography where he is mentioned. Circa 1667, Gerawa commissioned a thangka with a dedication on the back for which the Fifth Dalai Lama wrote the prayers.[16] In fact, Gerawa and his younger brother were both known to the Fifth Dalai Lama. The younger brother of Gerawa was head reciter (*chos mdzad*) at the Lhasa monastery of Phendé Lekshé Ling, which at the time was part of the Potala monastery of Namgyal Dratsang.[17] Sometimes the younger brother requested offerings of *snyan dar* ceremonial scarves with prayers.[18] The sölpön requested the text to learn by heart the ritual of the white Jambhala according to the system of Atiśa.[19] At times it is the official function of Gerawa in his capacity to organize the offering of tea (*mang ja*) to the assembly of monks.[20] Sometimes the two brothers participated at ceremonies such as the one in 1671, when the head reciter took part in the offerings to protectors of Namgyal Dratsang, which was followed by offerings of tea at Drepung.[21] When the younger brother became very ill with influenza and high fever (*bro nad dam pos*), the sölpön requested prayers on the offerings of the ceremonial scarves.[22] In the following year, together they request prayers and offerings to the protectors,[23] then upon younger brother's death, the sölpön requested prayers to be recited at the Jokhang.[24] It is in this context, shortly after his brother's death, that Gerawa requested in 1672 the sculpture portrait, with the personal dedication which the Fifth Dalai Lama records in his volume of dedications and in his autobiography.[25] Gerawa continued to serve the Fifth Dalai Lama for another two years

16. Ngag dbang blo bzang rgya mtsho 1989, 2:65. Ngag dbang blo bzang rgya mtsho 2009b, 1:233.

17. Personal communication from Ven. Dvags-po Rinpoche, cited in Heller 1992, 278n78.

18. Nag dbang blo bzang rgya mtsho 1989, 2:77–78.

19. Nag dbang blo bzang rgya mtsho 1989, 2:196.

20. Nag dbang blo bzang rgya mtsho 1989, 2:219.

21. Nag dbang blo bzang rgya mtsho 1989, 2:221.

22. Nag dbang blo bzang rgya mtsho 1989, 2:237, 1671, 11th month 15th day.

23. Nag dbang blo bzang rgya mtsho 1989, 2:279

24. Nag dbang blo bzang rgya mtsho 1989, 2:280.

25. Nag dbang blo bzang rgya mtsho 1989, 2:288.

or so, until finally he took his retirement and a substitute was named.[26] Even after retirement, Gerawa still participated occasionally in donations, such as his offering of two horses around 1693.[27] Roughly speaking, Gerawa served the Fifth Dalai Lama for twenty years, a long and faithful relationship, undoubtedly remaining somewhat close long after his retirement.

Earlier, among more public events in which Gerawa participated, it was in the context of the activities of the Potala close entourage (*potala'i drung 'khor*) where notably present in the entourage is a monk named Samling Gyalpo (Bsam gling rgyal po), This monk also had a close, personal relation with the Fifth Dalai Lama which we will soon examine in more detail, as Samling Gyalpo was the person who requested the Fifth Dalai Lama's portrait without the paṇḍita hat. As part of the same group of ceremonies, Gerawa was the organizer of a tea ceremony at Drepung.[28]

Turning to the second statue, the person who requested this portrait is known as Jangling Samdrup Gyalpo (Byang gling bsam 'grub rgyal po), who was also a member of the Potala close entourage. As far as I have been able to determine, he seems to have had a varied role in the entourage of the Fifth Dalai Lama. He is often referred to as the distributor of salaries (*sprod mi*). One of his tasks was the supervision of the artists and artisans of renovation work in 1658, as noted by Karmay: "Samgrub Gyalpo of Changling led the work for providing them [the artists] with fees and other necessities."[29] Although the precise circumstances of Jangling Samdrup Gyalpo's relation with the Fifth Dalai Lama are far from clear, he notably participated in the funerary offerings during the immediate post mortem period of Depa Sönam Rabten (Sde pa Bsod nams rab brtan), who died of a sudden stroke. In the Lhasa Tsuklakhang, he participated by offering earrings to the Jowo and a pair of Kongpo earrings to a special image of Avalokiteśvara, intended as a gesture of homage to the Depa, for which he requested the Fifth Dalai Lama write dedications. This offering occurred while the death of Sönam Rapten was still concealed.[30] Thus Jangling Gyalpo was among those aware of the information shared by the Fifth Dalai Lama.[31]

Very frequently, Jangling Samdrup Gyalpo is referred to by this term *phogs*

26. Nag dbang blo bzang rgya mtsho 1989, 2:480.

27. Nag dbang blo bzang rgya mtsho 1989, 3:189.

28. Nag dbang blo bzang rgya mtsho 1989, 2:257–58.

29. Karmay 2014, 388.

30. Karmay 2014, 400.

31. Ngag dbang blo bzang rgya mtsho 2009b, 1:130: *ces pa 'di ni sa skyong bsod nams rab brtan gyi dgongs pa rdzogs byed du lha sa byang gling ba bsam grub rgyal pos g.yas g.yon gyi rna rgyan gynis go sha'ka dang rang byon lnga ldan la phus dus kyi kha byang du za hor gyi bandes bris/.*

sogs dgos cha spros mi, the person in charge of distribution of salaries and such. This was one aspect of his activities. He was also responsible for allocation of taxes (*phogs sogs 'phral dgos sprod mi*), or sometimes tea and butter distribution (*phogs dang 'ja mar sprod mi*). In this respect, one of the most illustrious tasks was his supervision of workers and distribution of wages to the craftsmen working on the renovation of the Jowo chapel and throne of the Jowo sculpture in 1673—there were more than thirty carpenters and artisans for copper repoussé.[32] As a complement to his work, he is the person responsible for the donations of books such as the prayers for the new table of contents of the Collected Nyingma Tantras (Rnying ma'i rgyud 'bum)[33] as well as prayers for series of gold thangka of the Buddha,[34] for all of which the Fifth Dalai Lama made dedications.[35]

The dedication of this sculpture portrait of the Fifth Dalai Lama has been admirably studied by Jacqueline Dennis of Sotheby's in the initial essay in 2016 (excepting the misidentification of the person requesting the sculpture which is corrected in the present essay). Dennis reads,

> This statue of the great, omniscient, powerful, and victorious Ngawang Lobsang Gyatso was commissioned as an object of faith by Je Lingpa [sic. Jangling] Samdrup Gyalpo in Lhasa. This statue contains the relics of the Tathagata beings, blessed substances from the holy masters of Tibet and India, and mantra of the four classes of Tantra. *The statue was consecrated by the victorious powerful same... Sarva za yantu!*[36]

The inscription reads:

> rgyal dbang thamscad mkhyen pa chen po ngag dbang blo zang rgya mtsho'i sku snyan 'di lha sa byang gling pa bsaṃ 'grub rgyal pos brten du gzhengs pa 'di 'i nang gtsug su/ de bzhin gshegs pa'i 'phe gdung rgya bo mkhas grub rnams kyi byin rlabs brten / brgyud sde bzhi'i bzungs sngsaga [*sic*, read sngags] sngags sogs bzungs 'bul ba dang

32. Ngag dbang blo bzang rgya mtsho 2009b, 2:45–46.

33. Ngag dbang blo bzang rgya mtsho 2009b, 2:232–33

34. Ngag dbang blo bzang rgya mtsho 2009b, 2:66 (just before 1675).

35. Ngag dbang blo bzang rgya mtsho 2009b, 2:232–33.

36. See Dennis 2016.

> rab gnas kyang rgyal ba nyid rang gi gnang ba'i byin blabs can/ sarva rdza yantu // [37]

As the sculpture was consecrated and sealed at the time of consecration, it is understood to still contain the relics and blessings (plates 10–11). In the photo of the x-ray of the contents one may discern the white circles which are probably prayers rolled around small metal cylinders.

To conclude, the great technical skills exhibited by the masterful casting and embellishment of these two portrait sculptures of the Fifth Dalai Lama are testimony to the prowess of the still-anonymous sculptors and their ateliers in Lhasa. At present, the circumstances of the casting remain unknown. As Buddhist portraits of the Dalai Lama, these are sacred representations yet simultaneously human. The identification of the two men who commissioned these sculptures and the Fifth Dalai Lama's act of blessing them with his personal dedications bring these two portraits closer to the human realm, where the aspirations of these two men are graced by divine blessings bestowed upon them by the Fifth Dalai Lama.

Works Cited

Blo bzang rnam rgyal and Brag g.yab blo bzang bu khrid. 2017. *Ching rgyal rabs slabs kyi bod kyi lo rgyus yig tshags bdams bsgrigs*, vol. 2. Beijing: Zhongguo Zang xue chu ban she.

Cüppers, Christoph. 2017. "Eine Sammlung verwaltungstechnischer Regierungserlasse aus der frühen dGa'-ldan pho-brang-Zeit." *Zentralasiatische Studien* 46: 233–76.

Das, Sarat Chandra. 1969 (reprint 1983). *A Tibetan-English Dictionary*, reprint by Rinsen Book Company, Kyoto, Japan.

Dennis, Jacqueline. 2016. "The Million Dollar Inscription." Sotheby's. September 21. https://www.sothebys.com/en/articles/the-million-dollar-inscription.

Heller, Amy. 1992. "Etude sur le développement de l'iconographie et du culte de Beg-tse, divinité protectrice tibétaine," PhD diss. 343 pages. Paris. École Pratique des Hautes Études, IVe Section Histoire et Philologie.

Karmay, Samten G. 2014. *The Illusive Play: The Autobiography of the Fifth Dalai Lama.* Chicago: Serindia Publications.

Kossak, Steven M., and Jane Casey Singer. 1998. *Sacred Visions: Early Paintings from Central Tibet.* New York: The Metropolitan Museum of Art.

Macdonald, Ariane, Dvags po Rinpoche, and Yonten Gyatso. 1977. "Un portrait du cinquieme dalai-lama." In *Essais sur l'Art du Tibet*, edited by Ariane Macdonald and Yoshiro Imaeda, 119–56. Paris: Librairie d'Amérique et d'Orient J. Maisonneuve.

37. Ngag dbang blo bzang rgya mtsho, op.cit., 2:474 for the commission of the sculpture.

Ngag dbang blo bzang rgya mtsho. 1989. *Za hor gyi bande ngag dbang blo bzang rgya mtsho'i 'di snang 'khrul pa'i rol rtsed rtogs brjod kyi tshul du bkod pa du kū la'i gos bzang*, 3 vols. Lhasa: Bod ljongs mi dmangs dpe skrun khang.

———. 2009a. *Smon lam shis brjod brtan bzhugs sogs kyi tshigs su bcad pa rab dkar dge ba' chu glung glegs bam dang po*. In *Rgyal dbang lnga pa ngag dbang blo bzang rgya mtsho'i gsung 'bum*, 24:1–418. Beijing: Krung go'i bod rig pa dpe skrun khang.

———. 2009b. *Sku gsum thugs rten gsar bzhengs rin po che'i mchod rdzas sang bzang gi dkar chag dang tham phud deb khrims yig gi 'go rgyangs sde bzhi'i sgo 'phar phye ba'i skal bzang*. In *Rgyal dbang lnga pa ngag dbang blo bzang rgya mtsho'i gsung 'bum*, 19:25–404. Beijing: Krung go'i bod rig pa dpe skrun khang.

Nor bu don grub and Snying lcags rgyal, eds. and translators. 2019. *Bod kyi gces nor*. Chengdu: China Cultural Heritage.

Sotheby's. 2016. "A Gilt-Bronze Figure depicting Ngagwang Lobsang Gyatso, Dalai Lama V, Central Tibet, 17th century." https://www.sothebys.com/en/auctions/ecatalogue/2016/important-chinese-art-n09541/lot.161.html.

Some Observations on the *Buddhāvataṃsakasūtra* in Tibet*

Leonard W.J. van der Kuijp

An unknown Sanskrit manuscript of what appears to have been a composite work with the title *Buddhamahāvaipulyāvataṃsakasūtra* [= BAS][1] was translated into Tibetan in circa 800 by, so a later tradition has it, the Indo-Tibetan team of Jinamitra, Surendrabodhi, and Zhu chen [gyi] Lo tsā ba Ye shes sde [and unnamed others (*la sogs pa*)]. Contrary to several other Indian Buddhist sūtras, śāstras, tantras, and various tantra-related canonical treatises that were translated into Tibetan, the sūtra was, as far as is attested in the vast majority of sources, translated only once, and the Sanskrit manuscript on which it was based is lost.[2] That said, Klong chen Rab 'byams pa Dri med 'od zer (1308–64) must be among the very few to have entertained the notion, we do not know on what basis, that there was a circa 800 translation of the BAS by Vairocana and Sba or 'Ba' Sang shi, which they had prepared from a Chinese version that had been related to them by Hwa shang (< Ch. *heshang* 和尚) Mahāyāna from memory.[3] We will see below that he was not alone in holding the view that it was translated from a Chinese version.

*I happily contribute this modest essay in recognition of my colleague J. Gyatso's fundamental contributions to our common passion, Tibetan studies. An earlier version of this short essay was given during a conference on the *Buddhāvataṃsakasūtra* at Beijing University that was held in November of 2017 and was kindly organized by Prof. Wang Song 王颂. For this version, COVID-19 prevented me from fully using the library resources that otherwise would have been available to me. I also thank my friend Jonathan Silk for having looked through this essay and for pointing out some infelicities.

1. For state-of-the-art scholarship on the sūtra, see Hamar 2015.

2. For the place of the sūtra in the subcontinent, see Hamar 2007, 163–64, and especially Skilling and Saerji 2013 and the literature cited therein. That a composite work called the *Buddhamahāvaipulyāvataṃsakasūtra* circulated in the subcontinent is underscored in the notice in Vīnītā (2010, 557–93) that the *Anantabuddhakṣetraguṇaodbhāvanasūtra* was explicitly a part of the BAS. See also Skilling and Saerji 2013, 202n48, and Silk 2013, 64.

3. Klong chen 2009, 228; Barron 2007, 258. We know of Sba/'Ba' Sang shi from *inter alia* the *Sba bzhed*, for which see briefly below.

Knowledge of a Chinese translation of the sūtra and its transmission briefly insinuated itself into Tibetan intellectual circles toward the end of the thirteenth century and has had a life of its own ever since. For reasons that still beg explanation, a few Tibetans appear to have written on this "irregular" and thence "quite extensive" (*vaitulya/vaipulya, shin tu rgyas pa*) sūtra[4] in the fourteenth and fifteenth centuries, in particular. Several scholar-monks active in these centuries were also engaged in writing analytical surveys of the contents of large swaths of the entire Tibetan Buddhist canon, and their expositions of the sūtra in these surveys will be briefly discussed below. The sūtra also played a role in the Tibetan understanding of the hydronyms of the Himalayan Range. It is always cited in connection with expositions of "the world" (*loka, 'jig rten*) and cosmological accounts as well as with certain problems that arose with the identification and authentication of the river systems that originate in the vicinity of Mount Kailash and Lake Manasarovar.[5] Lastly, narratives from the sūtra were also translated into fresco and stone, and this essay concludes with a Tibetan notice to this effect from potentially around the year 800.

The Tibetan version of the sūtra figures as follows in the oldest available Tibetan catalogs of translated scripture, the *Lhan dkar ma* and the *'Phang thang ma* of, respectively, 812/824 or 818/830.[6]

1. Lhan dkar ma[7]

As for what is included in the *'Phags pa shin tu rgyas pa chen po sangs rgyas phal po che'i mdo sde*:

a. *'Phags pa shin tu rgyas pa'i mdo sangs rgyas phal po che* up to the forty-fifth chapter **Āryabuddhāvataṃsakamahāvaipulyasūtra*	39,030 *śloka* / 130 *bam po*, 30 *śloka*
b. *De bzhin gshegs pa phal po che le'u* **Tathāgatāvataṃsakaparivarta*	4,200 *śloka* / 14 *bam po*
c. *Byang chub sems dpa' rdo rje rgyal mtshan gyis yongs su bsngo ba* **Āryabodhisatvavajradhvajapariṇāma*	*3,900 śloka,* 13 *bam po*

4. For the terms and usage of *vaitulya/vaipulya*, see Karashima 2015.

5. Hartmann 2020 and the literature cited in van der Kuijp forthcoming.

6. See the discussion of these dates in Schaeffer and van der Kuijp 2009, 55.

7. Lalou 1953, 319–20, nos. 17–24; it is also often called *Ldan dkar ma*. For the Sanskrit of these titles and where to place the * for tentative reconstructions, see Skilling and Saerji 2013, 197–99.

d.	*'Phags pa byang chub sems dpa'i sa bcu bstan pa* *Āryabodhisatvadaśabhūmikanirdeśa*	2,400 *śloka*, 8 *bam po*
e.	*'Phags pa kun tu bzang po'i spyod pa'i bstan pa* *Āryasamantabhadracaryānirdeśa*	4,800 *śloka*, 13 *bam po*
f.	*'Phags pa de bzhin gshegs pa skye ba 'byung ba bstan pa*[8] *Tathāgatotpattisambhavanirdeśa*	1,500 *śloka*, 5 *bam po*
g.	*'Phags pa 'jig rten las 'das pa'i le'u* *Āryalokottaraparivarta*	3,300 *śloka*, 11 *bam po*
h.	*'Phags pa sdong po bkod pa'i mdo* *Āryagaṇḍavyūhasūtra*	9,000 *śloka*, 30 *bam po*

2. 'Phang thang ma[9]

As for what is included in the *'Phags pa shin tu rgyas pa chen po sangs rgyas phal po che'i mdo sde*:

a.	*'Phags pa shin tu rgyas pa'i mdo sangs rgyas phal po che* *Āryabuddhāvataṃsakasūtra*	145 *bam po*
b.	*'Phags pa 'jig rten las 'das pa'i le'u* *Āryalokottaraparivarta*	2,700 *śloka* / 9 *bam po*
c.	*'Phags pa byang chub sems dpa'i sa bcu* *Āryabodhisatvadaśabhūmika*	2,020 *śloka* / 7 *bam po*
d.	*'Phags pa dkon mchog ta la la* *Āryaratnolkā*	1,210 *śloka* / 4 *bam po*
e.	*De bzhin gshegs pa skye ba 'byung ba bstan pa* *Tathāgatotpattisambhavanirdeśa*	1,400 *śloka* / 5 *bam po*

Of the measuring words for indicating the quantity of text that we find in these catalogs—that is, *śloka* and *bam po*—only *śloka* is of obvious Indian origin. Here it is usually used in the sense of thirty or thirty-two syllables of Sanskrit text, whereas the term *bam po* is exclusively of Tibetan origin and can amount

8. Tacitly correcting Lalou 1953, no. 21: *Byang chub sems dpa'i sa bcu bstan pa*, Skilling and Saerji 2013, 198, correctly list here the *De bzhin gshegs pa skye ba 'byung ba bstan pa* [*Tathāgatotpattisa mbhavanirdeśa*].

9. *Dkar chag 'phang thang ma* 2003, 5.

to several different numbers of syllables of text.[10] These two quantitative terms were evidently used to gain an idea of how much a translator or scribe should be paid for the amount of work they accomplished.[11]

None of the five editions of *Lhan dkar ma*, four xylographs and one manuscript written in the cephalous *dbu can* script, make mention of the identity of the translator[s], and the same holds for the *'Phang thang ma*.[12] The circa 1275 title catalog of translated scripture by Bcom ldan ral gri (1227–1305) is by and large dependent on the *'Phang thang ma* for identifying and listing those texts that were translated during the early period (*snga dar*). But evidently following the *Lhan dkar ma* entry, he states that the quantity of the text of the sūtra amounts to 39,030 *śloka* or 130 *bam po* and 30 *śloka* units of text. But he remains tellingly silent on the actual composition of this large work and suggests that it had been subjected to many corruptions.[13]

Comparing these two entries, we immediately notice the difference in chapters[14] and lengths of the translated texts. Skilling and Saerji have much to say about the different permutations, units of textual lengths, and contents of the sūtra that are found in the different Bka' 'gyur collections, and I happily defer to their perceptive comments.[15] An idea of the numerous text-critical problems that even exist among the eight different xylograph editions of the text can be gleaned from the recent comparative edition of the Bka' 'gyur.[16] Now some thirteen years ago, Imre Hamar briefly discussed the lengthy post-colophonic note that was uniquely added to the Sde dge edition of the BAS.[17] Using the Indo-Tibetan designation of the year, *dge byed* (*śubhakṛt), and the Sino-Tibetan one, the water-tiger (*chu stag*) year, that is, 1722, this important note for the his-

10. See van der Kuijp 2009, 125, 127–29; a verse-*śloka* can have a number of different syllables, whereas in prose it consists of thirty-two syllables of text. Hamar 2007, 163, notes that Zhiyan 智儼 (602–68) had a Sanskrit manuscript of the sūtra for which he gave a precise description of its length in terms the number of pages, the number of lines per page, and the number of *song* 頌-syllables (*śloka*) per line.

11. van der Kuijp 2009, 130–31, and the secondary literature cited therein.

12. We also do not find these in the fragmentary BAS manuscripts of the Ta bo Monastery Bka' 'gyur and the Gondhla collection; see, respectively, Harrison 2009, 73–78, and Tauscher 2008, 3–7.

13. Schaeffer and van der Kuijp 2009, 118–19.

14. See the useful list of the chapters in the Chinese and Tibetan translations of the sūtra in Hamar 2007, 156, 160–67.

15. Skilling and Saerji 2013, 195–201; but see also Park 2016.

16. Bka' 'gyur 2006–9, 801–960.

17. Hamar 2007, 153–5 *ad* Sde dge 1991, 723–5 [= Bka' 'gyur 2006–9, 728–80]; a portion of this colophon formed the point of departure of Park 2016.

tory of the sūtra's transmission was apparently drafted by the monk-attendant Bkra shis dbang phyug,[18] who had been requested to do so by Bstan pa tshe ring (1678–1738), then king of Sde dge. Of interest is that he did so as an outcome of editing the text of the sūtra that was being committed to the printing blocks at the Sde dge dgon chen, that is to say, some eleven years *before* Si tu Paṇ chen Chos kyi 'byung gnas's (1699/1700–74) efforts of editing the entire Bka' 'gyur canon in which this edition of the BAS was included. The note places the ideological foundation of the sūtra squarely in the so-called third and last "turning of the Dharma wheel" (*dharmacakrapravartana*), that is, the last phase of the Buddha's teaching as enunciated in the seventh chapter of the Tibetan rendition of the *Saṃdhinirmocanasūtra*, the well-known sūtra that can perhaps best be described as a first, if somewhat partisan, attempt at writing an intellectual history of Buddhism. While the long colophon is on occasion by no means easy to understand, it does bear an attempt at a translation; it states:

> So, from among the sequence of the three cycles of the Sugata's pronouncements, here the synonyms for the perfect quintessence of the final ascertainment of the ultimate reality,[19] the **Buddhāvataṃsaka*, are many, such as the **Mahāvaipulyapiṭaka*, *Snyan gyi gong rgyan*, *Padma'i rgyan*, and so on.[20] The precious Bu ston Rin chen grub (1290–1364) and others averred that by dividing the text into seven sections—that is, into the *De bzhin gshegs pa phal po che'i le'u* (**Tathāgatāvataṃsakaparivarta*), the *Rdo rje rgyal mtshan gyi bsngo ba* (**Vajradhvajapariṇama*), the *Sa bcu pa bstan pa* (**Daśabhūmikanirdeśa*), the *Kun tu bzang po'i spyod pa bstan pa* (**Samantabhadracaryānirdeśa*), the *De bzhin gshegs pa'i skye ba dang 'byung ba bstan pa* (*Tathāgatotpattisambhavanirdeśa*), the *'Jig rten las 'das pa'i le'u* (*Āryalokottaraparivarta*), and the *Sdong pos brgyan pa'i le'u* (*Gaṇḍavyūhaparivarta*)[21]—the text has 39,030 *śloka*, or 130 *bam po* and 30 *śloka*. And in the catalog of the Tshal pa Bka' 'gyur it

18. He occurs a number of times in the writings of his contemporaries, but he remains a rather elusive figure and is not known as a Sanskrit scholar in spite of his remarks about Sanskrit grammar. He is said to have written a biography of 'Jam dbyangs [Byams pa] Tshul khrims dpal bzang po (1675–1710), the twenty-eighth abbot of Ngor Evaṃ chos ldan Monastery.

19. It is by no means a coincidence that the Buddha's interlocuter in this chapter is the bodhisattva named Paramārthasamudgata [= Don dam yang dag 'phags].

20. Eimer 1999, 123 lists *Shin du rgyas pa chen po*, *'Phags pa phal po che*, and *Mdo sde Padma gang 'chad* as alternative titles.

21. Ōtake 2007, 88, points to the following possible set of equivalences: Huayan 華嚴 – *Sdongs pos brgyan* – *Gaṇḍavyūha* – *Avataṃsaka*.

was made into 115 *bam po* and in the Ldan [=Lhan] dkar ma into 127 *bam po*.[22] The present-day texts appear to have a multitude of more or fewer *bam po*.

At first, the two paṇḍitas Byang chub bzang po [= *Bodhibhadra, 佛馱跋陀羅 (or: Buddhabhadra!)] (359–429) and Paṇḍita Dga' ba [= *Śiksānanda, 實叉難陀] (652–710) requested this text from Nāgārjuna; both translated it into Chinese.[23] The Chinese translation (*rgya nag gi 'gyur*) is said to have been thoroughly edited by Surendrabodhi and Vairocanarakṣita,[24] and as for the oral transmission, the transmission of the translation from China/Chinese: Samyaksambuddha – Ārya Mañjuśrī – Nātha Nāgārjuna – the two above paṇḍitas – and then Hwa shang (< Ch. *heshang* 和尚) Thu shu zhun (???), and so on. Sangs rgyas 'bum heard it from Hwa shang Gying ju (< Ch. *jiangzhu* 講主); thereafter it was transmitted from Lo tsā ba Mchog ldan[25] up to the present.

And the transmission of the translation from India/Sanskrit: Nāgārjuna – Āryadeva – 'Jam dpal grags pa [*Mañjukīrti], and so on. Ba ri Lo tsā ba Rin chen grags (1040–1111) heard it from Rdo rje gdan pa [= ?Don yod rdo rje, *Amoghavajra]; it is said that from him it was transmitted to Mchims Brtson 'grus seng ge, Rje btsun Sa skya pa chen po [Kun dga' snying po (1092–1158)], and so on.

However, aside from the translators' colophons (*'gyur byang*) of the above, I did not see an historical account of how this sūtra was rendered by other scholars and translators; nor did I see the[ir] manuscripts. The fact that the king of 'Jang sa tham[26] realized this very translation in his Bka' 'gyur xylograph on the basis of having made the Tshal pa Bka' 'gyur as his source text (*ma phyi*), I have now taken

22. This number is not what we learn from the Lhan/Ldan dkar ma catalog; see *supra*.

23. For their translations, see Hamar 2007, 159ff.

24. This is a strange statement. Lo tsā ba Vairocanarakṣita is only mentioned as an editor in the Snar thang and Lhasa Zhol xylographs.

25. Also, sometimes referred to as Lo Mchog or Lo Mchog pa, this elusive man whose full name is curiously Mchog ldan legs pa'i blo gros dpung rgyan mdzes pa'i tog—he had given himself this name—has a tiny capsule biography in 'Dar stod 1987, 299. I recall seeing a manuscript with a series of *snyan ngag*-style poems written by him in the Nationalities Library of the Cultural Palace of Nationalities, Beijing, under catalog no. 002381. One should hope that one day he can be led out of the antechambers of Tibet's literary history.

26. See Imaeda 1982a, which was reprinted in his publication of this Bka' 'gyur catalog in Imaeda 1982b. The king in question was Mu Zeng 木增 (1587–1646), alias Karma mi pham tshe dbang bsod nams rab brtan. Dating to 1621, the 'Jang sa tham Bka' 'gyur xylograph is the second oldest of the eight known xylographs of the Bka' 'gyur. The oldest one with an extremely limited circulation was the Yongle 永樂 Bka' 'gyur of 1410, for which see Silk 1996.

> the renowned Li thang vermilion xylograph to be authoritative and made it my source text. Yet, on this occasion, since there were many elisions (*chad*), interpolations (*lhag*), and misspelled (*brda ma dag*) expressions, I again made editorial corrections, having discovered many old expressions (*yig rnying*).[27] And furthermore, even if, with respect to a different Sanskrit manuscript and an inconsistent translation, I was unable to correct the wording of a single meaningful block of text,[28] it just seemed useful to correct the majority of its [the BAS's] manuscripts. However, since the different translations of ***bkod pa*** for ***brgyan***, ***rab 'byams pa*** for ***'byam slas***, ***tha dad pa yang dag par shes pa*** for ***so sor yang dag par rig pa***, ***dgongs pa*** for ***thugs***, ***nyin mtshan dang yud du yan man dang zhes dang*** for ***nyin mtshan dang zla ba yar kham mar kham dang zhes pa*** did not contradict the intent, I left them as they were. The fact that Sanskrit has many stems (*rang bzhin*, *prakṛti*), suffixes (*rkyen*, *pratyaya*), derivations (*rnam 'gyur*, *vikāra*), in Tibet, some translators and scholars with the eye of the Dharma made their translations based on the intent of the wording. And since tense (*dus*, **kāla*), case-endings (*rnam dbye*, *vibhakti*), and so on are quite difficult to understand, I took as my standard the manuscripts that for the most part agreed with each other. The presence of some places that were doubtful in others were standardized in accordance with Tibetan linguistic treatises.

I have difficulty in understanding the next sentence.[29] It *appears* to say the following. Archaic terminology (*brda rnying*) and evidence of the translation having been emended were absent from the majority of manuscripts he consulted. Manuscripts that only had archaic terminology would have been fine, but it would be quite detrimental were there a mixture of updated and archaic terminology (*brda gsar rnying*). And he ignored the fact that they had an inconsistent use of (Tibetan) punctuation.

Bkra shis dbang phyug's reference to Bu ston's view on things is found in the latter's well-known chronicle of Buddhism of 1323–26, where, however, Bu ston

27. At first, I took *yig* to mean manuscript, but then, at my peril, I decided on "expression," even though he uses the term *brda rnying*, "archaic expression," later on.

28. The text has: . . . *yin la / de'ang rgya dpe mi gcig pa dang / 'gyur mi mthun pa ni don gyi khog gcig kyang tshig la zhu dag mi btub na'ang* / . . . , and my rendition is quite tentative.

29. It reads: *dpe phal cher la brda rnying shas che ba dang / 'gyur bcos mdzad pa'i gsal kha mi snang bas / bod kyi brda rnying pa sha stag zhig byung na 'brel chags pa 'dra yang phyis su brda gsar rnying 'dres nyams che ba dang / shad bar gcod mtshams 'khrugs pa mang du snang yang cung zad skyon chung ba'i dbang du byas nas btang snyoms su bzhag* /.

mentions that the translation was edited by Vairocanarakṣita.[30] An early notice of its translation is given in the chronicle that is attributed to Nyang ral Nyi ma 'od zer (1124–92), where, given the mention of such translators as Ka ba Dpal brtsegs, Cog ro Klu'i rgyal mtshan, and Sna nam Ban de Ye shes sde, the implication clearly is that the sūtra was translated from a Sanskrit manuscript.[31] While Bu ston notes that the original sūtra had one hundred thousand chapters, just more than forty chapters (*bzhi bcu lhag tsam*) are extant,[32] but the "more than forty chapters" is difficult to square with the precise number of forty-five chapters that he mentioned in the previous quotation.

Now what, to my knowledge, is so far the earliest available notice of the Chinese transmission of the sūtra in a Tibetan work is found in Ngor chen Kun dga' bzang po's (1382–1456) undated record of his studies. He gives there the following line of transmission:[33]

> The transmission of the BAS in forty-five chapters: Buddha – Mañjughoṣa – Nāgārjuna – Āryadeva – *Bodhibhadra – a wondrous, volitional manifestation of Mañjuśrī – Chinese Zhu zhun – Gyim btsun ja – Tan zhi du go zhi – Tshang long go zhi – Gyi rde'u – Haṃ ssaḥ ho thi – Tshang las ta go zhi – Ha hi tha – Gyi ju – Song chen gyin – Gyang ju (< 講主) – Saṃ gya ru – he, having spoking Tibetan – Lo tstsha ba Mchog ldan – Slob dpon Ra sa ba Shākya brtan – Bla ma Gzhon nu tshul khrims – Bla ma Chos grags dpal bzang po (1283–?1363) – Paṇ chen Ma ti [Blo gros rgyal mtshan (1294–1376)] – Sa bzang 'Phags pa Gzhon nu blo gros (1358–1412) – me.
>
> The tradition of the transmission from India: Buddha – Maitreya – Asaṅga – Vasubandhu – Sthiramati – Paṇḍita Purṇavardhana – Ratnākaraśānti – Rdo rje gdan pa – Vairocanarakṣita – Don yod rdo rje [*Amoghavajra] – Ba ri Lo tsā ba – Lho pa Khyung ston – Gtsang pa Ston grags – G.yor po Yug ston – Nyang Bsod nams dbang po – Rgya ston Dharmashrī – Kong nag Ral gri – Shangs pa Grags pa seng ge – Slob dpon Ra sa ba Ston shag[34] – Bla ma Gzhon nu tshul khrims – Bla ma Chos grags dpal bzang po – Paṇḍita Ma ti – Sa bzang 'Phags pa – me.

30. Bu ston 1988, 217.

31. Nyang ral 1988, 334, 394, 422, 430. For a discussion of the problems with this attribution, see Hirshberg 2016, 141–75.

32. Bu ston 1988, 171.

33. Ngor chen 2010, 360–61.

34. I suggest he is to be identified as Slob dpon Ra sa ba Shākya brtan of the Chinese transmission.

It is by no means obvious, at least not to me, what might be entailed by the so-called "Chinese" transmission of the sūtra in Tibet. Even if not much can be deduced from it, a hint is given by what Ngor chen says of a certain Saṃ gya ru, namely that he spoke Tibetan (*'dis bod skad gsungs*)! Upon an examination of the possible historical environment in which the points of intersection between the Chinese and Tibetan exponents of the Chinese transmission of the text might have occurred, I can think of two possible scenarios, both of which date to the last two decades of the thirteenth century. The first coincides with the presence of Gongdi (r. 1274–76), the last emperor of the Southern Song dynasty who, upon his deposition, lived in exile as a monk near Sa skya Monastery and is known in Tibetan as Lha btsun Chos kyi rin chen (d. 1323).[35] It is possible that a member of his entourage transmitted the Chinese version, but one is then left to wonder about the mechanics of this transmission and how the work continued to be handed down. The other possibility is that transmission was a byproduct of the compilation of the Zhiyuan 至元 canon of 1285–87, in which a consortium of scholars of different nationalities compiled an edition of the Chinese Buddhist canon wherein, when pertinent, the Tibetan counterparts of the Chinese Buddhist texts were compared. As Huang and Hamar have observed, the *Zhiyuan fabao kantong zonglu* 至元法寶勘同总录, the catalog of this endeavor, does say that the Tibetan version of the sūtra was translated from the Chinese.[36] The person with the intermediate clerical official title *gying/gyang ju* (< Ch. 講主)[37] was the Chinese monk who formed the link between the transmission of the Chinese BAS with a certain Dbus pa Sangs rgyas 'bum, and Saṃ gya ru did the same with Lo tsā ba Mchog ldan. Neither Dbus pa nor the Lo tsā ba are reckoned to have been present during the compilation of the famous catalog in which Chinese translations of Buddhist texts were compared with their putative Tibetan counterparts. One can only speculate what such a transmission of the Chinese text of the BAS to these Tibetans might have looked like. As stated, a hint may be given in the gloss anent Saṃ gya ru—namely, that he spoke Tibetan. But I hesitate to indulge in any further speculation.

As is to be expected, the entry for the BAS in Si tu Paṇ chen's 1733 catalog

35. For references, see Hua 2018.

36. Huang 2003, 46. The catalog entry (*songti* 宋体) reads here: "The two sūtras on the right," i.e., the two Chinese translations of the BAS, "are different translations of the same text. The Tibetan text of this sūtra was translated from the Chinese; both are the same" (右二經同本異譯. 此經蕃本從漢本譯出, 對同). See also Hamar 2007, 166. However, Huang's editorial remark in bold (*heiti* 黑体) stipulates that this is incorrect; neither the Tibetan text nor its title show a resemblance with the Chinese text[s].

37. I thank my student Mr. Ma Zhouyang for sharing his ideas about this title and the competence of the one who holds it.

of the Sde dge xylograph of the Bka' 'gyur canon is in part based on Bkra shis dbang phyug's note. He begins by stating that the sūtra's alternate names are *Sangs rgyas rma ga chad* and *Snyan gyi gong rgyan*, which, he states belong to the old and dated terminology (*brda rnying*) of Tibetan:[38]

> *... shin tu rgyas pa chen po'i mdo sde sangs rgyas phal po che ni / brda rnying du sang rgyas rma ga chad du grags shing / yang snyan gyi gong rgyan du 'ang bsgyur ba yod de / de lta bu'i mtshan de'ang bye brag gi ming spyi la btags par gsal te / ...*

> ... the very extensive and large sūtra, the *Avataṃsakasūtra*, was known in the old terminology (*brda rnying*) as the *Sangs rgyas rma ga chad* and, furthermore, there is its translation as *Snyan gyi gong rgyan* as well; it is clear that such a title, however, is an instance of the name of a particular that is given to the general ...[39]

He then goes on by citing the *Lhan dkar ma* catalog entries but states that the original sūtra was longer and that parts of it were lost due to a fire at Nālandā Monastery in what is now Bihar state, India. He may have picked up this detail during his first trip to the Kathmandu Valley or from some earlier source. Si tu Paṇ chen then attributes the different sizes of the text to different ideas about the size of the *bam po* text unit, and writes that for Bu ston the *bam po* consisted of three hundred *śloka*, whereas for the authors of the *Lhan dkar ma* and the Tshal pa Bka' 'gyur—see below—a *bam po* comprised three hundred fifty and even four hundred *śloka*.

As for the different titles of the BAS, we already find something like it in Bu ston's notice of the sūtra, even if he does not make a judgment in terms of one of them being an archaic, dated expression (*brda rnying*). The two names of *Sangs rgyas rma ga chad* and *Snyan gyi gong rgyan* do not figure in Ōtake Susumu's valuable study on the origin and early development of the BAS. Be this as it may, four xylograph editions of the Bka' 'gyur—the Yongle, Li thang, Beijing, and the Co ne—used *Sangs rgyas rma[d] ga gcad ces bya ba'i shin tu rgyas pa chen po'i mdo* as the title of the BAS.[40] Some time ago, Mimaki Katsumi studied a manuscript of the very work by Dbus pa Blo gsal Rtsod pa'i seng ge (late 13th–mid 14th cent.), which has the entry for *rma ga chad* and gives *yang dag* as

38. Si tu Paṇ chen 1990, 428–29, and 2008, 432–34.

39. See here also the notices on *rma ga chad* and/or *Snyan gyi gong rgyan* in Hamar 2007, 155n109, van Schaik 2012, Martin 2012, and Skilling and Saerji 2013, 201–2.

40. Bka' 'gyur 2006–9, 801.

the updated equivalent.[41] Cognate with Dbus pa Blo gsal's work and attributed to Skyogs ston Lo tsā ba Rin chen bkra shis, the *Li shi'i gur khang* of 1536 goes several steps further and has *yang dag pa* as well as *phal po che* and *snyan gyi gong rgyan* as new, updated (*brda gsar*) equivalents for *rma ga chad*.[42]

In his 1519 catalog of a Bka' 'gyur that he himself had produced, Zhwa dmar IV Chos grags ye shes (1453–1524) basically says the same thing about these different titles, but he adds a note stating that his "all-knowing abbot" had suggested that *avataṃsaka* had also been rendered *snyan gyi gong rgyan* and *padma'i rgyan*.[43] He informs us in his autobiography that his abbot was the famous 'Gos Lo tsā ba Gzhon nu dpal (1392–1481), who ordained him a monk on February 26, 1476.[44] In the entry for the Tibetan translation of the *Avataṃsakasūtra* of the incomplete manuscript of his large-scale study of the corpus of Buddhist sūtras, he first gives a rough idea of the sections within the sūtra and the names of the translators.[45] He then cites the passage from Bu ston, indicates that some texts have as *sangs rgyas smag bcad* and *rma kha chad* as their titles, and then corrects these by quoting Dbus pa Blo gsal. I suspect that *smag bcad* is quite simply a misreading for *rma ga bcad*, where superscribed *r* and *s* [*ra mgo* and *sa mgo*] in most acephalous *dbu med* scripts are virtual homographs, an inter-syllabic dot (*bar tsheg*) between **sma* and **ga* was overlooked, and *bcad* and *chad* as homophones were confused. He follows this up with an inventory of the individual titles on the basis of the *Lhan dkar ma*. Citing Karma pa III Rang byung rdo rje's (1284–1339) *Phal po che'i bsdu ba'i rnam bshad*,[46] he notes that his learned predecessor divided the contents of the text into eleven different sūtra parts (*mdo*). Zhwa dmar IV then proceeds to give a

41. Mimaki 1990, 26, no. 60.

42. Skyogs ston Lo tsā ba 1981, 3; see also the edition of the text that A mes zhabs Ngag dbang kun dga' bsod nams (1597–1659) prepared on the basis of some four or five texts (*dpe bzhi lnga tsam*) in A mes zhabs 2012, 13, which also includes its purported Sanskrit equivalent of *a bla tampa ka*, that is, *avataṃsaka*. In certain kinds of cursive, acephalous *dbu med* script, the ligature of *bla* and the graphs of *wa*, and *pa* and *sa* are not easily distinguishable, hence the resulting *a bla tampa ka*!

43. Zhwa dmar IVa 2009, 893: *saṃ skṛ ta'i skad du / buddhā vataṃ sa ka / zhes sangs rgyas phal po che'i skad du byung ba la / snyan gyi gong rgyan dang / padma'i rgyan du bsgyur zhing / shin du rgyas pa sogs don las tshan du bya ba yin no // zhes bdag gi mkhan po thams cad mkhyen pa gsung ngo //*. This was not the first Bka' 'gyur that he produced, for he writes that he had another one prepared in 1513; see Zhwa dmar IV 2009a, 918. Unfortunately, neither are given details in his autobiographical *rtogs brjod*, since it ends with an entry for the year 1505; see Zhwa dmar IV 2009b, 994.

44. Zhwa dmar IV 2009b, 948

45. Zhwa dmar IV 2009c, 164–65.

46. This work is not found among his writings that have been made available by the Buddhist Digital Resource Center.

much more granular analysis of its contents by signaling the subject matter of the forty-five chapters (*le'u*) in some detail. To be sure, it is the BAS in forty-five chapters that we encounter in all the known Bka' 'gyur editions. The last of these chapters consists of the *Gaṇḍavyūhasūtra*. He also refers to a work by Karma pa IV Rol pa'i rdo rje (1340–83). An entry in the Karma pa IV's 1388 or 1400 biography by Zhwa dmar II Mkha' spyod dbang po (1350–1405) informs us that he had written a study of the story of Sudhana that was strictly based on the BAS.[47] The story of Sudhana and his travels and travails are of course very popular in the Buddhist world of Tibet and beyond. Illustrative examples include Sudhana's voyage as depicted on frescoes in Ta pho Monastery in Himachal Pradesh, India,[48] and Gro tshang rdo rje 'chang / Qutan 瞿曇 Monastery in Qinghai province, PRC, or rendered into stone in the Duobao 多寶 pagoda in Dazhu 大足, Chongqing, PRC, and the panels of the Borobudur complex on Java, Indonesia.[49]

We do not have firsthand information on the circa 1340 manuscript edition of the aforementioned Tshal pa Bka' 'gyur, but Dalai Lama V Ngag dbang blo bzang rgya mtsho (1617–82) signals some of its features in the massive record of his studies that is dated 1670.[50] He approvingly gives a nod to 'Gos Lo tsā ba's remarks—he calls him 'Gos Lo tsā ba Ye bzang rtse pa[51]—and writes that Zhwa dmar IV had explained the term *smag chad* in the sense of "because there is no darkness for un-knowing" (*ma rig pa'i smug rum med pas*). I do not know where the Karma Bka' brgyud pa hierarch might have written this, but he definitely did not do so in the sources that I have used. But the Dalai Lama does take issue with the explanations of this expression that Dka' bcu pa Padma bzang po (15th cent.) and a Chos rje Dpa' bo [= ?Dpa' bo II Gtsug lag phreng ba (1504–66)] had put forward. The first had apparently equated *smad chad* with *ma smad*, and the second suggested that *smad chad* is a dated term for *phal chen*. Both, he says, appear to be doubtful. He also gives the following transmission of the Chinese translation of the BAS in Tibet:

> Samyaksambuddha – Ārya Mañjuśrī – Nātha Nāgārjuna – Paṇḍita Bodhibhadra and Paṇḍita Ānanda [these two made the Chinese

47. Zhwa dmar II 1978, 298.

48. Steinkellner 1995.

49. For Gro tshang rdo rje 'chang / Qutan Monastery, see Sperling 2001 and Jin 2014; for the fifty-three panels in Dazhu, see the reference in Hamar 2007, 153; for Borobudur, see now Fontein 2012.

50. Dalai Lama V 2009, 245–50. Ehrhard 2012 studied this large work that occupies some four volumes of the Dalai Lama's oeuvre.

51. For the different names of 'Gos Lo tsā ba, see the preliminary study in van der Kuijp 2007.

translation] – Hwa shang Thu thu zhun – Gyim btsun ja – Ten zhi di go zhi – Tshing lang go zhi – Gyi hung – Ha'i hrī tha'i – Gyi ju Son chen gyin – Sing ga sang – Gying ju – Dbus pa Sangs rgyas 'bum – Lo tsā ba Mchog ldan – Bla ma Bsod nams bzang po. . . .

Some 230 years earlier, in perhaps 1444, Gong ma Grags pa 'byung gnas (1414–45), the Phag mo gru ruler of Central Tibet, ordered Pad dkar bzang po to write a survey of the contents of the Bka' 'gyur part of the Tibetan Buddhist canon. Pad dkar bzang po complied and completed his survey shortly before his lord's untimely passing at the royal monastery of Rtse thang.[52] In this survey, which he subtitled "The Fourth Council" (*bka' bsdu bzhi pa*), he gives summaries of each sūtra, a notice of their controversial points, and the philosophical point of view that lies at their base. As is to be expected, his survey of the BAS is rather detailed, and prior to giving an overview of the contents of BAS's component sūtras, he shows under the rubric of "connectivity" (*'brel pa*) how each of the sūtras or cluster of sūtras logically follow upon one another. If true, this suggests that the sūtras that make the BAS were not haphazardly thrown together, that the BAS had a systematicity of which at least some pockets of the Tibetan tradition were aware. And adding their philosophical orientation, he then goes through each of its eight sections (*skabs*) in the following manner:[53]

a. *De bzhin gshegs pa rma[d] ga chad kyi mdo*[54]	Yogācāra-Madhyamaka Ekayāna chapters 1–11
b *Byang chub sems dpa'i sde snod kyi mdo*[55]	Yogācāra-Madhyamaka Ekayāna chapters 12–27
c. *Rdo rje rgyal mtshan gyi bsngo ba'i mdo*	same as b chapters 28–30

52. See Pad dkar bzang po 2006. This work's editor unfortunately misdated it a hundred twenty years later to 1565!

53. Pad dkar bzang po 2006, 6–23.

54. As for its controversial point, he writes: "Why are the lay-out of the world (**loka*) that occurs in other sūtras and the lay-out of the world that occurs in this sūtra inconsistent? Their approach is not the same, because, while the other sūtras show the lay-out of but a portion of the world system (**lokadhātu*), in this sūtra, the lay-out of the superior realm of the ten directions and the three times were shown." (*mdo gzhan nas 'byung ba'i 'jig rten gyi bkod pa dang / mdo 'di nas bstan pa'i 'jig rten gyi bkod pa mi mthun pa ci zhe na / mdo gzhan rnams nas 'jig rten gyi khams phyogs re tsam gyi bkod pa ston pa yin la / 'dir ni phyogs bcu dus gsum gyi zhing rab 'byams kyi bkod pa bstan pa'i phyir tshul mi mtshungs pa'o //*).

55. Pad dkar bzang po adds that for this section "rational cognition and meditative equipoise have visible contents" (*rigs shes dang mnyam bzhag ni snang bcas so //*).

d. *Mdo sde sa bcu pa'i mdo*	same as b chapter 31
e. *Kun tu bzang po'i spyod pa bstan pa'i mdo*	same as a chapters 32–42
f. *De bzhin gshegs pa'i skye ba 'byung ba'i mdo*	same as a chapter 43
g. *'Jig rten las 'das pa'i mdo*	same as a chapter 42 is given
h. *Sdong po bkod pa'i mdo*	same as a no chapter number is given

No doubt more such manuscripts will become available for inspection as we begin to do more cormorant-like dives into the literature, but I accidentally happened to come across a brief retelling of the BAS. It was tucked away, and thus remained uncatalogued, after a manuscript of 'Gos Lo tsā ba's study of the three cycles of the Buddha's teaching that was catalogued. The manuscript in question was written in the cephalous *dbu can* script, and its author was Khrims khang Lo tsā ba Bsod nams rgya mtsho (1424–82).[56] The title page titles this work *Shin tu rgyas pa'i sde snod sangs rgyas phal po che las nye bar 'kho* [read: *mkho*] *ba btus pa'i zin bris kyi yi ge* and measures some twenty-nine folios. Zhwa dmar IV completed the biography of Khrims khang Lo tsā ba, his beloved master, only a month or so after his passing, and he notes therein that this still relatively underappreciated scholar had written his synopsis of the BAS in 1449.[57]

Finally, unlike in China, Korea, and Japan, no school of thought formed itself around this sūtra in Tibetan Buddhism, and in any event, the Tibetans always seemed to have been more interested in *śāstra* rather than in *sūtra* Buddhism. To be sure, this does not mean that sūtras, or that this particular sūtra, were completely ignored. On the contrary, we have plenty of indications that the sūtra was also used for artistic motifs when several of its main narrative stories were "translated" from text into fresco. This was of course especially the case with the famous story of Sudhana's quest for enlightenment that is taken from the *Gaṇḍavyūhasūtra*, itself an integral part of the BAS and, indeed, its forty-fifth and last chapter of the Tibetan translation. In the area dominated by Tibetan culture, the translation of narratives into frescoes already had its incep-

56. Khrims khang, no date. For a synopsis of his life and collection of his letters—some four of which he wrote [two each] in Sanskrit, as befits a Sanskrit scholar, to his teacher Vanaratna (1384–1468) and his re-embodiment (*yang sprul*)—see Ehrhard 2002a, 2002b.

57. Zhwa dmar IV 2009d, 294.

tion with the Buddhist decorative art of the late eighth century. The primary source for this is the *Dba'/Sba/'Ba' bzhed*, the *Testimony of Dba'/Sba/'Ba'*.[58] Originally written around the year 800, portions of the extant texts are no doubt this old, whereas other portions are, equally without any doubt, much later additions and interpolations. Be this as it may, the *Testimony* reads almost like a biography of Khri srong lde btsan (d. 800), the ruler under whom Indian forms of Buddhism were declared a national religion. Some versions of this work contain a lengthy passage that deals with the construction of Bsam yas Monastery, the first monastery of its kind in the Tibetan state. Khri srong lde btsan ordered Bsam yas to be built in the second half of the eighth century. All versions concur that the foundation (*rmang*) for the main structure was laid (*'dings*) in 763 or 765 and that it was consecrated in 775. The version that is titled *Dba' bzhed* contains a very brief narrative of the actual construction of the monastery, and while it mentions paintings (*ri mo*)—that is, frescoes—and statuary (*sku*) with which it and its adjacent chapels and stūpas were adorned, it does not go into specific details, such as what these frescoes depicted. On the other hand, the versions of the text that have *Sba bzhed* as their title do have a much longer narrative that includes the decorative art and the narratives from various scriptures that were used for its frescoes. Using one recension of the *Sba bzhed*, the following frescoes from the narratives of the sūtra as such or its component parts are indicated to have figured on its walls:

Sba bzhed[59]

a. The third of the three floors of Bsam yas' main structure, the so-called "Indian floor," contained narrative frescoes from the *Daśabhūmikasūtra*.
b. The large circumambulatory passage (*'khor sa chen mo*) contained narrative frescoes from the *Gaṇḍavyūhasūtra* and Sudhana's story.
c. The Mkhyen rab 'jam dpal gling chapel contained narrative frescoes from the BAS (*Phal po che*).
d. The Bdud 'dul sngags pa gling chapel contained narrative frescoes from the *Daśabhūmikasūtra*.

58. For state-of-the-art studies of this work, see Doney 2021. Biondo 2021, whose chapter occurs in Doney 2021, 75–87, provides a very detailed study of members of the Sba family, including Sang shi mentioned above.

59. Sba Gsal snang 1982, 45–47.

If we are to believe the implied date of these frescoes of the *Sba bzhed*, then they were painted prior to its consecration, so that these and a number of other texts that are mentioned in this connection must have existed in translation prior to it. This is hard to believe. The various histories of and notices about Bsam yas Monastery that are now available suggest that numerous renovations were carried out over the twelve hundred years of its existence, the last one I myself witnessed when I visited the monastery in 1982. Renovation always implies change. It will therefore be well to examine the contents of these histories and notices before any hard and fast conclusions are drawn about the date of its artwork.

So far, we have only evidence of the Tibetan version of the BAS that was translated from a Sanskrit manuscript in around 800. But we must not jump to conclusions. There is so much that we do not yet know about the untold manuscript riches that still lie unexcavated and thus uncatalogued in many monastic libraries. It is quite possible that we will be able to get a more solid grip on the influence it exerted on Tibetan cosmological speculations, especially from the side of the Rnying ma school, when we systematically go through, say, the collected tantras of this school or the writings of the great Klong chen Rab 'byams pa and others. There is still so much to do, and so many wonderful things to uncover.

Works Cited

A mes zhabs Ngag dbang kun dga' bsod nams. 2012. *Gsar rnying gi brda'i rnam dbye legs par bshad pa gsung rab kun la lta ba'i sgron me.* In *Collected Works*, edited by Si khron bod yig dpe rnying myur skyob 'tshol sgrig khang, 9:11–31. Lhasa: Bod ljongs dpe rnying dpe skrun khang.

Barron, Richard, tr. 2007. *Longchen Rabjam. The Precious Treasury of Philosophical Systems*. Junction City: Padma Publishing.

Biondo, Serena. 2021. "Narrative Sources of the Great Debate." In *Bringing Buddhism to Tibet*, edited by Lewis Doney, 75–87. Berlin/Boston: Walter de Gruyter GmbH.

Bka' 'gyur. 2006–9. *Sangs rgyas phal po che zhes bya ba shin tu rgyas chen po'i mdo*. In *Bka' 'gyur* [*dpe sdur ma*], edited by Krung go'i bod rig pa zhib 'jug lte gnas kyi bka' bstan dpe sdur khang, vol. 38. Beijing: Krung go'i bod rig pa dpe skrun khang.

Bu ston Rin chen grub. 1988. *Bu ston chos 'byung gsung rab rin po che'i mdzod*, edited by Rdo rje rgyal po. Xining: Krung go'i bod kyi shes rig dpe skrun khang.

Dalai Lama V Ngag dbang blo bzang rgya mtsho. 2009. *Zab pa rgya che ba'i dam pa'i chos kyi thob yig ganga'i chu rgyun*. In *Collected Works*, edited by Ser gtsug nang bstan dpe rnying 'tshol bsdu phyogs sgrig khang, vol. 4. Beijing: Krung go'i bod rig pa dpe skrun khang.

'Dar stod Dgra 'dul dbang po. 1987. *Tha snyad rig gnas lnga ji ltar byung ba'i tshul gsal bar byed pa blo gsal mgrin rgyan legs bshad nor bu'i phreng ba*. In *Bstan rtsis gsal ba'i nyin byed / Tha snyad rig gnas lnga'i byung tshul*, edited by Nor brang O rgyan. Gangs can rig mdzod 4:253–322. Lhasa: Bod ljongs mi dmangs dpe skrun khang.

Dkar chag 'phang thang ma. 2003. [and the *Sgra sbyor bam po gnyis pa*], edited by Bod ljongs rten rdzas bshams mdzod khang, 1–67. Beijing: Mi rigs dpe skrun khang.

Doney, Lewis, ed. 2021. *Bringing Buddhism to Tibet: History and Narrative in the Dba' bzhed Manuscript*. Berlin/Boston: Walter de Gruyter GmbH.

Ehrhard, Franz-Karl. 2002a. *Life and Travels of Lo-chen Bsod nams rgya-mtsho*. Lumbini: Lumbini International Research Institute.

———. 2002b. *A Buddhist Correspondence: The Letters of Lo-chen Bsod-nams rgya-mtsho*. Lumbini International Research Institute, Facsimile Edition Series 3. Lumbini: Lumbini International Research Institute.

———. 2012. "'Flow of the River Ganga': The *gSan-yig* of the Fifth Dalai Bla–ma and Its Literary Sources." *Studies on the History of Tibet and the Himalaya*, edited by H. Blezer and R. Vitali, 79–96. Kathmandu: Vajra Publications.

Eimer, Helmut. 1999. *The Early Mustang Kanjur Catalogue*. Wiener Studien zur Tibetologie und Buddhismuskunde 45. Vienna: Arbeitskreis für Tibetische und Buddhistische Studien Universität Wien.

Fontein, Jan. 2012. *Entering the Dharmadhātu. A Study of the Gaṇḍavyūha Reliefs of Borobudur.* Leiden: Brill.

Hamar, Imre. 2007. "The History of the *Buddhāvataṃsaka-sūtra*: Shorter and Larger Texts." In *Reflecting Miirrors. Perspectives on Huayan Buddhism,* edited by Imre Hamar, 139–67. Asiatische Forschungen 151. Wiesbaden: Harrassowitz Verlag.

———. 2015. *Buddhāvataṃsakasūtra*. In *Encyclopedia of Buddhism Online*, edited by J.A. Silk, O. von Hinüber, and V. Eltschinger. Accessed 17 February 2021 <http://dx.doi.org/10.1163/2467-9666_enbo_COM_0012>

Harrison, Paul. 2009. *Tabo Studies III. A Catalogue of the Manuscript Collection of Tabo Monastery*. Serie Orientale Roma CIII,1I. Rome: Istituto Italiano per il Medio ed Estremo Oriente.

Hartmann, Catharine A. 2020. *To See a Mountain: Writing, Place, and Vision in Tibetan Pilgrimage Literature*. PhD dissertation, Harvard University.

Hirshberg, Daniel A. 2016. *Remembering the Lotus-Born. Padmasambhava in the History of Tibet's Golden Age*. Somerville, MA: Wisdom Publications.

Hua Kaiqi. 2018. "The Journey of Zhao Xian and the Exile of Royal Descendants in the Yuan Dynasty (1276–1368)." In *Buddhist Encounters and Identities across East Asia*, edited by A. Heirman, C. Meinert, and Chr. Anderl, 196–223. Dynamics in the History of Religions 10. Brill: Leiden.

Huang Mingxin 黄明信. 2003. *Han Zang Dazangjing Mulu Yitong Yanjiu* 汉藏大葬经目录异同研究 [*A Study of the Similarities and Differences of the Catalog of the Sino-Tibetan Buddhist Canon*]. Beijing: Zongguo zangxue chubanshe.

Imaeda, Yoshiro. 1982a. "L'édition du Kanjur tibétain de 'Jang Sa-tham." *Journal asiatique* 270.1–2: 173–89.

———. 1982b. *Catalogue du Kanjur tibétain de l'édition de 'Jang sa-tham, Première partie. Edition en fac-similé avec introduction*. Bibliographia Philologica Buddhica, Series Maior, IIa. Tokyo: The International Institute for Buddhist Studies.

Jin Pingzhu 金萍著. 2014. *Qutansi Bihua Yishu Yanjiu* 瞿昙寺壁画艺术研究 [A Study of the Mural Art of Qutan Monastery]. Beijing: Zhongguo Zangxue Chubanshe.

Karashima, Seishi. 2015. "Who Composed the Mahāyāna Scriptures? – The Mahāsāṃghikas and *Vaitulya* Scriptures." *Annual Report of the International Research Institute for Advanced Buddhology at Soka University for the Academic Year 2014* XVIII, 113–62.

Khrims khang Lo tsā ba Bsod nams rgya mtsho'i sde. No date. *Shin tu rgyas pa'i sde snod sangs rgyas phal po che las nye bar 'kho* [read: *mkho*] *ba btus pa'i zin bris kyi yi ge*. 29 folios. The second text in bdrc.io, W3CN15338.

Klong chen Rab 'byams pa Dri med 'od zer. 2009. *Theg pa mtha' dag gi don gsal bar byed pa grub mtha' rin po che'i mdzod*. In *Collected Works*, edited by Dpal brtsegs bod yig dpe rnying zhib 'jug khang, vol. 15/26. Mes po'i shul bzhag, vol. 120. Beijing: Krung go'i bod rig pa dpe skrun khang.

Lalou, Marcelle. 1953. "Les Textes Bouddhiques au Temps du Roi Khri-sroṅ-lde-bcan." *Journal asiatique* 241.3: 313–53.

Martin, Daniel. 2012. January 26, 2012, online reaction to van Schaik 2012.

Mimaki, Katsumi. 1990. "The *Brda gsar rnying gi rnam par dbye ba* of Dbus pa Blo gsal: A First Attempt at a Critical Edition." In *Asian Languages and Linguistics. Festschrift for Prof. Tatsuo Nishida on the Occasion of his 60th Birthday*, 17–54. Tokyo: Sanseidō.

Ngor chen Kun dga' bzang po. 2010. *Thob yig rgya mtsho*. In *E vaṃ bka' 'bum*, edited by Dpal brtsegs bod yig dpe rnying zhib 'jug khang, vol. 1/20, 165–386. Mes po'i shul bzhag, vol. 132. Beijing: Krung go'i bod rig pa dpe skrun khang.

Nyang ral Nyi ma 'od zer. 1988. *Chos 'byung me tog snying po sbrang rtsi'i bcud*, edited by Nyan shul Mkhyen rab 'od gsal. Gangs can rig mdzod 5. Lhasa: Bod ljongs mi dmangs dpe skrun khang.

Ōtake, Susumu. 2007. "On the Origin and Early Development of the *Buddhāvataṃsaka-sūtra*." In *Reflecting Mirrors. Perspectives on Huayan Buddhism,* edited by Imre Hamar, 87–107. Asiatische Forschungen 151. Wiesbaden: Harrassowitz Verlag.

Pad dkar bzang po. 2006. *Mdo sde spyi'i rnam bzhag* [*bka' bsdu bzhi pa*]. Beijing: Mi rigs dpe skrun khang.

Park, Hyunjin. 2016. "The Recensional Variants in Several Versions of the Tibetan *Buddhāvataṃsakamahāvaipulyasūtra*." *Indogaku Bukkyōgaku Kenkyū*. 印度学佛教学研究. *Journal of Indian and Buddhist Studies* 64.3: 249–53.

Sba Gsal snang. 1982. *Sba bzhed*, edited by Mgon po rgyal mtshan. Beijing: Mi rigs dpe skrun khang.

Schaeffer, Kurtis R., and Leonard W. J. van der Kuijp. 2009. *An Early Tibetan Survey of Buddhist Literature: The Bstan pa rgyas pa rgyan gyi nyi 'od of Bcom ldan ral gri*. Harvard Oriental Series 64. Cambridge, MA: The Department of Sanskrit and Indian Studies, Harvard University.

Sde dge, 1991. *Sangs rgyas phal po che zhes bya ba shin tu rgyas chen po'i mdo*. In *The Tibetan Tripitaka: Taipei Edition*, vol. 8. Edited by A. W. Barber. Taipei: SCM Publishing Inc.

Silk, Jonathan A. 1996. "Notes on the History of the Yongle Kanjur." In *Suhṛllekha: Festgabe für Helmut Eimer*, edited by M. Hahn, J. U. Hartmann, and R. Steiner, 153–200. Indica et Tibetica 28. Swisttal-Odendorf: Indica et Tibetica Verlag.

———. 2013. "Review Article: Buddhist Sūtras in Sanskrit from the Potala." *Indo-Iranian Journal* 56: 61–78.

Si tu Paṇ chen Chos kyi 'byung gnas. 1990. *Bde bar gshegs pa'i bka' gangs can gyi brdas drangs pa'i phyi mo'i tshogs ji snyed pa par du bsgrubs pa'i tshul las nye bar brtsams pa'i gtam bzang po blo ldan mos pa'i kuṇḍa yongs su kha bye ba'i zla 'od gzhon nu'i 'khri shing*. In Collected Works, vol. 9. Sansal: Sherabling Institute of Buddhist Studies.

———. 2008. *Bde bar gshegs pa'i bka' gangs can gyi brdas drangs pa'i phyi mo'i tshogs ji snyed pa par du bsgrubs pa'i tshul las nye bar brtsams pa'i gtam bzang po blo ldan mos pa'i kuṇḍa yongs su kha bye ba'i zla 'od gzhon nu'i 'khri shing*, edited by Ngang tshang 'Bum skyabs. Chengdu: Si khron dpe skrun tshogs pa / Si khron mi rigs dpe skrun khang.

Skilling, Peter, and Saerji. 2013. "The Circulation of the *Buddhāvataṃsaka* in India." In *Annual Report of the International Research Institute for Advanced Buddhology at Soka University for the Academic Year 2012* XVI, 193–216.

Skyogs ston Lo tsā ba Rin chen bkra shis. 1981. *Brda gsar rnying gi rnam gzhag li shi'i gur khang*, edited by Mgon po rgyal mtshan. Beijing: Mi rigs dpe skrun khang.

Sperling, Elliot. 2001. "Notes on the Early History of Gro tshang rdo rje 'chang and Its Relations with the Early Ming Court." *Lung rta* [Aspects of Tibetan History] 14: 77–87.

Steinkellner, Ernst. 1995. *Sudhana's Miraculous Journey in the Temple of Ta pho. The Inscriptional Text of the Tibetan Gaṇḍavyūhasūtra Edited with Introductory Remarks*. Serie Orientale Roma 76. Rome: Istituto Italiano per il Medio ed Estremo Oriente.

Tauscher, Helmut. 2008. *Catalogue of the Gondhla Proto-Kanjur*. Wiener Studien zur Tibetologie und Buddhismuskunde 71. Vienna: Arbeitskreis für Tibetische und Buddhistische Studien Universität Wien.

van der Kuijp, Leonard W. J. 2007. "The Names of 'Gos Lo tsā ba Gzhon nu dpal (1392–1481)." In *The Pandita and the Siddha. Tibetan Studies in Honor of E. Gene Smith*, edited by Ramon N. Prats, 279–83. Dharamsala: Amnye Machen Institute.

———. 2009. "Some Remarks on the Meaning and Use of the Tibetan Word *Bam po*." བོད་རིག་པའི་དུས་དེབ་ / *Zangxue xuekan* 藏学学刊 / *Journal of Tibetology* 5: 114–32.

———. Forthcoming. "U rgyan pa Rin chen dpal (1230–1309), Part Three: Once More on His *Garland of Tales about Rivers*."

van Schaik, Sam J. 2012. "The First Tibetan Biographies?" In earlytibet.com/2012/01/11/tibetan-buddhist-biographies.

Vīnītā, Bhikṣuṇī (Vinita Tseng). 2010. *A Unique Collection of Twenty Sūtras in a Sanskrit Manuscript from the Potala: Editions and Translation*. In *Sanskrit Texts from the Autonomous Tibetan Region*, vol. 7. Beijing: China Tibetology Publishing House / Vienna: Austrian Academy of Sciences.

Zhwa dmar II Mkha' spyod dbang po. 1978. *Mtshungs med bla ma dam pa'i rnam par thar pa yon tan mi zad pa rab ru gsal ba'i me long*. In *Collected Works*, 2:203–319. Gangtok: Gonpo Tseten Palace Monastery.

Zhwa dmar IV Chos grags ye shes. 2009a. *Bka' 'gyur gyi dkar chag bstan pa rgyas byed*. In *Collected Works*, edited by Yangs can dgon ris med dpe rnying myur skyob khang, 6:875–920. Beijing: Krung go'i bod rig pa dpe skrun khang.

———. 2009b. *Rtogs pa brjod pa'i tshigs su bcad pa utpala'i phreng ba*. In *Collected Works*, edited by Yangs can dgon ris med dpe rnying myur skyob khang, 6:911–96. Beijing: Krung go'i bod rig pa dpe skrun khang.

———. 2009c. *Mdo sde'i spyi'i rnam par bzhag pa gsung rab rin po che mchog tu gsal bar byed pa'i snang ba*. In *Collected Works*, edited by Yangs can dgon ris med dpe rnying myur skyob khang, 3:11–353. Beijing: Krung go'i bod rig pa dpe skrun khang.

———. 2009d. *Rje thams cad mkhyen pa lo tsā ba chen po'i rnam par thar pa ngo mtshar rgya mtsho*. In *Collected Works*, edited by Yangs can dgon ris med dpe rnying myur skyob khang, 4:272–458. Beijing: Krung go'i bod rig pa dpe skrun khang.

Plate 1. At the International Association of Tibetan Studies conference, Paris 2019. From left to right: Heather Stoddard, Françoise Pommaret, Janet Gyatso, Per Kvaerne, Anne-Marie Blondeau, Matthew Kapstein, Samten Karmay. Photo courtesy of Olivier Adam.

Plate 2. At the Tibetan Women Writers Symposium, University of Virginia, 2022. Back left to right: Françoise Robin, Nicole Willock, Tsering Wangmo Dhompa, Janet Gyatso, Sangmota. Front left to right: Annabella Pitkin, Holly Gayley, Tenzin Dickie, Kelsang Lhamo, Dechen Pema, Tsering Dolkar. Photograph courtesy of Andrew Quintman.

Plate 3. Janet with Tobysan in Cambridge, MA, May, 2022. Photograph by Ronghui Tu.

Plate 4. Group photo outside of the first meeting of Mayum.
Front: (from left, white shirt with black traditional chuba) Pema Choedon, Nyig Tsema, Nyima Tso, Tenzin Choedon; Back: (from left, see only face) Peldon, Zungdu Kyi, Dolkar Tso, Tseyang, Min Nangzey, Tukar Tso, Gang zi, Tsering Lhamo Samling. Photograph courtesy of Nyima Tso.

Plate 5. Rigzin Jigmé Lingpa, Tibet, pigments on cloth, Private Collection. Photograph by Changling Rinpoché.

Plate 6. Portrait of the Fifth Dalai Lama, 1672, at the request of Gerawa, hollow cast in gilt brass alloy with gilding and pigments. Height estimated at 15 cm. Photo after Nor bu don grub and Snying lcags rgyal 2019, plate 23.

Plate 7. Inscription on the reverse of the portrait of the Fifth Dalai Lama in plate 6.

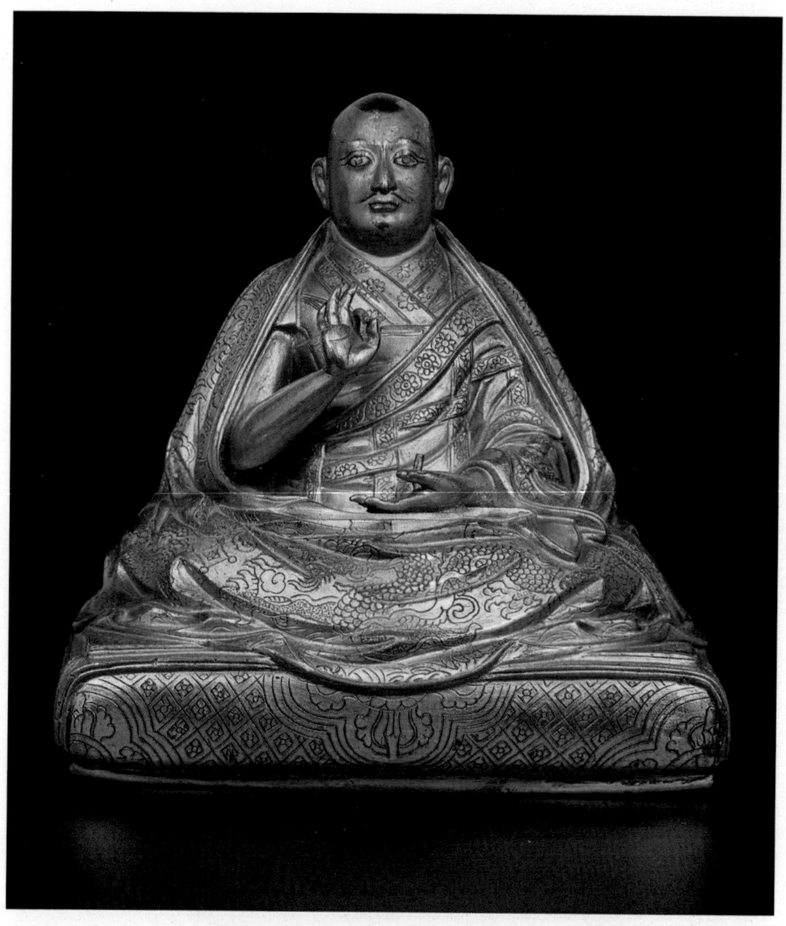

Plate 8. Portrait of the Fifth Dalai Lama, 1674, at the request of Jangling Samdrup Gyalpo, hollow cast in gilt brass alloy with pigments, consecration contents intact, height 15 cm. Photo courtesy of Sotheby's.

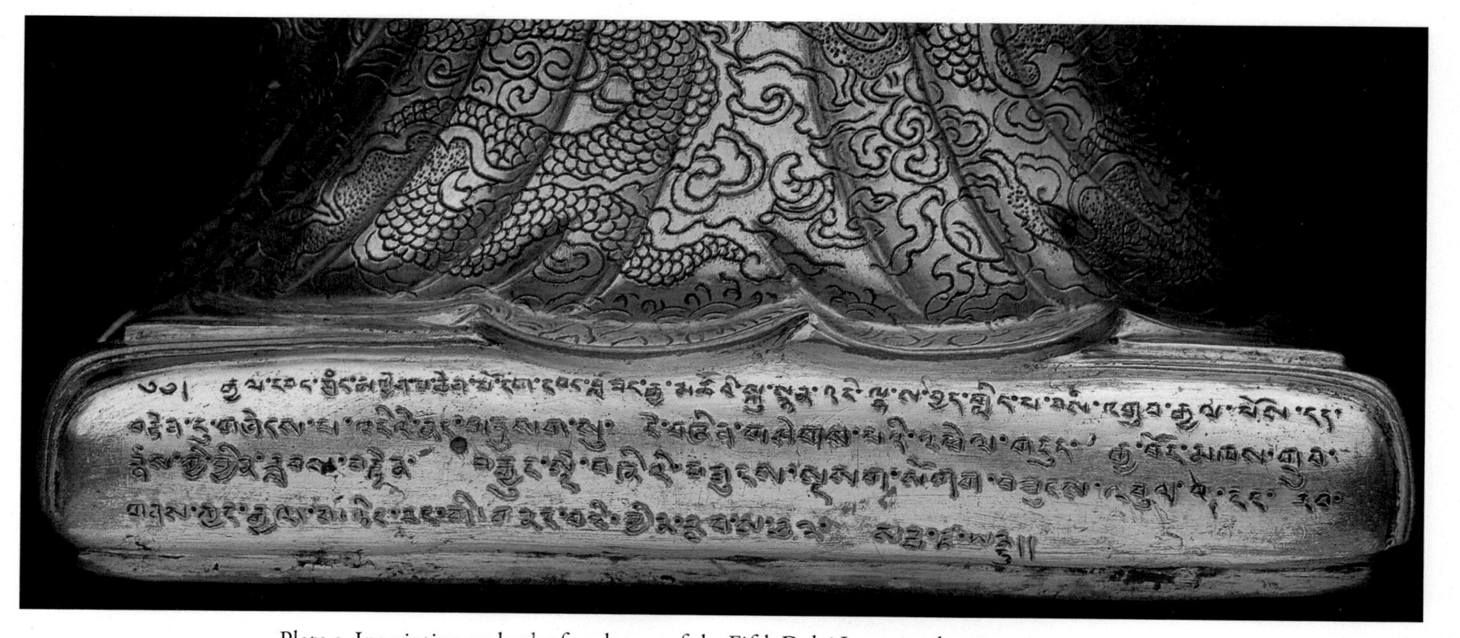

Plate 9. Inscription on back of sculpture of the Fifth Dalai Lama in plate 8.
Photo courtesy of Sotheby's.

Plate 10. Consecration plate of the sculpture dedicated for Jangling Samdrup Gyalpo with additional green stamp of Preziosi Oggetti d'Arte Z. Beldi, Torino. Photo courtesy of Sotheby's.

Plate 11. The x-ray of the consecration contents of the Fifth Dalai Lama sculpture commissioned by Jangling Samdrup Gyalpo.

V.

Early Modernity: Human and Nonhuman Worlds

Tendrel: Being Human in a More-than-Human World

Sarah H. Jacoby

THIS ESSAY DWELLS on a single Tibetan word, *tendrel*, as a theoretical paradigm, a term of art, and a reminder of who we are. *Tendrel* is a compound made up of two words: *ten* means "support, basis, that which holds," and *drel* means "connection, relation, link."[1] It is the Tibetan translation of the Buddhist theory of causality called *dependent origination* (Skt. *pratītya-samutpāda*), but it also has a broad range of distinctively Tibetan meanings pertaining to interpersonal and environmental relationality. Translations of these latter dimensions include "auspicious connections," "fortunate conditions," "favorable circumstances," and "good omens." In the process of exploring these varied meanings, I will retell a story about the most important sacred mountain in Golok, the ancestor of the Golok people named Amnyé (Grandfather) Machen, and the encounter of one extraordinary woman—Sera Khandro Dewai Dorjé (1892–1940)—with that mountain landscape. Through the story *tendrel* resonates deeply, reaching out like its unrelated near-homonym *tendril*, offering us a critical reminder that being human is only possible in relationship with the more than human.[2]

My thinking about the human and the more than human, as well as so much else in Tibetan Buddhist studies (tendrel, *namtar*, *terma*, gender & sexuality), is indebted to the scholarship and mentorship of Janet Gyatso. Her inspiration looms large in the field of Tibetan Buddhist studies and also in my head on a moment-to-moment basis as I write—her critiques and probing questions motivate me to dig deeper, and her far-ranging engagement with diverse scholarly domains serves as a model of humanistic scholarship. I will always be

1. Tib. *rten 'brel*, which is an abbreviation of *rten cing 'brel bar 'byung ba*. This essay began as a lecture I gave in 2018 titled "Interdependent Personhood and Relational Ethics: A Tibetan Perspective" (see https://www.bu.edu/ipr/video-jacoby/) at the Institute for Philosophy and Religion at Boston University. I thank David Eckel for this invitation.

2. "More than human" is not only a reference to the materialist turn in cultural geography (see Whatmore 2006) but also two specific titles: Janet Gyatso's *Being Human in a Buddhist World* (2015) and David Abrams's *Spell of the Sensuous: Perception and Language in a More-Than-Human World* (1996).

grateful for Janet's generosity in serving as a member of my dissertation committee even though we were not at the same university—her advice was invaluable then and continues to be now—I wish I could still send her all my drafts! Even the structure of this essay organized around a single word is influenced by Janet's work, specifically her essay on the semantic range of the word *certificate* (*byang bu*).[3] Her scholarship itself is a tendrel propelling new generations to continue exploring the worlds of Tibetan literature, medicine, and religion, riding on her coattails.

In modern usage, tendrel accentuates personal agency not derived from individual autonomy but from synergy among people, animals, plants, and minerals. The Seventeenth Karmapa Ogyen Trinley Dorje describes this as "interdependence," building in part on tendrel and in part on a Tibetan word for the world as "the vessel and its contents" (*snod bcud*). Without the vessel of the physical earth, its contents who are living beings could not survive, so they clearly need the support of the vessel. But the word for "contents" is also the Tibetan word for "nutrients," suggesting that living beings provide nourishment in return to the vessel that holds us by, for instance, the carbon dioxide we exhale.[4]

Some readers will hear strong resonances between these ideas and the Gaia hypothesis, and will interpret tendrel as a prescient form of environmental ethics.[5] Weaving in and out of this essay are ways in which tendrel does and does not relate to such domains. As we think about this, it is important to note that Buddhist teachings as they integrated with indigenous Tibetan conceptions of place and personhood over centuries do not prefigure environmental sciences, conservation, or sustainable development any more than Buddhist mindfulness practices anticipated the problems of the digitally mediated attention economy; to claim otherwise is anachronistic and manipulative, flattening tendrel into the metaphysics of secular modernity. In the same vein, the "green Tibetan" discourse, or the idea that Tibetan culture and Buddhism are especially environmentally friendly, has received considerable critique.[6] Bringing tendrel into contemporary conversations therefore requires careful attention to both resonances and dissonances; we must give tendrel breathing room to

3. Gyatso n.d.

4. Karmapa 2017, 21. On common mistranslations of *snod bcud*, see Yeh 2014a.

5. A large body of modern works on Buddhism and ecology reflect this inclination, including Badiner 1990, Batchelor and Brown 1992, Tucker and Williams 1997, Kaza and Kraft 2000, Cooper and James 2005, Kaza 2019, and Loy 2019.

6. Huber 1997; Yeh 2014b.

align with older ideas about Buddhist causality and soteriology as well as ricochet off into newer directions, such as ecology and systems theory.[7]

This is crucial because what is at stake now is breathing itself. The problems of our time—the global pandemic, racist murders of Black and Brown people, and human-caused environmental crises—are making breathing perilous, more so for some than others.[8] In their recent work, Judith Butler examines the factors that render some lives more grievable than others, calling attention to the "interdependency of life" as a key to realizing the radical equality of all people. Butler argues that "It may be, however, that the most persuasive reasons for the practice of nonviolence directly imply a critique of individualism and require that we rethink the social bonds that constitute us as living creatures."[9] Failure to recognize these social bonds, which according to Butler constitute the "overarching sense of the interrelational," enables the violence that disproportionately threatens Black and Brown lives, as well as those of women, queer, and transgender people.[10]

The recent posthumanist and materialist turns in critical theory also emphasize interrelationality, particularly with an eye toward troubling the binary between living beings and inert matter. For instance, Jane Bennett argues for the vitality of materiality "because my hunch is that the image of dead or thoroughly instrumentalized matter feeds human hubris and our earth-destroying fantasies of conquest and consumption."[11] However, the citational chains of such critical theorists draw from little outside of the domain of Euro-American intellectual history even as their arguments for interrelationality and a revision of the animate-being/dull-matter divide resonate in underexamined ways with Buddhist and Indigenous knowledges about human/more-than-human relations.[12]

As a gesture toward redressing this omission, this essay suggests that tendrel is worth taking seriously as a multilayered way of understanding humans'

7. Joanna Macy has written extensively on *pratītyasamutpāda*, ecology, and systems theory. For one example, see Macy 1991. For a more comprehensive retrospective on her career and environmental activism, see Kaza 2020. See also Meyers 2020.

8. Here I am referring to the "I can't breathe" slogan associated with the Black Lives Matter movement that developed after Eric Garner's strangulation via chokehold by a New York police officer in 2014, which was on my mind at the time of writing this essay in the wake of George Floyd's homicide in 2020.

9. Butler 2020, 15.

10. Butler 2020, 16.

11. Bennett 2010, ix.

12. Sundberg 2014; Gergan 2015; Larsen and Johnson 2016. A similar point can be made about the ontological turn in anthropology; see Todd 2016.

relationality with the vital world. In positing tendrel as an integral part of a theoretically significant episteme, I am inspired by decolonial thinkers such as Rauna Kuokkanen, who critiques "epistemic ignorance" and calls for "multiepistemic literacy," to which I add can and should include careful attention to tendrel as well as Tibetan practices of geopiety.[13] I am also inspired by Walter Mignolo's decolonial practice of "epistemic disobedience,"[14] meaning in this context that instead of presenting tendrel as a traditional (premodern) mystical cultural belief or even just as a subject for research in the history of religions, I posit tendrel as a valid knowledge system that can serve as a reminder in this time of multiple crises that human flourishing is dependent on relations with others, including other animals, as well as plants, air, water, soil, and rocks.

As this essay sounds the depths of tendrel's dimensions, three distinct and interwoven layers of meaning will surface—the first relates to Buddhist philosophy, the second to the ecology of revelation as part of a distinctively Tibetan geopiety, and the third to personal identity. In each layer, the line between dull matter and vibrant life, vessel and contents, scenery and salvation will fade, suggesting ways of being and knowing less harmful than those in favor in most of the world now, which we ignore at our own great peril.

Tendrel as a Buddhist Philosophical Term

Underneath the distinctively Tibetan territory of tendrel is its older Buddhist philosophical meaning as a translation of the Sanskrit term *pratītyasamutpāda*. Common academic translations for this foundational Buddhist theory of causality are "dependent arising," "mutual causality," and "interdependent origination." Put simply, tendrel in its Buddhist doctrinal dimension means that nothing exists on its own; everything and everyone is related through a type of causal dependence. The Pāli canon (Saṃyutta Nikāya 12:61) describes this as follows: "That being, this comes to be; from the arising of that, this arises. That being absent, this is not; from the cessation of that, this ceases." Initially pertaining to the formation of subjectivity and the perpetuation of suffering, over time this articulation of causal dependence became the heart of the Buddhist explanation for how the world and the beings within it, the vessel and its contents, came to be, as well as how the cycle can be reversed, leading toward liberation instead of rebirth.[15] The same Pāli sutta also includes a more detailed

13. Kuokkanen 2007.

14. Mignolo 2011.

15. Shulman 2008; Meyers 2018.

analysis of causality that includes twelve links beginning with ignorance, leading to the formation of the aggregates that make up personhood, and the resultant sensations, cravings, and attachments that perpetuate rebirth in saṃsāra. Practicing the Buddhist path reverses this causal momentum, leading instead to the eradication of ignorance and thus liberation from suffering.[16]

Placing the twelve links of dependent arising as presented in early Buddhist texts in conversation with environmental ethics raises a set of difficulties. For one, Buddhist causality is soteriologically oriented, intending to lead toward extricating oneself from entrapment in cyclic existence. The twelve links chart the perpetuation of suffering more than they celebrate the interconnected web of life sustained by the biosphere, rendering a dark vision of the interdependent world characterized by killing, devouring, and decay.[17] For another, the natural environment does not have much of a role in these links. Additionally, both dependent arising and the wheel of life more broadly are distinctly anthropocentric, in the sense that they explain the workings of rebirth from a human-centric stance. Human life is the best realm in which to be reborn, and reversing the twelve links requires human intellectual capacities. In conjunction with that, a conception of the natural world having intrinsic value makes little sense in a Buddhist frame since personhood and phenomena are characterized as being empty of essence, radically contingent, causally determined, and not self-sufficient.[18] But beyond whether nature is intrinsically valuable or instrumentally so to the degree it serves human needs, there is no comparable idea of "nature" as analogous to wilderness and opposed to "culture" or "civilization" in Buddhist canonical languages.[19]

For these reasons, critics have suggested that modern eco-Buddhists are "engaging in acts of eisegesis"—superimposing their own environmental ethic on to the Buddhist sources they selectively mine for evidence of such.[20] For instance, David McMahan finds that modern eco-friendly interpretations of Buddhist interdependence derive primarily from the legacy of European romanticism and transcendentalism and therefore have more to do with western fantasies than Buddhist roots. Of this eco-friendly bent, McMahan asks, "Is

16. For more information on the doctrine and iconography of the twelve links, see Sopa 1986 and Teiser 2007.

17. Schmithausen 1997; Harris 1994.

18. Ives 2009.

19. Eckel 1997; Harris 1997. See also Gurung 2020 for ethnographic analysis of Himalayan Buddhist conceptions of nature beyond a nature/culture binary, as well as his forthcoming article "(Un)seeing Like a Conservationist."

20. Ives 2016, 43.

it Buddhist?"[21] As we consider the possible answers to that, it is crucial to note that some of the most famous modern Asian Buddhist masters including Thich Nhat Hanh and the Dalai Lama respond affirmatively to that question.[22] Many other less internationally known Tibetan and Himalayan environmental activists and religious figures concur.[23] Surely these voices represent a conflation of modern ideas coming from within and far outside of Tibetan and Himalayan contexts. However, given that one of the oldest Buddhist doctrines is change, an argument can be made for constructively reimagining the ways that Buddhist conceptions of dependent arising can serve as a valuable resource for environmental ethics, whether their multi-millennia-old articulations prefigured that or not.

Tendrel as a Tibetan Term of Art

The scope of tendrel takes on a much clearer relationality with the earth as a vital participant as we turn to our second meaning of tendrel. On top of its earlier philosophical meaning as a translation of *pratītyasamutpāda*, tendrel is a term of art in Tibetan with a specialized significance in the Tibetan tradition of treasure revelation, illustrating how Tibetans domesticated Buddhist causality into their own densely animated spiritual geography. Ongoing from at least the eleventh century, the treasure tradition is found mainly in the Nyingma school of Tibetan Buddhism and in Tibet's indigenous religion Bön.[24] Treasure revealers (*gter ston*) discover earth treasures (*sa gter*) in the form of chests containing scriptures and sacred items such as statues, ritual implements, and medicinal substances hidden in nodal sites, and they discover mind treasures (*dgongs gter*) from within their mindstreams, which they access through visionary experience.

The process of revelation is predestined by the buddhas and enlightened figures from the golden age of the Tibetan empire, such as the eighth-century Indian tantric master Padmasambhava. At the same time, it is highly contingent, depending on an array of intermediaries and accomplices, including trea-

21. McMahan 2008, 177–80.

22. For a collection of the Dalai Lama Tenzin Gyatso's comments on the environment, see https://www.dalailama.com/messages/environment; among Thich Nhat Hanh's extensive writings on the environment, see Hanh 2004 and 2013.

23. There are many examples from Tibetan and Himalayan Buddhist communities. For the first-ever book on ecology written in Ladakhi, called *Rten 'brel Interdependence*, see Palden 1987. For references to ecological writings in Tibet, see Yeh 2014b.

24. The best academic scholarship on the treasure tradition remains Gyatso 1986, Gyatso 1993, and Gyatso 1998.

sure guardians (*gter srung*), who are very often territorial spirits associated with Tibetan mountain lifeways.[25] More accurately, these spirits are "masters of the territory" (*gzhi bdag*), "land deities" (*yul lha*), and other place-based forces. As can be ascertained by their names, these forces embody more than folk belief; they map territorial sovereignty in Tibet, and as such have as much if not more to do with Tibetan politics, society, and personal identity as they do with ritual or religion.[26] Tibetan mountain lifeways coexist with transnational Buddhist influence, at times in sync with Buddhist imperatives and at others ambivalent or even hostile to them. Treasures implant (mostly) Buddhist teachings in mountains and nearby lakes that, in many cases, were already considered sacred within Tibet's mountain lifeways.

Another element of the contingency of treasure revelation is that no matter how clearly prophesied, the process of successfully revealing a treasure requires the coalescence of a set of conditions, called tendrel. Best translated now not as "dependent arising" but as something more like "auspicious connections," "favorable conditions," or "fortunate circumstances," the five tendrel necessary for revelation are (1) being the right person, (2) at the right time, and (3) in the right place to reveal a given treasure, accompanied by (4) the right disciple, who will propagate the teaching (called a "doctrine holder," *chos bdag*), and (5) the right consort, who will enable the process of revelation (*thabs grogs*).[27] The last requirement articulates a shared space between sexuality and textuality, both dynamics that emerge from the smooth circulation of energies within the subtle body as articulated in tantric conceptions of the body.[28]

In an effort to listen directly to an example of how tendrel factors into a Tibetan treasure revealer's encounter with the living landscape, what follows is an account written by Sera Khandro Dewai Dorjé. First some context—the year is 1911, and Sera Khandro is seventeen years old. She is still finding her place in the vast nomadic pasturelands of Golok, which at this time is an independent territory not paying tribute to either the Dalai Lama's Tibet or the waning Qing empire. Three years earlier she was drawn to Golok out of fervent religious devotion to the Dudjom lineage masters of the Great Perfection,

25. More commonly referred to in scholarship as "the Tibetan mountain cult," the name "Tibetan mountain lifeways" builds on John A. Grim's (2008) description of Indigenous lifeways as knowledge systems operating "in shared and lived participation with the local landscape" (p. 94). Thanks to Natalie Avalos for directing me to this source and suggesting I find a word for Tibetan mountain relations that eschews primitivist tones.

26. Karmay 1998. See also Blondeau and Steinkellner 1996; Blondeau 1998; Yeh and Coggins 2014; Coggins 2019.

27. See Thondup 1986.

28. See Gyatso 1998, chap. 6, and Jacoby 2014, chap. 4.

the pinnacle contemplative teaching of the Nyingma school. On the eight-month journey on foot from her home in Lhasa to Golok, she nearly starved and froze to death. Once there, she worked for a few years as a maidservant for a local household tending their livestock, cooking, and doing chores. Finally, she had an opportunity to join a group of pilgrims setting out to circumambulate Golok's most sacred mountain, Amnyé Machen. Towering over 20,000 feet above sea level, Amnyé Machen is the extensive snow-capped fulcrum of the rolling grasslands of Golok. Standing guard over the territory, Amnyé Machen's full name is Machen Pomra, but in what follows Sera Khandro calls him Magyal. Together with his Queen Drakgyalma and their children, Machen Pomra is part of a broader kinship network comprised of a group of sacred mountains in the region who together map the jurisdictions of their human descendants, the sovereign leaders of the various parts of Tibet. In the autobiography Sera Khandro completed in 1934, she gave this account of what happened during her first visit to Grandfather Machen:

> That year Gara Gyalsé (Blacksmith Victor's Son) and some of his associates were preparing to go to Machen (Great Ma). The nun Samkar Drön (Lantern of Virtuous Intention) and I joined them and went to Magyal (Victorious Ma). When I arrived at Tachok (Supreme Steed) Pass, Magyal's minister Drendul Wangchuk (All-Mighty Enemy Conqueror) came to welcome me, actually riding a horse made of cloud. We went into Magyal's palace, where there was a sumptuous spread of food and drink. As if meeting someone he knew already, he was delighted, as were his queen, children, entourage, and servants. The palace gatekeeper Drala Dungkyi Torchokchen (War God with a Conch Topknot) said,
>
>> Great female bodhisattva, thank you so much for coming to our sacred land. Stay here for a few days; for the sacred land, offer a cleansing ritual and an auspicious vase that restores the earth's nutrients. For us, you must give us expansive Dharma teachings!
>
> I fulfilled all their desires, and our relationship as sacred land and guest was unified. I added, "I need to find a way to retrieve my *Zap Ter Tsogyal* (*Profound Treasure of Tsogyal*) and my *Phakmo Druptab* (*Vajravārāhī Liturgy*) treasures that I entrusted to the Seven Wangchukma (All-Mighty Goddesses).
>
> In an instant, Drala Dungtöchen departed like a lightning flash

for the sacred land of Magyal's western gatekeepers, the Seven Wangchukma. From them, he retrieved Tsogyal's profound pages together with a statue and the ḍākinīs' soul stones (*bla rdo*) and gave them to me.

He said, "Because the tendrel (auspicious connections) including the doctrine holder and consort for Vārāhī's profound pages have not yet coalesced, the Seven Wangchukma said that the time had not come, so I didn't retrieve the treasure chest."

Then I did whatever they needed me to do.

When I was preparing to return, Queen Drakgyalma (Fierce Victoress) spoke:

> Now that our sacred relationship (*dam tshig*) is unified, if you are able to come here to Magyal three times, your longevity and enlightened activities will be without comparison. If you do not do this, now and then you run the risk of experiencing undesirable things. In particular, since there is a massive obstacle to your longevity, it is important to be careful.

Then, as before, I rode the cloud horse through the air and arrived back to my land while the others were making some lunch.[29]

As sacred land (*gnas*), Amnyé Machen is not scenery forming the backdrop of human endeavor, nor is it a virgin peak waiting for some climber to summit, hauled upward by Indigenous porters whose names won't be remembered. Here Amnyé Machen is a vital, agentive force with demands and needs. Machen's icy peaks are a royal palace inhabited by a reigning king and queen, surrounded by their court. Sera Khandro is a guest on their ground, who must establish a rapport with these sovereign powers in order to accomplish her purpose. She calls this forging a "land-guest relationship" (*gnas mgron dam tshig*), using a word that has deep Buddhist resonances but is grounded in Tibet, for the beings she interacts with are the autochthonous sovereigns of Golok. Another way to translate this is "host-guest relationship," which de-emphasizes the sense of land as agentic but reinforces the connection between Queen Drakgyalma and Sera Khandro as one of hospitality. This relationship (Tib. *dam tshig*; Skt. *samaya*) is binding in that it connotes obligation, commitment, and promise. In Vajrayāna terms, *samaya* are the vows that a guru confers upon her disciple through Vajrayāna initiation. By protecting and upholding them, the disciple

29. Dbus bza' mkha' 'gro 2009, 164–66.

establishes a bond between guru and disciple through which enlightened realization flows. Break the bond, and obstacles block your path.

In Sera Khandro's visit to Machen, relationality and exchange are the currencies through which communication as well as mutual spiritual and material sustenance take place, linking tendrel to specifically Tibetan forms of geopiety. First the vitalized mountain makes requests of Sera Khandro, asking her to nourish the earth through the ritual intervention of offering a vase filled with blessed substances, which is often called an "earth nourishing vessel" (*sa bcud bum pa*). Only after she fulfils this request and gives Dharma teachings to everyone at Machen does Sera Khandro seek their support. Magyal's gatekeepers are intermediary figures empowered to guard Sera Khandro's treasures. Their identities disclose both Tibetan and Buddhist roots, for the One with a Conch Topknot is a non-Buddhist Tibetan war god, and the Seven Wangchukma are very likely a Tibetan adaptation of the Sanskrit *sapta mātṛkā*, a group of seven mother goddesses depicted together in South Asian religions.[30] From them she seeks to retrieve her treasures, but she is only partially successful. The reason is tendrel—because she does not have the appropriate doctrine holder or consort with her, she cannot reveal her Vajravārāhī liturgy. Instead this scripture remains hidden away in a treasure chest, waiting for a future time.

Perhaps this talk of flying cloud horses, mountain castles, and speaking earth spirits seems irreconcilable with a scientifically oriented conception of environmental ethics or ecology. Here the spheres of embodied sentience take on broader contours, but embedded in this relational exchange-oriented interaction is a discourse about human/more-than-human sustainability in which agency is distributed between an array of forces. Mountain deities such as Magyal Pomra of Amnyé Machen are sovereigns on many levels. They are environmental sovereigns in that they are the apex of watersheds; they are political sovereigns in that the local political leaders in Golok are their grandsons (and incidentally the word for politics in Tibetan is "water authority" (*chab srid*); and they are spiritual authorities in that they often have multiple iconographic representations, one as a transregional Buddhist bodhisattva and one as a Tibetan mountain deity to be propitiated by the local people (often only the men) whose ancestry is rooted there. These layers each involved sustained human/more-than-human negotiations in which the needs of the land and its people are mutually implicated. But ultimately, even if partially tamed by the civilizational forces of Buddhism and/or by human imperialist ambitions, the

30. On Tibetan "war gods" (*dgra bla*), see Nebesky-Wojkowitz 1956; on the *sapta mātṛkā*, see Kinsley 1986, chap. 10.

Tibetan landscape itself remains sovereign, unruly, and not fully under anyone's control.[31]

Additionally, the Tibetan treasure tradition cannot be fully extricated from a discourse on environmental ethics because the word for treasure, pronounced *ter* (*gter*), has two meanings. Treasures are esoteric revelations, but this same word also means mineral or natural resource. Although scholarship on the treasure tradition overwhelmingly focuses on the contents of the scriptures that treasure revealers mine from the Tibetan earth, which comprise a substantial portion of the most important Tibetan Buddhist liturgical, biographical, and historical texts, the process of revelation is not only one of extraction but also of exchange. When revealers remove a treasure, they replace it with what is called a "treasure substitute" (*gter tshab*), consisting of earth-nourishing substances. Antonio Terrone terms the reciprocal nature of this exchange "the ecology of revelation," finding more similarities in it than divergences with modern concepts of environmental sustainability.[32] Reciprocity is the means through which humans and the spiritually embodied environment establish balance in the treasure tradition, none of which is possible without the relational synergy catalyzed by tendrel.

Tendrel as Intersubjective Agency

The third layer of tendrel takes us into the realm of everyday Tibetan speech and out of the technical vocabulary of religious specialists. Now we move into a new dimension of causality not necessarily centered on Buddhist soteriology but instead toward the successful fruition of all types of actions, encounters, and plans in the here and now. Tendrel in this more colloquial sense refers to conducive connections, favorable conditions, good omens, positive coincidences, and synergies that coalesce in people's lives to make things happen. Tendrel manifests when a person shows up at the right place at the right time and something unexpectedly fortuitous unfolds, such as a meeting between old friends or a special religious empowerment. A sign of tendrel could be easily gathering the resources needed to complete a meritorious construction or publication project. It is like a coincidence, but not entirely random, because it occurs as a result of deep connections between people, places, and things fostered by karmic propensities inherited from previous lifetimes. The connections tendrel creates arise spontaneously, cannot be forced, and fade fast when

31. On the untamable nature of the Tibetan landscape, see Gyatso 1987.

32. Terrone 2014.

unfavorable influences interfere, like a dark storm cloud coming from nowhere and overtaking a placid blue sky.

Traces of the more formal religious meanings of tendrel as dependent arising and as a term of art in the treasure tradition persist in this more vernacular meaning, but now tendrel's valence has shifted from the causes that perpetuate suffering to the conditions that augur spiritual, social, and personal fulfillment. Perhaps this is not the same as eco-Buddhist delight in the interdependent web of life, but it is decidedly positive in tone, demonstrating that tendrel is not exclusively world-denying in Buddhist contexts.

Tendrel as the coalescence of favorable conditions appears pervasively in Tibetan life writing, as it does in Tibetan speech. For instance, in the autobiography of Sera Khandro, the term appears 177 times, mostly in this latter sense. When Sera Khandro's parents took her as a child to meet a renowned lama named Changdrong Druptop Rinpoché, he responded to their family's arrival saying, "It is good that you all came. Since it is a favorable circumstance (tendrel), you should stay here for a few days."[33] Tendrel is not only ethereal in the realm of ideas; it inheres in material objects, which absorb the blessing power of their owner. A good example of this is when the teenage Sera Khandro walked outside of her family's estate in Lhasa and found a special object left behind by the lama who would become her root guru, Drimé Özer. She narrates,

> I walked around the place where the tent had been and found one rosary bead. I thought, "What a positive connection (tendrel)! By invoking the essence of his personal deity, one day may I attain the mental realization of this lama." I tied the rosary bead onto my neck and returned home.[34]

Tendrel as tied to karmic propensities appears when, at the age of seventeen, Sera Khandro prays to a group of ḍākinīs headed by Yeshé Tsogyal, who appear to her in a vision. She says to them,

> By the power of auspicious connections (tendrel) from positive
> aspirations in former lives,
> today I meet with the assembly of mothers and ḍākinīs.
> Until the ocean of cyclic existence is empty,
> look after all of us sentient beings in existence.
> Ḍākinī Tsogyal, may we become inseparable from you![35]

33. Dbus bza' mkha' 'gro 2009, 15.

34. Dbus bza' mkha' 'gro 2009, 100.

35. Dbus bza' mkha' 'gro 2009, 136.

To speak of these dimensions of tendrel is to emphasize the intersubjective nature of agency, which derives from connections between people, places, and things as much as it does from forces within individual bodies. This interrelatedness appears in both Buddhist and Tibetan conceptions of personhood. The word for person in Tibetan is *gangzak*, a compound translated from the Sanskrit *pudgala*, made up of "to fill" (*gang*) and "to leak; drip down; flow out" (*zag*). Etymologically, personhood is thus process-oriented, porous, and characterized by swelling and leaking. More broadly, in Buddhist terms, it is a combination of parts that cohere temporarily and then dissipate. These parts are both material and mental, including form, sensations, perceptions, mental formations (will, karma, thoughts, emotions, and so on), and consciousness. These five coalesce in a bundle that sticks together for a while, even as this bundle lacks an inner stable essence we could call a "self." In Dungkar Lozang Trinlé's words, "The coarse selflessness of persons is their lack of permanence, singularity, and autonomy, and what is asserted to be the subtle selflessness of persons is their lack of material substance capable of being self-sufficient."[36]

While the extent of these Buddhist ideas about the selflessness of persons is pervasive in Tibet, it is crucial to note that non-Buddhist understandings of personhood are also salient. Often overlooked in the domain of Buddhist studies is the importance of Tibetan conceptions of the soul (*bla*) as a life force vital for a person's survival but not exclusively housed within that person's body. A person's soul can reside in particular elements of the landscape known as "soul dwellings" (*bla gnas*), such as a particular stone (*bla rdo*), tree (*bla shing*), lake (*bla mtsho*), or mountain (*bla ri*).[37] Tibetans perform a number of rituals to maintain their relationship with their soul dwelling, and if this environmental place is attacked by an enemy, it can lead to the demise of the associated person. These conceptions of human agency as part of a wider web of environmental forces wend their ways into Tibetan Buddhist ritual—note that in the passage we read in part 2, Magyal's retinue gave Sera Khandro ḍākinīs' "soul stones" (*bla rdo*) along with more transregionally recognizable Buddhist objects such as a scripture and a statue. Like the tendrel necessary for treasure revelation, conceptions of this vital principle (*bla*) within people are rooted in indigenous Tibetan logics of people and land as interdependent.

As we are propelled deeper into Earth's sixth mass-extinction event, many of us without even realizing it, and as climate change causes rampant wildfires, rising oceans, and ever more severe storms, tendrel is one richly resonant concept that can remind us that our delusions of autonomy are just that. Our human

36. Dung dkar Blo bzang phrin las 2002, 475.

37. Karmay 1998, 310–38.

potential has always been contingent on the web of causes and conditions, animals and plants, mountains and lakes, stars and space that make us who we are. We should avoid the pitfall of bracketing tendrel off as an outmoded traditional belief, or worse yet part of a worldview characterized by "primitive animism," as older religious studies theorists such as E. B. Tyler might have classified it.[38] Instead, we should explore tendrel as a valid relational epistemology, and in so doing contribute to decolonizing the field of religious studies.[39]

The reminders tendrel provides about human-nonhuman-earth interrelatedness have much to contribute to contemporary anglophone conversations in critical theory and beyond. Referencing Donna Haraway, Judith Butler argues, "The political concept of self-preservation, often used in the defense of violent action, does not consider that the preservation of the self requires the preservation of the earth, and that we are not 'in' the global environment as self-subsisting beings, but subsist only as long as the planet does."[40] Or Jane Bennett: "We need to cultivate a bit of anthropomorphism—the idea that human agency has some echoes in nonhuman nature—to counter the narcissism of humans in charge of the world."[41] What more could contemporary Euro-American theorists imagine if, in the spirit of multi-epistemic literacy, they ventured further outside the western canon to argue for the preservation of the earth and the vitality of matter, engaging with Buddhists as well as with their Indigenous neighbors, on whose ancestral lands American universities stand?

I write these words while located in the homelands of the Council of the Three Fires (Ojibwe, Potawatomi, Odawa), on the shores of Mishigami, Lake Michigan. As I reflect here on tendrel, I realize that as a descendant of European settler colonists, I don't even know the names of the local sovereign spirits. How does one repair the broken relationships caused by this legacy of genocide and cultural destruction? How does one repair the failed epistemology of neoliberal capitalism that has transformed the earth into inert matter available for exploitation? How does one respectfully engage with tendrel as a relational epistemology, without falling into cultural appropriation, even as elements of Tibetan geopiety described in this essay are threatened with state suppression in Tibetan areas of the PRC?[42] There is much more to be considered, because the relationships forged by tendrel don't stay bound by old wooden scripture covers in Tibet. They reach out to us today, tying us in dynamic webs of agen-

38. Bird-David 1999.

39. Meyers 2019; Avalos 2020.

40. Butler 2020, 199.

41. Bennett 2010, xvi.

42. Yeh and Coggins 2014.

tive forces, some human and others more than human. We would be wise to remember, as Sera Khandro did, that we are temporary guests hosted by this living land.

Works Cited

Abram, David. 1996. *The Spell of the Sensuous: Perception and Language in a More-Than-Human World*. New York: Vintage Books.

Avalos, Natalie. 2020. "Taking a Critical Indigenous and Ethnic Studies Approach to Decolonizing Religious Studies." *Contending Modernities: Exploring How Religious and Secular Forces Interact in the Modern World*, Oct. 14, 2020. Available online: https://contendingmodernities.nd.edu/decoloniality/critical-indigenous-approach/.

Badiner, Allen Hunt. 1990. *Dharma Gaia: A Harvest of Essays in Buddhism and Ecology*. Berkeley: Parallax Press.

Batchelor, Martine, and Kerry Brown. 1992. *Buddhism and Ecology*. London: Cassell.

Bennett, Jane. 2010. *Vibrant Matter: A Political Ecology of Things*. Durham, NC: Duke University Press.

Bird-David, N. 1999. "'Animism' Revisited: Personhood, Environment, and Relational Epistemology." *Current Anthropology* 40.S1: S67–S91.

Blondeau, Anne-Marie, ed. 1998. *Tibetan Mountain Deities, Their Cults and Representations: Papers Presented at a Panel of the 7th Seminar of the International Association for Tibetan Studies, Graz 1995*. Vienna: Verlag der Österreichischen Akademie der Wissenschaft.

Blondeau, Anne-Marie, and Ernst Steinkellner. 1996. *Reflections of the Mountain: Essays on the History and Social Meaning of the Mountain Cult in Tibet and the Himalaya*. Vienna: Verlag der Österreichischen Akademie der Wissenschaft.

Butler, Judith. 2020. *The Force of Non-violence: An Ethico-Political Bind*. London: Verso.

Coggins, Chris. 2019. "Sacred Watersheds and the Fate of the Village Body Politic in Tibetan and Han Communities Under China's Ecological Civilization." *Religions* 10.11: 600; doi:10.3390/rel10110600.

Cooper, David E., and Simon P. James. 2005. *Buddhism, Virtue and Environment*. Burlington, VT: Ashgate.

Dbus bza' mkha' 'gro. 2009. "Rnam thar nges 'byung 'dren pa'i shing rta skal ldan dad pa'i mchod sdong." In *Dbus bza' mkha' 'gro'i gsung 'bum* 1:1–547. Chengdu: Si khron mi rigs dpe skrun khang.

Dung dkar Blo bzang phrin las. 2002. *Dung dkar tshig mdzod chen mo*. Beijing: Krung go'i bod rig pa dpe skrun khang.

Eckel, Malcolm David. 1997. "Is There a Buddhist Philosophy of Nature?" In *Buddhism and Ecology: The Interconnection of Dharma and Deeds*, edited by Mary Evelyn Tucker and Duncan Ryūken Williams, 327–49. Cambridge, MA: Harvard University Press.

Gergan, Mabel Denzin. 2015. "Animating the Sacred, Sentient and Spiritual in Post-Humanist and Material Geographies." *Geography Compass* 9.5: 262–75.

Grim, John A. 2008. "Indigenous Lifeways and Knowing the World." In *The Oxford Handbook of Religion and Science*, edited by Philip Clayton, 87–107. New York: Oxford University Press.

Gurung, Phurwa. 2020. "'Mountains are Commons, Grasses are Divided': Indigenous Environmental Governance between Conservation and Democracy." M.A. Thesis, University of Colorado at Boulder.

Gyatso, Janet. 1986. "Signs, Memory and History: A Tantric Buddhist Theory of Scriptural Transmission." *Journal of the International Association of Buddhist studies* 9.2: 7–35.

———. 1987. "Down with the Demoness: Reflections on a Feminine Ground in Tibet." *The Tibet Journal* 12.4: 38–53.

———. 1993. "The Logic of Legitimation in the Tibetan Treasure Tradition." *History of Religions* 33.2: 97–134.

———. 1998. *Apparitions of the Self: The Secret Autobiographies of a Tibetan Visionary*. Princeton, NJ: Princeton University Press.

———. 2015. *Being Human in a Buddhist World: An Intellectual History of Medicine in Early Modern Tibet*. New York: Columbia University Press.

———. n.d. "The Relic Text as Prophecy: The Semantic Drift of Byang-bu and Its Appropriation in the Treasure Tradition." Unpublished paper.

Hanh, Thich Nhat. 2004. *The World We Have: A Buddhist Approach to Peace and Ecology*. Berkeley: Parallax Press.

———. 2013. *Love Letter to the Earth*. Berkeley: Parallax Press.

Harris, Ian. 1994. "Buddhism." In *Attitudes to Nature*, edited by Jean Holm and John Bowker, 8–26. London: Pinter Publishers.

———. 1997. "Buddhism and the Discourse of Environmental Concern: Some Methodological Problems Considered." In *Buddhism and Ecology: The Interconnection of Dharma and Deeds*, edited by Mary Evelyn Tucker and Duncan Ryūken Williams, 377–402. Cambridge, MA: Harvard University Press.

Huber, Toni. 1997. "Green Tibetans: A Brief Social History." In *Tibetan Culture in the Diaspora: Papers Presented at a Panel of the 7th Seminar of the International Association for Tibetan Studies, Graz 1995*, edited by Frank J. Korom, 4:103–19. Vienna: Verlag der Österreichischen Akademie der Wissenschaften.

Ives, Christopher. 2009. "In Search of a Green Dharma: Philosophical Issues in Buddhist Environmental Ethics." In *Destroying Māra Forever: Buddhist Ethics in Honor of Damien Keown*, edited by John Powers and Charles S. Prebish, 165–85. Ithaca, NY: Snow Lion.

———. 2016. "Buddhism: A Mixed Dharmic Bag: Debates about Buddhism and Ecology." In *Routledge Handbook of Religion and Ecology*, edited by Willis J. Jenkins, Mary Evelyn Tucker, and John Grim, 43–51. New York, Routledge.

Jacoby, Sarah. 2014. *Love and Liberation: Autobiographical Writings of the Tibetan Buddhist Visionary Sera Khandro*. New York: Columbia University Press.

Karmay, Samten. 1998. *The Arrow and Spindle: Studies in History, Myths, Rituals and Beliefs in Tibet.* Kathmandu: Mandala Book Point.

Kaza, Stephanie. 2019. *Green Buddhism: Practice and Compassion in Uncertain Times.* Boulder, CO: Shambhala.

———, ed. 2020. *A Wild Love for the World: Joanna Macy and the Work of Our Time.* Boulder, CO: Shambhala.

Kaza, Stephanie, and Kenneth Kraft, eds. 2000. *Dharma Rain: Sources of Buddhist Environmentalism.* Boston: Shambhala.

Karmapa, Ogyen Trinley Dorje. 2017. *Interconnected: Embracing Life in Our Global Society.* Edited by Karen Derris and Damchö Diana Finnegan. Somerville, MA: Wisdom Publications.

Kinsley, David R. 1986. *Hindu Goddesses: Visions of the Divine Feminine in the Hindu Religious Tradition.* Berkeley: University of California Press.

Kuokkanen, Rauna. 2007. *Reshaping the University: Responsibility, Indigenous Epistemes, and the Logic of the Gift.* Vancouver: University of British Columbia Press.

Larsen, Soren C., and Jay T. Johnson. 2016. "The Agency of Place: Toward a More-than-Human Geographical Self." *GeoHumanities* 2.1: 149–66.

Loy, David. 2019. *Ecodharma: Buddhist Teachings for the Ecological Crisis.* Somerville, MA: Wisdom Publications.

Macy, Joanna. 1991. *Mutual Causality in Buddhism and General Systems Theory: The Dharma of Natural Systems.* Albany: State University of New York Press.

McMahan, David. 2008. *The Making of Buddhist Modernism.* New York: Oxford University Press.

Meyers, Karin. 2018. "False Friends: Dependent Origination and the Perils of Analogy in Cross-Cultural Philosophy." *Journal of Buddhist Ethics* 25: 785–818.

———. 2019. "Decolonizing Dependent Arising." In *Buddhist Currents: Explorations in Socially and Ecologically Engaged Buddhism*, paper presented at the American Academy of Religion Meeting.

———. 2020. "Climate, Corona, and Collapse: The Dharma Was Made for These Times." *Insight Journal* 46: 9–26.

Mignolo, Walter. 2011. "Epistemic Disobedience and the Decolonial Option: A Manifesto." *Transmodernity: Journal of Peripheral Cultural Production of the Luso-Hispanic World* 1.2: 44–66.

Nebesky-Wojkowitz, René de. 1956. *Oracles and Demons of Tibet: The Cult and Iconography of the Tibetan Protective Deities.* The Hague: Mouton & Co.

Palden, Thupstan. 1987. *Rten 'brel Interdependence.* Leh, Ladakh: Ladakh Ecological Development Group.

Schmithausen, Lambert. 1997. "The Early Buddhist Tradition and Ecological Ethics." *Journal of Buddhist Ethics* 4: 1–42.

Shulman, Eviatar. 2008. "Early Meanings of Dependent-Origination." *Journal of Indian Philosophy* 36: 297–317.

Sopa, Geshe Lhundup. 1986. "The Special Theory of Pratītyasamutpāda: The Cycle of Dependent Origination." *Journal of the International Association of Buddhist Studies* 9.1: 105–19.

Sundberg, Juanita. 2014. "Decolonizing Posthumanist Geographies." *Cultural Geographies* 21.1: 33–47.

Teiser, Stephen F. 2007. *Reinventing the Wheel: Paintings of Rebirth in Medieval Buddhist Temples*. Seattle: University of Washington Press.

Terrone, Antonio. 2014. "The Earth as a Treasure in Tibetan Buddhism: Visionary Revelation and Its Interactions with the Environment." *Journal for the Study of Religion Nature and Culture* 8.4: 460–82.

Thondup, Tulku 1986. *Hidden Teachings of Tibet: An Explanation of the Terma Tradition of Tibetan Buddhism*. London: Wisdom Publications.

Todd, Zoe. 2016. "An Indigenous Feminist's Take On The Ontological Turn: 'Ontology' is Just Another Word for Colonialism." *Journal of Historical Sociology* 29.1: 5–22.

Tucker, Mary Evelyn, and Duncan Ryūken Williams. 1997. *Buddhism and Ecology: The Interconnection of Dharma and Deeds*. Cambridge, MA: Harvard University Press.

Whatmore, Sarah. 2006. "Materialist Returns: Practising Cultural Geography in and for a More-than-Human World." *Cultural Geographies* 13.4: 600–609.

Yeh, Emily. 2014a. "Reverse Environmentalism: Contemporary Articulations of Tibetan Culture, Buddhism and Environmental Protection." *Religion and Ecological Sustainability in China*, edited by James Miller, Dan Smyer Yu, and Peter van der Veer, 194–219. Oxford: Routledge.

———. 2014b. "The Rise and Fall of the Green Tibetan: Contingent Collaborations and the Vicissitudes of Harmony." In *Mapping Shangrila: Contested Landscapes in the Sino-Tibetan Borderlands*, edited by Emily Yeh and Chris Coggins, 255–88. Seattle: University of Washington Press.

Yeh, Emily, and Chris Coggins, eds. 2014. *Mapping Shangrila: Contested Landscapes in the Sino-Tibetan Borderlands*. Seattle: University of Washington Press.

The Poetry of Being Human: Toward a Tibetan Wisdom Literature

Christina A. Kilby

THIS ESSAY OFFERS the beginning of an excavation project: an effort to uncover the contours of a wisdom literature tradition from the vast treasury of Tibetan texts. Wisdom literature, as a genre classification stems from ancient Near Eastern and biblical literatures and there is no Tibetan genre name that seamlessly corresponds to the term "wisdom literature." To propose that the category of wisdom literature might be useful within Tibetan studies is not an obvious move, but its potential rewards may validate the undertaking. What might the category of wisdom literature contribute to the field of Tibetan studies? This Near Eastern genre signals and circumscribes a body of texts, as well as currents within and across texts, that center the human. The structural elements of these texts and the contexts of their production can further illuminate where, how, and among whom this centering of the human occurs. I see the idea of Tibetan wisdom literature as a heuristic that can carry forward Janet Gyatso's legacy of work to center the human within Tibetan studies .

Several of the guiding principles I propose for undertaking this literary archaeology are approaches that Janet Gyatso in particular has sharpened for our field: not only centering the human, but also engaging cross-cultural questions, attending to gender, and taking seriously the work of poetry, especially as it moves against the positions of classical religious doctrine.[1] After laying out a brief introduction, this essay borrows insights from Near Eastern wisdom literature in order to engage in sample readings of two Tibetan texts—against the grain of religion—in order to illustrate the kind of work that the notion of wisdom literature can do in our search for the human among Tibetan texts.

1. For example, in Janet Gyatso's presentation on "The Soul of Poetry" at the 2019 meeting of the International Association of Tibetan Studies, she examined the provocative use of the idea of "soul" in poetic theory despite its obvious challenge to Buddhist teachings on no-soul.

Wisdom Literature: The Shape of an Idea

Near Eastern wisdom literature is a body of writing concerned with a particular kind of wisdom, the "know-how of living" (Hebrew *hokma*),[2] which is the skill of successfully navigating a human life. The fruit of wisdom is a long and secure life, and so old age becomes a mark of authority in its own right in the transmission of wisdom. The authority of age is evident in the many Hebrew wisdom texts that style themselves as advice from a father to a son, or an elder to a youth (gendered masculine). Highly dependent on context, wisdom also tends to address an individual rather than a nation or group,[3] so dialogical conceit and direct address are common in the wisdom literature tradition. Because wisdom, *hokma,* is a skill that must be learned and developed, much Near Eastern wisdom literature includes exhortations toward the effort and patience required to gain wisdom. Such wisdom differs from scholarly knowledge and from prophetic revelation, although both book-study and visionary experience can contribute to one's development of wisdom. Training in wisdom necessarily involves discipline and restraint, attention and heed, but does not rely on belief. Wisdom literature is concerned with the world as it is rather than in mythic histories or promised futures. In fact, wisdom literature can be situated squarely within religious contexts of knowledge transmission while entirely ignoring or even challenging religion's soteriological concerns. *Hokma,* then, is a distinctly human wisdom.

In its pragmatic engagement with the contingencies of human life in the world as it is, Near Eastern wisdom literature has a strong resonance with the Tibetan category of *mi chos,* the way of humans or human dharma. As Gyatso has observed in her intellectual history of Tibetan medicine, *Being Human in a Buddhist World,* this human dharma is grounded in "material reality and the course of human life" as well as "the imperfectible human condition," and leads to worldly benefits such as skill, ease, reputation, and money.[4] For a physician, *mi chos* entails not only the medical expertise to make the right diagnosis, but also the human savvy to make one's diagnosis look right. Gyatso has also introduced the horizon of death as a defining contour of *mi chos* in medical practice:

> No talk of the patient's past life enters into the doctor's consideration, nor are there even hints in the physician's chapter of the patient's after-death experience, or miraculous reappearance, or

2. Weeks 2010, 2.
3. Weeks 2010, 1.
4. Gyatso 2015, 345.

> transcendent signs from beyond the grave, or imminent reincarnation, as are all so regularly seen in Tibetan religious narratives of death. [. . .] The place of death in the practice of medicine is one grounds upon which I would draw a critical distinction between the horizons of the human way of medicine and the soteriological aspirations of religion.[5]

The finality of death and emphasis on this human lifetime characterize *hokma* as well. When wanting to improve one's career, or win a war, or make friends, this life is what matters, not some theorized future existence. One of the hallmarks of wisdom literature is its refusal to minimize the challenges of this life within the larger frames of a cosmic past and future.

Gyatso's contributions toward examining the shape of *mi chos* in Tibetan literature comprise a foundation on which to define the features of a Tibetan wisdom literature. *Mi chos* is grounded in material and pragmatic realities: human bodies, the human life course (defined by the horizon of death), and human social dynamics (pride, shame, reputation, and competition). Although transcendent concerns frequently cross over into discourses on *mi chos*—for example, because karma is taught to confer tangible and proximal benefits as well as intangible and distal ones[6]—the ultimate horizon at work in the discourse is the most important criterion for distinguishing between *mi chos* and soteriologically efficacious forms of lived wisdom (broadly, *lha chos*). Wisdom literature conveys an ultimate horizon defined by the limits of this material world, this life, and this body, even when religious concepts are part of its construction.

The Near Eastern category of wisdom literature can help us further refine the contours of *mi chos* in Tibetan literature by the questions it provokes: how does age relate to human wisdom? How does success or prosperity? What kind of effort and training does the development of human wisdom require? What kind of world-as-it-is does human wisdom perceive? Is human wisdom best addressed to an individual or a group, and why? Finally, what literary forms does that address take, and what is their purchase?

5. Gyatso 2015, 395.

6. Discussions of karma make for a particularly slippery boundary between human and soteriological concerns because the mechanistic workings of karma look much like the "natural theology" (contrasted with divine intervention) that characterizes human wisdom in Near Eastern literature. See Weeks 2010, 114.

The Poetry of Human Wisdom

Martha Nussbaum reminds us to ask: "How should one write, what words should one select, what forms and structures and organization, if one is pursuing understanding?"[7] Near Eastern wisdom literature takes one of two specific literary forms that are deemed to enable the transmission of wisdom more effectively than others. One is aphoristic, consisting of proverbs that are pithy, poetic, and imagistic. The fact that they are easy to memorize is critical, for the authoritative power of proverbs lies in their shared currency; one cannot simply invent a proverb and expect it to persuade others. Examples such as the biblical Book of Proverbs gesture toward the genre of indigenous Tibetan proverbs (*gtam dpe*), whose shared currency is so strong that they have even been used in Tibetan legal literature as supports for judicial opinions.[8] The other major literary form that wisdom takes in the Near Eastern context is admonitory, consisting of dialogues and treatises of instruction.[9] These texts rely on the personal success and experience—including age—of the adviser for their currency.

In the Tibetan context, we can correlate these features to literary genres such as fine sayings (*legs bshad*), advice literature (*bslab bya*), political treatises (*rgyal po lugs kyi bstan bcos*), and letters (*spring yig*).[10] Each of these genres is typified by poetry. The scope of poetic forms in which *mi chos* takes shape is an area that warrants exploration and study, drawing on the intersection of Tibetan proverbial and folk traditions with Indian lyrical genres inherited through Buddhist lineages. Where there is poetry, there is persuasion: the poetic forms of both *hokma* and *mi chos* play on the imagination, the emotions, the lyrical ear, and the rhythm of the breath. They are pleasant to receive and easy to memorize. As Flannery O'Connor wrote of "good short stories," good *mi chos* literature "hangs on and expands in the mind."[11]

Admittedly, not all texts in these poetic genres are singularly focused on human wisdom, but collectively, these genres form a literary locus where currents of Tibet's human wisdom are more actively concentrated. Identify-

7. Nussbaum 1990, 3.

8. The Digitized Tibetan Archives at Bonn University (accessed at https://dtab.crossasia.org on March 6, 2021) contains a designated search parameter for proverbs within the legal texts gathered from Kündeling Monastery as well as from the Library of Tibetan Works and Archives.

9. Weeks 2010, 2.

10. The six-volume collection *Legs bshad bstan bcos phyogs bsgrigs* includes each of these categories except for letters. The advice letters of Nāgārjuna, for example, are instead included in Volume 1 on oral instructions, *zhal gdams.*

11. O'Connor 1970, 108.

ing these as exemplary genres of Tibetan wisdom literature may be useful for encouraging further attention to the way of humans.

Looking for Wisdom's Embodiment

In ancient Israelite society, the distinctiveness of *hokma* from other forms of knowledge was embodied not only in distinct genres of writing, but also in a distinct class of persons, the sages:

> Wisdom literature is usually associated with the sages who are mentioned along with priests and prophets as an important force in Israelite society. These gifted persons were recognized as possessing wide knowledge of the created world (see 1Ki 4:29–34), special insight into human affairs (as exemplified by proverbs) and exceptionally good judgment regarding courses of action to be followed to attain success in various enterprises (see 2Sa 16:15–23). In general, priests and prophets dealt with religious and moral concerns (proclaiming, teaching, interpreting, and applying God's word to his people), whereas the sages generally focused more on the practical aspects of how life should be guided in the created order of things (Proverbs) and on the intellectual challenges that arise from the ambiguities of human experience (Job, Ecclesiastes).[12]

This division of labor among sages, priests, and prophets does not neatly correspond to distinct Tibetan social roles. In some Tibetan epistolary manuals, however, the spheres of learning considered valid in the Buddhist world—the ten major and minor fields of knowledge outlined in the *Ornament of Mahayana Sutras*—are embodied in the roles of (real or imagined) people who are masters of those fields of knowledge. These letter-writing manuals give instructions about how to address religious scholars, grammarians, logicians, artisans, scribes, doctors, astrologers, and masters of poetics, synonymy, and prosody respectively. An 1806 epistolary manual by a monk and literary scholar named Mipam Dawa (1767–1807) surprises us by including instructions for how to address "those skilled in the speech of the way of humans" (*mi chos kyi gtam la mkhas pa dag*).[13] In these instructions, we learn more about how Mipam Dawa understood *mi chos* as well as the embodiment of its transmission. The manual reads,

12. *Zondervan NIV Study Bible* 1984, 725.

13. Mi pham zla ba 1986, 87.

> To those skilled in the speech of the way of humans, [write]:
>
> "To those masters of eloquence who, with full perfection in that eminent skill, the threefold art of speech,[14] accomplish the work of the great ones without difficulty;" [...]
>
> "To those great sages (*dpyod ldan*) of speech, cutting to the chase with sweet elocution, who because of their expansive vision, which probes the outer limits of worldly activities, are worthy ministers of great sovereigns;"
>
> "To those great worldly ancestors (*'jig rten gyi mes po chen po*), who lay out all counsel in the way of humans (*mi chos kyi 'dun ma*) as if in the palms of their hands [...]."[15]

Mipam Dawa locates the wisdom of *mi chos* primarily in the role of advisers, who are praised as broad-minded and broad-visioned. Furthermore, for these Tibetan sages, know-how in the art of living goes hand in hand with skills in rhetoric and oral persuasion, for wisdom only works when it can create an effect upon an audience. Mipam Dawa's descriptions of the sages of *mi chos* suggest that in our search for the human, we should attend to the lives of ministers, advisers, and other professionals (including physicians) as well as the oral literatures that they produce.

Inspired by Janet Gyatso's many contributions to gender studies, the question of wisdom's embodiment also leads us to critically examine gendered dimensions of *mi chos*. The reader may be familiar with Maya Angelou's life wisdom published under the title *Letter to My Daughter.* Maya Angelou never had a daughter. To her, it made utter sense that that transmission of life's deepest wisdom must take the form of an epistolary address from a mother to a daughter, so she shaped her book around the literary conceit of a daughter and invited her reader to inhabit that role. The social context that wisdom literature imagines for itself means something, makes its own argument about where wisdom is to be found—and knowing where to look for wisdom might be the whole point. As Gyatso observes about Tibetan medical training, "the virtue being advanced is rather about the student-teacher relationship itself."[16]

In the Near Eastern wisdom tradition, while discourses on *hokma* are sit-

14. According to the Tibetan-Tibetan-Chinese dictionary *Tshig Mdzod Chen Mo*, these rhetorical arts are a subdivision of the nine "manly arts" and include "eliciting virtue with stories (*lo rgyus*), eliciting humor with talk, and crushing the opponent with argumentation." Two of these three are mentioned in the following line from the epistolary manual.

15. Mi pham zla ba 1986, 87ff.

16. Gyatso 2015, 343.

uated in the literary conceits of male-to-male relationships of instruction, *hokma* itself is personified as a woman (Greek *sophia*) calling out in the streets for anyone who will heed her voice. Janet Gyatso has closely examined the gendered dynamics of Jigmé Lingpa's identification with his *dakini* in his secret autobiographies,[17] while the "threefold art of speech" that Mipam Dawa's manual mentions is defined as a subdivision of the nine manly arts (*pho rtsal sna dgu*). Why, in these contexts, is esoteric wisdom feminine and worldly wisdom masculine? Looking for gender markers in Tibetan wisdom literature is a promising direction for investigating the contexts of wisdom's transmission and potentially opening up new questions for biblical wisdom literature.

Jigmé Lingpa's Letter to a Young Renunciant

In Janet Gyatso's honor, I close with a brief reading of a text by the visionary Jigmé Lingpa (1730–98) through the lens of *mi chos* as sketched above. Jigmé Lingpa wrote a letter to a young student that was catalogued as "a letter to a youth, urging [him] to study hard, not to settle into action-abandoning laziness."[18] The title is provocative because this letter inhabits a world where the abandonment of worldly action, the yogi's renunciation, is upheld as a spiritual ideal and the goal of religious practice. Yet the youth in question seems to be in danger of abandoning too much: abandoning the effort required to learn and train, not only in meditation, but also in skills of literacy. At stake in this particular text is not necessarily his soteriology, but his success: *hokma*.

We can see the contours of *mi chos* in this letter's pragmatic and materialistic assessment of the capabilities of the human body and mind, as well as the nature of the human life course. Jigmé Lingpa appeals specifically to his elder age in this letter. As is customary when one opens a letter, he identifies himself with descriptive lines: "As for me, more than five decades old—/ blinded by far-advanced clouded vision/ having given up [distinguishing between] *bcad* and *gcad*."[19] In contrast, the student he addresses is endowed with "youth, with its thriving channels" that offer the possibility of great success in his meditative practice if only he will apply himself.[20] Even though this letter affirms the transcendental aims of meditation, its concerns and advice are rooted in an utterly

17. Gyatso 1998.

18. 'Jigs med gling pa Mkhyen brtse 'od zer 1988–89, 1240–43.

19. 'Jigs med gling pa Mkhyen brtse 'od zer 1988–89, 1240. *Bcad* and *gcad* are homophones whose orthography differs only by a single stem on the first letter. The implication is that because of Jigmé Lingpa's age, reading is becoming difficult for him.

20. 'Jigs med gling pa Mkhyen brtse 'od zer 1988–89, 1240.

this-worldly assessment of the young body in contrast with the elder body. This letter also makes a strikingly realistic assessment of how the human mind works and why studying the literary arts is important for a meditator. Jigmé Lingpa insists that the young student should study Dandin's poetics, the art of composing synonyms, and the other minor literary arts because "[meditational] manifestations are mental images (*rnam 'gyur sems kyi ri mo yin*). So, if we don't rely on mental knowledge (*sems kyi cho ga*), what [meditational] knowledge can there be?"[21] The meditator's loftiest aims depend on a basic facility with descriptive language and poetry because the human mind uses such language to make sense of what arises in meditation. Here, circumscribed by the limits and possibilities of the human body and mind, this letter from a master meditator speaks to the practical matter of doing one's homework.

Concluding Thoughts

In *Being Human in a Buddhist World,* Gyatso reflects on her process of tracing both human and soteriological threads in the *Four Treatises'* physician's chapter, even though the distinction between these two threads is "less than airtight."[22] She observes that "just because Buddhist terms and practices contribute to the cultivation of human dharma does not mean that their ethical and soteriological import remains unchanged in their medical guise."[23] In the end, to extricate *mi chos* from soteriology in Tibetan literature may require something like the *hamsa* bird's ability to separate milk from water—impossible for ordinary birds, such as most academics are—but Janet Gyatso's long and rich career provides a model for grappling with both *mi chos* and *lha chos* together, each on its own terms, and each changed by the other. With her example, as well as some inspiration from literary wisdom beyond the Tibetan Plateau, the search for the human in Tibetan texts does not seem quite so impossible after all.

21. 'Jigs med gling pa Mkhyen brtse 'od zer 1988–89, 1240.

22. Gyatso 2015, 350.

23. Gyatso 2015, 350.

Works Cited

Angelou, Maya. 2008. *Letter to My Daughter.* New York: Random House.

Gyatso, Janet. 1998. *Apparitions of the Self: The Secret Autobiographies of a Tibetan Visionary.* Princeton, NJ: Princeton University Press.

———. 2015. *Being Human in a Buddhist World: An Intellectual History of Medicine in Early Modern Tibet.* New York: Columbia University Press.

'Jigs med gling pa Mkhyen brtse 'od zer. 1988–89 [original not dated]. "Bya bral ba sos dal du mi 'jog par gzhon nu la yon tan bslab par rab bskul ba'i 'phrin yig." In *rtsom yig gser gyi sbram bu.* Volume 2:550–53. Xining: mtsho sngon mi rigs dpe skrun khang.

Legs bshad bstan bcos phyogs bsgrigs. 2006. Xining: Mtsho sngon mi rigs dpe skrun khang.

Mi pham zla ba. 1986 [original dated 1806]. *Phrin yig gi rnam bzhag dper brjod dang bcas pa padma dkar po'i phreng mdzes.* Xining: Mtsho sngon mi rigs dpe skrun khang.

Nussbaum, Martha. 1990. *Love's Knowledge: Essays on Philosophy and Literature.* London: Oxford University Press.

O'Connor, Flannery. 1970. *Mystery and Manners: Occasional Prose.* New York: Farrar, Strauss, and Giroux.

Weeks, Stuart. 2010. *An Introduction to the Study of Wisdom Literature.* T&T Clark: New York.

Zondervan NIV Study Bible. 1984. Peabody, MA: Hendrickson Bibles.

The Buddhist Aesthetic of Replication

Jonathan C. Gold

THE BUDDHA'S TEACHINGS, called the Dharma, are repetitive. Practically every chapter, section, paragraph, and turn of phrase is repeated—often. Throughout the early scriptures, topic after topic and event after event are described in formulaic, stereotyped language. Whether the Buddha is depicted speaking to a crowd or an individual, to a monk or a king, to a god or a ghost, he uses words that show up elsewhere. Within each speech, he often says the same thing many times, sometimes repeating a paragraph multiple times changing only one word each repetition. This is not to deny that there are many unique stories, statements, and structures. But they are the minority. Most of the Dharma is repetition.

It is regularly noted that early Buddhism was an oral tradition, and the literature of itinerant reciters the world over exhibits formulae and repetition.[1] It has been pointed out that terminological lists serve an essential mnemonic function.[2] These are not, however, incidental features of Buddhist literature. Even if the Buddha's teachings gained their formulaic, repetitive qualities and their systemic lists via monastic institutions of oral recitation, the question would still need answering: What were these reciters trying to express with all this duplication?

The repetition is not random, after all. It is structured and iterative. Take the *Aṅguttara Nikāya*, the *Numerical Discourses*, which is ostensibly a collection of teachings from the Buddha shaped around the numbers from one to eleven. Each section includes dozens of passages that do, indeed, reflect teachings found in other parts of the canon. In the "Book of the Sixes," for instance, you find more than one hundred teachings—Bodhi's translation has 139—on such "sixes" as six subjects of recollection, six ways to have a good death, six designations for sense pleasure, six unsurpassed things, six qualities of a thoroughbred, and on and on. The Buddha is depicted as someone who liked to teach with numerical lists. The reciters have collated, but not invented, these

1. Cousins 1983.

2. Gethin 1992.

citations. But then, each book from the "twos" to the "elevens" caps its collated scriptures with the so-called "Lust and so forth Repetition Series." In these series, a handful of the lists from the preceding book (in the "Book of the Sixes" it's six unsurpassed things, six recollections, and six perceptions) are each first described as a list of things "to be developed for the direct knowledge of lust." Then, the lists are each repeated with "lust" sequentially replaced in turn with *sixteen* other defilements. After that, we start again with "lust," but this time the whole sequence is re-run with "direct knowledge" replaced, in turn, with "full understanding." And then, that whole sequence of seventeen is run again with eight other accomplishments. This makes for a total of 170 (17 x 10) distinct discourses on each of the three lists of six—for a total of 510 iterations. The "Book of the Sixes" contains 649 scriptures (139 + 510), of which the "Repetition Series" makes up 79 percent.

This kind of iterative generation of scriptures out of formulaic material is not in any way covert. On the contrary, it is regularly praised by the Buddha and practiced by his immediate disciples as a method of understanding "in detail" what was "spoken in brief" (e.g., AN 6.69, and 10.26). And, to bring this home, it follows the basic methodology—the standard discursive mode—in the vast majority of the speeches attributed to the Buddha himself. It is difficult to locate passages from early Buddhist scriptures that are not iterations of one kind or another. This kind of mechanical production of expressive language based on abstract lists and memorized formulae could not have a better analogy than an automated weapon, the so-called "wheel" of Dharma: Just as the weapon subdues all enemies, the Dharma wheel produces language that establishes dominion in the mind on the Path of Seeing.

Buddhist scriptures are not just repetitive, they're *repetitions*. They have all been said before; in fact, for Buddhists everything is a repetition. The Buddha himself was really just *a* buddha. Look at depictions of the five, or seven, buddhas of our fortunate age, and they all look the same. Encounter the thousand buddhas of our fortunate age, or the countless buddhas in the miracle at Śrāvastī—they all look the same. The Buddha narrates his own life story through the life stories of previous buddhas. In Mahāyāna, buddhas are expressions of buddha nature, or the transcendent dharmakāya (whether Vajrasattva or Samantabhadra), or unified in their perception of the ineffable dharmadhātu.

So buddhas are iterations, the Dharma is iterative; finish off the set: The saṅgha—the Buddha's followers—also participate in repeating forms. It is backwards, I think, to say that iteration is a Buddhist reciter's strategy. Rather, we should say that the Buddhist worldview, with its expressive aesthetic of repetition, elevates the role of the reciter. Where the Hebrew Scriptures begin with the creation story, "In the beginning," and the Christian Scriptures begin with the lineage of Christ, and the Qur'an begins appealing to the name of Allah the compassionate, and merciful, Buddhist scriptures begin with the reciter's creed: "Thus have I heard."

The canonical literatures that present the most significant exception to my claims about verbal and conceptual repetition are the Jātakas and Avadānas. These are wonderfully complex morality tales, and they are structured narratively, and not at all (generally) bound to conceptual lists or doctrinal structures. Jātakas are bodhisattva tales, stories of the Buddha-to-be in his hundreds of previous lives, wherein he cultivated the virtuous qualities that would allow him to attain enlightenment in our age. Avadānas are tales of other beings' meritorious actions from the past, which have also brought fruit in the present world. Both types of stories are peopled by talking animals and terrifying monsters, and they recount acts of magic and moral extremes. How could this be the same tradition as that of the repetitive, machine-like doctrinal system?

One answer is that, however literary and narratively chaotic they are, Jātakas and Avadānas are depicted as holding lessons about the regularity of the karmic world, the world of rebirth (saṃsāra). What is called the "story of the past" is always connected back to a "story of the present," and in each case the Buddha explains something apparently unusual as being *not unusual at all*. The personal qualities displayed in one story, however fantastic the context or form of life, are quite exactly replicated in the other. It turns out that, in the long story of saṃsāra, these things happen all the time. So the royal advisor from the past is now Ānanda, the army is the saṅgha of monks, the enemy king is Devadatta, and the wise king is the Buddha himself—and everyone acted then exactly as they act now. The repetition is not in the internal narrative of a given story, but in people's moral characters and the karmic results their actions occasion. Such stories allow, simultaneously, for the appearance of complexity and the simple teaching that we are all forever repeating ourselves. The Jātakas and Avadānas lift us out of the meaning within an individual lifetime and reinscribe us within the cyclic repetitions of saṃsāra itself. It's like we're looking at Voyager I's picture of Earth from the edge of the solar system, which Carl Sagan described poetically as "a mote of dust suspended in a sunbeam."[3]

To see ourselves as iterations, as karmic inheritors, is the beginning of virtue in Buddhism. It is the beginning of the ability to accede to what is truly replicative within us, our buddha nature. To see the emptiness in our concepts is also to remove the particularity of our "dual" perspectives—our notion that things are specifically one way, rather than another. Buddhist faith, ostensibly

3. Sagan 2011, 6.

confirmed by practice, is about seeking buddha nature in oneself, discovering a convergence between one's own identity and the wall of repeating buddhas.

I first encountered Buddhism in a life-changing "Buddhist Scriptures" seminar taught by Janet Gyatso in 1988. Sometime shortly thereafter, I bought a used copy of Philip Kapleau's *Three Pillars of Zen*. In it, I was amazed by the story of "Mr. Y," the "Japanese executive, age 47," whose diary recounts his enlightenment "experience." Over several days, he writes such remarks as, "Am supremely free free free free free," and "I've totally disappeared. Buddha is!"[4] I recall being especially moved by the statement he shouts at the top of his lungs in the peak moment: "I've come to enlightenment! Shakyamuni and the Patriarchs haven't deceived me! They haven't deceived me!"[5] I remember feeling that this was surely evidence that there was something objectively valid in this path. I also remember, subsequently, in graduate school, being disappointed to learn that this was a stereotyped formula—a statement that Zen masters are *supposed to say* when they attain enlightenment. What could it show, I thought, about the truth of the individual enlightenment experience, if it was just a formula?

Now, I have begun to think that, for Mr. Y in that moment, only a formula would do.

Abbreviations

AN = *Aṅguttara Nikāya*. See Bodhi, trans. 2012.

Works Cited

Bodhi, Bhikkhu, trans. 2012. *The Numerical Discourses of the Buddha: A Translation of the Aṅguttara Nikāya*. Boston: Wisdom Publications.

Cousins, L. S. 1983. "Pali Oral Literature." In *Buddhist Studies: Ancient and Modern* edited by Philip Denwood and Alexander Piatigorsky, 1–11. London: Curzon Press.

Gethin, Rupert. 1992. "The *Mātikās:* Memorization, Mindfulness, and the List." In *In the Mirror of Memory: Reflections on Mindfulness and Remembrance in Indian and Tibetan Buddhism*, edited by Janet Gyatso, 149–72. Albany, NY: State University of New York Press.

Kapleau, Philip. 1989. *The Three Pillars of Zen: Teaching, Practice, and Enlightenment*. New York: Anchor Books.

Sagan, Carl. 2011. *Pale Blue Dot: A Vision of the Human Future in Space*. New York: Random House.

4. Kapleau 1989, 207.

5. Kapleau 1989, 206.

Knowing Knowledge: Geluk and Sellarsian Epistemology and the Emergence of Tibetan Modernity[1]

Jay Garfield

JANET GYATSO has contributed enormously to our understanding of the emergence and nature of Tibetan modernity, calling our attention to the seeds of modern thought in classical Tibetan metaphysics, literary practice, and medicine, as well as to the important interactions between Tibetan and other scholars that have supported the modernization of Tibetan thought. This essay addresses how to understand Tibetan modernity in the domain of epistemology. Has Buddhist Tibet *always* been modern, by virtue of its commitment to "inner science," as the Dalai Lama XIV sometimes suggests, or has Tibet only recently emerged into modernity by virtue of its interaction with the West following the exile of 1959? To what degree do Tibetan epistemological ideas and their evolution map onto Western epistemological ideas and their evolution? I will approach these questions in a roundabout way, beginning with some general reflections on epistemology and the modern, taking a detour through an instructive episode in twentieth-century American philosophy, and then turning to Geluk approaches to making sense of *pramāṇa* (*tshad ma*) in the context of Prāsaṅgika Madhyamaka. This tour will help us to understand current thinking about science and knowledge in the Tibetan world.

1. This work derives from a collaborative project addressing Geluk-Sakya/Kagyu polemics inspired by Taktsang Lotsāwa's critique of Tsongkhapa's approach to Prāsaṅgika Madhyamaka undertaken by the Yakherds, with the support of the Singapore Ministry of Education and the Australian Research Council. I thank these two funding agencies, as well as Yale-NUS College, the University of Tasmania, Deakin University, Smith College, and the Central Institute of Higher Tibetan Studies for supporting this research. The Yakherds are José Cabezón, Ryan Conlon, Thomas Doctor, Douglas Duckworth, Jed Forman, myself, John Powers, Geshe Yeshes Thabkhas, Sonam Takchöe, and Tashi Tsering. Thanks to Dan Arnold for comments on an earlier draft.

Two Approaches to Epistemology

The Yakherds distinguish two approaches to epistemology taken by Indian and Tibetan philosophers exploring the idea of *pramāṇa,* or epistemic warrant.[2] The first is what we might call *transcendental epistemology.* This is the most frequent register of epistemological reflection, both in the Indo-Tibetan world and in the West. When we pursue epistemology this way, we begin by thinking analytically about the nature of justification itself, bracketing actual human practices, and develop a purely prescriptive account of epistemic warrant embodying a set of standards that might or might not be met by actual human practice.

The second approach to epistemology is the *anthropological* approach. On this approach, we begin not with analytical reflection on the meanings of epistemic terms, but rather by asking what actual people *do* when they claim to be justifying statements, or when they certify statements by others as warranted. In this approach to epistemology, we bracket questions about whether those practices meet some transcendental standard, and develop a purely descriptive account of actual epistemic practices. On this approach, we take what counts as knowledge to be a social or institutional affair, like what counts as currency or as a legal vote, and then ask about the institutional conditions on bestowing that honorific on a cognitive or linguistic episode. We might, for instance, discover that those in some community count as knowledge only that which is endorsed by scientists, or that another community includes the deliverances of certain oracles as knowledge. If we take this approach, we take it for granted that there is knowledge, and ask only what leads us to classify some statements under that head.

There are broad reasons that might be adduced for favoring each of these approaches to epistemology. On the one hand, transcendental epistemology can be understood as conceptual analysis. We have a concept of knowledge—perhaps captured roughly by the so-called "JTB+ formula" of justified true belief plus some yet-to-be-specified Gettier-proofing condition—and it is the job of philosophy to reveal what is contained in that concept. Moreover, we should not presume of any concept that it is in fact satisfied by any instances, just as the geometric definition of a circle does not entail that any perfect circles have ever been drawn. So we should begin by understanding the concept

2. These terms are variously translated in English. Popular translations include valid cognition, means of knowledge, evidence, instruments of knowledge, epistemic instruments, epistemic warrant. I will use epistemic warrant when justification is at issue, and epistemic instruments when the means of acquiring knowledge is at issue, following the use of the Yakherds 2021.

itself, and then determine the degree to which we may or may not satisfy it in our epistemic life. Moreover, one might argue, since knowledge is an epistemic *ideal*, as goodness is, for instance in the moral domain, it is quite appropriate to represent it as something that nobody ever achieves, but yet stands as a regulative goal in practice. Only a transcendental epistemology can accomplish this task.

On the other hand, one might argue that inasmuch as epistemic activity is human activity—no different from speaking a language, playing a game, or dining with friends in that respect—any epistemology should characterize that activity. And, one might point out, since knowing is effectively like winning the epistemic game, not the achievement of perfection, and since we do often both claim to know and credit others with knowledge, an epistemology should tell us under what circumstances we in fact do that, and what the norms are that govern such attributions. Such an epistemology can only be anthropological.

Modernity and Epistemology: The Centrality of Science

It is widely recognized that among the important characteristics of modern epistemology as it emerged in seventeenth- and eighteenth-century Europe (and for better or worse, this is at least a paradigm case of the application of the term *modern*) are these: (1) the recognition of the individual rational subject as the knower; (2) the recognition of the responsibility of that subject to common standards of rational inquiry in order to count as a knower; (3) an understanding of the subject as immediately aware of their own inner states, providing an epistemic foundation for access to the external world. Knowledge of the external world is then regarded as mediated by our sensory and cognitive faculties, faculties which may be fallible and which may interpose a kind of veil between us and the external world. These are features of modern approaches to epistemology regardless of whether they are rationalist or empiricist, foundationalist or coherentist.

But a second, and perhaps ultimately more important characteristic of European modernity in epistemology derives from its origins in the Galileo affair. That is the installation of science as the paradigm of rational inquiry and as the final arbiter of truth regarding the nature of reality. This displacement of tradition, of collective wisdom, and of religious authority is what enabled the faith in progress, in reason, and in the power of the individual subject operating in the public sphere that constitute the heart of the modern sensibility.

This faith in science has several momentous consequences for epistemology as it has been understood in Europe since the Enlightenment. The first of these has been the introduction of a distinction between what Sellars has famously called the "manifest" and the "scientific" images of "man in the world."[3] That is, we distinguish a world as it appears to us in everyday experience from that revealed by scientific inquiry, replete with unobservable theoretical entities, and we take it that while both images of the world are accurate, the scientific image is capable of explaining and even correcting the manifest image. It has a *kind* of epistemic priority, but only a kind: whereas the scientific image may have epistemic priority with respect to the fundamental nature of reality and the causal principles that govern physical processes, the manifest is the source of the norms that govern scientific inquiry, as well as the home of the observations that vindicate its discoveries.[4] The important point for our purposes is that science is nonetheless granted authority over the basic structure of reality, and our own everyday experiences answer to it in that domain.

This dichotomy leads to a second, surprising, and little-remarked consequence: a subtle but pervasive transformation in our understanding of truth. Truth and trust are cognate notions. And a primary sense of *truth* in English is *trustworthy.* A true friend is one we can trust; a true coin is one we can use; to be true to a partner is to repay their trust, etc. . . . The application of the term to sentences or to beliefs was homologous: a true statement or a true belief is one on which an agent can rely in reasoning or as a ground for action. To say that a statement is true is to commit oneself to using it as a basis for investigation or as a reason for action.[5]

The rise of science as the measure of reality altered the semantic balance in our understanding of truth. Because science is now taken as the arbiter of the real, we end up adopting the attitude that the real is fully determinate, and independent of our own views or knowledge, the attitude we now call *scientific realism.* And since science is also taken as the arbiter of *truth,* truth comes to be understood as connected directly to the reality science delivers. It is no longer simply the property of being reliable in our everyday practices. This in turn introduces the idea that true sentences or true beliefs *correspond to reality,* a view we now call the *correspondence theory of truth,* another hallmark of modernity. (And note that nobody has ever proposed a contentful account of just in what that correspondence could consist.)

Finally, the manifest-scientific dichotomy, with its recognition of science as the measure (*pramāṇa*?) of reality leads inevitably to a kind of reciprocity between the manifest and scientific image that introduces a deep tension in

3. Sellars 1963a.

4. See Garfield 1988 and 2012 for more complete explorations of this reciprocal relation.

5. Note that this is consistent with many classical Indian accounts of truth as that which enables one to achieve one's ends (*puruṣārtha*). I develop this notion further in Garfield 2019.

modernity itself regarding self-knowledge, a tension that arguably contains the seeds of the postmodern attitude. Since our own bodies and minds are present in, and not external to, the real world, the final story about how they work is the scientific story, the story to be told by biology, neuroscience, psychology, and even the social sciences. That authority in turn reinscribes the manifest-scientific dichotomy in the domain of the inner. We now must distinguish our minds (and bodies) as they appear to us from our minds and bodies as science understands them, and this includes our sensory and cognitive faculties, our basic means of access to the world (once again, *pramāṇa*).

The fact of this dichotomy, and the fact of our introspective awareness of ourselves, like our everyday awareness of everything around us, means that we must jettison the view that we have immediate privileged access to our own inner states as they are. This is the foundation of Sellars' attack on the Myth of the Given in "Empiricism and the Philosophy of Mind."[6] Although the commitment to indubitable knowledge of our own minds as a foundation for possibly fallible access to the external world is a cornerstone of modernity, we now see that the commitment to *scientia mensura* or science as the principle *pramāṇa* undermines that very cornerstone, a tension that issues in the postmodern revolution in epistemology initiated by Quine and Sellars. The authority of science means that the nature of our minds, of our sensory apparatus, and of our access to any objects of knowledge is opaque to introspection. We are strangers to ourselves.

Responding to Carnap: Quine and Sellars

In the *Aufbau* (*The Logical Structure of the World*, 1967) first published in 1925, Carnap (1891–1970) proposes an account of our knowledge of the external world that takes as its foundations "the stream of experience," to which he also refers as "the given." (102) He emphasizes that his goal is "to construct the objective by starting with the stream of experience," a method he characterizes as "methodological solipsism" or "autopsychology." (107) These terms emphasize the first-person (singular) foundation of all knowledge on this model. Basic knowledge is independent of any knowledge of the external world or of other knowers. The idea is this: We have immediate knowledge of the given, the stream of experience, or what was later to be called by the logical positivists *sense data.* (Ayer 1963) This knowledge is achieved simply by virtue of their immediate givenness.

Concepts and external objects are then "logical constructions" out of actual

6. Sellars 1963b.

or counterfactual experiences or sense data. We form the concept of *redness* on the basis of red sense data; of an apple as that kind of thing which leads to red sense data when seen at a distance, white ones and sweet ones when bitten; of fruit as either an apple, an orange, or . . . ; etc. . . . , logically constructing both the world and the concepts adequate to it in a foundation of immediately known sensation. Meaning is grounded in reference: words refer ultimately to patterns of actual or possible sense experience. So, on this understanding of the structure of knowledge, knowledge has a foundation; that foundation is in individual first-person sense experience; the most basic known objects are sensations; all other objects and judgments are logical constructions therefrom.

I introduce the *Aufbau* framework not for its own sake, but because I am interested in the two most prominent responses to this short-lived (but, during its heyday, overwhelmingly popular) proposal, a proposal that those in Buddhist studies will note is intriguingly akin to ideas floated in the Indian Buddhist *pramāṇavāda* tradition of Dignāga and Dharmakīrti. Those are the responses of the two American philosophers Willard van Orman Quine (1908–2000) and Wilfrid Sellars (1912–89), responses that echo in fascinating ways those of Tsongkhapa and Takstang to Dharmakīrti. Sellars and Quine are each naturalists about epistemology, but their approaches differ sharply. We will see that Quine presupposes a transcendental understanding of epistemology and that Sellars advocates an anthropological account. And that difference generates very different attitudes towards the possibility of knowledge and of meaning.

Quine and Sellars each see that at least one fundamental difficulty of Carnap's program lies in its foundationalism. Carnap requires sensations, or basic experiences, to be *nonconceptual* and *immediate* and at the same time to constitute both *knowledge* and *semantic primitives* serving as the foundations for both the edifice of knowledge and the edifice of meaning. Although I want to begin with Quine's response to Carnap, he agrees with Sellars' diagnosis of the problem here, and given its clarity, it is useful to take the Sellarsian diagnostic account as our basis here.

In his "Empiricism and the Philosophy of Mind" (hereafter EPM), Sellars points to an inconsistent triad that lies at the base of all sense-datum theories, one that we will see Tsongkhapa anticipates. Sense data are meant to be *given,* that is, to be immediate and nonconceptual; all knowledge is expressible in language, and therefore conceptual; sense data are meant to constitute *knowledge,* indeed the most secure of all knowledge. Sellars and Quine each conclude from the inconsistency of that triad that nothing could satisfy the description that sense data are meant to satisfy, and indeed that it makes no sense to talk about foundations of knowledge, although their routes to this conclusion and the way they deploy it going forward are somewhat different.[7]

This argument against the possibility of epistemic foundations, which rests on the insight that nothing can be immediate and foundational and at the same time lie in what Sellars calls "the space of reasons"—the domain of justification that constitutes knowledge—lies at the heart of the epistemological attack on the Myth of the Given. But there is a semantic argument as well, which we will see is also relevant to the Tibetan debates to which we will soon turn. It is important to Carnap that sense data are not only epistemic primitives, known immediately without any justification or conceptualization, but that they are also semantic primitives, the denotations of the most basic terms in our language.

Carnap takes these to be observation terms, corresponding to immediately given sensory qualities, which might be rendered as *looks green, looks red, sounds like C#,* etc. . . . These observation terms, he supposes, get their meanings directly by referring to immediate sense experiences, or, we might say, by being connected as labels for those experiences. More complex descriptive predicates, such as *is green, is red, is a C#,* etc. . . . are then logical constructions from these primitively referential terms, denoting the properties of tending to produce the experiences of *looking green, looking red, sounding like C#,* etc. . . . And on to the rest of language. On this view—just as in the case of the epistemic side of the foundationalist program in which all of knowledge is grounded in the sensory given—all of meaning is grounded in the immediate referential relation between appearance terms and experiences. This entails that the constitution of meaning, like the constitution of knowledge, is *solipsistic* in Carnap's sense, that is, that a single knower or reporter could be a knower and a language user.[8]

This view also entails that appearance talk—predicates of the form *appearing to be F*—is logically and semantically prior to direct predication—the use of predicates of the form *is F.* Sellars put paid to this idea as well in EPM, pointing out that one can only learn such appearance predicates if one has already mastered the corresponding descriptive predicates, and that mastering those requires being socialized into linguistic norms and practices, just as learning to justify one's claims requires being socialized into epistemic norms and

7. There is insufficient space to go into the details of the complex argument of EPM here. But de Vries and Triplett 2000 presents an excellent overview.

8. It is noteworthy that this approach to semantics is akin to that of Wittgenstein in the *Tractatus*, and is also the target of the decisive attack on private language in *Philosophical Investigations.* I will leave aside the comparison of Candrakīrti's and Tsongkhapa's position on language and meaning to Wittgenstein's. But there are rich parallels there, also suggesting a postmodern turn in premodern Tibetan philosophy. See Thurman 1980.

practices. That is, one cannot know what it is for something to *look red* if one does not already know what it is for something to *be red.* One cannot know something to be a red sense datum unless one already has the concept of redness that is meant to be derived from knowledge of red sense data.

So much for what was wrong with the *Aufbau* program. Let us now turn to the very different conclusions that Quine and Sellars draw from its failure. Quine, as a transcendentalist, accepts Carnap's claims that meaning demands primitive, determinate referential contact with particular moments of experience, and that any normatively rich account of knowledge—one that generates the possibility of epistemic obligation, criticism, etc.—demands immediate contact with reality to ground those norms. He concludes from this that since there is no fundamental meaning-inducing relation between language and the world, there can be no such thing as meaning, that the very idea of linguistic meaning is incoherent. He also concludes that since there are no basic epistemic relations between minds and the world that could determine what one ought to believe, that normative epistemology is impossible.

Quine's proposal in this domain is to naturalize epistemology by making it a subdiscipline of psychology and the social sciences, that is, by adopting an anthropological approach to epistemology, eschewing any normative pretensions. On his view, we can ask what people say and do when they claim to pursue knowledge, but we cannot ask whether they are right to say and to do those things; we can ask about the regularities of uses of words, and about the conditions under which people approve or disapprove of their use, but not about their meanings. This is why he is both a naturalist and a transcendentalist.[9]

Sellars draws very different conclusions from the incoherence of Carnap's program. He concludes from the impossibility of primitive semantic and epistemic relations of language and thought to the world that neither language nor knowledge can have any foundations. By converting Quine's *modus tollens* into a *modus ponens,* he argues that neither meaning nor knowledge require foundations: meaning is constituted simply in the network of practices that constitute language use, practices that themselves induce the norms that govern syntax, semantics, and pragmatics; knowledge is that which is achieved by the appropriate use of epistemic conventions that themselves are justified by the knowledge they enable. He thus argues that we can make perfect sense of the norms that induce linguistic meaning as well as those that govern epistemic activity by attending to the power of conventions to induce normativity. Indeed, we can see Sellars' critique of Carnap's solipsism as leading him in this direction.[10]

9. See Quine 1960 and 1981 for the details of the arguments.

10. This point also connects Sellars' thought to that of Hume and Wittgenstein, each of whom

Sellars argues instead that empirical knowledge has no foundation (or as Wittgenstein puts a similar point so perfectly: "the foundations are held up by the walls of the house." [1972, ¶ 248]). We become knowers, on his account, when we come to participate competently in the collective social practice of justification and criticism; knowledge is just what we as a community of knowers take to be justified by our conventions of justification; no primitive world-experience relations are needed in order to constitute knowledge. We use language meaningfully, on this account, when we come to participate competently in collective social practice of language use; meaning is just the use of a word or a phrase by the members of the community of language users; no primitive semantic word-world relations are necessary to constitute meaning.

Sellars thus does not *deny* the normativity that governs meaning and judgment. Instead, he *explains* it. He explains that it derives from convention, the only possible source of normativity. Sellars hence joins Quine in his naturalism; but unlike Quine his approach to epistemology is *normative,* not *anthropological,* simply because he believes that we can naturalize normativity itself. Whereas Quine's naturalism leads him to deny that we can make any sense of the normativity presupposed by meaning and knowledge, Sellars' naturalism leads him to an explanation of how that normativity arises in nature.

Responding to Dharmakīrti: Tsongkhapa and Taktsang

It is hard to miss the parallels between the Pramāṇavāda account of knowledge and Carnap's. Digṅāga and Dharmakīrti (henceforth I will generally only refer to Dharmakīrti, as it was he who was influential in Tibet, not so much Digṅāga) also take knowledge to have a foundation in immediate sensory experience, or *pratyakṣa,* perception that puts us in direct contact with sensible particulars (*svalakṣana*). On their account as well, the macroscopic phenomena we encounter in daily life are logical constructs out of these sensory experiences, known inferentially (via *anumāna*) through the engagement of universals (*samanyalakṣana*). And Dharmakīrti also takes sense perception to be immediate and veridical, absent any conceptual mediation, and directly presenting

emphasized convention, or custom, as the source of normativity, as well as the fact that conventions are ungrounded, constituted only by the implicit agreement of those who participate in them, opening a wide avenue towards the naturalization of meaning and epistemology. See Garfield 2019 for a discussion of how this works in Hume's philosophy and Kripke 1982 for a discussion of how it works in Wittgenstein's philosophy. Note also that this connection forces one to take the Empiricism in the title of EPM very seriously. Many read this essay simply as an attack on the logical empiricism of Carnap and his followers in the sense data industry; but it is also the defense of an older form of empiricism found in Hume.

sensory experiences as they are. The possibility of error in experience enters with conceptual thought and the engagement with unreal universals. The foundationalism, the commitment to the given, the methodological solipsism, and the nonconceptual nature of perception we encountered in Carnap's program are all presaged in early Indian Buddhist epistemology.

The semantic side of Carnap's program also has antecedents in Buddhist Pramāṇavāda, although the homologies are not so tight in this case. This is because the Pramāṅavādins did not think that the sense experiences delivered by perception are expressible at all. They argue that language and conceptuality go hand in hand, and that language always engages with universals, not the particulars given to us in perceptual experience. Nonetheless, there is an important point of agreement: Carnap, as we have seen, thought that our ordinary language denotes things that are logical constructions from a sensory given, and that words get their meaning through a semantic relation to the world mediated in the first instance by reference to those objects, and in the final analysis by the particulars into which those macroscopic objects resolve on analysis. The only difference is that whereas Carnap takes the meanings of ordinary terms themselves to be analayzable in terms of terms denoting experiences, Dharmakīrti, because he takes that more primitive denotation to be impossible, does not adopt this analytic semantic foundationalism.

Because of his enormous impact on Buddhist (and for that matter non-Buddhist) epistemology in India, Dharmakīrti and his commentators attracted a great deal of philosophical attention in Tibet. Nonetheless, they were not without rivals. His Mādhyamika critic Candrakīrti had a very different epistemological perspective. Candrakīrti argues in *Clear Words* (*Prasannapadā*) against limiting the number of *pramāṇas* to two, adding at least testimony (*śabda*) and analogy (*upamāna*) to the list, suggesting that it is open-ended. He also rejects their foundationalism, following Nāgārjuna in taking the *pramāṇas* to be vindicated by the objects they deliver (*prameyas*) and by one another in a coherentist epistemology. In these two respects, we also see Candrakīrti rejecting the methodological solipsism shared by the Pramāṅavādins and Carnap.

Candrakīrti also diverges from the Pramāṇavāda tradition in his understanding of linguistic meaning. In a careful analysis of the idea of convention (*saṃvṛti/lokavyāvahāra*) he takes meaning to be constituted not by direct referential relations to extralinguistic reality, but by a network of customs for the use of words. This idea, championed in the twentieth century in Europe and the United States by Wittgenstein and Sellars, not only runs counter to Dharmakīrti's reductionism, but also to his methodological solipsism. For it forces us, if we want to understand the content of language and thought, to look to the community of language users and thinkers, and not to the individual speaker or subject.

This is particularly important in the present context because the towering Tibetan philosopher Tsongkhapa (1357–1419) and his followers in the Geluk tradition, as well as his most prominent critic Taktsang Sherab Rinchen (b. 1405) and his followers in the Sakya and Kagyu traditions, take themselves to follow Candrakīrti and not the Pramāṅavādins in their understanding of knowledge and justification in the context of Prāsaṅgika Madhyamaka. But just how they take themselves to do so is a matter of contention. They each reject Dharmakīrti's foundationalism, as well as his individualism. But while Tsongkhapa argues that this is consistent with a robust normative epistemology and the possibility of expressing a true Prāsaṅgika Madhyamaka position, Taktsang argues that at most it leaves us with an anthropological account of people's deluded epistemic practices and reduces Madhyamaka to inexpressibility. We hence see Tsongkhapa as following Sellars' approach to Carnap in his response to Digṅāga, and Takstang following Quine's approach in his very different response.

Let us begin with Tsongkhapa.[11] In the *Special Insight* (*lhag tong*) section of the *Great Treatise on the Stages of the Path to Enlightenment* (*Lam rim chen mo*),[12] Tsongkhapa explains how he interprets Candrakīrti's exposition of Prāsaṅgika Madhyamaka and how he interprets Candrakīrti's epistemology in this context. There are four central issues to which we need to attend: how he takes Candrakīrti's account of *pramāṇa* to differ from that of Digṅāga and Dharmakīrti; his account of knowledge as always conceptual; his understanding of conventional truth as *truth*; his argument that the Prāsaṅgika Madhyamaka position must be expressible.

Tsongkhapa notes that according to those in the Pramāṇavāda tradition, perception is an epistemic warrant because it puts us in direct, conceptually unmediated causal contact with particulars, which it delivers to consciousness nondeceptively, that is, with a mode of appearance congruent with their mode of existence. This is both why perception can serve as a foundation for knowledge, and why perception is nondeceptive, hence warranting. It is foundational because it depends on nothing else; it is warranting because it is always direct and nondeceptive. Candrakīrti, on the other hand, he argues, follows Nāgārjuna's account in *Reply to Objections* (*Vigrahavyāvartanī*), arguing that the *pramāṇas* and their *prameyas* are mutually dependent, and that the various *pramāṇas* also are mutually supportive, like the sheaves in a stack. We learn to

11. Those interested in Taktsang's side of the story are encouraged to consult Yakherds 2021.

12. Tsongkhapa 2004.

trust our vision when we are told that it is good; inference only gives us general knowledge when we can discern analogies between cases, etc. . . . Tsongkhapa is clear in the *Special Insight* section of the *Great Treatise on the Stages of the Path to Enlightenment* that he sides with Candrakīrti, not Dharmakīrti, in his understanding of epistemic warrant. He writes, "As to assertions about forms and such, we do not hold that valid cognition does not establish them; valid cognition does establish them."[13] And a bit later,

> . . . the logicians hold that a perception is a consciousness that is free from conceptuality and is nonmistaken . . . Therefore, it is in relation to the intrinsic character of these five objects that they consider such perceptions to be valid. . . . Candrakīrti does not accept even conventionally that anything exists essentially or by way of its intrinsic character. . . . Thus, how could he accept this claim that the sensory consciousnesses are valid with regard to the intrinsic character of their objects?[14]

That is, on this understanding, what generates epistemic warrant is not direct contact with things as they are, but rather a role in ordinary activity and confirmation by other warrants and the objects they deliver.

Moreover, Tsongkhapa and his Geluk followers argue, a *pramāṇa* may be veridical or trustworthy with respect to an object in some respects, but not in others. Perception, for instance, may be a warrant for the size, shape, or location of an external object, but might mistakenly deliver it to us as intrinsically real. There is thus a kind of fallibilism built into Tsongkhapa's understanding of epistemic warrant. He cashes this out by distinguishing between conventional and ultimate *pramāṇas* and emphasizing that conventional *pramāṇas* are nondeceptive with respect to conventional truth, in virtue of being confirmed by, and not being undermined by, other conventional *pramāṇas.* Yet they are nonetheless deceptive with regard to ultimate truth, a domain accessible only by ultimate *pramāṇas.* We thus end up with an epistemology grounded in interdependence and in collective epistemic activity. Warrant arises not from direct, nondeceptive access to reality as it is, but from participation in a set of conventions that are mutually supportive and that constitute conventional justification.

Tsongkhapa also rejects the idea that knowledge can ever be nonconceptual. Even perceptual knowledge, he argues, must be assertable and communi-

13. Tsongkhapa 2004, vol. 3, 163.

14. Tsongkhapa 2004, vol. 3, 165.

cable. Even nonconceptual meditative equipoise only yields actual knowledge in the postmeditative state when it can be verbalized, when it achieves a structure that can be assessed as *true* or *false,* and validated by appeal to appropriate *pramāṇas*. He writes that the point of uniting meditation and analysis is to "experience both serenity which observes a nondiscursive image and insight which observes a discursive image."[15] If this is so, even perceptual knowledge is *knowledge that,* and is therefore conceptually mediated. If so, once again, there are no foundations for knowledge, and what validates knowledge is not direct connection with reality, but rather the use of conventionally accepted epistemic practices, even if those practices are not always veridical. Tsongkhapa relies here on Candrakīrti's analysis in *Clear Words*:

> Since cyclic existence is also a concept (*rtog*), nirvana too must be a concept, for they both exist as mundane linguistic conventions. . . . [Ultimate truth] is called *ultimate truth* by means of mundane linguistic convention because its nature is not to deceive the world.[16]

This takes us straight to the issue of the nature of conventional truth. Candrakīrti famously notes that *saṃvṛti* can either mean *conventional* in all of its familiar senses, indicating *by agreement, ordinary, nominal, everyday,* etc. . . . or *concealing, obscuring.* So, we can gloss *saṃvṛti-satya* accurately either as *conventional truth* or as *concealing* or *obscurational truth.* One's attitude towards the status of conventional truth depends a good deal on which of these readings one takes to be primary. Tsongkhapa takes the first route, emphasizing that to be conventionally true is a way of being *true,* not a sham that conceals the truth. He leans hard on Nāgārjuna's doctrine of two truths, arguing that there can only be two of each of them, which is in fact a kind of truth. And since truth, or reality, and validation by *pramāṇas* are coextensive terms in this tradition, conventional truth is very much a way of being real, a way of being true, of being trustworthy. We thus see a tight connection between normativity and reality: what is real is what is warranted by normative practices.[17]

And this brings us to the issue of the expressibility of the Prāsaṅgika Madhyamaka position. The question gains poignancy not only because this is a central bone of contention between Tsongkhapa and Taktsang, but also because of the consensus that emptiness, or the ultimate truth, is a nonimplicative

15. Tsongkhapa 2004, vol. 3, 358.

16. Candrakīrti, *Prassanapadā,* 5cd, 7b.

17. See Cowherds 2010 for a more detailed discussion of the senses in which Candrakīrti and Tsongkhapa take conventional truth to be bona fide truth.

negation (*med dgag*) and Nāgārjuna's insistence in *Fundamental Verses on the Middle Way* (*Mūlamadhyamakakārikā*) that emptiness is not a *view,* (13.8) as well as his claim in *Replies to Objections* not to assert any proposition (29). These claims can be taken to suggest that if we really take Madhyamaka seriously, no claim about ultimate truth, and so no comprehensive assertion of any Madhyamaka position, can make any sense, that all would be self-refuting.

Tsongkhapa replies to this suggestion by arguing that even to deny a claim is to assert a negation; that even if emptiness is a nonimplicative negation, Mādhyamikas assert that all phenomena are empty. Moreover, since Nāgārjuna argues for the equivalence of emptiness as dependent origination, and since all Mādhyamikas assert that all phenomena—including emptiness—are dependently originated, we can certainly say things both about the conventional and the ultimate truth, and positively affirm the truth of the Prāsaṅgika Madhyamaka vision. This is enabled by Candrakīrti's understanding of meaning in terms of linguistic use. Even if we say that language does not latch directly onto the world and consider it only to be *upāya,* the fact that it is *upāya* constitutes its utility as language. And if use can determine meaning, then even in the absence of direct word-world referential links, there is no bar to meaning, even in the context of Prāsaṅgika dialectic. Tsongkhapa hence responds to the incoherence of epistemic foundationalism by reconstructing normativity in a coherentist, conventionalist framework, but without falling into the flat descriptivism of the anthropological approach endorsed by Taktsang. We have seen that Tsongkhapa, emphasizing that it is delivered by conventional *pramāṇas,* concludes that conventional truth is a kind of *truth.* And Tsongkhapa urges that we must be able to say what we mean and to endorse what we say when doing philosophy, and that the meaningfulness of the language we use derives from the conventions that govern its ordinary use.

So, on each of these issues, Tsongkhapa and his followers have a clear positive position: we can be warranted with regard to the conventional even though there is no foundation of empirical knowledge; all knowledge is conceptually mediated; conventional truth is a kind of truth; and the Prāsaṅgika Madhyamaka position is assertable. We now turn to Taktsang and his followers, who, we will see, will disagree with each of these positions.

In the fifth chapter of *Freedom from Extremes Accomplished through Comprehensive Knowledge of Philosophy* (*Grub mtha' kun shes nas mtha' 'bral sgrub pa*), Taktsang Lotsāwa adduces what he calls "the eighteen great contradictions in the thought of Tsongkhapa."[18] The vast majority of these concern what he sees as Tsongkhapa's illegitimate importation of the language of *pramāṇa,* which

18. See Yakherds 2021, vol. 2.

he sees as inextricably tied to Digṅāga's and Dharmakīrti's project, into Prāsaṅgika Madhyamaka, as well as Tsongkhapa's insistence on the expressibility of the Prāsaṅgika position. He summarizes the point nicely in this verse from the root text of *Freedom from Extremes:*

> 18. The reason for this heavy burden of contradictions
> Is their harping on a purely mundane and nonanalytic perspective
> While imposing rationality, they analyze and justify
> Because of their logic habit.

The "logic habit" and the analysis and justification to which Taktsang objects are the use of the conventional *pramāṇas* that the Geluk tradition takes to be essential to the project of understanding the two truths, and to be completely consistent with Candrakīrti's project. Taktsang, on the other hand, takes each of these to be inconsistent with Candrakīrti's articulation of Madhyamaka.

Taktsang is playing Quine to Tsongkhapa's Sellars. Like Tsongkhapa, Taktsang takes Dharmakīrti and his followers to be committed to a foundationalist understanding of warrant and of meaning and to methodological solipsism; like Tsongkhapa, he rejects both of these ideas. But whereas Tsongkhapa argues that epistemic warrant and meaning can be reconstructed through a realistic account of normativity grounded in convention, Taktsang argues that any commitment to warrant or to meaning presupposes the foundationalist, solipsistic framework in which they are articulated, and hence that neither in the end makes any sense.

For present purposes, among the more important of the contradictions Taktsang adduces against Tsongkhapa are these:

> All objects being false contradicts their subjects being nondeceptive. [13a]
> Accepting inference contradicts not articulating probative arguments. [13c]
> Things being true or false contradicts nothing being correct or incorrect. [15b]
> The nonexistence of floating hairs contradicts the existence of the rivers of pus. [14c]
> Refuting the foundation consciousness, reflexive awareness and other such doctrines . . . contradicts the recognition of epistemic warrants in one's own framework. [17]

Let us spend a moment simply explaining each of these, before turning to Taktsang's diagnosis of their common root. The first of these concerns the tension between the assertion that all conventionally real things are ultimately false (*rdzun pa*) by virtue of the discordance between their mode of existence (conventionally real) and their mode of appearance (ultimately real) on the one hand and the claim that they are nondeceptive (*mi slu ba*) conventionally, by virtue of being ascertained by conventional epistemic warrants on the other. Taktsang argues that the same thing cannot both be deceptive and nondeceptive.

The second in this sampler concerns the role of logic and reasoned argument in the Prāsaṅgika project. Tsongkhapa argues that a Prāsaṅgika is distinguished from Svātantrika in part on the grounds that the latter school admits the use of Indian probative arguments (*prayoga*) whose terms are understood in common by both dialectical parties, whereas the former—while it admits the use of reasoning, including both *reductio ad absurdum* (*prāsaṅga*) and argument acceptable only to the Prāsaṅgika herself in which there is no presupposition that any non-Prāsaṅgika interlocutor would use terms in the same way—rejects the use of those probative arguments. Taktsang argues that once one is committed to the validity of inference, it is inconsistent to admit some kinds of inference while rejecting others.

The third and fourth are each connected to the first. The third raises a very important issue relevant to the response to foundationalism: if there is no absolute standard of correctness or incorrectness—no foundation for such judgments—how can truth or falsity mean anything at all? And the fourth introduces the problem of relativism. Were a human being to see falling hairs in her visual field, she would be wrong; they would be an illusion caused by eye disease. And if she were to see pus and blood where there is really water, she would be equally wrong. But if a preta were to see pus and blood in the same location, he would be correct. How is it that the perception of water by a human being, and that of pus and blood by a preta are both correct, while the perception of hairs by the person with ophthalmia and the perception of their absence by everyone else are not? Let us now turn to the four issues we raised above, and see how Taktsang differs from Tsongkhapa on each of these.

First, there is the issue of the relationship between *pramāṇa* and foundations. As we saw above, Tsongkhapa responds to the incoherence of epistemic foundationalism by reconstructing normativity in a coherentist, conventionalist framework. Taktsang reacts very differently, accepting the entailment between a truly normative account of warrant and foundations to ground that warrant, he uses *modus tollens* to conclude from the incoherence of foundationalism that there is no possibility of a normative epistemology, asserting that we can only say in an everyday, nonanalytic context, what people say about justification, not what justification is. He writes:

> They might reply that they do not accept foundations. But not being foundational contradicts being epistemically warranted; for to be epistemically warranted means to be nondeceptive, and being nondeceptive means nothing more than being foundational.[19]

That is, he adopts what we have called an *anthropological* account of warrant, an account that pretends to nothing more than a description of deluded practice. When we move to a more sophisticated context, that of slight analysis, in which we engaged in Prāsaṅgika reflection, warrant has no place at all.

Second, there is the issue of the possibility of knowledge given that conceptuality always issues in some kind of falsification. We have seen that Tsongkhapa argues that even if when we cognize an object we are incorrect in some respects, we can nonetheless be correct in others, and that since knowledge is always expressible in a proposition asserting that an object has some property, it is always conceptual; nonetheless, assuming that we follow the epistemic practices appropriate to the conventional world, we can have knowledge of that world. Taktsang once again goes the other way. Since, he argues, knowledge must rely on infallible epistemic faculties and so must always be nonconceptual, and since there is no such access to the conventional world, there can be no genuine knowledge of conventional reality. This is articulated in the first several contradictions he adduces against Tsongkhapa. Here, for example, is the first:

> All objects being false contradicts their subjects being nondeceptive. (13a)
>
> Our opponents explain that unless one realizes that the object is false, one will fail to understand the meaning of relative truth. This is exactly right. In the Prāsaṅgika's own system, one indeed realizes that the relative is false. Therefore, it is contradictory to hold on the one hand that all relative objects are false and on the other hand that the cognitions that are their subjects can be nondeceptive and epistemically warranting.[20]

This is closely related to the third issue that divides Tsongkhapa and Taktsang in this domain: the very status of conventional truth. We have seen that Tsongkhapa, emphasizing that it is delivered by conventional *pramāṇas,* concludes that conventional truth is a kind of *truth.* Taktsang, on the other hand,

19. Yakherds 2021, vol. 2, 25.

20. Yakherds 2021, vol. 2, 33.

rejecting the validity of any conventional *pramāṇa,* and focusing on the concealing nature of convention and the deceptive character of conventional truths, argues that it is not truth at all, and hence that to talk about knowing it is utter nonsense.

We finally arrive at the question concerning the expressibility of the Prāsaṅgika philosophical approach, and so of the meaningfulness of anything we might say about reality. Tsongkhapa urges that we must be able to say what we mean and to endorse what we say when doing philosophy, and that the meaningfulness of the language we use derives from the conventions that govern its ordinary use. Taktsang, on the other hand, argues that since ultimate reality must be inexpressible, so must the Prāsaṅgika position; that since there are no truthmakers for our language, and no connection of language to the world, it is ultimately meaningless. All we can do is to talk about what people say; we never see through language to reality, and we never take our own utterances to be actual assertions. Taktsang's defender the Ninth Karmapa Wangchuk Dorje (1556–1603) puts the point this way:

> In [the Prāsaṅgika] context, unless a proposition is considered from the perspective of others, double negation elimination is never accepted. Hence, to deny existence is not to accept nonexistence; to deny nonexistence is not to accept existence. The law of the excluded middle fails.
>
> Some might propose the following reductios: "Because others say that there is a Madhyamaka system, there is a Madhyamaka system"; or, "Because others say that there is karmic causality, there is karmic causality." Neither follows. There is no proof of karmic causality, even though others accept it. This appears to be how we should formulate our response.
>
> If we grant that karmic causality exists and is a valid principle according to others, then we may also say that karmic causality according to others exists and is a valid principle. Does the karmic causality known to others exist or not? We accept neither. Does the karmic causality known to others exist according to others? It does. But to parse that proposition to mean that its subject is taken as "the karmic causality known to others according to others" amounts to sophistry.[21]

21. Yakherds 2021, vol. 2, 272–73.

Dignāga and Dharmakīrti—like Carnap—propose an epistemology grounded in direct perceptual access to particulars, individualistic in character, and one that offers a semantic theory grounded in direct referential relations of singular terms to independently real objects. Knowledge and meaning are, in each case, vindicated by foundationalism; collective practice is regarded as the sum of individual competencies in this domain. Taktsang and Tsongkhapa, as Quine and Sellars were to do, reacted against this foundationalism. As Quine and Sellars were to do, they each focused on the merely conventional character of language and the absence of any transcendent ontology that could ground knowledge and meaning.

Quine and Sellars, like Taktsang and Tsongkhapa before them, despite this broad agreement, disagreed vehemently about what this entailed, about whether *modus ponens* or *modus tollens* represented the correct response to this predicament. Taktsang and Quine took the negative route, conceding that any account of knowledge and meaning that is genuinely normative must be transcendent, and so rejecting the possibility of a normative epistemology and of linguistic meaning, settling for a merely anthropological account of epistemic and linguistic practice. Tsongkhapa and Sellars took the positive route, arguing that convention could—and indeed must—ground normativity, and so arguing for a naturalistic but normative account of knowledge and of meaning that is conventional and coherentist, not foundationalist in character. So, while there is agreement among the principals in each of these debates that no transcendent account of normativity is possible, there is substantial disagreement about whether this dooms the search for normativity *tout court.*

Tsongkhapa and Sellars are correct. First of all, we must make sense of the role that normativity plays in our lives. Perhaps the most significant characteristic of our shared humanity is our disposition to institute, to recognize, to enforce, and to conform to rules. This is true whether those are rules for the use of words that make language possible, rules for inference that make reasoning possible, rules for conduct that enable us to respect morality and the law, or rules or etiquette and religious observance that bind us more tightly into the communities that constitute these rules. The norms we live by are not *sui generis,* and they do not come to us from any transcendental source. As Candrakīrti and Hume each make clear, they derive from the way that our biological nature works itself out in the social contexts for which we are biologically tuned. Nonetheless, rules, and the normativity they require and induce, are real, as real is money, as real as governments, as real as thought, that is, as real as anything we encounter.

Any account of our lives that denies the reality of the norms that govern them therefore denies our very humanity. Moreover, any account that denies the reality of meaning or the authority of the arguments that establish that account denies its own cogency. And any account of expressibility that denies that it is expressible is a *reductio* on itself. Tsongkhapa and Sellars, by affirming the reality and the binding character of human norms, while grounding them in convention, manage to avoid the foundationalism that is their shared target, together with the essentialism that it entails, while embracing the naturalism that motivates it. They do not eliminate normativity, but show how to make sense of it as conventionally real.

Tibetan Modernity Revisited: the Dalai Lama XIV and Modern Science

I have been arguing that the debate inaugurated by Taktsang's attack on Tsongkhapa anticipates that between Sellars and Quine in the twentieth century. But, it is now time to ask, is this really an indication of *modernity* in Tibetan philosophy in the fifteenth century? Was Tibet, indeed, modern *avant a lettre?* I think not, and the reasons for this indicate a tension in Tibetan modernity even in the present.

Modernity, as I noted above, comes to Europe and infuses philosophical thought not simply through the advance of time, and not even simply through the advance of ideologies such as individualism, rationalism, or secularity, although these are critical components of the modern complex. The other critical component, I emphasized, is the deference to science as the arbiter of the fundamental nature of reality, as the ultimate epistemic authority. We might say fairly that European philosophy chose to be modern when philosophers sided with Galileo against the Church in the contest for that epistemic authority. The rest follows from that.

It is noteworthy that Carnap, Quine, and Sellars, despite the enormous differences in philosophical outlook that divide them, share this commitment to *scientia mensura*. Indeed, each grounds his respective position on an account of what science demands or does not demand. This commitment is notably absent in the work of Dharmakīrti, Tsongkhapa, and other Tibetan scholars. And no talk of Buddhist "inner science," of the kind made popular by the work of the Dalai Lama XIV and others such as Allan Wallace can undermine this claim.[22] For while it is true that Buddhist meditators and adepts in Tibet during that period developed great philosophical insight into the mind, it is not true that they deployed anything like the scientific method in that endeavor. There are

22. See Dalai Lama XIV 2006, Dalai Lama XIV et al. 2018, and Wallace 2009.

no controlled experiments; there is no third-person study of these phenomena, and no scientific suspicion of the veridicality of first-person report. Buddhist philosophical approaches to the mind—while they do embed a distinction between a theoretical and an observation language, and while they do appeal to theoretical entities to explain observations—do not subject their theories to the tests that constitute science.

We can fairly say that modernity enters Tibetan philosophy with the present Dalai Lama's engagement with science and with his explicit commitment to *scientia mensura*. He has repeatedly asserted that where science contradicts Buddhist doctrine, science trumps Buddhism. And his personal engagement with and endorsement of science have percolated deep into Tibetan academic culture, as evidenced not only by the Mind and Life dialogues, but more importantly by the recent revisions in Tibetan monastic curricula spearheaded by the Science for Monks program jointly administered by Emory University and the Library of Tibetan Works and Archives. To be sure, the heritage of philosophical reflection he inherits, by virtue not only of its systematic rigor, but also of its recognition of the distinction between observation and theory, and its attention to the important epistemological issues we have scouted, enables this venture into modernity. But philosophical modernity really only arrives with the serious engagement with science that we now see in the Tibetan community.

This is not to say that Tsongkhapa is not an important precursor to this developing modernity. His commitment to reason, his insistence on the fact that knowledge is discursive and conceptual, and that we can make sense of truth, knowledge, and meaning in the ordinary conventional world, are all necessary ingredients of a modern outlook, and indeed are necessary precursors to science itself. They make possible the engagement with science that is transforming Tibetan approaches to understanding reality today, and that usher in a genuine Tibetan modernity.

But this modernity is not yet complete. And paradoxically, it is much of the rhetoric about "inner science" that stands in the way of a true modernity. For too many involved in the rapprochement between the Tibetan Buddhist world and the contemporary scientific world—prominently including the Dalai Lama XIV—persist in the idea that the mind is directly accessible to itself in introspection, and the valorization of what has been called a "first person" science of consciousness. To do so is not only at odds with the scientific method, which demands intersubjectivity and which takes seriously the idea that all observation is mediated by potential distortion, but is also, paradoxically, to disregard the advice of Tsongkhapa. For to do so is to succumb to the Myth of the Given that he so astutely rejected long before Sellars named it. It is to suggest that our access to our inner space is conceptually unmediated, direct, and presents the mind and its psychological processes to observation *as they are,* as opposed to *as they appear to potentially erroneous introspective processes.*

To put the point most bluntly, if our goal is to understand the nature of the mind, we must presuppose that we do not yet do so. But if the mind is the very instrument by means of which we investigate the mind, we must confess that we have no idea how that instrument works, or how veridical its output is: is it the microscope that those who valorize this approach claim it to be, or is it the kaleidoscope as anyone convinced of the pervasiveness of cognitive illusion must suspect that it is? Without answering this question, we have no reason to be at all confident about any introspective methodology in cognitive science. This is why the idea that Buddhism has incorporated an "inner science" for millennia is so flawed. A systematic study of the inner is not yet a *science* of the inner, and that transition from philosophical reflection to scientific study is only happening in the last few decades.

Philosophical modernity is hence a work in progress in the Tibetan world. That is not to say that there is no progress, only that modernity is not yet fully here. But the modernity that is arriving, we have seen, has very old roots indeed, and emerges in a form not all that different from that which it has taken in Western philosophy.

Works Cited

Ayer, A.J. (1936). *The Concept of a Person and Other Essays*. London: MacMillan.

Cowherds. 2010. *Moonshadows: Conventional Truth in Buddhist Philosophy*. New York: Oxford University Press.

Dalai Lama XIV. 2006. *The Universe in a Single Atom.* New York: MorganRoad.

Dalai Lama XIV et al. 2018. *Where Buddhism Meets Neuroscience: Conversations with the Dalai Lama on Spiritual and Scientific Views of our Minds.* Boston: Shambhala Press.

deVries, Willem, and Tim Triplett. 2000. *Knowledge, Mind, and the Given: Reading Wilfrid Sellars'* Empiricism and the Philosophy of Mind. Indianapolis: Hackett.

Garfield, Jay. 1988. *Belief in Psychology: A Study in the Ontology of Mind.* Cambridge: MIT Press.

———. 2012. "Sellarsian Synopsis: Integrating the Images." *Humana Mente: Journal of Philosophical Studies* 23:101–21.

———. 2018. "Givenness and Primal Confusion." In *Wilfrid Sellars and Buddhist Philosophy: Freedom from Foundations,* edited by Jay Garfield, 113–29. London: Routledge.

———. 2019. "Belnap and Nāgārjuna on how Computers and Sentient Beings Should Think: Truth, Trust and the *Catuṣkoṭi.*" In *New Essays on Belnap-Dunn Logic,* edited by Hitoshi Onori and Heinrich Wansing, 133–38. Leiden: Brill.

Kripke, S. 1982. *Wittgenstein on Rules and private Language.* Cambridge: Harvard University Press.

Quine, W.V.O. 1963. *Word and Object*. Cambridge: MIT Press.

Quine, W.V.O. 1981. *Theories and Things*. Cambridge: Harvard University Press.

Sellars, Wilfrid. 1963a. "Philosophy and the Scientific Image of Man." In *Science, Perception and Reality*, 1–40. London: Routledge and Kegan Paul.

———. 1963b. "Empiricism and the Philosophy of Mind." In *Science, Perception and Reality*, 127–96. London: Routledge and Kegan Paul.

Thurman, Robert. 1980. "Philosophical Nonegocentrism in Wittgenstein and Candrakīrti in their Treatment of the Private Language Problem," *Philosophy East and West* 30.3: 321–37.

Tsongkhapa. 2004. *Great Treatise on the Stages of the Path to Enlightenment, Vol. 3*. Translated by the Lam rim chen mo Translation Committee. Ithaca, NY: Snow Lion.

Wallace, Alan. 2009. *Mind in the Balance: Meditation in Science, Buddhism, and Christianity*. New York: Columbia University Press.

Wittgenstein, L. 1972. *On Certainty*. New York: Harper.

Yakherds. 2021. *Knowing Illusion: Bringing a Tibetan Debate into Contemporary Discourse*. New York: Oxford University Press.

My Life as a Parakeet: A Bönpo Version of the Conference of the Birds

Charles Ramble

But fyrst were chosen foules for to synge,
As yer by yer was alwey hir usaunce
To synge a roundel at here departynge,
To don to Nature honour and plesaunce.
The note, I trowe, imaked was in Fraunce. . .
(GEOFFREY CHAUCER, *The Parliament of Fowls*)

THE IDEA of a conference of birds that gather to discuss human concerns has caught the imagination of authors in different lands and over many centuries.[1] Perhaps the best-known of these is the *Mantir al-Tayr* of Farid ud-Din Attar (ca. 1142–1220), introduced to Western readers as *Bird Parliament* in 1889, a partial English translation by Edward FitzGerald (who had also translated the even more famous *Rubaiyyat* of Omar Khayyam).[2] But there are others besides: English has its own native version, the *Parliament of Fowls* by Geoffrey Chaucer (ca. 1343–1400), who may have taken his cue from earlier works such as the *Owl and the Nightingale*, while one of the earliest is surely the *Birds* of Aristophanes (ca. 446–386 BCE). Tibetan has several such stories, one of which, the anonymous "Buddhism among the Birds: A Precious Garland" (*Bya chos rin chen 'phreng ba*) was translated into French by Henriette Meyer in 1953 and later into English by Edward Conze as *The Buddha's Law among the Birds*.[3]

1. In addition to authors, we should certainly include composers: Dave Holland's celebrated 1972 jazz album *The Conference of the Birds* is said to have been inspired by the morning birdsong outside his London home: See Cook and Morton 1992, 653.

2. For a more extensive translation, with a helpful introduction, see Darbandi and Davis 1984. I am indebted to Sarah Teetor for drawing this work, as well as several others cited here, to my attention.

3. For the Tibetan text of this work see *Bya chos* 1978. I am grateful to Naljor Tsering for informing me of this publication.

The similarity of the platform notwithstanding, the subject of the avian conference in each case is different. Attar was a Sufi mystic whose birds gather to choose a king but are told by the hoopoe that they already have one, the great Simorgh. They set off on a perilous journey to meet their sovereign only to find, on arrival, that the Simorgh is a composite of themselves. Chaucer's poem has the birds gathering on St. Valentine's Day to choose their mates for the coming year. (It has been suggested that the poem was later responsible for the association, unrecorded before the fifteenth century, between St. Valentine and romantic love.) In Aristophanes' play, two eccentric men persuade the birds to set up their own kingdom between the earth and heaven to intercept offerings on their way up to the gods. In "Buddhism among the Birds," a Kagyüpa work from the seventeenth or eighteenth century, Avalokiteśvara takes the form of a cuckoo and meditates under a sandalwood tree. The other birds come to receive teachings from him, and each in turn makes a short statement that enshrines a Buddhist truth.

The Tibetan account presented here appears in the fifth chapter of the *Ziji* (*Gzi brjid*), a Bönpo work of the fourteenth century (*Ziji*, 2:81–120). The setting is a grove in which the youthful Shenrab Miwo, regarded by Bönpos as the founder of their religion, is picnicking with his followers. As birds gather around them it becomes apparent that there is a connection between them and Shenrab that was forged in a previous life, and at the request of one of his followers, Öden Nyima, he tells them the story of this association: the tale of a conference of birds in which he himself had played a key role. The theme of this particular conference has less in common with "Buddhism among the Birds" than with the compositions by Aristophanes, Attar, and Chaucer, inasmuch as the main preoccupations are to create an orderly realm of birds and to appoint a king, with a subplot involving a quest to find brides for the protagonists, three parakeet brothers. The emphasis on law and statecraft is reminiscent of other early parts of the *Ziji*, notably the seventh chapter, the Sūtra of the Prince's Law-giving, which is entirely concerned with the principles of a just and orderly society.[4]

An annotated full translation of the episode presented here is a work in progress that I am currently undertaking with Khenpo Tenpa Yungdrung of Triten Norbutse Monastery in Kathmandu. Constraints of space do not allow me to present here even the basic translation of the episode, let alone a discussion of doubtful passages, textual parallels, and possible identifications of certain birds from their obscure names.[5] Nevertheless, having to reduce the story to a per-

4. For a discussion and partial translation of this sūtra, see Ramble 2006.

5. For a number of identifications I am indebted to David Holler, some of whose photographs

missible length is a perfect opportunity to gloss over its many uncertainties to produce a simplified paraphrase, uncluttered by scholarly baggage. While, like the bat in the story we are about to hear, I apologize for the deficiencies of this work, I am also honored to be able to offer it as the first fruit, the *phü* (*phud*), of this project to my friend and colleague Janet, to whom this volume is dedicated.

The Setting of the Story

The Teacher and his followers were sitting in a grove when birds started to gather from all around. There were vultures, eagles, falcons, kites, hawks, peacocks, pheasants, parakeets, snowcocks, geese and ducks, cormorants, cranes, ospreys, ravens, crows, owls, hoopoes, bats, roosters, cuckoos, larks, half-man half-bird shangshangs (*shang shang*), sparrows—all 360 kinds of birds gathered. They formed a circle around the prince, prostrating and offering flowers, plants, and fruits, singing sweetly, displaying their fine plumage, strutting, dancing, and fluttering. The peacock raised its train, the snowcock spread its tail-feathers, the pheasant laid out a seat, the shangshang offered him a bowl, and the parakeet made its carillon call. The Teacher's followers marveled at this display, and one of them, Öden Nyima, asked what aspirations might have been made in the past that had come to such a fruition.

The Origin of the Birds

The Teacher then proceeded to tell them the story. When the universe was coming into being, he said, the lord Künkhyab and the goddess Nangma Drösalma formed a mental union and produced four sons: Shechen, Shedag, Shebu, and Shelekye. From the union of Shelekye and the goddess Yisalma were born four sons: Dzutrulchen, Tobden, Öchen, and Drachen. Öchen coupled with the goddess Tsangdze, and she bore two creatures. One was Elder Brother Monkey, and the other had brightly colored plumage and wings and a decurved beak. This was Younger Brother the Winged Sky-Soarer, the king of the birds. From his mind he produced a partner, Jama Gungyal, with whom he coupled to produce four classes of birds: the raptors, the mud-feeders, the beauties, and the songsters. The raptors included the garuḍa,[6] the griffon, the eagle, the raven, the owl, the falcons and hawks, and the kite. Among the mud-feeders were

of Tibetan birds, together with remarks on their names, may be found on http://www.tibetbirds.com. He has also kindly drawn my attention to a field guide to Tibetan birds, *Mtsho bod mtho sgang gi bya rigs lta zhib lag deb*, that is however unavailable to me at the time of writing.

6. While we should usually be cautious about translating the Tibetan *khyung* and *klu* as garuḍa

various ducks and waders, the crane, and the cormorant. The beauties included the peacock, the black vulture, the snowcock, the rooster, and the flamingo; the cuckoo, the parakeet, the shangshang, the sparrow, and various finches made up the songsters.

All these birds gathered in the forest and played havoc with the fruits and flowers. The bigger birds fell upon the smaller ones, which in turn frolicked on the shoulders of the bullies; the dull ones plucked the plumage of the beauties, the melodious calls of the songsters were drowned out by the cacophony of their tuneless fellows, and the raptors persecuted the mud-feeders.

The Parakeets and Their Strategy

As the chaos continued, a pair of parakeets named Yuru and Laloma coupled, and Laloma laid three eggs from which three sons were hatched into the world: Yushok, Khala, and Puru Zhaö. Each was more beautiful than next, each finer, each lovelier, and each cleverer than the next. One flew to the land of gods, from where he gathered medicines; one descended to the land of the nāgas and gathered plant juices, and the third went to the land of humans and accumulated grain. Within a year they had acquired 500 bushels of rice, a thousand measures (*phul*) of juice, and 300 medicinal leaves. The parents and the three sons held a discussion. The eldest son, the first to speak, reviewed the results of their diligence and concluded that they should do something meaningful with all the riches they had accumulated, and asked his parents and brothers what they thought.

Father parakeet praised his sons as an exceptional trio, endowed with human intelligence in birds' bodies. Until now, he pointed out, there had been no custom of diligent hoarding among the birds. He proposed the establishment of a great estate, a lofty palace, a courtyard in front of it, and agricultural land to sustain it. Only we (he went on to say) can accomplish such a thing. The king of the birds may be great but he resents greatness among others; in spite of his nobility the griffon wanders around other lands; the scavengers are awesome but they're attached to charnel; the garuḍa has a keenly critical view of others but can't see the beam in his own eye; magnificent as the peacock is, his perception of himself is deeply flawed; the shangshang is a splendid creature but he does tend to be distracted as he wanders through the groves; the rooster is a pretty fellow, but very vain; the cuckoo has a magnificent voice, but for much of the year he is in the barbarous south; brave as he is, the falcon attacks the

---

and nāga respectively, the obvious Indic influence in this work—the *klu* are in fact referred to as *na ga* at one point—justify such a conflation here.

humble flocks, and the raven, for all his wiliness, craves the food of those black-headed humans. The owl is a fearsome beast, but he gets on with no one, while the geese and ducks are very proper but they are, well, lazy. The bat is the wise one, but is so ugly that he just cannot be seen in public. All the other birds are not worth mentioning. After all, he said, birds have small heads and their brains are weaker than water; since they have no ears to filter what comes in, they're gullible; they may fly in the sky, but their souls are firmly grounded on earth. Since they don't hoard, they're like the hungry ghosts, who circle around food and are caught in traps. Since we (he went on to say) aren't constrained by these limitations, we can accomplish whatever we set out to do. An estate such as this would be an enduring source of livelihood.

Mother parakeet, who was next to speak, began by quoting a proverb to the effect that the greatest challenge for any father is to establish a household that he can pass on to his beloved sons, while the greatest challenge for a son is to cherish and maintain his paternal inheritance. Our three parakeet sons are, indeed, she said, like the founders of three royal lines, and the family's priority should be to ensure a descendance; the sons should take brides from the snow-cocks, the pheasants, and the geese. Once the next generation has come along, the estate advocated by the father will take shape of its own accord, and virtuous deeds will be accomplished incidentally.

It was Khala, the middle son, who spoke next. If this great wealth we have amassed were now to be squandered, he said, it would be a terrible loss. Wealth that is not used for virtuous purposes is like a life-consuming demon, and multiplying one's offspring can also bring one low. Friends and relatives disperse like merchants leaving a trade-mart; a mansion and land are like the sloughed skin of a poisonous snake, while fame in this life is like brief thunder.

The youngest, Puru Zhaö, was next. On our visits to the realms of the gods, the nāgas, and the humans, we saw that all have laws—except the birds. In those realms, the king sits on high and keeps order, while his righteous minister sits beside him. There are judges, and councils where conflicts are resolved. The lowly obey the powerful, while the great protect the humble. The rich are measured in their indulgence, and everyone abides by the law. We birds, by contrast, have no parliament. We do not lay in stores but spend half our lives suffering from hunger and thirst. The mighty oppress the weak, the raptors ravage the mud-feeders, the finches ruffle the feathers of the beauties, the tuneless ones drown out the songsters—it's hardly a surprise that humans regard us birds as objects of ridicule. We must have a council. Without law, a realm falls into disorder. We must appoint a king whom everyone reveres to lead us, and a minister who is on good terms with everyone.

At last it was the turn of the eldest brother, Yushok, to speak. Our father is right that we need a dwelling place (he said), but a castle may not be ideal: if it's too splendid, we would run the risk of losing it to others. Mother, too, is right to say that our line should not be extinguished. But there is no imminent danger of that; and although the daughters of the snowcock, the pheasant, and the goose are very attractive, the world of women were better avoided. As our middle brother said, life is evanescent, and virtuous deeds are a true investment for the future. But as our youngest brother said, laws should be put in place, for without laws the kingdom will disintegrate and nothing can be achieved. Without a council we are no better than a swarm of insects. Creating a council will be a prelude to our father's wish of establishing an inheritance for his sons, since this will happen of its own accord. We should invite a *shen* (*gshen*) priest to preside over the conference, and we should share the work of convening this gathering.

And so, the father collected meat; the mother made beer; the eldest brother invited the divine *shen* Göse Khyungrum and his 500 followers from the realm of the gods; the middle brother invited Mabu Lekden from the human realm, and the youngest invited Luza Yumin from the land of the nāgas, and they feasted their guests with fine food and drink.

The question then arose of who should be entrusted to carry the invitation to the birds. Several birds volunteered, but the parakeets considered them to be unreliable. And so, the parakeet himself flew to the top of the wish-fulfilling tree in the realm of the gods and addressed the 360 kinds of birds. After summarizing the discussions the family had had, he explained that the prerequisite to the project of establishing order and prosperity among the birds was that there should be a council, a parliament, and he requested them to gather on the Seven Golden Hills.

The garuḍa was skeptical, doubting that the parakeets were strong enough to assemble requisites, and declaring that, without resources to offer the participants, any such gathering would be an embarrassing failure. And why was it necessary to go to the Seven Golden Hills when here, among the trees, was the natural gathering place for birds? And finally, he said, the discourse of parakeets may be very melodious, but it was after all just the chattering of birds, and how much truth can there be in that?

How the Owl and the Raven Became Karmic Enemies

The owl raised his feathered horns to indicate that he was about speak. He spread his brocade cloak, clacked his tongue against his palate, and addressed the gathering. There was, he said, an order of entitlement to speak: first, the garuḍa, who has true horns, and then he himself, who had feathered horns.

After him, what birds had any special features that might give them such an entitlement? And in particular, what qualities did the parakeet have that might make his words worth listening to? Did he have horns like the garuḍa? Or feathered horns like himself? Or the cuckoo's sweet voice? Or the griffon's wingspan? Or the peacock's radiance? Or the neck of the crane? Even all these birds, and the many others that he then went on to list, were not to be taken seriously. If a council were arranged, then it would be most proper if he, the owl, were chosen as sovereign. But if he got angry, he might punish even the garuḍa, and if the garuḍa were afraid of him, then all lesser birds would faint away in terror. And so, he concluded, it would be far better for everyone if he withdrew to a remote and solitary place.

The raven sneered at him. Because the owl had once been punished by the garuḍa, he said, he must hide by day and seek his food by night. He was an ill-omened bird that laughs his inauspicious laugh—*ha ha!*—in the darkness. Do you, he said, really think you could be the leader of the birds? Were it not for the presence of the garuḍa, the other birds would by now be adorning themselves with your feathers. Your horns would be the joke of the assembly, and your head would have been used by the *nangshen* (*snang gshen*) priest in one of his *jadang* (*bya sdang*) rituals;[7] your body would have been stuffed for use by the priest of the *tsen* divinities (*btsan bon*);[8] your blood would have been soup for the mud-feeders, and your claws playthings for children; and I, the raven, would have pecked out your eyes myself.

The owl flew into a rage. You cursed creature (he said) with your fine black face and fat beak—what qualities do you think you have? You bully the weak and fear the strong; you feign cleverness when you're actually stupid; you pollute food; you destroy the *tormas* of the tantrists; you peck the sores of enfeebled pack animals, and bring the wolves down from the mountains. You steal the breath of the weak, and you pluck out the eyes of the dying. Know that when you are sleeping I shall steal away the chicks from under your wings, and the food and wealth from your stores. And what is more, you the raven and I, and our children and our children's children, till the end of time, shall never be friends. Fortunately for you the garuḍa is present; otherwise, by merely clacking my tongue against my palate I would cause you to collapse senseless. From

7. A *jadang* is a construction used in rituals for the propitiation of certain categories of war gods. A *nangshen* is a priest who performs rituals belonging to the second of the Nine Ways of Bon, the "way of the *shen* of the visual world" (*snang gshen theg pa*).

8. The owl is closely associated with Abse Dungmar, the chief of the *tsen* category of protective divinities.

this day on, the enmity between the ravens and the owls shall be the stuff of proverbs.[9]

The parakeet stepped in and told them to stop their bickering. He pointed out that even if the parakeets were physically weak, they had strong minds; that if there were no council of birds they would continue to be derided by humans, and that the garuḍa should decide on the next steps. If the birds really didn't want a parliament, it was no great matter for the parakeets since they would use their resources for other virtuous purposes, and the birds were quite welcome to disperse and spend their lives as they wished.

The others conceded that the project was a worthwhile one, and that it couldn't be accomplished without the parakeets. And so, they all set off for the Seven Hills, where they were received with the lavish hospitality that had been prepared by the parakeets: rice, plant juice, oil, meat, beer, barley, sesame, peas, soft oily earth (for the mud-feeders), grapes, and other fruits.

The Wise Bat Makes a Speech

If such a fine feast were not introduced by a speech of just a few words, said the father parakeet, the revelers would not recognize one another, in the same way as you wouldn't be able to distinguish the entrance of a house from its innermost treasure if you didn't take a few steps in from the threshold. Someone should make a speech!

The eldest son replied that the humble repast they had prepared was not worthy of a speech. But the pheasant and rooster supported the father: beginning such a feast without some fine words would be a shameful thing to do in front of bodhisattvas and humans. All agreed that the only one able to do such a thing was the wise bat. But how could I do such a thing, replied the bat, hideous as I am? As you, who have feathered crests, rainbow-colored plumage, yellow-green crowns, know only too well, I am vile-bodied, and though I may be eloquent I am a spoiler of feasts. I can't do this!

The pheasant offered him a ball of rice and a bowl of beer. Drink this, wise one, he said, and make your speech. The bat cheered up and agreed to make the speech if he was given a turban, a cloak, a whip, and a mount. And so, the birds wound a piece of cotton wool around his head as a turban, covered his back with a leaf for a cloak, put a twig from an apple tree in his hand, and sat him

9. Owls and crows (including ravens) are regarded as "karmic enemies" (*las kyi dgra*). In certain exorcisms it is common to juxtapose a feather of an owl and of a crow to emphasize the conflictual nature of the ritual.

astride the flying squirrel. The rooster led his steed, and the peacock and the pheasant flanked him as outriders.[10]

Beginning by acknowledging the honor of addressing gods, nāgas, and humans, he went on to say that he would not make a speech that was as long as the ancestry of the birds, or as high as the glory of the heavens, or as far and deep as mid-space. But on this day, with the sun, the moon, and good fortune in the sky, and everything so well on this pleasant earth . . . and on he went. After a wonderfully florid overture, he praised the parakeets for providing such a feast; but since, as the saying goes, when one makes a gift of a horse one should also include all the trappings, so the feast should be accompanied by gifts for each guest. Saffron and silken robes shall be given to the *shen* Göse Khyungrum; the golden sun and moon shall be the crown ornament for the garuḍa; the bronze razor shall be for the griffon, who alone can cut through the blast of the Jet-stream. He went on to propose gifts and habitats for other birds, ending his list with the suggestion that the mango groves should be the home of the parakeets themselves.

And at last, he came to the main issue that was to be decided at the conference: the selection of candidates for the twenty-eight different offices in the society of birds, which he then listed. In concluding, he expressed the wish that this parliament would continue to meet regularly in the future, and asked the divine *shen* to bless the gathering with some auspicious words; he added coyly that there had been much unevenness and babbling in his speech, and besought his audience to be indulgent since it was, after all, nothing more than the chattering of a bird.

The *shen* reassured the bat that he was, on the contrary, a creature of great wisdom, and that the speech had been remarkable. Moreover, he must be very tired after that performance and was surely in need of a drink, at which the pheasant offered him another cup of chang and a bowl of rice. Moved by this reception, the bat dismounted from the flying squirrel and prostrated himself as the *shen* delivered his auspicious pronunciation. The *shen* concluded with the aspiration that the eldest brother of the parakeets might be reborn as a king; that his parents might be reborn as his parents; his brothers as his spiritual sons; the bat as a sign-reading Brahmin; the peacock, the pheasant, and the rooster as future disciples, and that the parliament of birds should end in accord.

The garuḍa thanked the *shen* and the bat for their speeches. I myself (he said) have no thought to go anywhere other than the top of the wish-fulfilling tree. And you, the parakeet, should make the appointments. Whoever is made lord

10. An extended paraphrase of the passage concerning the bat is given in Huber 2020: vol. 1, 108; the author's understanding of certain details differs slightly from my own.

of the birds, I too shall revere him, and anyone who challenges you shall fall beneath my talons; I myself shall arrange the estate that is the greatest challenge for a father on behalf of his sons and shall see to it that brides are found. The parakeet flew up to a high branch and addressed the assembly first in Sanskrit, then in the language of Singhala, and finally in his own rapid tongue.

The Allocation of Dwellings and Duties

Hear me, king and other birds! If there is no lord on high, the subjects below will be dispersed. If there is no Bön to lead us to liberation, we may wander in the lower realms. If the birds do not have a council, the king of the birds will be brought low, that the others will be borne away by the wind; the mangers of the raptors will be empty, the swamps of the mud-feeders will be drained, the colors of the beauties will fade, the voices of the songsters will be silenced, and the flocks of finches will cling to the distant crags. Since I have been authorized by the king, I shall delegate your respective tasks.

You, the garuḍa, as king of the birds, should remain aloof, lording it over the three worlds; the tamarisk bushes of the four continents cannot support you, and therefore you should dominate the top of the three worlds.

You, sweet-voiced cuckoo, shall be king of the birds. Your plumage is clearer than water, and your knowledge and intellect are sharper than those of humans. You shall also be revered by the garuḍa, and the ministers shall follow you, and all others shall support you. For the three winter months you shall go to the south, and for the three summer months you shall come to the north. Mark the boundary between north and south, and between summer and winter, and make the turquoise juniper your seat. The swallow shall be your minister, and the warbler your messenger. The raptors shall give you a share of meat as your due; the mud-feeders shall bring you the rich earth; the beauties shall welcome you, the songsters shall offer you reverence, and the finches shall pay you grain tax. The king of birds, the garuḍa, sits at the apex, but apart from him all birds shall obey you as their sovereign.

You, the griffon vulture, shall be the minister for external affairs. Only you can cross the ring of wind that encircles the world; soar in the sky, watch over all the realm, and make the white cliffs your dwelling.

The flamingo shall be the interior minister; make your home among the wish-fulfilling trees.

The black vulture shall be the minister for intermediate affairs and shall dwell among the thirty-three gods.

You, the sparrow, shall fetch guests from afar. Thanks to your companionship our guests will not notice the distance.

You, the eagle, shall go to the hard battle, and even if a hundred birds are arrayed against you, you shall prevail. Make your dwelling the fortress of the black cliffs and provide travelers with meat thrice daily.

You, the falcon, shall lead our lightning raids. Make three return journeys in one day, diving, flying fast, and hiding. Dwell in the fortress of the red cliffs.

White crane, you shall stage spectacular performances, stepping out the *gar*, *bro*, and stately *shon* dances. You shall provide a welcome distraction for the black-headed humans; make your dwelling the meadows and flatlands.

Yellow shangshang, travel through the four continents; your dwelling shall be the great reed beds and the flowery islands.

The blue *yöltse* (*yol tse*) shall be the judge. Make your dwelling the high impregnable cliff. Press down the heads of the lofty and raise the humble.

You finches shall occupy the streets of the town, and enjoy the granaries. You shall pay the sovereign a government tax.

The blue *yuphuk* (*g.yu phug*) shall be the priest—recite the sūtras and dhāraṇis, and take no more than three meals a day. Dwell in a pleasant and secure place.

The white-eared pheasant shall be the *nangshen*. After he has finished performing his ritual, he shall be accompanied to his own dwelling.

The eloquent bat shall be the speaker, since he can argue even with the Lord of Death. During the day you should hide in juniper groves.

The chough shall pay military tax to the *dü* (*bdud*) demons, who like him for his black plumage.[11] If it were not for you, the demons would overpower us, and the birds are indebted to you for that. Make your dwelling the northeastern crags.

The peacock transforms poison into nectar; dwell in the south. The pheasant enjoys the nourishment of white rice; make your abode the lowland plains. The rooster shall announce the stages of the night; make your abode the royal palace.

Geese and ducks, tread softly with the step of a lay-follower and set an example for humans. Dwell in the south for the three winter months and come north for the summer.

Let the flying squirrel purge the taint of all kinds of pollution. Dwell at the top and at the foot of trees.

Raven, watch and listen attentively, since you have some clairvoyance. Make your dwelling at the edges of the nomads' encampments.

Lammergeier, enjoy the food of the charnel ground and dwell at the foot of trees.

11. The chough is especially associated with Midü, chief of the *bdud* class of protective divinities.

Kite, go to the barbarous south, and when northern lakes melt come and collect salt.

Owl, utter your fearful calls; show your dreaded face to our enemies. Make your dwelling the fortified cliff, otherwise the birds will bind and drag you. Make friends with the otter; and though there is food to be had during the day, you should feed at night.

Raptors, soar in the sky; mud-feeders, dwell in the swamps; beauties, cling to the groves; songsters, live in the forests; finches, go to the low flatlands!

Raptors, beware the thin-necked arrow; mud-feeders, beware the lightning bolt; beauties, beware the finely primed trap; songsters, beware the predator; finches, beware gatherings of children!

The lowly should respect the great; the great should protect the humble. The wise should not steal ideas. The birds should assemble whenever needed, and when not needed, they should keep to their assigned places.

With these words, appointing to each their places, he established the parliament of the birds.

Then all the birds went off to their respective places. The parakeets went to the forests, where they occupied their mansion. The eldest brother trained in Yungdrung Bön with the divine *shen*; he translated the teaching into 360 languages, and became expert in the doctrine. The second became close to humans: he had the ear of the king, advised the minister, protected the person of the queen, acted as the moral conscience of the merchant, and acquired vast wealth. The youngest took as his wives the daughters of the peacock, the pheasant, and the rooster, and inherited the family estate.

Epilogue

When Shenrab had finished his account, he explained to his companions how the karma of those events had come to fruition in the present. In accordance with the *shen*'s aspiration, the mother and father parakeets were now Shenrab's own parents, while he himself was the reincarnation of their eldest son, Yushok. His two former younger brothers were now his chief disciples, Malo and Yulo, and the bat was the sign-reading Brahmin. The peacock, the pheasant, and the rooster would perpetuate Shenrab's teachings in a future time. As for the three guests of honor at the conference, Mabu Lekden the human was now the priest Trishe Khorlo; Lucam Yumin the nāga was his present interlocutor Öden Nyima; the former divine *shen* was now Tobum Trilokgi Chechen, and all the other birds were precisely these flocks of birds who had gathered around them now.

Work Cited

Bya chos: *Bya chos rin chen phreng ba*. 1978. In *Tibetan Didactic Tales on Animal and Bird Themes*. Vol. 1, 69–105. 2 vols. Dalhousie: Damchoe Sangpo.

Chaucer, Geoffrey. 2017. *The Parliament of Fowls*. With Modern English text by Greg Camp. Fayetteville, AR: Apollodorus Press.

Conze, Edward. 1955. *The Buddha's Law among the Birds.* Oxford: Bruno Cassirer.

Cook, Richard, and Brian Morton. 1992. *The Penguin Guide to Jazz Recordings.* New York: Penguin.

Darbandi, Afkham, and Dick Davis, trans. 1984. *Farid ud-din Attar: The Conference of the Birds.* London: Penguin.

Gzi brjid: Mdo dri med gzi brjid. 2000. Vol. 2. Edited by Pa sangs tshe ring. Lhasa: Bod ljongs bod yig dpe snying dpe skrun khang.

FitzGerald, Edward, trans. 1889. *Bird Parliament by Farid ud-Din Attar*. London/New York: Macmillan and Co.

Halliwell, Stephen, trans. 1998. *Aristophanes: Birds and Other Plays.* Oxford: Oxford University Press.

Huber, Toni. 2020. *Source of Life: Revitalisation Rites and Bon Shamans in Bhutan and the Eastern Himalayas.* 2 vols. Vienna: Austrian Academy of Sciences Press.

Meyer, Henriette. 1953. *Précieuse guirlande de la loi des oiseaux.* Paris: Cahiers du Sud.

Mtsho bod mtho sgang gi bya rigs lta zhib lag deb. 2016. (English title: *Field Guide to Bird-watching of Tibetan Plateau*). Lhasa: Krung go'i bod rigs dpe skrun khang.

Ramble, Charles. 2006. "Sacral Kings and Divine Sovereigns: Principles of Tibetan Monarchy in Theory and Practice." In *Power, Place and the Subject in Inner Asia,* edited by David Sneath, 129–50. Bellingham/Cambridge: Western Washington University.

From the Blue Lake to the Emerald Isle via the Kingdom of Sikkim: An Offering to Janet Gyatso, a Dear Friend in Mindful Travels Around the Land of Snows

Heather Stoddard

IT IS NO SECRET that Gedun Chopel (1903–51) has emerged over the last three decades as the most brilliant and controversial figure of twentieth-century Tibet. Since the first succinct biography written by a monk friend of his from Drepung Monastery in 1965, approximately twenty-seven life stories have been published, mostly in Tibetan from the Tibetan regions of the People's Republic of China, with several in other languages, French, German, Japanese, Czech, Chinese, and English, making him the most written-about figure in the Land of Snows during the first half of the twentieth century.

As is often said, his life embraces the first half of the twentieth century with heroic precision during what is arguably the most traumatic period of the history of the Land of Snows. Gedun Chopel was born by the wayside in Amdo, on May 19, 1903, just as Colonel Younghusband (1863–1942) was in the midst of massive preparations for the second British military invasion of Tibet, across the Himalayas from Sikkim (1903–4).[1] He died on October 11, 1951, a few weeks after watching the avant-guard officers of the Chinese People's Liberation Army marching around the Barkor in the heart of the holy city, announcing the end of traditional Tibet. Just a few months earlier he had been freed from three years in prison at the foot of the Potala Palace, thanks to a group of open-minded aristocrats and other allies who provided him with a small three-room apartment next to the Jokhang, a small stipend, and a (semi)-official government post.[2] His job was to write the first political history of Tibet in order

1. See *Bod kyi lo rgyus rig gnas dpyad gzhi'i rgyu cha bdams bsgrigs* 1985, volume 7 which provides detailed background and day-to-day reports from the Tibetan side, on the two British Raj military invasions of Tibet, in 1888 (pp. 4–62) and 1904 (pp. 63–163). See also Stoddard 2006.

2. Visit to GC's apartment by this author (2002) and private communications by Dobi Tsering Gyal.

to defend the Land of Snows in the post-WWII world. However, the gesture came too late. His liver was already destroyed by alcohol.

Born into a lay yogin family, he had followed both Nyingma and Geluk educational systems, but at the age of thirty-two, after a thirteen-year training as a dialectician in two of the best monastic-universities of Tibet—Labrang Tashikyil and Drepung (1920–34)—he felt himself drifting away from the debating arena, taking up painting and portraiture as a means of earning a living.

His focus was shifting from the inexpressible logic of Nāgārjuna's Middle Way philosophy into discovery mode. Indeed, he had been astonished, in the early spring of 1934, to notice an eighth-century Tibetan inscription on a tall stone stele just below the Potala Palace where he often sat chatting with monk companions on their way to and from the holy city. Around the same time, he fell in love with a girl and that meant he would have to give up his monk's robes. Then, in the summer of that year, just as he was about to take final exams in the debating arena, he was invited to accompany the Indian pandit-cum-communist adventurer, Rahul Sankrityayan, in search of the thousand-year-old palm-leaf manuscripts in Sanskrit, lost in their land of origin, yet safely kept in the ancient libraries of the Land of Snows. Gedun Chopel made up his mind. He abandoned a highly promising career and found himself exploring the monasteries of southern Tibet with Rahul, and from there walking down to Nepal and India where he would spend the next twelve years in self-imposed exile, roaming all over the sub-continent from the Valley of Swat to the Emerald Isle of Sri Lanka (1934–45).[3]

From the day he drank Ganges water for the first time on November 24, 1934,[4] right through to his return to Tibet in the winter of 1945, it seems that Gedun Chopel was researching, writing, and traveling non-stop, learning English, Sanskrit, Pāli and street Hindi, while taking any means of transport available to every corner of India. Apparently, he did not keep a diary but there are autobiographical passages in chapter one of his magnum opus, *The Golden Threshing Ground*,[5] and in some articles published in the *Journal of the Maha-*

3. The Sri Lanka of today was called by several different names during this period, including Singhala, Selan, and Ceylon.

4. Thanks to Prof. Charles Ramble for establishing the Western dates from the Tibetan calendar.

5. Cf. Gendun Chopel 2014. The translators Thupten Jinpa and Donald Lopez render the title of the book "Grains of Gold." This appears to be poetic license. Here the title is rendered following the correct meaning of *Gser gyi thang ma* in Gedun Chopel's own Rebkong Amdo dialect, *The Golden Threshing Ground*, or *The Golden Plain*. *Thang ma* means a flat stretched out area, for example a threshing ground of beaten earth (upon which grain is scattered). *Thang ma* is related to *thang–* as in *byang thang*, the Northern Plain; or *thang ka*, a Tibetan scroll painting, painted on a flat prepared ground, and usually spread out or unrolled to hang on a wall, or rolled up for

bodhi Society. What interested him was the rich historical environment he was suddenly experiencing and learning all about. The different chapters of his research notes unfold and reflect in remarkable detail his intellectual grasp and in-the-field exploration of a wide range of subjects—geography, history, botanicals, customs, ancient writing systems, the origin of the Tibetan script, rock inscriptions, the major dynasties of Northern India, and the history of Sri Lanka. That broad-based study was intended as the basis for a modern Tibetan encyclopedia of India, the very first of its kind. Chapter 14, "On the History of Singhala," is in a way the last chapter, while Chapters 15, "On the Circumstances and Customs of Tibetan People in Ancient Times," and 16, "On the Religion of the Tirthikas," that is Hinduism, appear as appendices.

Chapter 17, entitled "Conclusion" appears at first reading to have been completed in the year of the rabbit, 1939, yet there are at least two other later dates that show he was working on different themes at different times in the same chapter, using earlier or later dates to back up a particular statement.[6] In fact this may be one of the reasons why the book is considered to be unfinished. He did not have the time to comb through all the historical data to tidy up the chronology. Furthermore, taken as a whole, this "Conclusion" seems to be more of an opening rather than a closing to the multiple themes Gedun Chopel discusses on his way through the labyrinth of Indian civilization. Thus, the concluding chapter appears essentially to be a collection of jottings on new or controversial subjects, throwing them onto the page in a satirical or radical manner, planning no doubt to develop the themes at a later date.

The chapter begins with a deeply critical presentation of Europeans and their behavior as imperialists, going on to the failings of the "religion of Jesus," yet praising the prohibition by the British Raj of *suttee* or wife-burning in India. He cites modern inventions from the West, describing them as useful essentially for the educated and the rich, then going on to mention the Second World War that had just been launched, and which would have a profound effect on his own future plans. From there he goes on to discuss two or three new religious currents that he heard about and observed during his journeys across India, including the well-known Advaita Vedanta founded by the great Indian mystic Ramakhrishna (1836–86), who integrated anti-sectarian practices and a six-branched system of yoga into his teachings, revering the Buddha, Brahma, and

safekeeping and transport. *Thang* does not mean "grains." Grains come into the picture when they are spread out upon the "threshing ground."

6. Gendun Chopel 2014, 402, The two other dates are noted on p. 400, "this past rat year" (1936), and p. 406, on the subject of a great debate between a Christian and a Buddhist in Sri Lanka, which he notes was held fifty years earlier from the date of composition.

Allah, and spreading his universalist temples all over India, and even as far away as the United States. Indeed, by the time Gedun Chopel had written the conclusion to his *Golden Threshing Ground*, he had already been present during the World Congress of Faiths held in Calcutta, March 2–8, 1937, in honor of the centenary of Ramakhrishna's birth, and organized partly by Colonel Younghusband himself.

From that worldwide movement, Gedun Chopel introduces another ecumenical tradition, Theosophy, based upon mystical teachings that had spread from the United States in the second half of the nineteenth century, across Europe, and into India. This movement touched the alternative fringe of the British living and working in India, who used it to help develop resistance against the Raj, as well as to support the growing appreciation of classical India as a great source of spirituality, art, and literature. The founders of Theosophy were Helena Blavatsky (1831–91)—a lady of Russian origin who was much admired during the time of Anagarika Dharmapala—Henry Steel Olcott, and Khrishnamurti, whose championship of Theosophy was for a while seen as an open vision of human religious sentiment much needed to counterbalance the rigid emphasis on Christianity that pervaded the British Raj. Blavatsky freely combined her self-declared magical and mystical talents with "modern science" that Gedun Chopel refers to as *sa yan si*, or the "view of a new system of reasoning" (*da lta sa yan si'am rigs pa gsar pa'i lugs kyi lta ba*) . . . that is spreading and increasing in all directions."[7] A short discussion on Gandhi-ji's principles of *ahimsa*, or "non-violence," and *satyagraha*, or "holding firmly to the truth," is followed by a further digression on contemporary evidence for the survival of Buddhist Tantrayāna in India, and how it might compare with the practice of Secret Mantrayāna in Tibet. Ultimately that open market of raw materials is teasingly, lightly gathered-together to suggest the re-affirmation of a position according to which certain Buddhist and non-Buddhist concepts may perhaps be left undifferentiated and/or appreciated, with the basic proviso that Buddhism is the only religion whose view and practice remain steady and unperturbed by science. Indeed, among the religious leaders of humankind, the Buddha is the only one who follows the path of reason.[8]

According to his own affirmation in that last chapter, the *Golden Threshing Ground* was intended as a complete work, in need of minor additions or modifications. Moreover, it is widely thought that there were two manuscript versions, one sent to Amdo from Sri Lanka during his third visit, probably destined to be read by his long-distance friend, Gurong Gyalsey, who was one of

7. Dge 'dun chos 'phel 1990, ch. 17, 166–67; Gendun Chopel 2014, 402–7.

8. Gendun Chopel 2014, 404–5.

the two principal figures of the Ngakmang community in Rebkong. Indeed, their fathers had been close friends in a bond sealed as they traveled together to Central Tibet in 1887–88, where the tragic culmination of their journey was the scene of the bodies of 628 poorly armed Tibetans massacred by the British Raj army, at the beginning of the Earth Rat War.[9]

A second copy of the *Golden Threshing Ground* was given to Horkhang Sonam Pelbar (1919–95) when Gedun Chopel returned to Lhasa in the winter of 1945. However, it remained unpublished until much later on, after Horkhang managed to save it from the flames of the Cultural Revolution, by hiding it away until he had finished copying and editing the entire manuscript, publishing it for the very first time in Lhasa in 1990.[10]

When this author started doing research on Gedun Chopel's life and times in 1974, she began with fieldwork in India, at a time when one of the most learned Western Tibetologists, E. Gene Smith, was working in Delhi for the United States Library of Congress, publishing hundreds of classical Tibetan texts brought out by learned exiles as they fled from their homeland. Gene's refrigerator in Delhi was always full of delicious cheeses from France, and his home in Golf Links was a regular stopping place for traveling Tibetans carrying books to be published. Sometimes they would literally line up at his front door.

It was Gene who first told this author about Gedun Chopel's association with the Indian Pandit Rahul Sankrityayan, and more briefly about the Sikkimese-born Poet Laureate of Sri Lanka, S. Mahenda Thero, and his famous artist friend L.T.P. Manjusri. Among the three, Rahul, or Rahul-ji as he was often called, was well-known for his powerful multidimensional personality and his early escapades from his family to become a *sanyasin* renunciate. Instead, he became a learned Sanskrit scholar, the founder of Hindi travel writing, and an activist in the pro-Indian independence movement. He followed Gandhi's nonviolent *satyagraha* resistance, and during the coming decade when he was not in prison under the British, he traveled extensively, maintaining contact with Gedun Chopel by letter from time to time.

Indeed, during that initial period of fieldwork in 1974–75, this author visited Dharamsala and was shown a pile of correspondence letters and short notes sent between Gedun Chopel and Rahul, from 1934 to 1949, kept at the Library of Tibetan Works and Archives (LTWA). The then director Gyatso-la allowed the author to read and copy the letters, but unfortunately no photos were to be taken and furthermore, pressed for time and not properly realizing the value of that exchange, the author did only an immediate translation of some of the

9. Stoddard 2006.

10. Dge 'dun chos 'phel 1990.

letters into French for her Ph.D., rather than copy out the original English or Tibetan. Much later, during two following visits to the LTWA, when the new director was in place, regretfully no trace of that important historic correspondence was to be found, and information on the why and wherefore of the Amdo scholar's acquaintance with the two other remarkable "Singhalese" monks, Mahenda and Manjusri, had to be found elsewhere.

The first evidence came from a black and white photo known in Tibetan circles in the 1970s and 1980s (figure 1)[11] when it was thought the photo showed the two friends standing together with Gedun Chopel in the middle. All three are wearing the Singhalese monastic robe, and all three were born within one or two years of each other. Manjusri stands to the left and (supposedly) Mahenda to the right, yet no other context for the photo can be seen, and apart from Gene's emphasis on Rahul's membership in the Indian Communist Party, and his role as founder member of the Indian Peasants' Union, Kisan Sabha, in 1936, the American scholar made no comment on links between Gedun Chopel and the two "Singhalese."

Figure 1. Manjusri (left), Gedun Chopel (center), Jinorasa (right).

That photo was first published in this author's biography of Gedun Chopel in French, *Le Mendiant de l'Amdo*, in 1985,[12] and until recently no comment had been made on the identity of those present. There is no issue with

11. Stoddard 1985, fig. 20, misidentifies Gedun Chopel's two companions as T.P.N. Manjusri on the left, and S. Mahenda on the right. It is now known that the monk on the right is Jinorasa.

12. Stoddard 1985.

Manjusri's identification, but it is now clear that the monk on the right is not Mahenda, but another Sikkimese nobleman, born Pak Tsering and ordained Jinorasa, also within the Sri Lankan Theravadin tradition. Jinorasa became a generous ally and a reliable friend when the Amdo scholar was settling down for part of each year in the Sikkim-Darjeeling-Kalimpong region of the eastern Himalayas. Another similar photo (figure 2) shows the same Buddhist monk, Jinorasa, with his large head and short stature, dressed in Theravadin robes standing beside Gedun Chopel who is wearing a Sikkimese *chuba*. These two photos appear to be the only ones known of Jinorasa, founder and director of the Young Men's Buddhist Association (YMBA) in Darjeeling, and an active promoter of education in the region.[13]

Figure 2. Jinorasa (left) and Gedun Chopel (right).

The publication in 2017 of Alak Jetrul's book in Tibetan on Mahenda's life has once again brought the discussion on Gedun Chopel's travels in Sri Lanka

13. Hackett 2012, 318, fig. 11.1. S. K. Jinorasa and Gedun Chopel. Amnye Machen Institute Visual Archives (coll. T. Tsering).

to the fore.[14] Several well-attested photos of Mahinda are included. They show a slim figure with a large round forehead tapering down to a square chin, quite distinct from Jinorasa. In this way, securely identified images of Manjusri, Mahenda, and Jinorasa are now available. They all appear wearing Sri Lankan robes, showing their close connection in the context of the Emerald Isle and the Theravadin tradition, yet out of those three only Manjusri was born on the island. Mahenda and Jinorasa were from old Tibetan families settled in Sikkim, while Gedun Chopel was from Rebkong, to the north-east of the Tibetan plateau. Mahenda's birth name was Penpa Dondup, and Jinorasa's was Pak Tsering, as mentioned. It should also be noted that Pandit Sankrityayan's name Rahul is his ordination name, and although he later gave up his vows, he is still widely known by that name, Rahul, or Rahul-ji.

Questions arise from these two photographs. Where and when were they taken? Why was Penpa Dondup sent from Sikkim to Sri Lanka at the tender age of thirteen? Why did he take vows as the Theravadin monk Mahenda Thero, learning Pāli and Singhalese fluently, adopting the island as his own and living there until he passed away? Again, why did the famous Theravadin monk Walpola Rahula and other important Sri Lankans—including the Prime Minister R. Premadasa—recognize an ethnically Tibetan man as their poet laureate and "savior of the Sri Lankan people," with an official postage stamp created in his honor?[15] (figure 3). Sikkim is after all part of the Tibetan Buddhist world. Tibet is just over the border from Gangtok, and their language, culture, and religion have identical roots. Surely it would have been easier to take vows in one of Sikkim's own monasteries, or inside Tibet itself.

Figure 3. Postage Stamp honoring Mahenda.

14. A lags rje sprul Blo gros chos bzang 2017.

15. A lags rje sprul Blo gros chos bzang 2017. See the back cover of the book for a fine reproduction of the postage stamp, and the front cover for a portrait photo.

At this point it is necessary to explore Mahenda's career to try and link up strands of the story that led to Gedun Chopel's first visit to Sri Lanka in 1937. S. (Sikkim) Mahenda Thero (1901–51) was born just two years before Gedun Chopel, a scion of a noble eastern-Tibetan family settled in the sacred "hidden land" (*sbas yul*) of Sikkim in the fourteenth century, during the time of Sakya Pandita (1182–1251) and his nephew Drogon Phakpa (1235–80). Mahenda was the youngest of five children born from a second marriage and it is useful to go into his background here to see how it contributed to his development as a brilliant poet and orator, as well as our understanding of life in the satellite states of the Tibetan world.

Mahenda's eldest brother by thirty-three years was Kazi Dawa Samdup (1868–1922), a distinguished professor of Tibetan and Buddhist studies at the University of Calcutta, compiler in 1919 of the first extensive English-Tibetan dictionary, and a well-known pioneer translator of Tibetan literary classics into English. Before he passed away, he had been working for four or five years with the American anthropologist and writer, Walter Evans-Wentz (1878–1965), rendering the original Tibetan texts into English while Evans-Wentz reviewed and polished the translations. The series became known as one of the earliest collections of Tibetan literature in English: *The Tibetan Book of the Dead* (1927), *Tibetan Yoga & Secret Doctrines* (1935), *Tibet's Great Yogi Milarepa* (1951), and the *Tibetan Book of Great Liberation* (1954).

After the death of their parents, Kazi Dawa Samdup took responsibility for his five orphaned brothers and sisters, one of whom, Pem Chodar, went astray as a street urchin. He was soon joined by his brother Penpa Dondup, and the two lived together on the streets of Gangtok for two years. Fearing for their safety, the Kazi arranged for the young adolescents to be accompanied to Sri Lanka where they would be ordained and live their lives peacefully on the island as Buddhist monks of the Southern Theravadin tradition.

In 1914 when they arrived in Sri Lanka, Penpa Dondup was thirteen years of age. They traveled in the company of Jnanatiloka, a well-known learned German scholar and Theravadin monk who was later taken prisoner of war by the British and incarcerated in Dehra Dun till the end of World War II. Jnanatiloka was one of a number of Europeans who were converting to Buddhism as a rational nontheistic way of life, continuing their studies in Myanmar and Sri Lanka, where thanks to Anagarika Dharmapala (1864–1933) and other nineteenth-century personalities, the Revivalist school of Buddhism had been developing new critical apparatus for the chronology of the Buddha's life. A certain rejection of Vajrayāna as impure and influenced by Hindu Tantrism was part of the discussion. From the day they arrived in Sri Lanka, until 1931 when Mahenda became a fully ordained monk at the Matwatte Maha Vihara in Kandy, he studied and worked in various other viharas mastering the language of the Southern Buddhist scriptures, the Pāli Piṭaka, as well as the Singhalese language spoken by the population. Gradually he became known for his marvelous literary talent, winning several awards and "awakening the youth through poetical composition, and offering them guidance in the struggle for freedom from the British Raj."[16]

Mahinda's good friend Manjusri (1902–82) also played a key role in Sri Lanka as a modernist Buddhist monk painter, evolving through the twentieth century between tradition and the cosmopolitan world of international art. Born in a fishing village on the island, he took ordination at a young age before rising to become an exceptional Buddhist scholar in Pāli and Sinhalese. In the early 1930s, he went to study Chinese in Rabindranath Tagore's university of Shantiniketan,[17] where he turned seriously towards painting, dedicating his life to art, in particular to oil painting, and the making of inventories of Buddhist murals in Sri Lankan temples. He would go and stay for months at the Vihara of his friend Mahenda, spending all his time painting in traditional and modern styles. Gene Smith told this author that Gedun Chopel would also go and stay at Mahenda's Vihara, where he shared a room with Manjusri, and they would have lively discussions on the art of Buddhist murals that has played such an important role in educating the ordained and the lay people of Tibet. Gradually Manjusri made the art of copying Buddhist murals his own specialty, exhibiting alongside the great poet Tagore himself. Then in 1937, he was "especially invited" to Sikkim to study traditional thangka painting and Vajrayāna Buddhism with the Tibetan master artist Khenpo Uchenma, and another artist named Tashi, for several months in that same year.[18]

Gedun Chopel's First Visit to "Selan" ca. mid-March to end of April 1937

That invitation to Manjusri must have fit in well with events surrounding the World Conference of Faiths that was held in Calcutta from March 2–8, 1937, and although neither Manjusri's nor Mahenda's names appear in the minutes of the conference, "delegates from Sri Lanka" are mentioned, and it is likely

16. A lags Rje sprul 2017, 281–84.

17. A lags Rje sprul 2017, 222.

18. See Eventbrite.co.uk, 20 April 2021, 6pm-7.30pm, Manjusri – Sri Lankan Artist, a Zoom presentation by Friends of Sri Lanka Association, with Dr Shamil David Wanigaratne Manjusri author of the monograph, *L.T.P. Manjusri, Sri Lankan Artist & Scholar,* and the presentation of this new book.

that the two friends took part in the proceedings. In this case they would certainly have met Gedun Chopel, either during the conference or at the Mahabodhi Society in Calcutta. When it was over, they would have parted ways, with Manjusri going up to Sikkim to study thangka painting and Vajrayāna Buddhism, while Mahenda, or other Sinhalese delegates would have returned to the Emerald Isle accompanied by their new friend Gedun Chopel. His first visit to Sri Lanka, sponsored by the Mahabodhi Society, would have lasted only three weeks or so, during which time he began to familiarize himself with Singhalese culture and the Pāli language, with longer study visits in view.[19]

From March 2 to 8, 1937, roughly two hundred religious leaders from around the world had assembled in Calcutta to celebrate the World Congress of Faiths held in honor of the Indian mystic Ramakhrishna on the hundredth anniversary of his birth. This was a follow-up to the first Parliament of the World's Religions held in Chicago, September 11–27, 1893, during the World's Fair, in an attempt to create a global dialogue of faiths. Two of the highlights of that first gathering were a resounding speech by Vivekananda (1863–1902), principal disciple of Ramakhrishna, addressing the entire company, and the first face-to-face meeting between Zen and Theravadin Buddhists. The Japanese Zen master Soyen Shaku (1860–1919), teacher of the world-famous Zen master D. T. Suzuki (1870–1966), gave a speech on the law of cause and effect, while the Singhalese Buddhist reformer and leading figure in the Sri Lankan independence movement, Anagarika Dharmapala, found fame as the "first global Buddhist missionary."

In delving into this new area of research it was somewhat surprising for the present author to learn that one of the main organizers of the World Congress of Faiths in Calcutta was Colonel Francis Younghusband (1863–1942) the "last great imperial adventurer"[20] of the British Raj. Born in India, he became a great connoisseur of far distant territories, knowing Central Asia like the palm of his hand. It was he who organized both British military invasions of Tibet, the first in 1888 when he was chief scout leading the army into unknown territory, and again in 1904 as colonel and leader of the "Younghusband Expedition" that was in reality a hugely expensive and devastating military attack on the Land of Snows. Younghusband himself described the first battle at Chumi Shengo, the first violent conflict he had ever witnessed, as "pure massacre," leaving 628

19. Gendun Chopel 2014 mentions only one visit to Sri Lanka.

20. See the title and sub-title of Patrick French's 1995 book *Younghusband: The Last Great Imperial Adventurer.*

Tibetans dead and 220 wounded, with on the British Raj side, only "6 lightly wounded and 6 badly wounded," and none dead.[21]

Why was Younghusband there in Calcutta for the first time in thirty years, at the age of seventy-four, playing an active role as representative of the League of Nations in the organization of a week-long international discussion on peace and harmony between religious traditions? The reason was a deep and lasting spiritual experience the colonel had the day after signing the Treaty of Lhasa in 1904, when he rode off into the mountains carrying the bronze image of the Buddha offered to him by the abbot of Ganden Monastery, who had been left in charge of the government of Tibet by the Thirteenth Dalai Lama when he fled to Mongolia ahead of the invading army.[22] That spiritual experience had such a profound effect on Younghusband that after his return to the United Kingdom he dedicated the rest of his life to pursuing peace in the world (figure 4).

Figure 4. Colonel Younghusband grasping the bronze Buddha given to him by the Ganden Tripa, just after signing the treaty in 1904.[23]

21. French 1995, 222–25.

22. French 1995, 251–52; Hackett 2012, 134–35.

23. French 1995, List of Illustrations, Section II: Younghusband clutching the Ganden Tripa's bronze Buddha (OIOC).

On the second day of the conference an exceptional luncheon was held for Younghusband and Da Lama Ngakchen Rinpoche—the right-hand man of the exiled Panchen Lama—with whom Younghusband had shaken hands in Lhasa after signing the treaty in 1904. Several other personalities linked to the Tibetan world were invited to join. The host was Theos Casimir Bernard, an energetic doctoral student from Columbia University, New York, claiming to be the first to work on Indian religion and yoga as his main subject. Bernard was also attending the conference, trying to develop contacts to get a visa for Tibet. His plan was to acquire a library of "some repute" principally of Tibetan texts, including the entire Tibetan Buddhist canon, and establish a translation center he was calling "Tibet-Land" in the United States. He had already met Gedun Chopel in Darjeeling in September, 1936, and was planning to invite him to Tibet-Land as the principal translator.[24]

At that time, early in 1937, Gedun Chopel was also in Calcutta, waiting for his famous master of studies from Drepung Monastery, Geshe Sherab Gyatso (1884–1968), to come down from Tibet and take a boat to China, where he had been invited to teach Buddhism in the new Guomindang universities. Both were invited to the lunch, together with Da Lama and the trade agent David Macdonald, who was also chaperoning/accompanying two Guomindang agents on their way from Lhasa to the Calcutta docks. They too were returning home to China by sea. Furthermore, Younghusband was accompanied by his new American neighbors from London, the famous aviator Charles Lindbergh and his wife Anne. Since the kidnapping and death of their baby son, they too had been delving into spirituality and Charles offered to fly Younghusband on the last leg of the journey—from Mumbai to Calcutta—to attend the conference. Just a couple of days later, as the steamship was preparing its departure to Shanghai, Younghusband, David Macdonald, and Gedun Chopel accompanied the departing guests down to the docks with members of the Tibetan and Chinese communities in Calcutta, where they made speeches and waved goodbye.

Not long after the World Congress of Faiths had finished, Gedun Chopel wrote a letter to Rahul from "Selan," having been sent there by the Mahabodhi Society to study Sanskrit. He had already begun to make a translation of the Singhalese Vinaya, the code of monastic discipline, to send to a friend in Amdo, but as he wrote to Rahul,

> I have found a pandit for Sanskrit, but we have no common language in which to speak, so it is difficult to say anything. The heat

24. Hackett 2012, ch.11, 316–46.

> will soon arrive and I cannot stay, but I have no money. Should I sell drawings? Write to me quickly. The director [of the Mahabodhi Society in Colombo] says I can stay here for the winters and spend summers in Darjeeling. He has my good at heart. I have already been in India for two or three years and I really want to learn Sanskrit. Please, help me![25]

No date is given on the letter, but if Gedun Chopel had been in India for two to three years, the spring of 1937 would be the most logical period for the Mahabodhi Society to send him to Sri Lanka, right after the World Congress of Faiths when other delegates from Sri Lanka—perhaps including Mahinda—would be returning home.

Evidence of this short first journey comes in another letter sent to Rahul towards the end of April 1937, saying he had arrived in Kalimpong, *chez* Khunu Tharchin, and would be staying there through the summer. Tharchin was a Christian missionary and founder of the Mirror Press in Kalimpong, where he produced perhaps the first Tibetan newspaper and sent it around to all the important people in the Himalayas and beyond, including the Dalai Lama. Henceforth, Kalimpong became Gedun Chopel's main home and retreat during the hot summer monsoon season, and by the time he wrote to Rahul again, he had already joined another interesting translation project, working with Tharchin and Rani Chuni Dorje, wife of the prime minister of Bhutan, on a translation of excerpts from the life of the Thirteenth Dalai Lama, at the behest of Basil Gould (1883–1956) and Hugh Richardson (1905–2000), both British Raj officials working in Sikkim and Tibet. It is now clear that it was Tharchin and Rani Chuni who invited Gedun Chopel to join in the team, due to his excellent grasp of the dense classical style of the Thirteenth Dalai Lama's *Book of Activities*.[26] Indeed the fact that he was invited to join such a prestigious project shows he was becoming known among the international cohort of scholars working on the Tibetan and Himalayan world.

Around the same time, Gedun Chopel made friends with an Indian Buddhist monk and future director of the Mahabodhi Society, Jinaratana. They spent six months together at the College for Classical Indian Studies Kashibidyabitha in Varanasi, studying Sanskrit, Pāli, and English, and according to Jinaratana, Gedun Chopel went to Sri Lanka ("Selan") twice or three times

25. Stoddard 1985, 181. See note 2.

26. The Thirteenth Dalai Lama's official daily activities in two volumes. The short title is *Mzdad deb*.

during the period between 1936 and 1941. He also confirmed that between visits to "Selan," Gedun Chopel would be working on and off in the library of the Mahabodhi Society in Calcutta, or else traveling widely, studying, and writing his *Golden Threshing Ground*.[27]

Second Visit to Sri Lanka (between February 1940 and June 1941)

Gedun Chopel's second sojourn in Sri Lanka took place around two to three years later when he spent "one year and a few days less than four months" on the island.[28] Meanwhile, following the 1937 World Congress of Faiths, his circle of contacts had expanded considerably. He was increasingly in demand in collaboration projects, while doing his own research and writing. He had taken part in a second expedition to Southern Tibet with Rahul from April to September 1938, again in search of palm-leaf manuscripts and notably continuing his study of Sanskrit and Pāli, completing his own *Kama Shastra, Treatise on the Arts of Love and Desire*, in January 1939. It was sometime between the winter of 1939–40 on through to June 1941, Gedun Chopel informed his readers without giving any dates, that he had stayed on the island for one year and four months less a few days, while writing a chapter of around forty pages for the *Golden Threshing Ground,* entitled "On the History of Singhala."[29] He delves into the subject in his chatty critical way, with around half the chapter based on his own observations. He had borrowed a guidebook to the island from a man whose name he writes as Nangma Rauyi'patou, private secretary to the king. With that guidebook in hand, he had visited all the famous places, describing with delight some of his adventures as he "practically walked all around the island" taking one month to do it.[30] A mythological and historical account of the island completes that chapter, as well as a few charming poems on the Singhalese Sthavira monks, attributed to this period of deep reflection on abandoning his robes.[31]

27. Interview 1975 with Jinaratana at the Mahabodhi Society, Calcutta. See Stoddard 1985, 380.

28. Gendun Chopel 2014. Jinpa and Lopez (page 346) only mention one visit to Sri Lanka, lasting "one year and a few days less than four months."

29. Gendun Chopel 2014, ch.14, 305–47. This chapter 14 was later republished several times separately as a small booklet or guide to the Emerald Isle.

30. Gendun Chopel 2014, ch.14, 305–48. Gedun Chopel describes his adventures around the island and began to translate the Dhammapada. See colophon, Gendun Chopel 2014, 397–416. See also Rdo rje rgyal 1997, 68.

31. See Rdo rje rgyal 1997, 66–67; Hor khang Bsod nams dpal 'bar 1990, 2:73–74; Gendun Chopel 2014, 347.

Ganna Buys Two Estates in California, USA

By July 6, 1941, Gedun Chopel had returned from Sri Lanka once again to the Himalayas. We know this as he translated a short verse, "Tara the Quick," into English and wrote it down on the second page of the large dictionary George Roerich (1902–60) had given him in 1938, when that date had also been noted down. Theos Bernard too was back in contact, inviting him enthusiastically to the United States to join in his mega-translation project at Tibet-Land, for which one large and one small estate near Santa Barbara in California had been purchased by his wife Ganna already in June of that same year. Bernard was so sure that Ganna's lawyers would manage to get a visa for Gedun Chopel that he had already begun building a temple in the grounds of Tibet-Land, announcing the foundation of an "Academy of Tibetan Literature" and delivering his inaugural lecture in the grove where the new institute would be built.[32] By August 1941, a notice appeared in the *Journal of the Mahabodhi Society*, "Lama Geshe Chompell, with whom our readers are already acquainted, has returned from his sojourn in Ceylon. He has an invitation from an American scholar to visit New York, which journey though not without danger, he seems willing to undertake."[33]

Third Visit to Sri Lanka: A Period of Eight Months, Roughly between November 1941 and August 1942, or Later

Gedun Chopel's third visit to Sri Lanka must have taken place sometime after November 8, 1941, when final news came from the United States announcing that his visa had been refused. "Government refused visa. Pay $400, $300, or any amount you consider right for Geshe-la's lost time remaining to help your school. Hope it is only a short postponement."[34] The disappointment was deep and enduring, but hope was kept alive by Bernard insisting they should wait until the war was over and try again. Meanwhile Bernard began to settle seriously into Tibet-Land[35] while Gedun Chopel went on his third trip to Sri Lanka, where he spent some time polishing one of two drafts of the *Golden Threshing Ground,* writing a long conclusion, and sending one copy off to Amdo, perhaps to Alak Gurong Gyalsey[36] for perusal before leaving Sri Lanka

32. Hackett 2012, ch. 11, 316–23.

33. *Journal of the Mahabodhi Society* 49.8:3 (August 1941).

34. Theos Bernard papers, telegram dated Nov. 8, 1941. See Hackett 2012, 321–22.

35. Hackett 2012, 316–46.

36. Wiley: A lags Dgu rong rgyal sras.

for the last time.[37] His departure would have been some time before August 1942, at which time Gedun Chopel's artist friend LTP Manjusri was taking part in the first exhibition in Colombo of the modern artists of Sri Lanka. Manjusri was one of their leaders, and they called themselves the "43 Group" (figure 5). By that time Gedun Chopel had already left for India.[38]

Figure 5. A traditional ceremonial temple frieze by LTP Manjusri Thero.

On December 29, 1943, Gedun Chopel wrote to Rahul from the Roerich Urusvati Institute in Kulu Manali, mentioning his journeys to Sri Lanka briefly for the last time, adding eight months onto the total length of stay, "For two years I travelled in Lanka. An invitation to visit America also came but I was unable to go because of the war."[39] Rahul commented, "Geshe has now learnt a great deal of English and while in Naggar he was assisting George Roerich in his research. He has begun to translate Abhigyan Shakuntala."[40]

This rambling narrative is meant as a background to the exploration of roles played by widely scattered communities within the Tibetan, Himalayan, and Vajrayāna Buddhist world, in interaction with Southern or Theravadin Buddhism, itself in full transmutation since the mid-nineteenth century. The story raises a number of questions on the roles these four friends, Gedun Chopel, TPN Mahenda Thero, S. Manjusri Thero, and Kazi Jinorasa, played as leading intellectuals, artists, philosophers, and translators, navigating the troubled

37. Gendun Chopel 2014, 397–416.

38. The "43 Group" of Singhalese artists was officially founded the following year in Colombo, 1943.

39. This is an extract from one of the LTWA letters written by GC to RS.

40. Note from Rahul's Diary.

waters of pre-independence Sri Lanka. Three of those friends emerged from the vast ramparts of the Land of Snows.

Works Cited

A lags rje sprul Blo gros chos bzang. 2017. *Sing+ga la'i deb ther du 'khod pa'i rlabs chen Bod mi sna. Mahenda'i mi rigs kyi lar zhen dang Dge 'dun chos 'phel gyi gsang ba.* n.p.

Bod kyi lo rgyus rig gnas dpyad gzhi'i rgyu cha bdams bsgrigs. 1985. Volume 7. Lhasa Bod ljongs mi dmangs dpe skrun khang.

Dge 'dun chos 'phel. 1990. *Rgyal khams rig pas bskor ba'i gtam rgyud gser gyi thang ma.* In *Dge 'dun chos 'phel gyi gsung rtsom*, 1:3–426 and 2:3–188. Gangs can rig mdzod vols 10–13. Lhasa: Bod ljongs bod yid dpe rnying dpe skrun khang.

French, Patrick. 1995. *Younghusband: The Last Great Imperial Adventurer.* London: Flamingo.

Gendun Chopel. 2014. *Grains of Gold: Tales of a Cosmopolitan Traveler.* Translated by Thubten Jinpa and Donald S. Lopez Jr. Chicago: University of Chicago Press.

Hackett, Paul G. 2012. *Theos Bernard, the White Lama: Tibet, Yoga, and American Religious Life.* New York: Columbia University Press.

Hor khang Bsod nams dpal 'bar, ed. 1990. *Dge 'dun chos 'phel gyi gsung 'bum.* 2 vols. Gangs can rig mdzod. Volumes 10–11, Lha sa: Bod ljongs bod yig dpe rnying dpe skrun khang.

Journal of the Mahabodhi Society. 49.8:3 (August 1941).

Rdo rje rgyal. 1997. "Dge 'dun chos 'phel gyi byung ba brjod pa bden gtam rna ba'i bcud len." In *'Dzam gling rig pa'i dpa' bo rdo brag dge 'dun chos 'phel gyi byung ba brjod pa bden gtam rna ba'i bcud len*, Par gzhi dang po, 15–166. Lan kru'u: Kan Su'u Mi Rigs Dpe Skrun Khang.

Stoddard, Heather. 1985. *Le mendiant de l'Amdo.* Paris: Société d'ethnographie.

———. 2006. "The Forgotten Military Clash between British India and Tibet: The Great *Pi ling dmag zlog* of 1888, from the Tibetan Point of View." Paper presented at the Eleventh Meeting of the International Association of Tibetan Studies (IATS), Bonn University, Germany.

———. 2010. "The Relationship between the Thirteenth Dalai Lama (1876–1933) and *gter ston* bSod rgyal Las rab gling pa (1856–1926)." Paper presented at the Twelfth Meeting of the International Association of Tibetan Studies (IATS), University of British Columbia, Vancouver, Canada.

Janet Gyatso's Major Publications

Co-Authored and Edited Works

Bhum, Pema, and Janet Gyatso. 2017. "Condensed Tibetan Allusions." *Rivista Degli Studi Orientali* 90 (spring): 165–78.

———. Forthcoming. "*Mirror* on Fire: An Ardent Reception in Tibet and Mongolia" In *Daṇḍin in the World*, edited by Yigal Bronner. New York: Oxford University Press.

Buffetrille, Katia, and Janet Gyatso. 2008. "What Customs and Habits are There in Tibet" and "What Festivals are There in Tibet." In *Authenticating Tibet: Answers to China's 100 Questions*, edited by Anne-Marie Blondeau and Katia Buffetrille, 302–12. Berkeley: University of California Press.

Germano, David, and Janet Gyatso. 2000. "Longchenpa and the Possession of the Dakinis." In *Tantra in Practice*, edited by David White, 239–65. Princeton, NJ: Princeton University Press.

Gyatso, Janet. 1992. *In the Mirror of Memory: Reflections on Mindfulness and Remembrance in Indian and Tibetan Buddhism*. Albany: State University of New York Press.

Gyatso, Janet, and Hannah Havnevik, eds. 2005. *Women of Tibet*. New York: Columbia University Press.

Solo-Authored Works

1980. "The Teachings of Thang-stong rGyal-po." In *Tibetan Studies in Honour of Hugh Richardson*, edited by Michael Aris and Aung San Suu Kyi, 111–19. Warminster: Aris and Phillips.

1981. "The Literary Transmission of the Traditions of Thang-Stong RGyal-Po: A Study of Visionary Buddhism in Tibet." Ph.D., Berkeley: University of California.

1985. "The Development of the gCod Tradition." In *Soundings in Tibetan Civilization*, edited by Barbara Aziz and Matthew Kapstein, 74–98. New Delhi: Manohar.

1986a. "Image as Presence: The Place of the Work of Art in Tibetan Religious

Thinking." In *The Newark Museum Tibetan Collection III. Sculpture and Painting*, edited by Valrae Reynolds, Amy Heller, and Janet Gyatso, 30–35. Newark, NJ: The Newark Museum of Art.

1986b. "Signs, Memory and History: A Tantric Buddhist Theory of Scriptural Transmission." *Journal of the International Association of Buddhist Studies* 9.2: 7–35.

1986c. "Thang-stong rGyal-po, Father of the Tibetan Drama: The Bodhisattva as Artist." In *Zlos-gar, The Tibetan Performing Arts: Commemorative Issue on the Occasion of the 25th Anniversary of the Founding of the Tibetan Institute of Performing Arts (1959–84)*, edited by Jamyang Norbu, 91–104. Dharamsala, India: Library of Tibetan Works and Archives.

1987. "Down with the Demoness: Reflections on a Feminine Ground in Tibet." *Tibet Journal* 12.4: 34–46. Reprinted in *Feminine Ground: Essays on Women and Tibet*, edited by Janice Dean Willis, 33–52. Ithaca, NY: Snow Lion Publications, 1989.

1992a. "Autobiography in Tibetan Religious Literature: Reflections on Its Modes of Self-Presentation." In *Tibetan Studies: Proceedings of the 5th International Association of Tibetan Studies Seminar*, edited by Shoren Ihara and Zuiho Yamaguchi, 2: 465–78. Narita, Japan: Naritasan Institute for Buddhist Studies.

1992b. "Genre, Authorship, and Transmission in Visionary Buddhism: The Literary Traditions of Thang-Stong rGyal-Po." In *Tibetan Buddhism: Reason and Revelation*, edited by Ronald M. Davidson and Steven Goodman, 95–106. Albany: State University of New York Press.

1992c. "Letter Magic: A Peircean Perspective on the Semiotics of Rdo Grub-Chen's Dhāraṇī Memory." In *In the Mirror of Memory: Reflections on Mindfulness and Remembrance in Indian and Tibetan Buddhism*, edited by Janet Gyatso, 173–215. Albany: State University of New York Press.

1993. "The Logic and Legitimation in the Tibetan Treasure Tradition." *History of Religions* 33.1: 97–134.

1994. "Guru Chos-dbang's *Gter 'byung chen mo*. An Early Survey of the Treasure Tradition and Its Strategies in Discussing Bon Treasure." In *Tibetan Studies: Proceedings of the Sixth International Association of Tibetan Studies Seminar*, edited by Per Kvaerne, 1: 275–87. Oslo: Institute for Comparative Research in Human Culture.

1996. "Drawn from the Tibetan Treasury: The *gTer ma* Literature." In *Tibetan Literature: Studies in Genre*, edited by José Ignacio Cabezón and Rodger R. Jackson, 147–69. Ithaca, NY: Snow Lion Publications.

1997a. "An Avalokiteśvara Sādhana." In *Religions of Tibet in Practice*, edited by Donald S. Lopez Jr., 266–70. Princeton, NJ: Princeton University Press.

1997b. "Counting Crow's Teeth: Tibetans and Their Diary-Writing Practices." In *Les Habitants Du Toit Du Monde*, edited by Samten Karmay and Philippe Sagant, 159–77. Paris: Societe d'ethnologie.

1997c. "From the Autobiography of a Visionary." In *Religions of Tibet in Practice*, edited by Donald S. Lopez Jr., 369–75. Princeton, NJ: Princeton University Press.

1998a. *Apparitions of the Self: The Secret Autobiography of a Tibetan Visionary*. Princeton, NJ: Princeton University Press.

1998b. Introduction to *The Lives and Liberation of Princess Mandarava: The Indian Consort of Padmasambhava*, translated by Lama Chonam and Sangye Khandro, 1–14. Boston: Wisdom Publications.

1999. "Healing Burns with Fire: The Facilitations of Experience in Tibetan Buddhism." *Journal of the American Academy of Religion* 67.1: 113–47.

2002. "The Ins and Outs of Self-Transformation: Personal and Social Sides of Visionary Practice in Tibetan Buddhism." In *Self and Self-Transformation in the History of Religions*, edited by David Shulman, 183–94. Oxford: Oxford University Press.

2003. "One Plus One Makes Three: Buddhist Gender, Monasticism, and the Law of the Non-Excluded Middle." *History of Religions* 43.2: 89–115.

2004a. "The Authority of Empiricism and the Empiricism of Authority: Tibetan Medicine and Religion in the Eve of Modernity." *Comparative Studies of South Asia, Africa, and the Middle East* 24.2: 83–96.

2004b. "Compassion at the Millennium: A Buddhist Salvo for the Ethics of the Apocalypse." In *Thinking Through the Death of God: A Critical Companion to Thomas J. J. Altizer*, edited by Brian Schroeder and Lissa McCullough, 147–67. Albany: State University of New York Press.

2004c. "The Ultimate Couple." In *Buddhist Scriptures*, edited by Donald S. Lopez Jr., 488–94. London: Penguin Classics.

2005a. Introduction to *Women of Tibet*, edited by Janet Gyatso and Hanna Havnevik, 1–25. New York: Columbia University Press.

2005b. "Sex." In *Critical Terms for the Study of Buddhism*, edited by Donald S. Lopez Jr., 271–90.

2006. "A Partial Genealogy of the Life Story of Ye shes mtsho rgyal." *Journal of the International Association of Tibetan Studies* 2: 1–27.

2008. "Spelling Mistakes, Philology, and Feminist Criticism: Women and Boys in Tibetan Medicine." *Revue d'Etudes Tibétaines* (*Tibetan Studies in Honour of Samten Karmay* Part 1) 14: 81–98. Reprinted in *Tibetan Studies in Honour of Samten Karmay*. Dharamsala, India: Amnye Machen Institute, 2009.

2009. Introduction to *Body and Spirit: Tibetan Medical Paintings*, edited by

Laila Williams, 3–13. New York: American Museum of Natural History in association with University of Washington Press.

2010. "Female Ordination in Buddhism: Looking into a Crystal Ball, Making a Future." In *Dignity and Discipline*, edited by Thea Mohr and Jampa Choedron, 1–21. Boston: Wisdom Publications.

2011a. "Discerning Tibetan Modernities: Moments, Methods, and Assumptions." In *Mapping the Modern in Tibet: PIATS 2006, Tibetan Studies, Proceedings of the Eleventh Seminar of the International Association for Tibetan Studies, Königswinter 2006*, edited by Gray Tuttle, 1–37. Halle, Saale: International Association for Tibetan Studies.

2011b. "Experience, Empiricism, and the Fortunes of Authority: Tibetan Medicine and Buddhism on the Eve of Modernity." In *Forms of Knowledge in Early Modern Asia: Explorations in the Intellectual History of India and Tibet, 1500–1800*, edited by Sheldon Pollock, 311–35. Durham, NC: Duke University Press.

2012. "Looking for Gender in the Medical Paintings of Desi Sangye Gyatso, Regent of the Tibetan Buddhist State." *Asian Medicine* 6.2: 2017–92.

2013. "Buddhist Practices and Ideals in Desi Sangye Gyatso's Medical Paintings." In *Bodies in Balance: The Art of Tibetan Medicine*, edited by Theresia Hofer, 198–220. New York: Rubin Museum of Art in conjunction with University of Washington Press, Seattle.

2015a. *Being Human in a Buddhist World: An Intellectual History of Medicine in Early Modern Tibet*. New York: Columbia University Press.

2015b. "One Picture." In *Tibetan and Himalayan Healing—An Anthology for Anthony Aris*, edited by Charles Ramble and Ulrike Roesler, 273–78. Kathmandu: Vajra Books.

2016. "Turning Personal: Recent Work on Autobiography in Tibetan Studies." *Journal of Asian Studies* 75.1: 229–35.

2017a. "Did the Buddha Really Compose the Classic Tibetan Medical Text? A Critical Examination from *The Lamp to Dispel Darkness*." In *Buddhism and Medicine: An Anthology of Premodern Sources*, edited by Peirce Salguero, 602–8. New York: Columbia University Press.

2017b. "Recently, Under the Bodhi Tree: The New Bhikshuni Trajectory in Tibetan Buddhism." *Tricycle*, Winter: 88–93.

2018. Introduction to *Tibet and China: Revisiting Past and Exploring Future Possibilities* by Dawa Norbu, 1–12. New Delhi: Tibet Forum.

2019. "Seeing from All Sides: The Ethics of Multi-perspective in Śāntideva's *Bodhicaryāvatāra*." In *Readings of Śāntideva's* Guide to Bodhisattva Practice (*Bodhicaryāvatāra*), edited by Jonathan C. Gold and Douglas S. Duckworth, 99–133. New York: Columbia University Press.

Tabula Gratulatoria

Eyal Aviv
Geoffrey Barstow
Yael Bentor
Suzanne M. Bessenger
Pema Bhum
Lara Braitstein
Erik Braun
Briana Brightly
Yigal Bronner
Alexis Brown
Nina Bryce
Erin Burke
Kalzang Dorjee Bhutia
John Canti
Cathy Cantwell
Joie Szu-Chiao Chen
Wen-shing Chou
Michela Clemente
Lowell Cook
Sienna Craig
Rae Dachille
Tashi Dekyid
Jetsun Deleplanque
Karen Derris
Tenzin Dickie
Lewis Doney
Wendy Doniger
Brandon Dotson
Damchö Diana Finnegan
Renée Ford
Leren Gao
Alexander Gardner
Frances Garrett
Cheryl A. Giles
Natalie Gummer
Guttorm Gundersen
Amelia Hall
Charles Hallisey
Sarah Harding
Lauran Hartley
Kate Hartmann
Hanna Havnevik
David Hempton
Isabelle Henrion-Dourcy
Dan Hirshberg
Amy Holmes-Tagchungdarpa
Bryan J. Cuevas
Alison Melnick Dyer
Nisheeta Jagtiani
Sonam Kachru
Joseph Kimmel
Matthew King
Adam Krug
Derangala Kusalagnana
(Bhante Kusala)
Amy Paris Langenberg
Stefan Larsson
Amod Lele
Kelsang Lhamo (Chozin)
Jue Liang
Rory Lindsay
Cuilan Liu
Adam Lobel
Dawa Lokyitsang

Maisie Luo
Zhouyang Ma
Ian MacCormack
Ariana Maki
Charlene Makley
Jonathan Makransky
Dan Martin
Robert Mayer
Thomas Mazanec
Carole McGranahan
William McGrath
Shoko Mekata
J. Arya Moallem
Elizabeth Monson
Eric Mortensen
Reiko Ohnuma
Ryan Richard Overbey
Elena Pakhoutova
Adam Pearcey
Marcus Perman
Annabella Pitkin
Françoise Pommaret
Alyson Prude
Gedun Rabsal
Michael Radich
Dhondup T. Rekjong
Ulrike Roesler
Jann Ronis
Geoffrey Samuel
Lobsang Sangay
Vanessa R. Sasson
Miguel Sawaya
Joshua Schapiro
Kristin Scheible
Anna Sehnalova
Bob Sharf
Michael Sheehy
Joshua Shelton
Xianfeng Shi
David Shulman
Eviatar Shulman
Miranda Smith
Somtsobum
Priya Rakkhit Sraman
Upali Sraman
Penghao Sun
Dominic Sur
Andrew S. Taylor
Tulku Tenzin Gyurmey
Anh Tran
Yangga Trarong
Karma Lekshe Tsomo
Gray Tuttle
Roy Tzohar
Stacey Van Vleet
Lina Verchery
Xingyi Wang
Sherab Wangmo
Cameron David Warner
Eveline Washul
Christian K. Wedemeyer
Shan Wu
Carl Yamamoto
Emily Yeh
Devin Zuckerman

Contributor Biographies

Elizabeth Angowski is an assistant professor of religion at Earlham College where she teaches courses on Asian religious traditions, hagiography, ethics, and ecology. Her current research focuses on Tibetan biographical literature and the figure of Yeshé Tsogyal.

Willa Blythe Baker, PhD, is an author, teacher, and independent scholar. She is the founder of the Natural Dharma Fellowship and its retreat center Wonderwell Mountain Refuge in Springfield, New Hampshire. In early adulthood she spent twelve years as a Buddhist monastic, completing two consecutive three-year retreats. In midlife she entered graduate school, completing a master's in religion at the University of Virginia and a doctorate in religion at Harvard University under Dr. Janet Gyatso. She was a visiting lecturer in Buddhist Ministry at Harvard Divinity School from 2013 to 2017. Her books include *Essence of Ambrosia: A Guide to Buddhist Contemplations* (Library of Tibetan Works and Archives, 2005), *The Arts of Contemplative Care: Pioneering Voices in Buddhist Chaplaincy and Pastoral Work* (Wisdom Publications, 2013), and *The Wakeful Body: Somatic Mindfulness as a Path to Freedom* (Shambhala Publications, 2021). Her current scholarship interest is Tibetan experiential poetry (*nyams mgur*) and memoir (*rtogs brjod*). She is currently translating a memoir of Jikmé Lingpa.

Pema Bhum is the executive director and co-founder of The Latse Project. He served as the director of Latse Library for fifteen years. He holds an MA in Classical Tibetan from the Northwest Nationalities Institute (now known as Northwest Minzu University) in Lanzhou, Gansu Province, PRC, where he also taught Tibetan language and literature. After his arrival in India in 1988, he founded the first independent Tibetan language newspaper in exile, *Dmangs-gtso*, and the Tibetan literary magazine, *Ljang-gzhon*. From 1992 to 1996 he served as founding director of the Amnye Machen Institute in Dharamsala, India, and for two years taught Tibetan language and literature at Indiana University. He is author of two memoirs of the Cultural Revolution—*Six Stars* *with a Crooked Neck* (2001), and *Dran tho rdo ring ma* (2006)—as well as *Heartbeat of a New Generation*, which has been translated into three languages. He has also authored several articles, the most recent of which are published in issues of the Latse Library Newsletter. From 2015 to 2020, he taught students at Columbia, Yale, and Cornell Universities as part of the Shared Course Initiative, and from 2021 to 2022 he taught at Stanford University. He is currently a lecturer in Classical Tibetan language at Northwestern University, where he also offers an advanced readings seminar.

Benjamin Bogin is a scholar of Himalayan Buddhism. He is associate professor and director of Asian studies at Skidmore College. Bogin writes and teaches on the intersections of biographical literature, sacred geography, and visual art in Himalayan cultures. He is the author of *The Illuminated Life of the Great Yolmowa* (Serindia Publications, 2013) and the co-editor, with Andrew Quintman, of *Himalayan Passages: Tibetan and Newar Studies in Honor of Hubert Decleer* (Wisdom Publications, 2014). Other research interests include Buddhism and agriculture, death and dying, poetry, translation, and ghosts.

José I. Cabezón is Distinguished Professor of Religious Studies, and XIV Dalai Lama Professor of Tibetan Buddhism and Cultural Studies at the University of California, Santa Barbara. He has published nineteen books and many dozens of articles on Buddhism, Tibetan culture, and the academic study of religion. His most recent publications include *Sexuality in Classical South Asian Buddhism* (2017) and *Sera Monastery* (2019, with Penpa Dorjee). He served for almost twenty years as coeditor of Wisdom Publications' *Studies in Indian and Tibetan Buddhism Series*. His current research focuses on the "synoptic" literature of late Indian Buddhism. The recipient of many grants and fellowships, including fellowships from ACLS and the Humboldt, Guggenheim, and Rockefeller Foundations, he was Tsadra Foundation Distinguished Research Scholar from 2021 to 2022. Cabezón was elected to the Academy of Arts and Sciences in 2019 and served as president of the American Academy of Religion in 2020. Between 2018 and 2019 he made three month-long trips to explore some of the ancient Buddhist sites of Pakistan.

Jacob Dalton, Khyentse Foundation Distinguished University Professor in Tibetan Buddhism, holds a dual appointment in the departments of South and Southeast Asian Studies and East Asian Languages and Cultures at UC Berkeley. After studying with Janet Gyatso as an undergraduate, he received his PhD in Buddhist studies from the University of Michigan in 2002. He works on tantric ritual, Nyingma religious history, paleography, and the Dunhuang manuscripts. He is the author of *The Taming of the Demons: Violence and Liberation in Tibetan Buddhism* (Yale University Press, 2011), *The Gathering of Intentions: A History of a Tibetan Tantra* (Columbia University Press, 2016), and *Conjuring the Buddha: Ritual Manuals in Early Tantric Buddhism* (Columbia University Press, 2023).

Jay L. Garfield is Doris Silbert Professor in the Humanities and Professor of Philosophy and Buddhist Studies at Smith College where he chairs the Philosophy Department and directs the Buddhist Studies Program and the Tibetan Studies in India Program. He is also Visiting Professor of Buddhist Philosophy at the Harvard Divinity School, Professor of Philosophy at Melbourne University, and Adjunct Professor of Philosophy at the Central Institute of Higher Tibetan Studies. *Academicinfluence.com* has identified him as one of the fifty most influential philosophers in the world over the past decade. Garfield's research addresses topics in the foundations of cognitive science and the philosophy of mind, modern Indian philosophy, ethics, epistemology, philosophy of logic, cross-cultural interpretation, and Buddhist philosophy, particularly Indo-Tibetan Madhyamaka and Yogācāra. He is the author or editor of over thirty books and nearly 200 articles, chapters, and reviews. Garfield's most recent books are *Getting Over Ourselves: How to be a Person Without a Self* (2022), *Knowing Illusion: Bringing a Tibetan Debate into Contemporary Discourse* (with the Yakherds, 2021), *Buddhist Ethics: A Philosophical* Exploration (2021), *What Can't Be Said: Paradox and Contradiction in East Asian Thought* (with Yasuo Deguchi, Graham Priest, and Robert Sharf, 2021), *The Concealed Influence of Custom: Hume's* Treatise *From the Inside* Out (Oxford University Press, 2019), and *Minds Without Fear: Philosophy in the Indian Renaissance* (with Nalini Bhushan, 2017).

Holly Gayley is a scholar and translator of contemporary Buddhist literature in Tibet and an associate professor in the Department of Religious Studies at the University of Colorado Boulder. Her research areas include gender and sexuality in Buddhist tantra, ethical reform in contemporary Tibet, and theorizing translation, both literary and cultural, in the transmission of Buddhist teachings to North America. She is author of *Love Letters from Golok: A Tantric Couple in Modern Tibet* (2016), coeditor of *A Gathering of Brilliant Moons: Practice Advice from the Rimé Masters of Tibet* (2017), translator of *Inseparable Across Lifetimes: The Lives and Love Letters of Namtrul Rinpoche and Khandro Tāre Lhamo* (2019), and editor of *Voices from Larung Gar: Shaping Tibetan Buddhism for the Twenty-First Century* (2021). Her recent articles on gender and sexuality include "Revisiting the 'Secret Consort' (*gsang yum*) in Tibetan

Buddhism" (*Religions*, June 2018) and "Parody and Pathos: Sexual Transgression by 'Fake' Lamas in Tibetan Short Stories," co-authored with Somtso Bhum (*Revue d'Etudes Tibétaines*, April 2022).

James Gentry is assistant professor of religious studies at Stanford University. He specializes in Tibetan Buddhism, with particular focus on the literature and history of its tantric traditions. He is the author of *Power Objects in Tibetan Buddhism: The Life, Writings, and Legacy of Sokdokpa Lodrö Gyeltsen* (Brill, 2017), which examines the roles of tantric material and sensory objects in the lives and institutions of Himalayan Buddhists. Among his current projects is a history of the *maṇi* pill and other medico-ritual pill traditions in Tibet that incorporate the flesh and bodily remains of the Buddhist special dead.

David Germano teaches and researches Tibetan and Buddhist studies at the University of Virginia, where he is a professor, as well as directs the Contemplative Sciences Center and the Tibet Center. He has lived for years in Tibetan communities, where he has studied Buddhist philosophy and contemplation and done extensive community engagement work. Since 2011 he has explored contemplative ideas, values, and practices in relationship to scientific frameworks and creative applications in higher education in service of facilitating student flourishing. Currently he leads the Generative Contemplative Initiative, which explores contemplation as a generative capacity with distinctive lexicons, grammars, and contexts.

Jonathan C. Gold is professor in the Department of Religion and director of the Center for Culture, Society, and Religion at Princeton University. A scholar of Indian and Tibetan Buddhist philosophy, he is especially interested in Buddhist approaches to meaning, ethics, language, and learning. He is the author of *The Dharma's Gatekeepers: Sakya Paṇḍita on Buddhist Scholarship in Tibet* (2007) and *Paving the Great Way: Vasubandhu's Unifying Buddhist Philosophy* (2015). He is coeditor, with Douglas S. Duckworth, of *Readings of Śāntideva's* Guide to Bodhisattva Practice (Bodhicaryāvatāra) (2019). In his current work he is developing a Buddhist approach to politics and social thought.

Amy Heller teaches Tibetan art and architecture in the Institute for Science of Religions, University of Bern. Since 1986 she has been affiliated with the Paris CNRS Tibet team of the East Asian Civilizations Research Centre (CRCAO). She has earned a 1974 BA cum Laude at Barnard College in art history, 1980 Diplôme de Langue et Civilisation Tibétaine at INALCO, Paris, and 1992 Diplôme de l'Ecole Pratique des Hautes Etudes, IVe section, Philology and

History, Paris. She was a visiting professor at La Sapienza (2006, 2008) and the Centre for Tibetan Studies, Sichuan University (2007–2013). Her books include *Tibetan Art* (1999), *Early Himalayan Art* (2008), and *Hidden Treasures of the Himalayas: Tibetan Manuscripts Paintings and Sculptures of Dolpo* (2009); her edited books include *Discoveries in Western Tibet and Western Himalayas* (2007), *The Arts of Tibetan Painting* (2012), and *Visual Culture of Tibet and the Himalayas* (2020).

Lama Jabb was born and brought up in the Dhatsen tribe, a nomadic community in Northeastern Tibet. He studied in Tibet, India, and the UK and received his DPhil at the University of Oxford. He is currently a Supernumerary Fellow in Tibetan and Himalayan studies and the head of the Tibetan and Himalayan Studies Centre at Wolfson College and teaches Tibetan language and literature at the Faculty of Asian and Middle Eastern Studies, University of Oxford. Lama Jabb's research and writing center on the interplay between the Tibetan literary text and oral traditions, literary criticism, translation theory and practice, and contemporary Tibet. He is the author of the book *Oral and Literary Continuities in Modern Tibetan Literature: The Inescapable Nation* (2015) and many scholarly articles including "The Mingled Melody: Remembering the Tibetan March 10th Uprising" (2019), "The Wandering Voice of Tibet: Life and Songs of Dubhe" (2020), and "Currents of the Tibetan National Epic in Contemporary Writing" (2022).

Sarah H. Jacoby is an associate professor in the Religious Studies Department at Northwestern University in Evanston, Illinois. She specializes in Tibetan Buddhist studies, with research interests in Buddhist revelation (*gter ma*), religious auto/biography, Tibetan literature, gender and sexuality, the history of emotions, and the history of eastern Tibet. She is the author of *Love and Liberation: Autobiographical Writings of the Tibetan Buddhist Visionary Sera Khandro* (Columbia University Press, 2014), coauthor of *Buddhism: Introducing the Buddhist Experience* (Oxford University Press, 2014), and coeditor of *Buddhism Beyond the Monastery: Tantric Practices and their Performers in Tibet and the Himalayas* (Brill, 2009).

Sonam Kachru is an assistant professor in the Department of Religious Studies at Yale University, specializing in the history of premodern Buddhist and Indian philosophy and literature. His first book, *Other Lives: Mind and World in Indian Buddhism*, was published by Columbia University Press in 2021.

Matthew T. Kapstein is professor emeritus in the division of Religious Studies of the École Pratique des Hautes Études, PSL Research University, Paris, and former Numata Professor of Buddhist Studies at the University of Chicago Divinity School. He was previously director of the Tibetan studies research team of the Centre de recherche sur les civilisations de l' Asie orientale, Paris, and is a member of the American Academy of Arts and Sciences. Publications include *The Tibetan Assimilation of Buddhism: Conversion, Contestation and Memory* (2000), *The Tibetans* (2006), and the edited volumes *The Presence of Light: Divine Radiance and Religious Experience* (2004), *Buddhism Between Tibet and China* (2009), and, with Kurtis Schaeffer and Gray Tuttle, *Sources of Tibetan Tradition* (2013).

Samten G. Karmay was born in Amdo, Tibet, in 1936. He was educated in a Bonpo monastery. Later he studied Buddhist philosophy in Drepung until 1959. In 1961 he became a visiting scholar at the School of Oriental and African Studies, University of London, where he obtained an MPhil in 1976 and a PhD in 1985. After 1985, he was a visiting scholar in a number of academic establishments: Ecole Pratique des Hautes Etudes, Paris, University of Tokyo, University of Kyoto, and College de France, Paris. In 1981 he became a director of research in the National Centre of Scientific Research (CNRS), Paris. He was awarded the 1990 Silver Medal of the CNRS for his research in Tibetology with the mention of "high quality and originality." In 1996 he was elected president of the International Association for Tibetan Studies (IATS). He is the author of several books including *The Great Perfection (rDzogs chen): A Philosophical and Meditative Teaching of Tibetan Buddhism* (1988), *Secret Visions of the Fifth Dalai Lama: The Gold Manuscript of the Fournier Collection* (1988), and *The Illusive Play: The Autobiography of the Fifth Dalai Lama* (2014).

Christina Kilby is associate professor of Religion at James Madison University. She studied with Janet Gyatso at Harvard Divinity School, where she earned a Master's of Theological Studies before completing her doctorate at the University of Virginia. She has published research articles on Tibetan epistolary culture and on the documentary aspects of Tibetan letters, both manuscript and print. Her current research focuses on the intersection of religion and displacement. She regularly consults for the International Committee of the Red Cross initiative on "The Interface Between Buddhism and International Humanitarian Law: Reducing Suffering During Armed Conflict."

Nancy G. Lin is the Noboru and Yaeko Hanyu Professor of Buddhist Chaplaincy at the Institute of Buddhist Studies. Her research and teaching interests include poetics, narrative, karma and rebirth, world-engaging and world-renouncing elements in Tibetan Buddhist literature, visual and material culture, and history. Her recent essays include "Ornaments of This World: Materiality and Poetics of the Fifth Dalai Lama's Reliquary Stūpa," in *Jewels, Jewelry, and Other Shiny Things in the Buddhist Imaginary*, edited by Vanessa R. Sasson (University of Hawai'i Press, 2021) and "Karmic Affinities: Rethinking Relations Among Tibetan Lamas and the Qing Emperor," coauthored with Wen-shing Chou, in *Water Moon Reflections: Essays in Honor of Patricia Berger*, edited by Ellen Huang, Nancy G. Lin, Michelle McCoy, and Michelle H. Wang (Berkeley: IEAS Publications, 2021).

Donald S. Lopez Jr. is the Arthur E. Link Distinguished University Professor of Buddhist and Tibetan Studies at the University of Michigan. He is the author, translator, and editor of numerous works in the field of Buddhist studies. He has also written extensively on the European encounter with Buddhism. His recent books include *Dispelling the Darkness: A Jesuit's Quest for the Soul of Tibet* (with Thupten Jinpa); *Gendun Chopel: Tibet's Modern Visionary*; *Seeing the Sacred in Samsara: An Illustrated Guide to the Eighty-four Mahasiddhas*; *Two Buddhas Seated Side by Side: A Guide to the Lotus Sutra* (with Jacqueline Stone); and, as translator, *Beautiful Adornment of Mount Meru: A Presentation of Classical Indian Philosophy*. Among anthologies, he is the editor of the Buddhism volume of the *Norton Anthology of World Religions* and *Buddhist Scriptures* for Penguin Classics. He was the first scholar of Buddhism to deliver the Terry Lectures at Yale, in 2008. In 2014 *The Princeton Dictionary of Buddhism* (edited with Robert Buswell) was awarded the Dartmouth Medal of the American Library Association for best reference work of the year. In 2000 he was elected to the American Academy of Arts and Sciences.

Padma 'tsho (Baimacuo) is a professor in the Philosophy Department of Southwest Minzu University in Chengdu, China. She holds a PhD from Sichuan University in Chengdu and an MA from Minzu University in Beijing. She was an instructor at Front Range Community in 2016–17. Her areas of research and teaching include Tibetan Buddhism, ritual, and culture, as well as the education of Buddhist nuns in Tibetan areas. She has published numerous articles in several languages and two books. Her articles have appeared in anthologies such as *Eminent Buddhist Women* (edited by Karma Lekshe Tsomo) and *Voices from Larung Gar* (edited by Holly Gayley), as well as numerous journals, including *Religions*, *Contemporary Buddhism*, *China Tibetology*, *Journal of Ethnology*, *Sichuan Tibetan Studies*, and *Asian Highlands Perspective*. In the last decade Padma 'tsho has spent time at several North American universities as a visiting research scholar, including Harvard, Columbia, University of Virginia, and the University of Colorado Boulder.

Andrew Quintman is a scholar of Buddhist traditions in Tibet and the Himalaya and an associate professor in the Department of Religion at Wesleyan University. He writes, teaches, and lectures about Buddhist literature and history, sacred geography and pilgrimage, and visual cultures of the wider Himalaya. His book *The Yogin and the Madman: Reading the Biographical Corpus of Tibet's Great Saint Milarepa* (Columbia University Press, 2014) won the American Academy of Religion's Award for Excellence in the Study of Religion and the Heyman Prize for outstanding scholarship from Yale University. In 2010 his new English translation of *The Life of Milarepa* was published by Penguin Classics. He currently serves as president of the board of directors for the Buddhist Digital Resource Center.

Charles Ramble is directeur d'études in the History and Philology Section of the École Pratique des Hautes Études, PSL University, Paris, and director of the Tibetan studies research team of the East Asian Civilizations Research Centre (CRCAO). From 2000 to 2010 he held the position of university lecturer in Tibetan and Himalayan studies at the University of Oxford, with which he remains associated as a university research lecturer. From 2006 to 2013 he was president of the International Association for Tibetan Studies. He is currently director of the European Society for the Study of Central Asian and Himalayan Civilisations (SEECHAC). His research interests include the Bon religion, Tibetan pagan religion in the Himalayan region, the social history of Tibetan societies, pilgrimage, and biography. He is the author or coauthor of eight books, including *The Navel of the Demoness: Tibetan Buddhism and Civil Religion in Highland Nepal* (2008) as well as three volumes in a series entitled *Tibetan Sources for a Social History of Mustang (Nepal),* (2008, 2015, 2019).

Julie Regan is a scholar of Buddhist literary works in Sanskrit and Tibetan and an assistant professor of Asian religions at La Salle University. Her approach draws on doctoral studies of Buddhism and Religion, Gender and Culture under the supervision of Janet Gyatso (Harvard University, PhD, 2016) as well as training in comparative literature (secondary field, Harvard University, PhD, 2016) and literary arts (MFA, Brown University, 1995). Her work, which has appeared in *Feminist Studies in Religion*, *The Iowa Review*, *LIT magazine*, *Movement Research Performance Journal*, and *Religions*, takes an interdisciplinary approach to reading a variety of texts, performances, and rituals, from early

Sanskrit *kāvya* to contemporary works of Tibetan poetry and protest. "Pleasure & Poetics as Tools for Transformation in Aśvaghoṣa's *mahākāvya*" (*Religions*, 2022) introduces some of the themes of her book-in-progress, which explores the Buddhist literary text as a path to awakening.

Kurtis R. Schaeffer is the Frances Myers Ball Professor in the Department of Religious Studies at the University of Virginia. He specializes in the cultural and literary history of Tibet. He is the author of several books, including *Himalayan Hermitess* (2004), *Dreaming the Great Brahmin* (2005), and *The Culture of the Book in Tibet* (2009); translator of *The Life of the Buddha* (2015); and coeditor of *Sources of Tibetan Civilization* (2013) and *The Tibetan History Reader* (2013).

Heather Stoddard grew up in an alternative cosmopolitan community on the edge of London, traveled overland to discover classical India at Kalakshetra, Chennai, and then encountered Tibetan refugees in the Himalayas. Following the start of the Cultural Revolution she studied Chinese and Tibetan at SOAS Sorbonne in Paris. She later served as head of Tibetan studies at INALCO, Paris (1977–2012), during which time she undertook multiple missions to Tibet, the People's Republic of China, and Mongolia. She has conducted research into modern Tibetan intellectuals, writers, and artists, coupled with classical literature, history, and Buddhist art. She is author of *Early Sino-Tibetan Art* (2008) and cofounder of Shalu Association and Tibet Heritage Fund. She is currently completing a new biography of Gedun Chopel (1903–51).

Dominique Townsend is associate professor of Buddhist studies at Bard College. She is the author of *A Buddhist Sensibility: Aesthetic Education at Tibet's Mindröling Monastery* (Columbia University Press, 2021); *Shantideva: How to Wake Up a Hero*, an adaptation of the classic text for young readers (Wisdom Publications, 2015); and a collection of poems, *The Weather & Our Tempers* (Brooklyn Arts Press, 2014).

Leonard W. J. van der Kuijp (范德康) is professor of Tibetan and Himalayan Studies and chairs the Committee on Inner Asian and Altaic Studies. Best known for his studies of Buddhist epistemology, he is the author of numerous works on Tibet and Tibetan Buddhism. Recent publications include *An Early Tibetan Survey of Buddhist Literature* (2008), coauthored with Kurtis R. Schaeffer, and *Bcom ldan ral gri (1227–1305) on Buddhist Epistemology and Logic: His Commentary on Dignāga's Pramāṇasamuccaya*, with

A. McKeown (2013). Van der Kuijp's research focuses primarily on Indo-Tibetan Buddhist thought, Tibetan Buddhist intellectual history, Tibetan Buddhism, and premodern Sino-Tibetan and Tibeto-Mongol political and religious relations.

Nicole Willock is an associate professor of Asian Religions at Old Dominion University in Norfolk, Virginia. Translating from Tibetan and Chinese languages, her research examines the intersections between literature, Buddhist modernism, and moral agency. She is the recipient of FLAS fellowships, the Fulbright-Hays DDRA, and the American Council of Learned Societies' (ACLS) Robert H.N. Ho Family Foundation Research Fellowship in Buddhist Studies. Her articles include "Thu'u bkwan's Literary Adaptations of the Life of Dgongs pa rab gsal" in *Trails of the Tibetan Tradition: Papers for Elliot Sperling* (2014); "Maps and Territory in the 1950s: The Writing of the *Dan tig dkar chag—A Guide to Dan tig Monastery*," in *Trans Himalayan Tibet: History, Language and Literature, Traditional & Contemporary* (2016) and her latest publication "'*Avadāna* of Silver Flowers:' A Discussion on Decolonization and Anti-Colonial Translation Practices for Tibetan poetry," co-written with Gedun Rabsal, in the *Journal of Tibetan Literature* (2022). Her first book is *Lineages of the Literary: Tibetan Buddhist Polymaths of Socialist China* (Columbia University Press, 2021).

Studies in Indian and Tibetan Buddhism
Titles Previously Published

Among Tibetan Texts
History and Literature of the Himalayan Plateau
E. Gene Smith

Approaching the Great Perfection
Simultaneous and Gradual Methods of Dzogchen Practice in the Longchen Nyingtig
Sam van Schaik

Authorized Lives
Biography and the Early Formation of Geluk Identity
Elijah S. Ary

Buddha's Single Intention
Drigung Kyobpa Jikten Sumgön's Vajra Statements of the Early Kagyü Tradition
Jan-Ulrich Sobisch

Buddhism Between Tibet and China
Edited by Matthew T. Kapstein

The Buddhist Philosophy of the Middle
Essays on Indian and Tibetan Madhyamaka
David Seyfort Ruegg

Buddhist Teaching in India
Johannes Bronkhorst

A Direct Path to the Buddha Within
Gö Lotsāwa's Mahāmudrā Interpretation of the Ratnagotravibhāga
Klaus-Dieter Mathes

The Essence of the Ocean of Attainments
The Creation Stage of the Guhyasamāja Tantra according to Panchen Losang Chökyi Gyaltsen
Yael Bentor and Penpa Dorjee

Foundations of Dharmakīrti's Philosophy
John D. Dunne

Freedom from Extremes
Gorampa's "Distinguishing the Views" and the Polemics of Emptiness
José Ignacio Cabezón and Geshe Lobsang Dargyay

Himalayan Passages
Tibetan and Newar Studies in Honor of Hubert Decleer
Benjamin Bogin and Andrew Quintman

How Do Mādhyamikas Think?
And Other Essays on the Buddhist Philosophy of the Middle
Tom J. F. Tillemans

Jewels of the Middle Way
The Madhyamaka Legacy of Atiśa and His Early Tibetan Followers
James B. Apple

Luminous Lives
The Story of the Early Masters of the Lam 'bras Tradition in Tibet
Cyrus Stearns

Mind Seeing Mind
Mahāmudrā and the Geluk Tradition of Tibetan Buddhism
Roger Jackson

Mipham's Beacon of Certainty
Illuminating the View of Dzogchen, the Great Perfection
John Whitney Pettit

Omniscience and the Rhetoric of Reason
Śāntarakṣita and Kamalaśīla on Rationality, Argumentation, and Religious Authority
Sara L. McClintock

Reasons and Lives in Buddhist Traditions
Tibetan and Buddhist Studies in Honor of Matthew Kapstein
Edited by Dan Arnold, Cécile Ducher, and Pierre-Julien Harter

Reason's Traces
Identity and Interpretation in Indian and Tibetan Buddhist Thought
Matthew T. Kapstein

Remembering the Lotus-Born
Padmasambhava in the History of Tibet's Golden Age
Daniel A. Hirshberg

Resurrecting Candrakīrti
Disputes in the Tibetan Creation of Prāsaṅgika
Kevin A. Vose

Scripture, Logic, Language
Essays on Dharmakīrti and His Tibetan Successors
Tom J. F. Tillemans

Sexuality in Classical South Asian Buddhism
José I. Cabezón

The Svātantrika-Prāsaṅgika Distinction
What Difference Does a Difference Make?
Edited by Georges Dreyfus and Sara McClintock

Vajrayoginī
Her Visualizations, Rituals, and Forms
Elizabeth English

About Wisdom Publications

Wisdom Publications is the leading publisher of classic and contemporary Buddhist books and practical works on mindfulness. To learn more about us or to explore our other books, please visit our website at wisdomexperience.org or contact us at the address below.

Wisdom Publications
199 Elm Street
Somerville, MA 02144 USA

We are a 501(c)(3) organization, and donations in support of our mission are tax deductible.

Wisdom Publications is affiliated with the Foundation for the Preservation of the Mahayana Tradition (FPMT).